Cult Cinema

Cult Cinema

An Introduction

Ernest Mathijs and Jamie Sexton

A John Wiley & Sons, Ltd., Publication

This edition first published 2011
© 2011 Ernest Mathijs and Jamie Sexton

Blackwell Publishing was acquired by John Wiley & Sons in February 2007. Blackwell's publishing program has been merged with Wiley's global Scientific, Technical, and Medical business to form Wiley-Blackwell.

Registered Office
John Wiley & Sons Ltd, The Atrium, Southern Gate, Chichester, West Sussex, PO19 8SQ, United Kingdom

Editorial Offices
350 Main Street, Malden, MA 02148-5020, USA
9600 Garsington Road, Oxford, OX4 2DQ, UK
The Atrium, Southern Gate, Chichester, West Sussex, PO19 8SQ, UK

For details of our global editorial offices, for customer services, and for information about how to apply for permission to reuse the copyright material in this book please see our website at www.wiley.com/wiley-blackwell.

The right of Ernest Mathijs and Jamie Sexton to be identified as the authors of this work has been asserted in accordance with the UK Copyright, Designs and Patents Act 1988.

Wiley also publishes its books in a variety of electronic formats. Some content that appears in print may not be available in electronic books.

Designations used by companies to distinguish their products are often claimed as trademarks. All brand names and product names used in this book are trade names, service marks, trademarks or registered trademarks of their respective owners. The publisher is not associated with any product or vendor mentioned in this book. This publication is designed to provide accurate and authoritative information in regard to the subject matter covered. It is sold on the understanding that the publisher is not engaged in rendering professional services. If professional advice or other expert assistance is required, the services of a competent professional should be sought.

Library of Congress Cataloging-in-Publication Data

Mathijs, Ernest.
  Cult cinema : an introduction / Ernest Mathijs and Jamie Sexton.
    p. cm.
  Includes filmography.
  Includes bibliographical references and index.
  ISBN 978-1-4051-7374-2 (hardback : alk. paper) – ISBN 978-1-4051-7373-5 (pbk. : alk. paper)
  1. Cult films–History and criticism. 2. Sensationalism in motion pictures. I. Sexton, Jamie. II. Title.
  PN1995.9.C84M38 2011
  791.43'653–dc22
                                                                                    2010051053

A catalogue record for this book is available from the British Library.

This book is published in the following electronic formats: ePDFs ISBN 9781444396423; Wiley Online Library ISBN 9781444396447; ePub ISBN 9781444396430

Set in 10/12pt Bembo by Thomson Digital, Noida, India

1 2011

"*One has to be in a state of* euphemia, *cultic purity … Any religious ritual is arbitrary unless one is able to see past it to a deeper meaning …. It had to be approached on its own terms …. It was heart-shaking. Glorious. Torches, dizziness, singing. Wolves howling around us and a bull bellowing in the dark. The river ran white. It was like a film in fast motion, the moon waxing and waning, clouds rushing across the sky. Vines grew from the ground so fast they twined up the trees like snakes; seasons passing in the wink of an eye, entire years for all I know … Duality ceases to exist; there is no ego, no "I" … as if the universe expands to fill the boundaries of the self. You have no idea how pallid the workday boundaries of ordinary existence seem, after such an ecstasy. It was like being a baby*"

– Donna Tartt, *The Secret History* (1992)

"*Keep you doped with religion and sex and TV*
And you think you're so clever and classless and free"

– John Lennon, *Working Class Hero* (1970)

Contents

List of Figures

Acknowledgments

We would first of all like to thank our editors at Wiley-Blackwell, who have enthusiastically supported this book project from the very beginning and patiently extended the original deadline. In particular, we would like to thank Jayne Fargnoli for her encouragement, energy, and expertise.

We also want to express our gratitude to the three referees who provided feedback on different versions of the manuscript – Daniël Bilvereyst, Matt Hills, and Peter Hutchings. Their detailed and intelligent comments were crucial in improving the overall quality of this book, and we hope that we have honored the majority of their suggestions.

The authors would like to thank the academic departments that they have worked for past and present for their support: the Department of Theatre, Film and Television, Aberystwyth University; the Department of Theatre and Film, University of British Columbia; and the Department of Arts, Northumbria University. We also thank the Royal Film Archive of Belgium (www. cinematek.be) and the organizers of the Abertoir Horror Festival, the Brussels International Festival of Fantastic Film (BIFFF), the Cine Excess festival and conference, the Monstermania Convention, the Flashback Weekend Chicago Horror Convention, and Norwescon for access to their sites and materials. Further thanks go to Henry Ordway and the *Ginger Snaps* fan community.

For permissions to reprint images we are grateful to Kathleen Dow of the Library of the University of Michigan, Christoph Foqué and PeyMey Diffusion, Andrea Pereira and United Press International, Scott Shuffit and Lebowskifest, Jean-Paul Dorchain and the Royal Film Archive of Belgium, Shawn Marier and Norwescon, Debbi Berlin and Palisades Tartan, and Marianthi Makra and the British Film Institute. We explored every possible avenue to obtain permissions to reprint. We hope rights holders will recognize the spirit of appreciation within which images have been reprinted. Any new information from rights holders will be credited in forthcoming editions of this book.

Our work has benefited from discussions with scholars, trades people, students, and friends, both within and outside of the institutions that we have worked in. In particular we would like to thank Brenda Austin-Smith, Gareth Bailey, Martin Barker, Mark Bould, Brigid Cherry, Nathen Clerici, David Church, Joe Dante, Kevin J. Donnelly, Kate Egan, Mark Goodall, Jonathan Gray, Steffen Hantke, Joan Hawkins, Kevin Heffernan, Russ Hunter, I.Q. Hunter, Mark Jancovich, Alexia Kannas, Geoff King, Barbara Klinger, Harry Kümel, Eric Lichtenfeld, Xavier Mendik, Jason Mittell, Tamao Nakahara, Emily Perkins, Julian Petley, Murray Pomerance, Steven Jay Schneider, Iain Robert Smith, Justin Smith, R. Colin Tait, Rachel Talalay, Dirk Van Extergem, Constantine Verevis, and Jeffrey Weinstock. We also thank the many members of the cultmediastudies.ning.com network for their posts and input.

Introduction

Cult cinema is a term that is often met with some confusion. One of the problems of responding to the puzzled enquirer who asks "what exactly *is* a cult film?" is that the phrase has been adopted and employed in a variety of ways in its relatively brief lifespan. This book is an attempt to provide an overview of the predominant means by which cult cinema has functioned and been understood in all of its complexity, without simplistically contending that its instability is evidence of its redundancy as a valid concept. Such dismissals can only be accepted if one believes that words and terms can always be reduced to short, definitive explanations. Many words, however, have unstable meanings, often because their connotations fluctuate throughout time and also because they are used in different ways across varied contexts. David Lee has argued that "meaning is not an inherent property of words but is strongly influenced by contexts of use" (1992: 16), stressing the heterogeneous and complex nature of words.

To begin with, there is the range of meanings associated with the word "cult" proper. Generally speaking, there are two frameworks through which the word "cult" is approached, a sociological one and a religious one. The religious understanding refers to "cult" as the ancient or original procedures of practice that are externally present in the observation of a belief. These procedures of practice represent the care (from the Latin *cultus*) given to exercising a belief. The emphasis of these procedures lies on rituals, routines, and on material elements of the belief (idols, temples, shrines, attire).

The sociological understanding of the term "cult" also deals with religion, but it approaches it more as a degree of institutionalization. According to Ernst Troeltsch's (1931) typology of religious beliefs (which concentrates on Christian religion only) a cult is a form of religious behavior that is different from a church or a sect. Whereas a church claims its belief to have absolute truth and is geared towards the elimination of competitive beliefs, a cult is less concerned with universality of belief. Cults are also far less professional and bureaucratic in their organization than churches (with only a very small number of full-time salaried clergy), and they are not as closely allied with state-powers as churches usually are. Troeltsch also notes that like sects, cults promote a purity of belief. But unlike sects they do not usually advocate a return to purity. Instead, they embrace a new purity (this is why they are often called NRM: New Religious Movements), which makes their type of belief more open to esotericism and prone to mysticism. Cults are also different from sects in that they originate much more organically, whereas sects are typically break-offs from churches.

Troeltsch's typology was further refined by Howard P. Becker (1932) and Colin Campbell (1977), who emphasize that cults are usually small in size, that the observance of belief is of a private nature, and that their difference from churches means they are often portrayed as deviant – in opposition to mainstream culture. Cowan and Bromley (2008: 10–11) specify this last point by arguing that cults, like many religious beliefs, operate with a concept of 'unseen order' which acts as an incentive for the "harmonious adjustment" of behavior to a greater good. The unseen order motivates explanatory narratives that interpret its relationship to the everyday world (myths), and it acts as a sort

Cult Cinema: An Introduction. Ernest Mathijs and Jamie Sexton.
© 2011 Ernest Mathijs and Jamie Sexton. Published 2011 by Blackwell Publishing Ltd.

of compass for prescribed behaviors (rituals). For Cowan and Bromley a main difference between cults and established religious groups lies in the fact that culturally "their myths, beliefs, rituals, and practices . . . differ significantly from those of the dominant culture" (2008: 11).

Although cults have always carried a pejorative connotation, an organized resistance against cults has arisen in recent decades, especially since the second half of the 1960s (Cowan 2003; Beckford 2003: 30). Christian counter-cult movements have tended to regard all cults as deviations from orthodoxy, and therefore as heretical. Secular counter-cult movements too have increasingly opposed cults because of the perception that high-profile controversies (such as the Manson Family, Jonestown's People's Temple, the Solar Temple, or Heaven's Gate,) but also more moderate movements (such as Maharishi Mahesh Yogi's Transcendental Meditation, of which the Beatles were famed followers) have created cults using methods of conversion such as "brain washing" and "mind control," and that cult members are essentially slaves to charismatic leadership ("gurus"). For example, in "Why the Cults Are Coming", Marvin Harris (1981) argues that one reason for increased cultism is as a response to perceptions that society is too alienated in its post-industrial age. For Harris, this response is ineffective because cultism too runs the danger of alienation, of seeking solutions to spiritual crises through worldly means – economic and political. This is worth noting because of the immediate context it provides for the increase in use of the term with regard to cinema that occurred around the same time.

The phrase "cult cinema" – which has brought the connotations of the existing word "cult" to bear on the world of film culture – is a particularly knotty term, which renders it difficult to pin down in any definitive manner. It is subject to differing applications and battles over its meanings (as when disputes arise over which particular titles are cult films). Despite its contested nature, it is not totally elastic: its use has been influenced by historical and other contextual developments, so that when one looks at the ways in which the word functions within various contexts (i.e. in journalistic articles, in academic papers, on a variety of internet discussion platforms), there are a number of recurring themes which tend to be associated with it.

This book provides an overview of a range of topics which we believe are important to cult cinema. Within each of the chapters we attempt to describe the concept or category in question and to outline ways in which it has been important to cult cinema, to provide information on historical and/or theoretical features which centrally inform such categories, while also making reference to films where necessary to illustrate particular points. In this way, we hope to provide a thorough overview of cult cinema from a number of different perspectives, which we feel has the benefit of pointing to the diverse ways it has functioned within film culture. While we are aware of the contested nature of cult cinema, we nevertheless offer our own interpretation in the light of previous research. We also think that an introductory book of this nature should reflect the diversity of interpretations and designations involved in the field of cult cinema, and in this sense the book can be considered as following a "constructivist" approach to cult media (though of course we only focus on cinema) outlined by Philippe Le Guern, who posed the question: "Is it, in the end, the usage of the concept of cult, its mobilization, and its varying interpretations by audiences that should be examined, independently of the question of whether cult corresponds to an objective reality and a proven body of work?" (2004: 4) We certainly think that the usage, interpretations and values attached to cult are particularly important; yet while we do not think that any film is immanently cult, we do think that the ways in which the concept has been utilized in different contexts and developed historically has nevertheless led to a body of texts that are frequently referred to as cult films, and this is reflected in films that are repeatedly mentioned throughout the text. We have, however, also attempted to present a wide range of films here in order to point towards the large, and varied, body of work that has been termed cult. The large number of films mentioned and discussed in the book precludes us from being able to explain in what sense *every* film is to be considered cult, though we do frequently do so. If an explanation is lacking, we should stress that it has been discussed and/or listed as a cult film within print or online.

We should also mention our use of another concept that is difficult to pin down, and which is often used as a yardstick against which cult cinema is measured, namely the concept of the mainstream. The mainstream is referred to a number of times within this book and we would like to make it clear that we also use this term in a similarly constructivist manner as we use cult: it acts as an umbrella term which refers to a number of values, most often denoting the "norms" of film production, textuality, and consumption. However, what counts as the mainstream (and what counts as the norm) may differ according to context. For Jancovich *et al.* (2003a) the mainstream tends to be a rather fuzzily defined imaginary concept among a number of different "taste cultures," yet despite such imprecision it still functions as a crucial concept among fans who use it to define themselves against more "normal" or "average" film viewers (2003a: 1–2).

The History of Studying Cult Cinema

Considering our claim that cult cinema has been influenced by its historical and other contextual developments, we will provide a brief overview of the historical emergence of cult cinema as a subject, particularly within an academic context. Hitherto there has not been a great deal written on how cult has emerged and developed historically within film culture, though some works have contributed to this field. These would include the contextual introduction sections in Mathijs and Mendik's collection *The Cult Film Reader* (2008a) as well as Greg Taylor's history of "cultism" within American film criticism, *Artists in the Audience* (1999). Other historical work can be found in occasional articles or as fragments of larger works, which include Hoberman and Rosenbaum (1991), Jancovich (2002), Smith (2006), Sexton (2011), and Stevenson (2003e).

While the use of the word "cult" within film culture stretches back much further, it was probably in the 1970s that the term "cult film" or "cult cinema" began to be used (at least relatively frequently), and it tended to refer to films that gained repeat audiences and who would often indulge in behaviors considered "ritualistic," hence the adoption of the religious metaphor. Thus, in addition to the ritual of continually returning to "worship" a particular text, other rituals such as repeating the lines of the films (as was the case with *Casablanca*) or dressing up and talking back at the screen (as was the case with *The Rocky Horror Picture Show*) were observed as evidence of cult viewing practices. The 1980s saw the rise of academic studies of cult cinema, with most attention being paid to *The Rocky Horror Picture Show* (see, for example, Austin 1981a; Siegel 1980), but also including Umberto Eco's (1986, first published in 1985) canonical study of *Casablanca* as a cult movie. While the first two articles are largely sociological in nature, primarily focusing on audience responses as cult, Eco's article was an attempt to map out the textual nature of the cult film (albeit through a single example), noting that a cult film is particularly rich in *intertextual* detail; that it is an example of "living textuality," consisting of a large assemblage of characters and situations which draw upon archetypal characters and situations from other films. While he states that all movies do this to an extent, he claims that *Casablanca* does so excessively, so that it is not "one movie. It is *movies*." (1986: 208). He ended by claiming that this process of excessive quotation, which he did not believe was a deliberate strategy of the film's creators, was more recently becoming a self-conscious component of film production and that we were entering a "Cult Culture" (1986: 210). Several chapters in this book explore the importance of Eco's ideas: Chapter 17 discusses intertextuality in relation to classical Hollywood cults; Chapter 21 explores the importance of intertextuality more broadly, particularly through the strategies of parody and irony. Chapter 22 looks at the importance of "meta-cult," which Eco argued was culture that self-consciously draws on cult (1986: 210).

As academic studies of cult cinema grew Eco's arguments became questioned. J.P. Telotte, for example, claimed that Eco overstated what he described as the "imperfections" of *Casablanca*, thus "trivializing what the public perceives to be a classic of the American screen" (1991b: 44). Whereas Eco viewed it as a kind of incoherent patchwork, Telotte stressed how the film managed to unify all of its various, disparate elements. Barry Keith Grant, meanwhile, questioned Eco's stress upon the cult film as a "collagelike assembly of interchangeable parts" as he stressed that this was a general characteristic of *all* classical Hollywood genre films (1991: 125). Both of these articles appeared in Telotte's 1991 collection on cult cinema, which was the first academic book entirely devoted to the cult film phenomenon. This collection was also important for broadening academic cult studies: while the two films that had up to this point gained most coverage as cult films – *Casablanca* and *The Rocky Horror Picture Show* – featured prominently, a large range of additional titles were also included. These films were approached from a wide variety of frameworks, though among these different perspectives there was an assertion that the cult film came in two notable guises: the "classical cult" film and the "midnight movie." The former were films produced within the classical Hollywood system between, approximately, 1917 and 1960 (Bordwell, Staiger and Thompson 1985) and which had endured through being repeatedly viewed by particular audiences at repertory screenings or through frequent television appearances. Issues explored in relation to the classical cult film in this volume include nostalgia, the role of the cult star, and the function of camp, topics discussed respectively in Chapter 7, Chapter 8 and Chapter 17. The midnight movie phenomenon (discussed in Chapter 1) – which had already by this point led to two books on the subject (Hoberman and Rosenbaum 1991 [1983]; Samuels 1983) – was at this stage perhaps the most noted manner by which films were designated as cult, and was where *The Rocky Horror Picture Show* gained its cult reputation. Scholars in this section discussed issues such as transgression (covered in Chapter 9), performance (covered in Chapters 7 and 10), nostalgia (Chapter 17), as well as distribution/exhibition trends (Chapter 1). And yet, while midnight screenings still occur, this edited collection was published when their heyday was passing. In Gregory A. Waller's empirical survey of midnight movie screenings in Kentucky between 1980 and 1985, he notes the "shrinking market" for midnight movies and claims that one of the reasons for this is because "many once-popular midnight movies – and movies that might have become successful at midnight – became available on videocassette" (1991: 177).

The importance of the videocassette, and home viewing more generally, was only briefly mentioned in Telotte's edited collection, but it would soon become a central focus of academic studies of cult cinema. The idea of repetition – of viewing films again and again – became much easier when films were accessible on videotape. As Anne Jerslev noted,

videotape also enabled viewers to be able to have more mastery over films through functions such as fast-forward, rewind and freeze-framing (1992: 194). Videocassettes had a huge impact on film culture generally, and inevitably affected the processes associated with cult cinema. The domestic arena now became an important site in the construction of cult films: new "sleeper" patterns could be formed, for example, when films which flopped or disappointed at the box office found a new life on videocassette. Or, as was the case of the "video nasties" in the United Kingdom (see Chapter 4), new forms of censorship could lead to the formation of particular subcultures based around a corpus of videotapes. Video companies could also use "cult film" as a marketing label, releasing films that already had a cult reputation (or fitted vaguely into a cult-like genre such as exploitation) in order to sell films.

Novel viewing conditions and the expansion of cult discourses into marketing would feed into new approaches to cult cinema within academia. In 2000, Mendik and Harper edited another book-length collection on cult cinema, in which a variety of approaches to the cult text were evident, including theoretical analyses of films which had already established a cult reputation, the study of "transnational cult" films, cult stars and video nasties. Perhaps the best-known (and notorious) chapter in this collection was I.Q. Hunter's piece on *Showgirls*, much of which explored his own liking of the film and the politics of taste. The interrogation of cult in relation to taste – why people like particular works and for what reasons, and how these relate to particular social conditions – became particularly notable in the 2000s, with sociologist Pierre Bourdieu the most influential figure being drawn upon to analyze such issues. Bourdieu had already been drawn upon by Jeffrey Sconce in his influential 1995 article which investigated enthusiasts of a variety of exploitation films, a mode of ironic connoisseurship he termed "paracinema" (see Chapter 8). While Sconce's article did not discuss cult film as such, it certainly made an impact on subsequent studies of cult cinema, and paracinema tends to be considered a subsection of cult cinema. Work by Hawkins (2000), Hills (2002a), and Jancovich (2002) all extended research into areas of cultist taste (and other cult media in the case of Hills), and this was also evident in some of the chapters within another collection on cult cinema by Jancovich *et al.* (2003b). The growth in the study of taste and cult was undoubtedly linked to the rise in academic studies of fans (see Chapter 5), a research area that has often overlapped with cult studies (Hills' aforementioned cited work was a study of fan cultures) and which has also been influenced by Bourdieu. Another research area influenced by Bourdieu which also overlaps with cult studies is the study of subcultures, particularly those subcultures identified through intensive forms of media consumption.

While the mass consumption of video technology marked an important stage in the domestication of cult cinema, the increasing digitization of media technologies has arguably led to a new stage in such domestic trends. In particular, the increasing embedding of the internet into people's lives and the success of DVDs have led to new patterns being observed within cult studies. DVD, which usurped VHS as the dominant media upon which films were domestically consumed in the early 2000s, actually expanded the types of material available to view at home. As the discs were cheap to manufacture an increasing body of film material began to be released, with small companies emerging to cater towards more "niche" tastes. This was undoubtedly aided by the growth of the internet which in the 2000s was being used by an increasing number of people. This had a number of impacts for cult cinema, relating to areas including e-commerce, sites of consumption, as well as ways in which cultists could share information and communicate with other cultists. E-commerce meant that it was now easier to obtain a wide range of films; this would have been particularly important for those who lived outside of the metropolitan areas in which "specialist" films were more likely to be accessed (such as repertory cinemas and specialist outlets selling more exclusive videos). This is not to claim that cult films are *always* more obscure, marginal films (see Chapters 5, 17 and 20 for discussions of more "mainstream" cult films), but such fare does constitute a significant corpus within traditional canons of cult cinema. The virtual networks created by internet connectivity not only enabled people to search out and obtain films and film-related goods from a range of actual locations, it also created a wealth of accessible information on films so that people

could find out about new films, seek out production details about particular films, interpretations of films, or details about stars and actors, for example. The proliferation of information, whether through databases such as the *Internet Movie Database (IMDB)*, fan sites, online journals, blogs, or wikis, to name only a few notable examples, is important because of the ways in which cultists often want to know more about particular films. This eagerness to know more, or to "master" a film, manifests itself not merely through repeat viewings, but also through gaining knowledge of films in other ways, so that films become much more than just specific viewing encounters and feed into the cultist's broader cultural life in a variety of ways.

The significance of online culture for cult cinema first made itself present within Mendik and Harper's and Jancovich *et al.*'s edited collections but only as a marginal presence, most notably in Julian Hoxter's (2000) analysis of internet fan sites on *The Exorcist* in the former, and Harmony Wu's (2003) consideration of online cult material in relation to Peter Jackson in the latter. Yet a number of articles have been appearing over the past few years which consider the importance of network culture for cult cinema either directly or indirectly, including Brooker (2002), Jenkins (2006), and Telotte (2001). We discuss digital issues occasionally throughout this book, most notably in Chapters 4 and 5, where we point to some trends within cult fandom that have been sparked by new technologies and their uses, and in Chapter 22 where we consider the emergence of cultist DVD labels. The fact that technological change is increasingly accelerating and being used in novel (and often unsurprising) ways makes it difficult for academic work to keep abreast of such shifts. No doubt when this book is published there will have emerged new trends and a number of more recent articles that we will not have been able to consider. We have done our best, though, to at least indicate some of the debates engendered by technological changes and how these have impacted on the field of cult cinema.

At some point in the oscillation between availability and scarcity the conscious avoidance of easy access becomes an important attitude. Anecdotal evidence from studies of collecting, the long-term reception of the video nasties, and so-called "residual media" suggests transferable technologies impact on the "street value" of their reputations (Staiger 2005a; Egan 2007; Acland, 2007). Jancovich quotes director/cultist Frank Henenlotter:

> all those obscure films that I would have risked injury and death to see (literally, in some of those theatres) are now available at your local clean video store! It's a little unnerving. I'm wholeheartedly in support of this, but I'm still not used to the fact that those films that I spent my whole life trying to see are now *consumer items* (quoted in Jancovich 2002; our emphasis)

Henenlotter was speaking about the early 1980s, and things have accelerated since. We should, however, remain aware that new technologies do not displace older technologies and therefore render them redundant. Instead, they reconstitute relations between different types of mediated activities, whether watching films, writing about films or talking about films. Thus, public visits to the cinema to watch films may have been overtaken by domestic viewing, but they still remain important, and for some the cinema experience takes on ever greater value in relation to watching cinema on the home screen (whether this be a large, high-definition set or a small laptop screen). And while VHS has "officially" become an obsolete format, its marginal status can create a new set of cultists. Analogous to music fans preferring vinyl over compact discs these cultists trade or swap VHS cassettes, or post older videos or videotaped televised films of movies which are otherwise hard to get as digitized AVI files (on sites such as Cinemageddon and Karagarga). New technologies do not necessarily wipe out old technologies: they can co-exist in interesting ways, feeding into value judgments or new cultural patterns. The circulation of a low-fi quality VHS bootleg is of high significance for the cult surrounding *Superstar: The Karen Carpenter Story* (Davis 2008). The relations between old and new technologies, between the public and domestic film viewing site (and between mobile and static platforms), will undoubtedly continue to inform the future trajectory of cult cinema. It may be that cult cinema becomes increasingly difficult to distinguish between other forms of cult media, but we do not think that this is certain. In the age of "convergence" the distinctions between different media platforms may have become increasingly intertwined, sometimes murky, but we do believe that despite such overlaps many people do distinguish between cinema (films, movies) and, for example, television. It is for this reason that we think that cult cinema is worthy of an overview as a self-contained subject, albeit one that cannot be isolated from the broader, interconnected media sphere within which it exists.

Definition of Cult Cinema

Numerous attempts have been made to define cult cinema. Many of these approach the topic from a vernacular angle, highlighting elements that cannot be caught in a description and – hence – remain intangible and very subjective. If anything, this means that a definition of cult cinema can only be intersubjective. Many overviews of cult cinema give lists instead of definitions, in the hope that the aggregate of illustrations of how individual films are cult leads to an explanation of why they are cults.

If we look beyond lists, definitions of cult cinema come in four contexts: sociological studies, reception studies, textual interpretations, and aesthetic analyses. Sociological studies assume that a cult film is a film with an intense following, not unlike religious cults. It is a contested parallel, which we will explore further in Chapter 12. However, if cult cinema is seen as a form of cultism in which religiosity has been replaced by an intense mode of consumption, the kind Douglas Cowan and David Bromley have called "audience cults" (2008: 89–90), it offers valuable insights into how exactly cult followings develop and what kind of cultural status they take on. Similarly, cult film can be approached as a form of deviant subculture. The most strident example of the sociological approach is presented by Patrick Kinkade and Michael Katovich (1992). They define a cult film as one whose audience community intensely celebrates "themes that (1) place typical people into atypical situations, (2) allow for narcissistic and empathic audience identification with subversive characters, (3) question traditional authority structures, (4) reflect societal strains, and (5) offer interpretable and paradoxical resolutions to these social strains" (Kinkade and Katovich 1992: 194). This definition describes a double bind: these components are features of the films themselves as well as characteristics of what audiences experience. For Kinkade and Katovich, a contradictory attitude is essential. Cult audiences rebel against the mainstream and canon of cinema and hold that "nothing is sacred"; at the same time they present their own fandom as "sacred."

Reception studies investigate the trajectories through which films develop cult followings as part of their passage through markets. Such studies often offer theoretical outlines of cult films' place in culture, mostly through illustrations and case studies. For Hills (2002a) and Staiger (2005a), cults are a very visible form of fandom. For Jeffrey Sconce (1995, 2007) and Mark Jancovich (2002), cult receptions are to be understood as struggles for cultural positions, rooted in battles over taste hierarchies. Reception approaches also concentrate on the conditions under which cult followings are developed and maintained (Waller 1991; Hawkins 2000; Klinger 1994). In this view, cult films are films whose celebration or appropriation by cultists is the accidental consequence of their fractured reception trajectories. Often failures upon their initial release, and frequently encountering obstacles in their search for audiences, they develop committed followings during repeat screenings (often at fringe times) and they go on to enjoy long lasting fandom. For Danny Peary (1981: xiii), cult receptions are minority receptions, which means that they concern methods of distribution and consumption outside the mainstream. Mathijs and Mendik (2008b: 4–8) isolate active fandom, a sense of community, the liveness of the viewing experience, commitment and endurance, a sense of rebellion, a paracinematic desire for the deconstruction of canons, persistent legends of distribution, specialist or niche events, and a long-term presence, as characteristics of cult receptions. We will examine these concepts more closely in the first section of this book.

The textual approach follows closely on the reception studies approach. While the stress in this approach is on offering a definition based on the analysis of the films, there is a strong acknowledgment of the role of viewers. A central point of attention in these studies is the complexity of communication between text and viewer. A key component of that communication is the use of what is often called "allusions" or "inferences" (by Carroll 1998 and Bordwell 1989 respectively). These are salient moments or small clues within a film that are picked up by savvy viewers who relish their expertise in recognizing these "cues." Other central points in the textual interpretation approach are "nostalgia," "irony," and "camp." These concepts refer to hyperbolic uses of modes of representation, picked up by viewers eager to appropriate these in their enjoyment and celebration of the films.

There are a few attempts to define cult film from a uniquely aesthetic angle, as films whose reception is secondary to understanding them. Most of these are valuable because they emphasize issues of "exoticism," "rarity," "genre," "transgression," and "quality" (Grant 1991; Cox and Jones 1990, 1993). Often, these studies concentrate on specialized subgenres and formats (such as the giallo, anime, martial arts, vampire movies, sleaze movies). These studies are essential in outlining the stylistic components that trigger enthusiasm, aberrant reactions, or repeat-viewing devotion. We will explore many of these instances in the second section of our book.

At their narrowest, aesthetic approaches seek to understand cult films as so unique that they defy interpretation, and operate purely on an affective and visceral level (hyperbolic camp, pornography, extreme horror, weepies, schmaltz, or maudlin melodramas). These films are defined through their representational and stylistic excess, which frequently motivates their subsequent critical interpretation. Such definitions are most common in fanzines and specialist blogs, but echoes of this sentiment are traceable in academic studies as well: for instance, Jancovich et al. have defined cult via a "multitude of sins" (Jancovich et al. 2003a: 1), while Welch Everman refers to it as something "kind of offbeat, kind of weird, kind of strange" (Everman 1993: 1). Harper and Mendik have compared its intensity and physical impact to an "orgasm" (Mendik and Harper 2000a: 7), while for Allan Havis (2008: 2), the very nerve of cult film is related to "personal frisson," which he explains in the form of a recurring dream. Umberto Eco has perhaps come closest to a description of this elusive factor. He has explained the cult cinema experience as having an "archetypical appeal" that provokes a "sort of intense emotion accompanied by the vague feeling of a déja vu that everybody yearns to see again'" (Eco 1986: 200). Even though Eco is quick to separate the term archetype from any "mythic connotation" (1986: 200), and even though he shies away from invoking any reference to pontifical language, or to Carl-Gustav Jung's collective unconscious, his reference to a desire to relive some "magical moment" as a group is central to his argument.

Based on these previous attempts, and with the historical shifts in usage of the term in mind, any updated definition of cult cinema is both an amalgam of what has been said before and a departure from it. In our view, *cult cinema is a kind of cinema identified by remarkably unusual audience receptions that stress the phenomenal component of the viewing experience, that upset traditional viewing strategies, that are situated at the margin of the mainstream, and that display reception tactics that have become a synonym for an attitude of minority resistance and niche celebration within mass culture. In turn, filmmakers have used audiences' management of their "cult attitude" to consciously design films to include transgressive, exotic, offensive, nostalgic or highly intertextual narratives and styles. Although such opportunistic programming of cultism has created the impression that the term cult is now merely a marketing ploy, there continue to be receptions – especially in relation to the use of new technologies alongside traditional theatrical exhibition – that generate unexpected audience engagements which reconfigure the very notion of viewership.*

Structure of the Book

This book is structured into two main parts, each of which include a number of chapters on subjects that we feel are of particular importance to the study of cult cinema. The first part is "Receptions and Debates." Receptions are particularly important within the field of cult cinema, as the term emerged as a phenomenon that described particular reception patterns as opposed to specific textual features. In Chapter 1 we outline the important reception contexts which have been historically intertwined with cult status and move on to look at more specific instances of reception that can feed into cultism. In Chapter 2 we look at the importance of the marketplace in relation to cult cinema, an area that has been neglected in many studies of cult because of the way in which cult cinema has often been perceived as antipathetic to commercial strategies (a view which we do not share). Chapters 3 and 4 interrogate the institutions and mechanisms of prestige

and evaluation that govern films' immediate reception into public culture. Among the elements we discuss here are awards, festivals, conventions, censorship, and criticism. In Chapter 5 we focus on fandom and subcultures, both of which are interlinked with the study of cult cinema in important ways and which have increasingly gained academic attention in the recent past. Chapters 6 and 7 concentrate on two concepts that have attracted very specific forms of fandom, namely auteurs and stars. In Chapter 8 we discuss camp and paracinema: viewing strategies that have been labeled cultist because they are seen to diverge from normative viewing positions in order to create alternative evaluative criteria. The importance of differing from cultural norms has been a key theme running through debates on cult cinema and in the final three chapters we explore the idea of difference further. Chapter 9 analyses the concepts of transgression and freakery, Chapter 10 deals with issues of gender and sexuality, and Chapter 11 looks at issues of exoticism and transnationalism. In the final chapter in this part, Chapter 12, we look at how the historical bond between the concepts of cult and religion can inform modes of appreciation.

Part II of the book, "Genres and Themes," analyzes modes that have been prominent within discussions of cult cinema. We therefore identify the ways in which particular genres have been linked to cult cinema through exploring relevant historical and conceptual issues. In our discussion, we will first pay attention to motives, tropes, traditions, and genres that have been located outside of, and regarded as antithetical to, mainstream cinema, such as exploitation films and B-movies (Chapter 13), underground and avant-garde cinema (Chapter 14), drugs (Chapter 15) and forms of music such as rock, punk, or glamrock (Chapter 16). We will next discuss modes of cultism within genres and themes from films that use formulas and motives more firmly entrenched in traditions close to, or within, the mainstream. Chapter 17 looks at Hollywood cinema, Chapter 18 at the horror film, Chapter 19 at science fiction, and Chapter 20 at blockbusters. In each case, we will identify which films within these traditions are more likely to receive cult reputations, and through which means. Our last two chapters will focus on the notions of intertextuality (Chapter 21) and meta-cult (Chapter 22), and interrogate the increasing self-awareness and use of modes affiliated with cultism within discourses in the critical reception, production and marketing of cinema, a process that has impacted greatly on how films are identified as cult today.

The large number of chapters in the book reflects the many diverse threads that feed into the overall topic. Inevitably, there are overlaps between some sections. No one category is ever entirely isolated from others. The parts and the chapters are constructed to provide a structure which can be used by readers to navigate their way through this book. Within chapters, where there are overlaps with other chapters, we note this by referring to other chapters which provide further detail on the particular material under discussion. We hope the book thus allows readers to explore particular aspects of cult cinema and to map their own journey through this broad field.

As this book is primarily an overview of cult cinema studies up until this point (even though we would like to think of it as also extending current studies), it reflects some of the "blind spots" within such research. Perhaps the most important one that we are aware of is the very American-centric nature of cult cinema studies up until this point. That is, the focus on cult receptions has tended to focus on reception within the United States. It is true that there has been research on cult reception outside of the United States (primarily, but not limited to, the United Kingdom), but this is comparatively marginal. Following from this, the majority of films which get listed as cult films and discussed as such are also from the United States. There are certainly exceptions, and there are particular geographical areas that have become prime sites of cult production (notably Japan and Hong Kong, discussed in Chapter 11), but their films still tend to gain their cult reputations at least partly in the United States. While we have attempted to provide a range of cult films from different countries, we are bound by the state of research in the field up until now (although the growth of the internet has started to complicate, if not entirely eradicate, such trends). We hope that more research charting cult reputations in a greater diversity of contexts, such as Latin American cult cinema or Eurocults, will increase over the forthcoming years. Likewise, we anticipate that more research will be conducted into "female cults" (which we briefly touch upon in Chapters 6 and 10) and other areas that have hitherto fallen beneath the radar of cult cinema studies. This, we feel, demonstrates that there is a great deal of work still to be done within cult cinema studies, which signals a healthy and productive future for the subject.

Part I

Receptions and Debates

1

Cult Reception Contexts

We have proposed in our introduction that cult cinema is primordially known through its reception. In this chapter we provide a conceptual view of various elements that inform cult reception contexts. In order to illustrate how cult receptions differ from mainstream or normalized trajectories our attention first goes to the paradigmatic historical exemplar of cult cinema, namely the midnight movie. Next, we will outline the significance of a phenomenological approach to cult film reception. Subsequently, we will theorize the kind of experience cult receptions offer, and the value it generates.

Midnight Movies

Traditionally, the midnight movie is associated with New York. J. Hoberman and Jonathan Rosenbaum (1991: 310) observed that, on a worldwide scale, "New York is Palookaville when it comes to midnight movies," and there were vibrant late night scenes across North America and Europe.[1] Yet the New York scene is the only one thoroughly investigated and therefore we will use it as our key example.

Most scholars agree New York's midnight movie scene started when, in the late 1960s, underground and avant-garde theaters, with established clienteles and institutional affiliations, started programming risqué and exploitative materials. Mark Betz (2003) argues this shift was encouraged when "kinky" foreign art films and American underground films came together, near the end of the 1960s, in an exploitation/art circuit that emphasized the countercultural potential of cinema. Parker Tyler (1969) suggests a cross-fertilization between filmmakers who started to include more sex and violence in their films, and the demands of theaters catering to more permissive taste patterns, created a momentum in which practitioners and patrons encouraged each other to go ever further (Tyler 1969). The film usually credited with initiating the transition is the infamous *Flaming Creatures*, with its Dionysian theme and brutal rape-orgy. It was seized at several screenings and stunned audiences at others (for more on this film, see Chapters 3 and 14). Soon, other films with provocative aesthetic attitudes, and shocking or politically radical imagery drew similar receptions: *Queen of Sheba Meets the Atom Man*, *Blow Job*, *Sins of the Fleshapoids*, and *Chafed Elbows*, which Tyler describes as "the offbeat of the offbeat." It had a "marathon run at a small East Village theatre" (Tyler 1969: 53). Probably the most cultist trajectory was that of Kenneth Anger's *Scorpio Rising* and *Invocation of My Demon Brother*, both of which ran for long periods of time at late night slots in theaters East of Greenwich Village (Betz 2003; Tyler 1969). A constant reference in the receptions of these films was that of physical and mental liberation from repression – a function similar to that of ancient rituals.

At the beginning of the 1970s a string of New York theaters started midnight programming. The underground repertory was complemented with exploitation films with kaleidoscopic and apocalyptic motives, revivals of previously banned films, new and explicit horror, films pushing the boundaries of sexual permissiveness, and exotic and surreal foreign films (Figure 1.1). The acceleration was a sign of the

Cult Cinema: An Introduction. Ernest Mathijs and Jamie Sexton.
© 2011 Ernest Mathijs and Jamie Sexton. Published 2011 by Blackwell Publishing Ltd.

Figure 1.1   Midnight movie classics from 1970 to 2002: from left to right, *El Topo, The Rocky Horror Picture Show*, and *Donnie Darko*.

vibrancy of the counterculture, and of its widening into radical "outsider" films – the weirder the better. Topping them all was the visceral and symbolically heavy Mexican western-on-acid *El Topo*. Virtually unadvertised, *El Topo* sold out the Elgin theater for half a year. After a while, its screenings were described as a "midnight mass" (Hoberman and Rosenbaum 1991: 94). With the success of *El Topo*, the midnight movie really took off. Films as diverse as George Romero's zombie film and civil rights-metaphor *Night of the Living Dead*, Alejandro Jodorowsky's *The Holy Mountain* (a mystical adaptation of René Daumal's *Mount Analogue* to which Jodorowsky improvised a clever ending), and the mind-boggling surrealism of *Viva la muerte* attracted repeat audiences looking for "underground" thrills, and gusts of revelations – often aided by illegal substances. With these films, the midnight movie added an anti-establishment stance to its radical aesthetics; increasingly graphic depictions of sex and violence and explorations of immorality correlated with the audience's anxieties about the "violence engulfing the United States" (Hoberman and Rosenbaum 1991: 99, 112). Even if this feeling that the midnight movie exemplified a revolutionary attitude was more an impression than a fact, for midnight movie viewers the era's general unrest seemed to synchronize with what they experienced

on screen – as if it predicted "the end of the world as we know it."

As the 1970s progressed, the countercultural movement lost momentum. Midnight movies became ever more outrageous, but as their popularity widened across campuses, generic and aesthetic radicalism replaced ideological commentary. Art house and B-movie distributors such as Janus films and New Line Cinema became engaged in the midnight movie. Lesbian vampire movies, porn chic, blaxploitation movies, and foreign philosophical allegories such as *Antonio das Mortes, The Saragosa Manuscript*, or *WR: Mysteries of an Organism*, replaced the original batch of films. The most notorious among these films was *Pink Flamingos*, which tested viewers' threshold for revulsion – exactly the reason for its successful reception.

By the late 1970s, the midnight movie had become a staple of alternative cinema exhibition, the urban and college town equivalent of the drive-in. It was characterized by a hedonistic and wildly extravert context of rambunctious yet joyous celebrations. Many of the films championed in the circuit were as flamboyant as their audiences, with as figureheads campy rock musicals such as *Tommy*, or *The Rocky Horror Picture Show*. Proudly self-referential, these films were as much performances of cults, as cults themselves. Because of its endless runs *Rocky Horror* became a repertory in its own right (Weinstock 2007; Austin 1981a). Occasionally, "original" cults would still develop, around enigmatic films such as *Eraserhead*.

In the 1980s, much of the midnight movie attitude moved to VCR viewing, where "pause" and "rewind" functions on the remote control replaced the theatrical repeat viewing experience. What survived were nihilistic or flamboyant post punk movies such as *Heavy Metal*, the hardcore *Café Flesh*, or *Liquid Sky*. By the end of the decade many of the original midnight theaters had closed their doors, and filmmakers joined the burgeoning "independent" scene, or went underground again, with Abel Ferrara (*King of New York*) and Larry Fessenden (*Habit*) as crossover exceptions (Hawkins 2003). Only with large intervals would new midnight movie cults appear. The most prominent ones – *Priscilla, Queen of the Desert* and *Donnie Darko* – became the phenomenon's de facto eulogies. In 2001 "everything changed", writes Joan Hawkins:

> The World Trade Center in New York City was destroyed . . . The geography of downtown Manhattan has changed. So has the mood in the USA. And it's not at all clear what new avant-gardes and cult films might rise up to address what seems at this point to be a new era (one in which irony, for example, may not be considered an appropriate response to anything) (2003: 232).

For Hawkins, the cult of the midnight movie, a "moment when we believed that direct intervention in the country's spectacle would do some good," was over (2003: 232).

As befits cult receptions, the midnight movie did not really die. Since the 1990s the demise of the original phenomenon was balanced by three other trends. First, new films found their ways into festivals, which increasingly included midnight showings as part of their programs. Second, midnight premieres also became a feature of blockbuster releases vying for cult status. Third, the midnight movie phenomenon went into meta-mode. *Donnie Darko*, for instance, arguably the most famous midnight movie after 9/11, is also a meta-midnight movie. Its audiences at the New York Pioneer Theater, aware of the legacy of the midnight movie phenomenon, were not only continuing a tradition that had existed for more than thirty years, they also consciously knew they were contributing to

the heritage of the phenomenon by keeping it alive, or honoring the tradition by paying lip service to it. A decade after its first midnight run, college campuses, art houses, and festivals still screen *Donnie Darko* at midnight for this reason. Other instances of the meta-mode of the midnight movie include nostalgic revivals and queer celebrations of often overtly mainstream "classics" such as John Hughes's teen comedies (*Ferris Bueller's Day Off*), or sword and sorcery fantasy films (*Conan the Barbarian*). Their midnight success relies on the kitsch and camp attitude *Rocky Horror* had cemented as a core characteristic of the cult reception trajectory, and it reclaims some of the irony Hawkins claims it lost by exposing topical political attitudes through cheesy old movies. In its most recent form, this reflexive nostalgia has also included the original midnight movies, with relaunches of *El Topo* joining the never-ending runs of *Rocky Horror* and occasional newcomers, such as *The Room* (Bissell 2010).

In sum, the midnight movie highlights the key characteristics of a cult reception trajectory: films lumped together in a lively and "countercultural" exhibition context by their capacity to commit, through outrageously weird and explicit imagery, subcultural audience collectives, and to elicit performances of fandom and obsessions with the interconnectedness of elusive details intrinsic as well as alien to the films that enables allegorical and political interpretations that position themselves outside the realm of normalcy.

The Difficulty of Researching Cult Cinema

As the exemplar of the midnight movie illustrates, cult reception contexts are extremely heterogeneous. According to Mathijs and Mendik (2008a: 4–10), part of why they are called cult is because these receptions contain multitudes of competing and opposite discourses that stand in contrast of what a "normal" consumption process ought to be like. How does one begin to research such diverse contexts? At the basis of the cult reception context lies a fundamental philosophical question: does the value of a cultural product lie in its features and intentions or in the eye of the beholder? This question has important implications for the methodology of researching cult cinema.

Mathijs and Mendik (2008b: 15–16) distinguish between two schools of thought on this problem, with different implications:

> ontological approaches to cult cinema are usually essentialist: they try to determine what makes "cult cinema" a certain type of movie . . . Phenomenological approaches shift the attention from the text to its appearance in the cultural contexts in which it is produced and received. Such attempts usually see cult cinema as a mode of reception, a way of seeing films (2008b: 15).

In the ontological approach, the reception process is one that affirms the properties of the product. In the phenomenological approach the reception process negotiates these properties in the light of how they make themselves known – as a kind of phenomenon. Mathijs and Mendik refer to the work of Jerome Stolnitz as an effort that tries to solve the deadlock between these two positions. For Stolnitz (1960a, 1960b) any value is less a matter of the properties of the work or the viewer than of the experience generated by the flow of meaning during the process of perception. Stolnitz distinguishes between objectivist, subjectivist, and objective relativist views of experience. Objectivism, like the ontological approach, places the essence of value in the work itself – as if the work carries meaning within itself. This makes perception a process of detection. Subjectivism, on the contrary, identifies value as a faculty of the perceiver – as if the audience places its own meanings upon the work. This makes the work "empty."

Most reception studies of cinema embrace this approach. Janet Staiger (1992), for instance, explains that in order to understand how films work, and how the strategies through which they are given value operate, one has to distinguish between meanings generated through texts, through readers, and through contexts. Throughout, however, one has to accept

> that cultural artifacts are not containers with immanent meanings, that variations among interpretations have historical bases for their differences, and that differences and change are not idiosyncratic but due to social, political, and economic conditions, as well as to constructed identities such as gender, sexual

preference, race, ethnicity, class, and nationality. (Staiger 1992: xi)

Staiger argues that the best methodology for stressing contextual factors is to shift the focus of subjectivism from the mind of the spectator to the material conditions (the labor) involved in assigning meaning to a work – she calls this methodology a neo-Marxist approach. According to such an approach, studies of receptions should place emphasis on the use-value, exchange-value, and symbolic value of films (the latter being the value that is not expressed in material terms but in terms of the knowledge, expertise, kudos, and status, but also the dangers for exclusion and isolation any affiliation brings).

There have been several attempts to carve out procedures for this methodology. One attempt, by Barbara Klinger (1997), distinguishes between diachronic and synchronic approaches to film reception. The first stresses the materials that feature in a chain of events over time during a film's reception; the second emphasizes the materials from events that co-occur within the reception. The first method gives breadth, the second depth. Because cult reception trajectories are known to be volatile it is necessary to use both approaches simultaneously. Moreover, cult reception contexts are highly influenced by what Martin Barker (2004) has called unpredictable "ancillary materials": already existing artifacts and discourses that relate to the upcoming release that lead to polemics and legends and that prevent a nice match between expectations and the actual experience. The best example is probably the myth surrounding the troubled production history of *Casablanca*. Another good example is the abrupt way in which *Night of the Living Dead* was introduced to audiences, as part of a matinee double bill, before it became a midnight movie. This means that an essential part of the cult reception context is that it is "fractured." Its smooth running is interrupted or otherwise compromised, and audiences struggle to find an appropriate frame of reference for the newly released film.

Another attempt concentrates on the units of meaning that circulate in receptions. Each reception contains "intrinsic" and "extrinsic" references. Following David Bordwell (1989: 13), intrinsic references can be labeled "cues," elements of the film and its immediate production context used by viewers as tools in their construction of arguments about the film. Extrinsic references are "quotes," influences from outside the regular context that interfere with the reception. The degree to which a film's public course takes on the characteristics of a cult reception often depends on the abundance and the weight of extrinsic references. The longer a film's public visibility lasts (even in small communities), and the bigger the influences, the more likely it is to fracture a smooth reception. Controversies and moral panics are frequently a major part of the fractures in a cult reception trajectory.

There are some complications with the attempts we sketched. Topical events can penetrate so far into a film's reception they take over its direction. This is what initially happened to *Donnie Darko*. Even though it had been set for the Halloween weekend, traditionally a time for darker, more adult fare, *Donnie Darko* was too meta-generic to pose as a horror film, and the destruction of New York's World Trade Center on September 11th had temporarily eliminated audiences' appetites for dark materials and provocations. As one critic put it in hindsight: "why seek out talking rabbits warning of the end of the world when it already seemed to be happening?" Cult receptions also demonstrate psychological tendencies towards "insulation." Russ Hunter (2009, 2010) observes how subsequent to *Suspiria* (usually considered his best film) the reception of Dario Argento's films petrified into a series of mantras, which led to a refusal to include new achievements (or rather the lack of them) into reappraisals. The more Argento's reception became mantra-like, the more frequently it was called "cult." Such inoculation from new debates demonstrates how difficult it is to distinguish between instances of cultism that are convictions, and instances that are *performed* as attitudes, and if indeed there is a measurable difference.

Finally, there is the complication of a cult reception context's endurance. Films such as *The Wizard of Oz* or *Casablanca* have been enjoyed *as cult* by generations of audiences. The label cult is also instrumental to the long-term reputation of *The Rocky Horror Picture Show*, or *Pink Flamingos*, films that can be said to be on perennial release, as well as to the cult status of *Emmanuelle*, which played in theaters for a full decade. As figureheads for a certain period and style, their long-term receptions are imbued with a sense of nostalgia,

one that is equally often a nostalgia for a period (a zeitgeist or a popular myth) as a nostalgia for a kind of cultic experience. For years, *El Topo* was virtually unavailable – it only made it more cult. The search for bootlegged copies of *Superstar: The Karen Carpenter Story* quickly became a characteristic of its cult instead of an obstacle to it – as the vibrant illegal trade of VHS copies of it testifies.

As a result of these complications cult reception contexts ultimately remain exceptions to insights into how film receptions work. It is in this important sense that cult cinema is kept isolated from the mainstream – as an unresearchable, "fugitive" object with elusive receptions that don't "work" and that are in essence, dysfunctional and unproductive.

Cult Cinema as Phenomenal Experience

The way into investigating cult cinema receptions, and cult cinema, as an object of research lies in operationalizing that exceptionalism. This is possible through the third view Stolniz isolates, namely objective relativism. This concept assumes value and meaning lie in between product and perceiver – in the actual *phenomenal experience* of the spectator, and the mutual material environment of both. Adopting a phenomenological perspective, argues Dudley Andrew (1985: 631), attempts to make visible reason "on the run." When we look at the ways in which our exemplar of the midnight movie presents itself, a more matching approach hardly seems imaginable. There are several reasons why Stolnitz's practical form of phenomenology, objective relativism, and its focus on the phenomenal experience, provide a good framework for studying cult reception contexts.

First, the phenomenal experience is an aesthetic one. It is an experience that is sought for its own sake – as an end in itself. It sketches the experience as one that cannot be purposeful, that cannot be an end to a means. Otherwise the perception would shut down under pressure of the perceiver's desire to find functions for the work (Fenner 2008: 104–106). There are several advantages to outlining the reception of cult cinema as a phenomenal experience of an aesthetic kind. It offers the opportunity to balance traditional points of attention in a reception study (such as box office performance, critical reception, marketing, and so on) with a focus on elements such as emotive overtones, degrees of investment, or formations of attachment. It also offers a possibility to investigate terms such as loyalty, time-wasting, excessive idolatry, or enthrallment in a reception. These terms are exactly the kinds that are found time and again in descriptions of cult receptions as "useless."

A second characteristic of seeing cult receptions as a phenomenal experience concerns the space in between the work and the perceiver. A phenomenal experience implies closeness, and so does cult cinema. This spatial relationship is to be understood as both geographical and mental. The cult film experience is indeed often described as one of close proximity to the screen (enthrallment with the giant canvas), to fellow viewers (huddled together in communion), and to the subject matter (overly close-reading of themes and motives). The two most commonly employed metaphors are that of the darkness of the theater (much loved in lyrical assessments of the midnight movie), or that of being glued to a home viewing set. The mental closeness refers to the viewer as someone near to the film, someone with a connection and an investment in it, and, as we will see in our discussions of fandom, someone with a sense of ownership over the film. At the same time the closeness also assumes that the object itself (the film) has some agency in the relationship, not only as carrier of cues and clues, but also something that first receives its meaning from the viewer and then talks back. Often, the closeness makes it difficult for the researcher to clearly distinguish between viewer- and object-agency (for an elaboration, see Miller 2010: 42–78).

A third characteristic Stolnitz draws is that of disinterestedness. Disinterestedness needs to be seen here not as a refusal to engage with a particular reception, nor as a position of free or detached engagement towards it, but rather as a form of decontextualized commitment, a sense of focus. It is not in the film that the cult reception is disinterested. Rather it concentrates intensely on everything to do with the film, the properties and appearances of which are interrogated and elaborated upon with detail and repetitively. Repeat viewing, as a physical reliving but also as a reactivation of emotion, is a key component and

recurrent characteristic of cult receptions (Wood 1991: 156–166, Châteauvert and Bates 2002: 90). The parallel with a religious exegesis of sacred texts is an obvious one. This is not to say that any attention for the rest of world is absent, only that it is viewed through the lens of the text and its affiliate discourses. Norman Kreitman (2006) employs the term "cultural disinterestedness" to identify this form of attention. He adds that it operates with a keen sense of the "generalized other," and that it can achieve a feeling of liberation from immediate personal concerns. Jean Châteauvert and Tamara Bates (2002: 93) observe how film cultism always harbors the desire to know the other's experience. For cult receptions, this characteristic is essential, as it highlights the extent to which the perception is always part of a larger whole – never limited only to one individual.

Cult Cinema as Bad Experience

An important qualification governing cult receptions is their perceived status as "bad," as an inferior form of experience. Watching a film for its own sake, from really close up, and with an intense focus that channels everything else through that film's perception in order for it to achieve meaning, is generally regarded as something an enlightened or informed viewer would not do. Ritual repeat-viewing is regarded as childish, boring, compulsive, but not tasteful. It goes, for instance, against the template of the cinephile as someone with an omnivorous curiosity and taste for films of quality.

Many cult reception contexts explicitly refer to the films as "bad," as poor or distasteful filmmaking. This badness has moral as well as aesthetic components. In chapters throughout this book we will analyze instances of cult films that are celebrated because of their representations of transgression, abjection, freakery, grossness, gore, misogyny, or cruelty. Likewise, cult receptions are known to revel in exoticism, fetishism, idolatry, and repetitiveness. This badness is as frequently approached ironically as it is carried as a sign of pride.

The tendency to classify the cult experience as inferior depends largely upon the degree of rationality and freedom attributed to how people watch films.

Studies of receptions of cult films often deal with expert audiences (such as critics, connoisseurs, or taste leaders). Often this is for practical reasons: these groups are the ones who most visibly embrace the positive attitude, the direct access, and the obsession with detail typical for disinterestedness – they are the easiest to research. If one looks at some influential studies of film reception contexts, especially fan studies, that apply to cult cinema, one gets the impression there is an assumption all such viewers operate as perfectly rational agents, not affected by cultural or social conditions, and totally free to choose their affiliations (Peary 1981; Jenkins 1992; Sconce 1995, Taylor 1999). Not only is this an artificial form of rationality; it is also far removed from the reality of many cult receptions. The liberty to browse freely between kinds of receptions before electing one is balanced by personal inhibitions, and by the cultural and social conditions that influence the environment within which the phenomenal experience occurs. It seems obvious to state that choice is limited by the material conditions within a given time and place. Next to that, alignments and affiliations frequently come through certain cultural ties, such as class, gender, ethnicity, or heritage. To use Kreitman's terms: the sense of the generalized other often looms large. These conditions make concepts such as loyalty, affordability, and pride, *and* the connections between them (such as declaring a loyalty to an affordable item at a certain time and place as a source of pride) a key feature in cult cinema receptions. Yet many scholars of cult cinema and many researchers of film receptions overlook these conditions and consequences.

One of the most prominent scholarly efforts to address this limited freedom has come from Pierre Bourdieu (1984). According to Bourdieu, taste can be distinguished in "tastes of luxury" and "tastes of necessity." Tastes of luxury are typical of the kind of freedom and limitless choice assumed by rational agency, though they can depend on habit as much as conscious decision-making. Tastes of necessity are, Bourdieu argues, the result of a "forced choice" that is fulfilled not only because it is an economic necessity but also a cultural reflex of people who "are inclined to fulfill it, because they have a taste for what they are anyway condemned to" (1984: 178). Bourdieu's conceptualization of taste as socially conditioned has been

very influential. Yet his conclusions are often criticized by studies of cult receptions that continue to assume that cult viewers exercise free taste. In fact, the cult receptions of "tasteless" films (gore, pornography, rape-revenge, video nasties, trash) are regarded as choices of luxury by cult fans who thereby assert themselves as taste leaders because they can elect to apply aesthetic criteria to otherwise unredeemable movies. Reading protocols such as "camp" and "paracinema," which we will discuss at length in Chapter 8, are examples of this assertion.

One important exception to this view is the work of Mark Jancovich (2002). Paraphrasing Bourdieu, Jancovich sees these protocols as games of formalist sophistication: "As Bourdieu shows . . . the privileging of form over function asserts the 'superiority [of the bourgeois] over those who, because they cannot assert the same contempt for . . . gratuitous luxury and conspicuous consumption, remain dominated by ordinary interests and urgencies'" (Jancovich 2002: 312). In this sense, cult receptions display tastes of necessity as much as tastes of luxury. Cult reception contexts can thus be conceptualized as sites of struggle between choices of necessity on the one hand and games of luxury typical to bastions of middle-class luxury such as college towns or urban centers like Manhattan (locations where the midnight movie blossomed) on the other hand, with "taste" (and tastelessness) as the tool of distinction between kinds of cult receptions.

Cult Cinema as Collective Experience

A major way in which cult receptions are different from other forms of film receptions is that they are part of a collective process. We have already alluded to the fact that cult reception contexts work with a sense of the generalized other and that they are tied to social conditions of groups of people. Of course this notion is embedded in the very definition of the term cult as a community, a commonality of congregation that sees itself at odds with normalized culture. But it is not always this clear-cut. The collectivity of cult receptions is not just an aggregate of individual perceptions; it is more an impression of a collective effort that supersedes it. Put otherwise, the phenomenal experience is a shared one, even when the actual perception occurs individually.

This means that the collectivity of cult receptions is frequently a sensibility in addition to a material fact. There have been numerous attempts to describe collective processes of cultural reception of this nature. Siegfried Kracauer (1926) and other members of the Frankfurt School of sociology, employed the terms "crowds" and "masses" to describe movie audiences unaware of each other's presence yet attuned to the same points of interest. Throughout this book we will return to how film cultists and fans have been described through labels that stress collectivity. Overall, the intent was pejorative: by describing these audiences as groups they are denied individuality and agency – they are seen as an effect of their consumption rather than an active force shaping it.

Recent decades have seen a change in that patterning of collectivity. Benedict Anderson (1983) has used the term "imagined communities" to refer to autonomous and sovereign communities not based on face-to-face everyday contact yet sharing strong convictions and opinions. The conceptualization of community that comes closest to capturing the collectivity of cult receptions comes from Michel Maffesoli, who uses the term "affective communities" to describe what he regards as instances of neo-tribalism in contemporary society. According to Maffesoli (1996a: 40), such communities are active agents rather than powerless or passive recipients, even in their resistance to productivity. He observes how they place an emphasis on style and hedonism as a reaction against what is perceived as an increased instrumentalization of the world:

> the more one encourages a "utensilitarian" conception of existence, then the more, as if in response, a sociality asserts itself, one that, on the contrary, rests on the imaginary, on an existential casualness, a search for hedonism, a shared pleasure in living, and on appearance and the play of forms. (Maffesoli 1996a: 40)

Maffesoli stresses how this reaction is shared and social, a collective effort. Furthermore, his observation of how it relativizes utilitarianism acknowledges the aesthetic component of the collectivity – a core component of the phenomenal experience. Maffesoli's preferred metaphor for this conceptualization is the mythical figure of Dionysus (see Chapter 12). Maffesoli's description fits perfectly formations of fandom that have developed around cult receptions. It also matches the analysis of various subcultures (see Chapter 5).

Maffesoli (1993a, 1993c) further observes how collectivity is not always expressed in numbers, such as attendance figures. It often remains hidden ("imaginary"). The collectivity we speak of here is often an impression, a feeling of feeling together, an impression of solidarity and sharing that informs one's emotional attitude, and not necessarily one's material life (though it has effects in that material life). According to Maffesoli it is also a collectivity inspired by directness of experience, by hope, by a tendency to imagine other times (nostalgic pasts or utopian or even apocalyptic futures), and by a desire to dissociate itself from purposefulness. Instead of purpose it preferences "drifting" and the seeking of pleasure in what Maffesoli calls "the excesses of everyday life" (Maffesoli 2005; also see Mathijs 2010a). These elements certainly influenced the exemplar of the midnight movie, even in its post-heyday incarnations.

There is a tension between Maffesoli's conceptions of collectivity and those underpinning a lot of studies of fans and subcultures. Maffesoli's observations concentrate on radical degrees of collectivity that carry a deep suspicion of authority and an anarchist resistance to it, and that refuse to settle into "the real totalitarianism [of] interpretative systems [that] reinforce every social and political institution" (2005: 199). This is a collectivity of simultaneously active and passive opposition to dominant ideology that in its anti-intellectualism stands at odds with some more radical activist, utopian, and nihilist forms of cultism. It also stands at odds with more authority-friendly versions of cult reception contexts that see themselves less in opposition to dominant ideology and/or are co-opted into normalized patterns of consumption and behavior. Tensions between degrees of commitment in the collective experience, for instance between oppositional versus co-opted cult receptions, inclusive versus exclusive cult receptions, omnivorous versus univorous receptions, and sincere versus ironic or performative receptions, will inform much of our discussions of the cult experience.

At its broadest, for instance at moments when films such as *The Rocky Horror Picture Show* or *The Lord of the Rings* acquire a sort of cultural presence wider than their immediate niche appeal, the collective experience can be close to a sensibility that typifies a zeitgeist. At such moments it can be referred to as "part of the fabric" of society or a defining feature of the "social ambiance" (Maffesoli 1993b). When *The Lord of the Rings* films became a massive success some critics saw this as the result of the fact that its niche, which was frequently described as "geekdom," was now no longer a cultist, marginal position "but a formative force in the cultural imagination of our times" (quoted in Biltereyst, Mathijs and Meers 2007: 46). In this book we will analyze specific articulations of various senses of collectivity on numerous occasions.

Cult Cinema as Connected Experience

In some of his analyses of affective communities, Maffesoli (1996b, 2007) remarks that they give rise to "networks of relationships" whereby the network itself creates a feeling of belonging. The implication is that next to the collectivity the very notion of the network is of importance to maintain a sense of togetherness. This observation is not new. The idea finds its roots in the 1950s, when the concept of "para-social interaction" became a central component in attempts to understand how mass media could offer viewers a sense of close interaction with performers (Horton and Wohl 1956). In the 1960s the idea also appeared in media theories and semiotics (the work of Marshall McLuhan, Umberto Eco, and Jean Baudrillard).

The concept of connectivity fully entered onto the foreground in the 1980s and 1990s, when the idea of the network became the point of focus of Manuel Castells, who employed it to posit the idea of a "network society" (1996–1998). According to Castells, the end of the twentieth century (and of the millennium) is a moment in which a new kind of global society is coming into place, one that is based on three processes: the information technology revolution, a string of crises in capitalism and statism, and the coming of age of a range of social and cultural movements such as environmentalism, libertarianism, and feminism (what Maffesoli would call "neo-tribes"). Castells calls this emerging society one of "real virtuality" – a pun on one of its technological tools of imagination, virtual reality, but also an indication of how much of that new society exists as a network of links and connections between "cultural communes," which produce what Castells calls "global hypertexts," units of information in constant flow. Jean Baudrillard's concept of the simulacrum, the copy without original, is a powerful influence on this vision (Castells 1998: 336; also see Bell 2006: 55). Castells' network society is not a program for an ideal world, nor is it a dire forecast for a dystopic world – it explains how "bad" *and* "good" cultural communes exist in spite of public spheres that pressure them.[2]

If we apply the idea of the network to cult reception contexts the emphasis shifts from the "essence" of these groups (that what makes them unique) to the ways in which they establish and differentiate themselves in relation to the rest of the world (that what connects them) through the quantities and qualities of their connectedness. In theory, this allows for the mapping of cult receptions in terms of their proximities, alignments, or affiliations as much as in terms of their isolated identities. It is a perspective that is less concerned with the preservation of the essence of each group in alignments between communes or tribes (to use Maffesoli's term) and more with how the tangents through which they share contexts of action shape their existence.

Since Maffesoli and Castells presented their ideas there have been a number of attempts to apply them to cultist receptions. Joshua Meyrowitz (2002) uses the concept of connectedness in relation to fan obsessions and degrees of intimacy between fans and celebrities – what he calls the cult of media friendship. Diken and Laustsen (2002) discuss *Fight Club* as a film about cultural communities (for instance neo-fascist ones). Judith Halberstam (2003) and Angela Wilson (2008) use it to examine lesbian punk-rock and Riot Grrrl subcultures. Bernard Cova, Robert Kozinets, and Avi Shankar (2007) apply it to the receptions of goth subculture, surf culture, and *Star Trek* wikimedia. It also informs numerous studies of online fandom. What remains under-researched is how links *between* micro-groups fuel cult receptions. Early twenty-first-century cult films such as *Donnie Darko*, *Ichi the Killer* or *Ginger Snaps* have derived at least part of their cult reputation from crossing over between various cultural communities, and as such they are perfect illustrations of how the connected experience affects cinema cultism, fandom, and subcultures. For instance, the cult status of *Ginger Snaps* largely lies with how it links cultists from various cultural communities (horror, Goth, lesbian, feminist) around an affective catch-phrase ("morbid sisters") that allows the building or sustaining of bridges between each of these communes – it is a "facilitator" of crossovers (Figure 1.2). In that sense, *Ginger Snaps* is an exemplar of a new kind of cult reception, equally deep in its commitment, but less easily pinned down to just one type, and because of that more empowered. For the study of cult cinema this perspective can be of great importance. For one, the concept of connectedness

explains how a shift might be needed from studying cult receptions in function of finding their essence to studying them in function of how they connect to each other.

Cult Cinema as Surplus Experience

Cult reception contexts frequently upset protocols of meaning making. Next to generating values that can be understood in terms of the mainstream (i.e. in terms of productivity and functionality) cult reception contexts generate what Paul Ricoeur has called a "surplus of meaning and of value which is qualified but not exhausted by analysis" (quoted in Andrew 1985: 631). We would call it surplus experience.

In cult receptions, a connection equals an intimate affiliation, and what is connected acquires power. In a move to update Marxist methodologies of

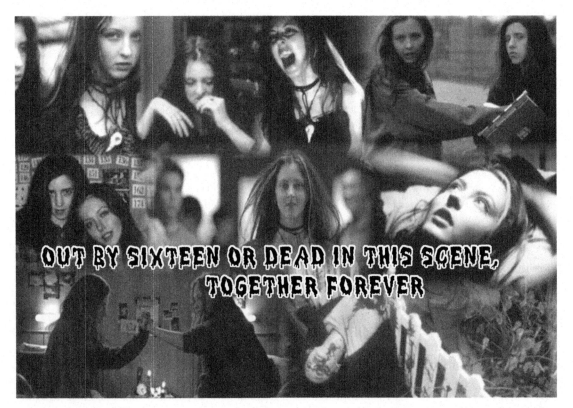

Figure 1.2   A collage of imagery from *Ginger Snaps* arranged around the "morbid sisters" motive and dialog: "out by sixteen or dead in this scene, together forever."

understanding material culture, Jean Baudrillard (1981, 1990) argued that objects – such as films – do not uniquely occupy a use value (their practical value) or even exchange value (their monetary value), but that they rely on symbolic value: they trigger needs and desires which attract cultist affections – such as investments in paraphernalia, antiques, or memorabilia. The connections of such objects, and object-signs, to each other generates a complex network of proxy seductions and fetishisms. One example of this is the appearance of an actor at a fan convention, where they sign autographs on posters and where, via exclusive meet-and-greet sessions, distinctions are drawn between those who can converse with the actor, and those who remain outside that circle. These networks of seduction, appropriation, and fetishism can be summarized as what Andrew Ross (1989: 210) has called a "cult of knowledge and expertise." In terms of value, these networks produce as a surplus value: they are the outcome of a form of labor in which the involvement of the perceiver is crucial, but which is not generally recognized as a productive effort, and does not render a direct profit. Therefore the surplus generated by cultist details is often called wasteful, a "geeky" self-indulgence that does not advance cinema, or improve the material conditions or cultural literary of the perceiver. The components informing these extensions of the perception process are furthermore elusive, obfuscated, and difficult to chart because they exist at the margins of what is accepted as evidence and material fact: gossip, trivia, hearsay, legend, prejudice, are often relegated as pieces of information, excluded from data as insignificant. Because of their contentious nature they pose a challenge to methods of analysis (they are almost impossible to codify, quantify, or qualify). In terms of a cult reception context it means cultists will always look for a further meaning, even when there is none, because connecting things gives the impression that one displays expertise and is, hence, powerful.

A complication is that not all elements of a cult reception are of equal weight. Nor does the physical film itself remain at the center of its reception. Klinger (1989) has called attention to the ways in which actions accompanying the reading of a film allow for "digressions" in which contextual information provides clues for enjoyment and communication with the text that compete with the ones in the text itself. This is at least in part informed by an ability to connect the (experience of the) text to an active knowledge of (and willingness to use) contextual or ancillary information. Some receptions disregard a film's features altogether. The video nasties (films whose UK video releases were caught up in a controversy in the early 1980s) are an example where a reputation of a group of films developed independent of their intentions or even their actual content: they were lumped together by the press, and subsequently by prosecutors, for their supposed impact on the viewer, not because they shared any common features (Barker 1984; Egan 2007). Furthermore, some meanings cannot be seen in separation of other texts, such as sequels, remakes, serializations, or re-imaginations. Trailers, double bills, directors' cuts, added footage, accompanying soundtracks, retrospectives, revivals, rediscoveries, restorations, prequels, spoofs, and new cultural sensibilities all impact on that reception. Literally anything can change public opinion on a film, as is demonstrated by Klinger's (1994) research on the changing status of the films of Douglas Sirk, and Cynthia Erb's (1998) study of the changes in the reputation of *King Kong* as a cultural icon after numerous remakes, appropriations, and parodies. Any research into a cult reception context, then, needs to integrate the complex patterns of influences and opinions operating in particular situations (synchronically), and maps them as processes over time (diachronically), all analyzed as types of "talk" – uttered by those involved in the production, presentation, and perception – in order to map the combinations of strategies used to forge (or fail) meaning. The obsessive mining for details and endless *kinds of talk* imply an *explosive* and *completist* frame of reference for cult receptions. For those outside that frame of reference any knowledge it generates is irrelevant, *only* surplus.

There have been numerous attempts to conceptualize the obsession with connectedness and cross-talk. According to Dana Polan (1978) they are part of an increase in "self-reflexivity" of cinema. Robert Stam (1985) has called it "reflexivity." Umberto Eco (1986) sees it as "intertextuality." Danielle Aubry and Gilles Visy (2009) label it "transtextuality." Whatever its label, early attempts regard the concept as a countercurrent to cinema's mainstream. Polan calls it Brechtian; Stam links it to Jean-Luc Godard's inter-rogations of film language. But in later discussions of the concept it is less seen as exceptional and more as a routine or protocol that has gradually been embedded into the very fabric of cult film, as well as into the range of expectations audiences have of cult films, so that every cult film becomes intertextual by default – that is how Mathijs and Mendik (2008a) present it. There are some small but significant differences between the various ways in which this cross-talk is discussed. We will address these in chapters that analyze the specific contexts in which they are used (see Chapters 2, 17, 18, 21).

There is some dispute over connectedness and cross-talk as surplus experience. One school of thought holds that the obsession with trivia is playful and revealing yet without relevance for the perceiver. The affilia-tions that connections allow are less causal than rhe-torical, circumstantial, or incidental. They can be made for the sake of it. For Robert Stam (1985), the way in which films can invite connections, and be reflexive, is a sign of their aesthetic maturity. It testifies of expertise in contemporary culture, of pos-ture to show off one's social standing within an existing cultural constellation, but also of a need to demonstrate some connections are indeed precious in a society that increasingly comes across as detached, specialized, and fragmented. But it does not do anything of a wider cultural relevance (see Chapter 21 for an elaboration). Against that view stands another school of thought, which claims that if one looks carefully at the moral and political consequences of the obsession with de-tails, it becomes clear that they can *also* be used to uproot existing constellations and instead promote revolutionary ideals (Ross 1989; Havis 2008). Think-ing through the ideological implications of the

"transgressions" of culture that occur in films said to be cult can create imbalances, provoke controversies, and stimulate utopian ideas. Through their fascination with details, then, the surplus experience that cult receptions generate allows audiences to "imagine" another world with other rules, and laugh at that world at the same time. It creates a rebellious attitude of defiance at odds with what dominant forces in a society endorse.

Conclusion: Cult as Performance?

In this chapter we have argued that cult cinema is best served by an approach that has its philosophical roots in a practical form of phenomenology. We have moved in this chapter from cult cinema's paradigmatic exem-plar, the midnight movie, and the smallest possible unit of perception, the spectator, to the largest possible, a society, and we have identified the cult experience on each of these levels. Needless to say all of these levels inform each other.

In conclusion, we would like to highlight one aspect that we briefly touched upon in our summary of the history of the midnight movie, namely the fact that in several cases the cult is less lived than performed. The distinction between an actual, sincere, and authentic cult experience and a performance of one is difficult to make and we will argue throughout this book that in many cases it is virtually impossible to make the distinction. In most of our chapters we will discuss instances of cult receptions and indeed of moments in cult films that can both be seen as authentic *as well as* a performance of an experience. We will tie some of those debates into an organized view on just how performative a cult experience and, by extension, the very notion of cult is.

Notes

1. In Paris, it is often associated with the ten-year run of *Emmanuelle*. In Los Angeles it has kept close links to the underbelly of Hollywood, with a special interest in reviv-ing "maudit" and "bad" Hollywood films such as *Plan Nine from Outer Space* or *The Room*. In London it is connected to the vibrant nightlife of Soho. In Antwerp cinemas like The Monty linked to the cosmopolitan attractions a port brings. In Ottawa it is still associated with the Mayfair cinema, whereas in Vancouver all original midnight movie houses have been replaced by multimedia centers such as

the Rio Theatre. San Francisco (with its Roxy Theater and Berkeley's Pacific Film Archive), Cambridge MA (with its Brattle Theater, which started the *Casablanca* cult), and Montreal (with its Rue St Catherine repertory theaters) also had lively midnight scenes. Many American college towns, such as Ann Arbor, MI, Madison, WI, Austin, TX, or Lexington, KY, also were, or are, at some point or another, thriving markets for midnight movie programming (Waller, 1991).

2. The concept of connectedness has been the subject of discussion for many decades, from the experiments of psychologist Stanley Milgram in the 1960s, to Malcolm Gladwell's musings on "Connectors" as people essential to setting trends. The concept of connectedness gained popularity in the early 1990s when it became the central metaphor of John Guare's play *Six Degrees of Separation*. In the play, a character declares: "I read somewhere that everybody on this planet is separated by only six other people. Six degrees of separation." (Guare 1994: 81). According to Gene Plunka (2005: 352), Guare's play exposes how in an attempt to "make a difference and feel we belong" the only thing one *can* do is *connect*. A revealing variation of the degrees of separation concept is the cult game *Six Degrees of Kevin Bacon*. The challenge is to connect actor Kevin Bacon to as many other celebrities in as few steps as possible.

2

The Cult Cinema Marketplace

When *Blues Brothers* director John Landis visited a cult film conference once as a guest of honor he was amazed at the attention cult films are accorded. "Back in the day, when someone called your film cult it meant it had bombed. Why study failures?" Like most other films, cult films are intended to provide a healthy financial profit in return for investment, even if the emotional component of that investment was a "labor of love." Landis's remark suggests cult films have a reputation of not delivering such profit. However, while it remains a very risky business, the label "cult" also has enviable commercial prospects, with potentially high profits margins. This chapter looks at cult cinema from the angle of political economy. It pays close attention to labor, funding and entrepreneurship, marketing, niche promotion, exhibition culture, and black markets.

Production Culture

Studying the production and business routines of films known as cult can provide valuable insights into the conditions that help shape the prefigurations of those receptions. This chapter aims to do that by painting the contexts of inception, labor, production, the aid of technology in the creation of films, and the attitudes, routines and practices as a culture in itself – a community very much like the kind anthropologists study. This community is what John Thornton Caldwell (2008) has called a "production culture."

The production culture of cult cinema is rife with attitudes of hyperbole and reflexivity, and it behaves as "a masonry" (Caldwell 2008: 36). Practitioners in the film and television industry display a high degree of self-importance (hyperbole), and self-consciousness about their profession (reflexivity). Some of this attitude is seen as inflated entitlement or arrogance, and as the "role-playing" of tasks (playing to "be" an industry professional). But these attitudes also reflect the degree of commitment, dedicated labor (and long hours), and professional care that goes into the production of films – a vocation more than a day task. It can lead to surprising innovations, often improvised under tense pressure, and to bursts of creativity in solving practical problems within strict financial constraints against looming deadlines. As Caldwell points out, the hyperbole and reflexivity cannot be separated from the perception of importance that the world accords to the film industry. The press, ancillary industries, and circles of fans, business associates, and dignitaries see being associated with the industry as important, and the industry sells its self-importance as a "culture" one wants to be associated with (2008: 10–11). "Genesis myths," "making-it sagas," "war stories," and gossip, rumors, buzz, and reputation play a crucial role in the sustenance of this culture. They provide a framework for the trade of the product that is delivered, and they establish career capital (2008: 37–68). Since much hinges upon the public delivery of a final product (a film), there is a careful balancing of presenting to that public rituals of trade and turf marking implied in this culture: occasionally on-set

Cult Cinema: An Introduction. Ernest Mathijs and Jamie Sexton.
© 2011 Ernest Mathijs and Jamie Sexton. Published 2011 by Blackwell Publishing Ltd.

troubles or "behind the scenes" revelations fit the profile, and are willingly leaked, but sometimes they are kept under cover.

Cult films differ from this system in that their attitudes of hyperbole and reflexivity seem to be more extreme than those usually accepted as normal. In jumping out of bounds they fit the reputation of cult cinema as "out of control." *Casablanca*, with its much-told production legends, is a famous example of this, but much of the production culture of Hong Kong cult cinema of the 1980s, or Italian horror of the 1970s operates in similar ways. The degree to which hyperbole and reflexivity are part of the production contexts is evidenced in the stunt work, the fight choreography, the work of crews and cast, and the professional approach to the subjects – always more over-the-top or self-aware than is the norm in Hollywood (Card 1991: 66–78; Reid 1994; MacCormack 2004). For Umberto Eco (1986), this quality is what makes *Casablanca* the archetypical cult film. It is also evident in products that become cult because of their failures, when the final product of labor is perceived as an abject fiasco, and the reason for that failure is seen as the result of inefficient use of skill and craftsmanship. This was the case with high-profile disasters such as *Heaven's Gate* and *Waterworld*, films known as megalomaniac and extravagant.

Another noticeable set of differences concerns scale and skill. While many cult films have had reasonable budgets, many of them are made for much less money than traditional cinema. This is a particular characteristic of exploitation cinema and B-movies (which we analyze in Chapter 13). Yet even in the classical poverty row and exploitation industries, and in the non-industrial cultures of avant-garde and underground cinema hyperbole and reflexivity remained a prevalent dynamic. Crew and cast working on films that became cult often display a "superior survivor" tactic – as if referring to an experience one has to be initiated to and graduate into. It is often associated with a "military-identity" complex, which Caldwell sees in particular with stunt and camera crews, with nomadic labor systems and working-class machismo (2008: 113).

The best example in that respect are special effects crews, in particular those of Tom Savini, Rick Baker, Rob Bottin, or Gary Zeller (also see Chapter 18).

To illustrate the similarity with cult audiences it is insightful to quote one of Caldwell's sources at length here:

> I would say that our company is a kind of "tribal" thing. Once you are in, and get the secret tattoos – we're then in there as a family operation . . . The core group that we have is intensely loyal. When work is slow they'll come in anyway . . . It's not just a paycheck issue. I'm old school. You just gotta love the work. And one of the bad things that happened when everything went digital was suddenly – compared to the old days – there were enormous sums of money thrown around . . . When this Hollywood cycle goes bust, we'll see a lot of these folks go away. And the nerds like us will still be there – doing the work. (2008: 127)

This attitude certainly helps sell products as "cult-like." Occasionally, companies and crews straddle the distinction between cult and mainstream: the KNB EFX company of special effects combines work for blockbuster Hollywood productions with smaller, more "streetwise" productions with lots of cult potential, like the *Ginger Snaps* films, *From Dusk 'till Dawn* or *Splice*. The creative challenge of accomplishing a vision within strict constraints and volatile conditions posed by these productions, and the war stories and street credibility that come with that, transfer easily into cult reputations. They become a point of pride.

Put together, next to a very high degree of reflexivity and hyperbole, the production culture of cult cinema appears to be more accidental, improvisational, renegade and subject to professional obsession than mainstream cinema, operating on a much smaller scale but with a notably bigger "family" influence (Caldwell uses the word nepotism).

Funding and Distribution

The spirit of independence of cult films is evidenced in their unique funding structure, complete with unsavory accounting tricks. The opaque financing and accounting practices of colorful figures such as Coffin Joe, or the dispersed funding of Alain Robbe-Grillet's films, have become legendary (Barcinski 2003: 27–38; Tombs 2003: 352–356). So is the impenetrable funding structure of *Daughters of Darkness*, evidenced in its seven production partners from six different territories

(Mathijs 2005b: 455). Other curious examples include the financing of *Caligula* by adult magazine *Penthouse*, the patched financing of Orson Welles's films late in his career, and the participatory, communal self-financing by the crew of *Mariken van Nieumeghen* (Agterberg 2004). The long incubation periods that several cult films went through contributed to their appeal, but were nightmarish in terms of financing. David Lynch started work on *Eraserhead* with a small grant, and worked stubbornly on it for a full five years. *El Topo* took four years to complete.

Two oppositions run through the funding of cult cinema. The first pitches commercial funding against state involvement. The overall majority of cult cinema is commercial in funding. Subject matter is partly responsible for this. Films such as *Emmanuelle*, *Behind the Green Door*, or *Café Flesh* would probably have never been possible if local authorities had to approve their funding. In some cases producers consciously avoided state involvement because of the associations of art house and "legitimate" filmmaking it brought with it. *Daughters of Darkness* is one such example. Director Harry Kümel wanted to produce "something nasty" and therefore chose to forego state-supported funding (Mathijs 2005b: 454). Yet state involvement is not uncommon in cult cinema, especially in Europe. State subsidy programs became well established in most European countries in the late 1960s and early 1970s, and they were frequently complemented by tax shelter systems that encouraged investments into cinema, exactly at a time of increased permissiveness, when state grants and funds would be less likely to declare ineligible the kinds of materials that would have been rejected a few years earlier. As a result, local authorities have been a substantial factor in funding films that acquired cult followings. In several cases this caused outrage, especially when the features of the films in question were deemed morally challenging. Canadian films from *Shivers* to *Ginger Snaps* have suffered (or benefited, depending on the view one takes) from such debates, as have Paul Verhoeven's *Turkish Delight*, in the Netherlands, the Belgian *Man bites Dog*, several of Pasolini's films in Italy, and the films of Dusan Makaveyev and Jan Svankmajer when Eastern Europe was still under Communist rule.

The second opposition is between single and multi-source funding. This is largely a historical distinction.

In the period before the end of the 1960s, the majority of films that became cults were financed through one main source, often the production company. It channeled all investments into the film. The careers of Roger Corman, William Castle, and Samuel Arkoff were built on this system. Because the system guaranteed some sort of continuous production gambles could be taken in terms of style and subject matter, as more profitable productions would cover less successful ones. It gave young filmmakers the chance to try their hand at movies. Though the system did involve presales, there was a relative independence; deals with distributors were not necessarily cut before the films were made (Schaefer 1999: 98–99). This also gave distributors the liberty to tailor films they purchased. Radley Metzger's company Audubon Films made several changes to European films they made available in the United States. New York distributor Sam Cummins even added a diary and voice-over narrative to the scandal film *Ecstasy*, in an attempt to get it approved without having to cut a sex scene. The attempt failed (Fischer 2001: 130).

This single-source situation first changed with the establishment of state subsidies in Europe, and the destratification of production, distribution, and exhibition in the United States. In many cases, funding opportunities across European countries enabled producers to look for small, hence less contentious, sums of money from a variety of authorities, and combine these with private investments to patch together a budget. In this system, presales to distributors played a crucial role. The result of having the distributor involved in the production meant that changes were made during production, rather than after the delivery of the print. But it made for less stable financing. Christopher Wagstaff notes how the majority of Italian spaghetti-westerns of the late 1960s and early 1970s were financed through an "extremely fragmented" model of advances and guarantees from distributors (Wagstaff 1992: 250; Eleftheriotis 2001: 92–134). Exploitation filmmaker Jess Franco made good use of such opportunities in securing small amounts of money from widely diverse sources, pulling funds from practically every European country, adding extra scenes of hard or soft material to meet local demands, and even taking on ethnic sounding pseudonyms for himself and his cast and crew in order to meet criteria for "regional" involvement. Until the mid 1980s overseas sales were usually excluded from this practice. It put US distributors of European cult cinema and European distributors of American cult films in the position to pick up films cheaply – a key feature of the midnight movie circuit. *El Topo*'s acquisition by Allen Klein of ABKCO, and *Even Dwarfs Started Small*'s acquirement by Robert Shaye of New Line Cinema, are among the most noteworthy examples because both cases concern filmmakers, namely Alejandro Jodorowsky and Werner Herzog, who were only just embarking on a career as filmmaker, and for whom the support from burgeoning distributors was more or less a guarantee that they could embark on new projects. In the case of Jodorowsky, that was *The Holy Mountain*, which was partly financed by John Lennon through ABKCO. As if to underscore the unpredictability of cult movies, and of course their niche appeal, *The Holy Mountain* did not receive wide visibility. It premiered in Cannes in 1973, and it had showings in New York and at various festivals but then it disappeared from circulation – at least until its DVD release in 2007.

Having to sell a film territory-by-territory, or city-by-city, had the side effect that word-of-mouth and reputation preceded the actual arrival of a film. The beneficial aspects of this free publicity have led to the tradition of staggered releases: distributing a film in a few selected venues first before making it available elsewhere. It helped *The Texas Chainsaw Massacre*, for instance, receive much press attention and it fueled the controversy around it (Peary 1981: 347; Staiger 2000: 183). These days, staggered releases are a well-known tactic to sustain a film's run across territories. In business terms, such films are known as "sleepers," and when they continue to attract good business they will be said to have "long legs." Needless to say, the long legs of *Emmanuelle* and *Donnie Darko* outrun most mainstream cinema's trajectories.

With the increased global trade in films, and the home-viewing market exploding in the 1980s, overseas presales opened up opportunities for increased funding and exposure. The travails of Roger Corman in Argentina, shooting productions there in order to benefit from local funding and distribution prospects, are one example (Falicov 2004). Another was the aggressive presales technique practiced by Cannon,

led by Menahem Golan and Yoram Globus, who had learned from Corman and Arkoff. Throughout the 1980s they financed camp classics such as *Bolero* and *King Solomon's Mines* shoulder-to-shoulder with art house films such as *King Lear* and *Barfly* (Beauchamp and Béhar 1992: 91–98). Eventually their system back-fired, but it extended numerous horror and soft-core franchises well into the 1990s. The advent of the internet opened up possibilities as well, though more in terms of marketing than funding or distribution. Online distribution (or internet retailing) enabled more direct contact with clients, and the niche culture of nostalgia made DVD re-issues of camp and cult classics a lucrative area, but the market remains small and profit margins are slim (for an elaboration on DVDs and cult, see Chapter 22).

Marketing: Causing and Containing Commotion

It is difficult to assess the effectiveness of marketing efforts, and distinguish between wanted and unwanted outcomes. Cult cinema forms an illuminating case in this respect. On the one hand it carries an abundance of production legends into its reception, ready to be distorted, abused and pulled out of context by slick marketeers. On the other hand, it has an audience that resists being told what to like and that is inventive in circumventing prescribed consumption. Film marketing needs to strike a balance between getting a film noticed and risk threading on communities' sensitivities (summarized in Earnest 1985; Staiger 1990; Jäckel 2003; Barker 2004). Cult films regularly upset that balance.

Many of the producers and distributors mentioned earlier in this chapter have become better known as publicity riggers than good businessmen or creative artists. They managed to bring their products under the attention of audiences by forcefully associating their films with topical fears, pleasures, and promises, and as such they generated what Thomas Austin (2002) has called "satellite texts," materials so closely associated with a film's public presence that it can be seen as part of the sales or production processes, developed to respond to and manage problematic discourses surrounding films. Whereas "making of" videos and programs, or notes in press kits function as attempts to streamline receptions, many other satellite texts allow meandering tangents of association, offering audiences the chance to "experiment" with meanings. Examples include the mentioning of sources of inspiration by stars and directors, of influences carried over from other films or the alignment of the film with certain causes and social issues – a favorite technique of exploitation cinema. In some cases, such as *The Lord of the Rings*, satellite texts are part of a subtle prescription of how the film should be read (Biltereyst, Mathijs, and Meers 2007). As Cynthia Erb (1998: 34) put it in relation to *King Kong*, however, there is a general willingness to let the "wild logics of the marketplace" determine the reading of a film.

The very term "cult" is finding increased application in marketing because of the rising awareness that it might lead to some revenue. Yet there is still some apprehension among publicists to plainly self-identify a product as "cult." *Snakes on a Plane* is an infamous example of a film that encountered resistance in being accepted as cult by audiences partly because it had boldly announced its own "cultishness" (or at least encouraged it). Most often, the use of the term "cult" is introduced into marketing campaigns indirectly, for instance through quotes from critics and reviewers predicting a film's cult reception. Though one would anticipate that the term "cult" is indiscriminately used, its occurrence is relatively selective. It occurs less in materials that are geared towards a mass public that is not automatically associated with the kind of movie-going and consumption linked with cult cinema. Put differently, the term "cult" is an exclusive one. That is also evident in its use in press books. It appears predominantly in press materials accompanying films by directors consistently linked to independent and exploitation cinema (Argento, Cronenberg, Lynch, Corman). In genre terms it is most heavily employed in relation to science fiction, horror, and fantasy publicity materials.

Indirect and auteur-related usage aside, relatively few films actually make an effort to market themselves as cult. For one, publicity budgets are usually tiny, and there is no consensus over what strategy is most effective, or over which elements of the film need to be highlighted. Quite the contrary, marketing campaigns accompanying films that became cults have

often found themselves struggling to achieve any direction at all, drowning as they were in a sea of numerous little, uncontrolled stories surrounding the films. Even films whose big budgets and strong backing would presume tight control over prefiguration, can succumb to legends and accidents which may lead to cult receptions. The distributors of *Hannibal*, the sequel to *Silence of the Lambs*, for instance, had made efforts to pitch the film as a "weird romance." But they had underestimated how the character Hannibal had sedimented into popular consciousness as a cult monster, and how circulating tales had already affected a Hannibal film's reputation. No Valentine's Day release was going to change that perception (Mathijs 2002).

One particular form of marketing associated with cult cinema is the presentation of material that is as persistent and remarkable as the stories surrounding the films. Stunts, rumors, scandals, and daring an audience to "sit through" an experience are key tactics in that effort. They have their roots in entertainment marketing, where as much effort went into adorning the front of house and canvassing the audience as in the stage show itself. To paraphrase one reviewer, the best show should be put in the lobby (Schaefer 1999: 102). Cult film learned from circus, vaudeville, burlesque theater, sideshows and roadshows how to attract audiences' attention. The releases of *King Kong* and *Psycho*, with carefully planted materials in lobbies (and in the media) are good examples (Erb 1998; Williams 1994). Producer William Castle equipped several of his films with gimmicks and accompanying gadgets that would incite audiences by way of antagonism – daring them into the theater as it were (Waters 2003; Brottman 1997). Castle's stunts were often too elaborate to work effectively, but the reactions they elicited still helped his releases gain attention. Roger Corman's publicity materials often latched themselves onto topical headlines to pretend they addressed hot topics, or were tailored to match local expectations (Pam Grier actually became Caucasian in some posters for *The Arena*). New World Pictures editors Joe Dante and Allan Arkush would liberally borrow shots from everywhere, or invent fake awards to link a coming attraction to "exciting promises" – usually drugs, sex or violence (Gray 2004: 107–109). Each of these marketing campaigns did not just poke audiences, they also disciplined them, and – as Linda Williams (1994) argues with regard to *Psycho* – they brought the prefigurations and expectations in reign. This did not always work. *The Rocky Horror Picture Show* was supposed to follow on the heels of the Broadway stage production. But the show was so savagely dismissed by critics that the whole promotion campaign for the film fell in disarray (Weinstock 2007: 18). In many cases the distinction between carefully planned strategy, disciplining effort, and accident become completely blurred *into* the kind of legend cults are known for. The recurrent streams of gossip that accompanied the films, and careers, of Judy Garland and Hedy Lamarr are excellent examples (Staiger 1992; Fischer 2001). An example of a "legend" that was planted in order to create a distinction between those who would react to it in disgust, and those for whom it would serve as an attractor, is *Scanners*. The film was presented to horror fans (and to the fan press) as a film exclusively about exploding heads, with the infamous head blasting off its shoulders present in virtually every story, in trailers, fanzines, and on posters. *Scanners'* strategy, devised by Avco Embassy employees Bob Rehme and Mick Garris, drew admiration from fanzines, and outrage from the general press. The division it created worked brilliantly, and it gave the film a lasting cult reputation as the "exploding head movie" (Mathijs 2008: 94–98). In sum, marketing efforts geared towards rumor and scandals have always found themselves in competition with other ancillary discourses.

More recently, the internet has given marketing new opportunities to emphasize little stories, and assert control over them – complicating the distinction between planted and genuine rumors or scandals even more. J.P. Telotte (2001) describes in his analysis of the marketing and release of *The Blair Witch Project* how the creation of a website that concentrated on the little stories and aspects of the film, such as elements of narrative, excess, or inventiveness aided the film in gaining attention, and helped it sell worldwide. In combination with endorsements in the form of blogs, straight from the core audience, it gave substance to otherwise empty claims of "something special." Ever since, films have tried to follow a similar strategy, and several blogging sites have grown into centers of gossip, rumor, spoiler alert, and prefigurative chatter. It has made them popular with cult fans seeking information

(especially the sites giving away details and spoilers, and in particular those of films with twisted narratives or special moments), but it has also created suspicion in the eyes of the "real cultists" – a common practice in subcultures eager for distinction. Ambiguity over the origin of stories of rumors and scandals can certainly help films achieve cult reputations, but the suspicion that marketing efforts are involved frequently clashes with cultists' preference for genuineness.

A final characteristic of marketing films received as cults involves niche promotion. Because of their extended reception trajectories, the marketplace of cult films contains a mix of new and old materials, and hot and cool reputations – the former referring to what is momentarily in the spotlight, and the latter to those products that are kept in circulation to meet demands of repeated consumption, either reruns, ongoing sales of DVD and video, or even reworked versions of old materials. Excellent examples are the many different cut versions of *Blade Runner*, the numerous edits of video nasties, and the different edits of the *Lord of the Rings* films. In such a chaotic environment it is essential to market a film to the right target audience, without wasting too much effort on the "wrong" constituency. As Matthew Ragas argues in *The Power of Cult Branding*, this means concentrating on the already established niche following:

> Using mass marketing to convert "pagans" is rarely where your company will find its true brand evangelists. The trick is, you have to preach to the choir. That's right. Focus your efforts on satisfying the happy customers in the "congregation" you already have! These are customers who already listen to your marketing messages, already know your product, already know your brand, and already feel real excitement for your company's product. Preach to them. Make them feel loved and accepted. (Ragas 2002: 61)

In other words, a film that wants to be cult needs to look for cultists. This strategy works best for homogeneous niches. It worked extremely well for the post-initial reception marketing of *The Blair Witch Project*. Well-directed messages to the known fan community of the genre were able to mobilize them and have them discuss the film to the point where fan excitement was noticed by other parts of the marketplace, whose curiosity then led to wider exposure and profit (Telotte 2001). *Paranormal Activity* too cleverly mobilized fans of the horror genre, and even rewarded them by issuing paybacks: it included audience reactions of a preview in a trailer, and it offered fans the option to put their names on the credits of the DVD. These paybacks were in turn used in further marketing efforts. In much the same way, cult "bibles" such as the *Psychotronic Movieguide*, *Video Watchdog*, *Mondo Macabro*, or *Canuxploitation* have veered from the banal to the outlandish in putting cultists on their way to new discoveries, or, as marketers prefer, purchases. Recent years have seen a steep increase in efforts to reach out to niches, and this has had repercussions on how the term "cult" has been understood as a meta-concept (see Chapter 22).

This increase has solicited the reaction that the situation whereby many products supposedly designed to escape classical market mechanisms (such as films belonging to "underground" or "indie" categories) but still operating *within* that market, demonstrate the ultimate failure of cult cinema to exist outside the market place. It is a comment powerfully voiced by Joseph Heath and Andrew Potter (2004) in their discussion of the dual cult and mainstream success of films such as *Fight Club* and *The Matrix*. In a sense, it is an extension of an argument started earlier, by authors such as Thomas Frank (1997), who claimed the separation between "hot" commercial markets and "cool" underground/indie products was essentially an artificial one, and that cult, like "hipness," is one of several categories that enables films to carve out a spot in the marketplace.

Exhibition Culture

Exhibition is one area in which the identity of cult cinema is undisputed. It is in the interaction between screen and audience that cults become solidified. The most significant exhibition contexts for cult cinema are midnight movies, film festivals, fan culture, underground and avant-garde exhibition, home viewing (DVD and late night television), and the black market. Because of its paradigmatic importance for the study of cult cinema, we have discussed the exhibition context of midnight movies, and the importance of the phenomenal experience in Chapter 1. Film festi-

vals are discussed separately in Chapter 3. Fan culture has intimate connections to contexts of auteurship and stardom, and will also be discussed separately, in Chapters 5, 6, and 7. We will devote specific attention to examples of exploitation cinema in Chapter 13, and underground and avant-garde exhibition in Chapter 14. Here, we will give an overview of the more general ways in which the exhibition of cult cinema has been organized.

The exhibition culture of cult cinema is twofold. On the one hand it refers to the screening of films outside mainstream venues, for niche audiences whose routines and practices of viewing are markedly different from "normal" audiences. On the other hand it refers to the unexpectedly different viewing attitudes that some films in regular exhibition contexts encounter. Since its earliest mentions this twofold is manifestly present. Harry Allen Potamkin (2008 [1932]) is among the early critics singling out the "special" behavior of cult audiences. Eric Schaefer (1999) and Jamie Sexton (2008a) on the other hand, give thorough overviews of how certain exhibition contexts helped determine not just the films that were available for audiences to view, but also narrowed down the kinds of reactions possible: the very fact a film was screened in, say, the Broadway cinema in Nottingham, equipped it with a certain audience that would see the film in specific ways, different from a multiplex viewing or television broadcast (Jancovich, Faire, and Stubbings 2003). Those ways differ from one locale to another, but some general tendencies do exist.

The pattern most commonly associated with cult cinema exhibition is borrowed from art-house exhibition. It relies heavily on a loyal audience that is heavily invested in film taste. Though such audiences will not always honor the "right" appreciations, and will display idiosyncratic local preferences (that vary from theater to theater), they are nevertheless prepared to attend screenings frequently (and even repeatedly). In a sense, their patronage is not dissimilar to that of theatre audiences including as it does such techniques as "seat reservations," "fixed seats" and "season tickets" – though these are often informally arranged. Barbara Wilinsky (2001: 6) refers to art house exhibition culture as one of "sure seaters," a term that amplifies the degree of loyalty of custom. Stressing the link with theater she quotes "It's like the Broadway theater.

They go on time. They like a small place that has no popcorn and no kids" (also see Smythe, Lusk, and Lewis 1953; Chamberlin 1960). Of particular interest is the research by Bruce Austin 1891a, 1981b, 1983, 1984), into both art house and cult film audiences. Above all, Austin notes the similarity in strategies these audiences use to decide on their choice of film.

Among the preferred exhibition techniques for cult cinema are staggered releases, double-billing, and re-runs. This pattern characterizes exhibition contexts from the late 1940s to the mid 1980s. It is the period that follows the Paramount decision, which saw a court rule forcing Hollywood studios to abandon their block booking practices and shed some of their tight control over the exhibition market (Borneman 1977). It opened up opportunities for exploitation, art house, and independent exhibitors to be creative in building an audience for their venues. The period ends in the mid/late 1980s when renewed vertical integration – this time augmented with suburban and city-limit multiplex exhibition, and video and television specialty viewing – replaced one-screen inner-city theaters and their practices of double and triple bills, matinees, and midnight screenings. Commercially, art house and cult cinema venues would be run in such a similar fashion that distinguishing between them from a business point of view makes no sense. What does matter is the difference in viewing strategy.

One thing the analogy with art house exhibition does not capture is the attitude associated with cult film attendance, the atmosphere. In an infamous article, Pauline Kael (1961) fulminated against what she saw as the snobbery and fake disdain displayed by art house patrons. Citing Dwight Macdonald's review of *Hiroshima Mon Amour*, Kael asked if the references to "a religious service," "hypnotic trances," and "incense-burning" were not a bit too hyperbolic to describe what was, after all, only a movie screening. She got particularly annoyed with the "repetition" of the film's main points, and the insistence that a "ritual mood" was necessary for the right reception of the film (1961: 6). What Kael failed to appreciate was the cult aspect of the screening. It was not so much the film that mattered, but the experience itself, and the images of the film were there to support that experience. The link with cult becomes more visible a little bit further in the article, when Kael takes offense to Kenneth

Anger and Lo Duca's books on eroticism, scandal, and cinema, especially to their portrayals of women as lust objects. As we will see in Chapter 10, the performance of such sexist imagery is a key feature in the culture of cult film exhibition.

The main pattern sketched above does not cover all of cult movie exhibition. In fact, it excludes the most wild and radical examples. Numerous other formats have existed, and are still in operation. Most of these include the liveliness absent from Kael's account. Drive-in cinemas, grindhouse theaters, porn venues, college theaters, and even vibrant cinematheques, roadshows, and screenings of films in vaudeville and burlesque settings, complement the art house model. When looked at in general, cult cinema exhibition is art house exhibition with a more lively, visceral attitude. Among the more prominent towns and cities for cult movie exhibition are cosmopolitan cultural centers such as New York, Paris, Chicago, San Francisco, Paris, Los Angeles, London, Brussels, Amsterdam, Turin, or Montreal, and a string of college towns such as Madison, Wisconsin; Ann Arbor, Michigan; or Boston, Massachusetts (see Wilinsky 2001: 6–7). Nottingham's Broadway, mentioned above, fittingly became the site for the first ever Cult Film Conference (Mathijs and Mendik 2008a: 20). Increasingly, however, such venues are competing with home viewing. Given the communal and lively aspect of cult receptions, home viewing needs to be seen in the contexts of small groups of viewers sharing a viewing experience in a context that is both lively and requires deep immersion. Examples are sleepover movies, either horror or chick-flicks, binge-viewing (understood as screening multiple films in a row: all the *Lord of the Rings* extended DVDs in one go, all three *Sissi* films, the twelve *Heimat* episodes, etc.), and special occasion viewing (bachelor parties, hen nights, hazing evenings, and so on). In this exhibition context, the formal and physical arrangement of the experience goes beyond technology, and even beyond the private boundaries of the "home," becoming a social, and in many cases semi-public event.

Piracy

A special case of cult exhibition is the black market. Overall, the loyalty of cult viewers virtually guarantees purchase (paying for entrance or products). Yet that obedience to the market is often balanced by a resistance to having their object of fandom commercially exploited to the point where cult viewers feel they are being "sold" as well as by an attitude of rebellion against corporate commercialization and of an attraction to the thrill and hipness associated with illegal trade. In that sense, the entire black market has a cultist connotation, as it is a sign of its position outside accepted practices of film viewing.

Next to references to other black market activities such as moonlighting (illegal trade in alcohol), smuggling, or music bootlegging, the most often-used metaphor is that of "piracy." This metaphor gives the black market of film a romantic ring, and also links it to qualities historically associated with piracy (and with the myth surrounding pirates of the Golden Age of Piracy), such as anarchism, anti-authoritarianism, lawlessness, grassroots democracy, equality, naïve idealism, a penchant for unrestricted high living and a libertarian resistance against vast and shady corporations or state agencies (Snelders 2005; Leeson 2009). As we have seen in Chapter 1, these are also qualities of self-perception associated with film cultism, and because of this similarity piracy and the black market speak to the imagination of cultists.

Until the 1980s, when home viewing became a notable component of film consumption, the black market was one of freeloading. Scholars such as Eric Schaefer (1999) have made note of illegal copying, trading and exhibition of films, but this often occurred in the margins of accepted practices rather than squarely outside it. Only rarely were such practices criminalized or prosecuted. Audience freeloading existed mostly in the form of trying to sneak into screenings without having to pay, or in attempting to watch films outside one's age bracket (with sneaking into adult screenings an activity associated with rituals of initiation). The only research on this form of freeloading is anecdotal, but if the numerous admissions by critics of cult cinema of having attended screenings illegally is anything to go by then it is certainly a practice closely affiliated with the cult experience. Still, it was hardly ever regarded as a threat to the industry. That changed when home viewing technologies became a dominant mode of exhibition. With the move towards portable, cheap and user-friendly technology the counterpart of the legitimate marketplace became

that of the under-the-counter exchange or the flea market: an act in a location where value is determined semi-independently of commercial market mechanisms and where clear distinctions between illegality and legality dissolve in a grey area. Among the most noteworthy elements of this form of black market were the trade in uncut VHS copies of video nasties such as *Last House on the Left* or *House on the Edge of the Park* (Egan 2007), and the trade in pornography (with the hardcore films of Radley Metzger or Traci Lords much sought after objects).

While this flea market model seems harmless, and is seldom prosecuted, it is far less tolerated by the regular industry. In fact, the industry's attitude changed so much that by the beginning of the twenty-first century the discourse of the flea market as one of small-scale entrepreneurs or modern-day Robin Hoods who made films (and thus culture) available to the public against the prohibitions of corporations or authorities was met by a competing discourse that regarded such activities as downright criminal, and even terrorist. Numerous critics have described this reaction as over-the-top, and argue that it has given piracy and the black market an unprecedented vitality and a political significance. Ever since large corporations started high-profile campaigns to push stringent copyright legislation and criminalize the hacking, downloading, copying, and sharing of marketable materials, piracy has become associated with a principle that sees the free and unregulated sharing and distributing of culture as an inalienable right of the public. This situation has reinforced the cultist edge of piracy, and it has made copy-culture an instrument in the struggle over the ownership of culture. Through anti-copyright organizations such as The Pirate Bay and concepts as the Darknet Theory (which holds that the internet's ability for peer-to-peer sharing renders copyright obsolete) copy-culture has intensified connections with the cultist overtones of cultural opposition that piracy already had.

Most instances of copy-culture concern popular and mainstream films, such as blockbusters. While such films are far from regularly seen as cult, the very activity of illegally accessing them *cultifies* their reception. Only in a few instances does this cultification move into a permanent mode of film cultism. The aforementioned video nasties are a good example, as are suppressed films such as Nicholas Ray's *We Can't Go Home Again*,

Figure 2.1 *Superstar: The Karen Carpenter Story* owes much of its cult status to peer-to-peer sharing and bootlegging.

or Elias Merhige's *Begotten*. Often, these films are not explicitly banned but after their initial releases they have been so difficult to get hold of that a vibrant bootleg trade has replaced their legal circulation. Much of their status is subsequently derived from their place in semi-illegality. Their cult is a copy-cult. Among the most legendary exemplars of a copy-cult is *Superstar: The Karen Carpenter Story* (Figure 2.1). The film tells the story of singer Karen Carpenter of The Carpenters through the use of Barbie dolls. Neither the rights holders of the Carpenters nor the Barbie brand had given permission to have their materials used. Consequently, the film was withheld because of a copyright infringement suit filed (and won) by Richard Carpenter. Nevertheless, it was eagerly copied and shared, and it even appeared on university courses. As Glyn Davis (2008) observes, this slumbering presence has made *Superstar* a symbol for an anti-corporate low-fi sensibility.

Conclusion

The place of cult in the marketplace remains problematic. Production costs are usually low, labor can be found cheaply, and funding is of a volatile nature, with much improvisation, and benefits from unexpected partnerships. There is room for maneuvering as well. The marketplace for cult cinema is the ideal terrain for individuals and companies with a less top-heavy administration than the big studios, and an aversion of overhead costs. It is also a market where shady entrepreneurs meet organizations with high-principled aesthetic and political aims. Spreading efforts towards exposure across a number of media platforms, with consumption of and access to those platforms ever extending across time, can deliver sustained profits over a longer period of time than mainstream cinema. On the other hand, cult cinema is too unpredictable to fit the contingencies of any business plan – too dependent on erratic and impulsive receptions. Volatile partnerships break down easily, and adventures can come to a disastrous end, leaving projects without a completed product, without distribution or exhibition, effectively prohibiting profit. Even without these dangers there is a real risk that profits will be less direct, and more difficult to guard – it is far from certain they will end up with the same person or company who initially invested in the project.

3

Prestige, Awards, and Festivals

Like most other films, cult cinema receptions inhabit a network of cultural valuation and distinction. This network is at its most effective immediately after a film's release, when opinions and evaluations can be made freshly. Unlike most other films, however, cult movies have an antagonistic relationship with this part of official culture. They belong to what Jonathan Rosenbaum (1998: 48) has described as an "esoteric network" that "commerce deems irrelevant … and that most mainstream reviewers prefer to ignore as a consequence." This alternative network of valuation exists parallel to – and occasionally *within* –circuits of institutionalized awards, prizes, and criticism. It also stretches over extended periods of time – concurrent with cult films' long runs. Chapter 4 will discuss censorship and connoisseurship as elements of cult cinema's relationship to this network. This chapter deals with cult cinema's relation towards event-based valuation. We will first detail how cult cinema receptions are affected by a cultural economy of prestige. Next, we will outline how cult receptions fare at one of the platforms of most significance in this prestige circuit, that of the film festival.

Awards and Prizes

Cult films largely stand outside what James English (2005) has called "the economy of prestige": the framework of valuation through award, ceremonies, and prizes. According to English, the last few decades of the twentieth century have seen a veritable frenzy in the establishment of prizes that designate cultural

esteem. There are now, he observes, "more film prizes awarded each year than there are feature films produced" (2005: 324). This has led to a rhetoric in which nothing appears to matter more than just winning: "it is almost as though winning a prize is the only truly newsworthy thing a cultural worker can do, the only thing that really counts in a lifetime of more or less nonassessable, indescribable or at least unreportable cultural accomplishments" (2005: 21). According to English, this has simultaneously given rise to a counter-rhetoric in which wining an award is seen as somewhat dubious. He quotes Woody Allen from *Annie Hall*: "Awards! That's all they do, is give out awards, I can't believe it. 'Greatest Fascist Dictator: Adolf Hitler!'" (2005: 18). At the same time as this counter-discourse develops, however, English observes how the attention to awards and prizes has set in motion a fascination with quantifiable means of measuring cultural value that perpetuates itself, leaving little or no room for anything else: "[prizes] continue to serve as the most bankable, fungible assets in the cultural economy" (2005: 22).

Cult cinema has a peculiar role within this tensed situation. Because it occupies a marginal position within the market of official culture, it mostly falls outside the economy of prestige. In this sense, cult film receptions act as the opt-out of the desire to quantify culture. It is a position that confirms the marginal status of cult cinema and exemplifies the pride its audiences take in standing in opposition to official culture. However, in recent decades there has been a proliferation of cult cinema that has seen it partly being co-opted by official culture. Therefore its position

Cult Cinema: An Introduction. Ernest Mathijs and Jamie Sexton.
© 2011 Ernest Mathijs and Jamie Sexton. Published 2011 by Blackwell Publishing Ltd.

these days no longer lies uniquely outside the economy of prestige, but partly inside it.

Cult films win few prizes, but if they do they are often mock prizes or prizes that fall within the afore-mentioned alternative "esoteric network" and are awarded through affective appreciations and niche recognitions more than widely publicized laudations. We will explore the latter as part of the network of festivals later in this chapter. Mock prizes are essentially awards created to ridicule the enterprise of issuing prizes in giving them to films that are generally seen as undeserving of awards or by inventing categories that are not sanctioned with cultural value. Histori-cally, mock prizes began to achieve attention as a counter-cultural and ironic form of discourse in the late 1970s, around the same time that film festivals were garnering momentum as sites of celebrations for films which would otherwise not find distribution in the ever shrinking theatrical market. The result was a wave of attention for bad cinema, and a cultism of "badness," steeped in irony. Two books, *The Fifty Worst Films of All Time* (Medved, Medved, and Dreyfuss 1978) and *The Golden Turkey Awards* (Medved and Medved 1980), are usually credited for instigating mock prizes. J. Hoberman (1980) lists three reasons to celebrate bad movies: the change of taste (what was once bad is now good), a pedagogical value (to learn from others' mistakes), and the fact that movies "have a life of their own." All three culminate in what Hoberman terms the "objectively bad movie," films "so incoherent they unmake themselves" (1980: 518). Through this classifier Hoberman separates sur-realist, delirious films, from films *maudits* and truly bad films, of which he sees Ed Wood's *Plan 9 from Outer Space* as the top. An important impetus to the cele-bration of badness came from satirical columnist Joe Bob Briggs, who set up the Hubcap Awards (the "Hubbys") in the early 1980s. These "so-called 'Drive-In Academy Awards' were presented at horror conventions or on college campuses and featured prizes for 'Best Slimeball', 'Best Kung-Fu', and 'Best Mindless Sex Comedy'" (English 2005: 93). As the mock celebration of badness became more prolific, however, it acquired and demanded esteem in its own right. English notes that the tone of the Hubbys Awards made it difficult to asses whether cultural hierarchies were being inverted, if the value of

mindless pleasure was being asserted, or if the very capacity of movies to rise to the level of art was being mocked:

> with the Hubbys we can't be sure whether a serious honor is being bestowed on a marginal cultural product judged superior of its kind (an especially entertaining drive-in movie), or whether a mock honor, amounting to a form of dishonor, is being bestowed on a mainstream cultural product judged inferior of its kind (an especially trivial and squalid film) or whether the mockery inherent in the award is ultimately directed at particular styles of consumption (low-cultural or bourgeois). (English 2005: 94)

English maintains it is the second possibility of these three that lies at the core of mock awards. He remarks that there is a "tendency for instruments of con-secration," which is how he sees awards in culture, "to take increasingly parodic and self-parodic forms without ceasing to function effectively as economic instruments in either the symbolic or the material sense" (2005: 97). This may well be true for the Hubbys. It certainly is for another award for bad cinema, the Raspberry Awards (the "Razzies"), which were instigated in 1981. The Razzies are clearly an example of English's second option.[1]

But when the mock celebration of badness takes on cult status, as it increasingly did since the beginning of the 1980s, it ceases to be mere mockery. It clashes, for instance, with the seriousness of genre-specific awards, such as the Saturn awards for fantasy, horror and science fiction, or the *Fangoria* awards for horror, named after the fan magazine, which also received cult status. *Fangoria*'s Hall of Fame, in particular, is hotly contested. One example English mentions, the AVN Adult Entertainment Awards, is perhaps a good test case. For English, its mimicking of the Oscars is part of its parodying of awards. But David Foster Wallace, covering the awards ceremonies, remarked that its protocols and procedures exude a desire to be taken seriously – only in the eye of official culture is it ridiculous, not on its own terms (Wallace 2006: 3–50). One symptomatic example of this is the fact that David Cronenberg's *Crash* won the award for "Best Alter-native Adult Feature" at the AVN awards. Awarding it a prize was AVN's plea to be considered as authentic, not as (only) parody. Furthermore, even those awards

Figure 3.1   Halle Berry holds her Razzie award for Worst Actress of 2004 in one hand and her Oscar award in the other at the 25th Annual Razzie Awards, a spoof of the Oscars, on February 26, 2005, in Los Angeles. Berry won for *Catwoman* (UPI Photo/Barbara Wilson/Golden Raspberry Award Foundation).

that are merely meant to mock achievements, such as the Razzie, have had to revise their perspective since directors such as Paul Verhoeven (who won for *Showgirls*) and actresses such as Halle Berry (who won for *Catwoman*) appeared in person at the ceremony, and held acceptance speeches (Figure 3.1).

In other words, simultaneously with the rise of cult cinema as a perspective not uniquely outside, but part of the economy of prestige, mock awards have evolved to become equipped with a degree of authenticity and seriousness (the first option mentioned in English's quote). In that respect it is worth noting that there exists, since 2007, an Award for Lifetime Achievement in Cult Cinema, issued by the festival/conference Cine Excess. Recipients include Roger Corman, Dario Argento and Joe Dante. It is also worth noting that Corman was awarded a Lifetime Achievement by the Academy of Motion Pictures and Sciences two years after receiving the Cine Excess award; a further sign of the increased convergence of cult and culture.

In that regard the third option listed by English (that of the mock award as a critique of a mode of consumption) should perhaps no longer be seen as merely a critique but as a celebration as well. Mock prizes are exemplified by an expository desire to unveil some of the worst films ever, partly in order to ridicule them, and partly to demonstrate the entertainment value of sheer badness, and to celebrate this badness as a mode

of reception. This so-bad-they're-good reason to champion bad films asserts that watching these films as valueless trash offers a form of phenomenal experience that is transgressive: it lifts the viewer out of the dreary normalness of everyday life and as such it operates in the same way religious cultism tries to accomplish epiphanies. With Maffesoli (1996a: 43) one could argue that celebrating badness alters everyday life as it elevates ordinariness and banality to a level where it can be actively enjoyed.

This mode has had some significant repercussions on the long-term receptions of several films, helping them achieve and sustain cult reputations. For the film the Medveds put forward as worst ever, *Plan 9 from Outer Space*, it meant the start of a second career. The film was picked up by several festivals, and became the showcase piece of numerous "nights of bad taste" that were being organized from the beginning of the 1980s onwards. Next to Ed Wood's films, *Manos, the Hands of Fate* and *Robot Monster* are among the most perpetually recognized bad films ever. Most of the films at the top of the canon of badness are American, an indication perhaps of that culture's perceived obsession with rankings of cultural achievements. Among the most noteworthy non-American films are the Italian horror film *Troll 2* and the Bollywood film *Aag* (aka *Flames*). The former is not a sequel to *Troll*, and does not even feature trolls (but it does have former *Black Emanuelle* Laura Gemser as costume designer); the latter is a failed remake of Bollywood cult classic *Sholay*.

Since the end of the first decade of the twenty-first century, the celebration of badness has been exploding. Numerous books celebrating the worst movies ever have been added to mock awards, and in some cases even replaced them, as an increasing number of films are showcased for their badness. One of the most consistent candidates on such lists, *The Room*, has been regarded as straddling the line between incompetence and clever exploitation of badness. Because of its integrity it is labeled a post-camp cult film, a label that obliterates lines of reasoning along which it could be understood (Bissell 2010; Adams 2010: 298–300). Such contradictions continue to affect the receptions of bad movies. In 2010, *Battlefield Earth*, a multiple Razzie winner, and a film often cited as one of the worst in spite (or because) of it being based on source material by the founder of the Church of Scientology

L. Ron Hubbard, exemplified the thin line between real scorn and ironic celebrations of badness when one of its screenwriters, J.D. Shapiro, issued a public apology to moviegoers for his involvement in what had just been declared the worst movie of the decade.

Festivals and Valuation

Film festivals form one of the most important platforms on which processes of cultural valuation take place. For English (2005: 283), festivals are about the localizing of cultural value – literally placing it in a geographical or symbolic context and assessing value on the basis of this localization. The forces that determine this process consist of colleges of influence that include juries, programmers, boards, subscribers, sponsors, policy-makers, charities, audiences, guests, fans, and local businesses. Historically, films that developed cult receptions have not done well in such contexts. That is because most of these films exist outside – even in opposition to – normalized routines and protocols of cultural valuation. As we have argued in Chapters 1 and 2, its values are less tangibly and mostly only indirectly felt within culture at large – that is why their circuit has been called an alternative "esoteric" network. Occasionally, however, there have been overlaps, moments when films with burgeoning or nascent cult receptions appeared at regular film festivals, and caused commotions, scandals and outrage. Such upheaval mostly involved the film's ability to upset and expose the otherwise neatly hidden processes of valuation. Over the years, as the legitimacy of cult cinema has increased, such commotions have been fewer and fewer. Below, we will detail examples from Cannes to illustrate this development.

Another, parallel, historical evolution that helped to accept cult cinema's valuation at festivals has been the establishment of festivals for cults – events designed to celebrate and evaluate the kinds of films normal festivals would eschew. As their popularity grew, and they gained cultural visibility and recognition, so did the invisible colleges through which the processes of valuation took place. In other words, with the rise of niche festivals, the esoteric network became less esoteric and more respected – at least as part of a niche that earned its place in the cultural landscape. In this section

we will first discuss the cultist aspects of film festivals in general, and next explore festivals that have played prominent roles in constituting and sustaining cult reputations for films.

The connection between festivals and cults goes back to Greek antiquity (see Chapter 12). With regard to film, this connection has been reinforced enough times to assume many critics see a sort of causal connection. Andrew Sarris famously cemented the link by quoting André Bazin: "No less a cultist than the late André Bazin had once likened film festivals to religious festivals" (Sarris 1970: 13). Actually, Bazin's article compared film festivals to religious orders, but there is a close link with cultism, especially in the observation of closely guarded rituals (Bazin 2009 [1955]). As Bazin's account demonstrates, to see festivals as a cultist experience is to rely on a sense of occasion of the event itself, where orotund rituals of presence and presentation such as "red carpet" walking are of equal importance to the appreciation of the actual films. Many festivals remain vague over the criteria of admission and valuation. This elusiveness has benefited the creation of myths, scandals, haphazard decisions, and rituals such as booing, hissing, and cheering (even ironically), as a result of which films implicated in such actions have acquired "legends" that have – in turn – facilitated their own cult status. In terms of the marketplace, the analogy is with the bazaar: crowded, bustling and unwieldy to the uninitiated eye but firmly structured to the insider. As mentioned, location matters greatly to these festivals. Cannes, at the French Riviera, Venice, and Locarno, are all known for their beautiful and awe-inspiring locations. Similarly, the festival of Sitges, near Barcelona, offers a large selection of horror and fantasy materials and draws a significant part of its appeal from its location and its proud self-presentation as Catalonian. More than inviting a parallel with the origin of the term cult, festivals' locations prepare audiences and attendants for a cultist-like appreciation (Harbord 2002; Koehler 2009).

The best-known festival that is a veritable cult in itself is the one highlighted in Bazin's account: Cannes. Sarris once divided the Cannes festival audiences into two categories: the moles and the moths: "the moles arrive, sniff suspiciously at the sunlight, and then plunge as soon as possible into the darkness.". The moths "are noted for fluttering about the gemlike flames, emitted by the stars. For the moth, Cannes is an around-the-clock adventure of seaside lunches, cocktail parties, and gala dinners, all preferably free" (quoted in Beauchamp and Béhar, 1992: 24). Cannes merges the cult of stardom with that of classical auteurism, and mixes the elegance of glamour with the decadence of the bacchanal. It lays claim to grandeur, be it in the promiscuity and illicitness of the starlet appearance at the Croisette (from Simone Sylva to Pia Zadora), the sculpted majesty of the maggiorata, with Sophia Loren as its ultimate symbol, or in the presence of great, archaic auteurs – which helped to establish the cults of Alfred Hitchcock and Luis Buñuel (Sarris 1970: 53). The exhilaration, the "rush of excitement," the suggestion of easy sex, and the tireless disputes between novices and veterans that cult cinema is known for are constants in the discourse of Cannes (Beauchamp and Béhar, 1992). Much of the cult of Cannes is encapsulated in the 1960 debate over La Dolce Vita, champion of an edition presided over by jurors Henry Miller and Georges Simenon that was described as "the most scandalous ever" (Grenier 1960: 15). The question whether Fellini's film was a milestone in art, a celebration of moral decadence, or a cheap exploitation of women, "a satire of the female", as Pauline Kael called it (1961: 6), highlighted a debate over taste that would inform cult cinema and film festivals ever since (French and French 1999: 75–76). La Dolce Vita also bared the aforementioned invisible colleges and their criteria, even adding to the critical vocabulary by introducing the term "paparazzi."

Let us briefly explore two examples of Cannes film receptions that demonstrate how the esoteric networks operating in the valuation of cult clash with those of normalized cultural valuation. In each of the situations the films received part of their cult status as a result of how they exposed some of the routines and protocols of the invisible colleges at Cannes. In 1992, the low-budget Belgian black and white mockumentary Man Bites Dog won the International Critics competition at Cannes, amid controversy and to the astonishment of commentators who felt that the film's depiction of gratuitous violence and its status as a collaborative debut film (with overtones of being a send-up of filmmaking in general) from a small film nation did

not warrant such an award (Lafond 2004; Mathijs 2005a). Several stories accompanied this controversy. One story tells of then unknown director Quentin Tarantino (who had his debut Reservoir Dogs to represent at the same edition of Cannes) fist fighting his way into the screening at Cannes; another story details the censoring of the original movie poster (which shows the main character killing a baby – something that is never alluded to in the actual film). The result of these two stories was that Cannes 1992 became known as the origin of the debate about a new wave of violent cinema, later known as new brutalism or "nouvelle violence." All of these stories created a situation that challenged the procedures through which films would normally be channeled at the festival, exposing part of their arbitrariness. As the involvement of Man Bites Dog as part of the "nouvelle violence" wave of film of the early 1990s spread, the functions of Cannes' award administration and cultural valuation became more fiercely interrogated. The combination of "violence," "Tarantino," "child killing," "mockery," and a self-reflexive critique of the media were enough to provide the reception of Man Bites Dog with a cult potential – mirrored in its subsequent receptions. As it turned out, Man Bites Dog would remain caught up in the "new brutalism" group of films said to exemplify a loss of morality in cinema. In fact, it became one of its exemplars (Hill 1997).

Another memorable example of the clash between the esoteric network that is the valuation of cult receptions and the "normal" processes operating at festivals is the reception of David Cronenberg's Crash, which was entered in the general competition in 1996. It was both booed and applauded at its screening, and it created a sharp division between audiences and commentators. This division articulated itself in the award it was accorded: under the presidency of Francis Ford Coppola, Crash was given the newly invented prize for "audacity." It was the only time such an award was ever given, and a clear sign of how the film's fast developing reputation along esoteric networks of appreciation was impacting on the procedures of valuation the festival felt it had to honor. Two of the key terms in this esoteric network were "cool" and "depravity." "Cool" referred to the film's ability to use detachment as a stylistic tool, and was used by both the film's opponents and its defenders. "Depravity" was a term uniquely employed by its opponents, who felt the film – much like *Man Bites Dog* a few years before – crossed boundaries of moral decency (Barker, Arthurs, and Harindranath, 2001; Mathijs 2008: 187–194).

Niche Cults and Festivals

One kind of film festival we want to highlight is the one where niche cults rule – where the interrogations of and confrontations with processes of valuation are built into the fabric of the festival. In that respect, we are no longer talking about cult receptions at festivals but about self-sustaining cult events. This is not to say these festivals are therefore cut off from the regular circuit altogether. While wary of interference with their devotion to certain films, such festivals remain curious for new experiences, ready to embrace them into their midst and appropriate them as "one of us."

Among the earliest such examples is a festival that was explicitly set up to champion films excluded from the regular festival circuit: the experimental festival of Knokke-Le-Zoute, in particular the editions in the 1960s. According to Parker Tyler, (1969: 165) this festival was one of several that gave expression to the "neuroticism of modern life with its new and unusually morbid accent on youth." The festival, started in 1949, and located at the casino of the affluent Belgian seaside resort of Knokke (a location similar to Cannes), focused on presenting underground and experimental films – of the kind that were also being shown on the burgeoning midnight movie circuit in New York – to critics in Europe. The festival received notoriety in 1963, when it first selected and then rejected *Flaming Creatures*, a film that had already caused upheaval in New York. Under the auspices of members of the jury, including Jonas Mekas, an improvised New Year's Eve screening of *Flaming Creatures* took place. It was interrupted by scuffles, discussions, and riots (see Broughton 1964; Garcia Bardon 2002). After the controversy was widely reported in European newspapers, the film eventually received a special *film maudit* prize (Hoberman and Rosenbaum 1991: 59). As Gerda Cammaer (2005) argues, the festival of Knokke was, at the time of this controversy, a "try-out festival, an event that was still searching for its true calling and shape." This in itself means it did not have the set

protocols of the regular festival circuit. That allowed for the pushing of alternative agendas. Cammaer (2005) also notes how the *Flaming Creatures* controversy actually became "an ambassador for the festival".

The best contemporary examples of niche cults and cult festivals are horror, fantasy and science fiction genre festivals that have inherited, or sometimes grown out of, the midnight movie phenomenon. Many of these developed firm cult reputations more because of the kinds of audiences they catered to than what they screened. The festivals of Sitges, Avoriaz (now defunct and replaced by that of Gérardmer), Brussels' International Festival of Fantastic Film, Fantafest in Rome, and Fantasporto in Portugal, which all started before the mid 1980s, became crucial for the development of science fiction and horror cult fandom in Europe. The attitude of these festivals towards taste and indicators of quality is at its least problematic here: their programmers and audiences share an agenda, and they demand more of the same – more blood, more gore, more full moons, more sorcery, more time travel, and more vampires. Yet, in much the same way genre cinema never only relies on repetition and recognition but also on variation and innovation, these festivals regularly relish films that stretch the confines of the genres they cherish. As long as the framework within which these new experiences are presented is the trusted environment of the festival and the peer viewers they have known for years, they are in for the ride. This creates opportunities for a delicate balance between tradition and novelty.

This commitment is proof of the strong alignment between viewer and programmer, as part of the same cultist alliance. Visitors to these festivals are seldom only visitors, but rather fellow believers. They are closely involved with the festivals' selections and organization, and are extremely vocal in offering their opinions. As virtual co-owners they can stage boycotts or disrupt ceremonies, or lift the entire experience to a higher level of excitement and appreciation. Instead of snubbing minor stars they champion them as groundbreaking artists (an attitude that many guests have difficulty responding to; see Hills 2010b: 95). They act reflexively, very aware of their active role in the festival, and they are not afraid to exercise their power – not only verbally but also in terms of their subscription to future editions (the fact many of these festivals

actually have subscriptions makes the audience a pa-
tron in the classical sense). While several such festivals
exist in North America, such as Fantasia in Montreal,
Fantastic Film Fest in Austin, Texas, and elsewhere in
the world (such as the Puchon International Film
Festival in Korea), the emphasis of this phenomenon
lies in Western Europe.

The most noteworthy network here is the European
Fantastic Film Festivals Federation (EFFFF), also
known as the Méliès network (www.melies.org).
Unlike the loose esoteric networks described above,
it is a close collaboration between Europe's major
genre festivals. Over the last few decades, this network
has represented 8 to 15 niche festivals across Europe,
with sustained presence in Belgium (BIFFF), Finland
(Espoo Cine), Italy (Fantafest), the Netherlands
(Amsterdam, AIFF), Portugal (Fantasporto), Spain
(Sitges), Sweden (Lund, LIFFF), and Switzerland
(Neuchatel, NIFFF). The network has its own council, board and rotating presidency. Annually, the network offers one top award, the Méliès d'Or, to one of
the films that were crowned in each of the individual
festivals (a sort of season playoffs alternately hosted at
one of the participating festivals). Through its network Méliès reaches 600,000 genre fans in Europe,
making it the biggest fan-based cult-network on the
continent. It furthermore facilitates a global network
of adherent members in North America, Asia, and the
United Kingdom. The festivals in the Méliès network
also take on the role that, in North America and
East Asia, fan conventions play. They are catalysts
for genre fandom. In terms of scope and appeal they
are on a par with conventions such as the World
Science-Fiction Convention, Comicon, Otakon,
or Fangoria's Weekend of Horror. But they are
decidedly less corporatized and more adventurous in
their programs.

Location plays a role here too. More even, the
choice of theater and the urban quarters it is part of
can be seen as crucial for the constellation of the
cultist audience. According to Hills (2010b: 98):

> there is a fit here between a venue with an established
> subcultural reputation, and the materials of the festival.
> Just as "midnight screenings" or "late-nighters" serve to
> distinguish cult and horror film screenings from a cinema-
> going "mainstream", so too does the screening of films . . .
> at specific, independent cult/subcultural venues.

Hills isolates several other components that set up these
niche festivals as cultist. They allow for an unusual
closeness between fans and producers. They also require the performance of subcultural capital in order to
overcome the threshold (a jargon, access to certain
venues, insider knowledge in order to feel welcome,
and so on) that equals prestige and status, and the
attending of premieres, and previews. Q&A sessions,
panel discussions, collectors' markets, autograph sessions, and costume parties can easily be added to this
list. It is equally important, again according to Hills,
that the industry that is the subject of celebration at
these festivals (the actual horror productions, the sci-fi
films, the fantasy games, etc.), acknowledges the labor
fans and festivals audiences put into their celebration
and, hence, into the establishment of a long-term
reception. More and more DVD releases of cult
movies include secondary materials that testify to
horror, fantasy and science fiction films' success and
cult appeal at festivals. The DVD collectors' editions
of *Ginger Snaps* and *Evil Dead* are two examples that do
so explicitly.

We want to conclude this discussion of niche cults
and festivals with a short case study of the Brussels
International Festival of Fantastic Film (BIFFF). It is an
exemplary instance of cultism, in terms of its pedigree,
franchise and networking, programming, and audience activity. The BIFFF started in 1983 (Figure 3.2),
and it is a founding member of the Méliès network. It
has a predecessor in Antwerp's festival of Fantastic Film
that ran from 1974 to 1977. That festival had *The
Wicker Man* as its first ever screening. *Rocky Horror
Picture Show* director Jim Sharman and the director of
Blue Sunshine, Jeff Lieberman, were among its prominent guests (Magiels 2004: 161). The last edition took
place in Cinema Monty, known for its midnight
movie screenings of *Eraserhead* (Apers 2004:
143–144). This midnight movie heritage remains
reflected in some elements of the BIFFF programming. BIFFF quickly attracted attention because of its
cultist programming. It introduced Dario Argento,
Luc Besson, and David Cronenberg to Belgian audiences. Cronenberg visited in 1984 and brought all of
his films, including the then unreleased *Videodrome*,
which became a small-scale cult among Belgian film
critics (De Kock 1983; Danvers 1984). It became the
start of a template that regularly saw new auteurs

Figure 3.2 The Brussels International Festival of Fantastic Film, a festival with a communal atmosphere that mixes art and exploitation. Clockwise from top left, the posters for 1983, 2010, 2005, and 1993 © BIFFF/Buzzelli, BIFFF/Sokal, BIFFF/Michetz, and BIFFF/Mauricet.

singled out for celebrations. Unique among festivals, the programming was done communally, by a team of eight full-time programmers. BIFFF's core audience quickly became heavily invested in the festival via annual subscriptions. Today, that audience is largely in its twenties to forties, university or college educated, and it has a 66/33% male/female ratio (previously that was 75/25%). The first editions drew about 30 000 viewers. Currently that number is up to 65 000, spread over two weeks. About 90 films are screened, many of them in European or world premiere. The BIFFF carved a name for itself internationally when it started programming outside the circle of American horror. It screened Shinya Tsukamoto's, Guillermo Del Toro's, and Alex de la Iglesia's films well before they were known widely, and it unceremoniously programmed unusual materials such as Kim Ki-Duk's *The Isle* and Vincenzo Natali's *Nothing* amid traditional fare thus stirring up debates. In 1999 the BIFFF was among the first to present Europe with the new wave of Japanese horror, and in 2002 it showed an uncut version of *Ichi the Killer* to non-suspecting audiences. Also since the end of the 1990s, and following a trend of cult nostalgia, the BIFFF has organized a parallel stream of screenings called "the Seventh Reel," in which camp science fiction is screened alongside notorious horror cult material (Lucio Fulci, Jean Rollin, or Jess Franco) – at midnight of course (Van Laer 2004).

Of particular significance to the cultist feel of the festival are some of its locations. For the first 25 years of its existence the main venue was a gigantic, gothic cinema theater, the Auditorium in the Passage 44, adorned with long curtains and creepy statues. An additional venue had the design of a small, concrete bunker-like theater. Equally cultist is the highly ritualistic start to every screening: an enthusiastically shouted back-and-forth dialog by the audience that features a loose imitation of the Muppet show's "Piiiiigs in Spaaaaace' tune, various chants such as a rendition of the 20th Century Fox tune, and a loudly declared invitation to murder ("Tuer encore!"). This ritual ceremony separates the novices from the veterans at the start of each screening. When stars or directors introduce their film to the audience it loudly demands not promotion-talk but "une chanson!" (a song!); organizers usually hasten to explain this request to guests as "good natured" and occasionally guests dutifully oblige and actually perform a song (needless to say it makes them immortal) with the crowd. During screenings heckling and shouting are commonplace, as is the cheering of sex and violence on screen. Each full moon that appears on the screen is greeted with howls, each room entered followed by the yell "Close That Door!" It is in these activities that the BIFFF presents itself as a pure blooded cult. As former programmer Dirk Van Extergem describes:

> [Just like] every cult constitutes a community, a group that worships similarly and regularly, and finds strengths

in that shared experience, it relies on a set of practices or conventions shared by the devotees. And the demonstrated knowledge of those things (the participatory action such as the shouting being the most evident example) certifies the initiated, binds them in their privileged knowledge to others . . . . (2004: 224).

This communal celebration suggests that the BIFFF is more about its audiences, more about itself perhaps, than about the films. That is also evident in the many side activities, the carnivalesque nature of which proves its cult to be extremely festive. Body-painting contests, parades of "film monsters," and crowd surfing precede screenings. Each press conference is open to the public. Each edition of the BIFFF is closed with a gala "bal des vampires," in which guests and audiences don outrageous costumes inspired by the history of horror, science fiction, fantasy, and cult cinema. The full compliance of attendees with the dress code makes it difficult to distinguish guests from pundits, thereby achieving the abandonment of traditional cultural status often associated with cults.

Conclusion

In conclusion to this chapter we would like to highlight how, in many cases, processes of valuation of cult cinema consist of a mixture of the main instances we have isolated, namely the interrogation of prizes and awards systems, the upsetting of protocols at festival where a nascent cult clashes with existing traditions of valuation, and the celebration of films festivals where a film's cult reception is the confirmation of a largely pre-existing cult sensibility.

A perfect example of this mixture is the festival career of *Ichi the Killer*. The film had its world premiere at the Toronto International Film Festival (TIFF), at 15 September 2001, as part of a midnight screening series called Midnight Madness. But a few days before the screenings the World Trade Center in New York had been destroyed by a terrorist attack. Many flights through North American airspace were still canceled. Miike was trapped in San Francisco. He commented: "I turned on the TV barely half awake. The situation was worse than I could imagine. This was real people. Real human beings with more stupidity, more violence, more sadness, and more pain than any movie could have" (Macias 2001: 216). In spite of gimmicks such as complementary "barf bags" with Ichi's Superhero logo on it and in the absence of its main guest the TIFF Midnight Madness series did not become a great success; no one was in the mood for exuberant violence.

After TIFF, *Ichi the Killer* was screened at about twenty film festivals before it became widely available on DVD. Most of those festivals were specialty festivals. In order to assess the cultism involved in viewing *Ichi the Killer* at these festivals, it is helpful to contrast two festival appearances: the International Film Festival of Rotterdam (IFFR) and the BIFFF. The IFFR is known for its cinephile audience, a position encapsulated in founder Hubert Bals' assertion that he wants "to find an audience for his films and not films for his audience" (quoted in de Valck 2005: 102). When the IFFR screened *Ichi the Killer*, in February 2002, as part of a series of eclectic films that shared its fascination with sex and violence the reception was positive but also somewhat restrained. Many viewers and critics felt uncomfortable with the film, not knowing where to place it, a confusion that was further heightened by the fact that Miike's other film at the IFFR, the *Sound of Music* parody *The Happiness of the Katakuris*, was nothing like *Ichi the Killer*. In short, there was admiration but not much enjoyment. At the BIFFF in March 2002, where *The Happiness of the Katakuris* again accompanied *Ichi the Killer*, the reaction was the opposite. A packed house welcomed Miike with a thundering roar, and the entire screening was enlivened by screams, cries, chants, loudly voiced wisecracks (mostly of the "ouch, that must hurt" variety), and loud bursts of applause. Each killing and most acts of violence were greeted with hysterical laughter. There was much enjoyment, but far less respect and admiration.

The audience reactions of TIFF, the IFFR and the BIFFF to *Ichi the Killer* can all be regarded as part of the film's overall cult reception, but in different ways, and through different processes of valuations. TIFF is an audience festival, and a market. Its interest is in *Ichi the Killer* as a novelty and as a film that can whip audiences into a state of frenzy. But those valuations were blocked because of the disaster of 9/11 that overshadowed the event. The IFFR is generally recognized as a leading festival for cinephiles, one where the serious valuation of film as art takes precedence over other forms of enjoyment. As such the IFFR's audience reaction is one that highlights the "uniqueness" of *Ichi the Killer* as a film in a class of its own. The fact it astonishes audiences and pulls them out of their comfort zones is what makes it cult. The BIFFF is a niche cult festival whose very reason of existence is owed to the cult of horror. The BIFFF's audience reaction demonstrates that if the framework of the audience itself (its ambiance) is robust enough, a film such as *Ichi the Killer* can function as a catalyst for the community it is unleashed upon, and heighten its already high level of cultism to a degree other films cannot.

This chapter followed a trajectory from the most mainstream events involving valuation, in which cult film receptions were isolated aberrations, over events such as festivals that by accident or design have become known to allow for "cult moments" – instances in which films with cult reputations and receptions (many of them only nascent or potential) exposed otherwise secure protocols and routines of cultural valuation, to niche genre festivals in which cultism is cemented into the fabric of the event. Throughout, the location and cultural place of events (i.e. their status in the wider landscape of public and commercial presences) has been instrumental in allowing or blocking cultist intervention. The next chapter will explore the presence of cult cinema with regard to methods of valuation in the contexts of censorship and criticism.

Note

1. The same could also be said for the pie-in-the-face anarchist mock awards (which were not limited to film). One of its most prominent activists was Belgian filmmaker Remy Belvaux, co-director of *Man Bites Dog*, who participated in the pie-ing of Bill Gates, and who later committed suicide.

4

Censorship and Criticism

This chapter discusses how the actions of two institutions in film classification, censorship and criticism, impact on cult reception contexts. The function of these institutions is to mediate the mechanisms of promotion and event-based valuation (which we explored in Chapters 2 and 3). This stage of intervention in the reception process is where the meaning of the term "cult" is most often seen as pejorative, and where films known as cult suffer a lot of adversity. Yet it is also where some of the consolidation of certain films *as* cults starts. In particular, we will isolate which roles controversy and connoisseurship play in forging cult reputations.

Censorship and Controversy

Censorship encompasses the efforts from regulators with political, legal, or moral authority to ban or withhold films from the public. At its strictest, this process entails the compulsory submission of films to boards of classification mandated by regional or national public services of a territory (such as a state) that result in legally binding rulings which can prevent films from being released in certain formats. In a looser sense it also includes negotiating the recommendations and complaints issued by religious and political pressure groups that operate through self-assigned mandates. Such groups see it as their duty to safeguard the sensitivities of communities from certain forms of harm. Negotiating the activities of pressure groups does not always lead to effective bans of films, but it

does regularly lead to controversies, public upheaval over the appropriateness of a film. Pressure groups can often muster a lot of vigilant support, expressed in boycotts or pickets of a film's screenings. Combined with inadequate policies to deal with this, and clumsy communications between policymakers and pressure groups, controversies can impact significantly on the public status of a film.

One look at the canon of cult cinema reveals that censorship and controversies are a constant in its history. From *Häxan*, *Un Chien Andalou*, and *Freaks*, via "deviant youth" films such as *Rebel without a Cause*, and instances of violence in *Enter the Dragon*, to the serial violence and sex eruptions of *Baise-moi* and *Ichi the Killer*, releases have been blocked, prints cut, and screenings picketed. There is, however, an evolution in the kind of roles institutions have played in objecting to films known as cult. Throughout, bans remain scarce, and they are mostly located in the periods that precede the 1960s. With the increases in permissiveness of the late 1960s and early 1970s, and the introduction of new platforms for film releases (video, DVD, internet), single-sided regulation was mostly replaced by debates *about* films' appropriateness. This, in turn, has led to an increase in controversies, enhanced by social network technologies that stimulate public discussion. In such a climate of constant negotiation cultism was likely to flourish. It might partly explain why recent decades have seen a steep increase in films laying claim to the label cult.

If we look at the kind of films embroiled in censorship and controversies, the emphasis lies on those

Cult Cinema: An Introduction. Ernest Mathijs and Jamie Sexton.
© 2011 Ernest Mathijs and Jamie Sexton. Published 2011 by Blackwell Publishing Ltd.

films containing explicit representations of sex and violence, and those with morally unacceptable imagery. As Mathijs and Mendik (2008b: 9) remark, representations of "animal cruelty, misogyny, non-Western ethnicities, small-town mentality, and the Holocaust" are among the depictions that most frequently lead to censorship or controversy. To these categories can be added children and people with physical disabilities. In some of the more extreme cases of such representations, there is a strong connection between a film's cult status and the censorship and controversies it attracted. Realistic "mondo films" such as *Cannibal Holocaust*, *Faces of Death*, rape-revenge films such as *Straw Dogs* and so-called "sick films" à la *Salò*, various Italian horror films (especially those of Dario Argento and Lucio Fulci), and several *Emanuelle* films (especially the *Black Emanuelle* series), are good examples. Without the opposition they have received their cult status would be far smaller.

The commotion over content is mostly a symptom of the awkward cultural position of these films. It is because cult films are films with fractured yet inoculated reception trajectories that they are ideal candidates for censorship and/or controversy. They come from outside the mainstream channels of distribution, often unaccompanied by canvasing strategies that pave the way for smooth classification processes; they are introduced to the public via niche and fringe festivals or have indeed upset protocols of valuation at mainstream festivals; and they come equipped with attitudes of hyperbole and reflexivity, with limitations in terms of nuance and skill impeding on their chances to be considered "normal." Therefore such films are more likely to be seen as at odds with what a film *should* be. It is exactly with such prescriptive modalities of audience reception that institutions such as censorship commissions operate.

A good example of this is the most infamous case of censorship involving the "video nasties" in the United Kingdom. Acting upon a request to provide video retailers with a list of titles likely to be impounded or seized if stocked (to save them from random raids by local authorities, but also to make retailers aware of their rights and duties), in 1982 the Director of Public Prosecutions published a list of 74 titles of films that had at one point or another had charges pressed against them. These films became known as the video nasties. It took until 1984 before a law came into place that gave the British Board of Film Classification the authority to regulate and censor videos – which led to the prosecution of 39 titles. In the meantime, campaigning groups and the British press had given the video nasties' list a lot of publicity. This created national media hysteria around the issue. In the course of these campaigns many titles not on the list, such as *The Brood* or *Taxi Driver*, were implicated. Such inclusion benefited their cult status. It also demonstrates how indistinguishable – and for the purposes of cult reputations, insignificant – actual and proxy censorship are.

Many of the films associated with the video nasties contain challenging, graphic, and disturbing imagery (Figure 4.1). However, as Martin Barker (1984) and Kate Egan (2007) have demonstrated, more important is that a great deal of the unease of the public lay with the cultural position of these films. Much of the concern over the shocking and spooky images of the video nasties can be understood as the result of the public's unawareness of rapid advancements in, and excessive use of, special effects, especially in the horror genre. The fact that that genre was, at the time, fast becoming a sort of grassroots, working-class cult in its own right, accompanied by particularly visible forms of fandom such as fanzines, heavy metal, and goth fashion, and various forms of merchandise and fan-art, made the concern only bigger – in the eyes of the mass media it looked as if the video nasties were the symptom of a subversive movement (see Chapter 18 for more on cult horror cinema). Moreover, there was the rapid and unwieldy expansion of the video industry, which took publics and lawmakers by surprise. There was also insecurity about labor relations in the ever-changing media industries, an anxiety that was regularly combined with worries over health and safety regulations. And there was a distinct unfamiliarity with the aggressive marketing techniques of new distribution companies such as Vipco (distributor of *Driller Killer*), Go Video (distributor of *Cannibal Holocaust*), Wizard Video (distributor of *Terminal Island* and *The Boogeyman*), or New Line Cinema (which released *Evil Dead*). Added to this were inadequate regulation guidelines for new carriers (such as cable TV or video), and laws ill-equipped to prosecute and/or protect consumers, employees, and the interests of the industry.

Figure 4.1   Several horror films that showcased the rapid advancement and excessive use of special effects offended moral crusaders and policymakers, and became known as "video nasties." Clockwise from top left: *Cannibal Holocaust*, *Evil Dead*, and *The Beyond*.

These factors became so intertwined a politically volatile climate emerged that allowed policymakers and self-proclaimed moral crusaders to lump actual and simulated, real and fictional, implicit and explicit, hyperbolic and reflexive representations of sex and violence together as an issue that commanded attention and repressive reaction.

Another example of how cult receptions clash with prescribed audience modalities is the pornographic film. One core reason for its cult status is the legal and public ambiguity of explicit sex in films, or strong suggestions thereof. Its consumption takes place in a context of semi-legality, where there are large overlaps between inconspicuous enjoyment of entertainment, geeky and cheeky fandom usages of popular culture, amoral and immoral behavior in defiance of society's norms and values, and downright illegal acts of obscenity punishable under criminal law. Distinctions between soft-core and hard-core, between suggestions of explicit sex and actual sex-on-screen have always existed, but have never really been followed through legally or in public perceptions. Hard-core pornography is tracked carefully, and often outlawed by censors. Richard Randall (1976), Linda Williams (1999) and Jacques Zimmer (2002), give extensive overviews of the censorship of pornography and its treatment by society, and comment on how this has helped create a reputation of rebelliousness. Zimmer (2002: 10–19) chronicles the history of pornography as that of a

struggle between the bourgeoisie and progressive libertarians. Films such as *Deep Throat*, *Behind the Green Door*, and *The Devil in Miss Jones*, all from the early 1970s, a period known as "porn chic" in which the pornographic briefly blossomed as a quasi-mainstream form of entertainment, all carry labels of rebelliousness in their receptions.

Randall (1976: 440–443) observes how, from a legal perspective, the category of pornography has problematized representations of sexuality because it allowed for a divide between illegal products (such as hard-core sexual materials that can be prosecuted as obscene under criminal law), legal products presenting themselves as illegal (marketed as though they are legally obscene while they are not, in other words "pandering" to or narrowly avoiding a certain status), and completely legal products that occasionally attracted accusations of obscenity because they got caught up in the mix. Even in the cases where easily identifiable hard-core pornography was prosecuted, confusions led to a wild variety in verdicts; Randall remarks how *Deep Throat* was once found obscene and *not* obscene in the same state. Such ambiguities have greatly enhanced the cult reputation of explicit sex and materials caught in, or trying to exploit, the associations the term brought with it. It has certainly aided the cult status of films such as *Heat*, *Last Tango in Paris*, *Caligula*, and *Emmanuelle*.

In some cases, situations like these have led cult films to become proverbial *causes célèbres* that ignite broader cultural debate on expressions of culture, and instruments that triggered regulations to change. However, in most cases such recognition is reserved for films with production credentials and reception trajectories closer to what is seen as respectable. A good case in point is the upheaval surrounding the NC-17 and R-ratings in the United States at the beginning of the 1990s. These two ratings were designed to replace the X-rating, which had lost much of its power as deterrent after hardcore pornography ridiculed the rating with its "triple X" self-assignations. In an attempt to re-regulate film markets, the MPAA hoped the NC-17 rating would allow a distinction between art house risqué material, and plain smut. Among the first films caught up in the confusion were *Atamé, Henry and June*, and *The Cook, the Thief, His Wife, and her Lover*. *Showgirls* became one of the first big budget Hollywood films to have the NC-17 label bestowed upon it (Sandler 2001). The stubbornness of director Paul Verhoeven in making changes to obtain an R-rating no doubt helped the film gain its cult reputation. The atmosphere of reception, exemplified by the ambiguity of distinctions between art house and exploitation, was as significant as the film's content.

If we assume that those in charge of classifications and those attempting to influence the process are knowledgeable about the cultural position of films, we can also assume chances will be taken to court controversy. In Chapter 2 we observed how many marketing campaigns attempt to stir up interest in films that would otherwise not stand out among the general supply of films. Trying to create a controversy by rubbing against the sensitivities of the moral majority is as good a technique as any other. Similarly, the media, policymakers, pressure groups, and other players involved in public communication can use controversies to promote their own causes. The medium of film seems to be a preferred instrument for such efforts. Talk about film always makes good copy. It is highly visible, draws lots of attention, and makes for easy cultural currency. In fact, since the 1920s, and more or less parallel with the advent of Hollywood, of the star-system, of fandom, *and* of cult movies, cinema has had a privileged relationship with the reporting of scandal. This relationship is most infamously described in *Hollywood Babylon*, a book written by cult filmmaker Kenneth Anger (which we detail in Chapter 7).

Because cult reputations are so heavily implicated in controversies, it has become a tradition among researchers of cult cinema to investigate periods immediately preceding increased regulation – on the assumption such periods must have had some scandals causing the introduction of stricter censorship and tax regulations for cinema. They are therefore often framed as eras of "decadence" before the restoration. The early 1930s, just after the introduction of sound, but before the installation of the Hays code of self-regulation in Hollywood, saw exploitation cinema make concerted efforts to court controversy and aim for cultist receptions. In the case of *Dracula, Frankenstein, Freaks, King Kong* and the first two Tarzan films (*Tarzan the Ape Man*, and *Tarzan and His Mate*) this aim was actually achieved. Thomas Doherty (1999) describes this period as a heady one. Similarly, the first half of the 1970s saw a steep increase in exploitation output and cultist appreciation combined with permissiveness in regulation and easy market access for independent productions.

In addition, it is worth noting the collective nature of controversies that have had significant impacts on, or created, cult reputations. Not every scandal or controversy, and not every act of censorship leads to a cult reputation. In fact, because there are so many controversies and scandals, and so many instances of censorship, singular cases might not pull a film's reception out of normality enough to account for a cult reputation. When cases run across an extended period of time, however, stubbornly refusing to go away and unnerving the public profoundly, there is a bigger chance they will amplify or establish a cult reputation. The several years that span the video nasties or pornography controversies, the recurrent upheavals around *Rebel without a Cause* (Biltereyst 2005) or the continued polemic between scholars over *The Brood* (Mathijs 2008: 79–83) are good examples.

In sum, censorship and controversy ignite curiosity and separate the reception trajectory of a film from the many others that are circulating in a territory. If the reason for the censorship is related to challenging representations of sexuality and/or violence, or to moral taboos, the film's chances of being isolated as an aberration are even higher, since it is more likely to fall outside what is considered "normal" and "acceptable." More important than a film's content, however, is its challenging position as a symptom of cultural discomfort, especially when a group of films is lumped together. If, on top of that, public adversity towards a film extends across a sustained period of time, it is more likely controversies and/or censorship will become a dominant factor in its cult status.

Cult Connoisseurship

The majority of critical routines ignore films with cult reception trajectories. That is because criticism, as it is classically understood, involves the making of distinctions between "good" or "bad," and the offering, through interpretation, of viewing advice based on the criteria used in arriving at such distinctions. The best example, and also the most institutionalized, is reviewing: an act of classification of cinema that is most commonly expressed through value-judgment, and managed by various publications and media corporations. Because their protocols are so focused on the mainstream of cinema, or on finding the new and novel, reviews are often unable to capture the particularities of cult cinema receptions, let alone appreciate them. Films with cultist reception contexts consistently receive bad reviews. Let us give two examples. When *Bring me the Head of Alfredo Garcia* was first released, *The Wall Street Journal* called it "grotesque, sadistic, irrational, obscene, incompetent" while to *New York Magazine* it was "a catastrophe" (Cooper 2011). *Bad Taste* was, upon its release in the United Kingdom, greeted as a film that had "nothing to commend it but its foetid imagination" (Barratt 2008: 38).

Classifications that are somewhat more sympathetic to cult cinema appear mainly in what David Bordwell (1989: 20) identifies as "essayistic criticism." The formal and informal institutions that govern it are less corporate than reviewing and geared more towards collective attitudes, assumptions, and circles. When Bordwell uses the term "invisible colleges" to refer to the informal institutions that back up essayistic criticism, he is referring to informal and diffuse circles of authorship and readership that are very much like the ones that operate within the esoteric networks that characterize cult receptions at festivals (see Chapter 3). As Bordwell (1989: 19–20) points out, these institutions, and the classifications they develop

to arrive at views on films, are often "riven by disputes," yet they also remain "consanguine by virtue of the concrete routines they employ." They admit wide-ranging differences but are united in what seems a cause. The metaphor Bordwell evokes is that of the medieval Christian church. Essayistic criticism often also attempts to devote attention to films ignored by the mainstream (so called "misunderstood" films) in order to expand or interrogate the canon. Films with cult reception trajectories are perfect examples. Above all, however, a substantial part of essayistic criticism is cultist in its own right in that it is inspired by *connoisseurship*: the skill and talent to be an arbiter of taste, and to deliberately pitch expertise against mainstream and middlebrow conventionality. Connoisseurship also includes the self-reflexive interrogation of skill, talent, taste, and expertise.

Cult connoisseurship, then, exceeds regular connoisseurship in celebrating films whose reception trajectories put them at the margins of what is culturally acceptable. It places itself in an oppositional situation, at the margins of the routines and practices commonly seen as key to criticism. According to Greg Taylor (1999: 16–17), this position is often a vanguard one, concerned with exposing critical gestures and attitudes with the aim of pushing aesthetic appreciation ahead. It is less about the films than about the critical writing itself. Cult connoisseurship tries to achieve a form of purist classification, untainted by demands of efficiency or timeliness. Because of its self-declared freedom from constraints, it cannot pertain to hold an objective or aggregate view. It has to be impressionistic, based on subjective judgment. It also has to be disinterested, never giving the idea that it approaches its subject with a purpose – the professional expression of the phenomenal experience detailed in Chapter 1. Below, we will summarize some of the most important occurrences of cult connoisseurship.

Surrealist Criticism

The first form of cult connoisseurship, surrealist criticism, is also the most notoriously impenetrable. Attempting to turn the tables on the dictates of taste, and inspired by the rebelliousness of the Dadaists, surrealist criticism attempts to make a case for films whose combination of immorality, sheer lack of quality and popular, lowbrow appeal would exclude them from any canon. Films that were "more often than not involuntarily sublime, scorned by the critics, charged with cretinism or infantilism," wrote Ado Kyrou, "anecdotal" and "demented" films "shown in local fleapits," were the ones best equipped for this turning of the tables (Kyrou 2000: 68–69). The best-known example of the kind of film surrealist critics thus championed was American slapstick comedy, the anarchy of which was regarded as a rebellion against the bourgeoisie. The films of Charles Chaplin ("Charlot") and Buster Keaton in particular were put forward as works of genius. Next to that, surrealist critics lauded the fantastic films of George Méliès, the popular serials of Louis Feuillade (especially *Fantômas*), and, occasionally, Hollywood stars. Paul Hammond (2000: 29), in his overview of surrealist writing on cinema, refers explicitly to the "cult of Louise Brooks" among the surrealists. Much of the ensuing cult reputation of *Pandora's Box* was connected to that (Peary 1981: 247–251). Of course, surrealist cinema itself, and the films of Luis Buñuel in particular, were also cultified (see, for instance, Jean Vigo's critical poem on *Un Chien Andalou* in Mathijs and Mendik 2008a: 173–174).

In its practices, surrealist criticism was extremely impressionist, effusive, and personal, and characterized by an aggressive tone. Its language attempted to escape rationalist argumentation and rhetoric, and was drenched with cultist references, such as "eroticism," "amorality," "pre-consciousness," "rejuvenation," or "vitality." A fetishism of commodities was prevalent throughout. Hammond calls it the "cult of kitsch" (Hammond 2000: 27). In arriving at classifications of "see" and "don't see" films, the surrealist critics often relied on three concepts: "dépaysement" (disorientation), aleatory (accidentality), and "photogenia" (a term from French critic Louis Delluc, capturing the "ineffable 'quintessence' or the magic of cinema"; Stam 1999: 34). All three referred as much to a quality intrinsic to films as to a position of perception, visible only through particular viewing practices. Buñuel (1927, in Hammond 2000: 61–62), in his praise for Keaton's *College*, listed photogenia as central to what

cinema should be. This uneasy ambiguity between essentialism and perception is typical for cult connoisseurship. As befits the phenomenal experience, the truth never only resides in the text, but equally in the beholder.

Adding to the cultism of surrealist criticism was its invisible college of the surrealist movement. Cult cinema connoisseurship flourished in surrealist criticism especially during what is known as the "intuitive period" (1919–1929) of the Surrealist movement, when the writing was confined to publications with small circulations (Hammond 2000: 25). As the movement developed and became better organized, and more institutionalized, especially in its affiliations with the political Left, it became less cultist.

Cult Cinephilia and MacMahonism

The second form of cult connoisseurship we would like to highlight revolves around cinephilia and what Robert Stam (1999: 83–88) has called the "cult of the auteur" of the 1950s and 1960s. In his study of American film criticism, Taylor (1999) analyzes how critics such as Manny Farber (who wrote for *New Republic* and *The Nation*) and Parker Tyler (who first edited the surrealist journal *View*, and subsequently did much of his writing for *Film Culture*), moved away from the kinds of classifications and evaluations their predecessors had been making about cinema. Dissatisfied with the influence of the heritage of New Criticism and Modernism on cinema, and keen to assert their own specific connoisseurship, they started to adopt what Taylor calls "cultist" and "camp" attitudes. They championed films from low repute (and increasingly from a countercultural sphere) that allowed them to promote a "vanguard" aesthetic perspective, one that was more pure (more directed towards the "essence" of cinema) and continuously fresh enough to challenge the status quo of "classical cinema" and to prevent canon-making from settling in. The fact that Farber saw himself more as a painter than a critic, and Tyler regarded himself very much a poet, meant that both exercised their criticism more as a hobby, from a position of passionate disinterestedness. Their goal was not so much to "rescue film culture," as Taylor puts it, but to "shoot from the hip" and to "delineate the oppositional margins of popular culture" (Taylor 1999: 43). Theirs was very much the position of the "solitary activist" (1999: 47), who sought to "liberate the spectator from the 'sweet fog' of mainstream culture and return him to an idealized, revitalized version of his own folk traditions" (1999: 48). Among the films Farber deemed worthy of discussion (though not necessarily of *liking*) were *Casablanca* and *All about Eve*. Among Tyler's key exemplars were Mickey Mouse and Charles Chaplin. But the actual movies mattered less than the "critical skill and an artistic imagination" (Taylor 1999: 73). As with so many other attempts to promote the "new," this joint cultism/cinephilia eventually exhausted itself. By the end of the 1960s and early 1970s, as the dissemination of underground and exploitation cinema grew, the vanguard perspective ran out of steam. Parker Tyler's scathing overview of countercultural cinema from 1969, *Underground Film*, observed an "intellectual bankruptcy in the name of chic [that] hindered informed aesthetic distinctions" (Taylor 1999: 118).

One instance of cinephilia that is particularly cultist in its connoisseurship is the MacMahonist circle. Located largely in France, it originated in the margin of the wave of auteurism, from the mid 1950s onwards. Against the highbrow and middle-class aesthetics that were being promoted by the Parisian establishment, a playful and cheeky reaction originated, dubbed MacMahonism. The fact that the MacMahoniens named themselves after the theater ("Le MacMahon," near the Place de l'Etoile in Paris) where they convened, and that they championed films because they went against what was deemed respectable, illustrates how here too the conditions of reception were as important as the actual films. It confirms the cultism of this invisible college.

The MacMahoniens are often mentioned in the same breath as disciples of André Bazin and the critics of the *Cahiers du cinéma*, with whom they shared many concerns (and many of the MacMahoniens did publish in the *Cahiers*). The main difference is the high degree of connoisseur-like gamesmanship and fetishism of masculinity. Instead, of constructing a canon consisting of John Ford, Alfred Hitchcock, or Howard Hawks (like many other critics did), the MacMahoniens trawled deep into what Hollywood dumped on the French postwar market to emerge with Fritz Lang, Otto Preminger, Raoul Walsh and Joseph Losey. Maverick directors such as Nicholas Ray, filmmakers courting

B-movie status such as Jacques Tourneur, a few biblical films with Charlton Heston, and several Italian and Spanish Hercules epics also received high praise, especially in attempts to provoke reactions. This critical gambling was not void of cheekiness. As Raphaëlle Moine (2008: 144) points out, the MacMahoniens introduced the word *peplum*, with all its dubious connotations of historical insincerity and camp masculinity, to cinema parlance partly because they coupled their cinephilia to "a rather affected taste for the trashy." The main outlet for the MacMahonists was the magazine *Présence du Cinéma*. Its editor Michel Mourlet was decribed as the "high priest of MacMahonism." Jacques Lourcelles and Fereydou Hoyveda (who also wrote for the left-leaning, surrealist inspired *Positif*) were among the most notable critics of the group. Later, Jean-Luc Godard and François Truffaut were counted among the "apostles of the MacMahonist faith" (Hoberman and Rosenbaum 1991: 26).

Even as it opposed canons, middlebrow and highbrow taste, and respectable filmmakers, the impact of cinephilic cult connoisseurship, especially its advancement of auteurism, was so great that it became constitutive of a new canon inspite of itself. The hysteria of the later criticism of Tyler, the ecstasy of some MacMahoniens, the praise for camp by Susan Sontag, the self-avowed "cultist auteurism" of Andrew Sarris, nor the irrational eccentric criticism of Jack Smith or Kenneth Anger could stop this evolution. During the 1960s, Pauline Kael, who had always been skeptical of the auteur theory, mourned the newfound seriousness of cinephilia on a number of occasions and pleaded for a return to "excitement" and "bad movies" (Kael 1969; see Sconce 2007 for an elaboration). But no new critical efforts revived New York or Parisian cinephilic cult connoisseurship. In fact, as the increased ritualism of the *Casablanca* cult celebrations in the Brattle theater near Harvard University and of the midnight movies indicated, cultism would move away from cinephilia altogether, at least for a while.

Fan Criticism

The final two forms of cult connoisseurship we would like to showcase are both instances of "niche criticism." With this term we mean a form of criticism that has a strong emphasis on closeness with the object of scrutiny, an alignment with its receptions, and an intensification of the commitment that has the cultist see pretty much all of the world through the lens of their object of fascination – an attitude shared by fan and marketer. We will discuss two of the most prominent exponents of this, namely fan criticism and Do-It-Yourself (DIY) criticism. Both display a desire to move criticism as close as possible to the experience of the naturally emerging audience and the non-expert viewer. Yet through their desire to come as close as possible to the films they love, and through their obsession with details, these forms of criticism also present themselves as forms of specialization. As forms of amateurism they have taken over the vanguard role of defining cinematic purism that was once held by cinephilia. Yet they occupy a radically different part of the critical spectrum. In general, their efforts are ridiculed because they are seen as amateurs addressing audiences with shallow interests and curiosity. Much like surrealist criticism they are also less preoccupied with the "rhetoric of the text." Often their arguments are made through bricolage and illustration instead of through academic reasoning. This includes a much more liberal use of fonts, punctuation, and lettertypes, and also some preference for visual illustrations – drawings, original artwork, and the production of amateur media work (documentaries, taped interviews, short films, montages of clips, re-stagings, and so on). In a sense, the niche critic is located in a sphere of opposition to the professional industry of film reviewing. Its invisible college is what Terry Eagleton (1984: 115–118) has called the "intimate sphere" of culture. This is the sphere of informal personal contacts, such as family, neighborhood, community, flea markets, sidewalks, chat rooms, parking lots or bars – a sphere in which the experience of subjectivity is essential. It is the sort of atmosphere Maffesoli sees as crucial to affective communities (see Chapter 1).

Fan criticism first became visible in the 1960s but blossomed from the 1970s onwards. It consists of two types of publications, prozines and fanzines. According to David Sanjek (1990: 152), prozines are periodicals that address the fan reader but that are produced as commercial, mainstream magazines. *Famous Monsters of Filmland* (started in 1958) and *Castle of Frankenstein* (started in 1962) preceded a wave of prozine magazines such as *Cinéfantastique* (1970), *Starlog* (1976) and *Fangoria* (1979). In France, a pioneering role was played by *Midi-Minuit Fantastique*. It was among the first fanzines to make a move from a niche newsletter to connoisseurship. *Midi-Minuit* was succeeded by *Écran fantastique* (from 1969 onwards) and *Mad Movies* (1972). Inspired by specific communities, such as the cult of *Star Trek* and the cult of horror cinema (for *Starlog* and *Fangoria* respectively), prozines are often closely affiliated with burgeoning fan cultures and they share with their fans a dedication to a narrow focus on one or two genres – or even subgenres. For example, when the abundant supply of horror films in the early 1980s warranted demarcations of various subgenres within the genre, *Fangoria* developed a spin-off, *Gorezone*, dedicated to horror subgenres in order to prevent other magazines from intruding onto its market. *Écran fantastique* launched *Vendredi 13* with the same intent.

While prozines are a very visible exponent of cultist criticism, they are usually seen as less deeply committed than fanzines. According to Sanjek, fanzines are amateur publications that "constitute an alternative brand of film criticism, a school with its own set of values and virtues. They aim not only to *épater le bourgeois* but also to root out obscure marginalia … and revel in the private consumption of outrage for outrage's sake" (1990: 153). Again, *Famous Monsters of Filmland* and *Castle of Frankenstein* provided a lot of the inspiration for fanzines, especially through the ways in which they experimented with tone and tenor in their reviews (often a mix of admiration and sarcasm), and through their tools of analysis: retrospectives and biographies create a sense of history; interviews play a key role in establishing the impression of semi-direct communication between artists, critics, and audiences/readers; mini- or capsule reviews give fanzines a sense of completism and archivist significance; the editors and letters pages are prominent places for continued discussion. These magazines also display a desire towards seeing films as part of collective sensibilities, as part of a "wave," a "movement," or a "new era," one of which the fan critic and the readership declared themselves an equal part. Among the most notable examples of fanzines are *Sleazoid Express*, *The Gore Gazette*, *Wet Paint*, *Le masque de Méduse*, and *Vampirella*.

The relations of prozines and fanzines to cult cinema are radically different from those of cinephilia. Their rhetoric is directed towards an appreciation of the collective effort instead of the solitary genius (though there is ample praise for the "crazy loner"). Sanjek observes a slight preference for the "cult of the technician" in prozines and a "cult of the auteur" in fanzines. Across the board, however, special effects make-up artists such as Tom Savini, or storyboard artists and production designers such as Dan O'Bannon (before he moved into writing and directing) receive as much attention as renowned directors, and their work is imbued with a form of working-class street credibility. Among the directors that owe a lot of their cult status to fan criticism are David Cronenberg (*Scanners*, *Videodrome*), Wes Craven (*Last House on the Left*, *Nightmare on Elm Street*), Larry Cohen (*It's Alive*), Lucio Fulci (*The Beyond*), Tobe Hooper (*Texas Chainsaw Massacre*), and George Romero (*Night of the Living Dead*, *Dawn of the Dead*). They formed the core of the "cult of horror" propagated by *Cinéfantastique* and *Fangoria* (see Chapter 18 for more on this). Among the many ingénue fan-critics were self-declared cultists such as Joe Dante, Frank Henenlotter, and Mick Garris, who were practitioners, fans, and critics at the same time. Numerous issues also contain DIY guides to special effects (Mathijs 2010b). Classified ads are often platforms for collectors to exchange fan-related materials – in this sense they function as an extension of the flea market model we sketched in Chapter 2.

Over time, the distinction between prozines and fanzines has become more pronounced. Prozines have developed less interest in cultist appreciation and moved into a more institutionalized kind of professional criticism, of which *Cinéfantastique*, *Fangoria*, *Starlog*, *SFX*, and *Starfix* have become the representatives. Yet they still maintain a niche interest through associations with parts of fan cultures, such as fan conventions, collector's weekends, specialist stores, or spin-offs. Fanzines, on the other hand, have become more radical in their cultism. In the 1990s they were represented by publications that were mostly one-man operations, such as Tim Lucas's *Video Watchdog*, Andy Black's *Necronomicon*, David Kerekes's Headpress, and Harvey Fenton's FabPress. The niche appeal of these publications actually helped films sustain cult reputations: it reinforced Mario Bava's and Dario Argento's reputations, spearheaded the praise for the films of Bigas Luna and Peter Jackson, and assisted in the rediscovery of the films of Radley Metzger, Harry Kümel, and Alain Robbe-Grillet.

In their political positioning too, fanzines have shown a tendency towards radical collectivity. Instead of the existentialism of cinephilia, it showed a preference for utopian and communal philosophies of society. Hiding behind straightforward descriptors of setting or storyworld, a lot of letters, editorials, and reviews of films such as *Blade Runner*, *Dune*, and *The Lord of the Rings* reveal a fascination with sometimes crude and naive but often also idealistic negotiations of democratic and totalitarian variations of governance. This function of interrogation makes fanzines "engaged"; it gives them a cause shared with much of cult cinema.

DIY Criticism

Since the rise of the internet developments in cult connoisseurship have shown a surge in criticism that, like fanzines, offers subjective, focused commentary with a penchant for trivia and details. We find those characteristics in abundance in what can be called Do-It-Yourself (DIY) criticism, a form of online commentary often formatted as "user comments," "threads," or "responses" that is widespread, though mostly directed to a small, niche readership. Among the most visible examples are the improvised user reviews and message board comments on the Internet Movie Database (www.imdb.com), and the various contributions of amateur reviewers to social network media such as Blogspot, Facebook, MySpace or Youtube. DIY criticism contains many characteristics of fan criticism: it preferences impressionist and subjective comments, it relishes focus, single-mindedness, and closeness, and it puts itself in opposition to professional reviewing while still claiming expertise. It is also decidedly peer-to-peer in its address (though not necessarily always in its readership) and, connected with that, it demonstrates a sense of informality of address – with much attention for hearsay, trivia, and conjecture.

While directors still receive a lot of attention in DIY criticism, there is less emphasis on their efforts than on other components of the films and their receptions.

This is undoubtedly linked to the fact that DIY criticism favors feature debuts, such as *Superstar: The Karen Carpenter Story*, *Tetsuo*, *Man Bites Dog*, *Cube*, or *Donnie Darko*, but it is also due to other factors. Among the most notable points of interest are speculations about the story world of the film (with ample elaborations on that world's plausible and improbable aspects), and observations about the simplicity yet ingeniousness of film styles (observations that are often approached as peer review, frequently with a "I could do that too" undertone). Next to this, DIY criticism appreciates wit, irony and mild nihilism, which it frequently mirrors in tone. A good case in point is the online reception of a film such as *Nothing*, which looks effortless and which invites audiences to speculate on issues such as user-friendly technology, pop-philosophy, and morality in a world where one can only trust one's closest friends.

Like fan criticism, DIY criticism has been suspected of maintaining a contentious relationship with the commercial or corporate sphere. According to Elena Gorfinkel (2008: 38), "media industries have embedded connoisseurship into online merchandising, for example, in the 'Users like you enjoyed...' recommendation feature of Amazon, Netflix, and Youtube." This suspicion of viral marketing, of being employed in a clever scheme, often affects DIY critics, and it has damaged some reputations such as that of super-blogger Harry Knowles. In most cases, however, the tension between suspicion and trust does not deter participants from engaging in DIY criticism. Quite the contrary, the activity has become widespread, so common in fact that the perception at the end of the first decade of the twenty-first century may no longer be that it is marginal or niche at all. In the form of "sweding" this form of cultist appreciation has even made its way into the film profession. Originally, a term used to refer to erased and subsequently recreated cinema in the period of VHS, sweding was re-employed as a result of its use in *Be Kind Rewind*, a film by Michel Gondry (who directed the deviously simple clip for the "Mad World" song that helped *Donnie Darko* reach its cult status). Thanks to *Be Kind Rewind* sweding has become a tool in discussions about different generations of "new media" and their user-oriented and deliberately artisan creations that carry limitations as a form of pride rather than an obstacle. In that sense it is similar to how lack of access and

professionalism became points of "authenticity" for the niche critic.

Through its use of video, DVD and the internet, DIY criticism has had a profound impact on the viewing contexts of cult cinema connoisseurship. The rituals of endurance that were core to repeat viewing of the 1980s have been complemented by a new fascination for short materials (this has led to the cultification of the video clips of Michel Gondry for instance). In addition, shortness of exposure is a key element in new tendencies such as summary viewing or compilation viewing. Summary viewing consists of what Elena Gorfinkel, via Michael Newman, calls "snippy viewing" – whereby only the worst and most embarrassing moments, or representative samples, montages or "bloopers," are actually viewed (Gorfinkel 2008: 38). Good examples of creative interventions in summary viewing are *Pulp Fiction in 5 Seconds*, *Scary Mary Poppins*, or the *How It Should Have Ended* animated video speculations on alternative endings of films (most often cult films). Compilation viewing supersedes this by combining snippets of films into compilations pulled from multiple films. These are not always homages, but frequently also compilations of errors – with again the assumption that the DIY critic is a peer to the filmmaker. Frequently, such compilations are shared through the internet on shared user content platforms like MySpace, Facebook, or YouTube. Augmented viewing involves the adding of material to the original film in order to comment on it. The running commentary, or "riffing," that the television show *Mystery Science Theater 3000* provided when it screened exploitation or B-movies has been a prominent source of inspiration for this practice.

Conclusion

To conclude this chapter we would like to address "word of mouth endorsement." Because this process belongs equally in the areas of marketing, auteur, and star showmanship (especially celebrity endorsements, such as those Quentin Tarantino and John Waters are known for), and the peer endorsement of fan cultures of cult cinema, it is only tangentially related to the institutions of reception we have outlined above. But it informs them nevertheless.

Overall, most institutionalized forms of film classi-fication, whether concerned with moral, legal, ideo-logical, or aesthetic norms, behave adversely towards films whose receptions are fragmented, fractured, and unhinged. Yet within the margins there are several components of the same institutions that do find reason to champion these films. In most cases, this is not so much out of a love for the films themselves, though that is often offered as the overt reason, but out of a desire to position oneself, as taste-maker, as critic, or as intellectual. All of these processes try to achieve a status of trustworthiness that is directly related to a self-perception of significance.

It is at this level that the desire for advocacy and the fear of insecurity meet. The best possible metaphor to illustrate this situation is the concept of "word of mouth endorsement." As a simple communication process between two sources, without much interfer-ence from other forces, word of mouth is squarely placed within the intimate sphere; it relies heavily on mutual trust and personal contact. Word of mouth endorsements give the feeling they are to be trusted because of the position of equality between receiver and communicator. One of the most legendary ex-amples is *El Topo*, a film whose midnight run in New York popularized the midnight movie phenomenon, and which relied almost uniquely on word of mouth endorsement (including that of John Lennon, who subsequently got involved in financing *The Holy Mountain*). Given the esoteric networks of connections cult films rely upon in their reception trajectories, personal endorsements have a fairly great importance – a single voice can make a distinct difference in the reception of cult cinema. To believe individual voices count is the prime conviction of connoisseurs and classifiers in a world filled with institutions.

5

Fandom and Subculture

While the study of media fans and cult media do not totally overlap, they do have much in common: cult media has often been identified through the fan devotion that it has given rise to. Our focus is, of course, on cult cinema. While we will draw upon broader media fandom in this chapter, we will consider its significance mainly in relation to cult film (though we will point towards the importance of other media, especially when non-film media consumption informs the manner by which films are framed by fans). We will chart the overlaps and interconnections between fan studies and cult cinema in relation to some of the key historical developments within these fields of study.

We focus primarily on the academic study of fans in this chapter. Some other aspects, such as fan criticism, and transnational fandom in the form of "otaku" are discussed in Chapters 4 and 11 respectively.

Fan Studies: Early Approaches

Within academia, earlier studies of fans within media and cultural studies have tended to engage with fans as particularly *active* audiences (Jenkins 1992; Fiske 1992; Bacon-Smith 1992). This was partly a response to the ways in which media fans had often been ridiculed and/or demonized within the media (for example, the constant stress upon fans with psychological problems who stalk and sometimes murder media celebrities). Thus, Jenkins argued that "to speak as a fan is to accept what has been labelled a subordinate position within the cultural hierarchy, to accept an identity constantly belittled or criticized by institutional authorities"

(1992: 43). Against such negative commentary, there was a tendency to stress the positive nature of being a fan through focusing on the activities and communities which emerged from fandom.

Many studies of fans tended to focus on fans as producers, as a way of distinguishing them from "ordinary consumers." Henry Jenkins, drawing on the work of Michel de Certeau, emphasized the notion of "textual poaching," whereby fans can appropriate elements of a popular text and inscribe it with their own meanings. Here, fans resist "official" ways of reading and instead "raid" (as opposed to respecting) the text: "Undaunted by traditional conceptions of literary and intellectual property, fans raid mass culture, claiming its materials for their own use, reworking them as the basis for their own cultural creations and social interactions" (1992: 18).

Jenkins was keen to relate fandom to cultural politics, a political emphasis that was undoubtedly influenced by the fact that academic cultural studies tended at this point to focus upon popular culture in relation to broader social and political processes. Therefore, studies of audiences often focused on what Nicholas Abercrombie and Brian Longhurst (1998: 15–28) have termed the "incorporation/resistance" paradigm, which looks at how audiences are incorporated into, or resist, the "dominant order" via media use. Within the study of fandom this was evident in the stress upon fans' various forms of activity, of engaging in resistant behavior in order to undermine dominant ideologies (Fiske 1989: 56). While not all fan activity was construed as resistant, there was a tendency to focus on fans as engaged in "micro-political" acts: not

Cult Cinema: An Introduction. Ernest Mathijs and Jamie Sexton.
© 2011 Ernest Mathijs and Jamie Sexton. Published 2011 by Blackwell Publishing Ltd.

large-scale, radical activity but small-scale, resistant behavior. So, for example, fans could be seen as progressive in the sense that they were opposing "official" culture, through challenging what types of culture were worthy of consecration or through acts of reading/production which conflicted with institutionally sanctioned readings. An example of the latter is when fans come into conflict with copyright holders when they produce fan texts, particularly when they produce subversive interpretations which a company may not consider suitable. (Slash fiction, which creates same-sex couplings between characters, is particularly prominent within debates over correct types of fan production.) We will return to some criticism of these approaches when we focus upon more recent developments in fan studies, but for now we will think about the study of cult cinema fans in relation to these developments.

Visible and Performative Fans

It is perhaps no coincidence that both "fan" and "cult" derive from religious nomenclature: through negative connotations, both terms spread to other areas of culture. Both the study of fans and of cult cinema within the 1980s and early 1990s tended to look at the more positive aspects of the categories in question, thus marking a period in which the concepts were undergoing serious revaluation.

The stress upon audience activity marks one of the most well-known cult films, *The Rocky Horror Picture Show*: through dressing up, talking back at the screen, and dancing and singing within the cinema auditorium, fans of the film were engaged in textual poaching because they "remade" the text within a broader community of fans. This active, performative fandom, however, was not on the whole a prominent pattern in terms of cult film audience responses. There were, nevertheless, people who would note that many cult film screenings – in particular midnight screenings – were distinctively communal spaces in which the audience would often chat, drink, sometimes smoke pot, and occasionally shout things at the screen. Such visible text-audience encounters could be observed to note how cult cinema offered an alternative to "normal" consumption, just as fans' active behaviors

could be contrasted to the consumption of "ordinary" consumers.

While *Rocky Horror* remains the most notable case of cult cinema as defined by its visible fan responses, a number of other cult films have developed visible and performative fandoms since then, and can thus demonstrate fans as active and communal agents. A more recent incidence of such fandom being linked to a film's cult status is *The Big Lebowski* (see Klinger 2010b, for an overview). In 2002, while vending at the Derby City Tattoo Expo, Will Russell and Scott Shuffitt were quoting lines from the film when other nearby vendors joined in. From this spontaneous moment of camaraderie arose an idea to organize a festival based around *The Big Lebowski*, and so was born the "Lebowskifest," a festival set in a bowling alley that features people in costume, bowling contests, and prizes (Figure 5.1). As the festival was popular, it spread: there have now been seven annual festivals in Louisville, as well as others in places such as

Figure 5.1   The fifth annual Lebowskifest.

Chicago, Los Angeles, and New York, and one in Edinburgh, UK. Many subsequent events have grown in size and attracted guests from the film. They have also given rise to an array of merchandise: posters, t-shirts and stickers, as well as a 2007 fan book (Green *et al.* 2007). There was also an academic symposium on the film as part of the fifth annual festival, which featured a couple of presenters in costume (Robertson 2006) and brought together people who were both fans and scholars, or in Hills' terms, "scholar-fans" (Hills 2002a: 16–21). There are, additionally, a number of other related sites that have grown around the film, such as "Dudeism.com," which is a mock religion based around the ideas of the Dude.

Earlier academic study of cult cinema is more similar to fan studies, however, in its emphasis upon the fan/ cultist as representing an alternative to the mainstream. As mentioned, fans were often valorized for the ways in which their activities could be seen as different from normal (and, by implication, mainstream) consumption practices through refashioning texts according to their own agendas, by using the text as a platform for communal purposes, and/or through challenging official taste. The cultist could also be seen as challenging taste and acting outside of mainstream consumption norms (through attending midnight screenings and repertory screenings, and repeatedly attending screenings of a single title) and of, in Sarris's words, loving films "beyond all reason" (Telotte 1991a: 5). Therefore, if we think about other modes of visible fandom, we can also associate these further to degrees of "alternativeness."

The fan pilgrimage, for example, has become an increasingly studied area (Hills 2002a: 144–157; Couldry 2003: 75–94; Sandvoss 2005: 44–66). These are not always necessarily related to cult texts, but those instances that are can be distinguished through the manner by which such texts embody alternative values for many of their fans. *The Wicker Man*, for example, has since its original release gained a dedicated following. Some fans of the film display their love for it in reasonably conventional ways, through purchasing the film and sometimes related memorabilia, and through gaining a good knowledge of the film. Others take this further by going on a pilgrimage to where the film was made, or collecting more obscure and hard-to-find collectibles associated with the film. Visits to the

locations where the film was shot have become so popular that the South West Scotland Screen Commission publish a "Wicker Man trail" for visitors to follow, while a local coach company organizes a guided tour of key locations (Smith 2006: 264).

Such information signals a response to the continuing fascination that the film plays within a number of people's lives, despite the fact that it was not successful when originally released. In this sense, fans are a conspicuous segment of the film's identity: they have been active in resurrecting it from commercial oblivion and have kept it culturally alive. The film also is an alternative text: it represents a pagan culture and appeals to some people who are interested in occult issues and unconventional beliefs. Smith interestingly notes how the tourist visits to the film's locations are in some senses similar to the popularity of heritage sites, including locations that have featured within heritage films and television programs. *The Wicker Man*, though, exemplifies a kind of alternative heritage, a cultural trend that has been on the increase over the past decade or so. This is represented by record labels such as Ghost Box, which publishes music by artists "that find inspiration in library music, folklore, vintage electronics and haunted television soundtracks" (from the Ghost Box website); the "English Heretic" organization, which is both a parody of English Heritage but also an occult-inspired alternative to it (and which has published a booklet and CD-R guide entitled *The Sacred Geography of British Cinema*); as well as Julian Cope's "Head Heritage," which is involved in documenting prehistoric sites and pagan lore. *The Wicker Man*, along with other cult British films such as *Witchfinder General*, has become part of this alternative heritage which has further fuelled its cult reputation.

The alternative and "non-mainstream" nature of cult cinema continues to be important, though we do need to be aware that even these aspects are being challenged by more recent studies within fan studies.

Revising Fan Studies

While the first wave of fan studies was important and influential, it has more recently been subject to critique and revision. While many aspects of fan studies have been elaborated upon, we will focus on challenges to the picture of the fan as a resistant, communal, and active agent. Hills, for example, drawing on the work of Crawford, has pointed out that the types of fans that Jenkins and Bacon-Smith focused on in their studies are not representative of all types of fandom. He notes that there exist a range of different types of fans and that the earlier wave of fan studies tended to focus on more excessive types of fandom, in the process overlooking more mundane instances (Hills 2006a: 104) Thus, more recent fan studies have sought to redress this imbalance. This, however, has fed into a need to rethink exactly what a fan is.

Contrary to the fan being distinguished through active productivity, it has been stressed that some fans may not actually belong to any fan networks (they may even confine their fandom to privacy) let alone engage in the production of fan-related texts. Rather than the existence of fixed distinctions between a fan and non-fan, Hills has suggested that "fan identity has recently been seen as context- and situation-specific" (2006a: 105). Some people may be termed fans by others, for example, for their particular consumption of a range of texts but they may not themselves identify as a fan; while Hills again cites Crawford in discussing how sports fans may be dismissed as not "proper" fans if they do not attend live games, but may be labeled as dedicated fans by those who do not have much interest in sport (2006a: 105).

Despite the context-specific argument about what constitutes fandom, it is necessary to outline a broad definition of fandom. Cornell Sandvoss provides such a definition, noting that fans are often considered to differ from more general audiences by nature of their *intense* or *excessive* interest in a particular, or a corpus of particular, cultural text(s). Sandvoss has felt the need to go beyond this particular definition, though, as he claims that intensity cannot be "objectively measured" (Sandvoss 2005: 6). He claims that the clearest behavioral indication of emotional investment in a particular text "lies in its regular, repeated consumption," so at its lowest common denominator fandom is "the regular, emotionally involved consumption of a given popular narrative or text" (2005: 7–8). Of course, what counts as "regular, emotionally involved consumption" may again alter according to particular contextual variables.

It is worth detailing the overlaps and distinctions between a fan and a cultist, considering our overall focus on cult cinema. There have been some attempts to distinguish between these appellations within academic literature. Greg Taylor, for example, argues that the cultist can be distinguished from the fan due to a more resistant position; that is, the cultist will appropriate elements from commercial culture in order to mark out an individualized space within that culture. While the cultist will denigrate the majority of commercial culture, he or she will focus on selected moments of excellence that occasionally appear within the mass media (Taylor 1999: 161). From a different angle, Abercrombie and Longhurst have distinguished between a fan, a cultist, and an enthusiast: a fan is a person who "becomes particularly attached to certain programmes or stars within the context of relatively heavy mass media use;" a cultist is more focused than the fan, revolving around more specialist (and "refined") tastes; while an enthusiast is predominantly activity-based, spending a large amount of leisure time dedicated to their enthusiasms and often involved in networks related to them (1998: 138–139). There are problems with such categories: for example, their definition of an enthusiast is closer to how a fan has been described in much of the previous literature on the subject. Their attempt to demarcate a fan from a cultist seems too neat in light of the need to be aware of the importance of context, and also differs from Taylor's definition of a cultist.

While Taylor and Abercrombie and Longhurst conceive of the term differently, they do seem to be differentiating a cultist from a fan as understood in its general sense: that is, a cultist seems to be positioned as a particular type of fan. The growth of fan studies has therefore seen the need to distinguish between different kinds of fans. This is possibly a result of the growth of fan studies and the impact that digital technologies – in particular the internet – have wrought, further complicating understandings of the fan. It is now the case that many people will engage in online community discussions about their favorite media, whereas previously the establishment of community fandom would have been less common. In this sense, more and more people can be identified as fans, which has led Jenkins (2002) to claim that fandom is moving "from cult status towards the cultural mainstream." The need to distinguish a cultist from other types of fans, therefore, could be considered an attempt to re-stress the non-mainstream nature of cult fandom. For the most part, this does seem to ring true: cult fans often stress the non-mainstream nature of their passions and a segment of cult fandom seeks out obscure titles that lie beneath the radar of mainstream media exposure. Nevertheless, in line with fandom's general mainstreaming, there have been arguments over whether cult cinema/cult fandom itself has become more of a mainstream process.

Cultural Capital and Subcultures

One particular figure who has been influential on more recent studies of fans is Pierre Bourdieu. Bourdieu has been an important reference point for those studying the politics of "taste cultures," both in terms of how fans make distinctions in order to differentiate themselves from others, and also how such operations are related to broader sociological processes. The most prominent aspect of Bourdieu's work which has been applied to subculture-related studies has been his outline of different forms of capital, particularly his notion of "cultural capital." Bourdieu (1986) outlines three main types of capital operable within society:

- *economic* capital – which is the most recognized form of capital, referring to a person's financial resources and material wealth;
- *cultural* capital – this refers to a person's educational status and their knowledge and skills related to different cultural fields;
- *social* capital – denotes the extent to which a person is connected to various social networks, for example.

Bourdieu argues that these forms of capital are interrelated, but not in any straightforward manner. It is, therefore, possible for a person to have significant economic capital but very little cultural capital: an example would be those derogatorily termed *nouveau riche*, who have come from a low-class background but who have accumulated substantial economic wealth during their lifetime. Despite being rich, their tastes (for example, in the way they decorate their home, clothes that they wear, entertainment they consume) may be considered "vulgar" by those who have a firmer rooting within a higher class and have therefore enjoyed a better education. Conversely, a person who has come from a background in which education is seen as important may be knowledgeable about a wide range of different cultural domains, but may have spurned the pursuit of money and pursued a relatively low-economic vocation: such a person would have high cultural capital but low economic capital. Social capital, on the other hand, refers to an individual's membership (which can be official or unofficial) within certain groups, which can therefore benefit them by helping them gain prestigious positions through the connections that they forge. Of course, the status of these particular groups within a broader social landscape may vary.

Sarah Thornton (1995), in her study of various underground dance cultures within Britain, coined the term "subcultural capital" to refer to the processes by which subcultures create specific forms of cultural capital. The term was used in order to mark out how distinctions are made and expertise valued within cultural areas that do not fit neatly into the spheres of "high art," which is the most common form of culture associated with cultural capital. Thornton writes:

> Subcultural capital confers status on its owner in the eyes of the relevant beholder ... Just as books and paintings display cultural capital in the family home, so subcultural capital is objectified in the form of fashionable haircuts and well-assembled record collections ... Just as cultural capital is personified in "good" manners and urbane conversation, so subcultural capital is embodied in the form of being "in the know' " (1995: 11).

Within social life people are able to assemble cultural capital through expertise within specific fields. The types of knowledge possessed may be differently valued according to the field within which it operates: thus, knowledge of science fiction comics may not be held in much esteem within, say, a group of Shakespeare experts, but among science fiction comics enthusiasts it could place the beholder of such knowledge in an advantageous position. (Of course, fields are not always separate, so that a Shakespeare expert may also be a science fiction comic expert, but such a person may play down their knowledge of comics when among other Shakespeare experts.) In the broader social field as a whole, however, Shakespeare has a higher cultural status than science fiction comics, and in this sense the latter could be seen as reflecting subcultural capital (as would cult cinema fandom) as opposed to more general cultural capital. The status and value of cultural phenomena can, of course, change: institutional recognition, for example, may be considered a means whereby a particular field becomes more widely validated, though it still may meet resistance. A very broad, general example is provided by the study of television within university: while such study enhances the reputation of the subject, it has nevertheless suffered a number of attacks (a subject, for example, not worthy of academic analysis).

Thornton's analysis of subcultural capital focused upon the media as a crucial mediator of subcultural status and cultural capital:

> [the media] are the main disseminators of these fleeting capitals. They are not simply another symbolic good or indicator of distinction, but a series of institutional networks essential to the creation, classification and distribution of cultural knowledge. (Thornton 1995: 118)

She argues that the media do not merely, as Cohen (1972) suggests, construct dominant ideas of subcultures after they have formed, but are crucial to the formation and development of subcultures. She distinguishes between three broad types of media that play a part in this process: micro-media (such as locally distributed fanzines, flyers, and listings); niche media (such as the specialist music press); and national mass media (the tabloids, the main television and radio stations). Regarding film, the categorization of different types of media may slightly differ from music, and the huge rise in internet communications since the mid 1990s will have also complicated such categories. Nevertheless, Thornton does point to the ways in which subcultures tend to promote and define themselves through niche media, while coverage of particular subcultural formations in niche media can help to

"crystallize" them into a "fully-fledged subculture" (1995: 152). Mass media, on the other hand, are often involved in creating moral panics around subcultural activities or stigmatizing them in other ways. For Thornton, such negative coverage in the mass media is often welcomed by subcultures, for they define themselves against the "mainstream" and revel in their "deviant" status. When a subcultural trend becomes increasingly part of the mainstream, however – through being accepted, reported, documented by the mass media – it may well be denigrated by subcultural groups, who may then perceive the commercialization of particular cultural artifacts as "inauthentic."

Mark Jancovich has investigated cult film fans using Bourdieu's theories about cultural capital and Thornton's notion of subcultural capital. He claims that cult fandom is rife with distinctions and claims about authenticity, and is characterized by its difference from the mainstream and the mass media. Yet, while the mass media/mainstream and academic approaches to film appreciation are disparaged within cult movie fandom, they are nevertheless constitutive of such cult communities: "these institutions also provide the very mechanisms, spaces and systems of communication through which a sense of community is produced and maintained" (Jancovich 2002: 308). Jancovich argues that cult fandom emerged out of the burgeoning art house and repertory scenes that proliferated within the 1960s: the art house scene, he claims, was associated with commerce (many cinemas in this era converting to art cinemas in order to remain commercially viable), while repertory cinemas emerged from the college scene, itself linked to the academic study of film and the revaluation of older, commercial films emanated from Hollywood. Such an argument overlooks, though, how art cinemas – while commercial – are not often designated as "mainstream"; in this sense, Jancovich conflates commercialism/the mainstream here. Certainly, cult culture is characterized by a complex relationship to commercialism, but it does not seem to be opposed on a frequent basis to commerce *per se*. Rather, it is excessive commercialism, or particular *types* of commercialism (corporate and conservative as opposed to independent and "renegade") that are opposed. The academic opposition, although evident within cult culture, is perhaps becoming less so in recent years, in line with an increased academic interest in cult media. There *is* still hostility towards academic approaches to cult (and other films) in some cult-related fan discourse, but it is certainly not as prominent as the opposition to "mainstream" values.

Jancovich cites various forms of media which help to sustain an "imagined community" using Thornton's categories of micro, niche, and mass media, though he also claims that niche media here is quite difficult to define: if tabloid newspapers, for example, constitute examples of mass media, where does this leave a specialist film magazine such as *Empire*? One answer would be that, considering Jancovich has already pointed out how the mainstream is an imaginary construct, it would depend upon the context within which the publication is perceived. From within a number of cult communities, for example, it will tend to be considered a part of the mass media, an example of a mainstream film publication. In this sense, we could distinguish between "generalized" and "specialist" aspects of the mass media. (If, on the other hand, it is considered by groups not particularly interested in film, it may be perceived as niche media.) Within niche media, we would have publications which tend to have a specialist focus *within* the field of cinema: magazines and prozines such as *Fangoria, Video Watchdog* or *Little White Lies*; while micro media would constitute fliers and programs distributed by specialist cinemas or related venues, listings, posters, etc. It is important to note, however, that "cult cinema" is not a single, reified object, but rather an imaginative concept which applies to, and is used by, a number of different subcultural film-related communities (which are not mutually exclusive). Jancovich writes that:

> cult movie audiences are less an internally coherent "taste culture" than a series of frequently opposed and contradictory reading strategies that are defined through a sense of their difference to an equally incoherently imagined "normality", a loose conglomeration of corporate power, lower middle class conformity and prudishness, academic elitism and political conspiracy. (2002: 315)

Homing in on a more specific example of cult cinema, we could apply Thornton's arguments to a particularly noteworthy controversy within the United Kingdom: the "video nasties" phenomenon, which emerged in the 1980s (see Egan 2007; Kerekes and Slater 2000, for detailed overviews of this phenomenon). In the early 1980s the nascent video retail business was dominated by small, independent ventures, and a number of controversial films were released on video cassette. The very lurid covers of a number of such titles (designed to attract attention, which they often did) could be seen to constitute a form of "micro-media" here, alongside the ways that such films were written about in specialist horror/cult fanzines (often in more positive ways than they were received in the mainstream and even niche press). It was not, however, until a moral panic broke out through mass media reports – particularly within tabloid newspapers but also, to a lesser extent, within broadsheets and within television and radio current affairs programming – that a particular subculture began to form. The labeling of people who enjoyed such films as somehow deviant, which was legally established through the banning of many films, only strengthened a sense of community among diverse citizens. From the moment that these films were banned, an underground network of trading and selling of illegal tapes was established through fanzines and specialist press. Within this network, (sub)cultural capital could be established through expertise (knowledge of different titles and their legal status, for example) and ownership (how many titles a person has in their collection). While most of the "community" as a whole would place themselves against the "mainstream" (which here would refer to the mass media's general perception of the films), there also existed inner-distinctions in which degrees of "authenticity" (established through performance of expertise and collections) were in operation (Egan 2007: 112–118). Such distinctions continue to operate as the "video nasties" have fed into the identity and marketing of previously banned titles on DVD, while collectors still trade and sell older video cassettes.

Mainstream Cult Fans?

Hills (2003: 185) has noted how some critics and academics – Peary (1981), Meehan (1991) – have considered the mixing of cultism and the mainstream a paradox. Yet the case of *Star Wars*, which also forms the basis of Hills' observations, would seem to prove otherwise. Whereas a more obscure cult film may gain such status through its rarity (so that even owning a copy of the film may defer cultural distinction), this is replaced in the case of the "cult blockbuster" by repetition. Owning a copy of a blockbuster will not confer distinction, but perhaps the amount of times that a viewer watches it and comes to display knowledge of it, will. Additionally, the film also takes on a life of its own through its passionate fan base, who incorporate the film as an integral part of their everyday lives. As Will Brooker has written:

> *Star Wars* . . . is not just a film or a trilogy, or a trilogy and two prequels. For many people, including me, it is the single most important cultural text of our lives . . . . Even in 1977, *Star Wars* was a phenomenon. For many people now, it is a culture; a sprawling, detailed mythos they can pick through with their eyes closed. (Brooker 2002: xii)

While *Star Wars* was a relatively expensive, mainstream "epic," it has nevertheless furnished many fans with a spiritual experience and an ethical system that "traditional religion has failed to provide" (Brooker 2002: 5). In this sense, it could be seen as providing an alternative to the mainstream (in terms of beliefs) while at the same time being a mainstream product. Further, many fans of *Star Wars* have formed communities which sometimes come into conflict with the official creators of the *Star Wars* franchise (by creating fan work that Lucasfilm disapproves of, for instance, or criticizing some of the newer films) and are thus in conflict with the mainstream in some respects. The film is therefore both mainstream and cult: it has enjoyed such a remarkable presence within popular culture that it transcends the cult/mainstream dichotomy and alerts us to the fact that these categories may not be as distinctive as was formerly believed.

We could also think of the cult blockbuster as a kind of epochal film: a film that becomes, for many of its first wave of fans, a key film in their childhood memories which has remained with them as an important text throughout their life; additionally, it can become significant as an epochal moment in film history. The first is the most important in terms of cult reputation,

but if this subjective importance is overlaid with a more "objective" significance, then this will perhaps increase the blockbuster's chances of attaining cult distinctiveness (also see Chapter 20).

The increasing proliferation of digital technologies within everyday life is further blurring the boundaries between cult and mainstream. One reason for this is that networked media, in particular the internet, make it much easier for researchers to find evidence of viewing communities that fit into existing frameworks of cult cinema. Previous to the domestication of the net, it would not have been as easy to find evidence of fans for particular films. Rather, more extraordinary cultural events would have constituted such evidence, including conventions, discernible audience patterns for specific films (as exemplified by some of the long-running midnight movies), and pilgrimages to film locations. Secondly, less direct evidence could be garnered by collecting traces of commitment for particular films, as well as tracking a film's overall reception trajectory, within film magazines, fanzines, and relevant newspaper columns. The internet massively increases the (virtual) public presence of film fans, many of whom leave online traces of their love for films via discussion forums, blogs, web sites, and social networking sites, to name some prominent examples.

Just as digital developments have led to fandom becoming more of a mainstream process (Jenkins 2002; Ross and Nightingale 2002: 143; Jennings 2007: 1), the same can be said of cult films. Cyberspace provides access to a vast social network that has been utilized by many fans and researchers of fans; discussion of cult cinema, too, has proliferated on the web, alongside activities that are demonstrative of cult reception. These processes have taken place alongside an increase in academic attention to both fandom on the one hand, and cult cinema on the other. Taken together they lead to an escalating reiteration of the concepts in question, so that being a fan is generally considered less derogatory than it once was while cult cinema is also less of an obscurantist field than previously. We can also add that the concepts of both performance and surveillance are important here, and also appear to reinforce one another. The internet and other network technologies enable people to perform their identity as fans on a more frequent basis, which leads to them leaving greater data traces of their fandom to linger virtually as analytical fodder for future researchers. It is no surprise that increasing opportunities to form communities, to perform as a fan, and to detect fandom, lead to a greater mainstreaming of both fandom and cult cinema, which in turn impacts on the growth of academic work covering these areas.

Another reason why both fandom and an interest in cult cinema have grown with the rise of the net is that it now becomes much easier for people to engage in activities that single them out as a fan of particular media objects, and to become interested in cult films. David Jennings has written how previously it was difficult to get hold of a wide range of music and films if one lived outside large cities (2007: 1–2). Thus, a limited provision meant that it was more difficult for people to discover new films and play a part in their reputations. Of course, it was not impossible: a large number of films have always played on television, while people who have lived outside of metropolitan areas have been able to read about more obscure fare and (since the emergence of video) been able to purchase films via mail order. The actual ability, however, to discover material outside of the mainstream was a lot more difficult. (Of course, as noted above, cult films are not necessarily non-mainstream, but they often are, and even the ability to form a cult following around a mainstream product has become easier with networked media.) As cultural commentators such as Jennings (2007) and Chris Anderson (2006) have pointed out, an increasingly digitized, global multimedia environment alters this state of affairs. Jennings cites three particular important elements that contribute to a "culture of discovery": first, *trying out*, which refers to the abundant opportunities to sample media material; secondly, *links*, which enable people to constantly link from one subject that they are interested in, to another (some of which they may not have previously encountered); and thirdly, new forms of *communities* enabled by digital networks now mean that word-of-mouth (traditionally a core factor in the creation of cult status) can travel freely and quickly among connected citizens (Jennings 2007: 15–19). Anderson has also drawn attention to how the "long tail" now assumes much greater importance in the digital world. While "niche" tastes have existed for a

long time, they are now becoming more important in an age where the costs of supply and demand are much lower, when it is far easier for consumers to find more obscure products and for retailers to reach customers (for an illustration of how instances of these developments in fandom have been linked to other discourses that operate in the evaluation of cult cinema, see the section on DIY criticism in Chapter 4 and transnationalism and orientalism in Chapter 11).

The growth of niche markets does not erode the boundaries between what constitutes mainstream and cult, but it does certainly alter the ways that these concepts become mobilized in relation to cultural trends. The increasing ability to spot processes that connect fan practices in relation to cult cinema, alongside the proliferation of choice and availability, means that we need to be aware that there are many different types of cult cinema fans, and that the actual status of cult cinema among such fans is very much contested: there are, for example, arguments between fans (and, perhaps, "non-fans") as to what constitutes cult cinema, which may depend on the type of film fan who is contributing to the discussion. We should also be careful to make distinctions between types of cult film and types of cult fandom. While some fans may only be interested in particular types of cult cinema (e.g. science fiction and horror), other fans will avidly consume a broader range of cult cinema (in addition to other films and other media). While it is possible to categorize some fans of cult cinema through the types of films that they are interested in, others may be more eclectic and may be more adequately categorized through their attitudes towards films and the ways in which they fit these films into their everyday lives.

Conclusion: Recent Trends in Cult Fandom

We will finish by discussing two examples of films that generated a substantial degree of cult fandom in ways which were very much connected to new technologies. The first is an extremely low-budget production that marshaled the web as part of its innovative marketing campaign, the second a large-budget spectacle that intersected with other media in interesting ways. *The Blair Witch Project* cost only around $60 000 and generated profits in the region of $150 million in 1999 (Telotte 2001: 33). Much of its success was explained through the innovative design of its web site, which attracted a significant fan base long before the film had even been theatrically released (Jenkins 2006: 101–102). We should not overlook the fact that the website operated in conjunction with a more traditional marketing campaign (including TV spots, posters, radio ads, magazine ads, etc.) which cost around $20 million after the film was picked up for distribution by Artisan (Telotte 2001: 33). Nevertheless, the web site, in line with its related advertising strategy, was seen as important for the ways in which it generated a story world that could be appreciated on its own (and could spark interest in the film before its theatrical release), but which also acted as an added attraction for those who had seen the film. This was because the site constructed a mythical story world (presented as real) which documented the disappearance of students who had gone looking for a witch, and provided information on witchcraft that created a background against which the film was just one particular artifact (presented as found footage accidentally discovered and pieced together by Artisan). Taken together, the film, the web site, the ads, along with other artifacts (such as a pseudo-documentary airing on the SciFi channel and a series of related comic books) were constructed to interrelate with each other, so each segment added to the experience of discovering more about this particular mythical story world. They allowed people to become immersed within an active search for information: each segment could add to this experience, but one did not necessarily have to experience all of these mediated *Blair Witch* modes to appreciate it.

The cult of *The Blair Witch Project* was a very significant phenomenon as it was an instance of what Henry Jenkins has termed "transmedia storytelling," which is not entirely new but is taking on greater importance in what Jenkins terms "convergence culture" (in which the digital mediascape intersects with older media and forms new relations). Jenkins describes the transmedia story as unfolding "across multiple media platforms, with each new text making

a distinctive and valuable contribution to the whole." He continues:

> In the ideal form of transmedia storytelling, each medium does what it does best – so that a story might be introduced in a film, expanded through television, novels and comics; its world might be explored through game play or experienced as an amusement park attraction. Each franchise entry needs to be self-contained, so you don't need to have seen the film to enjoy the game, and vice versa. Any given product is a point of entry into the franchise as a whole. (Jenkins 2006: 96)

If *The Blair Witch Project* represents a low-budget film that began to utilize the web as a transmedia device to add layers to its mythic story world (and which then enjoyed a large cash injection to expand this process across a broader range of more traditional marketing platforms), then *The Matrix* represents a much larger-scale example. Jenkins argues that it "can be seen as emblematic of a cult film in convergence culture" (2006: 98), in that its story world was disseminated across a broad range of media platforms. Each platform was carefully thought about and designed in order to exploit the specific strengths of the respective medium, so that the more platforms one encountered *The Matrix* upon, the more one knew about the overall *Matrix* universe. The story world of *The Matrix* was dispersed among three feature films, two games, a series of comic books, and a series of *Animatrix* animated shorts, with each singular piece itself containing a wealth of detail that was designed to encourage speculation and discussion. In this, it succeeded in generating a cult following of fans who discussed how bits of the story world fitted together, the wealth of references scattered within the story, and its philosophical dimensions.

Transmedia storytelling is thus an important process that can lead to the broadening of a fictional universe and produce new routes by which fans can engage with each other to create cult status for a film. It is only one way, however, that cult status can be built up through fan response in the current media landscape. Just as "new media" does not entirely replace "old media," but is overlaid upon it to create new configurations, so modern processes through which cult fandom forms are overlaid upon more traditional patterns. This means that cult fandom becomes more visible, complex and variegated.

6

The Cult Auteur

The notion of the "auteur" is inextricably bound up with the arguments published by François Truffaut and his contemporaries within the pages of *Cahiers du Cinéma* during the 1950s, though related polemics existed well before such formulations and continue to take place. The concept of the "auteur" is a very specific inflection of the broader notion of the "author," adapted in relation to the cinematic medium. While it specifically refers to particular definitions of authorship, it is often employed to denote "cinematic authorship" more generally, which is how we will be adopting it in this chapter. The word "auteur" seems more appropriate within the industrial world of cinema than "author" does, as the latter is more connotative of literary and/or solitary creation.

Within the world of cult cinema the auteur acts, like in many other areas of cinema, as a crucially important mode of evaluation and categorization. A browse through many cult film publications reveals the auteur figure as a commonly significant structuring principle. Both academic (e.g. Mendik and Harper 2000b; Jancovich *et al.* 2003b) and more populist texts (e.g. Vale and Juno 1986; Ross 1993) devote substantial attention to auteurist figures.[1] The cult auteur figure is also prominent across a number of cult publications and has proliferated with the rise of web-based resources: not only do many cult-based film sites focus attention on individual cult figures, there are also whole sites devoted to cult auteurs. In addition, the name of a cult auteur can be a useful marketing tool in the promotion of certain DVD titles.

The emergence of auteurism in the mid 1950s was itself a cultist provocation: while it had previously been common to attribute authorial status to directors of "art cinema" (including figures such as Ingmar Bergman, Akira Kurosawa and Roberto Rosselini), only a select few directors working within Hollywood had tended to gain such kudos (D.W. Griffiths and Charlie Chaplin, for example). A young bunch of critics (many of whom would become filmmakers associated with the French New Wave) at *Cahiers*, including Truffaut, Jean-Luc Godard, and Claude Chabrol, championed a number of Hollywood directors (alongside more respected European directors) as auteurs, many of whom had until then been considered only as skilled craftsmen (including Howard Hawks, Alfred Hitchcock, and Nicholas Ray). While many critics disputed approaches that singled out the "genius" of directors working within a highly standardized Hollywood system, such positions nevertheless proved influential. The most passionate advocate of this position was Andrew Sarris, an American critic who popularized auteurism as a mode of film evaluation, and also outlined the position in a more systematic way in his 1962 article "Some Notes on the Auteur Theory." Auteurism also made an impact in the United Kingdom, chiefly through the journal *Movie* and writers including Robin Wood, V.F. Perkins, and Ian Cameron.

Previous to auteurism – and as outlined by Greg Taylor (1999) – cultism tended to be identified with an elite cadre of critics (Taylor focuses on Manny Farber and Parker Tyler as exemplars) who were valuing aspects of popular culture and, in the process, individuating themselves as critical provocateurs. Auteurism was an extension of this, in that it valued selected aspects of popular culture in a discriminatory

Cult Cinema: An Introduction. Ernest Mathijs and Jamie Sexton.
© 2011 Ernest Mathijs and Jamie Sexton. Published 2011 by Blackwell Publishing Ltd.

manner, treating commercial films seriously through identifying the traces of authorial creativity within an industrial product. As such, a number of attacks were leveled at auteurist critics for promoting a "cult of the director" – in which "bad" films of privileged directors were given more credit than "good" films of directors who were not considered auteurs.

Auteurism became popularized throughout the 1960s and it also influenced the emergence of Film Studies as an academic discipline within that decade. In the 1970s, however, auteur study became either questioned or modified. As more rigorous, theoretical approaches to the subject began to increase, romantic notions concerning "genius" directors began to be questioned. While studies of directors did not cease, they were supplemented by a number of other approaches (such as genre studies and psychoanalytic analyses). Increasingly, the study of authorship began to be posed in more theoretical terms, in which the "author" within a text became seen as a functional device to activate a particular type of reading (Michel Foucault termed this the "author-function') , rather than a "creative genius" who has managed to express her/himself within a highly collaborative medium.

The more romantic approaches which focused on the "cult of the director" can be seen to have continued largely outside of academia, though here the stance of critics such as Sarris, for example, were somewhat expanded and modified. While Sarris's arguments about the constancy of individual personality shining through related film texts can certainly be considered important in the establishment of the cult auteur, his remarks on technical competence highlight an area in which cultist celebration has been expanded. Sarris wrote that "the first premise of the *auteur* theory is the technical competence of the director as a criterion of value. A badly directed or an undirected film has no importance in a critical scale of value" (Sarris 1962/2000: 132). Competence is not always a skill demanded for cult celebration, however. The celebration of individual creators within cult filmmaking can therefore be thought of as a variation on more "classical" auteurism, and it is towards a fuller elaboration of how someone gets celebrated as a cult auteur, as well as who some of the more renowned figures are, that we now turn.

One particularly important thread feeding into the status of many cult auteurs is the importance of extra-textual information. Unlike in many cases of more traditional auteurism, where the actual biography of the individual was far less important than the connections running through a cinematic oeuvre, the celebration of a cult creator is often highly dependent upon his or her reputation. Biographical information and other types of activities that promote the visibility of a particular figure may be crucial in establishing a cult status. Yet the reputation constructed through both cinematic and other means must be of a particular kind: it often tends, for example, to have connections with anti-establishment themes in some manner (though this is not always the case). In this sense, celebration of cult auteurs is often underpinned by a romanticist creed: the idea of a lone, heroic figure battling against the odds to create works that are taken to heart by outsider audiences. If academic approaches to authorship very much moved away from romantic notions, cult auteurism arguably expanded such romanticism. Further, cult fans do not always locate the director as the core of creativity (although the director is the most frequently acclaimed auteur figure). Rather, and perhaps more suitably in relation to the multiple roles afforded by film production, they can sometimes acclaim other creative forces. In relation to cult cinema, the other most acclaimed "creator role" would undoubtedly be that of the producer/ entrepreneur, because such figures have had a particularly important influence on cult cinema's developments and reputations. There are other important roles, too, such as special effects creators (think of the work of Ray Harryhausen, for example, or of Tom Savini), which we briefly discuss in Chapters 2, 18 and 19.

The "Romantic" Cult Auteur

While the cult auteur's reputation needs to be acknowledged by a wider cult audience, the actual auteur can also play a crucial part in building a reputation. John Waters, for example, is a figure who has carefully constructed his own cult image through carefully referencing other cult figures and texts (such as Kenneth Anger, Russ Meyer, Herschell Gordon Lewis), through carefully courting scandal through the press (in order to widely publicize his films via controversy) and through carefully cultivating a public persona which enhances his auteur reputation (through numerous media interviews, cameo acting appearances, writing books and compiling music CDs, and even appearing as a stand-up raconteur, one appearance of which was filmed and released as *This Filthy World*). Roger Corman, while perhaps not to the same degree, has also paid significant attention to promoting and manipulating his status, including attempts to "enhance the Corman image" through tactics such as planting bogus stories in the trade press (Gray 2004: 28). Corman is, of course, famous as a prolific producer of exploitation pictures, particularly during the 1960s when he produced a number of Edgar Allen Poe adaptations and "rebellious youth" films such as *The Wild Angels* and *The Trip*. He forged his reputation through the types of films that he made (exploitation films), but also through the sheer *volume* of films that he produced (some of which he also directed): a combination of aesthetic factors and sheer longevity has led to his canonization by a number of cult film fans. Corman is a man who has done things his own way, constantly making films on a shoestring budget and extremely short schedules. His status has benefited from the fact that he has given career breaks to a number of directors who went on to become established names, such as Joe Dante, Francis Ford Coppola, and Martin Scorsese, who subsequently name-check him and thus increase his general standing. He has also managed to maintain his productivity during huge industrial changes: in the 1980s, as the VHS market took off, he slowly began making straight-to-video films and now mostly produces either these or television films. On top of these status-building components, Corman has exploited his own growing cult image through writings and appearances. His book, *How I Made a Hundred Movies in Hollywood and Never Lost a Dime* (1990), plays upon his maverick and persistent nature. In addition, he has made a number of appearances at cult-related events and – until recently – maintained his own web site, where once his cult standing was trumpeted through slogans such as the "Reigning King of Independent Cinema" and, even more tellingly, inviting readers to "join the Corman cult."

Romantic cult auteurs can operate outside of the "system," like Corman. On the other hand, they may gain a reputation for individuality by working within, but at the same time battling against, the system. The former category would include avant-garde artists creating challenging "avant-garde" films, such as Kenneth Anger and Andy Warhol (see Chapters 12 and 14); or directors/producers working in low-budget, "exploitation" pictures, such as Edward D. Wood Jr, Herschell Gordon Lewis and Lloyd Kaufman (see Chapter 13). A figure like Anger has built a distinct reputation through being part of Hollywood (as a child actor) and then luridly exposing it through his *Hollywood Babylon* books, which is a crucial part of his cult status. His films are then a further rejection of Hollywood in terms of their experimentation and their sometimes controversial nature (*Scorpio Rising* was considered "obscene" and was sometimes impounded by police at screenings). The figure of Anger himself also fed into his films: his homosexuality and his interest in the occult further strengthened his outsider status. Contrasted to Anger's intentional rejection of the social mainstream is Wood Jr's less conscious creation of an "alternative" oeuvre. Rather than rejecting cinematic mores, Wood Jr was too incompetent to reproduce them successfully, which in turn created a kind of warped distortion of the mainstream. Biographically, his homosexuality and penchant for cross-dressing has also contributed to his cult standing. His merging of outsiderness in both life and art thus sets him apart; as Puchalski writes, "Wood was seriously demented in both his life and his work, and that twisted enthusiasm oozes through every sprocket-hole of his films" (1996: 126). His acclaim as one of the world's worst filmmakers has cemented his cult credentials, though this was unfortunately an accolade bestowed posthumously. Wood Jr's *Plan 9 from Outer Space* was voted the worst film ever in *The Golden Turkey Awards* (1980), which also awarded him worst director (see Chapter 3). He was remembered more affectionately in Burton's romantic celluloid tribute, *Ed Wood* (1994), which introduced him to a newer generation of cinemagoers.

While these figures do not belong to the Hollywood "system," others have been seen as important for the way that they have battled with the system to get their own way, sometimes succeeding, sometimes not. Perhaps one of the most notorious is Alejandro Jodorowsky, who has mostly worked outside of

Hollywood but who has also dabbled – often unsuccessfully – with the mainstream. His cult standing stems from his *El Topo* gaining the reputation as being the first midnight movie cult but is not confined to this film alone. He also directed the remarkable *The Holy Mountain*, a bizarre concoction of occultism, surrealism, and demystification. He subsequently encountered his first battle with the mainstream when directing an eventually aborted film of Frank Herbert's *Dune* (David Lynch, another cult director, eventually directed it but also had an unhappy time with it). Until the release of *Santa Sangre*, on which he managed to attain creative control, his film career has consisted of a single film, *Tusk*, which he disowned as a "compromised" film. Admirers of his work agreed; yet while *Santa Sangre* was seen as a return to form after *Tusk*, it was followed by what was seen as his most mainstream work, *The Rainbow Thief*, which he disowned and after which he has yet to make another film.[2]

Jodorowsky therefore stands as a cult maverick: a mad visionary who is able to make strange and remarkable films if left to his own devices, but who falters if compromised by too many external constraints. In this sense, he can be considered a cult, rather than a "classical" auteur, in the sense that many of the directors hailed in the first wave of auteurism tended to be admired for the ways in which they adapted to the compromises of the studios and retained a personal vision. His status is, as is often common, further fuelled by an extra-filmic reputation, in this case his extraordinarily prolific and diverse artistic output: he has worked as a theater producer, a mime artist, a comic artist, a circus performer, and a Tarot reader among other activities and thus fits the mould of a hyper-talented individualist. As Keesey writes of Jodorowsky, summing up his rebellious persona: "Say what you will about Alejandro Jodorowsky, but one thing is certain: he is not just another Hollywood director" (Keesey 2003: 15).

Other figures connected more centrally to mainstream filmmaking can gain a reputation for their battles with the studios, or for fiercely preserving an egotistical control over the creation of a commercial product: these directors are "mainstream mavericks." The latter is relatively rare but certainly applies to Stanley Kubrick, even though he did experience losing

battles in the earlier part of his career, most notably with *Spartacus* (1960), which apparently led him to exert greater "autonomy" on his subsequent directorial work (LoBrutto 1999: 193). He has gained a reputation among fans and critics for being meticulous and controlling, a status that is difficult to probe into deeply because he always managed to maintain high levels of privacy.[3] Like Kubrick, Orson Welles is a filmmaker who fits into both classical and cult auteur frameworks, thus emphasizing their similarities in certain cases. A child prodigy and, like Jodorowsky, a man of many talents, he astonished film critics with his premiere film *Citizen Kane*. Yet this was followed by a series of frustrating encounters with Hollywood. If some of these have been critically recuperated, Welles is nevertheless a figure who retains a tragic aura: a prodigious talent whose creativity and originality was crushed by Hollywood. Welles' films have often been called uneven and incomplete, grandiose failures (Tyler 1970), and his acting was often deemed "over-indulgent, over-bearing and over-blown" (Jancovich 2009). The two films that exemplify this best are *Citizen Kane* and *Touch of Evil*. *Citizen Kane* features prominently in overviews of cult movies because of its flamboyance, audacity, and boisterousness, but also because of its box-office failure (Peary 1981: 52). *Touch of Evil* was supposed to be the film that would rehabilitate Welles in Hollywood. Taken out of his hands before it was released, it has had a severely fractioned reception trajectory, its status oscillating between unequivocal masterpiece or *film maudit*. Its reception is still far from having reached a "final moment" (Peary 1989: 255–260). In the words of Parker Tyler, Welles "remains a Cult hero, a film artist of ambiguous successes; a lone wolf, as it were, whose egoistic failures have stacked up to make him both notorious and famous" (Tyler 1963: 381).

Both Terry Gilliam and Nicholas Ray can also be considered examples of mainstream mavericks. Gilliam's cult status was bolstered by his legendary battles with Universal after they decided to edit his *Brazil* into a more audience-friendly version with a happy ending (usually referred to as the "Love Conquers All" version). Gilliam wrote a full-page ad in *Variety* appealing to Universal's then chairman Sid Sheinberg to release his longer version and then began to privately screen his cut to critics. Universal eventually released a longer cut after Gilliam's cut gained critical acclaim, while the battles over the film were documented in the film *The Battle of Brazil*, which was released on Criterion's laserdisc (and then on the DVD) edition of the film. Gilliam has continued to work within Hollywood and, despite encountering a number of further obstacles, has been seen by many as managing to creatively express himself within the industry. He has continued to experience many problems working within the Hollywood system: *The Adventures of Baron Munchausen* was beset by production problems and eventually flopped, while he has also been involved with a number of projects that have yet to see the light of day, the most notorious being his attempt to film *Don Quixote*, which began filming but had to be abandoned as during the first week of shooting one of the principal actors suffered a herniated disc and a flood wrecked the set. Nevertheless, despite these problems Gilliam is seen as someone who can impose his creative vision within Hollywood, creating fantastical cinematic realms notable for their elaborate mise-en-scène, grotesque characters and frequent use of wide angles and tilted camera set-ups. Perhaps it is no coincidence that, like Kubrick, he is an American exile who has settled in Britain and therefore retains a sense of distance from Hollywood.

Nicholas Ray also had to endure adversarial studio interference with his movies, which eventually led him to become disenchanted with Hollywood. Unlike his contemporary Welles, Ray was never a superstar. Therefore Ray's were cult films often attributable to other factors besides his direction. For *In a Lonely Place* it was Humphrey Bogart; for *Johnny Guitar* it was Joan Crawford playing a female Western heroine; and for *Rebel without a Cause*, it was James Dean and the controversy the film caused in Europe (Biltereyst 2005). Still, as Alex Cox puts it "certain individuals become cult heroes on the basis of a body of work which has genuinely curious or idiosyncratic nature ... Nicholas Ray is one such director" (Cox and Jones 1993: 26).[4]

From these few examples it is clear that the mainstream therefore acts as a major framework *against* which the cult auteur is constructed. Within this framework there are three broad models: those working outside the mainstream; those vacillating between independence and commercial work (often demonstrating some kind of tussle with commercial forces), and those who manage to work within the system but who maintain what are viewed as excessive levels of control (the "mainstream maverick"). It certainly is in the latter area where the cult auteur tends to overlap with more traditional auteur conceptions. This is unsurprising considering auteurism was a critical intervention that aimed to locate creativity within the industrial restrictions of Hollywood cinema.

The Cult of the Dead Auteur

Within such broad models, there are further categories – or perhaps what we could call "career trajectories" – through which creative film workers can attain cult status. First, and this is particularly related to the aforementioned importance of biographical information, there is the director (or producer) whose life is cut short. The cult of individuality based around early death is something more established within the world of music, particularly rock music (see Thompson 1999), though it is a phenomenon that can be seen as spilling over to the world of movies. The romantic "live fast, die young" ethos that fuels the veneration of certain rock stars is probably more connected to actors than it is to directors or producers (see Chapter 7), yet there are some exceptions. An example is French director Jean Vigo, who was associated with the first wave of the French avant-garde, itself one of the first movements to be associated with cultist viewing practices (see Chapter 14). Vigo directed only two short films and two features before his early death, yet left behind a body of work that is considered to be particularly impressive. His film *Zéro de conduite* was a boarding school picture depicting rebellious children that laid the template for others to follow, in particular Lindsay Anderson's *If....*; it further gained cult credentials because it was banned in France until 1945. His association with anarchism also fuels an anti-establishment profile: his father, Miguel Almereyda, was a militant anarchist who died in prison in suspicious circumstances in 1917 (Le Cain 2002a) and critics have often read his films as reflections of these anarchic tendencies. The fact that his two features – cut and compromised – were complete failures on their release yet resurrected to great acclaim after his early death from tuberculosis at 29, further established him as a tragic cult figure.

The early death can often feed into the cult credentials of an individual, but it needs to intersect with other factors (i.e. death in itself is no guarantee). If a figure is marginalized or ignored during his or her lifetime, then the discovery itself of a significant body of work can imbue the "discoverers" with a sense of exclusivity via the process of righting past wrongs and drawing attention to previously hidden wares. It can also lead to speculation about the films that could have materialized if death had not so abruptly intervened (as is the case with Vigo). This would also relate to the life of British director Michael Reeves who, after directing the cult British horror *Witchfinder General*, died when it seemed he was approaching his prime. Once again, trouble fitting within the film industry – he was having difficulty following up *Witchfinder* – led to depression and a barbiturate overdose at the age of 24.

Speculation about the kinds of films that a director could have made is a form of discourse that can feed into cult kudos. This is not always the case with dead directors – as noted, Gilliam's attempt to film *Don Quixote* is an instance of a living director being subject to "what if" speculation – but it is more marked in this area, possibly because there is no longer any chance of such a film being completed (at least by this particular director). Thus, many Kubrick fans have discussed what his proposed *Artificial Intelligence: AI* would have turned out to be and how it would have been different from the actual version eventually taken over and directed by Steven Spielberg (whom Kubrick requested). More recently French director Henri-Georges Clouzot has been the subject of such "what if" speculations, largely stemming from a documentary based around his unfinished film *L'Enfer*, during the production of which he died. Serge Bromberg's film *Henri-Georges Clouzot's Inferno* is the result of the filmmakers' cultist obsession with this unfinished film, as Bromberg went to great lengths to track down all the negative reels shot for the film, much of it pre-production test footage. It also offers new cultist perspectives on Clouzot because the material indicates that this was going to be a daring undertaking, with Clouzot testing out optical effects to simulate a mescaline trip and also pushing the boundaries of sexual representation (Lucas 2010: 70–73). (The importance of drugs in cult cinema is discussed in Chapter 15; and sexuality is discussed in Chapter 10.) Similar cultist speculation exists around unfinished "daring" work of Alfred Hitchcock (*Kaleidoscope*) and Jerry Lewis (*The Day the Clown Cried*) (McCarthy 2003: 45–47).

Curt McDowell is another figure who died early and has a cult following, though he is certainly not as respected a figure as Vigo. Rather, his reputation stems from his more trashy output and his continual hand-to-mouth existence. Strongly associated with George Kuchar, who he often collaborated with, McDowell merged underground camp with elements of pornography in many of his films. McDowell's status is linked primarily to his feature-length film *Thundercrack!*, which Jack Stevenson has dubbed "the world's only Underground porno horror flick" (Stevenson 1996: 239–240). In addition to containing a very bizarre combination of generic markers at the textual level, *Thundercrack!* has also gained a real cult status because of its reception. It has gained the status of one of the most "walked-out-of" films, a reputation firmly established by mass walk-outs at its screening at the 1976 LA Filmex festival (Stevenson 1996: 241). After its cult popularity among midnight movie audiences in the late 1970s, the film became difficult to see because of scarcity of prints and the absence of a video release (Stevenson 1996: 229). McDowell's continual poverty also fueled his outsider status; he continually struggled to express himself via the medium of film and died of AIDS at the age of 42. With the release of *Thundercrack!* on DVD, it may be that McDowell's cult reputation filters down into a new generation of film lovers seeking something out of the ordinary.

Self-conscious Cultism and Cult Salesmanship

The "self-conscious cult auteur" is a figure who carefully manufactures her or his image through continual reference to broader aspects of cult film culture. Tim Burton is a key example here: through making the early short animation *Vincent*, based upon his obsession with cult actor Vincent Price, through to his cinematic homage to Ed Wood and onto the creation of a big-budget take on low-budget exploitation flicks, *Mars*

Attacks!, Burton's taste in cult cinema has defined his cinematic identity. He is a director who wears his cult tastes like a badge and this means that he is also seen as someone who makes very distinctive, idiosyncratic movies within the mainstream of Hollywood (with occasional exceptions, such as *Planet of the Apes*, which he was unhappy with). Another example would be Joe Dante, a cult film buff who constantly references other films in his own studio productions. (See Chapter 22 for more on Dante.)

The individual creator who self-consciously identifies with all things cult and therefore hopes to imbue his own personality with cult kudos is not destined to succeed, however. The self-created personality must also meet with broader recognition and acknowledgement if this cult identity is going to gain credence. Some figures may be accepted as cult figures by some but not others; battles around the notion of authenticity may occur when a cult persona is seen as too obviously manufactured. Such debates about authenticity and worthiness regularly circulate around Quentin Tarantino, a director who constantly refers to other cult films and directors: his work is worshipped by a number of fans yet despised by other cinema viewers and critics. (See Chapter 22 for more on Tarantino and self-conscious cultism.)

Within the cult film universe the construction of the auteur can sometimes veer between the heavily romantic notion of authentic individualism and the more artificial, campy notion of personality as a hyper-exaggerated performance. Sometimes, though seemingly at odds, these diametric ideas may co-exist through the combination of performance and backstory. For example, accrued information about the life of a figure may indicate that, despite the emphasis upon artificiality and performativity within the construction of a persona and cultural objects, there lay a real heartfelt commitment to this performance (or perhaps more correctly a series of performances). This would seem to be the case for an auteur like John Waters, whose films are marked by exaggerated camp performance but who is nonetheless often perceived as a director with a singular vision which grounds his work in discourses of authenticity.

The self-conscious construction of a persona links to the idea of the auteur figure as a marketable sign. Timothy Corrigan has pointed out that, from its inception, "auteurism had been bound up with changes in industrial desires, technological opportunities, and marketing strategies" (Corrigan 2003: 96), that it was often a way of singling out a work among a mass of industrially produced cultural objects. Corrigan was here discussing the ways in which auteurism had become increasingly commodified, so that the director was increasingly becoming like a star. Yet areas of cult cinema – in particular exploitation cinema – have been linked to commercial practices for some time. This was sometimes foregrounded through the role of the entrepreneur, who could actually gain a devoted following through creatively engaging in commercial salesmanship. Such figures are not self-conscious cult figures in the way that the previously mentioned directors are. Rather than drawing on cult traditions in order to imbue their own work with cult values, these personalities have gained a reputation for establishing commercial practices that have been embraced within cultish circles.

While Dwain Esper and William Castle both directed films, it is in the realm of showmanship that they have really gained their cult reputations. Esper, for example, used a number of gimmicks to "sell" films to patrons as he took them on the roadshow circuit, including hiring "freaks" to perform in theater lobbies to promote *Freaks* in 1949 (Stevenson 2003a: 22). Castle, meanwhile, produced gimmicks galore in order to market his films, including giving viewers a number of props (fangs, special viewing glasses, cardboard axes), while arriving in a hearse for the premiere of *Macabre* and then placing himself in a coffin (Stevenson 2003a: 23). For *House on Haunted Hill* he created "Emergo," in which cinemas were installed with a large black box placed next to the screen, out of which, at certain points during the film, a 12-foot plastic skeleton would appear and be wired over the audience. For *The Tingler* he created "Percepto," which involved installing small motors inside selected theater seats that gave small shocks to viewers at appropriate moments in the film. Such stunts have led to him being acclaimed as "King of the Gimmicks," while John Waters goes so far to claim that "William Castle was God" (Waters 2003: 14).

The lauding of certain salesmen within cult circles shows that the auteur can sometimes be venerated for commercial activities. Such tactics are still different from the "norms" of mass marketing, however. With-in a saturated marketplace, cult figures creatively draw attention to their films, often without a substantial budget. Salesmanship here combines with a fiercely individualist belief in standing out from the crowd via outlandish behavior, bolstered further by the "outsider" status of the "little man" doing what he can to earn money in a field dominated by large commercial companies.

Female Cult Auteurs

Finally, one regrettable area in which cult auteurism does not differ from more traditional forms of auteurism, or from mainstream values as a whole, is in its marginalization of female figures. While many women may feature prominently in cult films, few creative figures become cult auteurs. During the classical period of Hollywood cinema women directors only sporadically received any recognition, let alone achieve a cult status. Among the isolated exceptions are Dorothy Arzner, whose *Dance Girl, Dance* is lauded as a cult film by Danny Peary (1981: 59–63) and some of actress Ida Lupino's films such as *The Bigamist* or *The Hitch-Hiker*.

Outside Hollywood, the situation is largely the same. One of the few exceptions to have gained a sustained cult reputation is Doris Wishman (see Gorfinkel 2000; Luckett 2003; Modleski 2007), who made a large number of sexploitation pictures (including "nudist" films and the more explicit, darker sex films known as "roughies") and worked in a number of creative capacities (including writing and production, as well as directing duties). *Deadly Weapons*, usually seen as her seminal film, is often regarded as a sharp, reflexive comment on the exploitation of women in cinema. The work of a female auteur like Wishman working within areas of filmmaking often accused of their sexist attitudes has, though, troubled some feminists and further points to the problematic status of the female auteur within the world of cult cinema. Artists such as Maya Deren and Yoko Ono too have achieved cult-like status with their work, but its reach is usually limited to avant-garde circles (see Chapter 14). Outside the United States too, there is little or no cult recognition for female auteurs. Adrian Martin (2008:

42) lists Chantal Akerman as a cult figure but he immediately adds that her appeal, which he largely links to one film, *Jeanne Dielman*, is restricted to "the university circuit." Directors such as Agnes Varda (*Le petit amour*), Catherine Breillat (*Romance*), or Claire Denis (*Trouble Every Day*) have experienced similar restrictions of their cult appeal.

In recent years, there appears to be a slight change towards more interest in female directors as cult auteurs. Some filmmakers, especially those active since the 1970s, have seen their work acknowledged as cult. Among them are Stephanie Rothman (who was honored as a guest at a 2002 trash cinema conference in Berkeley), Kathryn Bigelow, Rachel Talalay, and Catherine Hardwicke. Still, in most cases this recognition is the result of an aggregate of their films being celebrated as cult, and less because they are seen as auteurs. For example, Rothman's films such as *Velvet Vampire* and *Terminal Island* are highly regarded but are consistently discussed in conjunction with the production work of Corman. Similarly, Bigelow's *Near Dark* and *Blue Steel* have attracted cult receptions (Powell 1994; Daugherty 2002; Redmond and Jermyn 2003), though they are discussed more frequently as "genre cinema" (the vampire film and the cop movie), or, in the case of *Blue Steel*, even as a special instance in the career of scream queen Jamie Lee Curtis. Her subsequent films, such as *Point Break* or *Strange Days* are often regarded as "masculine" in tone, while this stage of her career is often judged as a result of collaboration with James Cameron, her partner at the time. As for Talalay, the strong cult reception of *Tank Girl*, which is a favorite of the Riot Grrrl subculture as well as in lesbian circles, the equally strong cult reputation of the *Nightmare on Elm Street* series (of which Talalay directed episode 5 and produced 2, 3, and 4), and her productions of John Waters' *Hairspray* and *Cry-Baby* have not led to a discussion of her work through the lens of auteurism (Whelehan and Sonnet 1997). The case of Catherine Hardwicke, production designer on *Tank Girl*, but more commonly known for directing teen drama *Thirteen*, skateboard movie *Lords of Dogtown*, and the first film of the *Twilight* vampire saga is exactly the same: each of these films has a distinct cult following (see Le Breton 2009; Bode 2010) yet no efforts have been made to approach Hardwicke's oeuvre from an auteurist perspective. If one compares this to the rushed eagerness with which male directors such as Eli Roth or Quentin Tarantino are lauded through cult receptions, a picture emerges of cultism and auteurism as masculine (this is an element we will further investigate in Chapter 10).

Conclusion

Within film studies there has been a return to thinking about the importance of authorship (e.g. Gerstner and Staiger 2003; Wexman 2003). Previously, the excesses of auteurism had come under attack for the ways in which it simplified the complex collaborative environment of filmmaking, while poststructuralist ideas undermined the romanticized belief in artistic genius. If thinking about artistic creation in individualist terms may seem a relatively recent socio-historical phenomenon (Wexman 2003: 9), the possibility of it being done away with is not very likely, at least in the near future. Nicholas Rombes (2005) has pointed out that authorship within film culture has actually proliferated in the digital age, in particular with DVDs often coming with director's commentary, which may lead some viewers to assume the director as a more central creative force than she/he actually was. Catherine Grant has termed DVDs "auteur machines"; she claims that director's commentaries and other DVD extras tend to encourage a "comprehensive attentiveness or responsiveness to the film's authorial context" (2008: 111).

Authorship should certainly not be idealized; the realities of collaborative work, industrial limitations and socio-historical determinations need our acknowledgment. Nevertheless, some people do make greater creative contributions than others, and their status and impact deserves recognition. In addition, the broader role of auteur figures within filmmaking is important in both the marketing of some films as well as the reception of films by large numbers of people.

The auteur figure is therefore important to cult cinema: within a mode of film culture and reception contexts very much based around the discovery of idiosyncratic films that differ from the "mainstream" (or at least "discovering" hidden profundities within mainstream texts), and where viewers often seek out information about particular films, the need to locate creative human beings is often an inevitable outcome of such a quest. Certain films may attain a privileged status because of connections to a figure who has already gained cult status; on the other hand, a figure may gain cult status due to his or her connection with a film that becomes a cult phenomenon. Cult auteurism shares some similarities with more "classical" auteurism, but also differs in particular ways. It tends to exaggerate certain tendencies, so that technical waywardness or scandalous personal details can be perceived as a maverick disregard for the mainstream.

Notes

1. In addition, primarily cult-oriented film books that are marked by a pronounced auteurist angle include Mendik and Schneider (2002b) and Schneider (2003). Even Hoberman and Rosenbaum's *Midnight Movies* (1983), structured ostensibly around particular films, devotes extensive discussion to directors such as David Lynch, Alejandro Jodorowsky, George Romero, and John Waters.
2. He told the *Guardian* in 2007 that he was planning to make a $5 million gangster film starring Nick Nolte and Marilyn Manson but had thus far failed to raise the money (Brooks 2007).
3. This is now about to change as a vast array of archive material relating to Kubrick's work (comprising over 1000 boxes) has been donated by his estate to the University of the Arts, London. This will undoubtedly stimulate a new wave of Kubrick research and will possibly enhance his cult status even further.
4. Ray's last two films, *We Can't Go Home Again* (1976), made with his students at Binghamton University, and *Lightning over Water* (aka *Nick's Movie*) (co-directed by Wim Wenders, 1979) are cult objects mainly because of how they sketch Ray's last years: as a raging and frustrated eye-patched veteran, and a dying, musing artist respectively.

7

Cult Stardom

Analyses of stars have become increasingly prominent within film studies since Richard Dyer's seminal publication, *Stars*, appeared in 1979, though there have long been reflections on stardom included in biographies, sociological accounts, as well as poetic rhapsodies, to name a few examples. Actually defining a star, however, is not as straightforward as it may at first appear. Without going into too many of the complexities here, we shall nevertheless stress some important ways of distinguishing a star from an actor. We can think of an actor as a person performing a role (on the stage or on the screen). When audiences begin to identify the face of the actor and recognize her or his name, and thus form some assumptions about how the actor will perform, then they also become a public *personality*. Such distinctions did occur within the early years of cinema: first, a discourse on acting emerged within the cinema around 1907, and then "picture personalities" were discussed from around 1909 (DeCordova 1991). The "picture personality" referred to the naming of an actor and related knowledge about how that actor had performed within a number of films. Stars, though, surpass the personality in that their fame and personas are more extensive. DeCordova notes that whereas knowledge about "picture personalities" is limited to their onscreen activities, the star (which he claims arose around 1914) is formed by information about screen roles *and* their private, offscreen life (DeCordova 1991: 26). The star, then, can be thought of as a construction formed out of on-screen and other public performances, media discourses which purport to shed further light on the private individual, and the projected desires of audiences who invest in these personalities.

The Cult of the Movie Star

It could be argued that all stars have gained a cult following; by their very nature stars tend to provoke desire, adoration, identification, sometimes impersonation, which are often indicative of cult status. Stars will often elicit greater interest than any particular film that they are associated with, which is why they are so important to the industry in terms of promoting specific films. Nevertheless, we will delimit the scope of this chapter by focusing on a number of stars whose status is particularly relevant to cult cinema. Thus, when we do focus on stars whose celebrity has been very much part of mainstream culture, such stars will embody additional values that promote their cult status. The first of these is the idea of *precedence*, which brings us to a discussion of the rise of the star system within the film industry. We will focus on Hollywood here, as it is generally considered to be the most important industry through which the star system emerged. We should not, however, overlook the transnational nature of stardom. Not only did Hollywood import stars who had established themselves in other national contexts, but precedents to the Hollywood industrial promotion of stars, such as the Italian phenomenon of the "divismo," played an important role in the development of Hollywood's star system (Fischer and Landy 2004: 3).

Cult Cinema: An Introduction. Ernest Mathijs and Jamie Sexton.
© 2011 Ernest Mathijs and Jamie Sexton. Published 2011 by Blackwell Publishing Ltd.

The emergence of Hollywood stardom is now an oft-told story: early performers were anonymous, a state partly influenced by the fact that many actors wanted to establish themselves in the more respectable realm of theater and did not believe that cinematic appearances would be good for their careers (though it was beneficial to their short-term finances). However, many viewers began to develop a curiosity about recurring faces in the films that they viewed and wanted to know more about these mysterious figures. While film companies were at first resistant to the promotion of their star actors, fearing that this would lead to increased salaries, they soon realized that the marketing potentials of promoting star players could outweigh any economic disadvantages. Furthermore, the increasing demand for information on various actors from an emergent fan base would have made it difficult to perpetuate an anonymous system. In 1910, Carl Laemmle – head of the Independent Motion Picture Company of America – publicized the name of Florence Lawrence. Lawrence had previously worked for the Biograph Company and had become known as the "Biograph Girl." Laemmle, aware of Lawrence's popularity, lured her away from Biograph and promoted her name in a publicity stunt: first he circulated rumors that she had been killed in a tram accident, and then placed advertisements in newspapers uncovering the hoax and announcing that Lawrence was alive, well and filming a new production. Thus, the beginnings of the Hollywood star system were intimately connected with death (albeit a fake death), a theme that constitutes a major thread in cult stardom and which we shall address later in the chapter.

Lawrence's popularity was soon to be surpassed by an actress that Biograph had hired to replace her: Mary Pickford, who was the most popular star in the first decade of Hollywood stardom and had become "the best known girl in America" by 1915 (Barbas 2001: 49). Pickford was even hired by the McLure newspaper to write an advice column (actually ghost-written) and, importantly, contributed to the creation of the star persona: a carefully managed public personality whose onscreen and offscreen traits consistently mirrored each other. According to Barbas, she stood as an exemplar of modern personhood, adored by fans as an "ideal" individual. She therefore had a huge fan base that passionately watched her movies, sought information about her, and sometimes modeled their own lifestyles on her (Barbas 2001: 47–52). The only other star during this period to challenge Pickford in terms of star power was Douglas Fairbanks, whom she married in 1920. These stars were truly important in the development of a "cult of celebrity," which has remained with us to this day, albeit in varying manifestations.

Mainstream Cult Stars

While all stars could be considered cult in the sense that they provoke dedicated, passionate followings, the "cult star" or "cult actor" tends to be distinguished by a number of qualities. Once again, the idea of the mainstream acts as a broad, fuzzy yardstick against which the cult reputation is forged. A number of mainstream actors/stars have, though, also established themselves as cult figures, though this is often because certain factors enable them to stand apart from other stars, creating a double-tiered status (as both mainstream *and* cult). This may be because of the longevity of their star status and a particularly marked, passionate following; or it may be because their offscreen lives are marked by tragedy or activities that are considered to be unusual. One of the most notable mainstream stars who also enjoys cult status is Humphrey Bogart. Bogart's star status turned decidedly cultic when he became the subject of revivals and intense interest in the 1960s: in France, cinephiles adored him, while his films became staple features on the US repertory circuit. He has also become the subject of impersonation within films, particularly evident in Godard's *À bout de souffle* and *Play it Again, Sam*, written by and starring Woody Allen. These films testify to Bogart's iconic status as a cynical, cool figure whose image and gestures exemplified an "ideal" personality linked to rebellion and machismo. He was, for example, a key feature in the celebration of masculine values by the "MacMahonists" (Hoberman and Rosenbaum 1991: 25–30; also see Chapter 4).

Joan Crawford and Bette Davis were two mainstream stars who also crossed over into cult status. Both often played strong females and both were incredibly popular throughout much of their careers. Crawford was a popular star from the late 1920s until the 1950s, first at MGM and then at Warner Bros, and had a considerable, devoted fan base. Davis's popularity was also at its height during the same period, although she also gained a reputation for being a combative personality and was often at odds with Warner Bros because of the roles they offered her. It was after Davis and Crawford's careers were in decline, however, that their cult reputations really began to develop. In their peak, they never appeared together: they detested each other and would sometimes battle for roles. In 1962 they were eventually paired up in Robert Aldrich's psychological horror film *What Ever Happened to Baby Jane?* This movie, which was financially successful, became a cult film due to its camp histrionics and its self-reflexive plot concerning two ex-actor sisters who despise each other. Many read the film as mirroring the tensions between the two characters in real life, heightened when Davis was nominated for a best actress Oscar, which Crawford campaigned against. Their cult credentials were boosted further due to their appearances in low-budget pictures such as *I Saw what You Did* (starring Crawford), *Trog* (Crawford), *The Nanny* (starring Davis) and *The Anniversary* (Davis). Crawford also starred in *Mildred Pierce* and *Johnny Guitar*, both of which would develop cult followings. Her personal life was also increasingly beset by troubles: she became notorious for alcoholism, while the publication of *Mommie Dearest* by her daughter Christina after her death accused her of child abuse (this was later turned into a 1981 film that found its own cult following). Both stars' cult status would also be connected to their appropriation as camp icons (see Chapter 8).

Crawford and Davis had their cult status elevated through a number of processes which are important in enhancing cult reputations. The main overriding principle involved here is how it became clear to many fans that there were cracks behind the surface of their Hollywood-constructed personas, thus revealing the seedier underbelly of the Hollywood dream. Crawford, in particular, embodied a tragic life: though her onscreen heroines often had to deal with misfortune, her alcoholism and reputed abusiveness indicated a personal life in more turmoil than any of her celluloid characters. Davis was less tragic and more bellicose, although her reputation was enhanced by publicized clashes with the studios, which marked her out as a

maverick individualist unwilling to be easily molded. Both stars also revealed, in their later careers, the difficulty of aging actresses retaining their former status as they struggled with roles in films that were minor in comparison to the fare they had appeared in during their heyday.

Personal tragedy, unhappiness, decline, and scandal are all important factors which can feed into cult reputations. For those who are skeptical of the Hollywood dream factory, such stories reveal the rotten core at its heart, hidden by a veneer of mendacious optimism. For those alienated by Hollywood's narratives of happiness, they may reveal stories which are more in tune with their own lives and hence offer a point of identification or empathy. The cult fan, in seeking out difference, can thus find in such factors a way to justify their love of mainstream filmmaking, even as they denigrate the system responsible for producing such films. They offer stories of real, authentic individuals who resist the industry's tendency towards standardization and thus are considered important contributors to the moments of creativity and humanity within Hollywood films. Fortunately for such fans, there are plenty of scandals to hit Hollywood, which has led some to view it as decadent and immoral rather than virtuous. This view of Hollywood was most infamously recorded in Kenneth Anger's *Hollywood Babylon*, first published in Paris in 1959 (it was not officially published in the United States until 1975). *Hollywood Babylon* pieces together a large number of scandals to hit Hollywood, most notably death, drugs, and sex. The decade that Anger focused on in greatest detail was the 1920s, when scandal after scandal hit Hollywood and when it began to be perceived by moralists as a den of iniquity. This led to the intervention of Will Hays and the cleaning up of Hollywood, though scandal would never entirely desert its shores.

What separates *Hollywood Babylon* from other accounts of scandals is that it takes the "cult of scandal" as its point of departure. Instead of only identifying individual scandals, Anger, who had grown up in Hollywood and was able to recount firsthand information, gave the impression that Hollywood was intrinsically associated with scandals, and that sectors of the public held a morbid, cultish fascination for these scandals. *Hollywood Babylon* was deemed so unnerving that Anger could only get the book published outside the United States, in France. Fittingly, it has since received a cult reputation itself. Among the most noteworthy scandals mentioned by Anger are the 1922 Fatty Arbuckle scandal, which is usually credited for instigating Hollywood's reputation as a "cesspool," and macabre stories circulating around the sudden deaths and tragic demises of film stars such as Rudolph Valentino, James Dean, and Judy Garland (these have developed into what Mikita Brottman has called "cults of death," see below). Later editions of the book also included the slaying of actress Sharon Tate by the disciples of Charles Manson. By then, Anger himself had been courting controversy by associating himself with members of the Manson Family and Hollywood-located Satanists – a surefire way to sustain his own cult reputation (see Chapter 12).

The Cult of Death

Death, perhaps more than any other factor, has contributed to many a cult reputation, or intensified the status of those who already enjoyed devoted followings.

This subject has been analyzed by Mikita Brottman (2000: 103–119), who claims that the fascination with celebrity deaths is rooted in a dual fascination with the star as a "revelatory body" and the intensification of individualism within the twentieth century. The former point refers to the way in which the cinema, following photography, was seen to emphasize the connection between self and bodily gesture, and for stars this connection becomes heightened, as the public reads much into how their screen bodies reveal deeper meanings. The latter point refers to how identity has become increasingly individualized, moving further away from a more collectivist notion of self, which itself leads to a greater fear of individual death. Thus, for Brottman, celebrity death engenders fascination because of the way the individual celebrity relinquishes their "revelatory" power in one sense, but manages to retain it in another:

That public body, once so expressive and so intensely scrutinized, is abruptly transformed into a limp marionette... And yet somehow, paradoxically, this detached puppet still purports to be the eminently notable celebrity its strings once so publicly animated. Little wonder, then, that the death of celebrity ... should arouse such violent emotion, such voyeurism, such curiosity, such alarm. (Brottman 2000: 111)

The cinema embalms a performance in time, while performers themselves continue to be marked by temporal decay. Cinema therefore creates a visible disjunction between then and now, which is heightened by the number of photographic images of stars disseminated through promotional materials and the like. When a performer dies, this temporal separation becomes intensified and, for those investing in the star image, poignant. Chris Petit has argued that as cinema ages it becomes "a mausoleum as much as a palace of dreams," as an increasing number of dead stars are re-animated by film viewing (quoted in Mulvey 2006: 17). It is perhaps this morbid flip-side of the palace of dreams that appeals to cult viewers, drawn as they often are to the more perverse pleasures of film viewing.

Brottman discusses two stars in detail who have gained a particularly cultic presence due to their premature deaths, but who had already gained iconic status in their lifetimes: James Dean and Marilyn Monroe. For these stars, as with others, a number of materials revealing personal, previously unknown details, flourished after their deaths. Death is certainly good for sales, as various segments of the entertainment industry have discovered. The range of personal, often prurient, information that floods the markets after a star's death can then feed back into our readings of the films that they appeared in, so that the temporal disjunction previously remarked upon becomes a constitutive feature of the viewing encounter. We may begin to read into the films elements of their personal lives that have come to light, so that they become, in Brottman's phrase, "inadvertent documentaries on the subject of human mortality" (2000: 112).

A huge star in her time, Monroe's iconic status has shown little signs of diminishing. Immortalized in Andy Warhol's silkscreen prints in the 1960s, her image has continued to proliferate in popular culture, while many of the films that she starred in also continue to hold interest for modern audiences. Brottman examines *The Misfits* as a particularly interesting film in relation to Monroe, stardom, and death. The film was a critical and commercial disaster, but has continued to exert a morbid fascination for many because it was Monroe's, as well as co-star Clark Gable's, last completed film before their deaths. Monroe was in a depressed state during the making of the film and was reportedly difficult to work with. The combined effects of alcohol, pills, miscarriages, and breakdowns, and continual rifts with her husband Arthur Miller (who wrote the script) were reflected in the film, in which she played a confused woman going through a divorce. Montgomery Clift, who also starred in the film, was also undergoing personal problems and would die six years after the film was released. A rather tragic film therefore becomes loaded with personalized sadness when the cult of dead stars is read back into it.

James Dean's iconic status was also boosted by his early death. While, as Claudia Springer argues, many who came of age in the 1950s are likely to consider Marlon Brando the ultimate rebel, it is Dean who has come to symbolize "rebel iconography" in general. Brando, who influenced Dean, continued to evolve and change his image, whereas Dean's image became frozen in time, locked in place by the car crash that prematurely ended his life in 1955. It was at this point, argues Springer, that "James Dean was born – not the twenty-four year old man who had died on the highway, but the icon whose image would become instantly recognizable around the world" (2007:16). His death gave rise to an incredible outpouring of public mourning, led to his image selling a vast range of consumer items, and has inspired his more committed fans to visit the site of his death each year to commemorate his passing (Springer 2007). Dean's importance to subsequent "rebel iconography" is particularly associated with his most famous film, *Rebel without a Cause*. The film was released when Dean died and his portrayal of a young, sensitive, cool, and rebellious teenager became a figure of identification for many teenagers who were feeling alienated by the prevailing conformity of 1950s America. The chicken-run scene, in which Dean jumps from his car just before it speeds over a precipice, became a symbol of his real-life recklessness and took on a poignant edge. It went on to capture the imagination of many more viewers from different generations and in a number of countries, thus cementing Dean's status as a rebel cult icon.

Dean and Monroe are large-scale stars whose cult status is guaranteed by iconicity and a mixture of longevity (of status) with tragic brevity (of actual existences). Another cult icon who could also be grouped into this category is Elvis Presley, though his status is primarily as a musician. While his films do have a cult following, it is largely due to the reputation that he secured within his musical career, which then spills over to his acting roles (see Chapter 16 for more on music and cult cinema). In more recent times, young stars on the verge of breaking into the mainstream film industry and who seemed on the cusp of a glittering career have become the subject of particular cult followings. One notable example is River Phoenix, who died at the age of 23. A dedicated campaigner for environmentalism and animal rights, Phoenix died in a high-profile drug overdose at The Viper Room, a club partly owned by fellow cult star Johnny Depp. His background, too, marked him out from the crowd in a different way: his parents joined a cult religious group entitled the Children of God when he was young and his troubled life has been linked to his experiences within the cult. His death provoked intense media coverage and fan mourning, and he ticks a number of boxes that recur in various areas of cult cinema: drugs, religious cults, left-field political beliefs, and a tragically early death. More recently, the early death of Heath Ledger has led to an outpouring of emotion and it could be that he will also develop a particularly marked cult status.

While death may be the most important factor that elevates the cult status of certain movie stars, there are other features which allow mainstream (or previously mainstream) stars to attain a cult status. While space does not allow us to go into detail here, we should mention some of these. They include *scandals*, such as Fatty Arbuckle's heavily publicized criminal prosecution, in which he was accused of the rape of Virginia Rappe and of contributing to her death. Although Arbuckle was exonerated, the scandal effectively ruined his career, a tragic story which has fed his cult reputation. *Sexuality* can also feed cult status, such as the heightened sexuality of Mae West, whose risqué persona pushed at the boundaries of acceptability within Hollywood and who is thus seen as a daring, controversial figure. Or cult status may relate to *sexual* or *racial difference*: for example, gay actors whose orientation may only come to light at a later period due to the earlier illegality of homosexuality (Rock Hudson being an example here); or black actors who struggled to carve out a career, no matter how compromised, within a racially prejudiced system (such as Paul Robeson or, later, Sidney Poitier). There are also actors who, though not gay, become gay icons, such as Judy Garland (see Chapter 8).

Cult Actors

The cultification of the dead star can be considered one of three broad ways in which a mainstream star can gain a cult status. Alongside the mainstream star who gains a cult after they have died is the mainstream star who gains a cult status after they have faded from the mainstream (such as Bette Davis and Joan Crawford, who moved from the mainstream to the margins of the exploitation circuit after their mainstream heyday). Finally, a few stars seem to attain the status as both a cult star *and* a mainstream star at the same time. This can occur when a star with a rebellious or non-conformist persona moves into the mainstream but retains much of their cult fan base: while some fans may lose interest in the star for "selling out," others may identify a star who has entered the mainstream on their own terms and who has retained a non-conformist, idiosyncratic aura. Johnny Depp could be considered as a example of such a star: previously considered a rebel (through scuffles, fights, and drunkenness) who acted in a range of quirky films (he has acted for cult directors such as Tim Burton, Jim Jarmusch, and John Waters), he has now settled down and become a bankable Hollywood star through his turn as Jack Sparrow in the *Pirates of the Caribbean* films. Yet he still retains an aura of idiosyncrasy and exudes an air of uncompromising artistry for many.

In contrast to many of the mainstream cult stars mentioned thus far, however, are a number of actors much more recognizable as cult actors through and through, in the sense that they are not stars in the conventional sense. Some of these may have stronger connections with mainstream cinema than others, though most of them are better known as cult figures due to establishing reputations within "marginal"

cinemas such as exploitation, independent, underground, "Art House" cinema, or "B" movies (of course these categories also criss-cross at certain points). Some of these actors can be particularly obscure and gain a reputation through small-scale championing.

Maria Montez, for example, was a Dominican-born actress who appeared in a number of Technicolor "costume adventure" pictures, such as *Ali Baba and the Forty Thieves* and *The Cobra Woman*. She tended to play exotic, seductress characters and was known as "the Queen of Technicolor." While critics tended to dismiss her acting abilities (not often helped by the type of pictures that she appeared in) she developed a dual cult following. First, she was adored by the people of the Dominican Republic as a figure of national pride, and even has an airport in Barahona (her birthplace) named after her; secondly, she was also appropriated as a camp icon (see Chapter 8). Her camp appeal was stimulated by underground filmmaker Jack Smith, who penned an extraordinary eulogy to her entitled "The Perfect Filmic Appositeness of Maria Montez" (Smith 1962/3). Smith opposed the critical consensus of Montez as a "bad actress": "She believed and thereby made the people who went to her movies believe. Those who could believe, did. Those who saw the World's Worst Actress just couldn't and they missed the magic. Too bad – their loss" (Smith 1962/3: 28). Rather than judging her by the criteria of "acting ability," he asserted his own reasons to value her which were much more based around the *cult of personality*. For Smith, she encapsulated what almost amounted to a system of values, as though she were an essential reflection of the things that he believed in: "moldiness, Glamorous Rapture, schizophrenic delight, hopeless naivete, and glittering technicolored trash!" (1962/3: 28, capitals in original). This was clear in his own films, which were lo-fi attempts to recreate the exotic world that Montez, for him, captured.

In a similar manner to Smith's eulogizing of Montez, actress Rose Hobart also became the unlikely subject of an avant-garde artist's attentions. In 1936 artist Joseph Cornell made a film of Hobart after buying a film that she starred in – *East of Borneo* – for watching at home. He became so enraptured with her that he created a film, *Rose Hobart* (Figure 7.1), compiled entirely from moments in *East of Borneo* that she

Figure 7.1   Rose Hobart from *East of Borneo*, which was recontextualized in Joseph Cornell's *Rose Hobart*.

appeared in, and manipulated these original moments by slowing down the speed, tinting the print blue, and accompanying images with a musical soundtrack (thus dispensing with the original film's dialog). The film, then, tends to fetishize the image of Hobart and is a way of enabling viewers to pay sole attention to the movements and gestures of Hobart herself, and to perceive them in a new light, as though liberated from the original film that they appeared in. Further, as Janet Staiger argues, it is a way of "Othering Hobart by decontextualizing her from the film and yet locating her in the jungles in which everything else is 'other'." She further states that "Cornell's arrangement produces a withdrawal of meaning while investing Hobart's image with new sense and sensuality" (Staiger 2005b). This is in line with many other art works that Cornell produced, in particular the collection "boxes" that he is most reputed for, which were often based around images of stars, including Lauren Bacall, Greta Garbo, and Jennifer Jones.

As exploitation filmmaking, and particularly the fantastical-related areas of it, has strong links with cult cinema (see Chapters 13 and 19), it is no surprise that a number of actors heavily associated with such films have gained strong cult reputations. These actors include Boris Karloff and Béla Lugosi, primarily for their association with the classic Universal horror films of the 1930s (and, importantly, for their roles as Frankenstein's monster and Dracula, respectively), but also because of their subsequent careers within which they remained associated with exploitation material.

Karloff, for example, appeared in a number of Corman productions later in his career, including Bogdanovich's *Targets*, a remarkably self-reflexive film about Karloff's position as a cult actor. Lugosi, meanwhile, cut a more tragic figure as he became increasingly typecast. Falling into poverty and addicted to heroin, he ended up featuring in a number of Edward D. Wood Jr's micro-budget productions, including *Plan 9 from Outer Space*, which featured posthumous archive footage of him.

Karloff and Lugosi were employed by segments of the exploitation industry because of the cult values accrued from their iconic status as classic monsters, but the emerging exploitation circuit in the 1950s and 60s also created its own star figures. Vincent Price, for instance, is a good example of an actor who both William Castle and American International Pictures (AIP) employed because of his star value, which enabled them to create films likely to find larger audiences because of the presence of a recognizable icon (Heffernan 2004: 90–112). Price's connection with Castle – in films such as *The House on Haunted Hill* and *The Tingler* – and AIP – in a number of its Poe adaptations – bolstered his cult appeal. Such appeal was also heightened in some sectors because of Price's camp qualities (see Chapter 8) and his particular acting style. In terms of acting, Price is renowned for his "hammy" style, which denotes an over-exaggerated acting mode (Figure 7.2). "Ham" is generally a term of abuse that refers to actors who do not have a very broad range of acting skills, and who thus tend to compensate through excessive facial and bodily gestures, which can render particular scenes bathetic. Yet ham can also be celebrated by cult fans because, rather than viewing ham as a failure to match the criteria of "professionalism," they sometimes view it as an *alternative* form of acting that contains more personality than many more respectable performances. This is not the case with *all* ham acting, and here the filter of subjectivity must enter the unpredictable field of evaluation. As Jack Stevenson argues: "ultimately ham is in the eye of the beholder: one person's divinely inspired ham is what another might deem complete garbage. It's an area of total subjectivity, which is why it is such an affront to critics" (Stevenson 2003c: 71). Certainly, subjectivity is a crucial component of such evaluation, but we must also add to Stevenson's assertion that broader cultural considerations must also

Figure 7.2 Vincent Price hams it up as he pretends to undergo the impact of psychedelic drugs in *The Tingler*.

be taken into account here, in particular the notion of "cultural capital" (outlined in more detail in Chapter 5), for broader cultural and social systems will to an extent shape a person's subjectivity.

Artificiality and Individuality

Price is an actor who, if he does embody ham, would seem to do so in a self-conscious manner at times. In many of the Poe adaptations, for instance, it is as though Price is aware of how he is expected to act, and plays up to these expectations of himself. While such play acting may at times be dismissed as self-parody, there is more to be said about it: in such performances there can be a consideration of an audience which is important for the cult actor, who may well cultivate her or his cult status among a particular fan base through solidifying a public persona. Mathijs (2011a, 2011b) has noted how cult actors often create formalist, rather than realist, portrayals. Thus, instead of "authentically" becoming lost in the characters that they are playing, they retain the tics and quirks that specialized audiences expect them to display. According to Mathijs qualities constitutive of formalist acting such as copying and ostentation are part of *referential acting*: "Referential acting includes homage, quotation and allusion. It offers the opportunity to include the magician's tricks: winks, nudges, signature gestures or direct address" (2011a). Referential acting highlights self-conscious qualities, and allows audiences

"in the know" to register the ways in which the actor is referencing their own, as well as others', styles.

For a segment of cult fans, repetitious performances can provide pleasure rather than suggesting a lack of range. Pleasure can arise from viewing the same persona manifest itself in different filmic environments, in which subtle differences and qualities can be identified by avid, invested audiences. Certain actors become particularly cherished for acts or traits that evidence an identifiable style, a kind of authorial trace that they leave upon the films they appear in. These can include the manic tics and feral stare of Klaus Kinski, the quirky neuroticism of Jeff Goldblum, the physical athleticism of Bruce Lee, or the stately authority of Christopher Lee. Repetition can also prove pleasurable in terms of recurrent situations that some actors become entangled within. A key example here would be Giovanni Lombardo Radice, an Italian actor who has appeared in a number of low-budget horror films. A relatively obscure actor who is only known by sectors of horror fans, he has played a range of different character types, but has become known for his spectacular and gory deaths. As Patricia MacCormack (2004: 107) has observed, between 1980 and 1992 he appeared in ten horror films, of which seven included him being violently killed (while being mocked, wounded, and beaten in another). Any follower of the actor, then, becomes aware of him signifying not a "certain role, style or quality of acting, but a certain possible affect due to the probability of a visceral death" (MacCormack 2004: 108). In this sense, followers of Radice will watch one of his films with the expectation of a gory death, an expectation which may or may not be fulfilled.

The recurrence of performance gestures, role types and filmic situations can lead some fans to become highly conscious of intertextual connections evident within particular performances, which then leads to them being viewed in the context of a wider oeuvre (for more on intertextuality and cult film, see Chapter 21). This feeds into the aforementioned *self-conscious* performance style where actors will often reference other texts (which may or may not be their own performances). Bruce Campbell, who has gained a particularly dedicated cult following without ever becoming a Hollywood staple, is an actor who certainly is well aware of his own cult status. This is evident through the ways in which he will sometimes obviously reprise his over-the-top, comic style within numerous cameo roles, but is most marked by the fact that he has played himself within a film based around him, entitled *My Name Is Bruce*. In this film "Bruce Campbell" gets mistaken for Ash, the character that he played in *The Evil Dead* films, which catapulted him to cult status. The self-conscious nature of an actor playing his or her own "self" is also a salient feature of the cult film *Pink Flamingos*, in which Divine plays Divine, even though Divine himself was only a constructed persona. Divine also parodied other stars within his own performance, such as Jean Harlow, Mae West, and Jayne Mansfield (Harries 2004: 155). Such self-conscious performances often draw attention to the artificiality of acting, which sharply distinguishes them from "method" approaches, in which the actor attempts to lose her or himself in the character.

A particularly interesting cult actor who developed a self-conscious style is Peter Lorre. Lorre made his name in Germany, coming to prominence as a child killer in *M*, and who came to Hollywood in 1935. Even though he was promoted as a star he proved difficult to cast in leading roles, tending to play either bit parts in major films or bigger parts in cheaper films, often "B" movies. Yet, even though he was never a star as such, he did, as Sarah Thomas argues, possess "cinematic value and he remained an important screen commodity, partly due to his recognisable persona" (Thomas 2007). This status as a well-known personality who nevertheless never established himself in the way he had liked, undoubtedly fed his cult status. This status was also linked to the repetitious element of Lorre's acting, as mentioned above: his performances frequently drew on a limited range of recognizable traits and gestures, including abrupt shifts from meek to sinister, soft speech patterns juxtaposed with sudden outbursts, and the movement between a blank expression and exaggerated facial contortions (Thomas 2007). Thomas argues that these repetitive elements of Lorre's performances were particularly self-reflexive and were a means of compensating for his marginal status. Thus, in *The Maltese Falcon*, he develops a distinctly recognizable vocal style so that he is still a crucial presence within the film, despite spending much screen time with his back to the camera. Lorre's persona, then, was very much tied to his position within the industry and often refers to his own status as a performer.

Hammy, self-conscious, and formalist styles can be related to the notion of *excess*, in that they exceed particular norms (of professional standards, of realist modes). Another important excessive element in the repertoire of the cult actor is *intensity* and/or *insanity*, which can often carry over into the off-screen persona of the actor. Klaus Kinski, who we have already mentioned, is loved just as much for his reported antics on film sets as he is for the performances that make it into the final cut. His insane fits are legendary and were an important part of the appeal of the documentaries *Burden of Dreams* (which documents the making of Herzog's *Fitzcarraldo*) and *My Best Fiend* (in which Herzog focuses on his relationship with Kinski). Even his personal life seems to be exaggerated, as was the case with his (purportedly highly fabricated) autobiography *All I Need Is Love* (1989). In this sense, the cult actor's actual life becomes an extension of his or her on-screen persona (or at least vice versa). Other actors particularly known for their intensity and/or insanity include Dennis Hopper and Crispin Glover, who have both appeared within offbeat projects as well as more mainstream fare.

Excess can also inform the personas of cult actors in terms of the sheer amount of films that they have appeared within, and/or their association with a particular type of film. If an actor has appeared in a large number of films in a supporting or marginal role, it can provide cult fans with the potential to seek out as many appearances as possible, comparing nuances of performance in relation to the films as a whole. Often, actors predominantly associated with the fantastical/horror film tend to inspire interest in this regard, as fans of this mode of filmmaking are more reputed to seek out exhaustive details. Examples would include Mexican wrestler El Santo (Rodolfo Guzman Huerta), who crossed over into acting and starred in a large number of cult wrestling horror films; Barbara Steele, who became a fan favorite through her appearances in Italian horror films and for exuding an air of mysterious beauty; and Spanish actor Paul Naschy, who has appeared in a large number of horror-related films, and who has also written and directed a number of films in this genre. Naschy himself was a fan of the horror film, but other actors became associated with the genre more through accident: Donald Pleasance, for example, after appearing in more respectable material in his earlier career, featured in a great deal of low-budget horror movies. Fellow British actors Peter Cushing and Christopher Lee also became cult actors for their horror-related roles, in particular through the work that they undertook for Hammer studios between the late 1950s and 1970s (though Lee often bemoans that people frequently overlook his parts in other types of films).

Conclusion

A huge number of actors and stars can be linked to notions of cult due to the ways in which they exert fascination and often accrue fan followings (see Chapter 5). In contemporary society this is linked to a "cult of celebrity," in which celebrities in general often assume hyper-real qualities through intense media scrutiny. Undoubtedly, Hollywood stars have played a central role in the cult of celebrity during the twentieth century, and continue to do so into the twenty-first century. The star can take on a particularly cultic aura because of the personalized relationship that a fan constructs between themselves and a star image, and/or through the fondness for particular stars within cult communities. In the digital age an intense relationship between fan and star can be extended, as it is now easier to extract the star image from its surrounding environment. Laura Mulvey has argued that this leads to the notion of the *possessive spectator*, who can use video or DVD players to halt the linear narrative and gain a heightened relation to the body of the star: "Halting the flow of film extracts star images easily from their narrative surroundings for the kind of extended contemplation that had only previously been possible with stills. From a theoretical point of view, this new stillness exaggerates the star's iconic status" (Mulvey 2007: 161).

Despite the cult of stardom, cult stars and/or cult actors can still be differentiated from more general stars, although such demarcations can vary according to context. Such differences will often hinge upon a conceptual imagining of the mainstream, in which the actor/star represents values and/or styles that differ from – or perhaps transcend – the norms associated with the mainstream. While the cult actor may be most commonly associated with areas of filmmaking that exist on the fringes, or outside, of the mainstream, there are also – as we have shown – a number of mainstream actors who are also cult actors. The mainstream star can also become a cult star through a broad process of *double coding*, so that they have a more general star status, but also a status among niche groups for different reasons. This double coding often occurs at separate temporal junctures: so a cult following may develop around the star *after* their mainstream status has waned. Less commonly, a mainstream star can also attract a cult following during the height of their popularity.

8

Camp and Paracinema

"Camp" and "paracinema," alongside partially related concepts such "trash" and "kitsch," have frequently been used to refer to a range of cult cinema practices. Camp is a term that has a long history of usage which extends far beyond cinema itself, whereas paracinema is a word that more specifically applies to cult cinema. In this chapter we will outline some of the main concepts that have been associated with camp and briefly reference its applicability to cult cinema, before more fully investigating the concept of paracinema and "trash" film.

Camp

While camp as a term became well known during the 1960s, it has a much longer history. According to Cleto, it first entered the language in a Victorian dictionary of slang and referred to "actions and gestures of exaggerated emphasis . . . used chiefly by persons of exceptional want of character" (J. Redding Ware, quoted in Cleto 1999: 9). Deriving from the French term *se camper* ("to flaunt"), it became associated with homosexual subcultures in the early twentieth century, as a type of communication between people "in the know," which could signal their (at the time illegal) sexual orientation (Benshoff 2007: 202; Cleto 1999: 9). The act of role-playing, of performing in a deliberately exaggerated manner to communicate with a particular group of people who understand such gestures, is still important in understanding camp. It has, however, extended beyond such initial understandings to become a much more complex term: it is,

as Benshoff has argued "a confused and confusing term" (2007: 201); while Cleto claims that because it has different uses it should not be defined in a strict manner, as its meanings can alter according to the contexts within which it is operative (1999: 16).

One of the most well-known, and cited, articles on camp was written by Susan Sontag in 1964. This was a period in which camp was becoming much more visible within various sections of popular culture, and Sontag's piece helped to aid a particular understanding of camp. While earlier twentieth-century understandings of camp associated it with homosexuality, Sontag argued that it was much more than homosexual taste, even though homosexuals "by and large, constitute the vanguard – and the most articulate audience of – Camp" (2008: 51). Sontag articulated camp as both a mode of appreciation and a feature of objects. As a mode of appreciation, it is an approach that emphasizes artifice and exaggeration (2008: 43) and, as such, challenges dominant notions of *taste*: instead of appreciating what is considered to be conventionally "beautiful," or praising art works that contain deep meanings, camp transforms notions of beauty through stressing the importance of surface style. Camp privileges artificiality over the "natural," which stems from homosexuals' keen awareness, as minority outlaws, of gender being not a natural condition but rather something that is *performed*. Therefore, the camp persona adopted by many gay men exaggerates mannered gestures in order to foreground all gender roles as artificial constructions: that is, they are culturally learned as opposed to biologically inherent. Further, this mode of appreciation also has roots in gay men's

Cult Cinema: An Introduction. Ernest Mathijs and Jamie Sexton.
© 2011 Ernest Mathijs and Jamie Sexton. Published 2011 by Blackwell Publishing Ltd.

feelings of alienation from dominant social norms: as a minority, excluded group, they exert power through finding value within objects that have been devalued by prevailing regimes of taste. Andrew Ross has written that "Camp ... involves a celebration by the cognoscenti, of the alienation, distance, and incongruity reflected in the very processes of which hitherto unexpected value can be located in some obscure or exorbitant object" (Ross 2008: 56). This leads to a cultish celebration of marginal artifacts in which "those who are otherwise dominant are, for once, excluded" (Cleto 1999: 31).

Appreciation of artistic film works as camp, then, can privilege film genres which are considered to be very much opposed to realism, such as the musical, melodrama, and horror, or films which are cheaply made and therefore do not disguise their artifice very well (Benshoff 2007: 203). There are also a number of stars who were appreciated as camp, including Mae West, Joan Crawford, and Bette Davis, due to their "indefatigable drive and bigger than life personas" (in which performativity is stressed) and also because of their "subordinate (but often resistant) position within patriarchal culture, and their frequent romantic troubles with men" (Benshoff 2007: 2003). A particularly important camp-cult star is Judy Garland, who Richard Dyer (1986) has examined in detail. For Dyer, any star can be read *as* camp, but Garland was also a star "who expressed camp attitudes" (1986: 179). Garland's cult reputation revolves around her child and adult career, and the pathos surrounding her comeback in the 1950s. As Wade Jennings (1991: 94) writes: "After the success of *The Wizard of Oz*, a persona was established on record. Dorothy's wistfulness and childlike candor became permanently tied to the Garland screen persona." Peary's comments on Garland encapsulate the ambiguity encapsulated in this persona perfectly:

> Much of the Oz cult among adults is a result of Judy Garland, so young, so innocent, so pretty ... Watching Garland today, and knowing how scared she was at the time, how uncomfortable she was in her tight strap, and how soon after her body would become messed up because of a growing dependency on speed and sleeping pills, our feelings must waver – between *delight* in her dynamic yet touching performance under trying

conditions and *grief* that we are seeing the role that launched her into the world of superstardom she never was able to handle (Peary 1981: 393).

The cautionary tale of Garland's breakdowns, demise, failed comebacks, premature death, and quasi-sainthood, is a recurrent trope in camp. It pitches the poor defenseless child against an evil, faceless corporation, but it also portrays an irresponsible professional against the people who supported and cared for her (Kaufman 1994; Friedrich 1986: 346–349).

Camp followings, especially those of (former) child actors, are often deeply involved in identity-affirmation (Figure 8.1). Such involvements are combined with anxieties over the cultural appropriation of visual representations of child actors. In her study of the gay cult of Judy Garland, Janet Staiger details the similarities between public perceptions of Garland's adult "nervous exhaustion," "intensity," "insecurity," and "elf-like androgyny," and contemporaneous views of gays in American culture. She proposes that this similarity might be one of the reasons for the prominent queer cult appeal of Garland, articulated through organizations for gay liberation such as the Radical Faeries (Staiger 1992: 154–177). In more recent years, to the gay cult of Garland has been added, at least partially, a lesbian cult, one that departs from *The Wizard of Oz* and Garland's character of Dorothy, but which has increasingly focused on the "Wicked

Figure 8.1 Through the cult and camp following for *The Wizard of Oz*, the Wicked Witch of the West (Margaret Hamilton), Dorothy (Judy Garland), and Glinda, the Good Witch of the North (Billie Burke) have become identity affirmers for fans.

Witch of the West" Glinda. As Alexander Doty (2000: 51) writes: "I enjoyed the Wicked Witch of the West as another camp figure: she was a scary, tough butch dressed in black." The cult appeal of the theater musical *Wicked*, which takes the witches from *The Wizard of Oz* as its focus, has broadened this embryonic lesbian theme into a full-fledged mode of viewer engagement. These days, the lesbian appeal of *Wicked* and *Oz* is widely acknowledged (see Chapter 10). Tellingly, the Garland cults refer equally to her adult life and to the significance of her formative years – crucial in the formation of sexual identities. Similar anxieties can be found in the fandom surrounding Nathalie Wood and Shirley Temple, and the collectible-heavy fandoms of Deanna Durbin and Margaret O'Brien.[1]

Garland also became aware of her gay following and was well versed in gay culture, and these fed into her later performances. An awareness of her campness could, according to Dyer, be read back into her earlier film performances. They could do so in two main ways: first, knowledge of her working relations – in which the surface glamour of performativity clashes with her personal pain and hurt – became increasingly well known among sections of her gay followers; secondly, he argues that many of her performances can nevertheless be read as camp without this knowledge, as many of her roles – such as in Minnelli's *Ziegfried Follies* and *The Pirate*, and *The Wizard of Oz* – contain elements of theatricality, parody, and obvious artifice (Dyer 1986: 181). Garland's status as a camp icon became crucially heightened by the fact that her funeral (June 27, 1969) – attended by many gay men – occurred at a similar time to the Stonewall Riots (June 28, 1969), which have been linked to the emergence of gay rights activism (see Chapter 10).

Dyer's distinction between a star being read as camp, and a star embodying camp, deserves further consideration as it relates to how camp can be both a property of objects/people, as well as a mode of perception. Garland, and other stars, may embody camp because they are aware of the camp readings that have been inscribed upon them and they, in turn, actively incorporate camp into their persona as a willing participant in a kind of camp contract. Camp can also be considered to be a property of non-human objects, including films themselves. It is here where camp

partly overlaps with "kitsch," which generally refers to art that is aesthetically deficient, particularly mass-art objects which are seen to tastelessly mimic other – more valuable – works. As such, kitsch is a pejorative term which is often used to denote the opposite of genuine art (as it does, for example, in Clement Greenberg's 1939 article "Avant-Garde and Kitsch"; see Greenberg 1986). Nevertheless, since the growth of camp, kitsch objects themselves can be reclaimed through camp evaluations. So, even if kitsch is employed more frequently as a negative term, it is not always so (and neither is camp always used as a positive term): once again, the context of use is an important factor in the meanings of such terms. Kitsch, however, does tend to refer to the properties of an object, whereas camp is a broader term that, while it can be seen as existing within objects and as a trait of people, is more commonly thought of as a way of reading or communicating.

Susan Sontag actually identified two forms of camp, a distinction that has much commented upon: "naive camp" and "deliberate camp" (2008: 46). Naive camp refers to works which are not meant to be camp, but which are in fact attempts to create something straight, serious. However, such works are seen to fail in their attempts to be serious, and also contain a requisite degree of extravagance, ambition, and passion, which opens them up to camp readings. Sontag lists Busby Berkeley musicals such as *42nd Street* and *Gold Diggers of 1933* as examples of naive camp. The elaborate swimming pool choreography that follows from the song "By a Waterfall" in Berkeley and director Lloyd Bacon's *Footlight Parade* is among the most extravagant possible. Deliberate camp, on the other hand, is camp "which knows itself to be camp" (Sontag 2008: 46). Thus, if naive camp is camp purely by dint of its appropriation as a camp artifact, deliberate camp is intentionally designed as camp. The first is camp through its readings only; while readings inevitably must affect the second (people must be able to perceive its camp intentions for its status as such to be established), such readings are not the sole dimension of its camp identity. Films that have often been singled out as deliberate camp include *Barbarella*, *Beyond the Valley of the Dolls*, *Performance*, most of the films directed by John Waters, plus other underground works from filmmakers such as Kenneth Anger, George Kuchar, Jack

Smith, and Andy Warhol (see Chapter 13). However, neatly distinguishing between naive and deliberate camp can present occasional problems: if different people involved in a film quarrel over whether it was designed as camp, then how do we ultimately gauge whether it was deliberately produced as camp? Jack Stevenson has written how *Beyond the Valley of the Dolls* – often cited as an example of deliberate camp – was nevertheless not interpreted as such by all viewers: some just saw it as bad, while others perceived it as a serious melodrama on its release (2003d: 116). Thus, both intentions and perceptions are never entirely straightforward. For instance, films such as critic Roger Ebert's *Beyond the Valley of the Dolls* and writer Gore Vidal's *Myra Breckenridge* can both be interpreted as parodies of camp criticism (the novel *Myra Breckenridge* mentions critic Parker Tyler a few times explicitly). For Andrew Ross, these films are camp in attitude while also exposing that camp-ism (Ross 1989: 153).

Sontag also argued that time can play an important role in judging particular works as camp. The passing of time, she wrote, can provide us with the requisite distance to judge something as camp: "Time may enhance what seems merely dogged or lacking in fantasy now because it resembles too closely our everyday fantasies" (2008: 48). While we may judge more harshly failures in contemporary works of art, time can provide detachment and transform banality into the fantastic: "things are campy ... when we become less involved in them, and can enjoy, instead of be frustrated by, the failure of the attempt" (2008: 48). Jack Stevenson links this temporal aspect of camp to nostalgia, or at least – in keeping with camp's "artificial" sensibility – a simulated form of nostalgia: "camp is not just nostalgia, but rather a distillation of its pleasurable essence. It is the sweetness of nostalgia detached from the overpowering personal memory that drives one to tears ... It's an appreciation of the *feeling* of nostalgia detached from any specific personal memory" (2003d: 113).

The importance of distance, and time, to camp appreciation links camp to a love of "bad movies," movies which often date from an older time. In particular, the 1950s is a decade that has proven ripe for camp cultism, whether it is in the many sci-fi and horror movies which have been reappropriated as

camp texts, or whether it is through filmmakers – John Waters being an obvious example here – using the decade to feed into their own deliberate camp works. Alison Graham has written that the cultist embrace of the 1950s stems from "a kind of tragic irony. The perceived distance between the so-called fifties 'innocence' and a contemporary cynicism" (1991: 110). Certainly, this nostalgic distance is an important part of a camp celebration of bad films, though it is not the case that camp celebration necessarily entails such temporal distance. An example would be the more recent post-camp celebration of Tommy Wiseau's *The Room* (Bissell 2010). After a brief unsuccessful run in Los Angeles during which viewers ridiculed the film in the presence of its director, *The Room* found an unexpected audience across North America at midnight screenings in art house theaters and on college campuses, where viewers began celebrating it as an ironic masterpiece – an antithesis of professionalism and craftsmanship. During such screenings, people shouted at the screen (yelling "Alcatraz!" at stock shots of San Francisco), and threw spoons and footballs around. Wiseau, who kept occasionally attending screenings, wisely embraced the newfound following and has since claimed *The Room* was always intended to be a pitch-black comedy – as the DVD proudly labels it. And neither can camp be reduced merely to the "bad film subculture" that Ross identifies as a crucial aspect of camp (2008: 60). We will, however, continue the discussion of a "bad film subculture" as it is feeds into the concept of paracinema.

Paracinema

One of the criticisms that was sometimes leveled at Sontag's article was that she downplayed the homosexual aspects of camp and was seen to "de-gayify" the concept, thus leading to its appropriation by dominant culture (Cleto 1999: 10). While it is beyond the scope of the present chapter to probe this particular debate, the idea of camp continuing in a "de-gayified" form could be applied to the concept of "paracinema," although paracinematic taste tends to resist the tastes that are seen to characterize dominant culture, as we shall go on to discuss. In actual fact,

Jeffrey Sconce – who wrote the defining article on paracinema – has stated that the tastes and attitudes characteristic of paracinema are in some ways similar to camp. He argues that there are differences, though, in that whereas camp often referred to a process by which gay men could rework Hollywood codes to suit their own sensibilities, primarily through irony, paracinema is a more aggressive attack upon reigning notions of "quality." Whereas camp is a subtle tweaking of dominant codes, paracinema "seeks to promote an alternative vision of cinematic art"; it is not a "queer" undermining of the mainstream but is rather a "straight" attack undertaken by white, middle class, educated, and disaffected factions (Sconce 1995: 374). (It could be argued, contra Sconce, that paracinema is *less* radical than camp because it empties the sexual politics associated with it.)

Sconce defines paracinema as a term that not only refers to a particular corpus of "trashy" films – which include various forms of exploitation cinema, government hygiene films, sword and sorcery epics, Elvis films – but, more importantly, a way of reading films and the subculture that forms around such approaches (here it is again similar to camp). He writes that paracinema is:

> less a distinct group of films than a particular reading protocol, a counter-aesthetic turned subcultural sensibility devoted to all manner of cultural detritus. In short, the explicit manifesto of paracinematic culture is to valorize all forms of cinematic "trash", whether such films have been either explicitly rejected or simply ignored by legitimate film culture. (Sconce 1995: 372)

Paracinema therefore refers to films that have been deemed worthless by elite culture and which are taken up by particular subcultural formations to establish their outsider credentials.[2] At the time of writing, Sconce observed a growing number of critics who were adopting a "paracinematic" position regarding film viewing and criticism. This was evident in a number of fanzines and other publications, including *Zontar, Subhuman, Psychotronic Video, Trashola, Ungawa, Pandemonium* and the RE/Search volume *Incredibly Strange Films*.[3] He states that the most visible document of this film community is Michael Weldon's *Psychotronic Encyclopedia of Film* (1983). Many of the

views expressed within these publications, argues Sconce, are espoused by highly cine-literate, educated citizens who are reacting against the common canons of films and filmmakers established within high cultural circles. By valuing a number of films generally considered worthless within such circles they proudly differentiate themselves from cultural consensus. *Psychotronic Video*, which began as a Xeroxed zine, was thus produced as a guide to obscure films that could be found on late-night US television, inviting readers to become interested in a realm of filmmaking that fell outside of both the mainstream and critical canons.

Sconce further argues that paracinema has a political dimension in that it explicitly challenges "reigning aesthetic discourses in the academy" (1995: 380). It does this through the way that it reads films and concentrates on an aesthetic disposition characterized by the concept of "excess." This concept, previously explored by Kristin Thompson (1977), states that excess in a film exists when style ceases to serve the diegesis (the story world of the film) and instead exists for its own sake, as a purely aesthetic element. Moments of excess within a film, because they can disrupt absorption within the film's narrative, are able to draw attention to a film as an illusory artifact. Film academics had previously privileged films that disrupt the norms of classical Hollywood cinema and its principles of continuity editing because they were seen to distance the spectator from the text and alert said spectator to some of the filmic codes that were in operation. Such films were considered politically "progressive" and constituted a core of modernist texts favored within the academy around the late 1970s and for the most part of the 1980s.

According to Sconce, paracinema shares characteristics with academic approaches to "progressive" texts. Nevertheless, whereas academics tend to analyze films as intentional products of authors, the paracinematic viewer "often celebrates the unintentional production of different stylistic features, which may be more to do with budget constraints or incompetence than with authorial intention" (1995: 385). In this sense, these viewers focus upon moments of textual "excess" perhaps more so than many academics; they are not interested in the story worlds of these films, which are often trite and negligible, but are inclined to focus on the stylistic quirks that render such films distinctive.

Sconce further argues that paracinema communities often draw attention to the politics of taste, in that they foreground how taste and aesthetics are socially constructed. The introduction to *Incredibly Strange Films* explicitly outlines this disposition:

> This is a functional guide to territory largely neglected by the film-criticism establishment ... Most of the films discussed test the limits of contemporary (middle-class) cultural acceptability, mainly because in varying ways they do not meet certain "standards" ... At issue is the notion of "good taste," which functions as a filter to block out entire areas of experience judged – and damned – as unworthy of investigation. (Vale and Juno 1986: 4)

This is an aspect of paracinema that is particularly linked to Bourdieu's work on taste and its sociological dimension, which is more fully outlined in Chapter 5. As the work of Bourdieu has become increasingly influential within a range of cultural studies work since the publication of Sconce's article, the interrogation of taste has become a more central concern within film studies. Sconce himself noted that this paracinematic attitude was already beginning to infiltrate the academy and was partly responsible for challenging approaches to film research within a scholarly context. This is an issue that we will return to as we now review how the concept of paracinema has impacted upon subsequent work on cult-related cinema.

Critical Responses to Sconce

The number of academic articles which have drawn upon, or at least referenced, Sconce's article testifies to its importance within the field of cult cinema. As with many influential academic articles, it has also been the subject of debate, criticism, and revision. Joan Hawkins's work (2000), which itself has proven influential within this field, drew on Sconce's work and extended its focus. Hawkins actually begins her consideration of paracinema by claiming that it is a type of filmmaking which is heavily characterized by *affect*: films which impact upon the viewer in a physical sense (i.e. fear, tears), rather than intellectually. Hawkins therefore stresses Sconce's oversight of affect in privileging a "reading protocol" feeding into

the creation of cultural distinctions – against both the mainstream and high art (Hawkins 2000: 4). While Hawkins does not really pursue Sconce's neglect of affect, it is a criticism that others have leveled at him: that is, that his focus on how people read these films intellectually and ironically does not take into account the possibility that some people may actually become emotionally involved in viewing these films. This is a point that Sconce himself later admitted was a significant absence within the article (Sconce 2007: 8).

Returning to Hawkins, it is important to note that she also complicated the demarcations between "low" and "high," between "trash" and "art." So, looking at a number of "paracinematic" catalogs – produced by mail order companies selling the types of films discussed by Sconce – she notes some trends which complicate his assertion that paracinema places itself directly against high culture. Many of the films placed within modernist canons mentioned by Sconce, including films by Jean-Luc Godard, also find their way into paracinema catalogs. Hawkins further argues that many films considered high art actually trade on similar tropes and imagery as so-called "low brow" films. She mentions, for example, how Peter Watkins's *The War Game* and Stan Brakhage's *The Act of Seeing with One's Own Eyes*, while generally respected as works of art, nevertheless aim for a quite physical impact upon their viewers (Hawkins 2000: 5–6). It is also the case that many film directors have moved from the world of the avant-garde into more "lowbrow" exploitation territory. Hawkins mentions the work of Paul Morrissey, but we could also add filmmakers such as Anthony Balch, Curtis Harrington, and Walerian Borowczyk, to name a few other examples. The ease with which such filmmakers move from "high" to "low" filmmaking modes points to how such categorical demarcations perhaps tend to conceal a number of overlapping similarities.

For Hawkins, the paracinematic approach to film culture does not so much represent a need to celebrate low art in opposition to high art so much as it represents an attempt at cultural leveling; a need to break down high and low distinctions in order to create a more inclusive conception of culture (2000: 10). However, while on the one hand this paracinematic approach to film consumption is engaged in a form of cultural leveling, on the other hand it still creates distinctions by placing itself against the mainstream. Hawkins mentions this when she notes how paracinema enthusiasts feel a need to consume something different (2000: 7) but does not really pursue how this may complicate her points about cultural leveling. Perhaps we could add that it actually consists of a strange mixture of cultural leveling *and* the re-establishment of cultural distinctions: rather than "trash" being opposed to "art," what we are now faced with is "conventional" and the "mainstream" being opposed to the "deranged," "inspired," and "marginal."

Hawkins also notes that while there is a general process of cultural leveling apparent within paracinematic catalogs, there are still distinctions made within these catalogs between different films, so that not all films are treated in exactly the same manner. She points out, for example, that some films are treated as straightforward "art" (e.g., Dreyer's *Vampyr*), whereas others are described as enjoyable in a more ironic, "so-bad-they're good" manner (e.g. *Plan 9 from Outer Space*). This points to how such paracinematic cultures are actually composed of a number of competing discourses. It is because this broad cultural sensibility is composed of a number of different voices that there are sometimes identifiable particular subgroupings within it. This is actually mentioned by Sconce when he refers to infighting between "paracinematic factions," citing overt antagonism between the zines *Film Threat* and *Psychotronic Video* (1995: 375). He does not, however, pay substantial attention to this matter and, for the most part, focuses on the particular mode of "trash" cinema represented by the *Psychotronic Video*'s approach to "trash," as opposed to *Film Threat*'s.

This skewing of focus towards a particular notion of trash, as a cinema of the past that has been neglected – what Matt Hills has dubbed "archivist" trash (2002a: 61) – downplays how "trash" can be defined differently by different communities. Jack Stevenson, for example, though writing on a variety of subjects covering historical underground and exploitation, as well as more contemporary currents, nevertheless defines trash as related to an underground, rather than archival-exploitation, sensibility. It is true that the two terms are not entirely distinct, hence underground "trash" is influenced by historical exploitation, but for Stevenson this is a mode of film-making that is very

much manifested in low-budget "underground" films and practiced by filmmakers such as Jack Smith, George Kuchar, John Moritsugu, and Craig Baldwin. He argues that it is a form of *anti-art*:

> Like surrealism, it [trash] enables the film-maker, via a distorting prism of exaggerated stylisation, to use block humour to deal with shocking, horrifying or otherwise untouchable subject matter that would have been impossible to treat in a more conventional style. (Stevenson 2003b: 130)

For Stevenson, trash films self-consciously adopt a junkyard aesthetic, inverting the meaning of trash and adopting it as a badge of pride. These filmmakers collect cultural debris and construct a new aesthetic out of it; whereas Sconce's paracinematic subculture comprises critics who unearth and extol such debris and tend to find modern filmmaking wanting by comparison.

The archival bent within the paracinematic community can sometimes slip into a nostalgic tone (a tone, as mentioned, also evident in some accounts of camp). For some of these critics, the urge to delve into the more obscure and maligned recesses of film history can go hand in hand with a rejection of where cinematic culture, and often culture as a whole, currently stands. This also ties in with a rejection of the "mainstream" and an anti-corporate ethos: it is often considered that older cinematic culture allowed for a wider range of films to be seen because of the greater opportunities for small businesses to thrive. This often leads, in particular, to nostalgia for older "drive-in" "fleapit," and "grindhouse" cinemas and a distaste of the increasing, corporate-led dominance of multiplexes. This attitude is clear in Stephen Puchalski's following comments in introducing a collection of his criticism:

> More than just irreverent criticism, it's also a glimpse into a time long gone. Before the drive-ins I used to haunt during my college years were turned into mini-malls. Before the cool mom 'n' pop stores were buried by corporate-owned chains. Before 42nd Street – once renowned for its unsurpassed array of porno booths, convulsing junkies and gorgeous old theatres – was transformed into a Disney tourist trap. (Puchalski 2002: 9)

The link to films being consumed during a period of growth is explicit here, and this may well be a factor in other trash film connoisseurs' preference for films of a bygone era: they recall a formative period in their lives, when these types of films had particularly meaningful connotations, opening up as they did a vista to "another world."

This question of films being "meaningful" to particular viewers once again returns us to the question of "affect." As Sconce himself noted, the lack of focus on this particular angle was indeed a missing ingredient of his seminal article. And yet, this remark appears within an edited collection on "trash" cinema – *Sleaze Artists* – in which many contributors still tend to overlook this affective dimension. Many viewers, however, would not see themselves as gaining pleasure out of such films in a distanced, primarily ironic manner. Examples abound from people who are actually strongly affected by such films and approach them, sometimes write about them, in a serious manner. Tim Lucas's *Video Watchdog*, for example, is a consumer guide to "fantastic" cinema in which a number of such films are approached with a straight face. He and his contributors may not always acclaim such films as works of genius, and may not always maintain an entirely serious tone, but the "highly ironic" attitude identified by Sconce is not a particularly marked feature within the magazine. Likewise, Andrew Caine has written that although the "Beach Party" films made by AIP in the 1950s and 1960s have been reclaimed by some critics in ways that conform to Sconce's arguments, others – such as fans of Annette Funicello – tend to appreciate the films that she was in as "quality" products, related to ideals of "wholesomeness" (Caine 2001). Additionally, many people have recuperated these and related films in more ambiguous ways: while they may appropriate elements of them ironically, they also tend to value their soundtracks as "good." They therefore overlook the presence of music such as Frankie Avalon and Annette Funicello and instead focus on more "canonized" sounds:

Fans of Elvis Presley, Chuck Berry and the Beach Boys who relish *Jailhouse Rock* (1957), *Rock, Rock, Rock* (1956) and A.I.P. beach movies are arguably not engaged in "an overall aesthetic of calculated disaffection" (Sconce, 1995: 376), but rather cementing their own "good" taste

according to the canonical hierarchies evident within rock criticism. (Caine 2001)

This should alert us to the complexities at work within the consumption of films that Sconce includes within his paracinematic list. Different people will appropriate films for different purposes, hence Ed Wood biographer Rudolph Grey's distaste of those who enjoyed the director's work ironically. We should therefore remember that paracinematic viewing coexists with other ways to evaluate such films. Caine's argument also points to the ways that separate textual elements can be consumed differently, so that "ironic" and "earnest" attitudes towards a single film (or a set of films) can be both present in people's responses to films.

Another problem in focusing only on the ironic recuperation of these types of films is that it leads to a contradictory position. If such films are only ironically recuperated, if we can only appreciate them because of their unintentional deviations from aesthetic norms, then there is an implicit suggestion that they are actually "bad." This, at least to some extent, goes against the argument that Sconce makes about this viewing community challenging taste. In fact, it merely reaffirms taste if it accepts such movies are actually "bad" (even if it does expand the parameters of acceptability). Such an approach also places doubt upon Sconce's claims that this community challenges the types of questions that can be asked about the cinema; bringing into question not just *what* types of films should be studied, but *how* such films should be studied. On the contrary, it would seem to close down how such films can be approached. It is for this reason that Chibnall, in a subsequent article, argued that "we should be wary of dismissing cheap genre productions as 'paracinema', dumb sensationalism which can only be camply appreciated as 'bad film'" (Chibnall 1997: 98).

There is a further problem with Sconce's focus on a selected range of critical material: his occasional tendency to make broader assumptions about audiences that is never actually evident in that material. Mark Jancovich has drawn attention to how Sconce slips into making unwarranted assumptions about audience responses to these films. For example, Sconce claims that paracinema is potentially political when he writes that "it compels even the most casual viewer to engage with it ironically, producing a relatively detached textual space in which to consider, if only superficially, the cultural, historical and aesthetic politics that shape cinematic representation" (Sconce 1995: 393). As Jancovich points out, however, this argument "fails to see that these responses are not the 'effects' of texts but the products of different cultural competence and dispositions" (Jancovich 2002: 311). Jancovich argues that Sconce incorrectly claims that paracinema challenges "bourgeois" taste or "legitimate" film culture. Drawing on the work of Bourdieu, which Sconce also employs, Jancovich points out that paracinematic reading strategies privilege form over content, which Bourdieu had shown to be a "bourgeois" approach to art and which is a result of social inequality (2002: 311). Thus, this viewing community has much more in common with existing academic practice than it would like to admit, even if it does challenge some of its prevailing aesthetic tendencies. Ultimately, Jancovich argues, both "legitimate" film culture and paracinematic viewers privilege formal readings of film in order to place themselves in a superior position to "average" or "mainstream" segments of film viewers. He continues:

> far from serving as a reminder that "taste … is a social construct with profoundly political implications", paracinema is at least as concerned to assert its superiority over those whom it conceives of as the degraded victims of mainstream commercial culture as it is concerned to provide a challenge to the academy and the art cinema. (Jancovich 2002: 312)

This criticism is valid, though we should also be careful not to completely flatten out the differences between various segments of "educated" approaches to film art. While there may be similarities between these viewing "communities" – similarities that Sconce does not entirely overlook – their varying tastes and arguments also need to be acknowledged.

The point that Jancovich makes about paracinema communities being keen to assert their superiority over "mainstream" viewers should remind us of the earlier point made about how such viewers may on the one hand be engaged in "cultural leveling," but on the other hand produce exclusions. Matt Hills has looked at how some films and film communities beyond the mainstream can also be "othered" by paracinema *and* more "legitimate"

forms of film culture. Focusing primarily on the *Friday the 13th* franchise, Hills claims that a number of slasher films have "marked one limit to trash's classificatory elasticity" (Hills 2007: 219). He draws attention to the fact that not *all* neglected "cultural detritus" is accorded the status of trashy art within paracinematic canons. Some films, including a number of slasher films, are not only regarded as worthless within more traditional forms of legitimate film cultures, but also are maligned within a number of the paracinematic publications that Sconce focuses on. They are not, though, generally representative of the "mainstream" and, adds Hills, actually have their own "cult" followings on the fringes of film culture. This demonstrates that a number of separate film viewing communities compete in different ways to vouch for the cultural value of particular films. As a majority of slasher films have been neglected not only by established film communities, Hills terms them "para-paracinema":

> As para-paracinema – simultaneously other to trash and legitimate film cultures – it indicates that [sic] ways in which paracinematic and legitimate film reading protocols can become tactically aligned through a shared revulsion for the untutored, the artless, and the commercial turned cultish. (Hills 2007: 232)

The points made by Jancovich and Hills highlight how there are a greater number of competing communities battling over the status of different groups of films than Sconce originally acknowledged. Because of the ways in which individuals differ in their tastes from other individuals, we should also be cognizant of the ways in which viewers may not always imaginatively identify with the same film viewing community at all times. To cite a hypothetical example: a person could identify and "belong" to a paracinema community when participating in an online forum, but may differ from many of the other members in her or his keen interest in political documentaries, around which he or she has formed a separate community. It is also the case that different communities themselves may forge allegiances over issues of taste on some issues and diverge greatly over others. To add to the complexity of these cultural dynamics, such alignments and divergences are not static: they are forever shifting in relation to the different socio-historical contexts in which they exist.

Conclusion

In 1995, when "Trashing the Academy" was first published, Sconce wrote how the phenomenon of paracinema was making inroads into elite culture itself, including academic film studies. Since then, academic attention to "trash" has increased as a new generation of scholars with interests in exploitation-related cinema have undertaken scholarly research. Not only have PhDs and academic publications related to such topics increased, but there has been a growth of conferences and courses within this subject area. Sconce also noted how the phenomenon was infiltrating mainstream culture, pointing out the television program *Mystery Science Theater 3000* and the film *Ed Wood* as examples. This process has also increased, as evidenced by Tarantino's continual urge to make bigger-budgeted "exploitation" pictures and the increasing accessibility of once difficult-to-find "trash" items (the latter process no doubt having reached new levels due to the growth of the internet). This process, which Hawkins terms "mainstreaming trash aesthetics" (2000: 205), demonstrates how the status of cultural objects can shift over time and across space: yesterday's "trash" can transform into tomorrow's "treasure" (to borrow terminology from Egan 2007), as evidenced by the previously "low" cultural artifact *Godzilla* being released at cinemas (and then DVD) by the British Film Institute in 2005, as it was now valued for its cultural significance. Of course, not all trash has been recuperated and there will always be films that slip through the net of cultural revaluation. Potentially, however, any film is capable of being rescued from the cultural garbage heap and transformed into a valued artifact.

The excavation of previous attitudes predating paracinematic approaches to film has been occurring alongside the academic revaluation of trash. Sconce,

in his original article, noted a few predecessors to the phenomenon he was exploring: these included the surrealists, who attempted to buck the trend of bourgeois thinking by celebrating marginalized populist works, such as Loius Feuillade's serials and Max Sennett comedies. Joan Hawkins (2000: 18–20) has discussed "Macmahonism" as another crucial predecessor in this regard: named after the Cinema Macmahon in Paris, it refers to a number of French critics who lauded popular American cinema over more established "highbrow" fare and thus controversially challenged "legitimate" taste. Greg Taylor, in his book *Artists in the Audience* (1999), has identified "cult" and "camp" approaches to film art in the work of critics Manny Farber and Parker Tyler, and which fed into the work of Andrew Sarris as well as selected elements of the American Underground community (see Chapter 4 for more on Macmahonism and these critics). Despite their differences, what these critics shared was a celebration of "junk," which allowed them to display their own unique position through creatively transforming derided art works (Taylor 1999: 1–8). Sconce himself has more recently identified further paracinematic precedents in the work of Pauline Kael, whose 1969 article "Trash, Art and the Movies" extolled the AIP exploitation picture *Wild in the Streets* as a much more relevant film than the critically lauded *2001: A Space Odyssey*.

It is clear, then, that "camp" and "paracinematic" sensibilities have permeated the academy and the broader cultural fabric. This has marked important shifts in the legitimacy of what can be studied and how it should be studied. It should nevertheless be pointed out that a broadly ironic form of film appreciation is only one way of approaching neglected, derided works and should not lead us into thinking that we cannot evaluate such films from different perspectives (such as analyzing them as serious, aesthetic productions).

Notes

1. The ambiguities, anxieties and sentiments surrounding Hollywood's child cult are celebrated in Austrian artist Martin Arnold's *Alone. Life Wastes Andy Hardy* (1998), a short film of footage featuring child actors Rooney and Garland (in one of their many Andy Hardy pictures) that is alternately sped up or slowed down to highlight supposed innuendo in the relationships between the child actors and their adult counterparts.

2. We should note that there is a different way of describing paracinema which in fact precedes the use of the term by Sconce, but which has not gained such widespread currency. This refers to forms of experimental cinema that were attempting to expand cinema beyond its more common understandings, through – for example – creating works without film cameras, and which overlaps with other conceptual art practices emerging in the 1960s.

3. More recently, a small-circulation magazine entitled *Paracinema* – which focuses on "B-movies, cult classics, indie, horror, science-fiction, exploitation, underground and Asian films from past and present" – began publication in 2007. See www.paracinema.net for more information.

9

Transgression and Freakery

The apparent desire of cultists to experience something "different" can lead to strange forms of appreciation, as we have seen in the previous chapters. This chapter addresses how cult cinema's modes of reception are informed by debates around how they break boundaries of morality and challenge prohibitions in culture, how they dispute commonsense conceptions of what is normal and acceptable, and how in doing so they confront taboos. Among the most often mentioned instruments through which cult cinema is said to do this are "transgression" and "freakery."

Before we start, it is necessary to specify how perceptions and experiences of transgression and freakery lie at the heart of a particular range of cult receptions, namely *affective receptions*. As we have noted in previous chapters, aspects of perception such as curiosity, camp, and irony are of significance in sketching the cultist's interest. So are intense aspects of attachment such as fandom and idolatry. Those tools remain of high significance in how transgression and freakery are approached. Next to that, however, affective appreciation is a specifically crucial element in the perception and experience of transgression and freakery. In particular, cult cinema receptions negotiate *negative* forms of affect such as disgust, revulsion, and aversion. We noted in the previous chapter how Joan Hawkins' (2000) extension of Jeffrey Sconce's discussion of paracinema brought into focus the importance of *affect*, the impact of films upon viewers in a physical and emotional sense. She observed how affect played a role of importance in the cult reputation of films that traversed the distinction between high- and low-brow. The examples Hawkins gives are the silent

documentary on autopsies, *The Act of Seeing with One's Own Eyes*, and *The War Game*, a realistic imagination of the effects of a nuclear attack on the English population. Hawkins points out how the reception of these films was peppered with phrases such as "terrifying," "sickening," "destruction," "appalling," "haunting purity and truth," and she argues that rather than denunciations these terms actually were expressions of appreciation – appreciation for how, viewers claim, these films confront a sort of deep anxiety (2000: 15). As Mathijs and Mendik (2008b: 10) remark, such fascinations and framings also underlie the cult reputations for films dealing with traumas that defeat representation, such as the holocaust.

Why would anyone emotionally like films about autopsies, nuclear war, or the holocaust? It could be out of a sincere sense of rebellion against what is perceived as a suffocating pressure from dominant morality. It could be out of a performative desire to provoke reaction. It could also be out of an attitude that attempts to challenge intellectualizations of film viewing – and cultural appreciation in general. It could also be out of empathy and alignment with the margins of society. Kinkade and Katovich (1992) argue that one of the key components of cult viewing's oppositional attitude is its empathy with the "little people," with which not only is meant those in disadvantaged socio-economic and cultural positions, but also literally little people (the non-normative physical body) and, by extension, every example of the anomaly, the persecuted, the outcast, and the victim. In Chapter 1 we have used the term "affective communities" to describe the ways in which a

Cult Cinema: An Introduction. Ernest Mathijs and Jamie Sexton.
© 2011 Ernest Mathijs and Jamie Sexton. Published 2011 by Blackwell Publishing Ltd.

sensibility like this finds a grounding with a group of viewers and how it is part of a collective experience in which "the other" is always part of the consideration. The processes through which this occurs are the focus of our attention in this chapter.

Essentially, if we want to understand how the cult receptions of films that repulse or disgust viewers become tools for forging a feeling of community, we have to understand how these challenges to morality or confrontations of taboos work, how they reach viewers, and how these viewers articulate their fascination.

Taboo

A taboo is a cultural prohibition, an act seen as morally wrong. Central to understandings of taboo is the concept of "impurity" as an opposition to the normative "purity." Traffic *between* instances of purity and impurity challenges cultural systems and practices, thus leading to taboos. In the context of studies of cult reception, the concept of taboo has led scholars and critics to explore anthropological ideas to assess how cultism and (im)purity are linked to each other. Three of the main sources of inspiration in that respect have been Mary Douglas, Julia Kristeva, and Mikhail Bakhtin, all of whom have considered the body the central site for discussions of morality and taboo.

The work of Douglas and Kristeva concentrates mostly on how bodies perform a structural role in presenting or preserving a cultural order that is fixed into stable normality. As a result of this concern, they see taboos as a reflection on the contamination of perceptions of purity by impure mechanisms. Incest, for instance, is a form of violation of the established normality of intercourse and sexual contact between bodies. As a consequence the focus of what a taboo is moves away from the ways in which a taboo protects normality towards the forms of traffic and communication through which purity – and normality – are assaulted. In *Purity and Danger*, Douglas (1966) points out that the traffic between the inside and outside of the body correlates strongly with what cultures see as taboos. A crucial element here is that of any substance that allows for the crossing of borders between the inside and outside of the body. Mostly such materials are fluid, moist. If we look at the kind of fluids that traverse the

borders between the inside and the outside of the body, they are all, to some extent, subject to taboos. Some, such as tears and sweat are easily accommodated – though not in every situation. Others, such as spit, blood, pus, urine, semen, menstruation, lactation, or feces are much more severely sanctioned and regulated. In sum, the regulation of the transfer of bodily fluids forms the cornerstone of how groups of people perceive themselves, and how they act as a culture.

Kristeva (1974, 1982) applies the concepts of taboo and impurity to semiotics, especially those of texts of horror, which she sees as teeming with instances of impurity she calls *abjection*. Abjection, literally "the state of being cast off" is a concept that denotes the threatening "unsaid" by virtue of which meaning can be delineated. Abjection is where cultural meaning collapses. It is that which must be expelled for normal meaning to exist. Abjection is also what language fails to describe – hence the frequent usage of "yuk," "ouch," and similar terms to indicate moments of abjection. In terms of the law, the abject is that which fails to respect rules and against which the law gains meaning. In terms of identity, abjection is that which is not "I" and which threatens identity, often because it involves a fluid breaking through the skin, or because it involves bodies with missing parts. Traversing the border between the tightly regulated outside of the body and its messy and often uncharted inside (uncharted in semiotic terms) is often regarded as traumatic. Images such as blood, vomit, urine, and feces, and "monstrous" creatures with disintegrated bodies are abject in the sense that they do not respect borders: the aforementioned fluids continually spill out of bodies, thus passing from the "I" to the "not I"; the monster often signifies a collapse of boundaries, such as mutated bodies or bodies that are neither dead nor alive.

Like Kristeva's, the work of Mikhail Bakhtin (1965) approaches the concept of taboo through a discussion of the origins of language, meaning, and semiotics. But Bakhtin uses a different angle, that of the "carnivalesque." The term derives from the word "carnival," a seasonally recurring festive event that marks the overturning of the routines and regulations of daily, normal life. For Bakhtin, the carnivalesque is a unique instance in the social processes of meaning-making in which taboos are lifted and people are allowed to engage in what is otherwise culturally prohibited. During the carnival, amorality and immorality are condoned, and impurity and abjection are encouraged. Bakhtin argued that in the Middle Ages the carnival acted as a suspension of established order. While only temporary, it was a means by which to transgress the norms and regulations of official society, and hence an attempt to unhinge its rigid hierarchies (which kept the lower classes "in their place"). During the carnival, official icons, figures and rituals were mocked and ridiculed and an alternative, inverted society was acted out. The carnival, argued Bakhtin, was an expression of a worldview: a refusal to accept the certainties, and the seriousness, stipulated by the dominant order. The "grotesque" played a central part in the transgressions of the carnival: the flesh and the body – including those aspects often hidden by decorum – were celebrated. Objects of fear, meanwhile, underwent excessive distortion so that their power could be dealt with on a tangible level. Laughter, orgiastic pleasure, and grotesquery (especially grotesque bodies), which were both inimical to official culture, were celebrated as subversive acts, and the dominant order was rendered relative through its inversion. Umberto Eco (1984) qualifies the Bakhtinian take on subversion by adding that the carnival carries within itself the revenge of the established order, which governs the extent of the subversion in terms of time and the kind of rules that can be subverted. Still, the carnival may have been temporary, but it offered a glimpse of an alternative society and thus demonstrated that the current order was not eternal.

From Taboo to Cult?

There have been numerous attempts to link the cult appeal of films to theories of taboo. Robin Wood (1979) relied on ideas of Wilhelm Reich and on Marxist cultural materialism to draw up a categorization of horror films that represented monstrosity as either liberal or reactionary. Barbara Creed (1987, 1993) developed her ideas on the feminine as monstrous through the work of Douglas and Kristeva. Ideas of Bakhtin have inspired analyses of John Waters and Lloyd Kaufman's Troma films (Mendik and Schneider 2002). A lot of scholars and critics of cult

cinema are eager to point to abounding fluids and deviant bodies in order to suggest a film as a cult film: the disintegrated bodies in *Freaks*, *The Texas Chainsaw Massacre*, or *Cannibal Holocaust* (Brottman 1997), the bodily fluids abounding in porn chic films such as *Behind the Green Door* (Peary 1989), the liquid mirror (and fluid reality) in *Donnie Darko* (King 2007), the shower and blood in *Daughters of Darkness* (Mathijs 2004), or numerous scenes in the *Emmanuelle* franchise (Mendik 2004 singles out the scene in the squash court). *Showgirls* seems to have every scene constructed around the exchange of fluids by hyperbolically deviant bodies, the most infamous of which are perhaps the pool orgasm scene and the pole licking scene (Hunter 2000; Lippitt *et al.* 2003).

But where are the boundaries of such strategies of interpretation? The arguments of Douglas, Kristeva, and Bakhtin are extremely universalist. They are constructed in a manner that applies to all cultures, all actions, all meaning, to every cultural product and, by extension, every film. For one, they can function as barometers of degrees of cultism. They illustrate the cult appeal of a variety of films because they give reasons for *how*, among other explanations, some films are seen as bad, oppositional, or countercultural because of the ways they depict or confront taboos. Moreover, they offer cultists the opportunity to reinforce their cultism, as it were, by offering it a philosophical rationale and grounding in cultural history it might otherwise not achieve, simply through association with theories of taboo and deviance in culture.

Besides the positive role conceptualizations of taboo play in offering theoretical grounding for the study of cult films, the problem is that their universalism invites scholars to ignore the context-specific components of production and (especially) affectively experiencing certain films as "different" because they confront taboos and challenge morality and normalcy. Establishing direct links between conceptualizations and a film's properties also carries the danger of overlooking that producers and audiences are actively and self-consciously aware of the implications of instances of impurity, abjection, or the grotesque in films. Consider the act of licking, which we referred to earlier. It could easily be argued that such exchanges of body fluids triggers cultism – makes a film cult and allows audiences to use its shock value as a tool in seeing it as cult. During

Figure 9.1   The exchange of bodily fluids: licking in *Emmanuelle*, *The Brood*, and *Showgirls*.

her journey towards ultimate sex in the first *Emmanuelle* film, Emmanuelle (Sylvia Kristel) is instructed to lick the face of a sweaty martial arts fighter; in *The Brood*, Nola (Samantha Eggar) really shocks Frank (Art Hindle) by licking her bloodied fetus; and in *Showgirls*, stripdancer Nomi (Elizabeth Berkley) answers the provocation of Cristal (Gina Gershon), who licks her boyfriend's cheek suggestively, by licking the poledancing pole, up and down (Figure 9.1).

Douglas argues that strict governance over such behavior marks the enculturation of communities; using the act of licking is a provocation of this governance. Is viewers' obsession with them, then, one more sign of their refusal to act as a validation of such enculturation? Perhaps it is. But in order for this to be the case *equally*, the production and reception contexts of all three films would have to be identical. And they are not: *Emmanuelle* belongs to a different framework of presentation and reception than *The Brood*, and *Showgirls* is dissimilar from both, and each film addresses its context in its own way. For instance, the three films were made in contexts that had widely varying views on the representations of sexuality on-screen (encapsulated in tags such as "porn chic," "body horror," and "camp"), and they operated within production cultures that used hyperbole in distinctive ways. As a consequence, their grossness is of a different order and their receptions are marked by qualities that identify them as cults *in separation*.

In sum, in addition to turning towards universalist conceptualizations of taboo, research into film cults needs to give attention to context-specific ways in which films offer ways, formally and self-consciously, to make impurity, abjection, and the carnivalesque and grotesque detectible rather than just deducible. Scholars of cult cinema have made several attempts to theorize such ways, and it is to these we now turn.

Transgression

The most notable context-specific notion that informs the study of cult cinema's appetite for taboo, abjection, grotesquerie, and impurity is that of "transgression." Commonly understood, transgression is any act that violates law or morality; more broadly, it refers to the act of passing beyond any imposed limits.

Barry Keith Grant (1991) has argued that transgression plays a central role in the construction of cult films. He states that transgression can take place on the level of *content*, in terms of *attitude*, and in a *stylistic* sense. In relation to content, transgression occurs through the representation of acts or objects that may be considered threatening to social norms, or may be deemed obscene. Grant cites *Freaks* as an example of representational content that is transgressive. Grant also notes that the attitude of the filmmaker(s) may also be transgressive in that they may deliberately attempt to outrage. Such is the case with John Waters, whose early films such as *Pink Flamingos* often involved direct challenges to good taste. Thirdly, transgressive form involves stylistic excess, which can be understood as either competent excess (the use of kinetic pyro-technics in the *Mad Max* movies) or incompetence (the ineptitude of *Plan 9 from Outer Space*). In his analysis of transgression, Grant also addresses the issue of reception, in particular when he argues that recep-tion attitudes can undo some of the transgressive elements of a film. As such, the specific receptions of cult films can be equally subversive (in their flirting with taboo) and recuperative. For Grant they are actually more likely to be recuperative than subversive or taboo-challenging.

While Grant contends films such as *Night of the Living Dead* or *The Rocky Horror Picture Show* are ostensibly transgressive on a number of levels, they ultimately "reclaim that which they seem to violate" so that the cult viewer "ultimately gains the double satisfaction of both rejecting dominant cultural values and remaining safely inscribed within them" (Grant 1991: 124). In most cases, Grant sees little opportunity for transgression to touch audiences. Consider the 1979 Toronto Film Festival, which contained a ret-rospective of the films of George Romero. Before the screening of *Night of the Living Dead*, critic Robin Wood wanted to discuss with Romero how the film was ideologically subversive: "the audience, however, was impatient with such talk, became rude, and shouted for him to leave the stage so they could enjoy the movie" (Grant 1991: 128). Grant suggests that this means that the film's transgression, which Wood further analyzed in his article "An introduction to the American horror film" (1979), is recuperated by an audience attitude that refutes it in favor of "a good time." He writes: "the fact that the film can be read as a biting critique of the American middle class accounts for little of its cult appeal, although for those who can perceive it, this theme lends a degree of respectability to ... a real horrorshow" (Grant 1991: 128). We would argue that the audience's reaction does not preclude their perception of *Night of the Living Dead*'s transgression. In fact, their boisterous behavior, which for Grant is a sign of their desire "to see the good parts," could well be a sign of its affective impact with audiences, which may well harbor sentiments

that would include regarding the film as a biting critique – perhaps even triggered by the initial "ouch!" and "ew!" Grant presupposes audiences jump immediately to a level of interpretive sophis-tication without passing through an affective mo-ment. We would like to suggest such an affective moment is essential as a reaction to representations of transgression that then enable interpretations and analysis of exactly which taboos are challenged and how this makes a film (like *Night of the Living Dead*) a critique of morality.

Another complication to the audience reception of transgression is the fact it can be performed, faked. The way in which the fandom for *The Rocky Horror Picture Show* developed into a ritualized audience response with predetermined costumes and repetition of char-acter lines is, for Grant, a sign of how any transgression the film might have carried over onto viewers was now undone: "The performative nature of this audience response was scripted, predetermined; it discouraged spontaneous improvisation by newcomers and sug-gested that this community of readers was in its own way as conformist and repressive as the middle class satirized on the screen" (2000: 21). This argument is rather sweeping. Other accounts of the receptions of both films offer counter examples that suggest that the "truly trangressive experience" (as Grant calls it) *can* be achieved even when receptions are steeped in recu-peration as long as affective audience activities are not overlooked (see several of the essays in Weinstock 2008). Nevertheless, the observation on the perfor-mative nature of perceptions of transgression is valid and insightful.

J.P. Telotte (1991a) also claims transgression is a key element of cult movies, and he too relates the concept to both a film's textual properties and its reception (unlike Grant he sees it as an element of both in *equal* measure). Telotte asserts that the trans-gression of reason – the love for unreason – is a central trope running through cult cinema, most evident in the relationship between the film and its fans: "What the film cultist embraces is a form that, in its very difference, transgresses, violates our sense of the rea-sonable. It crosses boundaries of time, custom, form and – many might add – good taste" (1991a: 6). Like Grant, Telotte points to the fact that "the act of transgression may be little more than a gesture; it might only signal a kind of cook's tour of various formal and cultural borders that, in the end, simply returns us . . . to a world of reason where we can relish the feeling of transgression" (1991a: 6). Telotte describes here a kind of transgressive tourism, in that we vicariously delve into forbidden and dangerous territory only to return to a world of reason. Midnight movie screenings are the most obvious examples of outré viewing experiences that are positioned as transgressive because they cross the boundaries of time and custom, but at the same time are comforting for those who attend them precisely to enjoy the aura of difference. This double process could be related to Georges Bataille's writings, a theorist who is brought up frequently in discussions of cult cinema (Botting and Wilson 1997). Bataille argued that death was the ultimate limit, an existential full stop, and that our transgressive yearnings are self-destructive because they ultimately lead to death. Because of human capacity for self-destruction, societies restrain this damaging potential through the imposition of taboos. Thus, "transgressive" films are a means whereby we can act out urges in ways that do not endanger ourselves. Yet, even when taboos are channeled via film representation, the results can still cause social outrage.

In sum, cult films offer ways to enjoy transgression safely and can challenge conceptions of normalcy. We need to accept, though, that audience experiences can contain performative and ritualized *as well as* affective reactions to moments of abjection, impurity and grotesquerie that appear to challenge taboos and confront morality. Often cult fans believe this is one and the same thing *and* they act as if they believe it.

Freakery

The complexity of studying how cult films break or challenge taboos by pinpointing the process of transgression is further complicated by the notion of "freakery." While very similar to transgression, freakery is even more dependent on context-specific reception conditions, in particular because of its singular focus on deviant human bodies as sites of transgression. Human bodies provide a ready point of reference for audiences. Therefore, the high visibility

of freakery has attracted lots of analogies between freaks-on-screen and freaks-in-the-audience.

One of the earliest attempts to conceptualize the notion of freakery comes from Leslie Fiedler (1978). In his analysis, Fiedler goes further than the dictionary definition of "the freak" (as a fellow human whose physically anomalous features are stressed through exhibition) by asserting that freaks help establish the normality of those who witness the spectacle. He thus pushes the notion of freakery into one of perception. Similarly, Robert Bogdan (1988: 10) sees a freak as "a way of thinking, of presenting, a set of practices, an institution – not a characteristic of an individual." According to Rosemarie Garland Thomson (1996: xviii), "the freak is a historical figure ritually fabricated from the raw material of bodily variations and *appropriated in the service of shifting social ideologies*" (our emphasis). She adds: "the freak of nature [is] a freak of culture" (1996: xviii).

To the elements of perception and reception needs to be added that of performance. Fiedler (1996: xiv) refers to the success of *Freaks* by suggesting it found its audience among the "drug-obsessed generation of the sixties, young men and women who though physiologically 'normal,' liked to refer to themselves as 'freaks'." The suggestion here is that these audiences perform freakery – for Fiedler they are not really freaks but they like to be regarded as such because of their perception that their position at the margins of normalcy is akin to that of the disabled person. With that self-perception also comes an attention for ways in which freakery is culturally positioned, in particular for the abject, the grotesque, and the impure. For Fiedler it would be no coincidence that the attention for his work coincided with the cult appeal of films such as *Freaks*, *Eraserhead*, *The Elephant Man*, *Alien*, or *The Brood*, films to which he alludes. The element of performance of freakery is not uniquely one of reception and perception. As Carrie Sandahl and Philip Auslander (Sandahl and Auslander, 2005: 1–12) argue, it also concerns the presentation and, with it, the self-reflexivity of the performance in the text. Unlike "normative" acting, they state, the performance of disability can never fully move into a neutral mode in which the actor and character fall together. A final aspect of the performance aspect of the reception of freakery lies in how it allows audiences to take up positions of distinction and superiority. David Church (2011: 3) sees it as follows:

> freakery is premised upon unequal viewing and social relations. A nondisabled audience retains the power to subject the non-normative body (traditionally, that of a person with disabilities) to the ableist gaze as entertaining spectacle, enjoying a mixture of shock, horror, wonder, and pity.

In making this claim, Church follows a trajectory of reason not unlike that of Grant with regard to transgression: freakery confirms the position of superiority of the audience over the forms of instances of impurity, abjection, or grotesquerie in the film they are watching and in that process the potentially subversive aspects of those instances are neutralized, even recuperated into a system of normalcy. As we have seen with regard to transgression, this potential for recuperation, or even indeed its occurrence, does not preclude other non-recuperative modes of appreciation – for instance, by disabled audiences or advocates (such as disabled performance artist Mat Fraser, who has drawn on traditions of freakery as empowering and positive), whom Church here discounts as potential audiences.

Most studies regarding freakery refer extensively to *Freaks*, undoubtedly the best-known cult film that addresses the notion – and an inevitable example in any cursory overview of cult cinema. Originally released conventionally, it outraged people at the time and distributor Metro-Goldwyn-Mayer quickly withdrew it from circulation. It was censored in several countries. It was revived, however, on the exploitation circuit after being picked up by Dwain Esper. While it received a mixed reception, it was lauded by intellectuals in France and played in art house theaters, which led to it being resurrected internationally. It played the Venice Film Festival in 1962 and proved popular on the art house circuit during that decade (Hawkins 2000: 141–148). By 1970 it appeared on the midnight movie circuit. The film has since attained the status of a cult classic and continues to be viewed by new audiences. Much of the scholarly debate surrounding *Freaks* concerns the various strategies the film is said to employ to simultaneously present the freaks (such as the Hilton Twins, Johnny Eck, Prince Radian) as abnormal, to normalize them to the extent that the narrative can set them up as "good," and to re-ostracize them in scenes

such as the widely quoted Wedding Banquet. The latter scene is also at the center of studies of the film's reception (most of which are anecdotal and impressionistic), allowing as it does for analogies between the actors' performance of the chant "one of us" as a mantra ("gabba gabba gooble gobble"), and the audience's self-reflexive perception of this mantra as reflecting their own position as unorthodox film viewers (Hawkins 1996, 2000; Brottman 1997; Larsen and Haller 2002).

Besides *Freaks*, there have been numerous films whose receptions are explained as cult through their solicitation of freakery – both in their presentations of deviant human bodies as signs of how they challenge taboos, and in their receptions by audiences seeing themselves as outsiders to normalized viewing routines. *Häxan*, for instance, uses representations of old, weathered, disheveled bodies of women accused of witchcraft in opposition to those of corpulent monks who interrogate them to press a point about the ruthlessness of the inquisition. When such markers are acknowledged by audiences looking exactly for non-normativities (as many viewers of a William Burroughs narrated version of *Häxan* did when the film was re-released in the late 1960s), conflations between the film's argument and its function as a piece of exploitation create an ambivalence upon which a cult reputation can be hinged. *El Topo* is known for providing viewers with the widest and most eclectic samples of freakery. It combines disintegrating bodies (the first ten minutes of the film show an entire village littered with slaughtered people and animals) with disabilities, malnourishment, and non-normative representations of age such as nude pre-puberty children, and naked seniors. In a sense, *El Topo* explodes the concept of "freakery." Yet, as Church (2011: 15) observes, this does not necessarily have positive consequences for representations of disability:

> the freakish body remains read by cultists as a deviant and "transgressive" marker of otherness through which they can assert their oppositional aesthetic in a bid for subcultural cachet. . . . Following the binary logic of cult subcultures, actual social change that could gradually remove essentialist stigmas from the visually "abnormal" body would also remove the taboo and supposedly oppositional connotations of those bodies. Consequently, there would be little incentive for cultists to actively champion political change for people with disabilities without imperiling a major source of subcultural distinction.

One only needs to look at the long line of films with cult receptions that feature short-statured people whose easy association with exploitation and "little people," to use Kinkade and Katovich's (1992) term again, to find evidence of this sensationalism. *Freaks* and *The Wizard of Oz* have been followed by dozens of others: *Forbidden Zone*, *This Is Spinal Tap*, *The Rocky Horror Picture Show*, *Suspiria*, *The Brood*, *Wild at Heart*, *The Lord of the Rings*, and so on. A lot of films with cult receptions offer framing devices to display these representations. It is part of their ambivalent attitude towards the subject matter: part apologetic, part exploitation. Among the most popular such devices are circus and sideshow environments, ornamental or extravagant settings (a boarding school in *Suspiria*, a rock music stage in *Spinal Tap*, a clinic in *The Brood*). One of the framing devices of *Freaks*, the circus, not only corrals the subject matter, it also carnivalizes it, encouraging audiences to abandon the constraints of realism for their freewheeling and far-fetching interpretations because they would have no repercussions in reality – after all, it is a circus world (for an argument along these lines, see Brottman 1997: 15–48). Church adds, however, that when the cult receptions of these films address the fluidity of the very concept of "freakery," as a constantly shifting concept in itself,

> a small opening for (sub)culturally rethinking freakery in cult cinema can develop [whereby] the "freakish" body would still remain exhibited as spectacle [but] its unruly and excessive qualities would point toward the openness and indeterminacy of all bodies, remaining capable of violating the established boundaries of "good taste." (2011: 15)

The careers of filmmakers such as John Waters (*Pink Flamingos*), David Cronenberg (*Shivers*), Lucio Fulci (*The Beyond*), David Lynch (*Eraserhead*), Peter Jackson (*Bad Taste*) or Paul Verhoeven (*Robocop*) are littered with receptions that place their films as challenges to the idea that a human body can only be of a narrow range of normalcy. A film such as *Splice* charts the mutations through which bodies can go in presenting itself as a discussion on "transmutation," and triggering a reception that circles around what a human body is in the first place. As Church (2005) points out in another essay, films such as *Even Dwarfs Started Small* (or *Of Freaks and Men*, or *In Bruges*) have experienced

receptions that concentrate on how they manage to overcome the inclination to show disabled people only as "innocent victims"; they equally portray them as ill-tempered, arrogant, drunk, or in other situations still considered a little inappropriate but close to normative behavior. Iain Smith (2010a) has observed a similar development in the cult reception of the films of Philippine dwarf actor Weng Weng, known for his remakes of Bond materials (*For Y'ur Height Only*). In the case of Weng Weng, elements of "freakery" conflate with other modes such as the orientalist reception of the ethnic other (see Chapter 11) and the irony of camp. In such situations, the performance of freakery becomes a precarious exercise by audiences keen to destabilize processes of film perception.

There are two important complications for freakery. The first concerns gender, the second race. We will address gender separately, in our next chapter. Let us briefly expand on race here. The racialized body as a type of disability (or, occasionally, super-ability) and the complication of color-coding we find in the Tarzan and Kong films (see Peary 1981; Erb 1998) run through cult cinema as a constant thread but it is in the late 1960s that the portrayal of race becomes a real point of contention in cult cinema receptions. In *Night of the Living Dead*, the African-American protagonist overcomes extreme adversity, but in the final few minutes of the film he is killed by a posse of white cops and vigilantes who spot him, shoot him, and remark "here's another one." The abruptness of this ending, and the style in which it is shot (which invites comparisons with television footage of America's race riots of the 1960s) has caused critics like Robin Wood (1979) to see *Night of the Living Dead* as subversive and transgressive. As the aforementioned reaction of Grant (1991) testifies, not everyone agrees. Another example is the *Emmanuelle* franchise. As Xavier Mendik (2004) has observed, the *Black Emanuelle* series are a poignant counterpoint to the official franchise in that it exposes the underlying assumptions of racism and exoticism of the latter – which already held up a mirror of hypocrisy to audiences' taste for exotic sexuality. In each of these cases, a dark skin color is a signifier of a form of freakery.

In a few instances, this non-normativity has been appropriated, and turned into a performative quality, used by film and audiences alike to indicate awareness of the color coding. That is most notably the case with blaxploitation films (also see Chapter 13). The main articulation of this performative affirmation is the sexually assertive protagonist – a self-assured African-American urbanite whose knack for flair and style helps him/her achieve narrative goals. In many ways, the body in blaxploitation cinema is still non-normative, but in its hyperbolic combination of sexuality, athletic prowess (less so in chases or fights than in swanky posturing), fashion-consciousness (flouting moderation in favor of excess, particularly through exaggerated "Afro" hairstyles), and urban street-smartness (bringing class-awareness into the equation), it helps viewers position themselves in opposition to the kinds of antagonism usually associated with non-normativity. Instead of having to undergo purely affective reactions of disgust, upset, or outrage, blaxploitation's self-aware performativity allows viewers to actively perform those reactions. Examples of films following this mode are *Coffy*, *Foxy Brown*, and *Welcome Home Brother Charles*. Without doubt the most celebrated cult icon of this appropriation is Pam Grier. Her performance in *Black Mama White Mama*, from the disreputable subgenre of the women-in-prison films, pits her against the model of white female normativity (the blonde, big busted, white girl), a battle she wins through collaboration (Sims 2006; Dunn 2008; Walker, Rausch, and Watson 2009). In the late 1990s, a wave of homage to blaxploitation received cult receptions, most notably Quentin Tarantino's celebration of Grier in *Jackie Brown*, which pitches her as the ideal woman: independent, able, confident.

A final element worth mentioning in relation to "freakery" is the hyperbolic and oversized body of attractions – the super-able body that is too athletic, too muscular, too sexualized. Such bodies are often portrayed in contrast with the diminished capabilities of disabled and non-normative bodies, yet it is equally non-normative. In *Freaks*, the strongman Hercules is easily accepted as "evil" because of his excessive strength, and his sexist ideas. Angela Ndalianis (1994, 1995) has noted the cult fascination with the oversized shape of muscular bodies in superheroes cinema. In his study of the cult fascination for bodybuilding Adam Locks (2010) has observed how the reception of the "ripped" body consists not only of the "shock" of the grotesque deviation from the normative body, but also

the "pity" for the body-builders' body as a site of willful and wasteful destruction. Other, similar concerns can be found in the receptions of 1980s' action cinema (*Conan the Barbarian* and *Rambo*, for instance), in the bodily transmutations of performance artists such as Genesis P. Orridge, Orlan, Joseph Beuys Hermann Nitsch, or Jim Rose's Circus Sideshow (Kultermann 1970; Auslander 1997), or in pornography. The athletic porn performer is a sort of freak because of the "feats" they can perform. Here too oversized breasts or sexual organs are seen as a form of disability (see the receptions of the careers of Ron Jeremy, Chesty Morgan, Lolo Ferrari, or Mistress Rhiannon).

In sum, freakery is unorthodoxy made flesh. It is a tool that refers to the deviant body as one that is impure, abject, and grotesque. As a tool, it is used by groups in society that try to establish and defend normalcy, as well as by those that try and challenge it. The latter, among which we count cult audiences, use freakery in two ways: through association with the freak (encapsulated in the term "one of us"), and through affiliation with the potential that freakery brings to upset and challenge taboos. This makes freakery an extremely context-specific notion, which can be of great value in assessing the cult status of films.

Conclusion: Sick Films

In conclusion to this chapter, and to illustrate the ways in which transgression and freakery have operated in context-specific receptions and led to cult reputations, we would like to briefly discuss some kinds of films that owe large parts of their otherwise diverging degrees of cult status to their obsession with transgression and/or freakery. Most of these types of films we will discuss in some form at other points in this book, as belonging to cycles, themes, and/or genres. Here, we bring them together through a discussion of the ways in which they are said to sicken audiences via their confrontations of taboo through moments of abjection, impurity, and grotesquerie. The label of "sick" needs to be understood as containing both positive and negative connotations. For some audiences who identify themselves as cultist a sick film is something negative, while for others a sick film is not only a cult film par excellence but also a sign of admiration. In any case, "sick" is a tag that helps understand the reaction to a cult film. As such, all of these films' reputations as "sick" are identified through reception categories rather than textual classifications and the blurriness of the boundaries between the two is evidence of how they actually resist *any* categorization. Our goal is to demonstrate how these receptions are characterized equally by sincere, affective reactions of disgust and outrage as well as by self-reflexive modes of performative reception in the negotiation of the phenomenal experience of moments of abjection, impurity, and grotesquerie.

According to Church (2009), *Salò, or the 120 Days of Sodom* – based on the work of the Marquis de Sade – is generally considered the sickest film of all time. Its presentations of a wide variety of mutilations and penetrations include acts of rape, sodomy, torture, and eating feces. These acts deliberately challenged audiences and unsurprisingly led to many countries banning the film from public exhibition. *Salò* was the culmination of director Pier Paolo Pasolini's increasingly challenging portraits of human transgression, and can be related to his earlier *Porcile*, which featured human cannibalism and concerned bestiality. Both *Salò* and *Porcile* linked these provocative acts to the theme of fascism and were thus examinations of the limits of human barbarism – forcing viewers to confront the basic cultural question: where does humanity end? According to Church, "*Salò*'s displeasurable affectivity [is negotiated] through classist and masculinist reading strategies, but their performed anxieties reveal the instability of cultural distinctions premised upon displays of (sub)cultural capital" (Church 2009: 1). In other words, the term "sick" refers here to the inability or refusal of audiences to reach conclusions about a film's place in culture. Church's observation about masculinist reading strategies here is telling. It means viewers reject speaking to the misogyny of the film in favor of a relentless and perpetually cyclical debate on its "artistic" or "exploitative" features – as if anything is better than having to admit the film is misogynist. Such a strategy can easily be regarded as a mantra that is part of the insulation of cult receptions. We will return to this point in more detail in our next chapter, when we discuss the rape-revenge film.

Sickness has also played a vital role in the construction, promotion, and reception of John Waters' *Pink Flamingos*, one of the most notorious cult films that proved enormously successful on the midnight movie circuit. Discussing Waters' work in the context of more mainstream attempts to disgust, Mendik and Schneider argue that Waters' early films approach the level of *pure gross-out*:

> It was not merely the vast downward shift in production values, pacing, acting and effects work that distinguished his works from mainstream attempts to offend. Rather, it was the fact that his cross-gendered, orally-obsessed filth fetishists belonged to a wholly distinct order of transgressiveness. (2002a: 205)

Bakhtin's theory of the carnivalesque is used to interpret Waters here. Within the early features of John Waters – *Pink Flamingos*, and his next two films *Female Trouble* and *Desperate Living* – the material body, particularly in forms that are often repressed, are thrust into full visibility and often exaggerated. In fact, Bakhtin's term "grotesque realism" may be a perfect appellation for Waters' early films, particularly *Pink Flamingos*. The film is, because of its low-budget, "underground" look, connotative of realism. Waters said of this: "the very primitive (by which I mean 'bad') camerawork made people think [it] was like a documentary, and that really added to the scary part. I think the graininess and the cheapness of it all really gave it a further edge" (Kermode 1995: 19). At the same time, its characters and antics are larger than life, deliberately excessive. Additionally, the film is a litany of acts calculated to outrage, from the chicken-aided sexual intercourse to the "singing arsehole," from the slave who masturbates and then injects semen into kidnapped females, to Divine eating dog shit. Waters has claimed that his films are not political, but this is not entirely true. They are not overtly political in a didactic manner. But they are still all about challenging "taste," which is a politically charged motivation; as Waters has written, "To me, bad taste is what entertainment is all about" (Waters 2005: 2). The films also challenge peoples' attitudes towards size and gender by parading cross-dressers, transsexuals, and overweight people (Figure 9.2).

Both *Salò* and *Pink Flamingos* (and other films of their directors) are so commanding in their transgression and freakery that they have established their own, unique contexts of reception.[1] This is not always

Figure 9.2 Divine and Edith Massey (as "The Egg Lady") in *Pink Flamingos*: challenging attitudes towards size?

possible. In many cases, films and their receptions have to be negotiated within pressing and well-established frameworks of exhibition and production that force themselves onto any consideration of these films as taboo-breaking, thereby partially disabling the transgression. This is particularly the case with avant-garde and underground cinema, exploitation cinema, and the horror genre, all of which are seen to have it as their duty to transgress, shock, and sicken. For an audience to manage to pull a film out of such a framework is a sign of just how forceful the instance of impurity, abjection, or grotesquerie is, and also how important it is for that audience to achieve this liberation from the pre-established framework – as if the success of the effort liberates them too. Examples include the uneasiness with which a film such as *Flaming Creatures* is included in overviews of avant-garde cinema (see Chapters 3 and

14), the perennially special status of the video nasties (see Chapter 4), and various subdivisions of the horror genre that stubbornly refuse to be recognized as "just another form of horror" – among these, the gore or splatter films of Herschell Gordon-Lewis, such as *Blood Feast* and *2000 Maniacs*, as well as Peter Jackson's early gross-out films, particularly *Bad Taste* and *Braindead* take up a special place (Grant 2000).

Exploitation cycles such as the mondo film have long tried to emulate the cult appeal of the above-mentioned modes of representing bodies in extreme peril. Because of their reliance on artifice, often a result of their limited budgets and talents, they have largely failed to achieve anything close to that authenticity (Goodall 2006). This has not withheld viewers from performing their disgust with these films – as if they were rehearsing it. Probably because of their non-Western origin, Japanese Guinea Pig films, have remained an exception – effectively combining "authenticity" with "exploitation." Jay McRoy (2008: 15–30; McRoy, 2010) points out it has given them a sizeable cult following. Even exploitation films that do not explicate atrocities are frequently keen to reference them; hence the abundance of mondo films employing the terms "holocaust" or "apocalypse" in their titles, soliciting the performance of disgust from viewers.

It appears, then, that for every moment of pure abjection represented on screen there is a context-specific framework that allows not only for viewers to be genuinely disgusted and sickened, but also to perform such reactions – and thereby recuperate into a cultural order whatever challenge was posed.

Note

1. We would like to signal one more important example where we belief any performance or recuperation is extremely difficult and where displeasurable affectivity, to borrow Church's term, remains a core aspect of its cult reception. The film is *Sick: The Life and Death of Bob Flanagan, Supermasochist*. It is a fierce critique of the concept of sickness in the light of medical care, and in its treatment of freakery simultaneously a film that interrogates audiences' eagerness to perform modes of cultist viewing that embrace taboo-challenging instances of abjection, impurity, and grotesquerie. *Sick* shows a performance by terminally ill Bob Flanagan, whose entire life was affected by severe pain (he suffered from cystic fibrosis), that aimed to bring attention to the concept of "pain" – an element of bodily disintegration and of disability that is often overlooked in the world of medicine. In *Sick*, Flanagan ultimately hammers a huge nail through his penis – the ultimate act of de-masculinization (Perlmutter 1999; Sandahl 2000; Reynolds 2007).

10

Gender and Sexuality

Representations of women in cult cinema are complicated through the widespread acceptance in film studies of the notion of the male gaze. Most notably theorized by Laura Mulvey (1975) this concept holds that the female body is constructed for the pleasure of male viewership, as a tool for reproducing a patriarchic system of society. The notion of the male gaze also posits that female viewers will have difficulty finding anything in a film that allows positive, empowering identification, thus implying that a female viewer is powerless in her search for enjoyment – a victim, or someone passively undergoing the film. Next to that, there is also the prevalence of anecdotal evidence from cult reception contexts (such as the inner city fleapit theater, the genre festival and university campus theater) that testifies to boisterous audience activities regarding imagery of women, such as howling, hollering, whistling, or lip smacking, or muffled grunts of encouragements.

While the notion of the male gaze has been heavily criticized, and anecdotal evidence of audience receptions needs to be balanced against activities that are less easily construed as misogynist, there is no doubt that cult cinema has a worrisome reputation when it comes to gender equality. In this chapter, we address various components of this reputation as we sketch the most significant debates regarding gender, sexuality, and cult cinema.

Masculinity, Femininity, and Cult

Let us start with a macroscopic reflection on cult cinema and gender as articulated by Joanne Hollows (2003), who mounted a strong argument for a consideration of cult cinema as a masculine construction. The occasion of her intervention was the first international conference on cult cinema in Nottingham, UK, in 2000, and the publication of an influential study of fan-boy fandom of *Showgirls* (Hunter 2000). The *Showgirls* essay stressed how fan-boy fandom was as much a performative act as an admission of sympathy for the film's politics – with irony, camp, and hyperbole as instruments obfuscating differences between the two attitudes.

For Hollows, scholarly struggles such as those with *Showgirls* are symptomatic of perspectives that present all of cult cinema (including associated terms such as paracinema, trash cinema, or subversive cinema) as oppositional to the mainstream. The language used to draw this distinction, argues Hollows, is reminiscent of the ways in which distinctions are drawn between subcultures and popular culture – or indeed within subcultures, where degrees of authenticity are carved out. Hollows draws on research of subcultures by Sarah Thornton (1995) and Angela McRobbie and Jenny Garber (1991) to argue that such distinctions are drenched with gendered language (and the values such language imposes), whereby subculture is given a masculine identity of adventurousness, resistance, and heroism, and the mainstream is regarded as passive, homely, and feminine. According to Hollows, a similar distinction operates in cult cinema: "cult has been culturally constructed as masculine," she writes (2003: 39). Hollows's argument may be obviously evident in examples of how erotic and sleaze movies are targeted towards and received by fans. But her claim also reaches farther because it questions just how inscribed ideas of masculinity are in conceptualizations of kinds of cultural appreciation. For one, argues Hollows, the masculinity of cult works to "exclude 'real' women from some of the practices associated with cult fandom" (2003: 39). She adds that:

> *Titanic* might have a "cult" following, but its associations with a feminine and "mass" audience on one hand, and "middlebrow" discourses of "quality" on the other, mean that it is unlikely to be easily accepted into academic or popular cult canons unless the "dominant" and "conservative" meanings of the women's film can be subverted by the strategies of cult fans (Hollows 2003: 38).

Since the publication of her essay, Hollows's claim has been reiterated by numerous other scholars who have noted that films with female cult fans continue to be isolated from what is commonly understood as cult, being lumped together instead with the masses or the mainstream as if their form of fandom is indeed inferior. A good example is recent research on the fandom of the vampire melodrama *Twilight* (Click 2009; Bode 2010).

In the light of critiques such as those of Hollows one would expect cult receptions to adopt a more sensitive approach to representations of gender. This is partly the case. There is a decided increase in scholarly work that notes the presence of discourses around political correctness, gender equality, and feminism within cult receptions (we will detail some of these further on in this chapter). This does not necessarily mean that these discourses dominate the receptions. But their presence is certainly visible. Examples include Annette Hills's (1997) research into discourses of gender in the receptions of films such as *Henry, Portrait of a Serial Killer* and

Man Bites Dog, or various studies of the reception of *Carrie* or *Ginger Snaps* (Barker, Mathijs, and Mendik 2006). As we have noted in Chapter 6, there has also been increased interest for films with cult receptions that were made by female directors. The films of Dorothy Arzner (*Dance Girl, Dance*), Dorish Wishman (*Deadly Weapons*) or Stephanie Rothman (*Velvet Vampire*) for instance, have been celebrated as exceptions made, against the odds, in an industry largely dominated by exploitation, and their existence has been used to push debates about gender representation in cult cinema (Gorfinkel 2000; Luckett 2003; Modleski 2007). Increasingly, too, films such as *Baise-moi*, *Romance*, *Trouble Every Day*, or *Irréversible* – which are often associated with art cinema – have developed cult reputations of which gender concerns are an integral part.

There has also been some effort to isolate and analyze specifically feminist cults. Part of this involves research into the cultist receptions of activist films such as *Born in Flames*, *A Question of Silence*, or *SCUM Manifesto*, films made by women that concentrate on acts of violence against women, and on ways in which actions against such oppression can be taken (Lane 2000; Rich 1998: 319–325; Udris 2004). The most commonly mentioned example is Chantal Akerman's *Jeanne Dielman, 23 Quai du Commerce, 1080 Bruxelles*. Its style, structure, narrative, acting performances, and even its title are a deliberate challenge to mainstream cinema's androcentricity, and besides the genuine appeal it has with feminists (see Kinder 1977), much of its cult reception is hinged upon its status as an ambiguous work of art. This fits a pattern whereby visceral cult films are considered fan-boy material, while more abstract and intellectual films with cult followings are assigned a reception context that is seen as promoting supposedly more discriminative viewing strategies.

Even in the light of changes that have led to home viewing becoming the predominant site of consumption (hence closer to the femininity associated with domestication), much of Hollows' claim still stands. The core of cultism remains committed to a perspective that substantiates cultism as masculine. Hollows quotes David Sanjek's study of fanzines, which asserts that "self-conscious misogyny" and an "intentionally, juvenile, hard-boiled tone" go hand in hand because "only the most hardened sensibilities can bear the assault of offensive imagery" (2003: 45). Similarly, Brigid Cherry's (1999) analysis of female fans confirms how women continue to be excluded as part of the imagined community of cult consumption.

Anxieties of Cult Consumption

One reason for the persistence of cult cinema as masculine, and a way of understanding the complexity of the process through which the tag "masculine" is perpetuated in spite of accusations leveled against it is offered by the work of Jacinda Read (2003). Read builds on Hollows's argument. She investigates how the awareness of scholars of a gendered distinction between subculture and the mainstream (and of the efforts signaled above) complicates their ability or eagerness to engage with films (and receptions) that are said to draw much of their cultism from misogyny. An evident exemplification of this awareness has been the term "guilty pleasure," a phrase popularized in the late 1970s when *Film Comment* started a column celebrating critics' favorite films they felt they could not defend, thereby of course mounting exactly that, a defense. It is telling that this backhanded form of defending what was often sexist material originated exactly at a time when "bad cinema" was being re-appraised and the pornographic and horror genres rose to infamous prominence. Read asks if some of the allegations of chauvinism and misogyny leveled against these genres (and their defenses) did not disallow fans and users to find a cultural identity or to amass cultural capital. Do such allegations not take away the possibility of male, straight fans to take up a position from which they can speak to the subject? In other words, does the criticism directed against cult cinema not make it impossible for fans to publicly remain male and straight spectators that are supportive of this kind of cinema? (Read 2003: 58). At the very least it leads to what Read calls "anxiety of consumption" (2003: 58), an acute awareness that in approaching, say, an erotic film one might well be exposing oneself to ridicule simply because of the overtones associated with cultism (we too have had to answer the question "why would you study such woman-unfriendly material" several times). In that respect, it hardly matters that the study of a cult film's *reception* does not imply an

agreement with its politics. Attempts to justify, ratio-nalize, or spoof (in the case of Hunter's *Showgirls* essay) analyses are then akin to what Will Straw (1997: 11) called "an ageing male's strategies for survival in a cultural realm in which his place is no longer certain." It puts the male scholar at the same level as the fan-boy, and it chastises both for associating with a kind of cinema that has the reputation of being "wrong." References to camp, irony or hyperbole as instruments of that attempt to survival thus become equally suspect.

Read poses a very valid point, though she offers no solution. Instead, she observes how scholar after scholar fails to provide a sound rationale when they try to claim that "new" forms of approaching cult cinema might offer a way out. Jeffrey Sconce (1995: 379) notes the position of "limbo" and disempower-ment from which a lot of academics approach para-cinema, as a site for "refuge and revenge." Steve Chibnall (1997: 85) goes perhaps the furthest in sug-gesting that "psychotronic criticism [which runs] counter to dominant streams of political correctness" and which is "aware of feminism and the politics of difference," can offer "a reassertion of the right to look, to make anything the object of the knowing, sardonic, ironizing and frankly excited gaze." Both Sconce's discussion of paracinema and Chibnall's argument on psychotronic criticism describe efforts not to address the allegation of misogyny but to blow up the system of debate, reasoning, and discourse by embracing outra-geousness. Such descriptions certainly help us under-stand the tactics used by audiences that feel cornered in their right to align themselves with cultural products because of the dubious reputation those products have (rightly or wrongly so). By not taking into account the socio-economic and cultural conditions under which such audiences have to labor for their right to access and enjoy and cultify films, however, they fail to provide insights into just how forceful, demanding, and inescapable some tactics are.

There is also the problem that the very term "masculinity" is often used homogeneously. As Jan-covich (2002) has argued, not all viewers operate from the privileged position of the "educated, male, white, middle-class" (to use Sconce's terms as paraphrased by Read) – a position of uncertainty perhaps (as Sconce argues) but unquestionably also one of liberty of access. It is a position not enjoyed by a wide range of viewers that come from different constellations of class, ethnicity, and – indeed – gender. In fact, this is exactly the point Cherry made when she analyzed female horror fandom. Because there is a much wider range of audiences than those reflected in most research, it is not sufficient to merely describe and automatically dismiss the tactics used by viewers to regain their "right to look." There also needs to be an investigation of the material conditions that regulate the access to cult films those audiences have had, as well as research into the channels through which their cultism (of whatever degree of sophistication) is communicated.

The main implication of Hollows's and Read's work, and the consequence of our remarks above, is that many cult receptions take place in a context of anxiety, especially when it comes to mechanisms of (and receptions of) gender representation. Within these contexts it is absurd to assume that either "femininity" or "masculinity" are homogeneous concepts. Future approaches to gender in relation to cult cinema, then, would benefit by abandoning one-size-fits-all theories in favor of looking into context-specific cult receptions of gender representations – receptions by gendered, actual audiences that use their own *and* others' perception of "masculinity" or "femininity" to define themselves against mainstream culture. We will present some such efforts in the next sections of this chapter.

Non-Normative Sexuality and the Performance of Gender

In order to understand how cult receptions use concepts of gender and sexuality, it is necessary to analyze how these concepts have been embedded into the history of cult. More often than not gender and sexuality are fluid concepts, especially in the case of cult cinema. As Hoberman and Rosenbaum write (1991: 263), "Androgyny, transvestism, and gender blur have been major motifs in midnight movies from *Flaming Creatures* through the John Waters oeuvre to *The Rocky Horror Picture Show*." Following Grant (1991: 129) it then becomes "important to consider how the alternative [sexuality] is used or consumed by audiences." In the next few sections of this chapter we will look at how cult films

have overtly portrayed non-fixed or non-normative forms of gender and sexuality.[1]

For Judith Butler (1990), gender is always *performed*. It is the result of bodily routines, acts of stylized repetition managed through regulatory discourses: femininity, masculinity, and even the so-called "natural" and "biological" sex of a body are largely the result of cultural discipline. Breaking out of these regulatory constraints, then, is often seen as a subversive act of resistance against dominant ideologies and of liberation of the human body. This is very much the context within which much of cult cinema is discussed. The overt displays of cross-dressing, travesty, and queer sexuality in *The Rocky Horror Picture Show* (Figure 10.1), for instance, feature against a background in which Frank (Tim Curry) constantly comments on the attire and gender presentation of Brad (Barry Bostwick) and Janet (Susan Sarandon) (Weinstock 2007).

Similarly, *Showgirls*, which also has the word "show" in its title, contains a continuous stream of comments on "performing" to be a woman or a man, and the film has elaborate scenes in which women are "checked out" for their female sensuality. In numerous other cult films too, men and especially women comment upon performing gender roles: Ilsa in *Casablanca* does so explicitly when she muses over what kind of woman she is to Victor and to Rick; in *Emmanuelle*, characters continuously comment on Emmanuelle's performance as a liberated woman. Even Emmanuelle's rape is explicitly staged as a performance.

Figure 10.1 In *Fame*, Ralph (Barry Miller) and Doris (Maureen Teefy) perform with the audience of *The Rocky Horror Picture Show*.

There is a historical component to this link between cult cinema and the performance of non-normative sexuality. In their overview of midnight movies, Hoberman and Rosenbaum (1991) refer to the 1970 receptions of three films featuring drag, namely *Performance*, *Beyond the Valley of the Dolls* and *Trash*, as a point in history that highlighted how performances of ambivalent or unfixed sexuality and gender roles were fast becoming a common part of cult cinema. Even films with drag and transvestite performances produced well before the 1970s, such as *Glen or Glenda* or *Some Like it Hot* received new cult appeal during midnight runs in New York in the early 1970s. The cult success of *Rocky Horror* and *Outrageous!*, which featured Bette Davis and Judy Garland-impersonator Craig Russell, continued the trend. For Andrew Ross (1989: 135–136), the link between cult cinema and the performance of non-normative sexuality (especially drag) has its origins in late June 1969 when two apparently unrelated events (the funeral of gay icon Judy Garland and the Stonewall riots that followed the arrest of people attending the gay Stonewall bar in New York) virtually forced a connection between the performance of alternate sexuality and the performance of subversive film viewing (see Chapter 8 for an elaboration on how this influenced camp viewing practices). Before the riots in Stonewall, cultist receptions were usually regarded as straight. After Stonewall, they were increasingly associated with gay and alternate sexuality, and with a conscious awareness of how gender is performed.

According to Staiger (2000: 125–160), however, the link between the collectivity of the cult experience and the performance of non-normative sexuality has roots that precede 1969 or 1970. Staiger's analysis of the receptions of the scene of the New York underground cinema of the early 1960s and especially of films such as *Flaming Creatures* (which features an orgy and several scenes of explicit sexuality) and *Scorpio Rising* (which has gay overtones), sketches a gradual symbiosis, across the decade of the 1960s, between countercultural developments, such as gay culture (we use the term gay here to refer to homosexuality as well as lesbianism and transvestism), and underground cinema that eventually culminated in cult receptions of the kind Ross and Hoberman and Rosenbaum observe. Staiger's research claim has far-

reaching implications. On the one hand it demonstrates how cult cinema's development, in the guises of underground cinema, midnight movies and camp, helped find a community for a hitherto non-homogeneous gay culture. But it also suggests that for non-gay audiences who regularly attended cult screenings, and who felt themselves belonging to its subversive, subcultural or countercultural atmosphere, the performance of gender and sexuality of any kind became a notion they grew familiar with. Such a context-specific insight paints in a different light the discussion of the anxiety of male cult consumption we mentioned earlier in this chapter. For one, it signals that analyses of the anxieties of cult consumption receptions warrant placement in a historical context. Another implication is that the multiple lines of association and alignment make it near impossible for researchers to find evidence that justifies drawing a firm dividing line between so-called "innocently straight," "deliberately straight," "closely gay," or "gender performative" attitudes towards affiliations between counterculture, gay culture, and cult or underground cinema, *especially* when not only "identities are at stake," as Staiger puts it, "but a *movement*," too (2000: 126). It is therefore perhaps more practical to assume, at least in broad overviews of cult cinema, no such line exists (and indeed both naivety and performativity may collide within the actions and beliefs of a single fan). It would also seem prudent, then, to allow the notion of so-called performed gender receptions to be of equal significance as that of so-called frank or earnest ones.

While the developments sketched by Staiger explain how gay culture found an association with a film-viewing community, it does not offer a connection to the mainstream. Many performances of non-normative sexuality remained too adventurous, too openly gay and lesbian or too ambiguous to be considered anything else but "exceptional," "problematic," or "political." That counted for new releases (such as *Harlis* or *La cage aux folles*) as much as for the reappraisal of older films such as Jean Cocteau's *Orphée*, Jean Genet's infamous *Un chant d'amour*, *Mädchen in Uniform*, or *Belle de jour* (Rich 1998: 174–206; Dyer 2003: 63–88, Cairns 2006: 58). *Personal Best* became the totemic lesbian film for a wide audience; it made Mariel Hemingway, who also appeared in Playboy at the time of the film's release, an iconic yet controversial figure for the lesbian movement (Williams 1982). Within a smaller niche, the films of Monica Treut received a firm cult following (Straayer 1996: 23–41). For gay film cultism, the films of Derek Jarman were important (Richardson 2009).

The early 1990s saw a convergence similar to the one observed by Staiger in the 1960s, in which the performance of gender and non-normative sexuality underwent a further development and found a renewed connection with a film viewing community whose reception activities displayed cultist sensibilities. For the most part, this development is linked to the way in which so-called "New Queer Cinema" changed the narrative and stylistic frameworks through which performances of gender and non-normative sexuality were presented: stories about overcoming adversity became increasingly embedded in a context of "play" and the carnivalesque (with the circus a recurrent background). With the midnight movie circuit on the wane this renewed performativity found exhibition platforms in a growing number of LGBTQ-film festivals (LGBTQ stands for Lesbian, Gay, Bisexual, Transgender and Queer; see Gamson 1996, Rich 1999). Through the LGBTQ networks and communities, films such as *My Own Private Idaho*, *The Living End*, *Les Nuits Fauves*, *Priscilla, Queen of the Desert*, *Go Fish*, *When Night Is Falling*, and *Happy Together*, which combined anarchic, mocking, carnivalesque, and ironic attitudes received cult receptions across borders (Feigenbaum 2007; d'Allondans 2009). This change moved gay and lesbian cinema into a reflexive mode and in a permanent niche, a place that was still marginal culturally but that at least provided a secure position from where one could speak (to paraphrase Read's comments from earlier in this chapter). One result of this redirection were receptions that blended in nearly seamlessly with other types of cult receptions through shared stylistic tropes of hyperbole and irony, and shared narratives involving slacking and aimless young adults.

Since 2000, the emphasis on the carnivalesque has intensified to the extent that it has become the dominant lens through which performances of gender and non-normative sexuality are managed. To this has been added a self-reflexivity that roots many of these

performances as homage or persiflage of previous performances of gender and non-normative sexuality – with *Hedwig and the Angry Inch*, influenced by *Rocky Horror*, among its key examples (Havis 2008: 92–94; we will explore some of the mechanisms of this development in Chapters 21 and 22).

Erotica and the Performance of Gender

Performativity of gender and sexuality is at the center of many exploitation films with high erotic content – the kind of films that are said to reinforce dominant ideology. In fact, the explicit address of the performance of sexual acts and an equally explicit address of the act of observing that performance are key elements of the way in which audiences of erotic cinema are introduced to non-heteronormative forms of sexuality and gender role-playing, while the cultural sanction of this adventurousness is frequently absent. Among the most visible tropes these types of exploitation cinema employ is that of a setting that enables both performance and observation of sexuality – often a shower, a prison, a convent, or a brothel – and a quasi-automatic association of women with eroticism, most often evoked through series of scenes that revolve around female nudity and inferences of lesbian sex that is performed in the presence of (or spied upon by) a male or masculinized authority figure (a prison guard, a security guard, etc.).

A good illustration of this is the women-in-prison film, of which *Caged Heat* is an often-mentioned example (Peary 1981: 44–47). The performances of the film's stars, Erica Gavin and Barbara Steele, act as textbook illustrations of what Pauline Kael (1961) had called the "satire of the female" (Kael had Anita Ekberg's performance in *La dolce vita* in mind). We find similar routines of hyperbolic gender performance at work in nunsploitation films such as *Flavia the Heretic* and *Killer Nun* – with Ekberg in the leading role (Nakahara 2004). In the case of the soft-core erotic thriller too, the performance of female gender is constructed so it can be understood as performed. As Robert Eberwein (1998) and Linda Ruth Williams (2005) have pointed out, in the formula of the erotic thriller female sexuality is literally put on stage, its performance explicitly worked into a story in which it is surrounded by surveillance cameras and voyeurs. Examples include film such as *9½ Weeks*, *Basic Instinct* and *Scorned*. In this context too, the body of the female is a satire of femalehood. Soft-core erotic parodic films such as *Lord of the G-Strings* and *Spiderbabe* have continued this trend of spoofing womanhood even more explicitly (Hunter 2006; I. Smith 2010b).

Some exploitation films present performances of gender and sexuality in a context of death and destruction. Among the most infamous such cycles is nazisploitation. In the wake of *The Night Porter*, films such as *Ilsa, She Wolf of the SS*, *Salon Kitty*, and *Gestapo's Last Orgy* have used the stages of camps and brothels to display performances of sadomasochist sexuality within the wider framework of the Holocaust (see Leiva 2008). Such performances are also prevalent in Sade-sploitation, a body of films inspired by the work of eighteenth-century French libertine author Marquis de Sade. Its representations of sadomasochistic submission – in particular blindfolding, chaining, whipping, branding, and piercing – gave films such as *Justine de Sade* and *Histoire d'O* highly contentious receptions. In the case of the vampire exploitation film, performances of gender and sexuality contain strong elements of violence, including torture, rape, and orgiastic sex. Because of the long history of the vampire film, several scholars have suggested that its representation of the performance of sexuality and gender can be seen as a barometer of Puritanism in a culture (Tseëlon 2001). Milly Williamson (2005) argues that vampire fandom, and indeed the entire cult of fashion surrounding the vampire figure, are influenced by views of the Western female as someone "guaranteed to be at fault" with dominant culture, someone "unattainable," an "impossible creature" and a "timeless cultural phantasy" (2005: 144). In vampire movies, this view is pushed to the extreme: women are represented in highly stylized and fashionable modes, yet they are also inaccessible; they are sexual, but out of reach for the spectator. An object of desire and a warning against that desire for both male *and* female viewers, female vampires are *only* performance. Films such as *Rape of the Vampire*, *Fascination*, or *Vampyros Lesbos*, showed women as active hunters as well as passive prey. Harry Kümel's *Daughters of Darkness*, a film highly praised in cult receptions, is often regarded as an example of a vampire film that problematizes the representation and performance of gender and sexuality to the extent that it takes on feminist traits (Mathijs 2004, 2005b; Dion 2009).

Probably the most acute case of the performance of gender and sexuality in the framework of eroticism is pornography, and the porn chic cycle of the 1970s in particular. For Ross (1989: 172) porn chic marks the rise of filmic porn as a full-fledged capitalist industry, characterized among others by a professionalization that saw an increase of women as agents in its production and reception, as well as a stylistic change: explicit penetrative sex was shown in full detail and the performativity of the sex act became the center of the narrative – indeed "performing" this or that sex act was what porn chic was all about. *Behind the Green Door* is an excellent example: Marilyn Chambers is kidnapped and brought to a secret sex club where she is forced to perform sexual acts on stage, surrounded first by only women (dressed as nuns), then by only men. Chambers' performance is attended by an audience that, spurred on by her actions, engages in an orgy. Eventually, the sex acts culminate in an extreme close-up "money shot" that lasts several minutes – one that is frequently commented upon as so surreal in its color-saturated slow-motion that it becomes hyperbolic, even abstract (Peary 1981: 23). *The Opening of Misty Beethoven* and *Café Flesh* too incorporated elaborate stagings and performances, turning these films into comments *about* sex (see Smith 2007). After the heydays of porn chic, the performativity of sexual acts remained a key component of the pornographic film: it informed the cult receptions of *Caligula*, *Debbie Does Dallas* and *New Wave Hookers* and it was central to the crossover reputations of the films of Annie Sprinkle, who moved from being a porn star to a career as performance artist. Hyperbolic examples of performativity in pornography are the performance of Annabel Chong in *The World's Biggest Gang Bang* (which also became the subject of the documentary *Sex: The Annabel Chong Story*), and the collaboration of former Italian porn star Ilona Staller with "husband" artist Jeff Koons. In an attempt to disrupt the patriarchal and androcentric procedures governing sex Staller and Koons "performed" marriage, and ridiculed gender role-playing, sex, and dressing up.

The Performance of Gendered Reception

A complication of the performance of gender and sexuality that affects the reception contexts of cult cinema is that of the performance of gendered reception, or the degree to which audiences perform (i.e. *pretend*) affiliations or sensitivity towards one or another gender in reaction to various representations of, and allusions to, sexuality.

Many longer-term receptions of cult films of which the representations and performances of gender and sexuality had been the subject of controversy or of discussions of how they affected people (porn arouses or disgusts, Nazisploitation repulses, drag liberates, and so on) have experienced moments in which the performance of gendered reception is said to take precedence over any other form or mode of audience activity. In most cases, such performance causes doubt about how sincere or meaningful the reception is, at least in the eyes of the researcher. This is best exemplified by the wide range of analyses of the long-term receptions of *The Rocky Horror Picture Show* that try to assess how any of the film's initial liberal politics are forgotten or buried under the high degree of ritualization of the performance of its gendered reception (Wood 1991). As we observed in Chapter 9, there are several context-specific instances in which the performance of gendered audience activity can still be said to achieve some form of transgressive liberation. Nevertheless, the question remains whether multiple layers of performativity do not make it unnecessarily difficult for audiences to access any liberatory content that might lead to personal liberation. In an essay on configurations of femininity in midnight movies, Gaylyn Studlar (1991) asks if the revelation that very few cult films have effectively subverted oppressive norms means that the films are not perverse enough to elicit change, or if they are too easily assimilated. Perhaps, as Grant (1991: 129–130; 2000: 21) suggested, the high degree of ritualized performances of gendered reception is conformist indeed, precisely because it is seen as performed. For Jeffrey Weinstock (2007: 1), the consequence is that "*The Rocky Horror Picture Show* has never taken place . . . at least not for me."

But, as Weinstock (2008) goes on to show, this does not prevent communities from being established and anxieties from being reduced. Exposure to the multi-layered performances regarding films such as *Rocky Horror* does still generate debate and out of those debates grow understandings, solidarities, alignments, and affective commitments. Consider, for instance, the case of feminist cultism. Some of the films and receptions we have singled out earlier in this chapter and in Chapter 6 as examples of an increased attention for and sensitivity towards issues of gender representation (the films of Akerman, Arzner, Wishman, Rothman, or the *Ginger Snaps* trilogy), can also be said to have received part of their cult recognition as a result of critics and audiences "performing" feminism. As a result, debates have arisen over whether or not a cult film's "feminist" components are indeed "truly" feminist or partly the effect of the performance of feminist attitudes in its reception. *Tank Girl* in particular has been held up as a "real" feminist cult film, especially in comparison with the cult films of Kathryn Bigelow, which are said to be too masculine, or some of the films of Catherine Hardwicke, which are said to cater too eagerly to hetero-normativity (Powell 1994; Daugherty 2002; Le Breton 2009: 137–144). According to Whelehan and Sonnett (1997: 33):

> it is the "social organization of the relations between texts within *specific conditions of reading*" that work to define the postmodern circulation of meaning-making within contemporary media forms. This is important for assessing how heterogeneous audiences are addressed across the cultural sites which form the social context of reception(s) of *Tank Girl*.

To name a specific context: many fans will set up *Tank Girl* against *Twilight* through a comparison that will note that Hardwicke was the costume designer of *Tank Girl*. Equally, *Tank Girl* is used as example to complicate considerations of just how feminist Bigelow's films are – and if indeed these articulations of feminism in the films' receptions matters (Talalay 2010). What is at stake here is less the "truth" about these films' feminism – or even the feminism of the viewers – and more the heightened awareness of "feminism" as a tool of significance in perceiving films in certain ways.

Ultimately, the performance of gendered reception can become a tool that is applicable not only in cases where audiences see themselves confronted with films that harbor a clear desire to shock, transgress, or present performances of non-normative sexuality, but towards *any film*. This activity has been referred to as "queering." The concept of queering relies on the pun involved in merging the terms "queer" (gay) and "query" (investigation). It refers to the audience activity of reading against the grain, of willfully reinterpreting films by looking for performances of non-normative sexuality even against the intentions of the makers. Queer viewing strategies are aided by what Ross (1989) has identified as "camp aesthetics" (see Chapter 8). Most cult classics have been queered. *Casablanca*'s last line has become emblematic in speculations that see Captain Renault (Claude Rains) and Rick Blaine (Humphrey Bogart) commence (or continue!) a gay relationship. Alexander Doty (2000) outlines the queering of *The Cabinet of Dr. Caligari* as a closet gay film, *The Wizard of Oz* as lesbian fantasy, and *Psycho* as a gay film. Through queering, Jodie Foster's portrayal of Clarice Starling in *Silence of the Lambs* and Linda Hamilton's role of Sarah Connor in *Terminator II* have been turned into iconic examples of lesbian heroines (Staiger 2000). Harry Benshoff (1997: 230) remarks how much queering involves the horror film. He writes:

> one might think that after the release and cult popularity of a film like *The Rocky Horror Picture Show*, the idea of the monster queer would be a harder one to exploit, since audiences would already presumably have some awareness of the genre's queer undercurrents ... Yet the general public still maintains tremendous powers of denial about matters homosexual ("Don't Ask, Don't Tell"), and the filmgoing public has a seemingly short memory for cultish deconstructions of popular culture.

Note how Benshoff's reference to a distinction between cult and the mainstream is established through a separation of audiences that can queer "undercurrents," and audiences that are not capable of this. Among Benshoff's most cultist examples is *Nightmare on Elm Street II: Freddy's Revenge*, which he calls "exceptionally queer" (1997: 246–247).

While largely playful and seldom attempting to effectively alter the course of a film's reception,

queering has nevertheless impacted on the status of resolutely mainstream films, up to the point where it has ignited, rather than extended, cult status. An example of this, observed by Mathijs and Mendik (2008a: 375–376) and Sean Griffin (2009: 212–214) is the queering of *Top Gun*. Employing a variety of trivia such as the biography of flamboyant producer Don Simpson, the symbolism of imagery of locker room scenes, beach volleyball, jets as phallic symbols, and curious pieces of dialog, audiences have produced an entirely alternative meaning for the film – one that, by means of confirmation, found its way into a scene in *Sleep with Me* in which cultural authority and spokesperson for cultist sensibility Quentin Tarantino held a manic speech in which he painted *Top Gun* as a queer film. In the form of montages of "Gay Top Gun" such readings have found welcome audiences on the internet.

Hidden Strategies of Cult Enjoyment

But what if cultists will not articulate their performance of gendered reception as explicitly as the cases mentioned above? One important consequence of the performance of gender and sexuality in the receptions of cult films is that labels of enjoyment and pleasure, performed or not, automatically carry the implication of approval. Frequently, the difficulty of disentangling enjoyment from approval muzzles explicit articulations of receptions. We would like to illustrate this difficulty through the example of the rape-revenge film. Because of their foregrounding of the link between sexuality and violence films such as *Last House on the Left*, *I Spit on Your Grave*, *Thriller – A Cruel Picture*, *Ms. 45*, and *House on the Edge of the Park*, to name a few illustrious examples, have never managed to escape allegations of misogyny or sadism regardless of the opportunities for performativity they offer. Any articulation of appreciation is drowned out by criticism, and the result is often that cult fans of rape-revenge withdraw from debates altogether.

In his cross-generation reception analysis of *Straw Dogs* Martin Barker (2005, 2006) gives an insight into the complications of the cultist receptions of rape-revenge movies. He concludes that the film's troubled reception "arises from a series of things that the film *isn't* ... Audiences who loved the film, lived its ambiguities, its loss of moral or motivational certainties. Audiences who hated it, sought for a clear meaning in it, and became distressed when they couldn't locate one" (Barker 2006). Importantly, in his research, Barker used a method (first used in a study of the reception of *Crash*, see Barker, Arthurs, and Harindranath 2001) in which audiences were asked to map their reception of the film not only in terms of how they "liked" it but also if they "admired" it. By offering their viewers the choice to avoid equating "pleasure" with "approval" through the semi-affective audience position of "admiration" they were given the chance to highlight what they felt were important elements of their appreciation or fandom without the risk of offending notions of political correctness. It made it possible to see the extent to which committed viewers who knowingly engaged with films they knew had a bad reputation (such as second- and third-generation viewers) were able to separate and negotiate conflicting affections and interpretations towards the film. Among the views Barker managed to isolate were highly affective ones (such as the fear of physical overpowerment) as well as highly intellectual ones (such as an admiration for how *Straw Dogs* attempted to understand the presence of violence in civilization as part of a "primal instinct" or an animalistic imperative). Barker's method enabled the assessment of the ambiguities that viewing *Straw Dogs* brought with it, and it thus gave an explanation for its cult status as "volatile."

Formats such as VHS and DVD have further confounded the ambiguities associated with rape-revenge films. A research project, funded by the British Board of Film Classification, into viewers' attitudes towards and consumption of both cut and uncut versions of rape-revenge movies available in different regions in the world, found that there were strong nuances in the cultism of rape-revenge movies (Barker *et al.* 2008; Selfe 2008). Unsurprisingly, receptions of *House on the Edge of the Park*, *Ichi the Killer*, and the French *Baise-moi*, *Irréversible*, and *À ma soeur* showed huge discrepancies, depending on the kinds of aesthetic values and meanings that were ascribed to the films, the kinds of attitudes with which the films were approached, and the kind of opinions and presuppositions existed about actions of censors. In each case, however, audiences describing themselves as "admiring" though not necessarily "liking" the films, embraced opportunities given by the films' textual cues or their contexts in order to explain their deep commitment to these films. In the case of *Baise-moi*, for instance, its self-declared feminist intentions, its exploitative distribution, and its hugely controversial reception helped establish a context of "ambiguity" that fixed itself onto the film's viewing situations to the extent that it made it virtually impossible for viewers to "un-cultify" (for overviews of *Baise-moi*'s receptions, see Franco 2003; MacKenzie 2002; Reynaud 2002; Le Cain 2002b).

The various contexts within which the rape-revenge movie can be understood offer viewers the ability to shift the emphasis away from their supposed pleasure in the presentation of sexual violence towards a position in which they engage in an *interrogation* of sexual violence. Such interrogations of the sexual violence motive invariably led to debates and controversies and then to defenses, which in turn fueled cult receptions. Even if many rape-revenge movies were only sporting the revenge element as a rhetorical excuse to exploit opportunities to show sexual violence, many audiences would still accord importance to that rhetoric as a significant part of the film's meaning. In a sense, then, the rape-revenge movie holds up a mirror to cultists' desire to see disturbing and challenging materials. It even implicitly criticizes such interests (while of course still profiting from it). Yet it ultimately validates this viewing attitude because the interrogation also exposes the wider context of the struggle over meanings of problematic categories in culture and it points out how the "cultist" viewer is put in the same corner as the problem regardless of the actual reasons for viewing.

In some instances, this constant struggle to separate one's commitment to a film, genre, or director with a disreputable status when it comes to gender representation has led cult fans to withdraw almost completely from debate – not in the sense that they blow it up (like paracinematic viewers do) or that they hyperbolically perform receptions (thus obliterating the distinction between fake and sincere convictions), but in the sense that there is a refusal to explain one's choices and alignments. Russ Hunter (2009, 2010) calls such entrenched and muted resistance an "insulation trajectory." In a study of the cross-cultural reception of the films of Dario Argento, Hunter observed how

Argento established a cultist rapport with horror fans in the wake of the release of *Suspiria*. Subsequent releases of Argento's films failed to reach the same praise. At the same time, new criticism highlighted a lot of the underlying misogyny or sadosexuality in Argento's films (especially with regard to *Tenebrae* and *Inferno* – two Argento films that landed on the video nasties list). Or, at the very least, such studies brought into view Argento's so-called disrupted, fragmented, and ambivalent representations of gender (Mendik 2000; Needham 2002). But instead of causing a change in the cult reception of Argento, this only led to a more stubborn reclamation of Argento's status as "cult hero." As both Hunter and Peter Hutchings (2003) observe, there is a high degree of seriousness in how fans of Argento comment on his work.

> We seem a world away here from the camp aesthetics associated with some cult movies, notably *The Rocky Horror Picture Show*, or from the more aggressive counter-cultural maneuvers associated with what Jeffrey Sconce in an influential article has termed paracinema (Hutchings 2003: 134–135).

Hunter notes that this does not mean that Argento's fans are blind to changes. Quite the opposite, they are happy to concede that the director is making "inferior" films aesthetically. But they do *not* appear to be prepared to discard their fandom in the light of what Hutchings (2003: 136) has described as a move towards understanding Argento's work as symptomatic, "as a window on themes and issues that do not pertain to Argento alone." He notes how in the case of Argento advanced insulation coincides with increased mentions of the term "cult," as if Argento's supporters attempt to defend their fandom by repeating a mantra of oppositional reading they have learned and adopted. In Hunter's words, it offers "for those so inclined, a chance to 'rebel' conceptually" (Hunter 2009: 12). Conceptually, but also muted.

There is a regional element to the cult insulation trajectory as well. Next to the lack of a context of "art cinema," and the refusal to adopt a camp position or to accept insights generated by symptomatic criticism, the insulation trajectory of Argento is also affected by its cultural origin. Hunter demonstrates how time and again fans and critics refer to the fact that his films are

"giallo," a "typical Italian" format that is close to that of a Western but at the same time different – Mikel Koven (2006) calls it a vernacular category, Gary Needham (2002) calls it a discursive site of contestation, and several critics refer to it through the Italian term "filone" (literally: thread), thus eschewing any reference to genre (and its implication of debates over categorization). The confusion over the specific contours and components of the giallo, and its culturally specific status, has increased ambivalence over the status of the work of Argento on an international level. On the one hand it is an attractor (Guins 2005), but on the other hand it is equally often referred to as a component that blocks anyone not familiar with that context from understanding what Argento's films are "really about." This has the consequence that many Argento fans can easily point to any symptomatic criticism as "ignoring" the cultural context within which Argento's representations of gender take place, thereby blocking debate. We will further elaborate on elements of transnationalism in our next chapter.

Conclusion

To some extent the hidden strategies of cult consumption are performative as well. Insulation entrenchments and admiration-not-approval can be regarded as postures the same way the performers of female nudity, of erotic scenes, and of queer sexuality can be said to offer merely performances – as if they are playing along with the kinds of reactions and receptions the fans think they are supposed to have without actually meaning it, as if it was a directive from "mainstream culture" they are only too keen to subvert by pretending to adhere to it.

In this perspective, then, female fans protesting to being victimized by offensively misogynist horror films, queer fans subverting the masculinity in *Top Gun* by cheering on macho posturing, and fan boys reveling in downgrading erotic displays by howling and hollering, are part of the same reaction that typifies cultism: they are assumed to challenge mainstream culture without being so offensive as to cause direct sanction while also allowing those viewers to take up a position from where they can speak – to the films, and via the films to their peers, opponents, and the rest of culture. In other words, the separation of pleasure from admiration, the insulation trajectory theory, and the varying degrees of performativity all offer audiences of cult cinema a way of addressing gender. While such performances can also confirm the very behavior they are criticizing, the fact that it is often virtually impossible to distinguish between genuine reactions, and performed ones, gives the entire process an ambivalence that characterizes cult cinema's receptions.

Note

1. We use the term "non-normative" in its most neutral understanding, as any form of gender or sexuality that stands outside the pattern of heteronormativity, monogamy, and patriarchy that has dominated film representation since the classical era.

11

Transnationalism and Orientalism

There is an increased effort to study cult globally. It is largely the result of the obvious observation that cult cinema is – by default say some – transnational or cross-cultural. Like many other forms of cinema it enjoys the opportunities of what Toby Miller has described as "an international division of cultural labour" (quoted in Schneider and Williams 2005: 5). This is not only a commonsensical observation. Research has highlighted just how international cult cinema is. Consider, for instance, the transnational contexts of consumption of the giallo film (Guins 2005; Koven 2006; Lucas 2007), of Latin-American cult cinema (Syder and Tierney 2005; Reboll 2009), and martial arts cinema (Hunt 2000; Bowman 2010).

Let us use briefly illustrate how wide-reaching considerations of cult cinema's transnationalism can be through two examples: *The Gods Must Be Crazy* and *Godzilla*. *The Gods Must Be Crazy* presents conflicts between normality and the trangressive "Other" in the form of intercultural and international conflict: African versus European, revolutionaries from one country versus the authorities in another, civilized versus primitive, even in its self-identification as a film from Botswana while it is in effect a South African production that wanted to sidestep the apartheid boycott. Regardless of how the narrative ostensibly mocks but ultimately supports recuperation (Grant 1991: 133–135), their awareness of connotations of "African," "South-African," "native," or "the bush," and the mere presence in *The Gods Must Be Crazy* of a people, a language, and a region that are far away from what they normally encounter asks audiences that see this film in a downtown art house or repertory theater

to defamiliarize Western normality. Even in its quasi-transgressive guise it confronts idiosyncratic consumption patterns and non-effective use of time thus forcing audiences to treat their home culture as "temporarily different" or "temporarily useless." The cult of *Godzilla* also built on aspects of transnationalism and exoticism. Cynthia Erb (1998) suggests there is a strong link between the *Godzilla* cult and the cultism that had evolved around *King Kong*. Of course, a major difference lies in *Godzilla*'s post-nuclear, radio-active origin, a quality that – with the nuclear bombing of Japan fresh in viewers' minds – gives the monster a decidedly tragic characteristic, and which puts the distinction between friends and foes in a complicated light. According to Chon Noriega (1987), *Godzilla* found a following beyond Japan because it forces audiences to acknowledge the monster Godzilla, in its dual role of destructor and respected icon, as "Other" to both the indigenous population and to foreigners. To a large extent, *The Gods Must Be Crazy* and *Godzilla* are transnational because they are transgressive, *and* transgressive because they are transnational. They upset the binary us-versus-them opposition that Western cinema seeks to conform.

In this chapter, we tackle transnationalism via one region that was once considered an unlikely component of cult cinema, namely Asia. J.P. Tellote's seminal collection on cult cinema mentions only one Asian film: in Gregory Waller's market study of midnight movies, Bruce Lee's martial arts film *Enter the Dragon* is described as a "highly unlikely candidate" (Waller 1991: 170). *Enter the Dragon* is also the only Asian film discussed in several other overviews (Peary 1981;

Mendik and Harper 2000b). In recent years, however, Asian cinema has had a fundamental impact on cult cinema. It is therefore crucial we highlight the region in our considerations.

Orientalism: Curiosity versus Exoticism

One recurrent problematic of how fans, critics, and audiences express cultism of certain Asian films is that of a Westernized perspective. Mathijs and Mendik (2008a: 275–280) point out that this perspective involves *both* a cultural curiosity and a predetermined notion of exoticism. Often, the qualities that Western audiences find so attractive in Asian cinema are a result of Western viewers' curiosity for and confrontation with systems of representation they have difficulty understanding (and that therefore violate practices, routines, and habits). But this does not automatically mean that curiosity is equal to a cultist *desire* to find "exotic" and "extreme" imagery. A cultist lens only occurs when audiences expand their viewing beyond curiosity to focus on the interrogation of "tainted reputations": when aspects of the culture of origin are read as separate from its "typical" elements and are instead seen to point to that other culture's taboos.

Any such effort is inevitably affected by what has been called an "orientalist" perspective. According to Edward Said (1978: 1), who coined the term, the Orient is a Western invention that regards it as a place, to the East of Europe, "of romance, of exotic beings, haunting memories and landscapes, remarkable experiences." "Orientalism," then, is the concept of engaging with cultures and cultural products originating to the East of Europe from a colonial, imperialist standpoint. The concept acts as a self-affirmation of the colonizer. Said's initial analysis was largely directed at the Middle East, as well as the regions of Persia and India. Said acknowledged that for the Americas "the Orient" might have different associations, because it might relate mostly to the Far East, but overall his conceptualization has been applied to all regions East of Europe and on the Western edge of the Pacific Rim, generally known as "the East." Orientalism has also affected Eastern critical observations of the West. Mitsuhiro Yoshimoto (1993: 338) argues

misrepresentations are unavoidable: "the Other cannot be misrepresented, since it is always already a misrepresentation."

With regard to cult cinema, orientalism most often refers to the ambivalent attraction of the cultural "other" from the point of the view of the Western "self." That attraction is frequently subjected to fetishist idolatry. After all, to assign a cult value to an object is an act of fetishism in itself. The fetishism of the Orient is often visualized through a series of traits associated with both femininity and uncivilized, unindustrialized wildness. Some of the most visible expressions of this fetishism include sexual seduction, soft-spoken or ornamental language, deception, immorality, ritualized lethal force combined with solemnity, and the depiction of scars, veils, and robes as props of sex and violence. As Gary Needham (2006: 10–11) has observed, such attractions are affirmative of the superior position of the West yet also indicative of the realization that that superiority is hinged upon the kind of imagery associated with the "other." In order to maintain the superiority, then, all Asian products, be they animated series (*Pokemon*), videogames (Super Mario) or hardware (Nintendo) are persistently framed as "other," regardless of whether such presences are ubiquitous or marginal. As a result, the distinction between center and periphery of culture that informs so much of cult cinema is invalid when it comes to Asian cinema – where everything is "other," everything is potentially marginal.

Given such complications, the cross-cultural exchange of Asian cult cannot be measured simply in terms of degrees of inferiority/superiority or degrees of misrepresentation. On the contrary, any surplus generated in its receptions (through fetishism, curiosity, or otherwise) falls well outside the scales of measurement for traditional cultural trades and exchanges. Films such as *In the Realm of the Senses* – too radical to be tied down into any cultural "normality" regardless from whatever angle it is considered – did a lot to deconstruct the classic orientalist view, as did several of the films we will discuss more elaborately further on in this chapter. The most significant deconstruction of orientalism occurs through cross-cultural fan receptions and the cultural surplus they generate. Such developments are accompanied, or even propelled, by globalized and transnational streams of distribution and marketing (Morris,

Siu Leung Li and Chan 2005; Denison 2006, 2008). Rob Wilson (2005: 268) even refers to this over-saturated translocality as necessitating a new form of cultist critique, one he enigmatically calls "spectral."

In sum, the orientalism of Said might work in both ways, as self-affirmative but also as interrogator of cultural identity. Even though it weighs heavily on the reception – across borders – of all cinema, it affects cult cinema differently because of that cinema's defiance of being measured in terms of normalcy. Only within the context of specific receptions and international exchanges, then, can we determine with any semblance of exactness how these acts of transnational affirmation and interrogation work.

The Reception of Asian Cult Cinema

Prior to the 1970s, cult receptions of Asian films were limited to isolated instances, most notably the samurai films of Akira Kurosawa (*Seven Samurai*, *Yojimbo*) and various *Godzilla* films (Peary 1983: 63–65; French and French 1999: 174–175; Everman 1993: 114–118). Since the 1970s, there have been two waves in the reception of Asian cult cinema.

The first wave occurred in the beginning of the 1970s, and runs parallel with the magnetic appeal of Bruce Lee. At this time, Asian cult cinema was largely limited to martial arts movies, re-imaginations of the jidai-geki, or Japanese films of what David Bordwell (2000: xi) has called "Sadean violence." After Lee's death and the posthumous release of *Game of Death*, cultist interest in these forms of Asian cinema dispersed across numerous tiny niches, constructed through festival audiences and Western film magazines. Characteristic of this first wave was that it relied on existing networks of cult and exploitation cinema (such as horror) to reach its audiences. It was part of the same market that sought to attract viewers by offering exotic, fetishistic materials. Put differently, during this wave Asian films became cults almost uniquely as a result of their Western reception within already cultified networks. The cult following of US-produced compilation film *Shogun Assassin*, distributed through Roger Corman's New World Pictures, and the French adoration for King Hu are illustrations of this (Macias 2001: 62–76; Wong 2007: 182–183).

The second wave, which took place from the early 1990s onwards, is radically different, partly because it shows discrepancies between regions of reception that had hitherto been presented as a unity, but also because the cultification of the films occurred *both* in Asia and in the West. In Europe, niche festivals and specialist retailers played a pioneering role in offering audiences access to Asian cinema that had already been perceived as cultist or marginal by the home territory. Similarly, in the early 1990s, specialist import-retailers of comic books and pulp literature started to carry VHS tapes and laserdiscs of Japanese anime and Hong Kong heroic bloodshed films. David Desser (2005: 210) notes that films such as *Akira*, *The Killer* and *City on Fire* were being picked up by fans whose willingness to watch them "with neither an audio or subtitle track" was a clear sign of their emerging cult reputations. These specialty titles were soon accompanied by Jet Li and Jackie Chan films, soft-porn such as *Tokyo Decadence*, *Sex and Zen* and *Naked Killer*, the fairytale *Chinese Ghost Story*, Japanese yakuza thrillers such as *Violent Cop*, and occasionally by Bollywood films (though these relied more frequently on their separate networks).

Already inscribed with cultist credentials, anime and heroic bloodshed films made their entry on student campuses, and in independent theaters. In contrast to the 1970s, audiences seemed to be treating these films as instant-cultist genres and formats in their own right, no longer as add-ons to existing networks. By the middle of the 1990s, anime and heroic bloodshed films had developed tight networks of retailers that supplied a growing Western cult following. The only significant change in that mode of distribution came in the late 1990s when a string of European festivals (of the Méliès network, see Chapter 3) started introducing their fans to anime and Japanese horror films as a means of breaking away from the traditional horror fare they usually offered. This wave of J-horror led to a diversification of the cult appeal of Asian cinema. The efforts of distributors such as Tartan (and its Asia Extreme label) brought Asian cult films to "an enthusiastic audience that is receptive to innovative genre, regardless of country of origin" (Berra 2010: 7). In the wake of J-horror, Korean films became late-night favorites at festivals, especially titles such as *The Isle* and *Oldboy*. An important factor in this development was the attempt made by Korean festivals such as PiFan to connect to the network of European fantasy festivals.

Networks of Exchange: Otaku

Compared to Europe, North America's second wave receptions of Asian cult cinema were initially powered more by individual fans and the general dynamics of popular culture than by institutionalized networks of distribution (Brophy 2005: 1). The first attempts to chart Asian cult cinema were the reviews of Thomas Weisser in horror and trash cinema fanzines, and from 1991 on in the first fanzine dedicated to Asian cult cinema, *Asian Trash Cinema* – which later became *Asian Cult Cinema* (Weisser 1997: ix). Next to fanzines, prominent elements in this constellation were video retailers, specialty festivals, and fan conventions, especially for anime. The latter display the most visible form of cultism, particularly through what Susan Napier has called "anime nation's con culture," and in elaborate "cosplaying" (anime-themed costume parties) (Napier 2007: 149–167; Winge 2006). Universities and colleges too started paying attention to Asian cinema outside the canon (Bordwell 2000: x). Near the end of the 1990s, internet forums allowed for even more pronounced distinctions, especially between first-hand and second-hand, and pre-remake and post-remake fandom. As Matt Hills (2005: 166) notes, "individualized and psychologized notions" of cult fandom prevailed in these networks, especially through the manufacturing of distinctions between fans that had "discovered" Asian cults a while ago, and newcomers.

Perhaps the best exemplar of this development is the phenomenon of the "otaku." Originally an honorific pronoun and a word for "another's house," the term otaku commonly stands for "people who become particularly loyal fans of a subculture" (Newitz 1995: 4). Popularized by Akio Nakamori, and later also by Hiroki Azuma, the term was mostly used for predominantly Japanese male fans of video games, sci-fi, comic books, anime, and "idols" (heavily promoted Japanese pop stars). It initially carried a highly negative connotation, and like orientalism it also carries feminine associations of domesticity, passivism, ornamentalism, and shyness (Barral 1999). To these are added charac-

teristics of sexual immaturity and a "detachment from reality that prevents the otaku from participating in society and forming authentic relationships" (Bolton 2005: 70). It is tempting to see in this initial labeling of the otaku a reproduction of orientalism that not only denies representations their right of meaning outside the Western, male gaze (much like Madame Butterfly), but also reduces the Eastern male to a powerless victim of a system of representation (cinema, media) over which only Westerners could command power.

Recent research into otaku fandom of newer generations and outside Asia, however, complicates this picture. Often, otaku are savvier than these cursory descriptions suggest. They reach a "higher perspective" in which their knowledge of mediation becomes a powerful tool in performing the delineation between the "real" and the "fictional." Christopher Bolton (2005: 66–76) adds to this the observation that there are numerous exceptions to the strict gender-division sketched above, especially in anime horror's "phallic girls." These characters function simultaneously as a confirmation of the male gaze and as a challenge to it – defying grounding in cultural reality through their highly fictional mechanical bodies. Nor did the term otaku remain limited to the East. The term also found wide application in North America, and in Russia, where it shed some of its negative connotations and became synonymous with cult fandom of anime (Napier 2007). As Annalee Newitz (1995) points out, this cross-cultural transfer of fandom gradually changed its feminine connotations (however ambiguous these often are) into associations of miscegenation, especially when the fandom involved the fantasy-horror genre, or "mecha." Newitz singles out *Tetsuo, Man of Iron* as one of several cult films from Asia that achieved its cult status in part because of how it challenged its fans to consider multiculturalism, racial mixing and identity construction. *Tetsuo* tells the story of an otaku whose body is gradually converted into a machine. *Tetsuo* is often regarded as a meditation on cyberpunk and a post-industrial crisis of identity (Conrich 2005). Newitz argues that *Tetsuo* in fact addresses the question of what it means to one's own cultural identity to access, digest, and celebrate foreign cultural products in a cultist manner. As Newitz notes, American fans might "enjoy Japanese anime precisely because it criticizes American culture" but they might equally see it as a "respite from political correctness" in which America is blamed (quoted in Mathijs and Mendik 2008a: 316).

Discussions of transnational and cross-cultural otaku fandom and comparisons with Western fandom have had the effect that they pulled this form of fandom out of a frame of reference that saw it as uniquely childish, and that, by extension, associated at least part of that childishness with the fact that the form of fandom is essentially non-Western. Instead they have presented otaku as "active," "empowered," in other words as performers of their fandom – similar to the kinds of performances we have discussed in previous chapters. An unfortunate consequence of this has been a tendency to homogeneously blend both otaku fandom and Western fandom, a tendency whereby cultural distinctions that do matter get swept aside in an effort to see all fans equally empowered by a "shared technological culture." According to Hills (2002b), it has meant that debates over how otaku fandom shares characteristics with Western cultism have shed one form of infantilization (fans are undeveloped and immature as human beings) in favor of another (as mere performers, fans are undeveloped in their critical awareness of transcultural media technology). According to Hills, this problem can be solved by regarding otaku fandom as a form of transcultural homology to Western cult fandom (*not* homogeneity) that does not erase context-specific differences in its eagerness to demonstrate similarities in performativity and achieve equality between kinds of recognition for cult fans. This homology could even, suggests Hills, form the basis of cross-cultural forms of solidarity between cult fans, a form of "fan internationalism" (2002b: 6). While Hills is careful not to push this analogy too far, it is nevertheless through the solidarity that the homology between otaku and Western fanboys escapes from the threat of "techno-orientalism."

In its straddling of various degrees of fandom and professionalism, especially with regard to series in which otaku have actively participated (such as *Neon Genesis Evangelion* or *Otaku No Video*), the entire concept of the otaku becomes, according to Thomas Lamarre, "an evolution in human perception" (2009: 144), a new kind of connoisseurship, literacy or competency in reading images that is perhaps the closest possible description of what can be called a "cultist view" of cinema. It refuses to distinguish between center and margin of the frame, between storyline and setting, between foreground and background, between trivia and narrative, instead "demanding an attention to production details as so much 'data' [that it] has the effect of flattening the image into a distributive field of elements" (Lamarre 2009: 145). According to Lamarre (and he cites otaku animator Toshio Okada), otaku perception includes "isolating perceptual elements . . ., dehierarchizing layers, and flattening the production hierarchies" (2009: 149). If nothing else, the otaku intervention in fandom has heightened the attention of fans as "interactors whose pursuit . . . make him or her a cooperator in production and promotion" (2009: 153).

Since the beginning of the twenty-first century, the reception of Asian cult cinema has exploded. Joan Hawkins has described this as part of the "mainstreaming of exploitation," a development that is particularly visible with Asian cult cinema. Tellingly, the example she uses is Park Chan Wook (*Sympathy for Mr. Vengeance*, *Oldboy*), as she quotes reviewers' struggles to accept that "movies that were once relegated to midnight screenings at festivals – and, in an earlier age, grindhouses like those that once enlivened Times Square are now part of the main event" (Hawkins 2010: 126). As a result of this mainstreaming virtually each region has developed its specialty festival and most of them have become fairly well integrated into the international circuit. Specialist online and mail-order retailers, and distributors such as Media Blasters, Section 23 Films, Bandai Entertainment, and Animeigo, which continue to supply niches of the Asian cult cinema market, find themselves in competition with major distributors and mass-market retailers.[1] The success of J-horror and other Asian cult films released theatrically have ensured this market's sustained visibility.

In sum, the cross-cultural reception of Asian cult cinema appears to have moved away from the stigma of orientalism, and away from a singularly negative connotation of the term otaku, towards an understanding of transnational cult receptions as informed by instances of performativity – fandom across borders performed by fans from various cultures embracing their fandom as an international sign of solidarity. But as the fandom grows, so does the need for internal distinction. This need is acutely visible in increases in critical commentary that addresses particular constituencies. And as such distinctions are carved out complications of cult receptions arise, especially with regard to receptions that comment on references to intercultural and transnational traffic that many of the films themselves make. In order to sketch some of these complications the remainder of this chapter will outline the specifics of two regions that have supplied and propelled much of Asian cult cinema: Hong Kong and Japan.

Hong Kong Cult Cinema

Asian cult cinema's first highpoint in the 1970s developed around martial arts movies, or *wuxia*, coming from Hong Kong (Hunt 2003). The galvanizing moment of this cultism is the worldwide craze of Kung Fu and the cult of martial arts actor Bruce Lee. As Paul Bowman (2010: 8) argues, the films of Bruce Lee, and indeed the figure of Lee himself, present themselves as a series of clichés of what film should not be: "trivial and trivializing, violent, masculinist, orientalist stereotype; a mythologized commodification of alterity packaged for a fetishistic Western gaze; the mythological reduction of ethnicity into posters, t-shirts, nerds' film collections." At the same time, of course, Bowman explains, Lee is a challenge to all of those images. Above all, he provides an opportunity for viewers to elaborate endlessly on the clashes and mixes these images offer, a play with symbols that denies there is one single "body of knowledge" that can be gained from the international transfer of imagery but that nevertheless located Bruce Lee, not as part of this or that culture, but as a "shifting center of enduring intercultural and cross-ethnic representation" (Bowman 2010: 229).

To begin with, there is the idea of Kung Fu. *Fist of Fury* and *Enter the Dragon* Westernized Kung Fu before it was orientalized: they added realism to the choreography of fights by showcasing Lee's considerable athletic talent and his iconoclastic philosophy of fighting (Jeet Kune Do, "the way of the intercepting fist"), and by introducing exotic weapons (such as nunchakos or iron claws) and detailed ornamental props (Figure 11.1). They updated the storylines to

Figure 11.1 Bruce Lee in *Enter the Dragon*, with nunchakos, at the center of enduring intercultural and cross-ethnic representation. Image courtesy of Royal Film Archive of Belgium.

contemporary, postcolonial times – even adding some references that put Lee in opposition to former colonizers, such as when he kicks a sign that says "no dogs or Chinese allowed" in *Fist of Fury*. In *Enter the Dragon* this sentiment had been tempered and changed into an international setting – a setting that fitted the transnational profile of Lee (of mixed American and Hong Kong upbringing) while offering nods to contemporary forms of exploitation cinema. The hype that had started developing around Lee in Asia was complicated by the limited availability of his films for Western audiences – as well as the fact that they were known under a range of different titles, some confusingly close to each other. Lee suddenly died, in 1973, just before *Enter the Dragon* was put on worldwide release. Within a matter of months, film fans went Bruce Lee-crazy. But Lee was not really a star *until* he died. As Eleftheriotis and Needham (2006: 407) put it:

> the legendary status that Bruce Lee enjoys has, at least partly, been facilitated by the impossibility for European and American audiences of engaging with him as a star at any level that can go, even slightly, beyond mythical opacity. ... Bruce Lee entered the consciousness of international film audiences not as a "real" actor and star but as a "legend".

It was the first time a non-Western actor from a non-Western film industry received such a cult following. The difficulties producers, distributors, and audiences had in sketching a framework for the reception of a non-Western local martial arts star are indicative of the volatility of cult stardom (see Teo 1997; Hunt 2000; Bowman 2010).

The appeal of Bruce Lee catapulted the cult reputation of numerous Hong Kong films. *A Touch of Zen*, which predated Lee's films, but which did not receive visibility in the West until 1975, gained a cult following for its elaborate representations of fighting techniques and acrobatics, high doses of Jacobean violence of vengeance and humiliation, and inferences to Buddhist philosophies of self-defence, and because of that it stood as a firm counterpoint to contemporary Western flirts with Eastern mysticism. Because of its combination of spectacle and introspection, *A Touch of Zen* became as much of a template for cult cinema from Hong Kong as Bruce Lee (Teo 2007). Other post-Lee cult wuxia included *The 36th Chamber of Shaolin*, and – increasingly – pastiches such as *The Legend of the Seven Golden Vampires*, *Five Deadly Venoms*, and the posthumously produced Lee film *Game of Death* (in which he dons his black and yellow track suit). David Bordwell (2000) has observed that wuxia often evolve in cycles, in which periods of hyperbole are followed by periods of realism. The hyperbolic cycles were the ones that particularly drew cult receptions. After the hyperbole of the post-Lee pastiches, a period of realism arrived. That period of realism, in turn, spawned an even more hyperbolic wave of films in the latter half of the 1980s that again opened up Hong Kong cinema to international fandom. One part of this wave consisted of ghost stories and swordplay fantasy. Of these, a few films such as *Chinese Ghost Story* achieved cult status – especially through the ways they connected, at least in the eyes of their fans, mainland China's mythology to contemporary anxieties about the Western world and to Hong Kong's specific anxieties about the handover to China.

The most visible cult following went to a series of crime thrillers set in urban, modern Hong Kong, that pitched highly skilled, ruthless professionals such as hitmen, triad gang members, cops, and bodyguards against each other while simultaneously stressing their emotional bonds. Through close combat and choreographed fights, these films maintained the attractions of martial arts films, but they replaced tools with guns (kung-fu thus became gun-fu). Because of their high

level of visceral violence, their often melodramatic and tragic storylines, and the prevalent theme of male bonding these films received the nickname "heroic bloodshed." The most noticeable of these films is *The Killer*. A collaboration between two of the most prolific creative talents of the Hong Kong film industry at the time (director John Woo and producer Tsui Hark), and the breakthrough performance of new star Chow Yun-Fat, *The Killer* appealed to cultist audiences because of its storyline of failed redemption, its plentitude of gun battles, and its intertextuality, hyperbolic religious metaphors (especially referring to catholic martyrdom), and homoerotic overtones. It took *The Killer* some time to reach international audiences, but it became the ultimate heroic bloodshed cult film. It is now invariably described as the Hong Kong film with the most "secure cult status" around the globe (Sandell 1996; An 2001; Hall 2009). In its wake, action films such as *Hard Boiled*, and dystopic wuxia such as *Ashes of Time* also became cults.

In terms of their international reception, heroic bloodshed and wuxia also benefited, ironically, from their association with a late 1980s Hong Kong rating system that saw them lumped together with horror films and softcore sex in a "Category III." Julian Stringer (1999) describes Category III as the "repressed underside of more respectable cultural forms." During much of the 1990s, almost 40% of released films in Hong Kong were labeled Category III: "*Sex and Zen III* is right there on the same shelf as Jackie Chan's *Mr. Nice Guy*" (Davis and Yu 2001: 13). In the eyes of fans, video store patrons, and audiences-at-large this created the impression that all these films were connected through "classifications of style (exploitation/ cult film, art cinema, adult film) or genre (horror, gangster, martial arts)" (Davis and Yu 2001: 12). As a result, films with a Category III rating temporarily gave all of Hong Kong cinema a transgressive reputation, which in the context of the anxiety of the run-up to the region's reintegration to the nation of China, made Hong Kong cinema extremely ambiguous: "Category III is marked out as 'other,' not suitable for children; and yet, it is not stigmatized, segregated, or shunned by mainstream audiences. [I]ts transgressive, offensive qualities mark it as a 'come-on' and serve to integrate it into the market." (Davis and Yu 2001: 14). As several scholars note, this transgression often took on the form of farce (Williams 2005). In short, Category III helped extend the international cult appeal of heroic blood-shed and wuxia films, and it enabled similar receptions for campy softcore detective films such as *Naked Killer*. Much of the cult dynamism surrounding the appeal of wuxia and heroic bloodshed films dissipated after Hong Kong's return to China.

Some elements were incorporated into the main-stream (such as Zhang Yimou's films), and some were pushed off the global audience's radar.

Anime and J-Horror

From the 1990s on, a strong cultism developed around two specific forms of Japanese cinema, anime and J-horror. Celebrated at niche festivals and through a vibrant video and DVD market, but in the margin of Japan's and the world's mainstream cinema, anime and J-horror have developed some of the most ardent fan followings of cinema of the last few decades. At the core of this cultism are an admiration for the visual flam-boyance yet nihilistic morality of these two formats, and a fascination for their explorations of the themes of urban alienation and advanced electronic technology.

As a term, anime refers to Japanese animation cinema, usually adaptations of manga, comic books. The breakthrough of anime cultism lies in the 1980s, though its origins stretch back as far as the 1960s. In the 1980s, series and films such as *Akira*, *Nausicaa of the Valley of the Wind*, and *Bubblegum Crisis* attracted cult followings, which in the 1990s, as the formats and subgenres expanded, became more prominent and visible. The cult of anime consists of two partly over-lapping areas: naive and mystical anime, and horror and science fiction anime, or *mecha*. The first category is often regarded as the least cultist, because it falls outside narrow understandings of cult audiences. Yet the nostalgia with which baby-boomer audiences remem-ber 1960s films and series such as *Astro Boy* or *Magic Boy*, or the fondness with which 1980s youths recall the colored *Astro Boy*, the baby unicorn *Unico*, and *My Neighbor Totoro*, are strong indications of this area's ongoing cultist appeal (Brophy 2005: 36–37). As part of *kawaii* (or the cult of "cutification"), these products have established cross-generational fandom. Through

series such as *Kimba, the White Lion* and the films of Hayao Miyazaki and Studio Ghibli (*Princess Mononoke*) this area of anime cultism has also been inscribed with a strong sense of karmic, environmental, and ecological awareness (Brophy 2005: 134–135; Cubitt 2005). In essence, it creates a form of "soft" or even "new age" global cultism. Rayna Denison (2006, 2008) argues this appeal needs to be seen in the context of the global marketing and presence of Miyazaki's films. Napier's study of Miyazaki online-fandom uncovers this cult-ism as ambiguous in the meanings its ascribes to the films, yet unified in its conviction that it presents a "non-Western worldview in which good does not always triumph over evil and the only appropriate response is to continue to look at the world 'with eyes unclouded'" (Napier 2006: 62).

Mecha has a more edgy cultist reputation, especially because its fandom demographic invites comparisons with that of other cults, such as horror and science fiction. The late 1980s are the breakthrough of mecha. Films such as *Akira*, *Tetsuo*, and the hugely contro-versial *Legend of the Overfiend* (Buruma 1995), received cult followings for their depictions of post-apocalyptic, macabre, highly technologized urban story-worlds in which heavily armed androids or demons, assassins, and gangsters (often supported by sinister surveillance police) fight it out at the expense of teens caught up in the battles. It is not difficult to see the image of the confused and corrupted youth become an attractor for young otaku. But the elaborate presentations of hostile urban jungles in which gangs and crime abound, and in which storylines are allowed to become lost in nu-merous asides are equally attractive. During the 1990s, as female otaku became a more pronounced part of the cult of anime, mecha also began to upset the fairly strict gender-divided market. According to this divide, shojo-anime, such as *Sailor Moon*, are directed at girls and presented throbbing emotions channeled through kinetic and dynamic visuals and an emphasis on altru-ism and attractiveness (Brophy 2005: 198–200). Shonen-anime, such as *Fullmetal Alchemist*, focus more on action, hybrid-humans and muscular athleticism, and address fanboys. The mixing of both is visible, first in "babes with guns" films, and subsequently expanded in the cult success *Ghost in the Shell*. In its represen-tation of a dystopian urban technopolis it leans heavily towards shonen-anime. But it retains elements of shojo-anime in the graceful, light-footed, free-floating fluidity of the female cyborg Kusanagi – who bases her identity on her relationship to the infinite ocean that surrounds her (Orbaugh 2002; Ruh 2004; Gresset 2009). Brophy (2005: 107) writes: "*Ghost in the Shell* freely mixes the karmic with the psychic with the robotic." Its fans across the world also cheer its lack of political correctness, and, like fans of science fiction and fantasy, they engage deeply in its story-world, enjoying an "estrangement from a world that sometimes can become a little too familiar" (Napier 2007: 190). Since the middle of the 1990s, series such as *Neon Genesis Evangelion*, *Final Fantasy*, or *Vampire Princess Miyu* have deepened anime cultism by establishing niches for epic, horror, and fantasy, and by applying story-worlds to numerous platforms and media (comic books, video games, television series, webcomics). In spite of this proliferation criticism accuses anime continuously of misrepresentations through its persistence of presenting women and girls as "in touch with intense, even magical, forces capable of overwhelming male-dominated reality" (quoted in Bolton 2005: 67).

The term J-horror entered cult parlance in the late 1990s, when a new generation of Japanese horror films began to forefront a mix of traditional horror elements, such as those of the *tokusatsu* (the special effects monster genre) and *yurei* (traditional ghost stories), with themes borrowed from the techno-existentialism of the anime, such as the placement of horror within an environment of economic crisis, or the view of monstrosity as a consequence of modernity. According to Ramie Tateishi (2003: 295), these films' inspired cult following is the result of a nostalgia for a cultural heritage that is entertained opposite an active destruction of that same heritage (so that it will not burden the present generation in its progress). *Ringu* is the most literal exploration of this ambiguous urge. It also opened up Western audiences for J-horror, and it introduced them to a series of similarly inspired films such as *Cure*, *Dark Water*, and *Ju-on: The Grudge*. Each of these films sees environments of modern technology (media, medical, or care-technology) trigger seemingly supernatural appearances, which its receivers are unable to process because of their disconnection from their cultural roots. Two key examples of this millennial "urban techno-alienation" are the satirical *Battle Royale* and *Suicide Club*. They present a generation of

disillusioned teens who blame their ancestral culture for their desensitization. Only through cult-like arrangements opposing this parent culture do these teens find meaning for their own existence – and often they don't at all. Because of their imagery of dying teens and claims of parental culpability, *Battle Royale* and *Suicide Club* became engulfed in controversy, stirred up through speculation and agitation (in the case of *Battle Royale* fueled by the role of Takeshi Kitano, a figure with a cult reputation of his own). It caused interventions in the national parliament, calls for bans by politicians and educators, and hotly debated festival screenings abroad (Macias 2001: 149–152; Crawford 2003: 305–307).

The flagbearer of the cult of J-horror is Takashi Miike. His reputation is that of a prolific provocateur or agitator. His high and varied output flaunts the routines and practices of the industry, and of traditional authorship (Mes 2004). The difficulty with Miike lies, moreover, in his bold style: hard-hitting, flamboyant, nihilist, and above all, "cool." This coolness ties Miike to the particular reception context of "cool Japan." Miike's stylistic bravura, claims Aaron Gerow (2009: 34–35), offers a veil of superficiality that cloaks a visceral politics of diversity. Miike first rose to international prominence with *Audition*, a grand-guignol art house horror film that forever connected him to J-horror. But Miike's films are not uniquely Japanese but rather transnational. In their liminal settings (in-between places such as rooftops, tracks, streets), Miike's protagonists also find themselves hovering in between hero and coward. Characters in *Dead or Alive* claim to be "like Japanese but not Japanese, like Chinese but not Chinese"; Ichi in *Ichi the Killer* is both super-hero and cry-baby.

According to Jay McRoy, Miike's films are an interrogation of a trend of films within J-horror that have received cult appeal through their depiction of "dove style violence," a form of violence in which "human beings coldly abuse one another with a detached cruelty reminiscent of 'certain species of bird' who, when 'a flock member is *different* or weaker ... peck at the weakest bird dispassionately until it's dead'" (McRoy 2008: 103[2]). McRoy sees Miike's *Ichi the Killer* as an example of a film that is a send-up of a core theme of J-horror, namely *ijime* (buylling). *Ichi the Killer* shows not just the impact of the bullying, but the fallout as well. It does so in such a hysterically hyper-moralistic over-the-top style (borrowing heavily from anime) that it defeats its purpose as a critique. The result, according to McRoy, is a representation of violence that is both painful and playful, and a reconsideration of the transgressive violence of desire that largely explains the film's huge cult reputation (2008: 132).

The boom of anime and J-horror brought with it attempts to extend its heritage into the past. Filmmakers such as Nobuo Nakagawa ("the Japanese Roger Corman") or Seijun Suzuki (*Branded to Kill*, "too much even for that hyperbole-drunk factory Nikkatsu") were eagerly picked up by cult distributors (Rayns 2009: 30–32; Atkinson 2009: 34). Around 2009, after a few key distributors went out of business and some festivals started to report audience fatigue, the general appeal of J-horror appeared to stagnate, and shrink to a smaller yet more devoted cult in the margins of the mainstream (Berra 2010).

Conclusion

The cult status of Kung Fu, anime and J-horror is largely undisputed. There are many other films from Asia, and from other regions of the world, where that is not the case. In general, this is because they are presented through a binary perspective: they are labeled cults either because they suddenly achieve niche popularity in certain regions (and are caught up in hypes), or because they remain forever obscure, in which case their cultness is one of invisibility instead of a niche following.

There is a danger with such a sharp-cut distinction. It relies too much on stable assumptions of what is mainstream and popular in transnational receptions, and what is at the margins. A good example of this is Bollywood, a term that originated as a tongue-in-cheek expression that describes Mumbai's Hindi-Urdu language cinema (Desai and Dudrah 2008: 1). But Bollywood is more than that. It has also become shorthand for a flamboyant style and a specific form of fandom of ethnically Indian fans for this type of film. As a dominant force in a vibrant market, Bollywood is the center of cinema, not the periphery. Still, its avid fandom, visible as much in box-office figures as in

rampant piracy, equips it with cult characteristics. Furthermore, as Rachel Dwyer (2005: 1) argues, the "use of melodrama and heightened emotion" and the "grandiloquent dialogues and the all-important songs" give the impression Bollywood's production values are close to those of Hollywood cult classics. Imperial in its origins, but increasingly referring to a globalized culture industry, the very word Bollywood begs a comparison – not only one that pitches Hollywood as a standard against the derivative that are all other forms of cinema, but also one that exists only in the tensions of intercultural communication it throws up.

These complications of distinction, popularity and periphery also govern the reception of *Sholay*. This film is simultaneously regarded as the "greatest Hindi film of all time" (Dwyer 2005: 218) and as a cult phenomenon that started as a box-office flop and worked its way into the hearts of fans over the course of a number of years (Dissanayake and Sahai 1992). Lalitha Gopalan testifies to the cult status it has since acquired: "fans of this cult film extensively quote Salim Khan and Javed Akthar's script back to the screen; rumours abound on the existent variations of the closing sequence; and [Amjad Khan] became one of the most popular stars" (Eleftheriotis and Needham 2006: 325). The cult reputation of *Sholay* has also affected the remake *Aag* (aka *Flames*), albeit adversely – it has gained it the unenviable reputation of one of the worst films ever.

There is no reason not to see *Sholay* as an example of cult cinema on a par with Western cult classics. If audiences and critics of cult cinema would accept the complications of their reception contexts the way they accept those of *Casablanca* and *The Lord of the Rings*, it probably would be. Yet when confronted with Bollywood, different conditions and strategies appear to apply, and one of the most stubborn of these is that for Asian films Western audiences in particular do not appreciate ambiguities of popularity the same way they appreciate them for other forms of cinema. To put it in the words of Hills – for Bollywood any homology is not yet accepted.

A similar attitude underpins cultists' worldwide appreciation of obscurity. Even when there is little evidence of continued fandom or subcultural appeal, Western critics and audiences are keen to identify instances of Asian cinema as cult. This is for instance the case with Philippines and Thai horror movies, and a score of exotic genre cinema from East Asia (Tombs 1997; Tumbocon Jr, 2003; Knee 2005). In these explorations the emphasis is not on the cult following of these films, but rather on the discovery, for Western audiences, of a form of cinema hitherto hidden. As such, these studies have both a pioneering and an orientalizing function: they make available new kinds of films to curious cinephiles and potential fans (thus enabling a cult following) while also framing these films as perennial "curiosities" – stripping them of any possibility to present themselves as "normal," even within their own cultural perspective, let alone on the global stage. Typically, for the perspective of obscurity individual titles of films matter less in such studies than groupings of them as "weird" and "exciting" – and in that refusal to individualize films lies of course another orientalizing element. It is a variation of orientalism that has come under some criticism (Espinosa 2009; Imanjaya 2009).

There are only few exceptions to the model that treats Asian cinema, and non-Western cinema in general as either obscure or popular but culturally over-specific for global cult audiences. Such exceptions have in common that the films and their receptions address the West (and its values) reflexively – the same way the term otaku, or Hong Kong's cinema, were said to address the West, namely through a combination of appropriation and alienation. Examples of such exceptions are *Lady Terminator*, an Indonesian horror critique of Western modernity's influence on traditional Indonesian culture, with a possessed female killer castrating men who seduce young Indonesian girls (Gladwin 2003: 227–228), and *Ong-bak*, a Thai martial arts film that "challenges the Hong Kong action model" (Morris, Siu Leung Li, and Chan 2005: 2–3). These films' cult status is partly the result of the stand they take against Western or globalized business practices, in particular issues of cultural ownership, copyright, and exotic tourism. In offering resistance against such practices, these films have occupied a rebellious position among viewers, who feel they offer an exit out of suffocating cultural routines.

Notes

1. We owe gratitude to Nathen Clerici for his expert advice on these recent developments concerning Asian cult, and we regret that we are not able to expand on the phenomenon of the cult appeal of the "kogal" (the "blue sailor suit girls") and the "take-it-easy" attitude; we refer to the essays of Hiroki Azuma for further reading on this.
2. The in-quotes are from Thomas Weisser and Yuko Mihara's *Japanese Cinema Encyclopedia.*

12

Religion and Utopia

The previous chapters have emphasized how cult cinema is marked by deep alignments between fans and films, but also by performances of such alignments. In this chapter we would like to extend our exploration of these issues through a link with the religious meaning of the term. We touched upon the religious origin of the term "cult" in our introduction. Here, we will look more closely at areas where discourses on cinema cultism and religious cultism collide in an attempt to determine if any of the seriousness (and indeed graveness) with which religious cultism is associated is also found in film cultism, or if frivolity has replaced it altogether. Throughout, our focus will be on films depicting religion and religious cults from a minority position – in the margins or in opposition of institutionalized religion.

Discourses on Cultism and Religion

For William Sims Bainbridge and Rodney Stark (2003: 60), religions are "social enterprises whose primary purpose is to create, maintain, and exchange supernaturally based general compensators [sets of beliefs and prescriptions for action that substitute for the immediate achievement of the desired award]." By comparison, cults are "social enterprises primarily engaged in the production and exchange of novel and exotic compensators." This means that not all cults are religions, and that they often do not offer general compensators – they promise more immediate rewards (epiphanies or healing). When cults that refer to magic evolve towards more general compensators (such as

eternal life, or otherworldly benefits) they become "cult movements," which Bainbridge and Stark (2003) define as: "social enterprises primarily engaged in the production and exchange of novel and exotic general compensators based on supernatural assumptions."

The type of cult that comes closest to cinema cultism falls under what Marvin Harris (1987: 268) calls "communal cults." Bainbridge and Stark call it the "subculture-evolution model of cult innovation." They are either organized around rites of passage or rites of solidarity. The model assumes that cults can emerge without authoritative leaders, as expressions of developments and consolidations of novel cultures often inspired by essentially accidental factors (2003: 67). As an example, Bainbridge and Stark give the subculture of juvenile delinquency that caused so much upheaval in the 1950s. This example invites a link between ways in which lower-class backgrounds, forms of deviance, and religious cultism are viewed by society. We will come back to this link further on.

Matt Hills (2002a: 117) has warned that comparisons between the kind of discourses surrounding film cults and religious cults are "absurdly insensitive to cultural and historical contexts." Drawing upon work of Emile Durkheim, Peter Berger, and Thomas Luckmann, Hills nevertheless outlines a number of similarities and connections between developments in cult discourse from the perspective of studies of religion, and discourses on cult in media and film studies. For Hills, there are three main components to any comparison between cult cinema and religious cultism. The first is their marginalization: both religious cultism and film cultism seem to present an "embarrassment" to

Cult Cinema: An Introduction. Ernest Mathijs and Jamie Sexton.
© 2011 Ernest Mathijs and Jamie Sexton. Published 2011 by Blackwell Publishing Ltd.

enlightened culture (2002a: 119). They exist in the margins of what is deemed acceptable in society. The second is what Hills calls the "practical unconsciousness" of the cultist: "the things that fans do not know . . . but which nevertheless still allow them to 'go on' in their subcultural and subjective activities" (2002a: 123). One function of this practical unconsciousness is the ability of otherwise rational people to engage in "discursive mantras" and to submit to the surrendering of "proof" in favor of an affective communal faith that brings about a "relaxation of rationalizations and justifications which fans may otherwise be called upon to produce" (2002a: 122). Hills sees this component as important in disabling the potentially awkward "why on earth are you a fan of this?" question. The third component is the increased individualization of cult beliefs, a development observed both in religious cultism and in film cultism.

There is little or no dispute over the first component: every description of cinema that utilizes its connection to religion and religious cults stresses that it is a position in the margin of cultures. At their most generous such descriptions describe cults as "mini-cultures" and "protocivilizations." Often they are less generous. There is also little disagreement with regard to the third component. It is extremely tempting to see the evolution to increased individualization in religiosity and religious/cult experiences in parallel with the rise of attention for cult movies – especially the midnight movie. In fact, one could position cult cinema's history as an indication of an evolution towards individualist religiosity. It is an evolution neatly captured in what Stark and Bainbridge (1985) have called a shift from "cult movements" to "client cults" and "audience cults," the former being more strictly organized and the latter more loosely based on the consumer activity of participants who "often do not gather physically but consume cult doctrines entirely through magazines, books, newspapers, radio, and television" (1985: 26). To these media Douglas Cowan and David Bromley (2008: 89–90) add the internet; and we could add film, cult films to be specific. We will encounter examples of both the first and third component in the historical instances of the collision between religious cultism and film cultism further on in this chapter.

But there is some debate around the second component, because by concentrating on how cultists avoid being asked about the essence of their cultism, Hills himself avoids addressing the substance of the cult experience: what *kind of experience* exactly are cult audiences after that could possibly be in line with religious cultism? Overall, critics and scholars of cult cinema are vague about this component. The quasi-religious characteristics of late night screenings frequented by repeat viewers looking for epiphanies and "whiffs of immortality" are not lost on Hoberman and Rosenbaum (1991: 16) when they describe midnight movies, but they resist going into too much detail: "Emile Durkeim's description of the positive cult is a virtual prediction of the sort of behavior observable any weekend night", they write. Danny Peary (1981: xiii) refers to some form of religiosity when he writes that "cultists believe they are among the blessed few who have discovered something in particular films that the average moviegoer and critic have missed", but he fails to specify what that "something" is. In "Confessions of a Cultist," Andrew Sarris (1970: 13) describes his initiation into New York's film cult scene as one that was "pure" because it was "poor" – an apt summary of the marginalized position of cults across history. Sarris stresses how much his position was akin to that of religious cultists: "I realized that the quasi-religious connotation of the term was somewhat justified for those of us who loved movies *beyond all reason*" (our italics). One of the reasons for this vagueness is that it portrays the film cultist as a naive, poor soul, unable to marshal the abilities to deal with films in an equally sophisticated way as middlebrow audiences, someone hopelessly lost, over-invested in aimless searches for deep answers.

David Lavery (1991: 187–199), offers one attempt to look beyond the "discursive mantra" and answer the "why are you a fan of this?" question. In Lavery's argument, the role of the discursive mantra is played by "cool" cynicism, and by semiotics and intertextuality (the idea that films are chains of signs, often towards themselves). For Lavery, such constructions stand in the way of what cult cinema and its audiences really want, namely glimpses of "cosmic meaning," the kind of feeling of collective belonging that the individualization, commodification and enculturation of belief-systems is said to have pushed out of people's everyday reach. Lavery observes such an underlying desire in films such as *The Man Who Fell to Earth, Repo Man,*

Liquid Sky, and *Man Facing Southeast*. If one tracks the tropes and motives of such cult movies, Lavery argues, they share a common ground with early Christian Gnosticism, a religious philosophy stemming from ancient heresies that stress an escape from this world through the acquisition of esoteric knowledge (Lavery 1991: 193–194). Gnosticism has multiple incarnations. Lavery focuses on a variation that relies on the writings of Hans Jonas (who stresses the transcendental conception of salvation from a world that is essentially one big accident), Jacques Lacarrière (who emphasizes that Gnostics believe themselves to be "autochthons of another world"), and A.O. Lovejoy (who stresses "otherworldliness").

Lavery's argument is specific and speculative, but it is not unique. There is common ground between a view of cult cinema as rephrasing age-old esoteric, philosophical and spiritual questions, and one that stresses its marginalization in society, and it is caught up in a larger cultural development of the commodification, individualization, and secularization of religions and religious cults. In order to sketch this common ground we will outline a few concepts from the history of religion and cult movements. We will frame the characteristics of these moments in function of the semi-religious inspiration cinema cultism draws upon – as points of comparison but also as proxy explanations for the investments cultists make.

The Cult of Dionysus: Wasted Time and the Orgy

Our first point of interest is the cult of Dionysus, probably the most often-used metaphor for critics attempting to illustrate film cults and its affiliated social experiences through a link with the history of culture and religion. The cult of Dionysus is only one of many cults that qualify as exemplar. John Mikalson (2010: 53–65) lists seven Western cults that address the origin of culture with regard to the sacred, the divine, and that stress mystic rituals. There are numerous more from outside the West. However, because of its prominent place in the history of visceral, wild, and physical cultism and because of its permanent marginalized position in relation to legitimate cultural systems, this chapter uses the cult of Dionysus as a model.

The original function of cults was to offer people an encounter with the foundations of life untied to rules of everyday governance. The encounter was supposed to obliterate enculturation in an effort to "return" to or "elevate" into a "direct understanding." The tradition goes back to the pre-religious ways of worshipping, and especially to the tenth century BC cult of Dionysus in Near Asia. According to local lore, Dionysus was a demon who, suffering from holy madness, hid in the forest hills, where he lost himself in delirious chases in an attempt to become one with nature *as a whole*. Followers of the cult would gather at night in the woods, and engage in wild orgies, with music rousing them into dances, trances, and sex, until their hunger for a literal union with all of life would lead them to sacrifice – originally a random human, later a carefully selected animal like a goat or bull (Otto 1965; Kerényi 1976; Burkert 1987; Mikalson 2010). The ecstatic communion of the sacrifice and the devouring of its flesh would transfer divine powers to the worshipper, and would give the deepest possible pleasure of feeling united with all forms of existence (feeling *wide awake* and *alive*). In short, the Dionysian cult offered communities a way to grasp, through tacit, physical experience, the terrifying yet wonderful nature of life in all its forms (beginning and end, night and day, season after season), worship and appease the forces that control it (storms, fearsome animals, vast landscapes), make bearable through commemoration the many traumatic and horrific events that would threaten them, and celebrate the very fact they are alive, and life itself.

Centuries after its original run, the Dionysus cult has remained influential as a metaphor for a worldview in which the celebration of cosmic meaning is linked to everyday life, and not alienated from it and in which the cultic experience was essential to a full life, not a marginal addendum. One example comes from Harvey Cox (1969), who uses the Dionysian festival and the medieval festival of the Feast of Fools as a model to explore the potential of the cultic experience (and its connection with lower-class populations, which he stresses) to address core values of humanity without conforming to hegemonic systems. For Cox, the concepts of festivity and fantasy, which he sees very much in the activist and eschatological sense of Antonin Artaud (who is discussed at length), offer an alternative model through which the cultic experience (rituals, dance, comedy, drunkenness, radicalism) can act as an agent of social change in everyday life. Another example, in line with Cox's aims to offer alternatives to individualization and commodification, is Michel Maffesoli (whose work we detailed in Chapter 1). For Maffesoli, the figure of Dionysus is a model for the celebration of everyday life because its modes of activity ignore "productivity," "efficiency," and "purposefulness." This conceptualization sees Dionysus as a core element of phenomenal experience – of cult but equally of life as a whole. For Maffesoli, what society and economy call a "waste" is exactly what a Dionysian model cherishes.

Two key aspects of the metaphor of Dionysus resonate with the kind of experience film cultism is said to include, namely the experience of time ungoverned and the visceral experience of sexual energy. For the first, the convenient shorthand is that of "wasting time," for the second it is the "orgy." Both are commonly regarded as superfluous, frivolous, and unproductive forms of conduct, and that is exactly why they resonate with cultism. The aspect of wasted time reflects on the unwillingness of cultism to slot itself into a conduct of time as prescribed by society. Instead, the Dionysian experience is essentially presented as one in which one loses oneself and in which time, as a tool that measures experiences, becomes useless. Philosophical studies of the governance of time from a variety of approaches, such as Henri Bergson (Totaro 2001), Stephen Kern (1983), Eric Alliez (1996), or John Zerzan (1994) often share a distinction between "proper" uses of time and "resistant" uses of time. The Dionysian experience, like the cult cinema experience, is seen as resistant. Mathijs (2010a) uses this parallel to argue that: "one main implication of all the modes, tools and instances of media cultism, and indeed the purpose of the epiphanies cults chase, is the subversion of a steady progression of time." Among the examples Mathijs mentions are the numerous instances of "ruptured time" in cult films (*Donnie Darko*, *The Rocky Horror Picture Show*, *It's a Wonderful Life*, etc.) as well as cult receptions' improper uses of time – watching films repeatedly, ritually, at midnight, outside of the proper time frames. To those can be added aspects of nostalgia, and of re-imagining repeat viewings as if experienced "for the very first time."

The aspect of the orgy as a contentious yet core component of cult cinema and cult receptions, is

something we have alluded to a few times in Chapter 9 and 10, where we discussed within the framework of the challenging of taboos and the performativity of non-normative sexuality. The specific aspect of the Dionysian orgy in itself has been the subject of much philosophical debate. For Georges Bataille (Botting and Wilson 1997), violent eroticism is the full acknowledgement of life into death. It is primarily lustful, uninhibited, and exuberant, and only remotely concerned with procreation. It is forceful and violent in that it transgresses borders. For Friedrich Nietzsche (1968) too, the Dionysus cult stressed a vital connection between violence and sexuality that goes to the core of being alive, being human. For Leopold Flam (1973) and Hubert Dethier (1994–2002), who studied centuries of heresy and heterodoxy, the Dionysus cult, and indeed all cults, primarily concern the carnal solidarity between humans as the ultimate way to find solace and belonging. The sexual orgy is the main method towards this ever-fleeting moment of utmost satisfaction.

With regard to cult films, the references to sex and violence are often more tempered. Yet, in addition to several of the films mentioned in Chapters 9 and 10, they inform discussions of avant-garde cinema as cultist (especially *Flaming Creatures*), and they also feature heavily in debates of the cultism surrounding films such as *Häxan* and *Un Chien Andalou*. The visceral component of cultist viewing also informs a number of reception studies. Using a phenomenological perspective, Vivian Sobchack (2004) has made reference to "sensuous experiences" and "carnal modalities" to describe viewers' embodied reactions to representations of, among others, sex, violence, and death. Among the examples she uses are *Crash* and *La jetée*, both of which have received cult receptions. Sue Turnbull (2007: 181–189) analyzes cultist viewers of *The Lord of the Rings* who insist on "descriptions of affect registered in and through the body" that go as far as to count the physical "experience" of the film as the most important aspect of it, establishing what Turnbull calls a "felt connection."

The metaphor of the Dionysian orgy has even influenced some professional training. With regard to the link between film and audience, for instance, Artaud often blamed Aristotle's notion of catharsis, and other concepts of drama for that matter, for replacing audience involvement with passivity, for exchanging performance with observation (Bermel 1977: 34). Known as the actor in *The Passion of Joan of Arc*, but most notably famed as a theater theorist, Artaud called for a "cruelty" that would directly affect, and alter, the state of the audience, and through rituals would eventually obliterate the border between performance and audience. Cinema in its raw state, wrote Artaud, "emits something of the atmosphere of trance conducive to certain revelations." It is "really the real in its entirety" (Artaud 1928, in Hammond 2000: 103–104). In the 1960s, Fernando Arrabal, Peter Brook, Jerzy Grotowski, and Joseph Beuys launched similar proposals (Auslander 1997: 13–27). They drew a lot of criticism from acting coaches. Lee Strasberg called their wish to "return to some mystical womb" laudable, but the impact on the audience to which he was witness "disappointing" (Strasberg 1987: 178–182). One can read into Strassberg's comment the view that the religious conviction and ritualistic repetition that is necessary to arrive at the state of epiphany and gasp should really only survive as a "method," one that "softens" the suddenness of the experience, and that clearly separates practitioners from audiences – a method to make cult into culture.

Utopianism

The second concept we would like to isolate is utopianism. We would like to follow a largely historical argument to sketch the intersections between cult cinema and utopian thought. As the Dionysus cult spread across the Mediterranean area, its visceral and radical elements were exchanged for more moderate routines in a Hellenistic version of the cult that treated the state of exceptional experience as an embellishment of, or even inconvenience to, everyday life. In the variation ascribed to Orpheus, there was no longer an organic union through sex or slaughter, nor an abandonment of time, but rather artfulness and asceticism were proposed as means to achieve the same results. Of the Hellenistic cult of Dionysus, Robert Turcan (1996: 296) writes:

> the Dionysian mysteries preserved some features of the ancient orgy. Their liturgy incorporated the gestural,

vestmental, emblematic, symposiac, even omophagic appearances of classic Maenadism: dances, rhythmic swaying of the body, and prophecies, drunkenness and music, garments of animal skins, the brandishing of staffs wreathed in ivy.

But he also adds that the symbolic ritualism was a few steps removed from the actual, original orgies. By the time of Socrates and Plato, most of the legacy of the Dionysian cult had been sublimated into systems of representation (theater), belief (religion) and knowledge (philosophy, history).

This change caused a shift in emphasis. Emile Durkheim (1915/1995) for instance, distinguishes between cults on the basis of their rituals: "negative" cults were based on rituals of prohibition (such as exclusion or asceticism), and positive cults were based on rituals of exhibition (such as sacrificing or mourning). The ancient Dionysus cult was very much an example of the latter; the Hellenist cult of Dionysus, the moderate cult of Orpheus, and many of the organized religions, were part of the former. From the moment the original Dionysus cult was overtaken by newer, negative ones (who inevitably isolated themselves), and by efforts to build large monolithic cultural worldviews, cults ended up in the periphery of culture, persecuted and sidelined, and the positive connotations of cultism (experiencing all of existence, commemorating the union with nature) were lost. The term "cult" became equal to "outsider" – outside the normal circuit of culture and outside of modern life, unable to keep up with it.

This outsider status facilitates links between cultism and utopian thinking, usually via references to specific movements. Scholarship on cinema cultism occasionally refers to movements such as Sufism, Taoism, Catharism, Paganism, and Manichaeism to express the position of philosophical marginality associated with cultism, as well as more revolutionary movements such as the Taborites, or folkloric or erotic pantheism. These references often appear in relation to *El Topo* – a film that seems to attract such discussions. Through these references some other components of cultism emerge, in particular the class-background and utopianism at work in cultism. Lavery's reference to Christian Gnosticism is one example of this. Lavery is interested less in the religious elements of the

Gnosticism and more in its socio-economic make-up because this paints a more accurate picture of the film cultist, as someone at odds with the mainstream in an ideological sense *and* within a socio-economic framework. It is in this sense that we need to understand Lavery's (1991: 194) reference to the work of Karl Marx.

Let us look at one example of the connection between cultism, class and utopia more closely. In their analysis of the reception of *Judge Dredd*, Martin Barker and Kate Brooks (1997: 289–291) are discussing the class backgrounds of fan-boys of the special effects in *Dredd*, when they use the work of sociologist Karl Mannheim on the cultist utopianism of the sixteenth-century Anabaptists and of "orgiastic chiliasm" as a point of reference. In *Ideology and Utopia* (1936) Mannheim distinguishes between four forms of utopianism: orgiastic chiliasm, liberal-humanism, conservatism, and socialist-communism. Chiliasm, also known as millennialism, is a belief that holds that a penultimate age of a thousand years (hence the millennium reference) will occur right before the end of the world, in which the heavens and earth will merge, and a battle with Satan will occur, before the Last Judgment. On a somewhat broader scale it holds the belief that periods of time (such as a millennium) are book-ended by huge calamities. It is tempting to use this concept as a metaphor for some of the apocalypticism in cult cinema, but there is more. For Mannheim (1936: 190), chiliasm is associated with the Dionysian cult through its investment in "orgiastic" practices of abandon, trance, reverie, and revolution – all of which put it at odds with ruling culture, and indeed present it as a danger to society (though often more by reputation than by fact). Mannheim uses the example of the Anabaptist movement of Thomas Münzer (which speaks of "storm and vitality and a new lawless and consequently free world") to press this point, and to illustrate how orgiastic chiliasm is a more radical form of utopianism than the other three models, closer to anarchism, more embedded in "presentness" (1936: 196). Barker and Brooks pick up on this element to suggest that the special effects fan-boys of *Judge Dredd* are being painted in the same corner as the chiliasts: as lower-class members of a cult that threatens routines of cultural consumption: "as chiliasm was attacked,

suppressed, and misrepresented as 'irrational', 'dangerous', and 'heretical', so delight in 'violent' films is feared, condemned, and misrepresented" (1997: 290).

Another factor that emerges in comparisons between marginalized religiosity, utopianism, and cinema cultism is the concept of idolatry. It is in this sense that Walter Benjamin (1936) uses the term "cult." Benjamin is inspired by Karl Marx's use of the term "cult-value." Marx employs it to signal an alternative to use-value and exchange-value, namely fetishistic value. That is the value a commodity (or event, or expression) has that cannot be measured in currency or labor, but only in the value irrationally accorded to it by its consumers – who often feel like participants rather than clients (Marx 1976). It includes attitudes such as "idolatry," "superstition," "loyalty," "solidarity," "self-effacement" – attitudes that accord a value to a good or event that is often only visible through the religious rituals surrounding its consumption. In the eyes of the capitalist society Marx analyzes, the cultic experience was outmoded and useless. It obstructs ideas of progress by treating time as an impression of the human body instead of a universal, linear concept, and by resisting the notion of advancement over time – cults do not "project" or "prophesize" the way religions do (their moment of revelation is too near to remain un-falsifiable), nor do they promote the concepts of "acceleration," "productivity," "growth," and "accumulation" (faster, better, more) that are essential to trade. Cults are all the more pathetic in a context that increasingly preferences what Durkheim called "the cult of the individual" over collective and communal celebrations (Chriss 1993). Benjamin (1936) argued that idolatry and fetishism are particularly present in the world of art. Traditionally, the cult of a work of art pivots around its "aura," its sense of uniqueness, which is revered and worshipped. But with the rise of mechanical means of reproduction (print, photography, film), this aura had come under threat. Benjamin observed that the cult moved from the material properties of the object to the ways in which it could mobilize emotions usually felt during worship and communion. The idolatric cult of stardom is a good example of such a displacement.

Marx's and Benjamin's application of the term "cult" to commodities and art, and Durkheim's "cult of the individual," show that the term "cult" was, in their times, no longer uniquely reserved for religious worship. It referred to all kinds of worship that contained, either directly, or remotely and symbolically a longing for some deep emotional connection – through rituals with a celebratory and orgiastic exponent – with the profound meaning of human existence, and the union between the self and all other forms of being. By the beginning of the twentieth century much of that behavior was frowned upon, and condemned as unprogressive, or silly. Though they noted the cult behavior of audiences of *The Cabinet of Dr. Caligari*, Rudolph Valentino, and Charlie Chaplin, Benjamin and colleagues such as Siegfried Kracauer (1926) or Harry Allan Potamkin (1933) had little patience with such low forms of culture, and they dismissed them as false forms of emancipation. "Not until the audience ceases being part of the ritual does it become an audience," Potamkin writes (2008: 217). At the time when film cults began to develop the term "cult" was enjoying a far from enviable reputation.

In the 1960s much of cultism's negative reputation was challenged. Concurrent with the advent of midnight movies, and parallel with the increase in individualized religiosity, countercultural movements arose, and sensibilities associated with cults were rediscovered and resurrected. Festivals such as Monterey, Woodstock, or the disastrous Altamont attempted to reclaim ancient rituals as "progressive" and "transcendental," and free love and drugs were – at least rhetorically – promoted as tools towards a connection with life's mystery (documentaries of those festivals have become cult films: *Monterey Pop*, *Woodstock* and *Gimme Shelter*, see Chapter 16). At the same time, scholars showed renewed interest in utopian thought and in the function of religious rituals in the organization of culture, especially those referencing sex and violence.

Within this context, various thinkers argued for a reappraisal of the cultic experience and a revaluation of utopian thought. Herbert Marcuse (1966) saw the regulation of sexual impulses and instincts as the key to establishing civilization and culture. According to Marcuse, repressing our desires inflicts a suffering upon humans, but produces the benefits of culture. "The sacrifice has paid off well", he added, "in the technically advanced areas of civilization, the conquest of nature is practically complete, and more needs of a greater number of people are fulfilled than ever before"

(1966: 3). But Marcuse saw a danger in over-regulating repression, because it could lead to *surplus-repression*: the repression in a society that goes beyond what is needed to maintain order and that exists only to protect the power and privileges of the establishment (1966: 37). Marcuse's fear was that this might lead to what he called a "one-dimensional man," an uncritical and conformist acceptance of structures, norms, and behaviors as dictated by power-elites (Marcuse 1964). Though written decades earlier the eschatological work of Ernst Bloch (1918, 1949) on utopia and the dialectic between "being" and "being able to" received renewed attention. Often, utopian thought moved to discussions of how people could find truth in rituals. As we saw in Chapter 10, Mary Douglas (1966) pointed to the essential roles rituals played in the identification of cultural taboos and, hence, the organization of society. Mircea Eliade (1961, 1963), who developed the concept of "hierophany" (which splits the human experience into a profane experience of space and time and a sacred one), regarded rituals as equally commemorative and participative in hierophanies. René Girard (1972), on the other hand, saw rituals such as sexual and violent sacrifices as means to regulate unchained "mimetic violence," a struggle of everyone against everyone fueled by desire (Mathijs and Mosselmans 2000). Religious rituals prevent random violence, and substitute it for violence against one person, "a scapegoat." In the initial, radical version of the Dionysus cult this could be anyone but in subsequent variations this soon became someone whose symbolic death several people could unite around. After a while, argued Girard, the celebration of unison no longer requires the actual defeat (the sacrifice). Instead, rituals *representing* the act will replace the actual violence. In other words, the participative element disappears in favor of pure commemoration.

Midnight Movies and Satanism

In parallel development to many of the ideas described above, and also actively *using* them, ran increases in appreciation for instances of religious cultism surrounding films that were being described as cults – as if their cultism was not just the result of midnight screenings and devoted fandom but of their religiosity itself.[1]

Crucial in that development were perceptions of initiation into a "secret society," and of outsider-ship towards "mainstream" culture. Hoberman and Rosenbaum's remarks about Durkheim and religion need to be seen in this light. So does Sarris's invocation of cultism and religion quoted earlier in this chapter. In that quote we find the passion ("beyond all reason"), the thirst for direct connection ("purity"), the sub-version, and the battle against intolerance that had characterized the position of cults since the advent of monolithic systems of philosophy and religion. Sarris's views also exemplify the need for a unifying figure (Bazin as the substitute for Dionysus), the importance of the rituals of festivals as sites of celebration, and the desire for advocacy. It equally stresses cultism as a conscious minority position a few isolated figures embark upon but no one else. Sarris's confession also takes the mystical/religious experience of film viewing itself, and the ritualistic way in which this is organized, as the core elements of his cultism – it is *through* his experience during the ritualistic encounters that he felt a powerful connection with being alive and becoming a cultist. Films about cultism and religiosity can be said to not only channel that connection, but to enable it.

The most visible expression of this development is the midnight movie (see Chapter 1). To their detrac-tors, midnight movies were degenerated exploitation; to their defenders they offered opportunities of "awe and enigma" and the unique opportunity to experience all of life's thrills in one initiation. The advent of the midnight movie circuit around 1970 captured the *moment* when the inspirations from the Dionysus cult, the various marginalized (and working-class) cults of utopia through the centuries, and the more recent development towards idolatry and individualized and commodified experiences of religion *all* became a cen-tral component to certain ways of appreciating certain films. Prominent to this moment were movies in which rituals stood central: *Häxan* and *Freaks* were re-released for late night audiences in the late 1960s because they included, among other things, cultism as a theme within their stories. *Freaks*' "one of us" chant and *Häxan*'s meticulous descriptions of persecutions of cultism and marginalized religious beliefs were centerpieces of such themes (Stevenson 2006). Pier Paolo Pasolini's *The Gospel According to Matthew*, *Oedipus Rex*, and *Medea* started a trend of films that re-examined elements of

well-established and institutionalized religions and myths in function of their representations of margin-alized lower-class peoples, their ritualistic aspects, and their utopian and revolutionary potential – triggered and enhanced by sex and violence (Macdonald 1969).

Other films of the time were even more ambitious in their religious connections. Among these were two films of Alejandro Jodorowsky and two of Fernando Arrabal, two figures instrumental to the art collective "Panic Movement." The best known of these films was Jodorowsky's *El Topo*, generally regarded as one of the most prominent midnight movies. *El Topo* was said to evoke a "spiritual epiphany ... to the chosen" (Havis 2008: 59). *The Holy Mountain* was a more conscious attempt at a systematic criticism of organized religion that simultaneously promoted – at least in its receptions – alternative forms of religiosity. *Viva la muerte*, directed by Arrabal, was inspired by the Dio-nysian figure of Pan and Artaud's theater of cruelty. It contained explicit sex, a violent sacrifice, and multiple surrealist tableaux. Arrabal's next film, *I Will Walk Like a Crazy Horse*, was less rooted in political reality but in its taboo-breaking imagery it was all the more an attack upon organized religion and Western society.

In a variety of films religious cultism was effectively promoted. Most prominently among these are the films of Kenneth Anger, especially the ones that pre-sented occultist Alisteir Crowley's religious philoso-phy of "Magick," a form of Gnosticism that flirts with Satanism, and which exists in various degrees of formal organization, even occasionally regarded as a proper religion (for more on Anger, see Chapters 6 and 14). Prior to the late 1960s, Anger had already directed the "luciferian" *Inauguration of the Pleasure Dome*, a film poem attempting to visualize some of the ideas of Crowley through the representation of a number of rites attributed to Egyptian and Babylonian legends. Of crucial importance to Anger was that the part of the Whore of Babylon be played by occultist Marjorie Cameron (see Schreck 2002: 250). Anger's best-known midnight movie, *Invocation of my Demon Brother*, specifically references satanic rituals. It pulled much of its inspiration from Crowley's pop-cultural appeal with contemporary celebrities, such as John Lennon, Led Zeppelin guitarist Jimmy Page, and heavy metal band Black Sabbath (Lachman 2001). The film itself showcases a hypnotic mix of pop-cultural icons,

Satanic symbols, orgies, sexual violence, and meta-phors of various religious cults. *Invocation* featured a performance of self-declared Satanist Anthony LaVey (as Satan), and it starred Bobby Beausoleil, a friend of the Manson Family.

In *Lucifer Rising*, which was started before *Invocation*, but which continued as an unfinished project until it was released as a 30-minute film in 1980, Anger elaborates further on the philosophy of Alisteir Crow-ley and the cult/religion of Magick, exploring it through a range of occult symbols and metaphors, and making explicit connections to the Dionysus cult and ancient Egyptian religion. The film stars Miriam Gibril and Donald Cammell (co-director of *Performance* and *Demon Seed*, and collaborator on *The Man Who Fell to Earth*), and also features Marianne Faithfull. Beausoleil composed the music (from his prison cell, where he was incarcerated because of his involvement in the murder of Sharon Tate, see further). The receptions of *Invocation* and *Lucifer Rising* propelled Anger to the forefront of occultism in cinema, a status reflected in a high degree of critical attention. Though only few fans or critics take Anger's ideas seriously, *Invocation* and *Lucifer Rising* were used within networks of cult re-ception as provocative samples of a willingness to mix popular culture and religiosity in opposition to estab-lished churches, and to promote cultism as an exciting alternative. Rob Cohen's documentary *Mondo Hollywood*, which tried to analyze the appeal of esoteric cultism in Hollywood in the late 1960s, offers a glimpse of this excitement (Rowe 1974; Huag 1996; Brottman, Rowe and Powell 2001; Brook 2006).

Contemporaneous to Anger's explicit address of religious and satanic cultism a high number of films emerged that addressed Satanism either as a theme or a stylistic motif. To some extent, these films can be seen as a subgenre of production-line horror movies and an attempt to exploit what seemed like a niche sensibility with mileage. Most Satanic horror movies that received cult reputations followed in the wake of *Rosemary's Baby*, a film about a pregnant woman who believes her baby will be seized by her husband and be given as a sacrifice to Satanic cultists. *Rosemary's Baby* became a cult after director Roman Polanski's own pregnant wife Sharon Tate was among the victims of the Charles Manson Family killing spree in 1969 (De Piciotto 2003; Havis 2008: 52–55). This sad event

triggered a myriad of tangled reception tales linking the Manson Family to Polanski's film, to the murder of his pregnant wife, to other figures in "Satanic film cultism," all of which resisted "normal" comprehen-sion in favor of receptions that thrived on tangents, wild explorations, and myth-building. The Polanski case briefly turned Satanism (and cultism itself) into a "cool" viewing attitude that, in acts of fandom performance, many viewers were proud to declare themselves fans of in order to distinguish themselves from other types of viewers. With the performance of Satanism in demand, dozens of films took Satanic rituals as a key motive. They ranged from *Witchfinder General*, *I Drink Your Blood*, *Le Diable est parmi nous*, *Cry of the Banshee*, *Race with the Devil*, *Santa Fe Satan*, *Mariken Van Nieumeghen*, to *The Wicker Man*. The most successful culmination came with *The Exorcist*, which presented the rituals of the Catholic Church as a form of cult.

Contemporary Performances of Religious Cultism

Explicit explorations of Satanism and religious cultism in cinema continue to appear frequently in films, even thought the context has changed much since the early 1970s. Examples with sizable cult reputations include *Prince of Darkness* and *Prophecy*. The 1980s saw a short revival of the theme of voodoo in cinema, and some of the films of this wave linked it to Satanism. It brought cult reputations to films such as *Angel Heart*, *The Believers*, and *The Serpent and the Rainbow*. In a similar vein, a few films about fallen angels received cult receptions, most notably *Wings of Desire*. Around the year 2000 a stream of millennialist apocalypse and endtime films was released, some of which stretched connections between religion, cultism, and postmo-dernity (see Negra 1999). Probably the best example of this stream is *The Matrix* franchise, the fandom of which, according to Marc Corcoran (2009: 123–129), is a perfect illustration of how fans switch constantly between sacred and profane planes of hierophany (he calls it "cinéphanie"). In spite of *The Matrix*, however, the receptions of these films were characterized more by their ineptness as explorations of marginal religiosity (their failure in other words) than their honest interest in religious cultism. As such then, these films' receptions might be a further indication of a move within cult receptions towards ironic, performative celebrations of rituals that serve only to commemorate, nor participate in, some form of religiosity.

In each of these cycles, Satanism and religious cultism appear in opposition to institutionalized religion, and in that opposition they are either portrayed ironically, or dismissed as unequivocally evil and bad. The fundamental criticism of organized religion in *Life of Brian*, a film by the Monty Python comedy team about an innocent poor soul (Brian) whom everyone believes is the savior, is neutralized by the explicit parodic tone of the film. Though *Life of Brian* was banned in several regions, it had its release obstructed more because of the disrespectful tone of its humor than its presentation of alternative forms of religious cultism.

Since the 1990s, only a few films have managed to combine a sincere or non-antagonistic approach to religious cultism with a cult reputation of their own. Among the best-known examples are the obscure cult surrounding *Begotten* and the huge but controversial cultism surrounding *The Passion of the Christ*. *Begotten* makes perhaps the most serious attempt to visualize elements of Dionysian orgiastic cultism in combination with Gnostic and pagan myths. Bypassing narrative and traditional stylistics, the film features a collection of scenes with ritualistic and symbolist overtones in stark black and white colors. Among the scenes are a burial, a resurrection, an impregnation scene, the rape of the impregnated woman by a group of nomads, and a flowering of plants from a burial site. *Begotten* has long been difficult to obtain on DVD or video, and theatrical screenings are very rare. This has created an underground bootleg exchange circuit for the film, which in turn enhanced its cult reputation.

The Passion of the Christ became known for its purist approach, insisting on the explicit presentation of graphic violence, detailing the rituals of "the passion," and using sources from outside the established canon. Pushed by grassroots Christian movements, and promoted through a papal approval (though John Paul II's "it is as it was" can also be seen as a *performance of an approval*), *The Passion of the Christ* became the highest grossing non-English language film of all time. Within that mass-appeal also lingered a number of cult receptions at odds with the vox populi. Those receptions linked themselves explicitly to the film's proto-evangelical Christianity or "sectarian Catholicism." Through that controversial aspect, *The Passion of the Christ* has become a cult film that has allowed viewers a wide diversity of interpretations, a stubborn strand of which even focuses on its depiction of Satan (by Rosalinda Celentano). For Graham Holderness (2005), the film provokes audiences by putting them in the position of attendees of a liturgy. For David Fenner (2008: 250), it separates its audiences into devoted (devout) followers, and "those interested in what all the hubbub was about." In other words, part of the cultism around *The Passion of the Christ* is seeking to break the discursive mantra of the majority view and pull the film away from a fixed meaning by utilizing its open references to Satan, violence, rituals, and, even here, irony.

Conclusion

In this chapter we have tried to show how the major components of the connection between cult cinema and religion (marginalization, discursive mantras obscuring a thirst for cosmic meaning, and individualization) are complicated by the ritualistic, orgiastic, utopian, and fetishist ideals and routines that influence it. The refusal, or inability, of cultists to fully answer the question of *what kind of insight the cult experience brings* is tied up in its connection with conceptualizations and philosophies that refute the very existence of "explanations of experience." The closest one can come, it seems, is through the adoption of discourses on cultism and religion that suggest that film cults, like other forms of cultism, try to celebrate the breaking free of societal constraints by imagining a life unbound, untamed, and untimed that would provide direct knowledge of all existence. Thus, cult receptions set themselves up in opposition to society in ways that are similar to historical forms of cultism.

In its literal form, the desire towards unbound, untamed and untimed life is largely unobtainable and unwanted. Therefore the performance of rituals of the film cult experience offers a placebo. That placebo is invoked through constellations of togetherness, initiation gestures, shouting, dancing, noise, shock, astonishment, references to (or use of) illegal substances, imaginings of the dawn of time and the origin of culture, approximations of sex and violence (and both), midnight attendance, and an advocacy for "purity" "beyond all reason." Only in a few guises would such a myriad of ritual activities be condoned without sanction. Film cultism is one of them. It would be tempting to conclude that this implies a move from *slogans to mantras* – to borrow the phrase with which Stephen Kent (2001) described a contemporaneous social development from counterculture activism into religious cultism. Such a conclusion would presume that none of the ideas surrounding the Dionysus cult, or historical forms of utopian cultism, or theories on liberation and repression that explain the essence of desire and the significance of rituals, would be valid, or viable anymore. Perhaps this is true.

But if the observations of Barker and Brooks (1997) on chiliasm, or Lavery (1991) on Gnosticism, and several similar claims (such as those of Maffesoli in Chapter 1) are anything to go by then it is much more likely that mantras have not replaced slogans altogether and that their coexistence means that utopianism, liberation theories, and Dionysian desires for orgiastic release are still embedded within cult receptions and the cult experience of cinema. In that sense, the link between religion and cinema cultism still pertains to an experience in which co-occur simultaneously the small details of one movie, and an impression of the breeze of the bigger scope of all movies, all of culture, all of human existence.

Note

1. This development is far from unique to cult cinema. It is also articulated in theater and performance art, areas in which artists such as Genesis P. Orridge, Hermann Nitsch, Joseph Beuys, Friedensreich Hundertwasser, and several others explore the crossroads between religiosity, cultism, and utopianism through the tools of violence, orgy, and rituals. Several of these artists have made films, some of which have obtained cult status, and their work is occasionally cited by film cultists as an indication of a closeness with their own community.

Part II

Themes and Genres

13

Exploitation and B Movies

If you browse the web in search of cult film sites, you are likely to encounter a predominance of exploitation-oriented material. In fact, you may form the impression that cult cinema is actually synonymous with exploitation cinema. We would like to counter that assumption, as is indicated by the wealth of non-exploitation titles that permeate this book. Nevertheless, exploitation filmmaking undoubtedly forms a key component of the somewhat broader category of cult cinema. B movies, which also figure in many a cult film list, are often conflated with exploitation films, though strictly speaking there is a difference between the two forms. More generally, though, there are also overlaps between the two, hence their incorporation into this single chapter. As so many of these films feature within cult film lists and articles, we think it is necessary to think about some key historical and conceptual issues related to their development, as these in turn feed into their prominence within cult cinema discussion, while also contributing to a firmer understanding of the terms themselves.

B Movies and Classical Exploitation

While Roger Corman has gained the status as "King of the Bs," he was fond of pointing out that he did not actually make B movies (Gray 2004: 48). Yet he, along with other exploitation figures, tends to be associated with B movies.[1] The main reason as to why Corman – along with figures like William Castle, Samuel Z. Arkoff and David F. Friedman – are not technically producers of B movies is that the majority of the work

they are associated with hit cinemas after the B movie had ceased to exist. The B movie was a film paired with a bigger "A" picture and positioned firmly on the lower end of a movie theater program. This type of film flourished during the 1930s as, in a bid to recapture dwindling audiences during the Depression, many theaters began to adopt double-bill screenings in order to provide improved value for audiences. (While the B movie became a staple in various countries it has been most documented in the United States and is thus our primary focus in this chapter.[2]) Both major studios and smaller, independent "poverty row" studios produced these cheaply made pictures in response to the flourishing demand during the decade. This practice began to die out during the 1950s, though, as changes in the US industry – such as the rise of television, the move to the suburbs, increasing costs and a shrinking rate of studio productions – dictated against this exhibition strategy. As Doherty notes, the types of qualities that characterized B movies were now likely to appear on television, and thus lost their cinematic appeal. The consequence of these shifts was that many smaller theaters lacked product. A number of low-budget filmmakers then stepped in to fill the void with the production of exploitation pictures (Doherty 2002: 28).

Before focusing on the 1950s further, it is sensible at this point to rewind a little, for exploitation pictures also existed before the decline of the B movies. Summarizing the similarities and differences of exploitation and B movies during the same period will aid understanding of the later period of exploitation filmmakers and films. The B film, according to Taves, has

Cult Cinema: An Introduction. Ernest Mathijs and Jamie Sexton.
© 2011 Ernest Mathijs and Jamie Sexton. Published 2011 by Blackwell Publishing Ltd.

several characteristics that distinguish it from the A picture. First, and most obviously, it filled the bottom half of the bill at cinemas; secondly, it featured leads with "moderate, questionable or unknown box-office appeal"; thirdly, budgets and shooting schedules were more limited, so it was produced more rapidly than an A picture; fourthly, running time was often shorter, usually around 55–70 minutes (Taves 1995: 314). Nevertheless, Taves notes there was a certain degree of fluidity between the A and B picture, that "there are no clear lines of demarcation" (1995: 314). For example, if a B picture turned out to be an unexpected success at a theater, it could make its way to the top of the bill; likewise, a top-billed audience failure could be demoted to a B slot (1995: 315–316). While there were differences between the lower budget B films made by "poverty row" studios and the more prestigious studio productions, there was an aesthetic quality evident in a number of these films, argues Taves. As B films were shot cheaply and quickly, there was minimal consultation between various production personnel; sets were cheap and often sparse, while lighting tended to be uniformly high key, as there was little time available for elaborate lighting set-ups. Films tended to rely on formulaic, often repetitious, narratives with many of them drawing from pulp fiction, and they tended to highlight "pace and thrills" over "mood, coherence and characterization" (Taves 1995: 334). Nevertheless, Taves also points out that within the limits of B productions, there were opportunities for resourceful filmmakers to experiment with lighting, editing, and camera set-ups (1995: 334).

The low-production values, greater latitude for experimentation and the general "low" status of the B movie in relation to the more prestigious A picture has undoubtedly fed into the cult status of a number of such productions. In particular, small, "poverty row" studios – such as Republic and Monogram – were admired for their contribution to cinema by a number of influential French film critics associated with *Cahiers du cinéma* in the 1950s; Jean-Luc Godard even dedicated his debut feature, *À bout de souffle* (1960), to Monogram Pictures. The stance by many such critics/filmmakers was cultic in that it singled out areas of production generally considered unimportant within cinema history and staked a claim for their importance. There were also particular B films and filmmakers that

gained reputations for transcending their production origins and gained cult followings. These include Edgar G. Ulmer's influential road movie *Detour*, the criminal couple movie *Gun Crazy*, Val Lewton's horror/mystery productions for RKO (such as *Cat People* and *I Walked with a Zombie*), and many of the low-budget films directed by Sam Fuller. Both *Detour* and *Gun Crazy* are often termed as film noirs, one of the most "cultic" genres (or series) of the classical period, and one which was applied retrospectively by French critics to a body of films that were often (though not always) low-budget, B pictures (the term was coined by Nino Frank in 1946, see Frank 1999). Many noirs appealed because they were perceived as challenging the norms that characterized much Hollywood product, particularly in their expressionistic lighting and mise-en-scène, and their often cynical, sometimes fatalist tone.

In contrast to B films, a number of characteristics defined exploitation pictures, which Eric Schaefer has exhaustively detailed for the period 1919–59 (which he terms "classical exploitation"). In terms of production, these films existed even below the poverty row B productions: they tended to be run by extremely small numbers of people, had less money to spend on filmmaking, and did not own their own plants (Schaefer 1999: 5, 47). Eric Schaefer describes how in exploitation cinema "the division of labor was not always as strict as it was in the classical Hollywood cinema's mode of production," adding that the multi-tasking this implies often meant that "those who labored in exploitation films usually had not had the opportunity to hone their skills to a degree comparable to those working in mainstream pictures" (1999: 46). Still, while Schaefer acknowledges that "watching a few exploitation films might lead one to conclude that their producers were fly-by-night operators who were more accomplished at evading creditors than shooting movies" (1999: 44) he is also quick to point out how much pre-1960s exploitation cinema adhered to business models used by Hollywood's B-studios such as Monogram and Republic. Exploitation producers outside the United States emulated such practices, as is evidenced by the routines and protocols of Hong Kong's Golden Harvest, Ernst Hofbauer's *Schoolgirl Report* productions, and the sleaze turned horror company Cinepix (Fay 2004). They operated in quite flexible ways, but their core business emulated Hollywood's practices.

In order to cover up lack of skill and low production values, exploitation movies often reverted to "recycling." Schaefer points to this technique as one in which footage from other films, preferably of a shocking or astonishing nature, was borrowed to complete a certain atmosphere. Clips from *Häxan: Withcraft through the Ages* were used as inserts in *Maniac*; Ed Wood as well as Kenneth Anger used footage purchased from libraries or stock newsreel footage; Radley Metzger was known to revert to library music for the soundtracks of his porn chic films. The carry-over of characters between films meant not just a familiarity on the side of the audiences, but on that of the performers as well, eliminating expensive rehearsal time (Schaefer 1999: 57). The use of Bela Lugosi and other actors in Ed Wood's productions is exemplary in this respect. Roger Corman was not beyond adding a few extra shooting days and footage to a film that had already been released and releasing it again as if it was new; blaxploitation failure *The Final Comedown* thus became the equally unsuccessful *Blast!* (Gray 2004: 107). Repeat techniques and references to other films were later also portrayed as "allusions" (Carroll 1998). Ironically, recycling later became a key production value in the eyes of cult audiences, which led to its revaluation as a form of homage, intertextuality, or reflexivity (see Chapter 21). It determined the acting, effects, and production design of the films of Dan O'Bannon (*Return of the Living Dead*) or the neo-gothic wave of the early 1990s (especially *Bram Stoker's Dracula*, which heavily referenced exploitation techniques) and helped turn them into veritable cults of pastiche (Austin 2002: 116–119).

Exploitation movies were distributed in two main ways: first, on the state's rights system, where the producer sold the exclusive film rights to an independent exhibitor within a particular territory for a specified period (usually 3–5 years). The exhibitor would then be responsible for presenting the film, which meant that sometimes the title could be changed or footage subtracted. The second main exhibition strategy was *roadshowing*. This entailed either a single person (sometimes the producer) or a small number of units, transporting the film from territory to territory

in order to exhibit it. Either they could hire out a theater for a period (known as "four walling") or, occasionally, they could set up temporary large tents in which to screen films (Schaefer 1999: 96–101; Stevenson 2000: 24). Perhaps the most distinctive nature of "classical exploitation" pictures, however, was their content and promotional strategies. The films often dealt with forbidden topics, such as sex, vice, drugs, nudity, and anything considered to be in "bad taste." As these films were made on extremely low budgets, dealing with such lurid material was a way to give them an edge, in that they were providing material that could not be found in other types of films. The name of exploitation stems from the fact that filmmakers exploited such material in their promotional campaigns, moving beyond typical film trailers, posters, and ads. They would play up the sensational aspects of their stories, and often complement screenings with extra-filmic practices such as lectures, slide presentations, sales of related materials, as well as gimmicks (such as the presence of uniformed nurses to help in case anyone fainted during screenings) (Schaefer 1999: 4–6).

Schaefer also outlines some of the predominant aesthetic features of exploitation films, which were closely linked to their economic status. Like B films, they are marked by an "impoverished" look, though to an even greater degree, with spare sets and minimal decoration frequently characteristic. In addition to low budgets, the speed of production and paucity of skilled actors and filmmakers led to a recurrence of stiff acting, bad lighting, and continuity errors (1999: 47–48). Though a number of "post-classical" exploitation films have gained more solid cult followings than their classical counterparts, there are a few classical exploitation films – such as *Narcotic*, *Maniac*, and *Tell Your Children*, aka *Reefer Madness* – that have built up cult reputations (Figure 13.1).

While – like B films – their marginal production status feeds into such reputations, these cult films are not celebrated so much for transcending their economic origins as testifying to them in a manner which spilled over into the ridiculous. That is, they tend to be enjoyed for their incompetence and unintentional hilarity, which marks them out as "bad" films (see Chapters 3 and 8 for more on the celebration of bad films).

"REEFER MADNESS," made in 1936 at a time when the government was pushing an elaborate campaign to make marijuana illegal (up to then it wasn't!), is now re-released in toto by New Line. Hopeless addicts smoke grass so strong they get high just by blowing billows of thick smoke—they don't seem to inhale; and after a couple of puffs they run around like crazed speed freaks on a terrible bender.

New Line considers the incredible acceptance of this film among young people a good sign. We point with pride to what its high grosses may be doing to Stem the Weed Tide across the Nation.

REEFER MADNESS. Directed by Louis Gasnier. Starring Dave O'Brien and Dorothy Short, 16 & 35 m/m, 67 minutes.

Figure 13.1   *Reefer Madness*, a classical exploitation film.

As previously mentioned, the B movie died out during the 1950s, at least in its original form. The use of the term has continued partly because many of the exploitation films made during this period, and beyond, shared a number of features with these movies. They were shot quickly, on low budgets, usually without recognizable stars, and often relied on for-mulaic narratives as well as an emphasis on pace and action over coherent narratives. Doherty notes that, during the 1950s, two main features distinguished the new range of exploitation pictures from the older B films: the subject matter became more exploitation-oriented with films aimed more at teenagers (Doherty 2002: 30–31). In one sense, the older exploitation pictures and B films merged somewhat in this decade, as was evidenced by Monogram's (an independent provider of B films) move towards exploitation tactics towards the end of the 1940s (Tzioumakis 2006: 139–41). In another sense, exploitation cinema would splinter into many different generic and sub-generic shards from now until the 1970s at least.

Teenpics and Youth Culture

Doherty has identified a number of key types of teenage exploitation pictures produced in the 1950s. The main categories were the "juvenile delinquent" film, the rock 'n' roll teenpic, the "clean" teenpic, and the "weirdies" (cheap horror and science fiction films that catered to the youth market). A number of independent film companies produced increasing amounts of such films in order to meet the demand for product created by the studios' drastic reduction in output.[3] Doherty mentions that, in response to the threat of television, cinema could deliver two main things that its little rival could not: first, larger images and expensive sets; secondly, controversial content (2002: 20). The independent companies were not in the position to provide the first of these, hence their move to specialize in, and exploit, controversial sub-ject matter and to aim this at the audience that was going to the cinema more frequently during this period: teenagers. The three types of films were tar-geting this age group in a way that had not happened before. The juvenile delinquent picture, for example, exploited scares about teenagers causing trouble, which were increasingly prevalent within the media. While the need to avoid trouble from potential critics led producers of such films to provide overarching moral frameworks warning against delinquency, they nevertheless tended to wallow in the excitement that such behavior gave rise to. The rock 'n' roll pictures, meanwhile, often featured stories that dramatized the place of rock 'n' roll in the broader cultural fabric: a force loved by youth and condemned by parents. The "clean" teenpic was a safer type of film that depicted teenage life in a less controversial manner. Finally, the "weirdies," though less explicitly about teenage life-styles, could be seen as metaphorically relevant to the alienation and bodily changes experienced by teen-agers, particularly in the guise of the monster figure (as argued by Doherty 2002: 119). Occasionally, the "weirdie" would explicitly concern teenage life, as indicated by titles such as *Teenage Zombies* and *I Was a Teenage Werewolf*.

A number of new independent companies and figures emerged during this period, many of who are feted within cult circles. These include American

International Pictures (AIP), their sometime producer/director Roger Corman, William Castle Productions, Sam Katzman, and Albert Zugsmith, to name just a few. The exploitation nature of these companies is made clear through some of the tactics that they used. Katzman, for example, was alert to the appeal of *Blackboard Jungle* and immediately attempted to replicate its success. As the use of Bill Haley's "Rock around the Clock" at the opening and closing of the film was seen as particularly noteworthy, and as rock 'n' roll was popular with teenagers, he produced a teenpic entitled *Rock around the Clock* featuring Bill Haley and the Comets playing themselves. Not only was it a huge hit, it signaled the glut of exploitation teenage movies to follow (Doherty 2002: 57). Exploitation producers would survey the market for exploitable popular themes and build films around them. They were in a good position to jump on a topical wave because their rapid production schedules meant that they could get a film onto the market while the topicality of the exploitable element(s) was still current. The whole ethos of exploitation filmmakers during this period is summed up by AIP's approach to marketing, codified in the following principles:

> OBSERVE trends and emerging tastes. KNOW as much as possible about your audience. ANTICIPATE how you will sell your chosen subject. PRODUCE with prudence, avoiding expense for what won't show on the screen. SELL with showmanship in advertising and publicity. USE imagination. Have good luck: even if you do everything else right, you'll still need it. (Quoted in Tzioumakis 2006: 152)

Within this type of filmmaking, a concept and title would come first, while frequently the script was developed *after* the marketing campaign had been devised. As in the classical era of exploitation, the role of marketing often-controversial content was extremely important in the absence of selling points such as familiar stars. And this was no surprise in an age when teenagers, who constituted the prime exploitation market, were claiming trailers to be the primary reason they went to see a picture; while interest in the persuasive psychology of advertising was also on the rise (Heffernan 2004: 68–69). Thus, there was renewed emphasis on sensational, eye-grabbing posters, trailers, and other paraphernalia, plus ear-grabbing radio spots and a host of other extravagant gimmicks.

The rise in teenage exploitation pictures occurred in tandem with a number of exhibition patterns, which have also played a key role in cult movie lore. The main trend was the huge increase in drive-in theaters. While conventional "hard-top" theaters were struggling, drive-in theaters, or "ozoners" as they were commonly known, grew massively. Between 1946 and 1956, the number of drive-ins increased from 500 to almost 5000, a growth spurred by the move to the suburbs and the increase in car ownership (Taylor 2002: 251). The drive-in was cheap to construct and appealed to both families – who could take their children with them – and teenagers, who were often tempted by the romantic potentials of this exhibition context. Drive-ins tended to specialize in double-features (or sometimes more), which provided added value-for-money for customers, but also proved profitable for the exhibitors as the longer people were at the drive-in, the more concessions they purchased, which is where the real profits lay. The fact that many exploitation pictures were shown on double bills may have added to their "B" status, but these programs usually screened films on an *equal* billing. The double bill also became increasingly popular within "hard tops," as did the increasing tendency to show screenings later, thus planting the seeds of the "midnight movie" (which would become more frequent in the late 1960s and early 1970s).

Exploitation filmmaking continued to flourish into the 1960s and 1970s, but it did undergo some notable changes. Though exploitation films continued to be consumed by a predominantly younger audience, the *teenage* demographic itself broadened. In the 1960s "teen" culture was supplanted by "youth" culture; whereas the former was strictly delineated by age, the latter was, Doherty argues, an "experiential realm" (Doherty 2002: 190). Youth became a state of mind, a "concept" that, as the 1960s progressed, became very much associated with the counterculture (a term which itself began to replace "subculture" in its usage). Films themselves began to reflect the themes and tastes associated with the new counterculture: rock music, sex, drugs, and a new form of politicized rebelliousness. This mode of rebelliousness did not constitute a radical break from earlier teenage alienation so much as an extension of it. Thus, Corman's *The Wild Angels* deals with themes similar to some of the "juvenile delinquent" films, but here the protagonists are not identified as teenagers: they are Hell's Angels and, as such, have joined a specific group and adopted a creed. Their anti-authoritarianism, symbolized most visibly by the police and the church, is less nebulous than that of their predecessors, but they still seem driven by a reaction against constraints that limit their hedonistic pursuits. They lack, unlike some of the countercultural protagonists that would follow in their wake, idealistic alternatives to the current system and thus seem content to remain a thorn in its side. This lack of any alternative dawns on Heavenly Blues (Peter Fonda) at the end of the film as he waits to be caught by the police, claiming that there is nowhere to go. (*Easy Rider*, a film indebted to *The Wild Angels*, ends on a similarly pessimistic note, though in this film the main protagonists do encounter alternatives before meeting their bloody end.)

Many exploitation films would draw more specifically on the politicized counterculture and feature protagonists seeking an alternative mode of living. In many of these films, youth is associated with hopes for a new age, with the elder generation represented as negative, greedy, and out of touch. Perhaps the apogee of such filmmaking is *Wild in the Streets*, which depicts a world in which a young pop star wins the presidency, lowers the voting age to 14, and decides to retire all people over 30 into special homes and force them to take LSD. The film draws on many of the recurring exploitative counterculture tropes – music, generational tension, drugs, and political alternatives – with obvious satirical intent, lampooning not only the cynicism of the establishment, but also the fascistic undercurrents of countercultural consciousness. Many movies depicting various countercultural movements and dramatizing the generational gap would follow, including *Psych-Out*, *Alice's Restaurant* and *Gas! – Or – How it Became Necessary to Destroy the World in Order to Save it*, all of which have featured in cult lists and discussions.

Many of these teen and youth exploitation films have gained cultist reputations. At the time that they were released, they were being lapped up by younger viewers in particular, and could therefore be consid-ered cult because they were appealing primarily to a "deviant" subculture who believed these films were communicating with them. Of course, much of the status of "delinquent youth" was constructed through exaggerated press reports, but this nevertheless led to *perceptions* of deviant groups consuming deviant films (films which were often considered tasteless by more conservative social factions despite their ultimate moral tone). A number of such films still continue to enjoy cult status, mainly through being part of the broader exploitation repertoire that serves as such an important mode of production in cultist circles. Some of these may be still loved for being innovative films which communicate ideas that contemporary audiences respond to; others may be enjoyed in a more mocking way, as "bad" films (see Chapter 24) which hold particular interest for how they depict social tensions within a specific era.

Nasty Trash: Exploitation in the 1970s

Not all exploitation fare in the 1960s and early 1970s directly concerned the counterculture, however. A number of different genres and cycles marked the period, including sexploitation films, beach party films, and mondo films. The latter were ethnographic documentaries that portrayed strange rituals and practices from around the world (the generic label stems from the film *Mondo Cane*, which established the blueprint for later such films). Often featuring liberal doses of violence and nudity, as well as a number of reconstructed scenes, these "shockumentaries" were often criticized for supposedly prioritizing sensation over education. (Goodall 2006). Most of these films hailed from Italy, pointing to another trend in the 1960s: the rise of exploitation films from other countries. In fact, there have long existed exploitation films from around the world, though the sheer number of films produced in America, and the wealth of research on American production and the reception of films in this country, has inevitably led to our current survey of exploitation cinema being skewed towards this country. Nevertheless, recent work has started to redress this imbalance (e.g. Tombs 1997; Mathijs and Mendik, 2004; Schneider 2003), while DVD labels such as Mondo Macabro are uncovering international exploitation fare for Western audiences. Currently, though, the most recognized non-American exploitation films are those that established themselves in the American marketplace. Italy is a key purveyor of non-American exploitation due to the size of its market as well as the links forged between American and Italian film companies (as well as between Italian and UK companies) from the late 1950s onwards. In the 1960s and 1970s, the Italian film industry was in a position of considerable strength, which aided the international distribution of many of its films (Eleftheriotis 2001: 103–108), and a number of films from this period have established themselves as cult movies. Filmmakers, including Dario Argento, Mario Bava, and Sergio Leone, established themselves in this period, as did cycles such as the spaghetti western and the peplum. It is arguably the horror film, however, which has proved the most enduring mode of Italian filmmaking to international cult audiences. There has also been a growing body of work emerging around the British postwar exploitation film, particularly regarding horror (e.g. Wathen 1994) and sexploitation (e.g. Hunt 1998), and focusing on the work of cult directors such as Pete Walker (Chibnall 1998) and producers such as Tony Tenser (Hamilton 2005).

The 1960s and 1970s saw the horror film move in new, nastier directions and it became the most prevalent exploitation genre. Sexploitation also continued to be a key exploitation production area as increasingly explicit material screened in public cinemas. Previously considered outside of the exploitation market because it was limited to private or underground settings, pornography hit the public cinema screens during the 1970s with the development of the "hardcore narrative feature" (Schaefer 2002). The biggest porn hit was *Deep Throat*, which caused a sensation when it was released, though other films – such as *Behind the Green Door* – were also popular during the "porn chic" phase and continue to attract a cult following (see Chapter 10).

The 1970s also saw the emergence, and rather rapid disappearance, of several other cycles of exploitation. In each case, controversies or scandals surrounding a more or less respectable but risqué art house production gave rise to numerous attempts to cash in on the more exploitative elements of these films (the ones the film got in trouble for) and address through these elements cultist audiences. Nunsploitation tried to capitalize on the upheaval associated with *The Devils*; nazisploitation attempted to cash in on the scandal around *The Night Porter*; *Deliverance* led to some examples of hicksploitation; notable scandal-films from specific regions such as Canada (*Cannibal Girls*, *Shivers*), continental Europe (*La grande bouffe*), or Spain and Latin-America (*El Topo*) led to subgeneric modes such as canuxsploitation, Eurotrash, or latsploitation. It provoked cult reputations for films such as *Killer Nun*, *Ilsa, She Wolf of the SS*, *My Bloody Valentine*, *Successive Slidings of Pleasure*, and *The Cannibal Man* (we examine some of the tropes and politics of representation of these cycles in Chapter 10).

One of the most notable exploitation cycles was that of Blaxploitation films. After it became clear that a significant African-American audience existed who were willing to pay to see productions concerning black protagonists, a glut of black-oriented, exploitation films flooded the market. Melvin Van Peebles' low-budget *Sweet Sweetback's Baadasssss Song* is generally considered the key film which kick-started this trend, though this film's experimental aesthetic was not indicative of subsequent films following in its wake. Many films, utilizing familiar themes and images – most notably crime and drugs, pimps and private eyes, action scenes, sexually assertive protagonists, ghetto locations, and the use of soul and funk music on the soundtrack – emerged in the early 1970s. Both Hollywood majors (such as MGM and Warner Brothers) and independents (in particular AIP) produced a number of such films, which include *Shaft*, *Super Fly*, *Blacula*, *Black Caesar*, and *Foxy Brown* (Figure 13.2).

Despite the huge glut of blaxploitation films that flooded the market, the success of *Shaft* and *Super Fly* was rarely repeated, despite these films spawning sequels such as *Shaft in Africa* and *Super Fly T.N.T.* Black audiences were apparently more interested in attending "event" movies such as *The Godfather* and *The Exorcist,* hence signaling an end to the short-lived, yet influential, exploitation cycle in the mid 1970s (Cook 2000: 265). Nevertheless, a number of blaxploitation films – such as *Coffy*, *Black Caesar*, and *Super Fly* – can be considered cult films as they still attract devoted followers even though they may fall beneath

Figure 13.2 Pam Grier as the sexually assertive protagonist of blaxploitation film *Foxy Brown*.

the radar of many filmgoers' choices. In particular, the films' soundtracks (as evidenced by a number of blaxploitation compilations released over the past decade), and their now "retro" styles and attitudes, have contributed to their niche appeal.

Exploitation in the Video Era

Since the 1980s, the exploitation market has changed and become somewhat murkier. The traditional exhibition outlets, such as drive-ins and grindhouse theaters, began to disappear, which made it more difficult to get cheap films shown in cinemas. Video created a new market, yet while cheap exploitation filmmaking certainly existed to fill this market, straight-to-video titles rarely become cult hits. This is perhaps because such films tend to slip beneath the net of many people's radar. Nevertheless, there is a small, yet growing, trend for people to laud straight-to-video, trashy films on the net, particularly low-budget sequels such as *Starship Troopers 2: Hero of the Federation* or *Freeway Mad II: Confessions of a Trickbaby*. The situation in Japan is somewhat different in this regard: more respect for the video market (known as "V-cinema") is perhaps a reason why more cult films emerge from this sector. One of the most prolific and lauded cult directors, Takashi Miike, has made numerous films for this market, including *Full Metal Yakuza* and *Visitor Q*. Contrastingly, in Nigeria, the video market has fed into a growing industry, as video technology has greatly reduced both production

and distribution costs. Cheap, "trashy" films based around voodoo and witchcraft are popular and are now gaining a dedicated following in the United States, giving what is interchangeably called Naija Cinema or Nollywood, and equipping films such as *Mortal Inheritance*, *Living in Bondage*, and *Owo Blow: The Genesis* with burgeoning cult reputations (Gray 2003).

The proliferation of sequels is certainly a notable characteristic of contemporary exploitation filmmaking. It is important not to overstate the "newness" of sequels, as they have existed for a long time in various guises. Nevertheless, modern exploitation filmmaking sometimes spawns franchises with unlikely longevity. Two striking examples are the *Friday the 13th* and *Nightmare on Elm Street* series, which between them have produced twenty films, if the film that combined their two anti-heroes – *Freddy vs. Jason* – is included (and there is another *Friday the 13th* film in production). In the case of these films, the main characters become such cult objects that they are capable of generating a proliferation of products, though fans do not receive all of these warmly. More recently, some figures are setting themselves up as exploitation filmmakers in a particularly self-conscious manner, referencing and revisiting older exploitation pictures and in the process heightening their cultural value. Eli Roth and Rob Zombie are particular examples of such filmmakers, though this tendency reached its apotheosis with Tarantino and Rodriguez's *Grindhouse*, which was packaged as a double-bill and even included fake trailers in between the two features (*Planet Terror* and *Death Proof*). If Bogdanovich, Scorsese, Coppola, *et al.*, were the original movie brats – drawing on, and often referencing, cinema history in their filmmaking – then Roth *et al.* could be thought of as exploitation brats, a second generation of self-conscious (and self-appointed) film viewers turned makers who largely draw on less respectable areas of cinema history. (See Chapters 6 and 22 for more on self-conscious authorship.) The fact that many of the more "classical" movie brats actually started out making exploitation films adds a somewhat ironic twist to the contrast.

One other notable trend in exploitation filmmaking is the art film/exploitation crossover. Of course, this is not a new phenomenon. Betz (2003),

Heffernan (2004), Hawkins (2000), and Wilinsky (2001) have all, in various ways, drawn attention to the ways in which these spheres have previously overlapped and are less distinct than formerly assumed. "Art films," for example, have notoriously been subject to exploitation marketing strategies and editorial interference, so as to play up their angles of nudity, sex, or violence. Exploitation films, too, have drawn upon art cinema because of creative reasons and/or a need to differentiate themselves from other exploitation fare. Over the past decade, however, a trend in European cinema to make art/exploitation hybrids does seem apparent and distinctive. This is particularly the case with French cinema – what James Quandt terms the "New French Extremity" (Hagman 2007: 32–33) – and includes films from Catherine Breillat (e.g. *Romance*), Gaspar Noé (e.g. *Irréversible*), Claire Denis (*Trouble Every Day*, 2001) and the film *Baise-moi* (which is perhaps more egregiously exploitation-oriented and less art-inflected than the others). Hagman (2007) has argued that such exploitation tactics are increasing within "art house" films as a way of drawing attention to product in a global marketplace. Alex Cox's (2006) contention that funding bodies and film festivals are encouraging the incorporation of greater amounts of explicit sex and violence would seem to support this argument. Nevertheless, one should not overestimate the extent to which this trend is new: Argento, Cronenberg, and Pasolini are all directors who have previously explored such hybrid territory.

Conclusion

Exploitation filmmaking continues to enjoy currency as a concept within contemporary cinema cultures, though it is arguably a less distinct area than it once was. The contours of the exploitation film have never been secure, but demarcations between the exploitation

film and a typical studio production did previously exist. Paul Watson has argued that Hollywood's contemporary promotion of concepts and promises is evidence that exploitation has become part of the mainstream (Watson 1997: 79–80). This does seem to be the case with modern blockbusters, though we should also be aware that this does not constitute the totality of Hollywood cinema. We should also be careful not to overestimate the newness of this trend, as Hollywood has often been involved in exploitation. For example, in the 1950s a major company such as Warner Bros was investing in "weirdies" such as *The Beast from 20,000 Fathoms* and *Them!*, and releasing them on a saturation basis alongside aggressive advertising campaigns (Heffernan 2004: 35). We should also remember that major studios produced and/or distributed a number of blaxploitation films. Perhaps we can argue that Hollywood previously only dabbled in such exploitation tactics, whereas now they are central to its operations. Yet this points to the dual nature of exploitation cinema as a concept. First, and more broadly, it stems from a purely commercial manner of exploiting a property for as much money as possible. In this sense, all commercial cinema is, and always has been, exploitation cinema. Secondly, as a category circulating within film culture, exploitation more specifically relates to a *type* of cinema that existed on the fringes of the mainstream, dealing with themes and images that the mainstream would not tolerate and exploiting taboo topics as a key appeal of the films. It is this form of exploitation cinema that tends to be most relevant to cult cinema due to its taint of outsiderness and danger (dealing with content in ways that the mainstream still tends to avoid). Today, there are still filmmakers attempting to capitalize on sensational material that pushes the limits of acceptability. At the same time, Hollywood is often willing to capitalize on such themes and images if they prove popular, hence the constant shifting and slipperiness of "exploitation cinema" as a concept.

Notes

1. This is even implied in McCarthy and Flynn's 1975 collection, *Kings of the Bs*, even though they distinguish between "classical B" pictures and the "exploitation B" pictures. They do, however, only tentatively call the latter

types B films, occasionally calling them "B-type pictures" (see McCarthy and Flynn 1975: 13–43).

2. More recent work is now expanding knowledge of the B movie beyond the United States. For example, Chibnall (2007) has recently written extensively on the British B film. Nevertheless, the "A" and "B" distinctions did generally have greater currency within the United States.

3. The studios did not entirely ignore such pictures, producing a few "adult" pictures, including *Rebel without a Cause* and *Blackboard Jungle*; while *The Wild One* was distributed by a major. Doherty does not really go into any detail as to why the majors did not produce more pictures along these lines.

14

Underground and Avant-garde Cinema

Cult cinema is often considered to be a different entity than underground and avant-garde cinemas, but these two spheres commonly intersect. The majority of cult films may tend to be more populist than the esoteric marginalia frequently associated with avant-garde and underground film, yet a number of key films belong to both domains. Perhaps of greater importance, the viewing contexts established by avant-garde film cultures bled into underground cinema and, subsequently, became important sites in which some cult films established their reputations. The avant-garde and the underground, then, are crucial components of cult cinema on the level of both particular films and the broader arena of film culture.

Avant-garde and underground cinemas are often difficult to distinguish, though the underground is generally thought to be a development of, but also a slight deviation from avant-garde film, which fully emerged in the 1960s within the United States and which soon spread to other countries. It is very much associated with the social and sexual liberation that characterized the more libertarian factions of the 1960s, and a move away from the more rigorous, politicized avant-garde that characterized the interwar period (O'Pray 2003: 7). In response a new, even more rigorous avant-garde formation emerged in the 1970s (especially associated with structural filmmaking), which often became housed within academic institutions and later became a staple of gallery exhibitions. While this distinction is certainly crude (and necessarily has to be because of the actual ways in which these terms often overlap), it does point to the key ways in which they have been distinguished. The underground currents of the avant-garde were of greater importance to cult cinema, so it is this area, along with its avant-garde antecedents, which we will primarily cover here.

Cult and the Avant-garde of the 1920s

Cult viewing practices are frequently linked to the emergence of art house and repertory cinemas that flourished in the late 1950s and 1960s within the United States. For example, Jancovich writes that "Cult movie fandom and academic film studies may have historically diverged into relatively independent scenes, but they both emerged through the art cinemas, college film societies and repertory theatres of the post-war period, and hence employ similar discourses and reading strategies" (2002: 308). This is true to an extent, but overlooks how these postwar developments were themselves building upon foundations instituted in the interwar period, when a number of film societies and repertory cinemas were established in various parts of the world. These viewing spaces, which offered alternatives to the majority of mainstream commercial cinemas, were themselves heavily linked to avant-garde film culture.

The main areas in which avant-garde or "alternative" film cultures emerged were in the major metropolitan areas of Britain, France, Germany,

Cult Cinema: An Introduction. Ernest Mathijs and Jamie Sexton.
© 2011 Ernest Mathijs and Jamie Sexton. Published 2011 by Blackwell Publishing Ltd.

Holland, Japan, the Soviet Union and the United States, although selected activities also occurred within other countries. The types of activities usually overlapped, though there were also differences that marked them. For example, one of the main differences was between societies that took a predominantly aesthetic orientation in regards to film, and those that took a more political line, in that they saw films as tools for use towards left-wing political goals. In reality, while arguments were often exchanged between political film societies and broader, artistically oriented societies, there were areas where such boundaries blurred. For the purposes of this chapter, we should stress that we will focus on the societies that were not explicitly organized for primarily political purposes (such as workers film societies, which were widespread by the 1930s), as it is the broader film societies that fed more directly into cult viewing contexts. Nevertheless, many of the so-called aesthetic societies also screened films that were political in the sense that they challenged broader social mores and ideologies.

The emergence of film societies in the interwar period was a key factor in the development of cult cinema. It is here that a broad number of people began to band together in order to create a passionate cinema culture that explicitly aimed to offer alternatives to the dominant ways in which film was promoted and consumed. Around the establishment of these societies, or "cine-clubs," emerged a series of other cultural activities in which people discussed artistic issues in relation to film: the publication of film journals, magazines, and program notes; the organization of conferences and lectures on film culture. This flurry of cultural activity around various parts of the globe marked the first sustained and systematic attempt to establish cinema as an extremely important new art form, and to promote a wide variety of different approaches to filmmaking. Thus, these societies distinguished themselves from commercial cinemas through screening films not according to a purely commercial agenda. Instead, they would program films that: first, exemplified what they regarded as the most artistic films; secondly, represented interesting experiments on the fringes of, or outside of, the commercial industry; and, thirdly, represented interesting moments of film history. This was, therefore,

the first real flowering of cinephilia, an intense love for film which has often been associated with cultism.

It was France, and more specifically Paris, where cinephilia most extensively flourished during the interwar period – and remains the capital of cinephilia even to this day (Hagener 2007: 79). Following the publication of specialist film journals in the latter part of the 1910s, cine-clubs began to appear in the early 1920s. The first major club was CASA (Club des amis du Septième Art), established by Riccioto Canudo in 1921, and this led to the establishment of "specialized" cinemas such as the Vieux Colombier, established by Jean Tedesco in 1924. (Specialized cinemas were commercially run cinemas that nevertheless attempted to balance art and commerce in favor of the former more than mainstream venues; film clubs or societies were, on the other hand, usually member organizations and therefore run through subscription fees.) London was the venue for the long-running Film Society, a members-only organization that began in 1925, while New York film society activity started in the same year when Symon Gould established the Screen Guild (Horak 1995: 20). By the end of the 1920s, a number of film societies and small, specialized commercial cinemas had been established in several countries.

The establishment of these film societies and specialized cinemas were important precursors to the emergence of the phenomenon of cult cinema for a number of reasons. First, this was a time when people were creating a cultural environment for like-minded people to view films they were passionate about, and to extend this passion for films through discussions, writings, and other extra-filmic events. In this sense, they were going against the dominant trend of films as ephemeral objects to be consumed and then forgotten about, and instead establishing films as enduring cultural objects. The importance ascribed to specific films, in tandem with the communal cultural spaces created to view films, can be related to Telotte's contention about cult films "speaking meaningfully to a select group" and to his point that the cultist's love for film speaks of *difference* from, for example, "normal marketing practices and viewing customs" (Telotte 1991a: 7).

Although it was not employed frequently during this period, the term "cult" did occasionally feature in writings to describe audience behaviors. American critic Harry Allan Potamkin discussed "film cults" in an article on prominent taste patterns evident among cine-club patrons. He used the term in a predominantly negative sense, suggesting that the "herd-like" behavior intellectual cineastes often accused the "mass audience" of also marked various trends within their own circles. Thus, for Potamkin, a number of "fads" marked cult audience behaviors and some people were too keen to latch onto the latest cult – which here included Charlie Chaplin and Mickey Mouse among others – in an "unthinking" manner. Thus, for Potamkin, film cults were marked by snobbery, laziness, and a lack of intellectual substance (Potamkin 2008: 28). In a similar manner Kenneth Macpherson, editor of the British film journal *Close Up*, excoriated Parisian cinephiles for "intellectual kowtowing" (1930: 2). What these interventions demonstrate is that, while these cine-cultures established in various parts of the world were generally supportive of one another, they were not devoid of tensions. The ways in which Potamkin and Macpherson attempted to distinguish themselves from other currents within alternative cine-culture, anticipate the broader and more fragmented in-fighting that has often characterized cult fan cultures. In contrast with the tendency for the word "cult" to be used positively in more recent fan discussions, it was used negatively in these instances. Such distanced critiques of cult viewers, including Potamkin's accusation that cults are never self-critical or objective (2008: 28), could nevertheless be seen as foreshadowing the more Bourdieu-inflected analyses of distinctions among cult audiences within academia (Jancovich 2002).

It is reasonable to label films that gained particular adoration in these cultural circles as the first examples of cult films: cinephiles hailed such films because of their assumed importance, part of which emerged from their *difference* from the mainstream. Even if a film itself was a product of a commercialized industry, it could still become a cult object if its aesthetic properties represented a divergence from commercial norms and pointed to new artistic routes. In the 1920s, *The Cabinet of Dr. Caligari* (Figure 14.1) was perhaps the biggest cult film and was labeled "the cult *par excellence* of the little cinema" by Potamkin (2008: 27). Initially, the film was released on the commercial (or mainstream) circuit and was successful in the United

Figure 14.1 *The Cabinet of Dr. Caligari* was described as "the cult *par excellence*" by critic Harry Allan Potamkin.

States, but it later became resurrected when small cinemas emerged in the mid 1920s (Thompson 1990: 139–149). In Paris, Louis Delluc had to overcome an exhibitors' ban on German films by sponsoring a single screening of *Caligari* as part of a Spanish Red Cross benefit program at the Colisée cinema on November 14, 1921 (Thompson 1990: 151). This led to the film becoming a popular success within France, before emerging as a staple on the cine-club circuit where, as Thompson points out, a "devoted fan would have been able to see it almost every year throughout the decade" (1990: 157).

Another film made within a very different industrial context but which was also subject to intense cinephile devotion was Eisenstein's *Battleship Potemkin*. The film's status benefited from the increased interest in Soviet films both across West Europe and in the United States in the late 1920s, which were becoming increasingly available for viewing. Many of these, particularly films by Eisenstein, Pudovkin, and Vertov, represented examples of advanced cinematic art for a number of cinephiles. It was *Potemkin*, however, which tended to be hailed as the greatest example and it was screened repeatedly within film societies. While the film today is canonized as a prime example of respectable cinema, this was not the case at this temporal juncture, which points to the ways that previous films' reputations can shift over time. In the late 1920s and early 1930s it even had the cachet of being a "forbidden" film, banned as it was in many countries.

Many societies were able to circumvent such legal restrictions because their members policy meant that they were not, strictly, public screenings. Nevertheless, in Britain, while the prestigious London Film Society was permitted to exhibit *Potemkin*, the London Workers Film Society was twice refused permission to screen it. The London County Council thought that the film would have been politically inflammatory if shown to working-class audiences in a way that would not affect the more bourgeois audience members of the Film Society. Even the Film Society screenings aroused suspicion from the government, though, which led to a discussion of the Society's activities within the House of Commons (Sexton 2008a: 28).

One other film particularly worthy of mention that was first screened within the international cine-club circuit is Luis Buñuel and Salvador Dali's *Un Chien Andalou*. The film was planned to outrage and shock, though it largely failed to do so, much to Buñuel's chagrin (Koller 2001). The ability of a film to confront taboos and cause a public scandal is a key contributor to cult status, yet was more successfully achieved by the film that Buñuel and Dali made next, *L'Âge d'or*, which led to audience protests and soon found itself banned (Williams 2000). Nevertheless, *Un Chien Andalou* arguably attained a greater cult status through its longevity, as it was repeatedly screened in a number of contexts. Not only did it enjoy an eight-month run in Paris (Koller 2001), it has continued to play within niche viewing contexts across international spaces at different times. For example, in the United States it was screened on a number of occasions at Amos Vogel's Cinema 16, a key postwar film society that would feed into the 1960s underground circuit. The underground circuit itself would then play a key role in the rise of the midnight movie phenomenon, where *Un Chien Andalou* continued to play, often paired with features such as Tod Browning's *Freaks* (Hoberman and Rosenbaum 1991: 295). Thus, though the film may have failed to outrage audiences at the time of its release in the way it intended, it has continued to matter to different audiences existing on the margins of the mainstream. Its confrontational power is undiminished, with its eye-slicing scene still managing to make many contemporary viewers wince.

The American Underground of the 1950s and 1960s

While Manny Farber used the term "underground film" in 1957 to refer to low-budget adventure films (Farber 1998), a new group of critics and filmmakers actively challenging mainstream norms of film production, distribution, and exhibition, would soon appropriate the concept in a more determined fashion. The key figure within this movement was undoubtedly Jonas Mekas, a Lithuanian who emigrated to the United States in 1949 and became a passionate spokesperson for a new cinema. Mekas established the journal *Film Culture* in 1955, which would become a key promoter of underground cinema, and wrote on film for the New York paper *The Village Voice*. While initially hostile to experimental work, Mekas soon began to champion it and in 1960 formed the "New American Cinema Group." This primarily supported a number of filmmakers working on lower budgets, who wanted to produce features of artistic interest outside of the Hollywood "system." Within its orbit were filmmakers such as John Cassavetes, Richard Leacock, and Shirley Clarke. The group's first statement forthrightly declared its intention to go against mainstream cinema, seen as glossy and insincere. In contrast, the new cinema claimed to be authentic, truthful, and spontaneous: "We don't want false, polished, slick films," it announced, "we prefer them rough, unpolished, but alive; we don't want rosy films – we want them the colour of blood" (New American Cinema Group 2000: 83). The group also adopted a firm anti-censorship stance, proposed to create a cooperative distribution center, and announced that the New Yorker cinema, the Bleecker Street cinema, and Overbrook theater in Philadelphia, had already agreed to exhibit their films (2000: 81–82).

The establishment of the New American Cinema Group was not an isolated phenomenon, but emerged in tandem with a flurry of small-scale film production, distribution, and exhibition. Lightweight 16 mm cameras became easy to get hold of as surplus war equipment was sold off and the amateur film market exponentially grew. Cheaper film stock and an increase in film laboratories meant that filmmaking was open to more people, while the affordability of 16 mm projectors led to a proliferation of cine-clubs and college film societies. At first, Mekas and the New American Cinema Group were trying to differentiate themselves from the precedent set by Amos Vogel and Cinema 16, the film society that ran from 1947 to 1963. Whereas Cinema 16 typified an avant-garde ethos, the New American Cinema Group attempted to forge a path that lay somewhere in between the micro-budget short film and the Hollywood feature. This would be a short-lived movement, however, and it was superseded by the more enduring, and influential, Filmmakers' Cooperative, formed in 1961.

After the establishment of the Filmmaker's Cooperative, Mekas began to champion much lower-budgeted avant-garde and experimental films. Unlike the earlier American avant-garde, though, the underground avant-garde of the 1960s became associated with a less rigorous attitude towards filmmaking. The Cooperative was a distribution facility that aided the exhibition of small-scale films and, unlike many previous alternative distribution units, did not have any selection criteria (a policy shared by San Francisco's Canyon cinema). As Paul Arthur has noted, Mekas began to reject tenets of professionalism; in contrast, he regarded ignorance and poverty as positive terms and associated them with authenticity and spontaneity (Arthur 2005: 18). As the 1960s unfolded, this low-budget, "anything goes" ethos became connected, in particular, to the broader social counterculture as well as a camp aesthetic. In relation to the former, it appealed to, and was taken up by, many people involved in campaigning for greater freedoms, be they sexual (e.g. the rise of gay rights), artistic (e.g. freedom of expression), or sensory (e.g. the right to partake in illicit substance consumption). A camp aesthetic (Chapter 8), meanwhile, became an important artistic thread running through many of the films made within the underground milieu. As opposed to the earlier American avant-garde's modernist rejection of popular culture, many films now began to engage with a range of populist works. These included Jack Smith's *Flaming Creatures*, Kenneth Anger's *Scorpio Rising*, and Mike Kuchar's *Sins of the Fleshapoids*.

The movement towards populism and away from professionalism came under attack from many for abandoning any standards whatsoever. The critic Parker Tyler, who had previously practiced a camp approach to film criticism, was one of the most vociferous critics of the underground and voiced his complaints at length in his *Underground Film: A Critical History*, first published in 1969. For Tyler, many of the films being shown within this milieu were marked by a self-indulgent infantilism and retarded the efforts made by previous avant-gardists to create new cinematic art. Greg Taylor has argued that Tyler's criticism failed to acknowledge how Mekas and the underground were actually challenging restrictive aesthetic freedoms:

> Underground freedom was more than simply freedom from repressive moral standards. It was also freedom from taste conventions and aesthetic niceties, the freedom to appreciate without criticizing, to enjoy all culture, and on one's own terms. These were radical and unabashedly vanguard ideas. Mekas was brazenly liberating the artist and spectator, throwing out the old guidelines for effective art, throwing into question the very importance of valuative criticism. (Taylor 1999: 112)

This argument ignores, however, the extent to which Mekas did actually erect discriminatory criteria; it was just broader and of a different order. If he completely abolished all such criteria then he would not have been so damning of Hollywood productions. Within the underground, Hollywood was acceptable when it constituted material to be plundered and transformed through a low-budget lens, but it was to be opposed on the level of *practice*. This broad "us against them" criteria fueled the alternative community and marked many underground currents as cult, as indicated in the following quote by Greg Taylor: "Less important than the formal or hermeneutic sophistication of a particular film was its existence as an experience to be shared, praised, explored" (1999: 99). Taylor also argues that cultist and camp approaches in the writing of critics such as Farber and Tyler, were evident in the filmmaking of underground filmmakers. Cultism, for Taylor, is characterized by a selective reading of popular culture and a transformation of that culture into a more exclusive form of cultural connoisseurship; while he argues that camp is similar but less selective: it "celebrates *any mass object* that is capable of being re-created aesthetically" (1999: 16).

If the underground constituted a film community of outsiders, then a fraternal spirit was consolidated by police raids of various screenings. These, in turn, aided the cult status of the actual films involved. *Flaming Creatures* and *Scorpio Rising* arguably constitute the two main cult films that emerged from this culture and both were subject to police interventions. Shot on outdated army surplus film stock, which gives it a washed-out, otherworldly feel, *Flaming Creatures* depicts a transvestite bacchanalia. Director Jack Smith gathered friends and constructed a cheap set on the top of the Windsor cinema in New York. With its attempt to mimic exotic Hollywood B-movies on a threadbare budget, the film embodies a kind of junk-shop glamour. This aesthetic is important to the film's cult reputation, but its controversial reception is undoubtedly central in this regard. Screenings left audiences stunned; as Ken Kelman wrote, after one of the first shows at Bleecker Street Theatre:

> When the first show was over, a clique, a claque of six or so, back on the west side applauded. And I, all alone, east of the aisle up frontish, applauded, amid the numb and blind. Amid the tame, I halted, oppressed by their inertia, paused, vacillated, considered for two beats of silence or three, before I clapped solo and thus no doubt branded myself a clappy pervert, crap happy degenerate, slobbering sadist, or, even, perhaps Jack Smith. (Kelman 1970: 284)

Kelman's description captures a key aspect of the midnight movie, and of the cult reception trajectory: the sense of a truly unique, forbidden experience that would pitch oneself against the rest of the world; a countercultural feeling. Soon controversy followed. In December 1963, the Tivoli Theater in New York refused to screen the film on the evening that Smith was to be presented with *Film Culture*'s Independent Filmmaker Award, due to pressure from the city's bureau of licenses (the film had not been submitted to the New York State Board of Regents for licensing). As we have noted in Chapter 3, controversy surrounded the film again shortly afterwards when an experimental film festival in Knokke-le-Zoute in Belgium refused to screen it. It was then, along with Jean Genet's *Un Chant d'Amour*, subject to a crackdown by New York authorities in 1964 as they attempted to clean up the city's image in preparation

for the World Fair taking place later in the year. Police often raided cinemas screening the film, impounding it along with projector equipment, while theater staff were sometimes arrested and jailed. This placed the film and the underground movement more generally within broader cultural debates and further politicized the movement. As Arthur has noted: "the *Flaming Creatures* affair briefly placed avant-garde film on the cultural map, stimulating support from quarters previously oblivious to or even hostile to the movement" (2005: 10). *Flaming Creatures*' cult reputation arguably endures: it has never enjoyed an official DVD release so that people wishing to view it have to obtain low quality bootleg copies or watch it through specialist websites such as UbuWeb.

It was into this melting-pot atmosphere that Kenneth Anger's *Scorpio Rising* was released. A homoerotic collage of biker subculture images and pop music, it was reported to be "the most widely seen experimental movie of its time and the most frequently rented title in the repertoire of the Filmmakers' Cooperative" (Suarez 2002: 115). The film premiered at the Gramercy Arts Theater in 1963 and went on to play in a number of different venues, including art cinemas and more mainstream outlets (Suarez 2002: 115). While it is not as explicit as *Flaming Creatures*, it still did not sit well with the authorities. The film therefore was subject to legal proceedings: Mike Getz was charged with screening an obscene film at the Cinema Theatre in March 1964, because of a brief flash of frontal male nudity (Hoberman and Rosenbaum 1991: 60). Unlike *Flaming Creatures*, however, the film's status as obscene was eventually overturned. While controversy certainly informs its cult credentials, other reasons also inform this reputation, including Anger's broader cult status, its aesthetic originality, and its coverage of marginal subcultures.

Andy Warhol is possibly the only filmmaker connected to the underground who has a larger cult following than Anger, though this is due not only to his filmmaking but to his larger profile within the art world. Warhol's films range from his early, extremely minimal works such as *Sleep* and the extremely long *Empire*, to the double-screen, more situation-driven *Chelsea Girls*, and into more narrative-focused works that Paul Morrissey directed under Warhol's aegis, including *Flesh* and *Trash*. Warhol's celebrity reputation, allied with his often very challenging films and the fact that they have become difficult to actually see, have imbued most of his films with cult value. Warhol withdrew his films from public circulation in the early 1970s and they were not publicly available until after he died (in 1987). Even since then they have been quite difficult to see: they appear sporadically on VHS and DVD, often through obscure labels (such as the Italian label RaroVideo), while public screenings are still rare. As such, they continue to attract considerable public interest, despite the challenging nature of the material. A film such as *Empire*, meanwhile, has the cult value of being a long, live experience, something that not too many people are able to endure (an eight-hour, static view of the Empire state building), so that it becomes a communal experience for those that do (Mathijs and Mendik 2008b: 4).

Warhol was fixated on stars as cult objects (Chapter 7), as was evident in many of his screen prints as well as his screen tests; and he himself managed to foster a kind of alternative star system through his film production. Joe Dallesandro and Edie Sedgwick are two of the most well-known examples of Warhol stars who themselves became cult figures. Dallesandro was a former hustler and model who went on to appear in a large number of Warhol's films, including films that Paul Morrissey made under the Warhol moniker (Figure 14.2). He became a kind of underground sex symbol in the late 1960s/early 1970s and went on to sustain an acting career, albeit mostly in smaller roles.

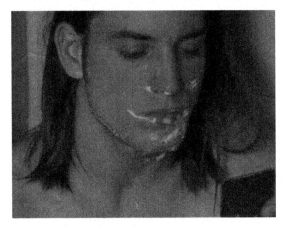

Figure 14.2 Joe Dallesandro became a cult figure primarily through his appearances in Paul Morrissey's films made under the aegis of Andy Warhol.

His cult reputation has been heightened by his appearance on record covers: his crotch formed the basis of the Warhol-designed sleeve for the Rolling Stones' *Sticky Fingers* (1971), while a still of him in *Flesh* adorns the cover of The Smiths' (1984) eponymous debut album.

Sedgwick was a particular favorite of Warhol's, at least around the mid 1960s, as he saw star potential in her. Making her debut in *Vinyl*, she appeared in a number of Warhol films around this time and became one of the most glamorous underground figures. Despite wanting to break into larger acting roles, she became increasingly beset by drug and mental health problems, which led to her early death in 1971 at the age of 28. Her last film, *Ciao! Manhattan* has proven to be a fascinating document because Sedgwick's real life is mirrored in the character that she plays (Susan Superstar), who is a washed-up star suffering from mental illness.

Underground Goes Overground: The Midnight Movie

A particular reason why US underground film culture during this period is important is that it fed into the rising popularity of midnight movie screenings, at which many cult films attracted their dedicated followings (see Chapters 1 and 12 for discussions of midnight movies beyond their relationship with the underground). Mekas himself ran weekend midnight screenings at the Charles Theater in Manhattan, where he programmed a number of underground movies before the cinema closed in 1962 (it reopened in 1963 as a more conventional operation) (Hoberman and Rosenbaum 1991: 42). Mekas then started another series of midnight film screenings entitled "Underground Midnights" at the nearby Bleecker Street cinema in 1963 (Hoberman and Rosenbaum 1991: 46). Midnight screenings were not new, but the 1960s saw them enjoy an unprecedented popularity and this carried on into the 1970s, a decade generally regarded as the heyday of the midnight movie. Samuels, for example, has written that the rise in midnight screenings was kick-started by the underground and the huge amount of films made on low budgets. By 1972, it had "become an established part of theatrical film exhibition" with an estimated \$35 million a year being collected at midnight screenings (Samuels 1983: 10–11).

The move from underground to overground is worth noting, yet despite this trend, many of the big "hits" of the underground circuit are still considered to be underground and/or avant-garde, including *El Topo*, *Pink Flamingos*, and *Eraserhead*. In a sense, the midnight movie phenomenon, while becoming hugely popular, was still marginal in the sense that many of its audience members felt outside of mainstream culture in various ways (through sexual orientation, political beliefs, etc.). The midnight movie explosion in the 1970s saw a number of independently made films gaining a cult following through repeated viewings. Many of these, though, were of feature length as opposed to the shorts that had (albeit not exclusively) characterized underground filmmaking in the 1960s. In a sense, the avant-garde/underground of the 1960s splintered into two broad pathways: first, a more serious, rigorous direction typified by "structural" filmmaking; secondly, the more populist, narrative-centered, yet occasionally experimental direction typified by the films mentioned above. Such films in many senses are difficult to categorize because they straddle numerous boundaries: they could be called underground, independent, or sometimes (as with *El Topo* and *Eraserhead*), avant-garde.

It is the second direction that is most appropriate to cult cinema because the former strand generally remained somewhat too restricted to gain cult followings. Thus, while underground and avant-garde screening venues and distribution networks proliferated on an international scale from the 1960s onwards, it is difficult to establish cult films within such environments for two particular reasons. First, many films screened within such venues quickly vanish; secondly, unlike the US underground of the 1960s, documentation of these underground nodes is sparse, so it is often difficult to establish screening and viewing patterns with any precision.[1] It is only when underground films emerge from micro-niche environments and impinge upon broader cultural radars that they begin to gain cult value. This can happen in a number of ways, but perhaps the most important are controversy and exceptionality. Controversy can link a film to current social debates (as with *Flaming Creatures*) and

lead to debate within mainstream media channels; exceptionality can see a film play so many times within micro-niche settings that it becomes recognized by outsiders and will then play other types of venues, or be spread throughout a wider niche community (often beyond a national border).

The Underground Today

The lack of extant documentation on underground viewing contexts complicates a proper sketch of more recent activity in this area. Suffice it to say, there has existed from the 1960s to the current day a great range of underground screening outlets, distribution networks, publications (e.g. zines, manifestoes, web sites), festivals and other initiatives around the world. Many have led transient existences, though others have managed – despite great practical challenges – to attain longevity. This is complicated further by the looseness of the term itself. Of course, it was never a simple concept but in hindsight at least, the US underground of the 1960s is associated with the term in a relatively unproblematic manner, mainly because it constitutes a kind of fulcrum point to which subsequent instances refer. Generally, though, it now refers to any film not picked up by a distribution company for a conventional theatrical release, as is argued by Hall (2004: xiv). Others would suggest, however, that there should be some form of radical, perhaps even transgressive, attitude embedded within the film. The controversial filmmaker Nick Zedd, a New York underground filmmaker, openly states that "To me it's not underground unless it's transgressive" (Sargeant 1999: 75; see also Chapter 9 for more on transgression and cult cinema). While it is not possible to fully freeze the concept, we can posit that underground films attempt to challenge through various means (e.g. through attempts to shock, attempts to challenge on the level of form, attempts to propose radical political ideas), and do not enjoy conventional cinematic releases (they either bypass mainstream cinemas and art houses, or they perhaps play them either sporadically or long after they are initially released).

Since the 1960s, a number of underground films have gained cult status, but it is only possible in the remainder of this chapter to mention some of these and how they moved from mere underground films to underground cult films. Controversy, which has been linked to underground cults throughout this chapter, is still a chief factor in leading to cult status, though it must be mentioned that controversy alone will not guarantee such a reputation. Low-budget films, because they are not designed to play at mainstream theaters and are rarely submitted to formal censorship boards, often have greater latitude to deal with extreme or risky material. The Japanese film *Emperor Tomato Ketchup*, for example, has gained a cult following due to its controversial content, which depicts children condemning their parents to death for depriving them of sexual freedom and features sexual acts between children and adults. The 1971 version of the film (a longer 1976 version also exists) was produced for European audiences and played in a number of underground venues. It has continued to garner interest, with rock group Stereolab releasing an album named after the film in 1995, and its controversial content imbuing it with rarity value. More recently, the web has increased chances of seeing this film; not only can one find DVD-R copies for sale, but it is also possible to see the film on UbuWeb and clips of the film on YouTube. Similar reception contexts exist for films such as *Nekromantik* and *Begotten*, which stand out because they try to offer a transcendental as much as a phenomenal experience through grainy, distorted, and blurry depictions of violence and transgression. In doing so, they reinforce the impression that underground cinema's cult appeal is also one that evokes a religiosity. Elias Merhige's *Begotten* carries the motto that "a time is depicted that predates spoken language, communication is made on a sensory level." Jorg Buttgereit's controversial *Nekromantik* movies have gained a cult status following their controversial reception in Germany. *Nekromantik* was released directly into cinemas without submission to the coding board and while not immediately subject to external restrictions, it was subsequently banned after *Nekromantik 2* was deemed illegal to watch, own, or screen (Blake 2004: 195). The films subsequently gained a cult following in other parts of the world, especially the United States, and are now available to purchase on DVD (though not through mainstream channels such as Amazon, which adds to their cult cachet).

Today the number of underground films produced, and the venues in which they can play (in particular the rise of specialist festivals), has continued to increase. The internet has also provided a new platform for the dissemination and screening of underground films through specialist sites such as Underground.com, while the relatively low cost of issuing DVDs has allowed a growing number of such films (as well as older underground films) to disseminate in this manner. The rise of films produced, though, will mean that more and more films will struggle to gain recognition, let alone become cult films. Nevertheless, the ever-shifting and increasingly digital mediascape will afford new routes and opportunities for the next underground cults to emerge.

Note

1. For example, the London Filmmakers' Co-Op, formed in 1966 has been well documented, though it is doubtful that any film emerging within this milieu subsequently attained cult status.

15

Cult Cinema and Drugs

A high number of cult films have links to drugs, either through featuring drugs in the plot, by referencing them abundantly, or by gaining a reputation for ideal viewing in a drugged state.[1] There are some important connections between drugs and their users on the one hand, and cult films and their audiences on the other. For example, cult film viewers have often differentiated themselves from mainstream film viewers and, by extension, mainstream society as a whole via attachment to films expressive of such difference. Bruce Kawin has written of the cult film "as a deviant or radically different picture, embraced by a deviant audience" (1991: 18), while Jancovich *et al.* have argued that the cult film is formed through a "subcultural ideology" that places films and/or filmmakers and/or audiences in opposition to the mainstream (2003a: 1). Drugs have also played a crucial role in many sociological accounts of deviance and subcultures (see Chapter 5). In various, often youthful, subcultural groupings, different drugs have often played important roles as agents of altered consciousness that can erect barriers between "us" and "them" (i.e. "straight," conventional society). This was particularly evident within the various hippy or "head" subcultures that emerged in the 1960s. In his ethnographic study of hippies, Paul Willis wrote that "the importance of drugs did not lie in their direct physical effects, but in the way they facilitated passing through a great symbolic barrier erected over against 'straight' society" (1976: 107). In particular, it was hallucinogens – most notably marijuana and LSD – that facilitated an appropriate altered state far removed from dominant cultural rhythms.

Hippie subcultures had their roots in the earlier beat generation, another subcultural movement that used drugs – along with literature, jazz, and Eastern mysticism – to place itself against straight society in favor of extolling expressivity, spontaneity, and creativity (Brake 1980: 91). It is perhaps no coincidence that the beats had connections to underground film culture, which established midnight movie screenings as a cult ritual. Amos Vogel, for example, has described midnight viewers at the Charles Theater as a "properly bedraggled beat audience spitting in the face of the bourgeoisie" (quoted in Hoberman and Rosenbaum 1991: 42). Many of the films connected to the underground were also examples of Beat Cinema and include: Alfred Lesley's *Pull my Daisy*, which was narrated by Jack Kerouac and featured Allen Ginsberg and Gregory Corso; Ron Rice's *The Flower Thief*, featuring poet Taylor Mead; and shorts by beatnik artist Harry Smith. Midnight movie screenings became popularized throughout the 1960s and 1970s, established on the 16 mm college circuit and in repertory theaters, whose audiences were heavily represented by students (Austin 1981a: 44). Many involved (either centrally or tangentially) with the hippie culture were also either students or student dropouts, whose dope-smoking proclivities were permitted within a number of such venues. Therefore, a significant overlap between the audiences associated with midnight movies and hippie subcultures existed, which resulted in the elevation of films with drug connections. We should make it clear, then, that this chapter is significantly concerned with drug films connected to midnight

Cult Cinema: An Introduction. Ernest Mathijs and Jamie Sexton.
© 2011 Ernest Mathijs and Jamie Sexton. Published 2011 by Blackwell Publishing Ltd.

movie viewing, youth countercultures in the 1960s and 1970s, and hallucinogenic drugs, as this triumvirate of factors interlocks to constitute the most significant body of drug cult films. Nevertheless, a number of important films exist outside of this remit and we will consider some of these in the latter section.

Cult Movies and Drug Depiction

Films depicting the use of drugs stem back to the earliest days of cinema. In 1894 Edison made a 30-second kinetograph (a film that could be viewed on a kinetoscope, a pre-cinematic viewing device) entitled *Chinese Opium Den*, which featured opium smoking (Starks 1982: 13). Up until the 1920s, when Hollywood began to take measures to defend itself against outraged moralists – leading to the advent of the Production Code in 1930 (not strictly enforced until 1934) – and with drug laws less prohibitive than they would later become, drugs featured in many films. The effects of drugs (such as the experience of being under the influence of opium) sometimes provided an excuse to indulge in experimental shots, including superimpositions and unusual angles. Not until we get to the 1930s, however, do we encounter films that would subsequently gain a cult status. In particular, some films released by exploitation producer Dwain Esper would gain cult followings in the 1970s.

Esper was among the many exploitation film producers who emerged after the Production Code was passed (see Chapter 13 for details on exploitation cinema). Esper's first film as an independent producer was *Narcotic*, the story of a doctor who becomes addicted to both opium and heroin. While the film was framed as a moral tale – with the doctor eventually committing suicide – it nevertheless wallowed in its graphic presentation of drugs, as well as sex. According to Stevenson, the film played over two thousand engagements before it hit the road-show circuit, where it played sporadically into the 1950s (Stevenson 2000: 25). Esper later purchased and reissued a film he titled *Reefer Madness*, which would become a huge cult favorite. He had purchased the rights to the film, originally titled *Tell Your Children* and produced by an LA church group (directed by Louis Gasner). While the film did not enjoy much success in the 1930s it was

revived in the early 1970s on the midnight movie circuit, where it gained a real following among pot-heads, who took ironic pleasure from the film's almost demented anti-drug propaganda.

Between the 1930s and 1950s, films about drugs tended to be exploitation pictures sensationalizing the impact of drugs and warning of their dangers. As the 1950s progressed, however, things began to change as the Production Code was gradually relaxed. A key moment in the celluloid depiction of drug use came with the 1955 release of Otto Preminger's *The Man with the Golden Arm*. The film, starring Frank Sinatra as a heroin user, and produced by a major studio, was released without a seal and yet widely screened. Fearing the loss of authority, in line with a number of other films challenging its mandate, the PCA appended the Code in 1956 to allow treatments of drug addiction, prostitution and child birth as long as they were "treated within the careful limits of good taste" (Stevenson 2000: 38). As the stringent Production Code gradually eroded in the late 1950s and the 1960s, there emerged a number of more daring cinematic depictions of drug use, many of which would become cult films. Of particular importance was the emergence of a youth market.

The youth market came to prominence in the mid 1950s, particularly in the United States, but also in other parts of the Western world. At this stage, audiences for movies began to drop with the rise of television, the middle-class exodus to the suburbs, and a host of other competing leisure activities. Major studios started to produce fewer films as a result, which meant that some theaters lacked sufficient product. To fill the gap, a new batch of independent filmmakers stepped in with films that were often "cheap, regular and exploitable" (Doherty 2002: 28). Around the same time, the rise of the teenager as an identifiably distinct, self-conscious and affluent category had emerged (Doherty 2002: 34), so a number of these exploitation films were catering to this audience. As many of these films exploited controversial themes, it was no surprise that some of them featured drugs, such as *The Cool and the Crazy* and *High School Confidential!* Many of these films, like their exploitation forbears, were moralistic in nature, but in other ways looked forward to a number of more important drug films that emerged in the 1960s.

Counterculture, Drugs and the "Head" Film

If teenagers constituted a broad subculture in the 1950s, then the 1960s saw an extension, but also a splintering, of this phenomenon. In particular, a marked self-conscious generation gap and anti-institutional attitudes fed into a burgeoning counter-culture, in which drugs became a symbol of pride and subversion. Hippie factions, as mentioned above, were so conspicuous (through media reportage) that it was only a matter of time before films were made to capitalize upon some of the tropes associated with them, one of which was drugs (mainly LSD and marijuana). With the media increasingly reporting upon the consumption and (often-supposed) effects of LSD around the mid 1960s, a number of exploita-tion films featuring this drug subsequently appeared. Like a number of the older drug exploitation films, many of these films were moralistic at core, poaching hysterical tabloid reports about LSD (that it led to suicide, psychosis, murder) and reveling in the excess of the condemned antics that transpired: such films included *Hallucination Generation* and *The Acid Eaters*. Other films utilized the spurious reports that LSD lowered inhibitions to embed druggy frolics within sexploitation comedies: for example, *Alice in Acidland* and *Wanda, the Sadistic Hypnotist*. It was not long before Hollywood entered the fray, most notoriously with Otto Preminger's outrageous LSD comedy *Skidoo*, starring Jackie Gleason, Mickey Rooney, and Groucho Marx among others. This disastrous comedy has since become a cult film, though is not currently easy to get hold of, probably because it has always been a source of embarrassment to most people involved in its production.

Some of the above movies featured small scenes translating the supposed effects of an LSD trip onto the screen, but such scenes did not often constitute a substantial proportion of the films' running time. The cult status accorded such films often relates to their campy nature, an outrageousness of tone and a failure to achieve any kind of "authentic" expressiveness. On the other hand, a number of films have achieved cult status through either implicitly or explicitly represent-ing some of the experiential properties of drugs such as

LSD, or sometimes marijuana. Such films tend to be labeled "head" films, as well as "headsploitation" films (Haas 1983). Benshoff has summed up the head film as:

> a type of movie that is either specifically produced to be experienced on drugs or that has subsequently become identified by drug users as a film that can be pleasantly enhanced via the ingestion of mind-altering chemicals, most usually hallucinogens such as marijuana, LSD and their analogues. (Benshoff 2001: 31)

He goes on to add that head films emerge "through the ongoing discussion and experience of them within a community of drug-using cineastes" (Benshoff 2001: 31) Thus, a niche community – often with shared values – flocking around a film for a particular reason and with a ritualistic drug of choice to ingest for the occasion, fits comfortably into a movie cult. Moreover, within the "head" drug world, there are certain films that seem to capture cinematically the head experience and lock into the drugged viewer's perceptual appara-tus. For example, Benshoff has argued that the head film can be allied to Gunning's idea of early cinema as a "cinema of attractions," a cinema that is more geared towards providing pleasurable visual moments rather than tight, linear cause-effect narratives (2001: 31). As hallucinogens tend to heighten spatial awareness and the immediacy of sensation, temporal matters are fre-quently downplayed; hence, for Benshoff, the head film often revolves around "spectacular aural and visual effects," focusing on color, movement, and abstractions (2001: 31).

A film that straddles the dividing line between the campy, moral exploitation drug picture and the more serious, exploratory head film is Roger Corman's *The Trip*. It was made for exploitation producers AIP but they were uneasy with the film because it was a positive depiction of LSD. In the film Paul (Peter Fonda), an advertising director having a mid-life crisis (disillu-sioned with his commercial work and undergoing marital problems), uses LSD in a therapeutic manner under the supervision of John (Bruce Dern), a figure modeled on real-life LSD advocate Timothy Leary. The manner in which the film depicted this trip as largely positive led to AIP placing a disclaimer about the dangers of taking drugs at the beginning of the film and an insistence that a cracked image be placed over

Peter Fonda's face at the end of the film, to indicate irreparable damage resulted from ingesting LSD. It still proved controversial: in the United States, many reviewers were outraged and its initial advertising had to be redesigned in order to placate broadcasters and publishers. In the United Kingdom the British Board of Film Classification (BBFC) refused it a certificate after psychiatrists deemed it "meretricious, inaccurate in its representations and therefore dangerous" (Starks 1982: 60). Its controversial nature in the United Kingdom fueled its cult status even further as a *film maudit*: many more knew about it than were able to see it. (It was not granted a UK certificate until 2003 and was released on UK DVD in 2004.)

Despite this controversy, *The Trip* – released in 1967 – can be seen as opening the way for the growth of more positive depictions of drugs. It is also, in its rather loose plotting and emphasis on subjective drugged experiences, an important head film. Using a combination of techniques, such as liquid and carousel projectors, strobe lights, special lenses, superimpositions, focal changes and camera movements, this was one of the most sustained attempts to recreate subjective elements of an acid trip in an American feature film. Many of the effects are not actually representations of an acid state as such, more the creation of a type of generalized hallucinatory state. As psychedelics are capable of enhancing interest in abstract patterns, and of giving the impression of visual movement, abstract imagery therefore appears in a number of sequences.

The late 1960s and early 1970s was a period when youth countercultures with strong drug predilections were particularly marked, and which saw the emergence and/or extension of cult viewing spaces (drive-ins, grindhouses, art cinemas and midnight-movie screenings), it is therefore no surprise that this was the strongest period of the cult head film. Some head films explicitly featured drugs and would use the drugged experience of characters – particularly LSD – to create an audiovisual representation of the head state: films falling into this category include *Easy Rider* and *Performance*. However, films did not need to represent drug use in any explicit manner. Some films, for example, could imply the head state through knowing winks and resolutely non-linear plots: *Head*, featuring the pop band The Monkees, is a key example of this kind of film; obvious to those in the know, but perhaps

working on a different level for those who do not cotton onto the drug references. (The key advantage of this type of "double entendre head film" is that it is less susceptible to censorship controversy.) Other films work in different ways: *2001: A Space Odyssey*, for example, is perhaps not an intentional head film in the manner of *Head*. Nevertheless, its spectacular space scenes, often standing alone as immersive experiences irrespective of their narrative framework, created sequences analogous to the drugged experience and (for some) proved pleasurable to watch in such a state. In particular, the "Stargate sequence" was required viewing for viewers under the influence of LSD, due to its abstract depiction of a type of "cosmic consciousness" (Figure 15.1). In fact, because the film was about space, cosmic issues, and travelling beyond known perceptual realms, it was no surprise that it was appropriated as a head film. While Kubrick has downplayed the drug connection, it nevertheless fed into its marketing campaign, with one poster proclaiming it "the ultimate trip" (Castle 2004).

Some of the more abstract films that emerged within the US underground (see Chapter 14), notably films by Harry Smith, Jordon Belson, and James Whitney, undoubtedly influenced the Stargate sequence. A great deal of activity was occurring on the fringes of the cinema industry, as artists created personal, low-budget films. During the 1960s, a number of artists were creating films that either directly reflected their psychedelic experiences, or were perceived as psychedelic in nature. Harry Smith cited both marijuana and other hallucinogens as influences for a number of films that he made, including abstract and geometric

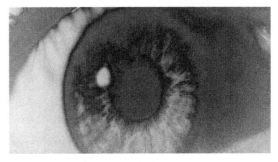

Figure 15.1   Still from the "Stargate" sequence of *2001: A Space Odyssey*, which became known as a "psychedelic" sequence.

hand-drawn films, as well as collage films. Whitney, meanwhile, made a few psychedelic films, such as *Yantra* and the more intricate, "mandala" film *Lapis*, whose raga soundtrack further lent it a drug-tinged edge. Whitney and his brother John were innovators in computer animation and *Lapis* was the first computer-aided film that James completed. Belson, meanwhile, made an increasingly complex set of abstract films based upon inner consciousness – sometimes drawing directly from his hallucinogenic experiences, but also upon meditative states – which he merged with "outer" space concerns to create a form of cosmic cinema. His statement regarding his 1961 film *Allures*, for example, demonstrates how his filmmaking would have appealed to "head cineastes": "It's a trip backwards along the senses into the interior of the being. It fixes your gaze, physically holds your attention" (quoted in Youngblood 1970: 160). Youngblood actually notes that *Allures*, and Belson's next film, *Re-Entry*, have similarities to the Stargate sequence in *2001*, although they both preceded the Douglas Trumbull designed sequence (Youngblood 1970: 162, 167). Youngblood has also claimed that many of the sequences in *The Trip* were inspired by abstract films being shown on the underground circuit (Benshoff 2001: 37). While these films would not have gained huge audiences, they did accrue smaller cult followings within the underground movie circuit which – as mentioned above – fed into a broader cult film culture via the establishment of midnight screenings in rundown inner-city areas; and they were an important influence on the head film.

There are a few psychedelic movies made outside of the United States that also seem to have developed cult followings in some quarters. One of the most notorious, and interesting, is Coffin Joe's *Awakening of the Beast*. Coffin Joe was the alter ego of José Mojica Marins, a Brazilian who had created a horror figure bedecked with a cape, hat, and particularly long fingernails. In *Awakening of the Beast*, Joe serves as a focus for four drug users who are being subject to a scientific experiment. Given doses of LSD, they descend into a psychedelic nightmare world hosted by Joe and signaled by a shift into color from black and white. This remarkable film, which is beautifully surreal yet distastefully misogynist, had its cult credentials boosted by its controversial reception; banned in Brazil, Marins

found it difficult to work for some time. After fading into obscurity, his reputation has been recuperated by cult film fans over the past decade or so. Another film worthy of mention is Federico Fellini's *Toby Dammit*, a segment from the portmanteau of Poe stories, *Spirits of the Dead* he co-directed with Roger Vadim and Louis Malle in 1968. The Fellini segment is by far the most celebrated part of the film. Though not overtly mentioning drugs, it creates a psychedelic environment through which its addled protagonist (played by Terrence Stamp) stumbles, created by the stylized use of light, sound, framing, and mise-en-scène. Fellini himself told Stamp that his character should act as if he had been at a drug and sex saturated party the night before and had been given a large tab of LSD in the morning (Lebbing and Van Der Put 2000: 156).

When the cult of midnight movie screenings flowered in the early 1970s, they often allowed people to smoke dope within their premises and also screened a number of head films. As such, many films attained cult status through their popularity within such contexts. These include, among many others, *Performance*, *El Topo*, *The Harder They Come*, *200 Motels*, and *Magical Mystery Tour*. It is no real surprise, considering that head films are often based around spectacle and nonlinear elements, that many of these films feature prominent use of music and contain musical set-pieces (see Chapter 16). This would fit in with Timothy Corrigan's assertion about cult films more generally as containing a "proleptic rock video form":

> Anticipated by older musicals and anticipating television shows like *Miami Vice*, these narratives often seem to undermine their own narrative structures through loosely connected nonnarrative events whose excessive display either of the visuals or the music becomes a perceptual or aural format for the audience's own performance. (Corrigan 1991: 31)

With the rise of the VCR, the midnight-movie phenomenon began to wane, but people could continue to take drugs and watch films in the more secure environment of their own homes. More recently, it has been marijuana more than LSD that has been the drug of choice to accompany film viewings. This is reflected in guides such as *Baked Potatoes* (Hulme and Wexler 1996), which provides a guide to some of the best films to watch stoned and includes a marijuana-leaf rating scale plus a key to the type of film reviewed (e.g., "Best watched alone," "Feel-good movie," "Subtitled"). Related to stoned viewing is the phenomenon of "stoner films," which often revolve heavily around the use of marijuana (usually in a positive fashion) and thus appeal to dope-smoking film buffs. The series of Cheech and Chong comedies – most notably *Up in Smoke* – are archetypal examples of this type of film, which is often comic in tone. More recent examples include Linklater's *Dazed and Confused* and the Coen Brothers' *The Big Lebowski*, both of which have steadily built up a cult following after initially disappointing performances at the box office.

Beyond Psychedelics

The head film mostly appealed to stoned perception, and occasionally LSD-aided states. Marijuana in particular is well suited to watching films: a relaxant, it aids contemplation and immersion. No other comparable subgenres exist; for example, there do not seem to be any film cycles aimed at the viewer under the influence of heroin or amphetamines. These drugs tend to aid conscious states that are either below or above the threshold suited to watching films. This is not to say that people do not watch films under their influence, but it does partly explain why no cycle comparable to the head film exists in relation to other drugs. Nevertheless, some movies do attempt to approximate other drug states, while there are a number of cult films that feature different drugs.

The use of heroin in particular has featured within a few cult films of note. Importantly, the films of Andy Warhol and Paul Morrissey often featured heroin use (frequently in tandem with other drug intake). Morrissey's *Trash* is one of his most sustained depictions of heroin addiction. The film depicts the lives of two junkies: Joe (Joe Dallesandro) and Holly (transvestite Harold Danhaki), who aimlessly drift from one situation to another. The film is significant because, as claimed by director Paul Morrissey, it was a riposte to the glamorization of drugs evident in many of the 1960s head films. While there is not a heroin equivalent of the head film, this film could perhaps constitute the basis for such a subgenre. With its directionless plot and a main character (Dallesandro) who blankly seems to sleepwalk through the entire movie, it can be seen as a filmic analog of the heroin state (disinterestedness, lack of motivation). The camera also aids this tone by steadily documenting the unfolding performances without the aid of any flashy embellishments. In this, Morrissey continues the aesthetic example of his mentor, Andy Warhol, who was noted for his blankness and an "affectless gaze" (Shaviro 2004: 138). Whereas the head film, then, was often trying to capture the sensational pleasures of drugs via spectacle, Morrissey here downplays spectacle in preference for the mundane, and rejects subjective illustration in favor of an objective gaze. Thus, in a similar manner to how fellow Warhol-affiliated group the Velvet Underground differentiated themselves from the peace and love philosophy espoused by hippy musicians, so Morrissey's film seems to hint at a comparable nihilist sensibility within cinema.

A further factor in the cult status of *Trash*, at least in the United Kingdom, is the controversy surrounding it. The BBFC initially refused to grant the film a certificate in August 1971 because of its possible impact upon susceptible minds, in particular fearing that its explicit drug-taking scenes may prove instructive. The Greater London Council also denied the film a local certificate in September of the same year. It was not until November 1972 that it was passed "X"-rated, though on the insistence that nearly three minutes of material be cut from the film, one of which was the first heroin injection scene. A further twist was added to the saga when distributor James Vaughan added further cuts before it was theatrically released, so that the version British cinema-goers saw was eleven minutes shorter than Morrissey's cut. This was the version that made it to video in 1982, and it was not until 2005 that British film viewers could actually see a full cut of the film when it was released on DVD by Tartan (Lapper 2005). Such a troubled trajectory, partly related to its drug content, further fueled its cult status.

Despite Morrissey's avowed intention of making an anti-drug film, this was not entirely clear in the finished product, as evidenced by the nervousness shown by the British film censors. If the title "Trash" was meant to denigrate the characters within the film, viewers enamored by the sleazy, anti-authoritarian antics depicted could just as easily invert its meaning.

Much like the way hippies adopted the negative term "freak" and wore it as a positive badge of difference, likewise with "trash." In this sense, heroin films can have a wider appeal beyond mere users of the drug; they can also appeal to anyone who feels dissatisfied with the conventional parameters of everyday living. Arguably, such factors feed into the cult status of a film like *Drugstore Cowboy*. This film *does* attempt to convey some sense of the junkie's subjective drug experience, though the broader appeal of the film is arguably linked to a humanist depiction of an outsider community. While it does not glorify heroin users, it nevertheless expresses some of the excitement of choosing, and living, an alternative lifestyle. The appearance of cult writer William Burroughs in a cameo undoubtedly heightens its cult credentials. Other cult films featuring heroin use include Shirley Clarke's documentary satire *The Connection*, which involves a filmmaker attempting to film junkies making a deal; *The Panic in Needle Park*, which stars Al Pacino and Kitty Winn playing two addicted partners; *Christiane F*, Ulrich Edel's stark film about drug addiction; and *More*, Barbet Shroeder's bleak depiction of a young couple's descent into heroin (kicked off by a lighter tone and lighter drugs), which features a Pink Floyd soundtrack. The most recent cult film depicting heroin addiction is *Trainspotting*, the adaptation of Irvin Welsh's novel that caught on with British youths in the mid 1990s. Though it was primarily concerned with heroin use, though, the film also featured the use of other types of drug use (alcohol, amphetamines, ecstasy, and marijuana). Its cult success is explainable partly by how it incorporates a story concerning heroin use into a broader canvas that appealed to the then thriving youth club cultures. A story shot in a strikingly stylistic manner, concerning a bunch of young people taking drugs, feeling they are social outsiders, and with a soundtrack merging older "indie"' hits and newer club sounds, was obviously meant to appeal to a broad range of younger people (elder teenagers and upwards); and in this it succeeded.

Other types of drugs also sporadically feature within a number of disparate cult films. In particular, many blaxploitation films featured narcotics as a central plot component: drug dealers and drug gangs populated many of these films, such as *Super Fly*, *Gordon's War*, and *Foxy Brown*. While some of these films adopted a condemnatory stance against drugs, others, such as *Super Fly*, were more ambiguous. That film's ending, in which a cocaine dealer roams free, led to much criticism from the more socially active strands of the black community (who often criticized blaxploitation films for their lurid and stereotypical depictions of black people). Nevertheless, the soundtrack by Curtis Mayfield lends a critical tone that counterpoises the unfolding action on the screen. A later breed of black, urban-set films echoed this earlier cycle, though crack cocaine replaced "straight" cocaine, and there tended to be a less sensationalist approach to the subject matter. Films such as *Boyz N the Hood*, *New Jack City*, and *Clockers*, all exemplify such a move.

Conclusion

The affinities between elements of the cult audience and certain drug users has resulted in a number of drug-related films becoming cult items, a trend that is likely to continue. The changing modes of film viewing and sociality, as well as broader social trends, will inevitably affect how and why viewers celebrate certain films. For example, the heyday of the "midnight movie" occurred in run-down movie houses at a time when cinemas often tolerated drug consumption, a situation that very rarely occurs today. Currently, drug use is more likely to occur at home, where new technologies have enhanced the experience of film viewing in the domestic space, as well as the variety of films available. Social sharing of drug film viewing, then, is likely to occur at a relative micro-scale now, though the variety of platforms available through the internet enable broader, virtual forms of social connectivity to exist (and thus offer new spaces where talk about drugs and films can be found). Wider social developments, also, play a part: different forms of subcultural communities emerge in response to changing socio-cultural conditions, and the types of valued drugs within subcultures change.

Cult movies featuring prominent drug use do not appeal merely to drug-using subcultures, however. Often, they will have broader appeal, and the presence of drugs within certain films may be an incidental quality for some. For others, though, such presence may constitute a central appeal. When drug films connect with drug subcultures in a particularly resonant manner there is sometimes a marked cycle of cult films with drug connections. The period of the late 1960s and early 1970s and the emergence of the head film was undoubtedly the most significant of such cycles to date. The stoner film is perhaps the next most important cycle, though one that spans a longer duration and is still current today. In fact, stoner comedies such as *Harold & Kumar Go to White Castle* and *Harold & Kumar Escape from Guantanamo Bay* are modern attempts to update the *Cheech and Chong* cycle. The presence of broad, identifiable, drug-associated subcultures does not always lead to a significant corpus of related cult films, however. The rave and club cultures that emerged in the 1990s did have a few films that were latched onto by frequent clubbers – such as the aforementioned *Trainspotting*, *Human Traffic* and *Groove* – though not perhaps as many as

would have been expected. (There were a lot more made that did not seem to attract a substantial audience.) *Human Traffic* is one of the most notable in its relation to rave culture as it was actually premiered at the Homelands dance festival, which took place a few miles outside of Winchester, UK, and was attended by around 20,000 people. The film played in a tent with about 200 attendees, many of whom had taken ecstasy and who would talk back to the screen and sometimes dance along to the on-screen dancing (Sorfa 2000: 258). Yet this was a generally rare occurrence of a film tapping into the rave/ecstasy culture which was a significant phenomenon in the 1990s, particularly within Britain. Whether this was down to the properties of the drugs involved (mainly ecstasy and amphetamines), the social constitution and habits of the subcultures, broader industrial and social factors, or the "quality" of the films, is a subject that would require further investigation.

Note

1. We use the term "drugs" here in the meaning of illegal mind-altering substances. We exclude alcohol and other legal drugs from our overview, as well as some of the more specialist performance enhancing drugs that feature in the professional sports and entertainment industries. In a sense, then, we are dealing with drugs as understood by their subcultural reputation.

16

Cult Cinema and Music

Academic coverage of music and film has expanded rapidly over the past decade or so, but consideration of music within cult films is still relatively scant. This is surprising, bearing in mind the number of cult films in which music performs a key role. There are many links between film and music: industrially, a number of film and music companies belong to the same parent conglomerate, and cross-promotional tie-ins between the two media forms are common. In this sense, the music and film industries often partake in active attempts to encourage cross-media consumption. Music artists do not only provide soundtrack material for films, they also sometimes appear within films as actors. Films themselves often feed into music lyrics, titles, and videos, while film actors and other personnel occasionally move into music production. These interactions are certainly not comprehensive, but they do point to the strong links between these two forms and these are often particularly marked within the world of cult cinema.

Rock Movies

The most obvious examples of music-related cult films are movies which primarily attract a following due to the cult reputation of the musical artist(s) who feature within the film and/or provide a significant contribution to the soundtrack. Thus, if a particular group or artist enjoys a dedicated fan base, this may in turn constitute a core audience for a particular film title heavily connected with said group/artist. In his survey

of midnight movies in Lexington, Kentucky, between 1980 and 1985, Gregory A. Waller (1991) found that such films were a frequent staple of this mode of exhibition (which is crucially interlinked, though certainly not synonymous, with cult cinema). Waller uses the term "rock movies" to account for a number of films in which rock music serves a crucial role, and which include: rock music documentaries and concert movies; films based on music albums; films featuring actual musical performers; and films which feature fictional rock performers. The most popular films in this survey that have gained a cult status on a broader level drew on the huge fan base of the artists involved. They include Led Zeppelin's *Led Zeppelin: The Song Remains the Same*, a concert film incorporating fantasy sequences; *Pink Floyd: The Wall*, based on, and featuring music from, Pink Floyd's album of the same name; and *Tommy* and *Quadrophenia*, both based upon concept albums by The Who.

The concert film and/or music documentary based around a particular artist/group, is most reliant on an already existing fan base for its appeal. A concert film of a single band, for example, is unlikely to attract many viewers who are not particularly interested in that band unless other factors enhance its appeal. While *The Song Remains the Same* may have attained a cult status because of the huge popularity of the rapidly disbanding Led Zeppelin, a film such as *Stop Making Sense* accrued a reputation not merely as a Talking Heads concert film, but because of the imaginative stage designs and choreographed routines that set it apart from "routine" concert films. In this sense, while it

Cult Cinema: An Introduction. Ernest Mathijs and Jamie Sexton.
© 2011 Ernest Mathijs and Jamie Sexton. Published 2011 by Blackwell Publishing Ltd.

primarily appealed to Talking Heads fans, it also managed to interest others who were not particularly familiar with the band's music (and who may have become interested in the band through the film). Films based on the music of particular artists, however, will often attempt to target a broader audience than the band's fan base, even though this group may constitute the most dedicated audience for such films. *Quadrophenia*, in particular, is a film that certainly appealed to a number of The Who fans, but its cult status was not solely dependent on this particular segment. Rather, the film was a historical document of British mods in the 1960s, and thus appealed to those who were involved, or interested in, this phenomenon. It also tapped into a burgeoning "mod revival" in late 1970s Britain, and has been credited with feeding the growth of this revival (Catterall and Wells 2002: 177–179). A 1997 re-release of the film intermeshed with the latter stages of the partially mod-inspired Britpop phenomenon to find a new audience. *Quadrophenia* appealed not only to fans of The Who, but also to successive generations affiliated with the "mod" (or neo-mod) subculture, and more broadly to alienated youths for its depiction of young people disaffected with conventional social life.

The importance music plays in cult films often relates to the manner by which films appeal to recognizable subcultures. As Gina Marchetti has noted, documentaries such as *Monterey Pop*, *Gimme Shelter*, and *Woodstock* appealed to the subcultures depicted in them, providing the subcultural audience "with a chance to see their favourite rock group on the big screen" (Marchetti 1985: 74). A number of different musical acts appeared in *Monterey Pop* and *Woodstock*, alongside other activities surrounding the festival, including substantial footage of concertgoers. These films were able to connect with a general countercultural audience in which a variety of different music importantly linked with a lifestyle that was opposed to dominant American ideology of the time. *Gimme Shelter* was more focused on one particular act (the Rolling Stones), though it did also feature other acts and was, more importantly, documenting an event (the Altamont music festival) that for many symbolized the dark side (and perhaps the death) of the 1960s counterculture. These films are all associated with

direct cinema, a style of documentary filmmaking that attempted to capture events spontaneously through utilizing lightweight equipment and available light. Another direct cinema film, *Don't Look Back*, is also a key cult film. Following Bob Dylan on his 1965 tour of England, its main appeal is undoubtedly among Dylan's substantial (and often very passionate) fan base, though its presentation of Dylan as a hip and savvy iconoclast also presents Dylan as a kind of representative symbol of a particular generation (as well as documenting the attendant strains of being perceived in such a manner).

The intersection between cult films and identifiable subcultures arguably stems from the rise of youth-oriented exploitation films in the 1950s (see Chapter 13). This was a period when "youth," at least when combined with "delinquency," constituted a subculture in itself. Importantly, music – in the form of rock and roll – was a chief signifier of how youths differed from their elders. Following *Blackboard Jungle* and *Rock around the Clock*, a slew of rock and roll "teenpics" emerged, including *Shake, Rattle and Rock!*, *The Girl Can't Help it*, and *Love Me Tender*. The latter was one of the many Elvis Presley vehicles produced until 1969, most of which now enjoy a cult status because of the huge cult surrounding Elvis himself, but also because they enjoy a certain "kitsch" appeal (see Chapter 8). The success of films based around musical artists would continue into the 1960s, and importantly includes the Beatles' films *A Hard Day's Night* and *Help!*. Richard Lester's direction in these films has been credited with creating a number of audio-visual sequences that presage the aesthetics of the music video (Smith 1998: 159), which further bolsters their appeal as innovative texts.

In the latter part of the 1970s another recognizable youth subculture – punk – also impacted upon filmmaking and created a few notable cult films. Film such as *The Blank Generation*, *The Decline of Western Civilization*, *The Great Rock 'n' Roll Swindle*, *Jubilee*, *Repo Man*, and *Smithereens* all, in different ways, represented punk subcultures. Some of these films – such as *The Blank Generation* and *The Decline of Western Civilization* – are documentaries which gained small cult followings among those interested in the musical scenes represented; *Repo Man* is a film that features punks within it, and which is fueled by a punk attitude, but which is not centrally about punks and gained a cult following outside of punk subcultures. *Jubilee*, on the other hand, is a film that gained a cultish following among some "underground" audiences but which was also vilified by some punks. Other films, like *Repo Man*, had cross-cultural appeal. One example is *The Harder They Come*, a film based around the music industry in Jamaica and which appealed not only to Rastafarians but also to punks (as well as skins) in late 1970s/early 1980s Britain. This reception was boosted by the actual connections forged between some punks and Rastas in Britain during this period: Rastafarianism appealed to elements of the punk subculture through its militantly rebellious stance (Hebdige 1979: 62–70). Another cult film with cross-cultural appeal is *Space Is the Place*, a low-budget science-fiction film based around the philosophy of maverick jazz musician Sun Ra. Ra was influential on some punks because of his uncompromising, DIY approach to music (he self-issued a large number of records). He has also intersected with a wide range of other musical cultures including protopunk (playing a concert with MC5), funk, and hip hop. While *Space Is the Place* was not widely seen on release, it has since become a cult film primarily among Sun Ra fans (see Sexton 2006), but also because of it being viewed as a seminal film related to Afrofuturism (a blending of science fiction and African American politics). If Rastafarianism imagined the future as a return to roots (African heritage) and if punk was declaring that there was "no future," Afrofuturism posits African Americans using technology to engineer a more positive future.

Cult Cinema and the Visual Economy of Rock Music

Lawrence Grossberg has argued that rock itself is a visual form, in that its fans often encounter it through live or mediated performances, or through the visual containers of record sleeves. He also notes how different types of rock fans will often adopt specific dress codes and other stylistic markers. It is this visual economy within the world of rock, he further argues,

that adds to its power within the lives of its fans (2002: 83). In studying the performances of glamrock, Philip Auslander comes to a similar observation. The visual aspects of the performers such as David Bowie, Bryan Ferry, and Suzi Quatro go well beyond those of their real selves as individuals or musicians. They add layers of characterization and role-playing to the music so that posturing and posing develops into little narratives to which the music is a witness as well as its source (Auslander 2006).

The visual nature of rock music perhaps meant that its incorporation into cinema was inevitable. More importantly, this cinema/rock combination created a powerful combined force, directly appealing to fans with particular musical tastes and in the process generating a number of cult films. Rock music, for Grossberg, is a site where ideological and affective maps intersect (2002: 91). If this is the case, the transposition of rock music into films could doubly intensify the ideological and affective power of such music, through not only attaching these sounds to more concrete ideological narratives, but for placing them in a context with particularly affective potentials. According to Kevin Donnelly, non-diegetic sound and music can physically affect viewers; this power relates to its status as something both a part of, yet apart from, the filmic world, imbuing it with a kind of supernatural presence (2005: 13).

Rock music arguably enjoyed its most ideologically loaded period in the 1960s, and this combined with its visual and affective dimensions to create a rather powerful cinematic tool, contributing to a glut of 1960s cult movies in which rock music took center stage. One of the most iconic of such movies is *Easy Rider*, a studio-released feature rooted in low-budget, exploitation production (Chapter 13). *Easy Rider* employed rock music that reflected its countercultural attitude. At times, particularly in the scenes where the two main characters are travelling on the road, music dominates the attention and provides added meaning in the absence of narrative drive. Importantly, the film's soundtrack was also popular and paved the way for the use of popular music as a means to identify and tap into pre-existing taste cultures. Yet that film followed a number of other independent, exploitation pictures, such as *The Wild Angels*, *The Trip*, and *Wild in the Streets*. All of these films used rock music as a symbol of countercultural attitude, even though these were songs written for the movies (as opposed to *Easy Rider*'s compilation of largely pre-existing songs). *Wild in the Streets* centrally incorporated music into its plot: the main character, Max Frost, is actually a rock singer turned political figure. He ultimately manages to lower the voting age to fourteen, consigns everyone over 35 to concentration camps and forces them to ingest LSD. Music, drugs, and youth here all combined into one heady, subcultural brew.

One of the most interesting 1960s films to use pre-existing popular music, however, was the "underground" film *Scorpio Rising*, directed by Kenneth Anger. Predating *Easy Rider* by five years, the film is often cited as a key moment in discussions of the "pop compilation" score in feature films (e.g. Smith 1998: 160). Whereas the films mentioned above used rock music – whether specifically produced for the film or already present within the cultural landscape – in order to reinforce and expand the subcultural nature of the films, Anger used songs that cut against the images and created an almost alchemical audiovisual collage. As the film itself features no dialog, and no inner sense of unfolding narrative, the songs help to provide a vague sense of semantic commentary. Images of leather-clad bikers are not driven by rock 'n' roll but by an audacious blend of melodic pop, including such well-known staples from the erstwhile hit parade as the Shangri-La's "Leader of the Pack" and Martha and the Vandellas' "Heatwave," as well as songs with strong sexual innuendo, such as Bobby Vinton's "Blue Velvet" and Kris Jensen's "Torture." At times, this music does seem to bolster image events, but elsewhere it combines with the visual track to create meanings that may not have been otherwise apparent. In particular, the death, danger, and fetishism glimpsed in the visual sequences imbue these "innocent" songs with a dangerous edge, revealing, according to Philip Brophy, "that which has been covertly inscribed underneath their labelling, exposing a universe of transgressive desire" (2004: 206–207). Importantly, the use of music by Anger in this film would inspire Martin Scorsese and its influence can be detected within Scorsese's *Mean Streets*, as well as David Lynch's *Blue Velvet*, films which themselves have also gained a place within cult canons.

Cult Cinema and the Musical

Not all cult films with strong musical support are dependent on rock music, however. A number of musicals have gained cult status, including *Footlight Parade, The Wizard of Oz, Singin' in the Rain* and *The Sound of Music*. The cult appeal of musicals can vary, though nostalgia and camp are key concepts often associated with the genre. The former in the sense that many of these films are "classical" cult films (Telotte 1991a): films from the classical era that were exhibited conventionally, but which have retained cultural currency among certain viewers because they evoke pleasurable memories. While all classical cult films are potentially valuable in this sense, the musical could be considered a particularly cultish classical genre because it belonged to, yet pushed against, classical narrative conventions through its emphasis on spectacle. And, as musicals are often self-consciously artificial, they are prominently associated with a "camp" aesthetic (Sontag 2008; see also Chapter 8).

Ian Conrich has written that the cult film and the musical share a number of common characteristics such as "performances of extravagance and exuberance, obvious energy and ability, open emotions, fantasy and sudden explosions of spectacle" (Conrich 2006: 115). As such, it is perhaps no surprise that one of the most written about cult films, *The Rocky Horror Picture Show*, is also a musical, albeit one that is informed by rock music. It is in this respect that its appearance in yet another musical, *Fame*, makes sense. In fact, the scenes in which students of the Fame school attend a *Rocky Horror* screening give a good indication of the difference between mainstream and cult usages of music. While attending the *Rocky Horror* screening (presided over by Rocky über-fan Sal Piro), the students strip their clothes, smoke pot, shout and cheer, and improvise on-stage chorus dancing. The on-screen audience is very much part of the set up. The contrast with the "normal" scene spliced in between the two *Rocky Horror* scenes is telling: it shows a lonely musician gently singing a love song in his room to no one in particular. More recently, following the "participatory" nature of *Rocky Horror*'s cult screenings, a number of musicals have been screened as part of a performative "package" in what are called

"Sing-a-Long" events. Stemming from a "karaoke"-type screening of *The Sound of Music* at the 1999 London Lesbian and Gay Film Festival, these events encourage people to dress up and sing along with the film, with the song lyrics being displayed at the bottom of the screen (Conrich 2006: 117). These shows have expanded beyond London and other parts of the United Kingdom to the United States, Canada, Australia, New Zealand, Sweden, the Netherlands, Norway, Switzerland, Belgium, and Malaysia. Films shown at such events include *Annie, Hairspray, The Sound of Music*, and *The Wizard of Oz*. Conrich himself, though, debates the extent to which such events can be thought of as constituting a cult phenomenon:

> while *Sing-a-Long-a Sound of Music* has seemingly become the contemporary model of the cult film musical experience, the event is highly staged, manufactured, packaged, and controlled. Beyond the core venues, such as London's Prince Charles cinema, the film is often consumed in a conservative manner, the apparent conformity of the audience members challenging the notion that at such screenings the audience is essentially spontaneous and transgressive. (Conrich 2006: 118)

The assertion that London audiences are less conservative than those living outside the capital is problematic; there is no explanation how this decision was arrived at (with the possibility that this is merely an assumption), or in what sense they are considered to be more conservative. It is also questionable to claim that these events are not cult because of their commercial nature, leading to a conformism which cuts against a supposed "spontaneous and transgressive" audience. This argument conveniently downplays how even audiences at midnight screenings of *The Rocky Horror Picture Show* were often marked by levels of conformity and control: even if they did initially emerge spontaneously, such spontaneity was soon overtaken by more structured participatory activity in which newcomers to such screenings had to follow strict rules (Weinstock 2007: 38–39). It is noticeable how in the *Rocky Horror* screenings portrayed in *Fame*, the audience obeys various rules with minute precision. Events that are "manufactured, packaged, and controlled" should not necessarily be regarded as negating cult value. As will be argued in Chapter 22, cult is a concept which has

infused a wide range of commercial practices, and it may now be more sensible to think of cult, following Matt Hills' argument (2008a: 449), as a kind of "generic contract" between promoters/publicists and audiences/consumers. If this is the case, the audience still needs to play its part within this contract, to make up its own minds whether to accept the cult "invitation."

Conrich has also looked at a number of more modern, self-consciously "cult" musicals, such as *Joe's Apartment, Alfred Packer: The Musical*, and *The Happiness of Katakuris*, all of which combine elements of horror with the musical. The latter in particular is interesting as it is the product of cult Japanese director Miike Takashi and is partially inspired by *The Sound of Music*, which some promotional images for the film deliberately invoked as did the tagline: "The hills are alive with the sound of screaming!" (Figure 16.1).

A number of other musicals fit into Conrich's more "self-conscious" cult variety of films and are worth mentioning. These include *Rock 'n' Roll High School*, which features The Ramones, often cited as the first punk band; *Streets of Fire*, which features among others The Blasters; and the eccentric *Forbidden Zone*, directed by Richard Elfman and featuring the music of his brother Danny (who also plays Satan). Both *Rock 'n' Roll High School* and *Streets of Fire* reference the rock 'n' roll exploitation narratives of the past, especially the 1950s (*Streets of Fire* announces in an opening statement it is set in "another time, another place"). In that sense they are very much in tune with what in Chapter 17 we identify as the nostalgic fabrication of history (also see *Grease*, below). The images of The Ramones and The Blasters as bands also rely on that reference. Yet in both cases the nostalgia is offset by an edgy, subcultural tone that shows protagonists, music, and the rock bands themselves still in firm opposition to law and order (even if they are morally on the right side), and a narrative based around the subcultural appeal of rock music as a symbol of youth resistance against adult restriction. These offsets are aided by the cult credentials of *Rock 'n' Roll High School* producer Corman (and his screenwriter Joe Dante) and *Streets of Fire* director Walter Hill (whose *The Warriors* had already obtained a firm cult status). *Forbidden Zone*, on the other hand, is a bizarre film based upon The Oingo Boingo band's theatrical shows, which blended

Figure 16.1   A still from *The Sound of Music*, and a DVD cover of *The Happiness of the Katakuris*, the image and wording of which clearly draws on *The Sound of Music*, which famously includes the sung words "The hills are alive with the sound of music".

gothic comedy visuals with a broad repertoire of musical styles, including cabaret and punk. Danny Elfman's subsequent status as a distinctive soundtrack composer for cult-related fare including *The Simpsons* and the films of Tim Burton and Sam Raimi, also provide this film with a post hoc cult dimension. Another cult figure, John Waters, has made a couple of musical films. *Hairspray*, set in 1962, revolved around a teenage dance show and featured a number of dance-based set pieces, though not in the traditional "song and dance" sense. The film built up a cult following on video and then spawned a Broadway musical and then a more conventional, and expensive, musical film remake in 2007. Waters' next film *Cry-Baby*, which starred Johnny Depp, was a more conventional musical (it featured song and dance numbers) that parodied earlier musicals and teenpics, most notably *Grease*.

Grease, a fantasy-like recreation of the 1950s as a utopian playground of sounds and images, has itself developed into a cult. The film was a huge success on its release, particularly among teenage girls, with the associated music singles from the film also selling extremely well. For a hardcore group of original fans, the film has continued to play a key role in their lives. Therefore, a film that was originally nostalgic about an imagined past has now itself become an object of nostalgia for a personalized past. Furthermore, the film continues to attract new fans, as shown by the sales of its DVDs and connected memorabilia. If *Grease* is a "mainstream cult," then *Grease 2* has become a cult film via a more recognizable – and some would argue more "authentic" – trajectory. Critically panned and a box office failure on its original release, the film has steadily gained a following of fans who claim it a superior movie to its more famous predecessor, and who have formed a "Son of Grease" web site and fan group.[1]

Cult Soundtracks

While musicals do not enjoy the status that they did in their heyday, the increasing use of popular music on film soundtracks, as well as the rise of music video culture (symbolized by the arrival of MTV in 1981) has led to the proliferation of "musical moments" (Conrich and Tincknell 2006: 1) within many films. These are sequences of explicit musical performance within the film, or segments when the highlighting of soundtrack elements may, in relation with visual style, temporarily disrupt the linear momentum of the narrative. A particularly vital area of filmmaking that featured such moments is the phenomenon known as blaxploitation cinema, which flourished briefly between 1971 and 1974 (see also Chapter 13). In order to appeal to African-American audiences, these films very much relied on established musical artists who already enjoyed popularity. Thus, the soundtracks of many of these films was an area where potential audience attractions could be located, and indeed such music has often constituted the most lauded aspect of the films themselves. As Kodwo Eshun has noted, "the musical presence of *Shaft* and *Super Fly*, for example, completely overshadows that of other, more lauded genres of the period" (Eshun 1995: 53). Prestigious artists such as Isaac Hayes (*Shaft*, 1971), Curtis Mayfield (*Super Fly*, 1972), Marvin Gaye (*Trouble Man*, 1972) and James Brown (*Black Caesar*, 1973), were hired to create new music for these films, and the respective soundtracks bolstered their mood and attitude, in which a proud assertion of "blackness" was paraded. Many of the musical sequences in these films have become iconic, such as the theme song in *Shaft* accompanying John Shaft's walk down a New York street. The music becomes an immersive aural fabric, both for the audience and the character, denoting the laid-back cool of the lead character. Somewhat different is Mayfield's score for *Super Fly*, which lyrically counterbalances the main character Priest's actions, critiquing them and thus producing a dialectic in which music/vision intersect in contrasting ways.

While blaxploitation films employed well-known artists, they nevertheless featured newly recorded scores. A number of more recent cult films, by contrast, have tended to rely upon music already in public circulation. One particular cult director who has exploited such music in particularly noteworthy ways is Quentin Tarantino. Although Tarantino's music has differed in its use and range from film to film, it has tended to rely on an eclectic range of music that mostly dates from before the 1980s. Ken Garner has pointed out that many of Tarantino's characters not only discuss music, but also select particular music at certain moments (for example, on a jukebox) (Garner 2001: 190). This not only highlights the importance of the music for these characters, but for Tarantino himself. While music-dominated scenes within Tarantino films often become memorable, they also tend to serve different purposes. The infamous ear slicing scene within *Reservoir Dogs*, for example, is a prime example of effective juxtaposition in that the brutal image is underpinned by a sugary pop song, whose lyrics then take on new import. The beginning of *Pulp Fiction*, however, uses Dick Dale's "Misirlou" as an effective audio-adrenalin rush, plunging the viewer into the midst of the filmic world without mercy. At other times, Tarantino's music can serve as a referential aid, nowhere more so than when he uses music from other soundtracks, so that particular film genres or individual films are evoked. An example is the use of Bobby Womack's "Across 110th Street" in *Jackie Brown*, which was used in the 1972 film of the same name and is indicative of how the film draws upon blaxploitation (strengthened by the appearance of Pam Grier in the lead). The referentiality of Tarantino's music, in conjunction with his tendency to use songs of a certain age, also combines with visual iconography to create an atmosphere of analog fetishism. Characters within his films tend to play music on vinyl or cassette, or select tracks from a jukebox, as in *Death Proof*, which is his own personal item. The fact that the more recent songs on Tarantino's soundtracks tend to avoid overt digital markers, in line with broader characters' discussions about digital technology as cold and soulless (see again *Death Proof*), may partially explain why he needs to keep revisiting older genres more generally: he is mired in a past world, nostalgic for that which has already slipped away.

A cult film that also recalled a past world, but which conjoined this with the present in particular through its musical soundtrack, was the British film *Trainspotting*. To some, the sophisticated marketing that fueled the promotion of the film – the manner in which its different posters and its musical numbers, for example, targeted a range of key audience sectors – has, for Catterall and Wells, placed doubt upon the cult status of the film. They write:

> *Trainspotting*'s promoters pushed all the right buttons. They colluded with its target audience in a way few British cult films had done before, utilising already homogenised cults – such as those surrounding Britpop, the burgeoning Retro craze, the Rave scene and Irvin Welsh's novel – to add a synthetic veneer of cultish credibility. (2002: 234)

However, as mentioned earlier in this chapter, this ignores the extent to which cult has infused marketing and promotional discourses. When the market value of cultism is recognized, it is not a surprise that it becomes adopted by commercial agents. Nevertheless, a film being marketed towards particular demographics does not guarantee the adoption of the film by such audiences as important, meaningful texts. Cattterall and Wells's use of the phrase "push the right buttons" downplays how many films may be promoted in "savvy" ways and yet be refused by the targeted audiences.

Trainspotting's music track, as Murray Smith has pointed out, actually cross-references a number of musical periods, which may have helped in its appeal to different audience types. Smith notes how the film makes connections between dance and guitar music, as well as between different decades (the 1970s, 1980s and 1990s), and between the United States and Great Britain (2002: 66). He also notes how important this music is to the film's aesthetic in that, rather than providing mere "aural wallpaper," "the film makes the music itself palpable. It would be hard to over-estimate the 'value added' by the songs to the meaning and emotional force of the film" (Smith 2002: 65). Similar mechanisms underpin at least part of the cult appeal of *Donnie Darko*. In this case, the film itself stood outside the cultural context of the music's appeal: the film was American, its music mostly

British. Yet that did not prevent a cult connection. After *Donnie Darko* had failed to attract good business as a film, its soundtrack became popular at British campuses and among teenagers interested in its retro-sound of the 1980s (featuring Tears for Fears, Echo and the Bunnymen, and Duran Duran). This popularity helped propel the film's cult revival. Since then, films such as *24 Hour Party People* and *Control* have deepened the interest in British pop as a cult of nostalgia. Certainly, the variety of the music used in these films, and the ways in which it draws upon a range of cultural associations and blends these with visuals and narrative, can be seen as crucial ingredients in their cult appeal.

It is not only soundtracks created from pre-existing popular music or created by already established pop musicians that can add to a film's cult appeal. A number of artists have actually gained reputations predominantly for their soundtrack work and have themselves gained cult followings as recording artists. Specific soundtracks can also become cult items, cherished by dedicated collectors of soundtracks or through becoming particularly influential within specific cultural communities. There is often a pronounced transnational nature to soundtrack collecting, in which the exoticism of the music is often valued. Examples include the Romantic spiritualism typifying German group Popol Vuh's soundtracks to Werner Herzog's movies (such as *Aguirre, Wrath of God* and *Heart of Glass*), or the Buddhist-influenced minimalism of Philip Glass's score to *Koyaanisqatsi*.

One country that has been the subject of much cult interest in terms of film soundtracks is Italy; in particular, Italian exploitation cinema (or *filone*, a word used to refer to populist genre films) from the 1960s and 1970s (a productive period for Italian film production). Composers such as Fabio Frizzi, Bruno Nicolai, Riz Ortolani, Pierre Piccioni, Nino Rota, and Piero Umiliani, as well as the rock band Goblin, have all gained followings from soundtrack collectors. In line with the rapid production of the films themselves, these composers created a large number of scores for a range of genre films including horror, police thrillers, sci-fi, sex films, and spaghetti westerns. Despite the limitations of having to produce so rapidly, the work of these composers has been celebrated by a growing number of soundtrack collectors for their innovative blend of avant-garde, pop, rock, jazz, and other musical styles. While some of the soundtracks they have created are for films with established cult reputations (e.g. Frizzi's score for *Zombie Flesh Eaters* or Ortolani's score for *Mondo Cane*), others are more regarded than the actual films that they accompanied and it is sometimes easier to obtain the film soundtrack than it is the actual film itself.

By far the most regarded of such composers, though, is Ennio Morricone. While Morricone eventually went on to compose for larger Hollywood pictures and also modified his style to fit into a more classical tradition, his prolific output for Italian *filone* has gained a particular reputation. His work for directors Sergio Leone and Dario Argento is probably his best known within cult circles, yet the number of releases of his soundtrack work – including compilations which collect recordings from different films – testifies to his cult reputation. In addition to specific film soundtracks and compilations based around a composer's work across films being released, there are also a number of broader compilations linked to Italian exploitation cinema of this period, which include *Beat at Cinecitta* (three volumes), *Delirium of the Senses: Psychedelia in Italian Cinema* and *Italia Violenta: The Best Music of the Italian's Police Movie* [sic] (two volumes).

British horror cinema – particularly between the late 1950s and the 1970s – is another area of exploitation filmmaking linked to soundtracks that have gained a cult following. Hammer's horror films, in particular, have gained a following within areas of soundtrack collecting, with the work of James Bernard being most prominent, but also including the soundtracks to *Quatermass and the Pit* (Tristram Carey) and *Blood from the Mummy's Tomb* (Basil Kirchin). Carey and Kirchin are among the relatively obscure composers who have more recently gained a following among a number of musicians interested in British soundtracks, electronic and folk music, and a number of other – often horror-related – cultural artifacts. In terms of soundtrack collecting, this interest is most saliently represented by Trunk records, a small British record label that releases TV and Film soundtracks from yesteryear and other obscure music. Its releases include the soundtracks to *Blood on Satan's Claw* (Mark Wilkinson), *Psychomania* (John Cameron) and *The Wicker Man* (Paul Giovanni). Its release of *The Wicker Man* has

been seen as especially important for its influence; while the film had already gained a cult following its soundtrack had never officially been released before Trunk released it (as its first release) in a limited edition in 1998 (it was further issued by the label Silva Screen in 2002). Since then, it has itself become subject to fan devotion and the original pressings of the vinyl album have become rare collectors' items within the second-hand marketplace. It has also been credited by many musicians as sparking an interest in folk music and has thus been implicated in the recent resurgence of folk music, including subgenres known as "neofolk" (emerging from the post-industrial music scene and usually with interests in ancient paganism and the occult), and the "Freak folk" movement (which combines psychedelic influences with inspiration from British folklore) (Pitzl-Waters 2007).

A number of other cult films contain soundtracks which have themselves been subject to cult followings. These include Vangelis's ambient, synth-led score for *Blade Runner*, the cult of which was spurred by its unavailability until 1994, at least on an official level. In lieu of the official release a number of bootleg recordings of the soundtrack proliferated, and these continued to do so after the official release as they contained extra material. In 2007 a new, three-disc edition was issued that contained extra tracks and outtakes, though there were still grumbles among some fans that this edition still left out material. *A Clockwork Orange* is another cult film whose soundtrack has accrued its own cult reputation in its own right. Composed by Wendy Carlos (at the time named Walter Carlos) it made extensive use of the Moog synthesizer (still relatively new in the early 1970s), an instrument she had helped popularize with her 1968 *Switched-On Bach*, which featured covers of Bach played on the electronic Moog. The recordings for *A Clockwork Orange* led to two albums: the first was a mixture of Carlos's tracks with other classical tracks and Gene Kelly's "Singin' in the Rain"; the second, released in the same year, contained solely material recorded by Carlos, some of which was not used in the film. The soundtrack's future-oriented synthetic sounds had a pronounced influence on 1980s New Wave synthpop music such as The Human League and Heaven 17 (whose name comes from the name of a fictional pop group from *A Clockwork Orange*).

Both *Blade Runner* and *A Clockwork Orange* are cult films which have also attained a level of critical appreciation. Other cult soundtracks, however, may attain a greater respect than the actual films that they stem from (and in turn play a major part in cultifying the film itself). This is arguably the case with *Forbidden Planet*; while the film is reasonably well regarded critically, the status of the soundtrack has far outstripped that of the film itself. The main reason behind its cult status is that it is seen as particularly innovative: composers Louis and Bebe Barron were early pioneers of electronic music and the soundtrack is considered to be the first all-electronic soundtrack. Creating their own electronic circuits and drawing inspiration from Norbert Weiner's work on cybernetics, the Barons created dissonant, otherworldly sounds which had a large influence on many areas of electronic music that emerged in its wake. Another soundtrack whose status perhaps surpasses the film which it is attached to is *Vampyros Lesbos*. Although not actually recorded specifically for the film – music was taken from Manfred Huber and Sigfried Schwab's *Psychedelic Dance Party* (1969) and *Sexadelic* (1970) albums – the music gained a cult following when it was issued as the soundtrack under the title *Vampyros Lesbos: Sexadelic Dance Party* in 1995. Its blend of Eastern instrumentation and kitsch pop fitted into the vogue for easy listening "lounge music" in the late 1980s/1990s and was frequently used to soundtrack people's own parties.

It is also worth mentioning that there are some directors who have also gained a cult following for creating music for their films. One of the most notable here is John Carpenter, a cult director who has composed a number of his own soundtracks. It is his earlier, sparse synthesizer-based scores which have gained most of a following, including *Assault on Precinct 13* and *Halloween*, both of which have been extensively sampled by a number of hip-hop and electronic artists. Herschell Gordon-Lewis is another director whose own soundtracks have something of a cult following. While Lewis's soundtrack work is not often regarded as great music, the homemade, sparse music for *Blood Feast* and other tracks that he created for his films were released on a compilation in 2002 as *The Eye Popping Sounds of Herschell Gordon Lewis*. Finally, it is worth mentioning David Lynch as important in this regard. Lynch's soundtrack to *Eraserhead* (which he created

with Alan Splet) was an arrangement of found sounds mixed into a suitably harsh flow of drones and hisses. Meanwhile, one of the actual songs composed for the film, "In Heaven" (performed in the film by "The Lady in the Radiator") has been frequently covered by musical artists including Bauhaus, Devo, and The Pixies. Lynch's films have since become notable for their soundtracks by Angelo Badalamenti, which themselves have a cult following, though Lynch himself has continued to be closely involved in soundtrack work and has written music and lyrics for a number of tracks featuring within his films The ability to get hold of different soundtracks or to access information about them has undoubtedly increased over the past decade or so. Web sites about soundtracks, blogs devoted to them (some of which upload actual albums from the blogger's collection) and specialist soundtrack sellers are easy to access online, while a new wave of specialist labels are emerging to cater to the increasing interest in this area. It is not, therefore, only the use of pre-existing music with subcultural appeal which is important to music and cult cinema; there is also a following for work that is specifically made for, or at least primarily connected with, a particular film. This can either gain a status through its association with a film that has already gained cult status (and may be an integral component of such status), or – as is increasingly becoming common – soundtracks can gain a kind of independent cult status regardless of the film they were produced for.

Musical Performers and "the Musician" in Cult Cinema

A number of films featuring musical performers playing lead characters have also gained cult status. These can include performers as their selves – as in the previously mentioned Elvis and Beatles pictures – or as fictional personae. As Ben Thompson has pointed out, many attempts by pop stars to forge an acting career have been the subject of ridicule (1995: 33). Occasional performances have captured the imagination of viewers, though, and this is often when the pop star is actually playing a version of their extant celebrity persona. A particularly striking example here is Mick Jagger's role in Donald Cammell and Nicholas Roeg's

Performance, in which he played a washed up rock star. Combined with its psychedelic trappings, its non-linear editing and speculations on identity and performance, the film has proved to be an enduring cult and has even fed into subsequent pop music culture, having been sampled on Big Audio Dynamite's "E=MC2" (1985) and the Happy Mondays' "Mad Cyril" (1988). Nicholas Roeg also directed another cult film featuring an international pop star: David Bowie in *The Man Who Fell to Earth*. In this film, Bowie's androgynous and alien-obsessed persona, combined with his acting inexperience, imbued his performance with a sense of remoteness that suited the role of an actual alien. A sense of remoteness also characterized the performances of James Taylor and Dennis Wilson in Monte Hellman's cult road movie *Two Lane Blacktop*. The musicians' inexperience was once again expertly employed by Hellman here to convey a sense of existential anomie and was contrasted with actor Warren Oates more exuberant performance.

One particularly interesting cinematic employment of pop artists is within films that are about the music industry. Such depictions are often rather critical about the machinations of the music business, stretching back to the early days of the "rock 'n' roll film." Ben Thompson has written that there was never an "age of innocence" regarding the rock 'n' roll film, that it emerged fully cynical, possibly because "the idea of a new branch of the entertainment industry more venal than itself was just too good to resist" (1995: 38). Two noteworthy cult films about the music business and featuring musical artists certainly fit this bill: *Head* and *The Harder They Come*. The former was The Monkees' audacious deconstruction of their own manufactured image: a nonlinear, psychedelic attack on the inauthentic pop world (and a stake to move forward into autonomous artistry). Unsurprisingly, it alienated their fan base and confused many, but developed its own niche following. The latter was Perry Henzell's Jamaican film in which Jimmy Cliff starred as an artist exploited by the ruthless record companies and ended up a criminal. The film mirrors the very real exploitation of many reggae artists and highlights the social ills that many experienced in Jamaican life.

Films highlighting the cynical operations of the music business contain critical elements that tap into broader ways in which cult films (sometimes) speak to marginalized groups. Disaffection with the music industry can be representative of broader social alienation and this can combine with cult musical appeal to heighten a film's cult potential. One film about the music business deserving mention, but which does not quite fit into this cynical mould is *This Is Spinal Tap*, which featured fictional rather than real music artists. *Tap*'s cult status is due much more to its comedy value than for any social attitude. While it does share the distance of the more cynical films mentioned above, it uses this distance in a more loving manner to mock the antics of a heavy metal band and their travails. Ethan de Seife has noted how the film parodies both rock 'n' roll *and* "the semi-parasitic people and industries that have emerged to promote and valorise it" (2007: 100). In this sense, it does not take sides but treats all characters as worthy of humor. It also, importantly, adopts a mock documentary style that, in line with its acutely observed characters and surrounding paraphernalia, creates a rather uncanny effect (to the extent that some musicians have thought that some of the movie's ideas were stolen from them).

Conclusion

To conclude, it is clear that music is an important contributor to many a cult film's appeal. This can work on a number of levels: the music used on the soundtrack; the ways in which music (especially the music industry) can become the subject matter of the film; or through actual musical artists appearing within the films. Musical appeal can also cut across forms and genres: from the documentary to the musical, from exploitation to avant-garde, and from drama to comedy. The cult status of a musical artist can feed into a film to create cult value, though such cult value will often increase if the actual film contains a number of common cult film traits. Though these can never be exhaustively categorized, in music-related films these tend to include: nostalgia; alienation and deviancy; kitsch and camp qualities (Chapter 8); irony and parody (Chapter 21). They will also tend to provide immersive, affective spaces that the cult viewer can become lost in and moved by, as embodied in films that privilege spectacle and performance, such as the musical or the concert film, or within the "musical moment" of innovative audio-visual synthesis. Or films may be largely forgotten about bar the continued interest in their soundtracks, the influence of which can far outweigh the overall products they were once only a single component of.

Note

1. Their web site is at www.sonofgrease.org, while they have a Yahoo fan group at http://movies.groups.yahoo. com/group/sonofgreasefanclub.

17

Classical Hollywood Cults

Even the narrowest interpretations of cult cinema cannot ignore the cult movies Hollywood produced during its classical era, roughly between World War I and the 1960s. In their list of only thirteen films that confirm to a tight sociological definition of cult cinema Kinkade and Katovich (1992) still include three classical Hollywood productions: *Freaks*, *The Wizard of Oz*, and *It's a Wonderful Life*. There is no clear-cut definition of a classical Hollywood cult film, but there are plenty of films that have had that label bestowed upon them. An illustration that comes close to a definition is offered by Danny Peary, the critic who has given the most attention to Hollywood movies as cults:

> the typical Hollywood product has little potential for becoming a cult favorite because it is perceived by everyone in basically the same way ... Although *Gone with the Wind* and *Star Wars* have fanatical followings [they still] attract the masses rather than devotees on the fringe of the mass audience; the word *cult* implies a minority, and the studios are well aware that *Gone with the Wind* and *Star Wars* still attract the *majority* of the movie audience. Once these two pictures join such films as *All About Eve*, *Singin' in the Rain*, *Casablanca*, and *The Wizard of Oz* – all popular with the mass audience but today distributed primarily for their hardcore fans – on repertory theater schedules and on the midnight movie circuit, they, too, will be classified as legitimate cult movies. (Peary 1981: xiii)

The main complication that faces classical Hollywood cults is that it concerns films that seem, at the same time, mainstream and marginal, center and periphery. Peary excludes *Gone with the Wind* as a cult film because as the ultimate classic it is too popular, and its fandom is too much that of regular moviegoers ("the masses"). The qualification of having a hardcore base of followers *within* a mass audience is important, as it delineates a distinction between the audience as a collective and the audience as an aggregate of individuals. For Peary, it is the feeling of being part of a collective that makes a community a cult. *Gone with the Wind* would be a classical Hollywood cult as long as someone would identify its hardcore fandom as a cultish community. J.P. Telotte (1991a: 9) does exactly that when he argues that the appeal of *Gone with the Wind* lies in the way it unites an otherwise heterogeneous audience around "a fondness for conventions."

In this chapter we will discuss a variety of routines and themes that have led to cult reputations for films from Hollywood in its classical era. Our first point of attention will be nostalgia, which we identify as the overarching characteristic of classical Hollywood cults. Next, we will devote attention to a few forms of labor within Hollywood that have attracted cult receptions. We will also analyze the tropes of intertextuality, gaiety and violence as contributing to classical Hollywood cults. In conclusion, we will

Cult Cinema: An Introduction. Ernest Mathijs and Jamie Sexton.
© 2011 Ernest Mathijs and Jamie Sexton. Published 2011 by Blackwell Publishing Ltd.

elaborate on aspects of cultism towards classical Hollywood after its demise.

Nostalgia

"There's no place like home", sighs Dorothy (Judy Garland) at the end of *The Wizard of Oz*. Much of the appeal of classical Hollywood cult films comes from an elusive sense of "home," a home carrying only the good characteristics of the term. As Mathijs and Mendik (2008b: 3) observe, cult receptions are drenched with a nostalgic yearning for an idealized past, a sense of belonging that can only be located outside of the present reality. For Mathijs and Mendik, this nostalgia is the result of two factors: the emotional impression of nostalgia that is part of a film's reception, and nostalgia as a component of the film's story.

The storylines of most classical Hollywood cults embody a strong yearning for a past, better time. In *The Wizard of Oz*, that past includes Dorothy's home, and – in her search for it – her innocence. In *Gone with the Wind*, it is the yearning for Tara, the manor of the family. In *Casablanca*, it is the time before the German troops marched into Paris. Peary (1981) points out how Rick's (Humphrey Bogart) initially cold and callous attitude gradually changes to reveal a "sentimentalist" view on life when that past Paris returns in his life (in the form of Ingrid Bergman's Elsa), more powerfully every time he hears the song "As Time Goes By". In *It's a Wonderful Life*, the nostalgia is for the missed chance of enjoying what one has in life while being preoccupied with other plans. In *Harvey* it is the longing for a time away from reality altogether. As Elwood Dowd (James Stewart) puts it: "I've wrestled with reality for 35 years, and I am happy to state I've finally won out over it." In *Singin' in the Rain* it is the longing for truthful entertainment, which means the recognition of skill and talent over celebrity status. In each of these films, characters get a second chance, and in most cases they take it. Only in classical Hollywood cults from the mid 1950s and later (*Rebel without a Cause*, *The Searchers*, *Touch of Evil*) is no such choice available, or it is not taken. It is as if with the mid 1950s nostalgia stops having an impact on the present and from then on only relates to the definite past.

Frequently, the sense of nostalgia is reinforced by time travel. Characters travel literally through time (*It's a Wonderful Life*), or are pulled out of the normal passage of time (*The Wizard of Oz*). Locales are presented as timeless (*Top Hat*), or stuck in limbo while for the rest of the world time goes by (*Casablanca*). Any straightforward passage of time is furthermore interrupted by frequent stops (for a song or for elaborate flashbacks), and within the mise-en-scène numerous props and atmospheres refer to multiple ages and eras; it is almost as if the surroundings of circuses, cabarets, or theater stages, littered with assorted materials from bygone eras clutter the story to the point it can no longer progress functionally (*Meet me in St. Louis, Touch of Evil*).

Another recurring characteristic of the nostalgia in classical Hollywood cult films is its suspicion of modern technology and progress. It is a characteristic shared with many forms of secular and religious cults. Technology is represented as an obstruction to happiness, bringing only anxiety and alienation, and tearing communities and families apart. As is the case in *Miracle on 34th Street*, but also in *Casablanca*, *It's a Wonderful Life*, *Harvey*, *Touch of Evil* and many others, nostalgia is frequently inhabited by a gentle but persistent criticism of capitalism, consumerism, commodification, and the pinch these have put on close-knit communities. New York, as embodiment of capitalism, frequently gets a bad rep in these films. The classical Hollywood cult film that encapsulates this sentiment best is *Meet me in St. Louis*. In the film, the Smith family finds new means of transport, communications, and artificial lights threatening their cohesion as a family, in their home, in their trusted corner of the town. It takes the combined antics of the female family members, especially young Tootie (Margaret O'Brien), to persuade the father to change his mind. The structure of *Meet me in St. Louis* is that of seasonal cycles, not of progress. It offers in the song "Have Yourself a Merry Little Christmas" a rationale for nostalgia as an embrace of the repetition of the past (Kaufman 1994).

The nostalgia of these films is paralleled by the nostalgia in their receptions. On a very particular level, the nostalgia that accompanies the reception of classical Hollywood cults is partly that of the audience's yearning for a form of film consumption that has passed, namely that of the cozy inner-city neighborhood theater where young and adult couples could catch double bills, matinees, and premiere-evenings alike. As Wheeler Winston Dixon observes: "one went to the movies to see the stars, but also to be with one's friends . . . You would see your friends and neighbors a few rows down and wave to them" (Dixon 2006: 181). Next to that, the element of nostalgia in the receptions of classical Hollywood cults is one that lifts audiences out of specific conditions of time. According to Telotte (1991a: 9), films such as *Casablanca* and *Rebel without a Cause* display a "remarkable ability to live on through and, in effect, outside of history." They are unstuck in time. Telotte links this displacement in time to the nostalgia with which cult audiences approach these films. At its simplest, this nostalgia is the yearning for the initial impression the film left on the viewer, or, a little broader, a desire for a "first time" exposure to a film – the part of the phenomenal experience of viewing that regards every session as "original" (Barker and Mathijs 2007; Card 1991: 66). The ability to position the viewing as a continuous "first time" with all its emotional impact and aura of uniqueness intact, and to embrace the nostalgia that memories of such a first time evoke, is what sets classical Hollywood cult viewers apart from other cultists. Simultaneously, the nostalgia in the reception of classical Hollywood cults operates as a desire for innocence, or for an indefinite "other" time where the day-to-day troubles that occupy daily routines do not exist. Classical Hollywood cults "represent what Christopher Lasch has termed 'ego-ideals': 'admired, idealized images', in a most fundamental sense, *loved ones*" (Telotte 1991a: 9). Such images offer not only consolation to audiences, they also provide an imaginary release from the tensions of real life.

In combination, the re-creation of a "first time" and the search for innocence and idealized icons keep much of the nostalgia in the receptions of classical Hollywood cult films free of irony. In that sense it is different from the receptions of many other types of cult film. The combination also creates legends of receptions, whereby particular instances are singled out as markers for a "true" capture of a film's meaning. These instances become directives for moments of nostalgia in subsequent receptions. This was the case with several instances in the immediate reception of *Rebel without a Cause*, after the death of its star James Dean, and amid some upheaval over the film's place in a controversy over how it was contributing to the corruption of "deviant youths" – a perception that led to the film being banned in France (Biltereyst 2005). After the shock over Dean's death had passed, and moral panics about deviant youths had subsided, the long-term reception of *Rebel without a Cause* was accompanied by a nostalgia for that initial reception – when it seemed to matter to watch the film (McKelly 2005; Shary 2005; Springer 2005).

At its broadest, the nostalgia surrounding the cult reputations of classical Hollywood also transfers into a cultism for much of the period of classical Hollywood, and for the cultural certainties and excitements it is said to offer. Classical Hollywood *itself*, with its image of glamor, stardom, and glory, but also with its perceived decadence, abuse, and sleaze, has a cult reputation. Of course, many eras attract their own nostalgic reminisces. But what sets the classical Hollywood period aside is that the nostalgia for it is often expressed through the same media of film and television that helped to establish this cultural mythology in the first place. It was mainly in films from the 1980s that the consumption of nostalgia took on a cultist quality in its own right, expressed and fueled by films such as *Back to the Future*, *Peggy Sue Got Married*, and *Dirty Dancing*. For Vera Dika (2003), such nostalgia is in effect a fabrication of history, and part of the 1980s mode of "recycled culture." Mathijs (2007) argues that the cultism surrounding 1980s films recycling cultural consumption patterns of the 1950s is part of a broader development wherein audiences' longing for a better future has given way to a yearning for a better past. Both Dika and Mathijs stress how with this development nostalgia for Hollywood cultism is transformed into a consumption pattern itself – exactly what the original classical Hollywood cults implicitly criticized.

Routines of Labor

There is a certain relationship between nostalgia as the overruling concept for classical Hollywood cults, and some of the routines of labor associated with the system of classical Hollywood, specifically kinds of labor (and perceptions thereof) that are prone to attract fan devotion through their imperfect fit within, and challenges to, the system.

In Chapters 6 and 7 we analyzed the cult appeal of stars and auteurs. Let us add to those considerations a few Hollywood-specific elements. The most significant observation is that discussions of the labor of stars and auteurs with cult reputations of the classical era are drenched with the impression that they stand for a "truer" kind of professionalism, sophistication, glamor, or charisma from a time when such qualities were said to be of a more pure constellation. Larry Vonalt (1991: 59) calls it "artful glamour." It is an observation repeated in virtually every biographical study of Humphrey Bogart, Judy Garland, or James Dean. Such repetitions of a mantra amplify much of the nostalgia surrounding classical Hollywood cults. A second observation is that the labor of stars and auteurs with cult reputations in classical Hollywood would be labeled as "maverick," because they often evidence a less-than-smooth and fractured career – a career cut short by adversity, disrepute or early deaths.[1] Actors and directors with liberal political profiles, such as Abraham Polonsky or John Huston, or stars and directors with high-profile careers in disreputable genres such as horror, such as James Whale or Tod Browning, would also often be considered mavericks (Curtis 1998; Herzogenrath 2008). While cultism of classical Hollywood stars shows equal interest in male and female stars (though there can be much discussion over the kinds of properties cultists wish to accentuate in their fandom of male or female stars), cultism of classical Hollywood maverick directors is almost uniquely male-centered (see Chapter 6 for a discussion of female cult auteurs). At the same time, however, the masculinity of the mavericks is contested. Many have had gossip about their sexual identity become part of their reputations. The ambiguity accompanying these stories helped solidify their cult reputations.

Stars and auteurs aside, excellent examples of cults that have arisen around instances of Hollywood labor include crew whose profession invites perceptions of daredevilry, risk of bodily harm, and "street credibility," such as stunt people (immortalized, for instance, in *Singin' in the Rain*), athletes, and special effects artists (see Chapters 2, 18 and 19). One category of labor in classical Hollywood that pushed that perception of conflation between the professional and personal the furthest, and thus also received the biggest cult appeal particularly in terms of the nostalgia it incited, was that of the child actor. As Diana Serra Cary, also known as 1920s child star Baby Peggy, observes in *Hollywood's Children* (1979), the 1920 to 1940s can easily be described as the era of the "child star cult." The situations these actors ended up, or maneuvered themselves in, oscillate between "dreams" and "nightmares," swerving from boy wonder or America's sweetheart over stubborn genius to perennial exile – but never are they just simply mainstream. Child actors have always been a point of fascination for film audiences. There is nothing more universally adored than a child star. At the same time, there is a sense they are out of place, their physical and mental well-being endangered by the machinery of Hollywood. Conflicts between perceptions of child labor (exploitative, slave-labor, exhausting, damaging, and so on) and perceptions associated with children (pure, naive, innocent, playful, cute, asexual, impulsive, cruel etc.), put child acting outside of normality and open films with such acting up to wide-ranging interpretations and comments, leading to unstable receptions. Frequently, such debates have fueled cult reputations in which admiration for child acting is precariously negotiated against concerns about labor conditions. These concerns permeate the cult reputations of Jackie Coogan, Shirley Temple, Mickey Rooney, Deanna Durbin, Nathalie Wood, the many other child actors in *Meet me in St. Louis*, *It's a Wonderful Life*, *Miracle on 34th Street*, *Night of the Hunter*, and *The Sound of Music*, and, most famously, Judy Garland (see Chapter 8 for an elaboration on the Garland cult).

The most commonly mentioned classical Hollywood cults combine high degrees of exceptionality of production and reception with presentations and conditions of labor deemed unusual for the Hollywood system – hence provoking production and reception legends or even spark entire mythologies. A perfect example is *Casablanca* (Card 1991). Umberto Eco (1986: 197) refers to its production as "a hodge-podge of sensational scenes strung together implausibly," with incredible characters and mannered acting. Because of this, Eco adds, it is "a palimpsest for future students of twentieth-century religiosity" (1986: 197). In terms of reception, there was equally much confusion over the kind of film *Casablanca* wanted to be, and what it eventually became. Films now regarded as evergreens, such as *Singin' in the Rain* and *The Wizard of Oz*, too, were seen as exceptional to Hollywood (Higashi 2005: 73; Maland 2007: 243–244). Ultimately, the superstructure of Hollywood, its collection of rationalizations and self-beliefs endorsed by the corporations leading it and publics consuming its product, has managed pretty well to contain these films and explain them away as one-time exceptions. As such, they present not an alternative to Hollywood, but oddities within it.

Intertextuality

On the basis of Hollywood's system of routines it would seem logical to assume that genre plays an important role in the characterization and reception of classical Hollywood cults. But that does not mean it is a cinema of genre. Like cult films in general, classical Hollywood cults relate closely to issues of genre in that they consistently strain, over-play, or ridicule notions of generic categorization while simultaneously relying heavily upon formulas and conventions of genres. Mathijs and Mendik (2008b: 2) name *Gone with the Wind* and *The Sound of Music* as examples when they argue that cult films "shatter all existing genres." Eco asserts that Hollywood films that mix genres are likely to have cult followings. *Casablanca* is his favorite example (Eco 1986). Alex Cox too observes "a tendency to slosh over from one genre into another" (Cox and Jones 1993: 1).

Instead of being generic, then, classical Hollywood cults are meta-generic, or, intertextual. Intertextuality has connotations that stretch well beyond genre and classical Hollywood. We explore those in Chapter 21. Within the context of classical Hollywood cultism the concept of intertextuality is usually understood along Eco's definition, as a framework of data-structures (such as a film) that consists of "stereotyped situations derived from preceding textual traditions and recorded by our encyclopedia" (Eco 1986: 200). Intertexuality consists of macroscopic textual situations and stereotyped iconographical units, the latter more or less the equivalent of formulaic imagery and narrative, immediately recognizable by audiences. By breaking up

genre in a number of situations and acknowledging their travel across texts, intertextuality avoids discussions of genre as "accomplishment." According to Stam (1999: 201), intertextuality surpasses the problems of taxonomism and essentialism that the concept of genre tends to become embroiled in. But it retains, and indeed highlights, the importance of how films relate to other systems of representations through clichéd or stereotypical formulas.

Classical Hollywood cults are highly intertextual in two ways. First, they are intertextual in their self-conscious application of clichés. It creates the impression that these films use as well as subvert or deconstruct the very situations they are setting up (Peary 1981; Cox and Jones 1990, 1993). The intertextuality of classical Hollywood cult movies thus becomes a way of bypassing the conditions of quality genre imposes – a way of not having to live up to the pressure of having to "be" a good genre film, but to be appreciated on "another level." A staple example is the use of story backgrounds such as the circus or the theater backstage that function as ready-explanations for eccentric behavior (which consequently does not need to be addressed through character development or plot). Among the most frequently mentioned such films are *Freaks*, *Footlight Parade*, *Hellzapoppin'*, *Sullivan's Travels*, *Singing' in the Rain*, *All about Eve*, *Sunset Boulevard*, *A Star Is Born*, and *Imitation of Life*, all of which are set in the world of entertainment, where "stereotypes," "stock characters," and "sudden changes" are not only to be expected, but through their full display also become motors to the narrative and its meaning. The framed worlds in films such as *The Wizard of Oz*, *Meet me in St. Louis*, or *Touch of Evil* too have been analyzed as highly intertextual. Through their intertextuality classical Hollywood cults offer audiences a way of enjoying what would otherwise be either less than fully accomplished genre exercises, or merely just good genre films.

Secondly, intertextuality invites audiences to "make up" interpretations that add to the film's richness, and its cult reputation. Audiences can use intertextual prompts to mine films for references and connections they might not even knowingly contain. The various references to *Casablanca* in *À bout de souffle*, *Play it Again Sam*, or *When Harry Met Sally* have fortified the cult reputation of *Casablanca* by adding interpretations beyond the film's intentions (Maltby 1996). A famous example, researched by Barbara Klinger (1994), concerns the films Douglas Sirk made with Rock Hudson, which found renewed followings, and renewed cult receptions after the actor had died of AIDS in 1985, and audiences started to revisit his films to look for clues and cues for his homosexuality. Another example is the renewed cult followings for Joan Crawford triggered by the release of *Mommie Dearest*. This audience-driven intertextuality has had significant repercussions for classical Hollywood cults' long-term receptions. We have mentioned in Chapter 1 how reception contexts are known for their obsession with details, and their interconnectedness. This mining is a sign of this. It really became a part of cult readings of cinema from the late 1960s onwards, concurrent with the demise of classical Hollywood. In the years since, as classical Hollywood cults gradually lost their original audiences, they were replaced by audiences trained to look for ulterior motives and symptomatic meanings, for bits and pieces of intertextual referencing films carried unknowingly, that were simply added on to the films, or that were only noticed after they had been spoofed or referenced by other, newer films. As such, intertextuality, and its use by audiences, offers explanations as to why some classical Hollywood cults remain cult films, while others have disappeared.

Gaiety

When classical Hollywood cults are described in terms of nostalgia it is often noted that they offer a "gay ole' time." The term "gay" has changed meaning over the course of its application in the receptions of classical Hollywood cults. That change reflects a development many classical Hollywood cults experienced.

Initially, the term refers to a mood that stresses frivolous, flirtatious atmospheres in enclosed, artificial settings that highlight their entertainment and leisure functions – such as hotels, bars, ballrooms, dressing rooms, luxury estates, yachts, casinos, theaters, or film studios. Gaiety abounds most visibly in stories that upset "cheery problemless world[s] where gentlemen have valets and dress in top hats and tails and ladies have maids and dress in evening gowns" (Peary 1981: 103). The genre most commonly associated with gaiety is

the musical. Among the most commonly listed Hollywood cult musicals are *42nd Street* and *Footlight Parade*, *Top Hat*, *Meet me in St. Louis*, and *Singin' in the Rain*. Gaiety also informs much of the appeal of sentimental fantasy films such as *Harvey* and *It's a Wonderful Life* – films in which the joy of living forms the main drive for the narrative. These films owe much of their cult appeal to the joyful mood they establish with their audiences, to their relentless belief in a fun time, and to the self-reflexivity of "a story inside a story inside the industry" (which functions as an intertextual tool through which the joyful mood is established).

Several critics argue that the cult appeal of gaiety lies in how it presents a world that does not gel well with reality. *Top Hat* seems oblivious to the real-life Depression. Rick's Café in *Casablanca*, the backdrop of the theater in *All about Eve*, or the background of the film industry in *Singin' in the Rain* appear disconnected from reality, consciously so (Peary 1981: 4–8; Higashi 2005). Often, there is a tension between the high-society entertainment setting and the working-class backgrounds of the characters – stuntmen, chorus dancers, piano players, bartenders, pirates and outlaws – who are presented as quasi-egalitarian collectives of guys, gals, and pals. Conflicts remain light-hearted, and are carried with a smile – as if life is merely a frivolity.

In its more modern meaning, the term "gay" also carries overtones of camp and queer sexualization. The above-mentioned films often contain "battles of the sexes," with sexual identity at stake. Such battles are accompanied by a "pratfall" – a fall from grace of the protagonist that forces him to abandon his disavowal, acknowledge his attraction to the heroine, and give up his roving ways.[2] Because these films address both a leisurely and a sexualized connotation of the term "gay" the phrase has become representative for a turn in the modes of reception of films with gaiety – a turn that has affected the long-term cult receptions of these films. Since the 1960s, savvy audiences have been more vocal in identifying or attributing queer or lesbian subtexts to Hollywood films, in particular with regard to musicals, screwball comedies, and swashbucklers. Anything from the male bonding between teens in *Rebel without a Cause*, the flirting and cross-dressing within the vaudeville troupe in *Sylvia Scarlett*, the reversal of dominant gender roles in films with Marilyn Monroe, Joan Crawford, or Rock Hudson, or the restrained, domestic tensions in some of the films of Douglas Sirk (*All that Heaven Allows* in particular) have been reinterpreted along this sexualized understanding of gaiety (Peary 1981; see Klinger 1994 for a study of Sirk's reception). As camp and queer readings became more prevalent parts of cultism (see Chapter 8), gaiety gradually became understood as a reference to queer or promiscuous subtexts, planted and hidden in films in order to bypass the strict self-censorship of Hollywood, but detectable for those with the right arsenal of subtextual implications and inferences.

The change in application of the term "gay" illustrates a change in the long-term reception of classical Hollywood cults. This change is often reflected upon in nostalgic reflections as a perception of a loss of innocence. The cultist reattribution of the motive of gaiety in musicals, swashbucklers, and screwball comedies was paralleled by Hollywood audiences' abandonment of these genres. However, in the case of the musical such nostalgic reflections mix with camp and queer readings without too many obstructions. This mix has made the model of the musical an almost uniquely cultist type of film, especially in the period after the demise of classical Hollywood. *The Sound of Music* is generally considered the end-point of the classical musical. Its current cult reception is characterized by sing-a-longs that highlight audience participation, what Ian Conrich (2006: 117) has called "karaoke cinema" (also see Chapter 16). Fittingly, this reception, and the comments of "silliness" it elicits, can be regarded as a struggle between the initial understanding of "gay" (as frivolous fun) and the post-1960s queering of it (as repressed sexuality being outed).

Violence

Many cult films present instances of violence as a way of opposing mainstream modes of representation. Violence is also abundantly present in classical Hollywood cults, often in the guise of perpetual anarchy, toughness, or frontier liminality – in fact we can say that in classical Hollywood cults violence is routinized, made part of the fabric of storytelling and style.

Routines of violence are a particular characteristic of the zany slapstick film and its unattached, uncivil tramps and wanderers. As Harry Allan Potamkin (2008) noted, the 1920s slapstick film used to form a cult all onto itself, celebrated exhaustively by the surrealists (see Chapter 4). Because of the quantity, size, and speed of gags (pie fights, chases, crashes) within these films, and the ridiculing of figures and institutions of authority, the zany slapstick film was often seen to contain a political subtext of anarchy. Many of Chaplin's films end with the tramp setting off on the road, to nowhere in particular. The overt links between violence and zaniness in the films of the Keystone Cops, Laurel and Hardy, Buster Keaton, the Marx Brothers (especially *Duck Soup*), and several pirate films (notably *Captain Blood*) gave them solid cult reputations. In 1941, *Hellzapoppin'* encapsulated the traits of zaniness in an overtly intertextual and self-reflexive tale about filmmaking that paved the way for parodies (see Chapter 21).

Routinization of violence is also prevalent in the hardboiled *film noir* with the femme fatale. Such films have frequently been called nihilist, for their preference for dodgy locales (in bars, cabarets, on the road, in halfway houses of low repute), their avoidance of the presentation of women in fixed routines and domestic environments, and their violence against women (comedic or not) – in these films, men are dangerous, women are lethal, and adventures are doomed. The most visible instances of such routines of violence were far more concerned with formalisms and mannerisms of violence (such as menacing poses or sudden outbursts, like Lee Marvin's infamous hit in *The Big Heat*) in shabby locations than with plot-driven storytelling. Among the most frequently mentioned hardboiled cults are *The Maltese Falcon*, *The Big Sleep*, *Detour*, *Out of the Past*, and from the fifties, *Gun Crazy*, *The Big Heat*, *Kiss me Deadly*, and *The Killing*. *Touch of Evil* is usually regarded as the epilog of the hardboiled cult. Each of these mostly low-budget films is noted for its expressions of physical and emotional violence (often against women), for its labyrinthine plots of betrayal, and for an overall tone of cynicism, factors that gave them a heightened sense of liminality, and contributed to their cult reputation.

The most renowned routinization of violence in classical Hollywood cults, however, is the kind associated with the frontier. A metaphor for the edge of civilization, the frontier stands as a key component of the kind of cultural mythology Hollywood is said to promote (the American Dream and its "wide horizons"). In classical Hollywood films with cult followings any crossing of the frontier appears to be impossible. Instead, characters and stories get stuck on the frontier – they linger in no-mans' lands. As a consequence violence is everywhere. Steven Schneider describes the eponymous city of *Casablanca* as "hovering" in between worlds and cultures, stalemated by the war (Schneider 2006: 91). The border town in *Touch of Evil* or the observatory in *Rebel without a Cause* are also locations in which characters are stuck and violence ensues.

The forms of classical Hollywood cult that push this notion of the frontier furthest are the exotic adventure film and the western. In the figure of the "frontier hero" simmers a dilemma between civilization and wilderness: the hero is unable to function within the civilized world but equally unable to live in the wild. That conflict inevitably erupts in violence. The biggest cult reputations are for adventures and westerns whose entire narrative is set in the frontier zone, where violence becomes a mode of existence rather than a functional tool. In the pre-Hays Code adventure film this violence is often linked to sexual attraction. In *Tarzan and his Mate* and *King Kong* love is expressed in a very physical way, as befits their position of "uncivilized" beings. With regard to the western, the frontier violence is probably most iconically illustrated through the image of Ethan Edwards at the end of *The Searchers*. Peary (1981, 1989) lists the following films as cult westerns: *My Darling Clementine*, *Johnny Guitar*, *The Searchers*, *Man of the West*, *Rio Bravo*, and *Ride the High Country*, and the Randolph Scott westerns *The Tall T* and *Ride Lonesome*. Most of these westerns are called revisionist, from the period near the end of classical Hollywood when the genre started to shed its blind loyalty to the myth of the conquering of the frontier and, instead, films such as the above-mentioned get stuck on the border. In a sense, this intertextual exposition of the genre's constructedness, expressed in an increase in formal mannerism, ignited its downfall. It helped destroy some of the mass appeal of the western. At the same time, the formal subversion helped the genre gain a cult reputation.

The cults of the zany slapstick, the hardboiled film, and the Hollywood western are largely a thing of the past. Peary aside, very few studies of cult movies even refer to Hollywood western cults (Cox and Jones 1990, 1993 is an exception). But some traces of their cult are carried over into the present in the form of homage. Contemporary films such as *Pulp Fiction* and *Crash* eagerly reference the hardboiled femme fatale and the western, thus enshrining their routines of violence into cult fandom. The best example of this are European spaghetti westerns such as *Django*, *A Bullet for the General*, *The Good, the Bad and the Ugly*, *The Big Silence*, or *Once Upon a Time in the West*, or post-classical westerns such as *The Shooting* and *The Wild Bunch*. These films' routinization of violence goes a few steps further, especially in their focus on the spectacle of indiscriminate violence and on the collectivity of its perpetrators. More men than ever before get stuck in the frontier zone, and not even the most extreme violence gets them out. Their cynicism actually turns these films into send-ups of violence. It has given these films greater cult reputations than their Hollywood predecessors, ones that persist to this day. At the same time, the spaghetti western's appeal virtually erased any cult followings for classical Hollywood westerns (for more on the spaghetti western, see Chapter 20).

Classical Hollywood Cults on Television

Rio Bravo and *The Sound of Music* are often listed as the last examples of classical Hollywood cults. As we have outlined above, the cult of the violent spaghetti western erased the cult of the Hollywood western. The increasing tendency to mine musicals, screwball comedies, and melodramas for their camp and queer subtexts – and to see every mention of "gay" as something else – drastically changed their cult appeals too. In general, nostalgia for classical Hollywood pushed specific cult followings for nostalgic films out of the spotlight. But on television, classical Hollywood cults found a new home. From the 1960s onwards, and particularly through the 1970s and 1980s, television gradually replaced the repertory theater: its reruns of beloved films made re-releases superfluous. Network television became the quintessential form of family entertainment, and it also became the medium classical Hollywood cults migrated to.

In fact, television perpetuates the cult of classical Hollywood through the nostalgia it embraces. The major proof for this is what can best be described as seasonal cults: the fervent cultism around specific, recurrent periods and dates in the year linked to cultist behavior and to specialist television programming involving classical Hollywood cults. This is how Peary introduces *The Wizard of Oz*:

> I flashed back to the fifties when *The Wizard* entered the lives of us children across America via annual television screenings that we watched religiously year after year after year. Few of us can deny how important to our lives *Wizard* was; its annual TV presentation was as comforting as our birthdays, holidays, a cup of hot chocolate (with a marshmallow), and even the opening day of the baseball season (Peary 1981: 390).

The Halloween period has a special significance for the horror film, as a dedicated release date, but also as a slot for classical Hollywood horror on television (Mathijs 2009). Valentine's Day too has, through *Casablanca*, become a slot with cultist overtones.

The most important seasonal cult is the *yuletide cult*, the avid following for, and ritualized viewing of, a group of classical Hollywood cults broadcast on television during the end-of-year celebrations (Mathijs 2010a). Among the most frequently programmed films are *Holiday*, *The Wizard of Oz*, *Meet me in St. Louis*, *It's a Wonderful Life*, and *Miracle on 34th Street*. These films share an emphasis on family union, intimate song and dance routines, and naive beliefs in love and happiness. They provide mild criticisms of capitalist modes of consumption and distribution. They are also characterized by the prominent presence of children in the story – *It's a Wonderful Life* and *The Bishop's Wife* even cast the same child actors. Above all, they transcend cynicism by highlighting maudlin sentiments, feelings of nostalgia for "olden days of yore," as Esther (Garland) puts it in "Have Yourself a Merry Little Christmas."

Perhaps more than *Miracle* or *Meet me in St. Louis*, *It's a Wonderful Life* is the quintessential yuletide cult film from classical Hollywood (Figure 17.1). Its message of

Figure 17.1   Championing family and community values over capital gain: the yuletide cult of *It's a Wonderful Life*.

championing family and community values over capital gain and ruthless business is mirrored in its reception trajectory. The film had not been a success when it was originally released. Ever since its copyright lapsed, and it became public domain, it had been cheap for networks to put it on their holiday season schedules. This enabled regional television stations to program the film, and these localized appearances helped solidify the film's reputation as a "small town" favorite, a film that demonstrated the robustness and indispensability of closely knit communities. In larger cities, broadcasts would be supplemented with fervently attended theater screenings (Peary 1981: 162).[3]

Seasonal television re-runs, and occasional theatrical re-releases, add to the already nostalgic-heavy long-term receptions of classical Hollywood cults. Two means through which this added value is expressed are crying and imagining. As with *Miracle*, the long-term receptions of *It's a Wonderful Life* abound with references to weeping and crying. As Peary remarks: "There is no shame in crying while watching *It's a Wonderful Life*, admittedly one of the most sentimental pictures of all time" (Peary 1981: 163). Eric Smoodin (2004: 183–199) details how inmates of the San Quentin prison referred extensively to crying and, indeed, anticipations of crying (being "ready-for-the-river") when discussing a screening of *It's a Wonderful Life* in January 1947. Similar observations, usually of anecdotal nature, can be found in the long-term receptions of *Singin' in the Rain*, *Casablanca*, and *Harvey*. Even more hard-nosed classical Hollywood cults do not seem immune to it. Sue Harper and Vincent Porter (1996) have argued that crying at the movies, and indeed at certain movies ("weepies") needs to be seen in the context of immediate postwar society, as a mechanism to be understood not just in relation to the film being screened but to the wider cultural atmosphere and its audience's sensitivities. Both Smoodin and Harper and Porter allude to the fact that crying is connected with audiences' re-imaginations of history. What crying at the seasonal re-runs of classical Hollywood cults indicates, then, is the performative – though not less sincere – articulation of nostalgia.

Conclusion

As classical Hollywood cults moved from the theater to television, new cults occupied the slots they left open at inner-city repertory theaters. Even staunchly traditionalist bastions of classical Hollywood reverence, such as cinematheques or film museums, saw themselves gradually open up their schedules to newer cults. When home-viewing media made their entrances, they drew on fringe and niche specialist cults at the expense of classical Hollywood cults. By and large, classical Hollywood cults remained stuck in the television medium. Since 2000, prestige up-market editions of classical Hollywood cult films have propelled a wider availability, but this has not yet led to a systematic revival.

The consequence of this development has been a gradual disappearance of classical Hollywood cults

from studies of cult cinema. Peary's first volume of *Cult Movies* (1981) lists 41 classical Hollywood films, out of a total of 100. In his subsequent collections that ratio declined drastically. Umberto Eco's (1986) seminal essay on *Casablanca* was still largely aimed at classical Hollywood cults. A few years later, J. P. Telotte (1991b) balanced discussions of the classical cult film (*Casablanca, The Wizard of Oz, Beat the Devil*) with that of midnight movies. So did Anne Jerslev (1992), who drew equally on *The Big Sleep* and *Pink Flamingos* to argue her case that cult movies are intertextual.

Over the last decade, overviews of cult cinema have tended to further reduce their attention to classical Hollywood cults. Apart from *The Wizard of Oz, Casablanca, It's a Wonderful Life, Singin' in the Rain, Rebel without a Cause, The Sound of Music*, and a few others, there remains little or no consensus about classical Hollywood cults among recent studies and overviews of cult cinema. This narrowing of the perspective also affects how some of the themes classical Hollywood cults highlighted, such as gaiety, or nostalgia, are remembered.

As a result, we should perhaps worry for what Svetlana Boym (2001) has called the limited "future of nostalgia." The danger exists that classical Hollywood cults will soon be cast out of considerations of cult cinema altogether. Before long, the current nostalgia *within* classical Hollywood cults may soon be replaced by a longing *for* classical Hollywood cults.

Notes

1. One of the most recent directors of classical Hollywood to receive a European cult following is Edgar Ulmer (Isenberg 2004; Herzogenrath 2009; Rayns 2009). Ulmer's cult status has led to an annual convention, the *Ulmerfest*, in his hometown in the Czech Republic.
2. Probably the most notorious example is one of Cary Grant's outbursts of frustration in *Bringing up Baby* (the film can be seen as one extended pratfall). Forced by

circumstances to wear a lady's negligee, he bumps into a respectable, elderly woman who confronts him with the peculiarity of his outfit and asks him why he is wearing these "idiotic clothes." He shouts: "Because I just went gay all of a sudden."
3. When the Pickwick Theatre near Chicago invited one of the child actors to a screening of *It's a Wonderful Life*, 3000 people attended.

18

Cult Horror Cinema

The term "cult" is probably at its most mobile, and in the most danger of being over-used, when it is discussed in relation to the horror genre. As a descriptive or critical category, a historical tradition, or a set of routines, "cult horror" is simultaneously a very slippery concept as well as a site of partisan entrenchment. In this chapter we will try to offer accounts of both, conflicting, positions, by approaching cult horror from three angles: cult horror as a subcategory within the horror genre (i.e. as a label that some horror films receive); cult horror as a specific historical tradition and cultural sensibility with repercussions for both the horror genre and the concept of cult (i.e. as a moment within the history of both cult cinema and horror cinema); and cult as an asset of a number of ways in which viewers have used opportunities created by producers to cultify certain horror films (i.e. as a sort of elevation of the cultural status and value of horror movies).

Cult Horror as a Subgenre of Horror

Approaching cult horror as a subdivision of horror, as a distinction within the genre, creates a big complication, namely that for a lot of vernacular surveys, overviews, and reports, the terms cult and horror are almost synonymous – even if this is not always articulated explicitly. There is a historical aspect to this conflation between cult cinema and the horror genre, that goes back to the early 1920s and *The Cabinet of Dr. Caligari*. As we have seen, Potamkin (2008: 27) calls it the "cult film par excellence." Peary (1981: 48) praises

it as the "first *horror* film of real, lasting quality." To many, *Caligari* is horror because it is cult and cult because it is horror. The controversies it caused in several markets etched its reputation as a "wretched story" deep into the minds of viewers who felt at odds with mainstream cinema. When surrealist René Crevel wrote on his admiration for *Caligari* in 1927 the phrase "Caligari's madness" had sunk into both cult and horror parlance. (Hammond 2000: 57–58).

Ever since *Caligari*, numerous other conflations have persisted, with the confusing result that sometimes there is no longer a distinction between "horror" and "cult." The conflation is not helped by the fact that academic studies of the effects and impacts of horror films on viewers employ arguments and language that are also used to describe cult audiences – both in negative views (that see these viewers as addicted victims) and in positive ones (that see these viewers as empowered agents). Moreover, hardly ever do such studies appear to offer examples of horror that are not also widely recognized as film cults. A cursory look at web sites, blog sites, and online criticism delivers a plethora of illustrations of the continued presence of this conflation.[1]

If we look at attempts that place cult horror within the genre of horror as a subdivision that does not conflate with the entire genre, two interconnected characteristics appear: cult horror films are bad and break taboos. For Bartlomiej Paszylk (2009), cult horror films are a "genre within a genre," or horror outside the mainstream of horror. Their uneasy fit within formats, failure to provide programmatic pleasure, and lack of easy availability makes them cult. Paszylk also notes that cult horror film punishes viewers "by reveling in its own vulgarity or badness" (2009: 1). For Welch Everman too, cult horror films are first and foremost "bad horror films" (1993: 1), which he initially sees as an aesthetic judgment of under-achievement coupled with low production values and small budgets. Yet he immediately adds that some cult horror films are so bad they are good, and that much of the badness lies in how they subvert politics of representation. He thereby moves the focus from the aesthetic quality of the picture to its political position.

Like so many critics and scholars, Everman asserts that most horror films are essentially conservative in their message. Monsters are threats to cultural order and they must be destroyed through extreme means. Cult horror films, however, add subversions, ambiguities, and contradictions so that it becomes unclear whether or not restoration of the order is a good thing, or the ends justify the means, or the film itself is actually siding with its story. Decades after its original release, Siegfried Kracauer used this line of reasoning to attack *Caligari* for its reactionary ideology (Kracauer 1959: 66–67). Although Kracauer's interpretation was later nuanced, it decalibrated the status of *Caligari* for a long time. In his analysis of horror, *Danse Macabre*, Stephen King (1981: 154–230) arrives at the insight that cult horror movies have conflicting political leanings; their politics are not tabloid editorials but rather muddled, confused utterances. Paszylk, Everman, and King devote considerable attention to illustrations of how cult horror films push the boundaries of taste by breaking taboos. For King, they are "a sort of picture that doesn't want to score political points but to scare the hell out of us by crossing certain taboo lines" (King 1981: 156). For Everman, this means that these films are "all kind of offbeat, kind of weird, kind of strange" (Everman 1993: 1). Or even "too weird," as Paszylk remarks (2009: 1).

The focus on breaking taboos is also a central element of other uses of the term cult horror. Such uses most frequently occur in the margins of works on extreme horror cinema. Their appearance in these works illustrates the close affiliation between high degrees of explicit violence, fear, and bodily mutilation and the cult status of a horror film – the more radical a horror film's depictions of bodily harm, and the

bigger the taboo it is breaking (or the "weirder" it is), the more likely it is to attract a cultist audience and be labeled cult. A good example is Mikita Brottman's (1997) analysis of "cinema vomitif," which concentrates on extreme horror films that have elicited a visceral reaction from audiences. Although Brottman argues for a distinction between the offensive films she analyzes and "cult bad movies," the way she approaches case studies such as *Freaks*, *Blood Feast*, *The Texas Chainsaw Massacre*, and *Cannibal Holocaust* nevertheless positions these films as cults. Similar approaches can be found in David Kerekes and David Slater's (2000) critical overview of "death cinema from mondo to snuff." In fact, the application of superlative adjectives such as "shocking," or "nasty" has become a proxy indication of the cult status of some horror films.[2] Publishing houses such as Creation Books, Headpress, and FAB Press, and fan magazines such as *Fangoria*, *Cinefantastique*, *Ecran fantastique*, and *Gorezone* employ the term cult regularly when discussing taboo-breaking horror.

Cult Horror as a Historical and Cultural Sensibility

A more specific use of the term cult horror refers to one period in the history of horror cinema that has become a cult in itself. This period runs roughly from the mid 1970s to the late 1980s. During this time horror cinema developed such a rabid cult reputation that it caused a radical change in the components that characterize the general term "cult." At the same time, it was a period in which the horror genre as a whole was so visibly prominent within popular culture discourse (yet so reviled) that it almost became a synonym for cult cinema in general. Following Lawrence O'Toole's (1979), this period is often described as the *cult of horror*.

The cult of horror comes out of a sensibility that is strongly linked to the 1960s counterculture. Vilified by reviewers, eschewed by large theaters, and most difficult to distribute, films such as *Carnival of Souls*, *Blood Feast*, *Rape of the Vampire*, and *Night of the Living Dead* appeared in niche markets seemingly out of nowhere. The independent origin of these films, produced in defiance of industry routines and practices, gave them a flavor of countercultural resistance, which was bolstered through their alignment with campus radicalism and the burgeoning subculture of comic books.

Through the 1970s, this alignment developed into the cult of horror. It was spearheaded by a relatively small cohort of high-profile controversies, in particular those involving *Night of the Living Dead*, *Last House on the Left*, *The Texas Chainsaw Massacre*, and *Shivers*. Facilitated by increasingly lenient censorship regulations, these films presented themselves as radical, political, and independent-minded. Their horror involved starkly realistic depictions of the detailed, explicit, and abusive violation of bodily integrity – with rape and cannibalism taking a prominent place. One of the most powerful elements of the films spearheading the cult of horror was that literally anyone could become a monster, within an instant, and most characters would at some point become monstrous. This meant that audiences had no recourse for their emotional investments into characters (there were no heroes to save the day), which added a very bleak tone to the films' endings. The stories ceased to be about defending normality (white, middle-class, individualist, capitalist, patriarchic, monogamous, meritocratic society) against an outside threat (often a seductive, egalitarian, hereditary, communal collective, such as a sect, a coven, an orgy, or socialism). Instead, stories emphasized the defense of oneself against a threat within, which often led to sacrificial death or suicide.

As Robin Wood (1979) has remarked, such presentations of violence appeared to claim direct cultural relevance for a generation of viewers that wanted their anxieties about the Vietnam war, civil rights riots, the breakdown of the nuclear family and traditional role models, and the uncertainties caused by the economic crisis, addressed in uncompromising terms. In all their directness these films remained ambiguous – with open endings, undefeated monsters, unresolved trauma, and an overall tone of despair about the possibility of survival in a world gone mad. In addition, much screen time was devoted to building a close attachment to the monster (and its values of unrepressed desire and sexuality), and to showing in precise detail its crimes and destruction. In films such as *Suspiria*, *Day of the Dead*, or *City of the Living Dead*

explicit imagery of death and flesh wounds, aided by special effects, emphasized every detail of the violent abuse of the human body, and the literal violation of bodily integrity (the last frontier of humanity) – thus blurring the border between good and evil, man and monster. On top of this, these films added the assumption that the source of evil was directly connected to historical and contemporary forms of waste, such as warfare, pollution, excess, over-consumption, gluttony, and greed – combating the idea of progress. The fact that these films were also rife with references to the legacy of the genre gave them a reach beyond any immediate appeal.

At least as important as their content and style was the way these films found their audiences. Without elaborate publicity campaigns, and distributed outside regular markets, they shocked audiences because they appeared out of nowhere, at matinees, inner city theaters, on the midnight movie circuit, and on college campuses. These sudden receptions provoked reactions from authorities that led to political backlash, bans, and police seizures. Before long, each of these films acquired a huge cult reputation (Peary 1981; Skall 1993: 307–309; Staiger 2000; Heffernan 2004; Mathijs 2003a: 109–126).

These films caused a paradigm shift for both the horror genre and the concept of the cult movie. All of a sudden, *Daughters of Darkness*, *The Blood Splattered Bride*, or *The Wicker Man* were no longer merely exploitation movies, but explorations of modern man's paranoid victimization by a civilization gone berserk. The change led to numerous imitations and a drastic shift in modes of practice towards much more grisly realist and cynical horror with a single-minded investment in mutilating normalcy (Holthof 1980). Above all, it gave horror cultism a pressing purpose and cultural mission, aligning it with counter-cultural dissidence as well as aesthetic vanguardism. By the end of the 1970s, at the time when O'Toole coined the phrase "cult of horror," the change had impacted on all of popular culture. O'Toole argues that North America was "hell-bent for horror," and that the popularity of the scary movie genre reached gigantic proportions: everything from *Halloween*, through *Suspiria*, *Dawn of the Dead*, and *The Brood* to *Alien* seemed a big success and also appeared to touch a cultural nerve, especially with younger generations of avid moviegoers, devouring horror with insatiable appetite. Beyond movies, horror imagery found public release, and wide fandom, through comic books, heavy metal music, punk rock, and literature (Stephen King, Ann Rice). Nor was the change limited to a few countries. American, Italian, Canadian, and French horror may have stood out because of the international distribution of the films of George Romero, John Carpenter, Dario Argento, Lucio Fulci, David Cronenberg, and Jean Rollin, but markets around the world were affected by the new development. O'Toole even connects the cultist adoration for horror with contemporary religious cults (like the Jonestown one, but also underground gatherings of real-life vampires), and threats of real horror (Skylab falling from the sky, industrial pollution, nuclear meltdown, cancer), inferring that they are signs of a society looking for certainties where there are none. For O'Toole, that fear explains much of the appeal of horror *as a cult*. He quotes Romero: "the rationale is, since this is the way we're going why not celebrate it" (quoted in Mathijs and Mendik 2008a: 259). O'Toole sees as the cult of horror's main components the emphasis on body horror (the monster comes from inside, or near you), the refusal to provide a comforting ending (either everyone dies or there is a "big question mark"), and the exposition of fanaticism (not just in the portrayal of characters, but also in the relentless drive of horrific events happening on screen – there seem to be no more rest points).

Throughout much of the 1980s, this arrangement of subculture, counter culture and popular culture around horror extended into a veritable cult industry. New production, distribution, and promotion practices, combined with innovative modes of reception, helped establish a worldwide fascination with the horror genre that spawned celebrations of the most diverse kinds. Companies such as New Line Cinema produced wildly successful franchises. New Line first made its name distributing *Pink Flamingos* and *The Hills Have Eyes* across campuses throughout the 1970s, then distributed the splatter cult phenomenon *The Evil Dead*, and finally became "the house that Freddy built" – producing the *Nightmare on Elm Street* franchise. The rise of video saw specialty labels such as Vipco make horror even more widely available. Many distribution companies started out in video, such as

Vestron, which started out by releasing films such as *House on the Edge of the Park* on VHS. Hollywood studios followed suit, financing the *Halloween* and *Friday the 13th* franchises and bankrolling a score of Stephen King adaptations. There was also a dramatic increase in specialist festivals, such as those of Sitges, Avoriaz, Porto, and Brussels (see Chapter 3). These festivals became instrumental in extending the reach of the cult of horror and giving it a historical grounding through the re-appraisal of older horror films (thus appropriating much of the genre's legacy into the cult, without much distinction in terms of quality, as the newfound cult appeal of *Plan 9 from Outer Space* testifies). Fanzines such as *Fangoria*, *Gorezone*, and *Halls of Horror* became hugely popular, partly as outlets that defended the cult of horror against its detractors (especially policymakers anxious to regulate the video market), but also as platforms on which distinctions within the cult of horror would be explored. Ian Conrich observes how disagreements between fans of monster characters such as Michael Myers (*Halloween*), Freddy Krueger (*Nightmare on Elm Street*) and Jason Voorhees (*Friday the 13th*) would be fought out in the same magazines that promoted the cult of horror, and how this combination of discourses is a sign of the cult-ness of all horror of the time (Conrich 1997, 2000). Similarly, Kate Egan (2007: 106–109) notes how a newcomer fanzine such as *The Dark Side* would place itself and its readers in opposition to other fanzines (such as *Fangoria*), thus establishing what she calls a "reader/editor collective."

Fan publications also promoted interest in aspects of production culture previously under-appreciated. The most important of these was the craft of special effects. Within the cult of horror special effects became the most celebrated production value, a logical consequence of the cult's investment in explicit depictions of injuries and bodily mutilations. Their elaborate effects made films such as *Suspiria*, *Scanners*, *The Beyond* or the remake of *The Thing* objects of cult fascination. Make-up and creature artists such as Tom Savini, Rob Bottin, Dick Smith, or Chris Walas became heroes of the cult of horror (Mathijs 2010c). The cult of horror furthermore extended into areas usually unaffected by cultism, such as academic scholarship. Spurred on by fanzines' aesthetic vanguardism scholars and critics started to bestow auteurist interpretations upon directors such as Argento, Cronenberg, Craven, or Romero. In 1979, the festival of Toronto was among the first to hold a horror-film retrospective (during which directors debated scholars). Soon, other festivals followed suit. By the middle of the 1980s academic presses were printing scholarly essays and books on the "new horror film" (Grant 1984; Brophy 1986).

By the second half of the 1980s, sequels, remakes, television spin-offs, and highly mannerist exercises in gore began to overshadow the subcultural and countercultural aspects of the cult of horror. Extremely violent and highly intertexual homages such as *Re-Animator*, *Return of the Living Dead* or *The Hitcher* continued to attract cultist receptions, as did attempts to re-radicalize the politics of the cult of horror through films such as *Hellraiser* or *Nekromantik*. But by the beginning of the 1990s the cult of horror had largely dissipated across numerous niches and subgenres, such as zombie horror, voodoo horror, body horror, giallo horror, Euro trash, serial killer and slasher horror, neo-gothic horror and postmodern pastiches of horror, some of which, such as *Edward Scissorhands* and *Man Bites Dog*, would *still* find cult followings.

The impact of the cult of horror continues to skew debates. Its ferocious appropriation of the history of the genre has made it difficult to assess the cultural contexts of cult horror prior to the 1970s. Its long tail of sequels, remakes, pastiches, and re-imaginations has added an emphasis on reflexivity to cult horror discussions (as we will see further on), but also an impression that it is virtually impossible to escape the framework of the cult of horror even after it passed its prime.

Cult Monsters

In between a perspective that sees cult horror as a subgenre engulfing part of the horror genre, and one that sees cult horror as one specific moment in the history of both cultism and the horror genre, lies an angle that attempts to pinpoint modes of operation and reception that the horror genre and cultism share, and which would explain why certain horror films gain cult reputations and some do not. The issue in identifying these modes is less one of aesthetic or cultural analysis, and more one of isolating the uses viewers make of opportunities offered to them by the practices (of films) that give them the chance to identify a film as cult horror. Sometimes, the study of these uses and practices offers only acquaintance-knowledge, but occasionally it offers deep insights in the kinds of processes that equip certain horror films with (degrees of) cult reputations. We will start with uses and practices that are usually more closely associated with the textual properties of films, namely modes of monstrosity, and modes of reflexivity and hybridity, and then move on towards more reception-oriented ones.

One of the defining traits across all instances of cult horror is the attention that fans and critics give to its monsters. Visit any horror fan convention or festival and invariably the monsters achieve most of the attention and praise. Cosplay and costume dress parties accentuate that appeal in very visible ways. There is a lot of mileage in discussing particular instances of representations of monstrosity and the specific cult reputations they achieve separately, especially since over the decades there have been wildly different responses to them, which have often been linked to either specific aesthetic innovations or particular cultural anxieties. Examples of the first instance are the cult appeal of the acting performances of Lon Chaney ("the man of a thousand faces"), whose portrayals of disfiguration and madness in films such as *Phantom of the Opera*, *The Unknown* and *London after Midnight* caused furor (Havis 2008: 6–8), and the cult reputation of a film such as *I Walked with a Zombie* that did not contain a marketable monster, and that was almost void of explicit violence, showcasing instead long, dreamlike and silent passages with lyrical background ambiance rife with sexual suggestion (Havis 2008: 26–28). Examples of the second instance are the cultist adoration for dehumanized creature monsters such as those in *Invasion of the Body Snatchers*, *Godzilla* or *Them!* as symbols of social fears and reflections of Cold War anxieties and xenophobia (Hentzi 1993; Jancovich 1996), or the cult appeal for depictions of monstrosity such as those in *Videodrome*, *Man bites Dog*, *The Blair Witch Project*, *Ringu*, or *Paranormal Activity* that focus on the complicity of audiovisual media, especially user-friendly video cameras, in determining what exactly constitutes a monster. As Brigid Cherry (2010: 185–199) points out, the marketing of these films via social network media that rely on roughly the same technologies as the ones on display in the films appears to make the very consumption of these films an accomplice in the processes of representation they are critiquing.

While such monster-specific interpretations certainly help explain specific cult receptions, it is equally useful to look at what holds all of these appeals together, and to investigate which kinds of processes underlie all modes of use and practice involving monsters that lead to assignations of cult for horror films. Generally speaking, there are six kinds of monsters that are regarded as significant in triggering cult reputations: "creatures," "werewolves," vampires," "serial killers," "zombies," and "the media." What all of these share in their monstrosity is that they desire to consume humans. They literally threaten the disintegration of the human body through anthropophagy – the act of being devoured by another human body. As we saw in Chapter 9, it has frequently been argued that such moments of abjection – instances of violent penetration *and* metaphors for sexual penetration – are key to any cult reputation of movies. What we would like to add with regard to their occurrence in horror films is that the way in which the consumption of humans is portrayed by monsters – for instance through the biting of humans by vampires, zombies, or werewolves or the "sliming" of humans by creatures –makes the act of devouring humans the center of attention in the uses and practices that lead to cult horror reputations. It becomes the dominant mode, cue, or clue around which cult status is organized. We noted in Chapter 1 how cult receptions are often arranged around contentious nodes of extrinsic and intrinsic references. "Consumption of humans" is one such node, of overriding importance.

This is most infamously the case with a slate of Italian mondo films that depict or suggest cannibalism quite directly. The most notorious of these is *Anthropophagus*. It features a scene in which a serial killer strangles a pregnant woman, pulls the fetus (actually a skinned rabbit) out of her womb and devours it. The scene landed the film on the "video nasties" list (Egan 2007). It also fueled speculations that the film was a snuff movie. This controversy greatly aided its cult reputation. A number of cannibal-mondo films, such as *Emanuelle and the Last Cannibals*, *Cannibal Holocaust* and *Cannibal Ferox*, have become renowned for their radicalism in

special effects (which are unusually convincing for films with such small budgets) (Goodall 2006).

Even in less radical form the trope of consumption of humans tends to dominate modes of practice and use – it simply cannot be pushed to the side of a story without viewers picking up on it and making it the centerpiece of interpretation. The cannibalistic motive in *The Texas Chainsaw Massacre* overruns several other tropes of violence, disability, and sexual violence in the film, and, as Brottman (1997) shows, in doing so it pushes to the fore an interpretation of the film as a criticism of how industrial modes of production push rural communities out of business and into abjection – an interpretation that even achieves portraying the violent family as victims of progress. *The Texas Chainsaw Massacre* has become paradigmatic in setting the tone for such interpretations. Similar considerations have also affected the cult receptions of *The Tenderness of the Wolves*, *The Cannibal Man*, and *The Fan*, to give a few examples that demonstrate that this is not a region-specific mode of usage – even if it can be explained as such (Hantke 2005; Mathijs 2006).

A motive that often occurs in connection with the consumption of humans is that of the serial killer. Mark Seltzer (1998) discusses how serial killers negotiate (or fail to negotiate) a "leaky self" through the possession and consumption of humans. In doing so, Seltzer shows how the phenomenon of the serial killer – and the public's fascination with it – needs to be seen in the wider context of the perception of the public sphere as pathological, dominated by the development of impersonal and inhumane "machine violence" unleashed by industrialization. Seltzer notes how serial killers move in the margins of such developments – on the borders of rural and urban centers, dependent on systems such as assembly-line labor, fast-food chains and postal systems that are simultaneously modern and outdated. Brian Jarvis (2007) makes the link between consumption, serial killers, and cannibalism more overtly, and stresses how it affected the ways in which the *Hannibal* films, *Se7en*, and *American Psycho* were read by audiences, and how these readings led to the cultification of these films. In his analysis of German serial killers' American reputation, Steffen Hantke (2005) develops a similar argument. Much of the cult reception of *The Hitcher*, too, focuses on the parallel between fast food (a burger) and cannibalism (a finger in the burger), both of which it cleverly links to the mutilations of bodies through torture.

Various instances of cult horror demonstrate how uses and practices of the mode of consuming the human body can be widened to include self-consumption, media consumption and capitalist consumption (and even greed), and the parallels between these (Guerrero 1990; Mathijs 2003b; MacKinnon 2005). For some critics such practices and uses amount to tangents and conjectures rather than insights. But the backgrounds of distinction, taste, and connectedness against which these uses and practices operate are instrumental for how cult reputations are arrived at. To put it bluntly, *even* if an interpretation of *Bram Stoker's Dracula* as a metaphor for AIDS would be incorrect epistemologically, the very existence of such interpretations, and indeed their prevalence, is evidence of how discourses surrounding certain horror films are cultified – affected by processes that draw them into connections and link them with beliefs that become true through the very fact that they are made and defended. Such practices and uses have influenced – for instance – interpretations of *Night of the Living Dead* and *Dawn of the Dead* (Heffernan 2004; Loudermilk 2003), and helped them achieve cult status. Similarly, they have helped werewolf movies such as *I Was a Teenage Werewolf* become a cult (Jancovich 1996); and they have aided the cult reputations of vampire films such as *Near Dark* (Powell 1994).

There are numerous complications affecting the mode of the monster's consumption of humans – for instance the degree of humanity a monster is given. Often, monsters are given human-like emotions, or made to look romantic, lonesome, and tragic rather than merely menacing. Such complications can feed or obstruct the processes described above. It is also worth noting that processes pushing a mode of practice and use occasionally wear off, or become hyperbolically reflexive or even parodic. This happened in the wake of films such as *Twilight* and *Shaun of the Dead* and books such as *Pride and Prejudice and Zombies* (Grahame-Smith 2009). In such instances, however, processes of determining the degree of cult of a horror film move into a different frame of reference, namely reflexivity and/or hybridity.

Reflexivity and Hybridity

A second mode of uses and practices governing the degree of cultism assigned to horror films that we want to single out concerns reflexivity and hybridity – or the self-conscious ways in which horror films that comment upon their own status as horror plays a role in the kind of cult appeal they have.

The point of departure here is that horror films obtain and maintain cult reputations by stretching and bending categories and by alerting audiences that they are doing this. Sometimes it seems such stretching and bending is merely a form of going against expectations. Vampire and werewolf subgenres, for instance, go through cycles of stagnation and innovation, with cult status bestowed upon films interrupting the flow of development – *Rape of the Vampire* and *Ginger Snaps* are two cases in point. It is important to note that the vitality of discourses surrounding these perceptions of interruption is more important to the cult reputations of the films than the degree of accuracy they contain. In other words, there only needs to be a discussion about how and if films are effectively rupturing the flow of development, but that discussion does not require either a resolution or indeed a change in assessment in comparison to prior discussions. Argento and Fulci's films remained associated with the giallo even after they had moved away from it, and their increasingly uneasy relationship with the giallo enhanced their cult status. Similarly, the *Friday the 13th* series remained for many cultists *the* totemic slasher franchise, even after it had started incorporating supernatural elements – and even crossed over into the *Nightmare on Elm Street* franchise with *Freddy vs. Jason* (Hills 2007). The *Nightmare on Elm Street* franchise, on the other hand, increased its cult potential by overloading its sequels *Freddy's Revenge* and *Wes Craven's New Nightmare* with queer subtexts or self-reflexivity (Benshoff 1997: 246–249). Equally, films such as *Snuff*, *Faces of Death*, and *Gimme Shelter* are forever fenced together as "snuff" even if their differences outrank their similarities, and the evasiveness of the very category snuff adds to their cult status.

At the same time as stressing their contested place within microscopic niches, most critics also note the generic hybridity of horror films known as cult.

While conforming to standards of subgenres and factions within the genre the cult horror film also appears to cross over between these subdivisions. This is best illustrated by what Joan Hawkins (2000) calls "art-horror," namely films produced and received as art-cinema *as well as* genre cinema. In many cases, the term art-horror relates to the inability of – mostly non-American – films with features of the horror genre to fit within existing routines of marketing, distribution, and reviewing.[3] Their isolated appearance in the market greatly reduces, and sometimes eliminates, the canvassing functions of these routines, giving audiences "unprepared" and "direct" access to the movies, thereby enhancing their chances of attracting uses and practices that show characteristics of cult receptions. Examples of art-horror go back to the very beginnings of horror. In the immediate wake of *Caligari* several European films with expressionist styles and horrific themes received cult reputations. *Nosferatu: Symphonie des Grauens* and *Häxan* attracted special attention for pushing boundaries in representing the macabre (their characters Dracula and Satan were deemed particularly grotesque), for their explicit sexuality and cruelty, and for their strong suggestions that evil was grounded in nature at large. The surrealists adored *Nosferatu* and *Häxan*. Because each of these films also played fast and loose with their source materials, controversies quickly arose, leading to bans, cuts, and confusions over final versions of the films. This only added to their cult appeal (French and French 1999: 151; Hammond 2000: 154; Stevenson 2006).

Hawkins further isolates film such as *Freaks*, *Eyes without a Face*, and some films by Paul Morrissey and Jess Franco, as key examples of mixes of horror and the avant-garde. *Freaks*, in particular, refused to be pigeon-holed. Its seemingly classic story-within-a-story portrayal of a troupe of circus "freaks" enacting revenge upon their bullies caused outrage, inverted so many production standards, and was so politically volatile that it caused a controversy that led to numerous bans, until a rediscovery as a midnight movie at the end of the 1990s. *Freaks* went further than all other horror films of the time (and many years later) by distributing aspects of physical monstrosity across virtually all characters in the film and challenging the audience to decide for themselves if any of the ensuing violence can be justified.

As Kevin Heffernan (2004, 2007) observes, Mario Bava's films *Black Sunday* and *Lisa and the Devil*, and Michael Powell's *Peeping Tom* also cross over between various subdivisions of the horror genre. This made it much more of a challenge to market them. It also proved a hurdle for reviewers, who often dismissed them. As a result, these films gave the impression they happened upon audiences, which further aided their cult reputations. A similar hybridity affects the status of films such as *Baise-moi* or *Salò*, which in spite of protest by critics are co-opted into cult horror because of their extreme imagery and taboo-breaking themes. In some instances, this hybridity has been used as a conscious strategy by filmmakers, to help films stand out from the rest of the market. A good example of this is *Daughters of Darkness*, whose cult reputation comes from being repeatedly labeled the most artistic vampire film (Everman 1993: 68–71; Mathijs 2005b).

Cult horror is further known for its extreme relationship to reflexivity, a mechanism associated with hybridity. It has been abundantly argued that reflexivity is a staple characteristic of horror that comes with the high degree of formulaic-ness and genre-mixing found in the genre (Wood 1979; Brophy 1986). In general, a horror film is more likely to be received as cult when it digresses from the contemporary degree of reflexivity. Cult horror is therefore usually either highly reflexive, or has a very low degree of reflexivity. In the latter case the emphasis is instead on the realism or directness of the horror – which amplifies the impression that the film is breaking taboos. It invites receptions of the film as even more shocking. Examples include the early receptions of *Night of the Living Dead* and *Henry, Portrait of a Serial Killer*. These films do include reflexive moments (think of the camcorder scene in *Henry*) but such instances were ignored in receptions that saw the films as shockingly realistic. High reflexivity is often regarded as a key characteristic of sequels, prequels, spoofs, remakes, and franchise features. The quintessential example here is *The Rocky Horror Picture Show*, whose reflexivity is so recognizable that the film ceases to be seen as horror at all. Other examples include *Return of the Living Dead*, *Man bites Dog*, and *Tesis*. In many cases, discussions about the cult status of a horror film revolve around the degrees of reflexivity that can be attributed to it, at various points during the reception trajectory of the film. Janet Staiger found, for instance, that many of her students viewed *The Texas Chainsaw Massacre* as a highly reflexive film, even treating it as homage to *Psycho*, whereas earlier receptions had treated it as a misogynist and insensitive critique of changing labor relations in rural America. As Staiger concludes, both receptions are not in opposition with each other. Instead, they typify the cult status of *Chainsaw*'s status, with the reflexivity acting as a *mediator* of the initially strongly received offensiveness of the movie (Staiger 2000: 179–187).

Reflexivity is applied in cult horror films in two major ways: as a framing of the narrative as a story-within-a-story, and as the presence of media reflecting on media. Examples of the first, which found its ways into the horror genre from *Caligari*, include *Freaks*, *Snuff*, and *Cannibal Holocaust*. Early examples of reflexivity through the presence of media include the film crew in *King Kong*, and a late-night bill of cheap movies in *The Blob* (Kawin 1992: 247–253; French and French 1999: 36). Frequently, cult horror films combine framing with media reflexivity. A good example of an in-depth exploration of this combination is *Videodrome*. Its cult reputation is largely dependent upon its reception as a treatise on reflexivity and media (Lucas 2008). At its broadest, reflexivity features the use of clichéd characters or the use of cameo roles, such as Barbara Steele in *Piranha* or *Shivers*. At its most specific – and most challenging – it features the use of objects planted for detection by committed fans. Masks and chainsaws are among the most totemic props.

Cult Horror Receptions

In conclusion we will look at some of the reception uses and practices that govern the labeling of horror films as cult. As the above discussions demonstrate, the role of the audience in determining the cult status of horror films is high, even in efforts that only want to consider cult horror through its textual properties.

Above all, cult horror receptions are noisy. The release of horror movies that go on to develop cult appeal is often met with outrage and controversies, be it for their crude depictions of monstrosity or their threatening, absurdist, or nihilist atmospheres. This has been the case from *Caligari* over *Night of the Living Dead*

and *The Texas Chainsaw Massacre* to *Ichi the Killer* (Budd 1990; Peary 1981; Mes 2004). Such aversion is in no small way helped by the fact that horror cinema in general remains reviled by moral majorities, eschewed by policymakers, and dismissed by critics. Partly in reaction to this, fans' appreciations of horror have become more exclamatory and superlative. There is a historical distinction here that needs to be addressed. Until the 1970s, this procedure of adversity, often followed by rallies to a film's defense, was a major mechanism through which horror films achieved cult status. It gave fans the chance to proliferate themselves as a subculture, with its own taste formations and canons independent of the impositions of mainstream culture. With the acceleration that became known as the "cult of horror" in the 1970s and 1980s, however, and in the wake of the far-reaching controversy over video nasties (see Egan 2007), these reactions and subversive attitudes became so entrenched that they led to a systematized cultism that no longer existed uniquely in a playful opposition to mainstream culture, but that also acted as a counter culture that held up a mirror to hypocrisies in society – especially those regarding moral panics, gender struggles, and xenophobic fears. The economic viability of the cult of horror also meant cultist appreciation of horror could function on itself, separate from the mainstream, which it did not need anymore. Before long, however, the same mechanisms that had once separated cult horror from mainstream horror were being replicated *within* the cult of horror, with subgenres and subdivisions pitched against each other as much as in reaction to objections and moral panics from outside horror culture. To some extent this means that cult horror receptions mimic receptions of genre, and that issues of "purity" and distinctions between "hardcore" and "pseudo" fans – distinctions between center and periphery in other words – continue to be performed on the smallest possible levels of mirco-cultism. The loud rhetoric used by fans to separate "gore" and splatter from each other is a good indication.

Secondly, and as a consequence, cult horror receptions refuse to disappear. After their initial noisy receptions, subsequent generations of fans reassess and celebrate the cult status, either by highlighting its formal qualities in defense of any reactionary criticisms, or by isolating newly found subtexts with political and cultural significance. The fact that cult receptions remain volatile for long periods of time aids such re-evaluations. Re-releases for niche markets and retrospectives at festivals accompany them. For instance, around the time when the midnight movie phenomenon started gaining momentum thanks to *Night of the Living Dead, Freaks* and *Häxan* were also being re-released. About a decade later, New Line Cinema, which had its finger on the pulse of campus cults, captured the rights to redistributing *Night of the Living Dead* and *The Texas Chainsaw Massacre*, exactly at a time when these films were being recognized as inspirations for the cult of horror.

The endurance of cult horror's receptions ultimately enables canonization, and the referencing of these films' iconography as homage in newer horror films. Again, it was at the end of the 1970s and the beginning of the 1980s that significant accelerations in this process occurred. The popularity of horror in the burgeoning video market, but also the birth of numerous horror festivals, helped establish mechanisms for continued reassessment that immortalized numerous cult horror films. Television, too, helped a great deal to sustain cult reputations. Decades after their initial releases many of the 1950s creature movies saw their cult status reinforced as a result of late-night cable television programming. For American audiences, the show *Mystery Science Theater 3000* (or MST3K) became instrumental in resurrecting horror exploitation from the vaults and reintroducing it to new generations of fans. MST3K hosts provided voice-over commentaries of the films, mocking them for their badness while praising their audacity. Before long, "MST3K" became a marker for the cult reputations of 1950s and 1960s exploitation horror.

Thirdly, horror cultism is very recognizable, because of the steadfastness of its symbols, and the visibility this gives to its fandom. Cult monsters, an important set of symbols, are instantly identifiable. Vampires, werewolves, mad doctors, phantoms, zombies, serial killers, giant bugs, and knife, razorblade, and chainsaw wielding maniacs like Freddy, Jason, Michael Myers, and Leatherface have spearheaded an array of monster designs easily marked by a small number of defining accessories such as fangs, fur, or masks. In other words, there are fixed templates for most cult horror monsters, most of which received a set

identity – and matching talents and looks – before the 1960s. These templates have also given cult horror fandom a high visibility, not only in illustrations in fanzines but also at conventions, festivals, fan gatherings, or rereleases, where costumes, accessories, and paraphernalia mimicking favored monsters are celebrated through dress-up contests and vampire balls (Van Extergem 2004; Hills 2010b), and even within popular culture in general, where these monsters and their iconography have received shorthand recognition (if not always respectability). In general, cult receptions are more strongly associated with horror films that have established templates for monsters (the original *Frankenstein*), or that have deviated ostensibly from such templates (*I Walked with a Zombie*, or *The Bride of Frankenstein*, especially in its representation of "the bride"). Once more, the period of the cult of horror changed the parameters of this recognizability, as horror films that took chances in renewing the iconography became attractors for cult appreciation (Nakahara 2010). Films such as *Martin* and *The Brood* owe a great deal of their cult reputation to the ambiguity that was the result of blurring representations of monstrosity with realistic features. This left the original Universal horror films with the respectful status of "elders of the tribe" – a respect that is neatly illustrated by the enduring appeal of the label "Universal horror," an admiration for the original actors (Bela Lugosi, Boris Karloff, Elsa Lanchester), and an absolute reverence for "original Frankenstein" or "original Dracula" dresses at costumed galas at festival and conventions (Van Extergem 2004). Ironically, the enduring cult reputation of the original monsters had the effect that many of the films in which they appeared are now excluded from cult horror overviews, often with the excuse they are too popular.

Finally, horror cultism has a distinct ritual quality – a tradition of repetitiveness that has clichés eagerly anticipated and loudly cheered, but that also has a distinct thrill of "newness." This is exemplified in cultist reception traditions such as the "initiation viewing" experience, "sleepover scary movie" traditions, and "midnight" events. The cult status of films such as *Last House on the Left, I Spit on your Grave, Cannibal Holocaust, The Evil Dead*, and *Ringu* depends on the sustained re-establishment of such instances across generations of horror viewers. This repetitiveness has led researchers and policymakers to express concern over the effects of repeatedly watching horror. Rape-revenge movies and mondo films in particular have consistently been under scrutiny for allegedly promoting misogyny, misanthropy, and violence. So have films whose viewing has been associated with violent crimes (such as *Child's Play III*) (Hill 1997; Goodall 2006; Mathijs and Mendik 2008a: 371–372). In his overview of horror theories, Matt Hills (2005) challenges this form of criticism profoundly. Andrew Tudor (1989: 212) argues that to blame horror films for violence in society would be "pernicious scapegoating, since ... we simply do not live in a world in which discrete cultural experiences have dramatic measurable effects. We live, rather, in elaborate interlocking systems, the elements of which are in constant inter-action." The latter part of Tudor's reasoning stresses exactly the function repetition has played in cult horror. The repetitiveness of its receptions has enhanced the recognizability and, therefore, cultural sedimentation and canonization of sub- and countercultural viewing strategies of cult horror into near-mainstream practices, perpetually enhancing opportunities for an enduring visibility of cult horror. A good example of this is the cross-generational passing on of the cult of horror. As the editors of *Cineaste* put it in 2009: "The illicit thrill of the macabre unites the generations weaned on *Famous Monsters of Filmland* magazine and pre-cable telecasts of the legendary Universal pictures of the Thirties with the generation that grew up on *Fangoria* and DVDs of Michael, Jason, and Freddy" (*Cineaste* 2009: 1). Through mechanisms associated with repetition, cult horror amplifies both the potential for desensitizing effects and the ability to take charge of complicated networks of meaning across generations.

Notes

1. The fast-changing nature of many of these sites and online presences makes it difficult to single out examples, but here are a few: monstersatplay.com (accessed July 26, 2010), the online debate on cult horror movies hosted at helium.com (accessed July 26, 2010).
2. See, for instance, books by Curci (1996), Schoell (1985), Godin (1994), and Balun (1992).
3. We acknowledge there is a competing use of the term art-horror, as proposed by Noel Carroll (1990). Because Carroll's discussion of art-horror refers exclusively to textual properties and is geared more towards a systematic understanding of the aesthetics of horror, we do not include it in our debate here.

19

Cult Science Fiction Cinema

Along with the horror film, science fiction cinema is a genre that has often been closely connected to cult cinema. Rather than delve too deeply into the quite complex issues related to definitions of the science fiction film, we will here include films that have largely been received as science fiction texts (although it is not always the case that films are categorized within one particular generic framework). We will nevertheless emphasize a few important traits that have distinguished science fiction as a distinctive genre before moving on to more specifically cult-related issues. Science fiction is commonly associated with speculative fiction based around current scientific theories and/or technologies; it is concerned with themes including space exploration, time travel, alien encounters, and humans' relationships with machines. It can also be concerned with questions about what it is to be human (Telotte 1995) or attempts to reconcile man with the unknown (Sobchack 2001: 63).

The first part of this chapter will also treat fantasy as a related genre, especially with regard to the public presence of both science fiction and fantasy. Even though fantasy has sometimes been distinguished from science fiction in the sense that the former deals with impossible worlds while the latter deals with possible worlds (Grant 1999: 17), they nevertheless share a number of overlaps, not just on a textual level (their status as speculative fiction) but also on the broader cultural level (many awards ceremonies, festivals, and fan conventions will cover science fiction and fantasy). We will further address some of the other elements of fantasy in Chapter 20, when we analyze the story worlds of blockbusters.

Dedicated Followers

Science fiction and fantasy have become heavily associated with dedicated followings by a number of fans, perhaps more so than any other genre (with the possible exception of horror). While fandom in general is covered in Chapter 5 (with references to *Star Wars* and *The Matrix*), it is necessary to add some details of the relation between science fiction and fandom here. While our focus is on cult film, science fiction is nevertheless a genre that has given rise to fandom across other media platforms, including fiction, comic art, gaming, and television, and these sometimes overlap. Joe Sanders has noted that English-language science fiction fans had organized into communities by the 1930s, creating networks with their own publications, social norms and vocabularies (cited in Karpovich 2007: 7). Publishing ventures among science fiction fans led to the development of a number of fanzines, and then to the establishment of conventions, both of which emerged in the 1930s (Hansen 1994; Bacon-Smith 2000: 12). Today a large number of science fiction conventions exist, including those that address the genre across different media (such as the *Worldcon*, which started as a literary convention but has broadened to encompass other media), or those that are based around a particular media platform (such as the network of European Fantastic Film Festivals discussed in Chapter 3). There are also those which address a specific title, such as *Star Wars* conventions (e.g. *Star Wars Celebration Europe*), and some revolving around a particular segment of science fiction fandom (such as *Wiscon*, a festival devoted to feminist issues within the genre).

Conventions and fanzines have long provided visible manifestations of science fiction fandom: the former in allowing fans from different areas to convene in a common location to attend events and converse, the latter in providing a platform for fan expression and knowledge (see Chapters 4 and 5). The large amount of fanzines related to science fiction have been supplemented by a number of more "professional" magazines, whose market presence also testifies to a dedicated fan base wanting to gain information and opinion related to the genre. Fanzines have been produced regularly within the science fiction community and have often included content such as articles, reviews, fan art and letters. In their dissemination of knowledge and opinion they have demonstrated a passionate commitment to the expression and sharing of expertise. As Michelle Pierson has argued in discussing the fanzine *Photon* (devoted to the "fantastic" film and running between 1963–1977): "Cultures of connoisseurship and fandom cultivate an attentional complex in which it not only becomes important to 'pay attention' at the movies but also to attend to discussion and evaluation after the fact" (Pearson 2002: 71–72). The sense in which many science fiction and fantasy fans have not only treated cultural objects with avid seriousness, but have done so within a generic area that has traditionally been held in low esteem by the critical establishment, has heightened the cult aura sometimes attached to this broad and loose community. As Tulloch and Jenkins have pointed out, science fiction fans have often been "pathologized" within mainstream media and the academy (1995: 10–18). This can lead to the strengthening of bonds between like-minded fans, though this should not disguise the fact that many subgroups exist within the science fiction fan community.

One important area in which science fiction (SF) cinema has gained close fan scrutiny is the field of special effects. Within formal critical circles special effects have often been dismissed or overlooked as filmic moments less central than more conventional critical topics such as narrative, drama, and character development. Within serious SF and fantasy publications, such as *Photon* and *Cinefantastique* (1967–2006), however, there developed a close analysis and appre-

ciation of special effects work. Out of this, visual effects creators could gain a reputation; one of the most prominent in the history of science fiction and fantasy cinema has been Ray Harryhausen, who even had a fanzine devoted to him (*FHX*, which ran for four issues between 1971 and 1974). Other notable effects creators who have contributed distinctive work to SF films include Dennis Muren (who co-directed monster movie *Equinox* before supervising the miniature special effects for *Star Wars* and *Jurassic Park*), John Dykstra (who worked most notably on *Star Wars*), Douglas Trumbull (*2001: A Space Odyssey*, *Close Encounters of the Third Kind*) and Stan Winston (*Aliens*, *Predator*). Much of the close scrutiny of visual effects among segments of fan communities would eventually feed into an increasing tendency (both within academia and, to a lesser extent, among critics) to treat special effects work as a serious aesthetic realm in its own right. Such attention has grown in tandem with both the movement of SF cinema towards a more central position within mainstream cinema production, and an increasing respectability for the genre (which still, nevertheless, sometimes carries with it the taint of disreputability).

Even as science fiction filmmaking has become a more prominent staple of mainstream cinema since the 1980s, fans can still play a crucial role in maintaining a cult following by distinguishing their understanding and appreciation of the text from those more "mainstream" elements which tend to be associated with consumerism and which are perceived as catering to a more general audience. As Nathan Hunt has argued in analyzing the reception of *Star Wars Episode 1: The Phantom Menace* within the fan-oriented magazine *SFX*, fans could create ownership of the film "through supposedly superior textual and extra textual knowledge of the film, and this ownership was itself used to distinguish the magazine's appreciation of the film from that of mainstream publications" (Hunt 2003: 190–191). A text can thus become the site of both mainstream success and enjoyment, yet still retain a cult following through a more particular following by fans utilizing trivia and connoisseurship to distinguish their appreciation from more "general" pleasures. On a more obvious level, some SF films can accrue cult value through a clear identity outside of the mainstream in terms of their budget and box office, by gaining smaller followings from people who may claim that such films offer greater intellectual and/or emotional rewards than their mainstream generic counterparts.

One particular field in which fans have been able to proudly proclaim their obsessive knowledge and expertise is in relation to Japanese *anime* science fiction, which has gained particular cult followings in America and Europe. Anime in general has given rise to large numbers of specialist clubs, fanzines and networks devoted to the mode, with many fans trading information and materials. Science fiction anime films are a particularly significant component of this mode of production. *Akira* generated a particular cult following and triggered an international fan base for the medium, despite the fact that it was a commercial flop on its original release in Japan. *Ghost in the Shell* is another notable cult sci-fi anime entry, a cyberpunk adaptation of Masamune Shirow's manga which also spawned a sequel with a cult reputation, *Ghost in the Shell 2: Innocence* (for more on anime and its fans see Chapter 11).

The possession of expertise and the participation in fan-based activities can also extend to the production of "fan art," which includes fiction, paintings, songs, and other related creative artifacts. Of particular importance to this chapter is the increase in fan films, which often use favored texts as springboards from which to spin new fictions. These films are very much cult-flavored in that they are not only (often) expressions of love for a particular film, but are also made for a like-minded community. Fan films, which according to Gwenllian Jones have existed since the early 1970s, tend to be shown at private gatherings, conventions and, more recently, online (2002: 169). Online distribution of fan films – in line with the increased access to film production via relatively affordable digital filmmaking tools – has increased the previously limited networks by which such films gained exposure. Henry Jenkins (2003) has argued that the Web "has made it possible for alternative media productions of all kinds to gain greater visibility and to move beyond localized publics into much broader circulation." While online fan films remain largely seen by other fans, some can cross over to a broader audience through the buzz surrounding them on the Web. Films that do this are cults not merely in their relation to a source text (or texts) and dissemination amongst a community, but also through gaining their own cult followings as

"small" films that gain enthusiastic audiences principally via word-of-mouth. Two particularly notable fan films that have achieved this status are the *Star Wars* fan films *Troops* and *George Lucas in Love*. Both films employ intertextuality in order to create parodic effects: *Troops* mixes *Star Wars* with references to the television documentary *Cops* in order to create "an ironic explanation for events that remain enigmatic in the original film" (Brooker 2002: 185), while *George Lucas in Love* mixes parts of Lucas's biographical history with *Shakespeare in Love* in humorously speculating on the creative origins of *Star Wars*. The success of both films led to Kevin Rubio and Joe Nussbaum entering the industry and working in a "professional" capacity, a process that, according to Will Brooker, many fans aspire to, thereby conceiving of their films as "calling cards and potential springboards to careers in the movie industry" (Brooker 2002: 175). Thus, although the science fiction community constitutes the core audience for such films, this community is never hermetically sealed from the broader culture and can feed into it in important ways. A mainstream film such as *Galaxy Quest* takes the fan adoration for science fiction as the core point of its narrative – with *Alien*'s Sigourney Weaver reprising her role as the strong female astronaut (a role she also resumes in *Avatar*).

Pulp Fictions

While many science fiction films were made previous to the 1950s, their actual status as science fiction is sometimes debatable as they would not have been termed as such at the time; thus Christine Cornea labels such pre-1950s films "proto science fiction" (2007: 9). The 1950s witnessed the first real "boom" in SF film production, particularly in the United States, where it tended to have a reputation as a "lowbrow" genre. Many such productions were low-budget pictures, though there were exceptions to this: medium and larger budgeted science fiction pictures – such as *The Day the Earth Stood Still*, *The War of the Worlds*, and *Forbidden Planet* – were produced by the studios, for example. On the main, however, such productions were generally expensive risks for the studios. Low-budget science fiction pictures, alongside horror pictures, could often count on an eager teenage audience and proved a more reliable source of revenue (Doherty 2002: 118–119). It is because this first sustained wave of science fiction films was generally associated with negative qualities – low budgets, cheap sets and effects work, wooden acting – that a number of films which emerged from it have come to be loved as cult objects. Much of the cult attachment to these films, then, is connected to celebration of enjoyably "bad" films, a phenomenon which is covered more fully in Chapters 3 and 8.

Enjoying "bad" science fiction films from the 1950s can be attributed to a number of factors. Obviously, the idea of celebrating marginal products condemned by the mainstream may well be one crucial factor: it is, for example, common for such films to be celebrated in a generally condescending manner, as texts that can be laughed at as opposed to culturally "worthy" objects (though there will be exceptions to this). Other factors may include the gulf between reality and fantasy that feeds into these films in particularly marked ways. A number of science fiction texts can be seen to revolve around a fantasy/reality axis, but in many of the cheap SF films of the 1950s this tension becomes overtly evident: it is inscribed upon the product not just on the level of content, but also economically. That is, attempts to create an audiovisual world of the imagination conflict with the financial realities of production, and in many films this gap between practical reality and imaginary fantasy is emphatically underscored by, in particular, cheap mise-en-scène and effects work. Hence the cult affection for films such as *The Giant Claw*, the Sam Katzman production in which a giant alien bird is realized through a rather clumsily controlled puppet; or for the now infamous *Plan 9 from Outer Space*, which marries its low-budget with emphatic incompetence, and by doing so has provided ironic pleasure for many. The affection for such low-budget SF fare may also be related to nostalgia: for a period when imagining the future was more quaint and innocent, or before science fiction had fully entered the mainstream and turned sophisticated and serious.

Both the above films' cult status is heightened by their relation to auteur figures (see Chapter 6), even if Ed Wood and Sam Katzman have gained a status for their incompetence and opportunism more than for their artistry as such. Other auteur figures can help to raise the profile of cheap SF films through being centrally involved in their productions. Roger Corman is one of the most notable examples here, helping to elevate the status of films such as *Day the World Ended* and *Attack of the Crab Monsters*. In the 1960s, however, Corman began to produce and direct slightly more ambitious movies that, while still modestly budgeted, gained more respect as serious works. Thus, in 1963 he made the acclaimed *X: The Man with the X-ray Eyes*, which starred Ray Milland as a scientist whose experiments led him to see through objects. Later, in 1975, he produced the cult SF satire *Death Race 2000*, which revolves around a race in which drivers run over pedestrians in order to gain points. Edgar G. Ulmer is another B-movie "auteur" who is judged to have created some distinctive films despite the rather paltry budgets he often worked with. Though more noted for his horror film *The Black Cat* and, in particular, his bare-budget noir *Detour*, he also produced a number of science fiction films including *The Man from Planet X*, *The Amazing Transparent Man*, and *Beyond the Time Barrier*. Unlike a figure such as Wood, both Corman and Ulmer have often been judged talented creative figures, particularly when the budgets of their films are taken into account. Thus, while Ulmer's science fiction films are not typically heralded as great works, moments from them can be extracted by critics and presented as evidence of his talent, which manages to make itself felt even when handling the most hackneyed material. For example, Erik Ulman writes of *Beyond the Time Barrier*:

> Ulmer uses the insistent triangles and inverted pyramids of the interior of Texas State Fairgrounds to invent consistently interesting compositions and environments. In addition, Allison's arrival at the ruined base is beautifully shot, and its genuine desolation creates an interesting contrast with the unreality of Allison's first view of the citadel. (Ulman 2003)

There are other low-budget SF films from this period that have gained a more canonic place within film culture but which nevertheless assumed such a position through first gaining attention in more cultish circles. One particularly notable example is *Invasion of the Body Snatchers*, which began life as a drive-in movie and became, in the words of Michael Sragow, "one of those tribal teenage totems ... that got passed from town to town through pop cultural osmosis" (2008: 75). From such humble beginnings the film became an important entry into science fiction cinema, its status elevated in line with Siegel's subsequent auteur credentials and three remakes that are often unfavorably compared to the more modestly budgeted 1956 version (Philip Kaufman's *Invasion of the Body Snatchers*, Abel Ferrara's *Body Snatchers*, and Oliver Hirschbiegel's *The Invasion*).

Siegel's film concerns the story of human beings being replaced by aliens, who assume the outward appearance of the bodies they have colonized. It has been interpreted both as an anti-Communist parable *and* as a text critical of the red scare mentality pervasive during the Cold War climate when it was both produced and initially released. These "contradictory" interpretations are an important reason why the film gained cult status (Peary 1981: 157) and they point to how significant social events can often produce interpretive frameworks by which films are valued and contested. It is also the case that there is an ambiguity at the heart of the film: a textual indeterminacy that aids fan speculation and can be considered a contributory factor to its cult status. In addition to it being read as a Cold War parable, it can also open out to more general speculation that is not so rooted in a particular historical context. The themes of paranoia and conformism which run through the film, for example, can relate to a number of fears that individuals experience within variable social contexts, and these have arguably become more relevant in contemporary social life.

Science Fiction Spaces

One particular appeal of SF films is the creation of detailed environments that are strikingly different from those that we experience in our daily lives. As Vivian Sobchack has argued, science fiction enjoys "particular representational freedom as a genre of the fantastic" and "concretely 'real-izes' the imaginary and speculative in the visible spectacle of a concrete image" (1999: 124). The creation of imaginary spaces can lead to cultic followings through inducing a sense of wonder and leading to subsequent investigations of such spaces through re-readings, in which the detailed mise-

Figure 19.1 The "hyperdetailed" world of *Blade Runner*.

en-scène excites "reflection or speculation about the diegetic reality and the text's underlying ideas" (Britton 2009: 344). As Matt Hills has written in relation to the cult response to *Blade Runner*: "Its hyperdetail also textually incites a desire to see more – to identify the mass of design objects jumbled within the frame; to catalogue and comprehend special effects sequences" (Hills 2011). The "hyperdetailed" worlds created by particular science fiction films may therefore engender a push-and-pull between being awed and overwhelmed by the audiovisual spectacle, and a mastering of that world in order to better understand how its magic is materially produced (Figure 19.1).

The dystopian space of the future is one of the most important types of alternative world-making within science fiction films, and characterizes a number of cult films emerging from the genre. One particular type of dystopian city is the "dark city," as outlined by Janet Staiger (1999), which characterizes a strain of science fiction filmmaking that intersects with film noir. Staiger argues that such films are also marked by a sense of postmodern conflation – that is, they incorporate motifs relating to the past, the present and the future – and decay (1999: 100). Perhaps most importantly, she notes that the darkness and generally chaotic design of many such filmic environments "permit labyrinthine cities where only overhead schematics provide a sense of orientation" (1999: 100), a point that relates to the idea of a "hyperdetailed" world. Further, Staiger also notes that science fiction films using dark cities are often critical of consumerist lifestyles: space in many such films is often presented as commodified (littered with advertising boards and screens, and corporate logos). Such broad social commentary may also contribute to the cult status of some of these films, in that cult cinema has often (though not always) been connected to anti-establishment themes and appeals. Three films featuring "dark cities," which have also gained a substantial cult following are the aforementioned *Blade Runner*, *Brazil*, and *Dark City*. *Brazil* is set in a futuristic (or possibly alternate), Orwellian universe marked by clunky technology and a complex bureaucratic structure which leads to general chaos and inefficiency. Its status as a cult film was very much heightened by the tussles Gilliam had with Universal over its decision to release a truncated and lighter version of the film in the United States, and this was further heightened by a five-disc Criterion laserdisc release of the film, which featured two versions, documentaries and a host of other material (this was subsequently released on DVD). *Dark City* features a world that cannot be fully grasped because it is subject to alteration by a group of beings called The Strangers. The Strangers not only alter the environment, they also control the lives of the inhabitants of a city that is always dark because people fall unconscious during daytime. *Dark City* was also a film that suffered cuts and, partly in response to its cult following, was subsequently released on DVD in a "director's cut" version.

Many dystopian, hyperdetailed SF films have been linked by critics and commentators to *Metropolis*, a film that has gained a cult status for its seminal position within the history of science fiction cinema, and which could be considered a "canonical" cult film. While it has enjoyed a prestigious position within cinema as a whole (not just within the science fiction genre), it has accrued added cultic values through the following means: as a film that is often referenced within a large number of texts including films, television programs and music videos (in addition to its numerous mentions within reviews); as a film which many science fiction/fantasy followers feel the need to refer to and watch as a crucially important part of their generic heritage; and as an "incomplete" film that exists in a number of different versions. The version of the film which premiered in Berlin was considered too long and so edits were subsequently made for its theatrical release. Different versions have since proliferated, but more recently new footage was discovered in an archive in Argentina, leading to a restoration project and the creation of what many excited film buffs are anticipating as the "definitive" version. The film's mise-en-scène, in particular its effects work and architectural designs, continues to fascinate numerous viewers and filmmakers to this day and is undoubtedly a crucial factor that has led to its cult position.

For Sobchack, science fiction films can not only visualize the impossible or the speculative, they can also envisage things that exist yet which are beyond the confines of normal vision, such as elements that are too small or too distant:

> The SF film gives us images – even if manufactured – of the immense and the infinitesimal. Extrapolating from known and accepted science, these film images derive their power to induce wonder in the viewer not from the imaginativeness of their content, but from the imaginativeness of their stance and their scope. (Sobchack, 1999: 101)

The creation of such imaginative worlds can produce films which do indeed "induce wonder" in particular viewers, sometimes leading to repeat viewings and a desire to find out more about how these films were created. One such film is *Fantastic Voyage*, in which a team of specialists are shrunk in order to enter a scientist's brain and perform an operation. The film creates a speculative environment of an enlarged brain, through which characters have to navigate. This inner geography was created through miniatures, wirework, and light displays; the latter drew from the psychedelic light shows gaining popularity within countercultural environments and which were used in clubs and rock concerts.

An interesting cult film which provides a speculative insight into what could possibly lie beyond the confines of normal human vision is John Carpenter's *They Live*. In this film, construction worker George Nada (Roddy Piper) finds a box of sunglasses and, after taking a pair, finds that they enable him to see the world in new ways: subliminal messages on magazines and billboards are revealed (such as "obey," "consume," "marry and reproduce"), while he is also able to detect that a number of human beings are actually aliens in disguise. *They Live* also, crucially, provides a very blunt anti-consumerist, anti-authoritarian message which is a frequent theme across a number of cult SF texts. Made in reaction to the Reagan administration that was in power at the time of production, the film allegorizes the conformist, consumer-driven ideology of Reaganism as an alien invasion which has succeeded through subliminal brainwashing techniques.

Other cult SF films notable for their creation of virtual spaces include *Tron*, which takes place inside of a video game and *eXistenZ*, which takes place within a virtual reality (VR) environment. *Tron*, though a flop at the time, has since become appreciated within specialist circles for its imaginative visual look but was considered too unusual at the time of release to be embraced by large audiences; while *eXistenZ* can be considered cult because of its director's broader cult standing.

Art/Independent Science Fiction

While we have mentioned how the low status of science fiction has often strengthened its cult pedigree, there are also a number of more serious and/or respected films that have been made within the genre "Art" films and/or films emerging from the low-budget, independent production sphere that may also gain cult status through various means. One such appeal, outlined by Cornea (2007: 74–102), is an appeal to countercultural sensibilities. She claims a cycle of "new art" science fiction films emerged in the wake of the success of *2001: A Space Odyssey* and that many of these films were influenced by a new wave of science fiction literature (including Michael Moorcock and J.G. Ballard). *2001* itself, while including a journey to outer space, also concerned the effects of such a journey upon consciousness, including experiential time-space disruptions, the inclusion of abstract effects, and ambiguous moments that led to a number of speculative interpretations. The film adhered more closely to conventions associated with "art house" cinema – such as its slow pace and its refusal to arrive at any neat conclusions – than it did to mainstream cinema, even though it was produced by a major studio on a significant budget. Kubrick is a director who has been recognized as creating an authorial art cinema from within the studios and this has enhanced his cult reputation. Two other SF films

he made can also be considered cult films: *Dr Strangelove or: How I Stop Worrying and Learned to Love the Bomb* and *A Clockwork Orange*. The former transformed Peter George's novel *Red Alert* (1958) into a satirical romp and was embraced, in particular, by college audiences who enjoyed its absurd critique of Cold War politics. *A Clockwork Orange*'s cult value was heightened by its withdrawal from circulation in the UK by Kubrick himself, following reports of copycat violence in relation to the film. It could only be seen through illegal screenings and, later, through pirated video cassettes; it only became legally available in the UK for public viewing in 2000.

Another noteworthy cult SF art film released in the 1970s was Nicholas Roeg's *The Man Who Fell to Earth*, which starred David Bowie as an alien (Thomas Jerome Newton) visiting earth to set up a corporation so that he can fund the building of a rocket ship which can distribute water back to his drought-ridden planet. This story, however, increasingly fades into the background of a film which is more concerned with examining the mutual interactions between the alien and a few human characters. It is, as Justin Smith has written, an "example of an oblique, unorthodox take on the sci-fi genre" (2010: 146). The rather elliptical narrative and perplexing temporal transitions led to some critics dismissing the film when it was initially released, yet it has grown in status with age and through repeated viewings. The film's puzzle-like narrative and its lingering, poetic images fused with a consumerist critique in showing Newton's quest being undercut through succumbing to human vices such as alcoholism and media-addiction, the latter memorably visualized by a wall of TVs with which he surrounds himself. The cult status of the film is also enhanced by the inclusion of David Bowie, who appears in a role that gelled with his public persona at the time: an otherworldly and enigmatic presence.

A later film which shared *The Man Who Fell to Earth*'s focus on a human-looking alien attempting to adapt to life on earth is *The Brother from another Planet*. The alien, known as "Brother" (Joe Morton) is, like Newton, subject to the projections of the humans that he encounters in the film. As he is also mute, his identity is being constantly constructed by others throughout the film. As the film is set in Ellis Island – the official gateway for immigrants arriving in New York harbor between 1892 and 1954 – and includes a multiracial cast of characters, it uses a science fiction framework to explore racial issues overtly. The Brother himself is black *and* an escaped slave (although it is established that there is no actual differentiation between skin colors on his native planet). The film has been embraced by many as an example of "Afrofuturism," the fictional blending of SF and the addressing of racial issues from an African-American perspective. Such interest has grown in order to counter the largely white nature of the majority of science fiction texts in the past. Another cult film which has been hailed as an example of Afrofuturism is *Space Is the Place*, a cheap film which was based around the world-views of, and also starred, the colorful and uncompromising jazz musician Sun Ra.

The Brother from another Planet is also notable for its rather unremarkable mise-en-scène: it is not a film that creates an elaborate spatial universe. Instead, the film uses recognizable and "realistic" settings and distinguishes itself as science-fiction through occasional, and often low-tech, special effects (the spaceship landing at the beginning, the Brother taking his eye out in order to use it as a monitor) and the presentation of other significant narrative information. A number of other films which include what could be termed "mundane" settings are also commonly identified as cult films. Often the mundane nature of the sets within such films is connected to budgetary restraints, which is also why they will often feature effects work only occasionally, if at all. Yet mundane sets can also play an important part within the film as a whole. Thus, in Jean-Luc Godard's typically perverse take on the genre, *Alphaville*, the future city portrayed looks exactly like 1960s Paris: this can be seen either as a deflation of utopian techno-futurist speculations, or/and it can act as a satiric critique of contemporary society, as Alphaville is a dystopian, surveillance-saturated metropolis in which emotion has been extinguished.

Repo Man also incorporates SF elements and takes place within a mundane, shabby part of Los Angeles. In fact, the unspectacular environment is a central motif of the film. The run-down neighborhood blocks and derelict spaces are bland geographical markers which impact upon the psyches of the characters, fueling, in particular, the nihilist aggression of the punks. The blandness of the environment is mirrored by the delib-

erate strategy to label all food and drink in uniform designs, shed of any brand names (also a sly critique of consumerism). The main character Otto (Emilio Estevez) finds a purpose in this environment through becoming a car repossession man, fueled by amphetamines and excitement, which places him apart from "ordinary" people (his mentor, Bud (Harry Dean Stanton), at one point exclaims "ordinary fucking people, I hate 'em"). This leads to him getting caught up in a plot involving a very strange 1964 Chevy Malibu (whose trunk contains mysterious properties, in a nod to *Kiss Me Deadly*, one of its many popular culture references) and ultimately acts as a time machine. Once again, the low-tech effects are highlighted here in that the Malibu's glowing properties were created through reflective paint. Another punk sci-fi cult film made around the same time, which like *Repo Man* became a popular staple of the early 1980s midnight movie circuit in the United States, is *Liquid Sky*. The film revolves around the New York "New Wave" scene, in which heroin consumption is rife. Among this junky scene lands an alien looking for its own heroin fix, but who finds its needs can be satisfied by a chemical released by the human brain during orgasm. As with *Repo Man*, punk lifestyles and attitudes are meshed with science fiction motifs to depict outsider lifestyles and embrace deviance.

A more recent example of a low-budget sci-fi with a "mundane" setting is *Primer*, which was made for a staggeringly low cost of $7000. (The production of this film is already becoming a part of its cult stature, made as it was on 16 mm film without hardly any wasted film because of cost restraints; it was nevertheless blown up to 35 mm for theatrical release and this added $30 000 to its budget (Taubin 2008: 80).) Arguably the most cultish component of the film, however, is the manner by which it creates a dizzying vortex of a narrative via its time-travel inside time-travel sequences, which cumulatively spiral into perplexing configurations and invite speculative interpretations. This links to two modalities that Hills has argued are recurrent across a number of cult films: first, "explicitly addressing questions of identity in a 'philosophical' or existential register" (through the proliferation of the same people existing in different temporal moments, which leads one to question if one version of a character is more or less "authentic" than any other); secondly, the ability to "provoke moments of 'ontological shock' which can be, in one example, 'characterized . . . by plot twists reorienting the viewer's understanding of narrative events" (Hills 2008a: 444).

The use of time-travel as a basis to explore particularly philosophical questions can be seen as a key feature in many "art house"/cult sci-fi films, and a particularly renowned example is Chris Marker's *La Jetée*, which has shown daily within a Parisian theater to a small clique of dedicated fans for a number of years (Cohen 2003: 150). This short film –described by Marker as a "photo-roman" – consists of still pictures bar one exception. It concerns a man who is captured in a post-nuclear, underground world, and subject to time-travel experiments. It presents a narrative which includes speculation upon memory and identity, but also extends this philosophical tone to explore the paradoxes of time travel. As Jonathan Romney (2007) has argued, its narrative is "a Möbius strip, returning paradoxically to its point of origin to swallow its own tail and engender itself once more." And, of course, the meditation on time is formally explored in a manner that leads audiences to encounter cinematic time in a much different manner than they are accustomed to, through the slow unfolding of continuous still images combined with voice-over narration and occasional sound effects. This film itself inspired cult director Terry Gilliam's more conventional, yet still rather labyrinthine feature *Twelve Monkeys*.

There are a number of characteristics which recurrently feature within the independent and/or "art cinema" areas of cult SF cinema, some of which overlap with cult SF more generally. While not every such film will share all of these characteristics (that there is no exact textual formula for a cult film means that we have to allow for contingency), the frequent textual features that typify art/independent cult SF films are: mundane and realistic settings, which are often (in the lower-budget bracket of such films) related to budgetary constraints and can be signified through predominantly location shooting and/or through stripped-down studio sets, and also through cinematographic markers such as grainy footage, hand-held camera work, and/or monochrome film stock; philosophical speculations about problems such as the nature and future of human existence or the complexities of theoretical problems (e.g. the possibility and consequences of time travel); and a willingness to embrace narrative experimentation, particularly through a heightened *ambiguity* which can open the film to multiple interpretations.

Conclusion

As we have shown, science fiction cinema has been a particularly important genre within cult cinema. Yet, while we have pointed to a number of significant elements that have led to its embrace by fans and other avid viewers, it is not possible to pin these down in any definitive manner. Certainly, the speculative nature of SF filmmaking is important: it can create spaces for people to explore and map details, think through philosophical issues, and to become immersed in fantastical worlds. Yet not only can this occur in a variety of forms – both low-budget and high-budget, serious and camp – it also does not exhaust the processes by which cult status is secured. Not only do social, technological, and aesthetic developments lead to fresh avenues by which cultism can emerge, but cult cinema has always consisted of films that seem to buck general patterns, prove exceptions to norms.

Nevertheless, as science fiction is a generic mode that has been frequently concerned with technologies and their social applications, it is very likely that it will continue to be produced and consumed. As technologies continually change and, in their turn, impact upon social formations in complex ways, films will continue to reflect upon such changes through imaginative fictions. New technologies impact upon the field of production and consumption, generating new tools to produce and distribute films, and new modes of receiving films and networking with others in order to respond to them. As mentioned in Chapter 5, the notion of "transmedia storytelling" – in which fictional universes from one media form spill over into other media – is a particularly notable example that enables cult followings to materialize. It is expected that a number of new formations will also emerge in the coming future, though the shape of such configurations and their social consequences is perhaps best left to SF creators to imagine.

20

Cult Blockbusters

The tendency to include blockbusters in discussions of cult cinema is often at odds with more classical analyses of cults, and there is some debate about whether or not bringing blockbusters into considerations of cult cinema makes the whole enterprise redundant (Stanfield 2008). After all, if something as intuitively antithetical to cult cinema as a mainstream Hollywood blockbuster can be studied as a cult, then why not accept that all kinds of films can? Does it not invalidate the term cult as a category? This line of argument is often found among critics and scholars of cult cinema who limit their definition of cult cinema to certain periods (preferably the 1970s) or to certain offbeat properties of films (preferably those countering dominant tastes).[1] Against that stands a school of thought which asserts that if one takes into account some of the salient features of the production, content, style, and receptions of blockbusters, and study how these interact to form reputations and cultural statuses, we not only see the same mechanisms as with cult cinema, we actually observe cinema cultism at work. Matt Hills has repeatedly argued for the inclusion of blockbusters in discussions of cult cinema, as part of a particular process of "cultification." He writes:

> Cult responses can inhabit the "mainstream" (as do *Star Wars* fans), treating blockbusters differently, and living with them over time rather than merely occupying an evanescent moment of multiplex omnipresence. Fan devotion and "excess and controversy" need not be articulated, they can be two distinct lines of cultification. Cult is "in" the mainstream now; within its terms of reference even if the two labels haven't fully collapsed

together. Supposedly "mainstream" films can become cultified by the "unfolding consumption" of online fans who anticipate a release, follow production rumors and news, attend screenings, download material, and then debate meanings, await DVD versions, and so on. (Hills 2008b)

As we have observed throughout this book, the term "cult" is no longer necessarily avoided by mainstream industries. More and more, producers openly court the status, hedging their bets on both mainstream and cult receptions, hoping it will bring in unexpected surplus revenue – unpredictable but equally welcome. For Hills, it does not make sense to create distinctions between the kinds of receptions classic cult films receive and the kinds some blockbusters get – both attract cultist celebrations, and the differences between them are more those between insistencies on categorization than between the characteristics of products or audience reaction. If one looks at the following of the *Star Wars*, *Indiana Jones*, or *The Lord of the Rings* films there is, according to Hills, no reason to not see them as equally close to cult cinema than to traditional cinema. In fact, Hills suggests, one can even see internal distinctions within cult blockbusters, typified by attempts to separate "legitimate" cult blockbusters from hyped or inauthentic ones (Hills 2006b: 160–171).

Supersize Cult

One of the most visible reasons to bring blockbusters into a discussion of cult cinema, and to discern a type of

Cult Cinema: An Introduction. Ernest Mathijs and Jamie Sexton.
© 2011 Ernest Mathijs and Jamie Sexton. Published 2011 by Blackwell Publishing Ltd.

film that would be the cult blockbuster, is their disproportionate size. This may seem counterintuitive. Usually, cult films are thought of as small in budget, tiny in their market share, and niche in their appeal. Blockbusters, on the other hand, have big budgets, a huge market share (often programmed to either swallow or avoid competition and to maximize exposure), and aim for the greatest common denominator with immediate availability to as wide an audience as possible. Small cult films demand to be liked by a few (and are often demanding in *how exactly* they would like to be liked at all). Blockbusters do not even require admiration or appeal, they merely want admissions and aggregates. Based on these oppositions there is no reason why blockbusters would become cults. Yet when discussions around blockbusters become dominated by a preoccupation with exaggerated size, to the extent that they are seen almost uniquely as deviant, obese monstrosities they have de facto become ready to be treated as cults. In short, blockbusters are big; cult blockbusters are too big.

A first issue here concerns budget and revenue. Blockbusters are expensive to make – this is part of the reason why they are called blockbusters. But when the size of the budget and the operation exceeds that of what is considered appropriate or acceptable, when boundaries of moderation and modesty in the making of a film are trampled and outstrip the rhetoric of efficiency – what Jerome Stolnitz (1960b) has called the "economy of action" – the production is often referred to as a "monstrosity." Similarly, blockbusters are measured according to their success – it is another reason to call them blockbusters. But whenever the achievements of a blockbuster surpass expectations well beyond what studios are anticipating (and that means beyond the kind of ready-statements of exceeded expectations studios are all too keen to release), when they do not just reach the top but go "over the top," or when the gross taking has become "too gross" (to use two preferred metaphors of industry commentators), they are prone to attract a kind of attention that is equal to cultism. This not only applies to successful films but also to those that have become disproportionate failures. The inability of films such as *Heaven's Gate*, *Last Action Hero*, and *Waterworld* to become the successes they were supposed to become has created cultist followings partly because of the

magnitude of the failure, and of the way in which this failure was commented upon – often encapsulated in the phrase "just what were they thinking?" In sum, whenever budget and revenue take on grotesque characteristics, and can only be described in exaggerated terms, they become deviations from normal consumption and appreciation patterns. They become exceptional in much the same way smaller cult films do.

Beyond budget and profit, the culturally most tangible aspect of cult blockbusters' supersized-ness is that they are everywhere. They are what Thomas Austin has called "dispersible texts":

> the dispersible text is … at the hub of a triple movement: a centrifugal dynamic of aperture and extension via satellite texts, mirrored by a centripetal force which refers consumers from these texts to the film, and a further impetus to buy spin-off goods after leaving the cinema. These processes of dissemination, recruitment, and ancillary consumption are anticipated and enabled by the particular construction of the dispersible text. [They] multiply and complicate the promises, interpretations, and invitations-to-view offered on behalf of the film (Austin 2002: 29–30).

In a "normal" reception the centripetal force eventually wins out, converging all views into a few preferential and acknowledged meanings, and consumptions, of a film. But in some cases the "talk" generated by the centrifugal dynamic of aperture and extension prevents such convergence. Research into films such as *Judge Dredd* or *The Lord of the Rings* (Barker and Brooks 1997; Barker and Mathijs 2007) has demonstrated the extent to which the centrifugal dynamic can take over a film's reception up to the point where the film itself seems to matter no longer and hype appears to perpetuate independently from feeders by the industry.[2] In the prefiguration of *The Return of the King* industry attempts to control the hype were met, and occasionally obstructed by a "chaotic diversity" of centrifugal discourses fanning out in all kinds of unexpected directions, each with its own high degree of investment (Biltereyst, Mathijs, and Meers 2007: 48–49, 57). Whenever the subsequent dispersion stretches beyond what is considered "hype," and a film's popularity is sustained beyond release-related periods of time, and whenever such chaotic diversity becomes a force equal to the efforts of the marketers and producers, it becomes a strong indicator of a blockbuster's cult appeal. Again it is the extremity of the size of dispersion that makes the real difference. When the consumption of a blockbuster is not merely accompanied but in fact *constructed* through satellite texts and dispersed discourses it develops characteristics strikingly similar to those of cult viewing, such as multiple exposure, immersion, and the invitation to create interpretations far beyond the single film-text. In such a case, the dispersion is cultist.

Added to these mechanisms of dispersion are issues of length, of the film, the franchise, and of the audience reaction. Blockbusters are often longer in duration than regular films, which makes going to see them an endeavor of bigger proportions: queues are longer, and their visibility attracts more attention from other media, who are subsequently eager to label the phenomenon as a hype, a craze, or a cult. The effort to go see such a phenomenon is easily presented as one that requires "endurance," leaving much room for reflection on the physical aspects of watching such a film. Likewise, the aspect of immersion is described more often as "total." Amplifying those associations are marathon screenings or serialized franchises in which all of the episodes are viewed in succession, "extended" cuts with "new previously unseen" bonus materials, and the persistent or repeat viewing attitudes of audiences who return to see these movies more than once – an attitude confounded of course by the fact that blockbusters' bigger market share reduces the choice to go see other movies. As with budget, revenue, and satellite texts, the difference between a cult blockbuster and a "normal" one lies in the degree to which the size of the endeavor is one of the key features in its reception.

The supersized aspects of budget, revenue, dispersion, and length became tropes in the reception of blockbusters since the mid 1970s, and they have been eagerly linked to the films' contents. From early examples onwards, such as *Towering Inferno*, *Jaws*, or *Close Encounters of the Third Kind*, to so-called high-concept blockbusters such as *Die Hard*, *The Abyss*, *Jurassic Park*, and *Speed*, critics and audiences drew parallels between the size of the operation, their reception, and their content (big towers, big shark, big dinosaurs, big spaceships, big bus, etc.). It might not merely be a coincidence that one of the most popular scenes from *Jaws* contrasts the supersized shark with the boat hunting it: "You're gonna need a bigger boat" says a stricken Martin Brody (Roy Scheider) upon first seeing the shark. He even says it twice. A few years later, the X-wing fighters in *Star Wars* are equally direct in pointing to size as a marker of attention when they approach the enemy Death Star: "Look at the size of that thing!", one exclaims.

Until the late 1990s remarks about size were offset by other observations, so that the oversize trope did not come to dominate the discourse of blockbusters. But the late 1990s started a trend to have the size of some blockbusters become the *only* noteworthy point of attention. As we have observed above, it coincided with the introduction of cult blockbusters as a noteworthy albeit contentious part of cult cinema. This evolution is best characterized by the production and reception of *Titanic*, a film about a big boat and a big catastrophe, which was almost uniquely described along metaphors of its oversized dimensions, its mass. Kevin Sandler and Gaylyn Studlar (1999: 1) single out size as the predominant factor of the phenomenon; in fact they use the term "most" four times in the first two sentences of their introduction: twice to refer to the size of the boat, and twice to refer to the reception of the film. In his discussion of *Titanic*, Martin Barker (2001: 88) describes it as a "bloated leviathan" before detailing its epic proportions. Before it was released, *Titanic* was predicted not just to be a flop but to become "the turkey to out-gobble them all" (Shone 2004: 251). When it became evident the film was an unparalleled box-office success, the tenor of comments changed, but not the metaphors or rhetoric: super-size still dominated the debates. The size of the audience and the size of its repeat-viewing appetite, the often-commented on super-inflated budget that required the collaboration between two major studios (20th Century Fox and Paramount), the size of the risk, and director James Cameron's triumphant shout "I'm the King of the World" when he picked up a record number of Academy Awards (biggest possible of any film awards), all contributed to this impression of oversized-ness. If we look at the long-term reception of *Titanic*, its oversized-ness has remained a key factor, now no longer in attempts to praise the film, but rather in efforts to diminish its significance: too long, too bloated, too self-indulgent, it is frequently cited as one of the worst films ever exactly because of its gluttony – a sort of cult reception trajectory in reverse.

Retrospectively, the trope of supersized-ness also helps explain some of the cult reputations of films that have stood at odds with other cults: Hollywood films such as *Gone with the Wind*, or, outside Hollywood, *Metropolis*. Perhaps most symptomatic for this retroactive application is the cult reputation of *King Kong*, of which Cynthia Erb shows just how much it hinged on the motive of size, or "scale" as a contemporary critic referred to it: a mammoth of an ape, big showmanship, barnum promotion, and huge success (Erb 1998: 49–63).

Supersized-ness thus becomes a key identifier for cult blockbusters. Since *Titanic*, it has characterized the receptions of franchises such as the *Pirates of the Caribbean* and *Harry Potter*, and films such as *The Dark Knight* and *Avatar*. Their receptions contain references to disproportionate size at virtually every level of debate, from the ones mentioned above (length, dispersion, revenue, and so on) to details such as the size of the appeal of a star (Johnny Depp and Heath Ledger), the expansion of a bosom (there were numerous discussions about the increase in size of Keira Knightley's chest in *Pirates*), or a segment of the audience (too young, too loud, too hyper). Above all other examples stands what is, next to *Titanic*, the XXL in cult blockbusters, namely *The Lord of the Rings*, a films whose epic scale of operation, exposure, length, and appeal eclipsed that of nearly every film before it. Fittingly, in an article discussing the upcoming release of the first *Lord of the Rings* film, the *Village Voice* connected its supersized-ness to its cult status when it remarked that: "hype easily self-assassinates, but *LOTR* may be immune to excess … Because of its extra-cinematic life, it can't escape being a monument to its own built-in cult, which is roughly the size of humanity" (Atkinson 2001).

Content and Style of Cult Blockbusters

Cult blockbusters have in common with cult cinema that they present illogical, unhinged stories with lots of visual excess, offering manifestations that invite visceral instead of interpretive reactions. Because of this they are often called meaningless: void of relevance for our world, escapist or mere spectacle.

Let us start with the story-worlds, the fictional universes within which the stories unfold. Most movies known as cult blockbusters have what could be called built-in cult potential. In many cases this means that they are based on source materials that have already developed cult followings. Adaptations of comics and books are the most common examples, with *Batman*, *Harry Potter* and *The Lord of the Rings* among the best-known cases in point. *Titanic* was based on the sinking of the actual ship *Titanic* in 1912, an event several critics have described as having a cult reputation in popular memory (Barker 2001; Kern 1983). *Pirates of the Caribbean* was based on a theme park ride which itself was inspired by the cults of pirates, Maroons, yardies, and Rastafaris. In the case of *Star Wars* and *Indiana Jones* inspiration was drawn from an amalgamate of sources, many of which had cult status – ranging from previous cult films (Kurosawa's samurai films, westerns, adventure movies of the 1930s, etc.) to comic books (*Tintin*). The adaptation of cultist source materials necessitates the compression, elimination, or addition of many elements of the original story-world for transfer to the screen. Debates about which parts of the source material are truthfully transferred, part of what we have labeled the centrifugal dynamic of the dispersible text, often expressed in public forums, ensure that the screen adaptation quickly becomes a feature of the cult of the original material regardless whether the adaptation efforts are appreciated or not. It sneakily penetrates it as it were – before the actual film is released.

The second aspect of the cult blockbuster's story-world that we would like to touch upon is its "mythical" nature. We analyzed the connection between cults and myths in Chapter 12, and we addressed story-worlds in science-fiction in Chapter 19, but some elaboration is required here. Cult blockbusters invariably hint at worlds – or world systems – that are lost in time, either locked in a certain historical era decidedly not ours, far in some fictitious past or future time, or outside conceptions of history altogether. Yet, at the same time, there is the perception that there is some spillover into the present, some ephemeral impact in that the story-worlds appear to present foundational narratives for our world – the same way myths are foundational stories for the ideologies and morals of civilization. In attempting to achieve this spillover, these story-worlds weave a fair lot of history (and pseudo-history) into their fabric, especially of instances in which tensions between a largely disorderly but appealing world and a highly ordered but unattractive world run high. Through this method, cult blockbusters' story-worlds present an ideological framework that pertains to expose the problems of "our times" by offering purity of vision and by presenting a snapshot of unsullied time not yet tainted by real-politics. In terms of visual representation, the story-worlds are often shrouded in mystical symbolism. They consist of an amalgam of apocalyptic, utopian, and dystopian thought, an assembly of Western myths, legends, and religious beliefs (Christian, Jewish, and Buddhist in particular, but also various pantheistic beliefs), a mix of aesthetic heritages (romanticism, Greek antiquity, Gothic styles of the Middle Ages, expressionism), and a variety of political philosophies. With regard to politics, cult blockbusters' story-worlds show a preference for small-scale participative democracy and class collaboration, enlightened absolutism, eco-logism, and tribalism. They favor a fair degree of anti-hegemonic sentiments (even anarchism), often in romanticized form, especially in the form of bands of pirates, rangers, or rebels. Generally, vast organizations and collectives such as empires and bureaucracies are seen as evil. Furthermore, people and groups are often reduced to the skills and functions they perform ("warrior," "priest," "pirate," and so on), which, incidentally, puts them in a skilled-laborer class. Selected individuals are often endowed with super-powers and magic ("the ring," "the force," "the grail," "the mark," etc.), aided by secretive, sectarian organizations who guard "true knowledge" – models of inspiration here include a wide variety of militia and orders, from the Praetorian guards and the Knights Templar over wandering samurai, the SS, and buccaneers, to Tibetan monks. These alternative universes are not uniquely populated by humans either; they frequently include alien creatures and part-human life forms, a further reference to mythological conceptions of the world, from before history began, when humans would still share the world with beings that are not human – dryads, nymphs, elves, fauns, satyrs, centaurs, titans, gods, demons, trolls, orcs, talking bugs, and shapeshifters.

Put together, these imaginings attempt to evoke a "past" or "future" time when "pure" instances of mystical experiences are possible, and they ask audiences to "imagine" the deep connection between these worlds and an "original" cult feeling, and experience, if only remotely, some of the exhilaration of being connected with "true life force." The films that go the furthest in shaping an entire alternative universe and a coherent world system (complete with alternative historiography) often get the biggest cult following. Examples are *Batman*'s Gotham City, *The Lord of the Rings*' Middle Earth, *Harry Potter*'s parallel Muggle and Wizard worlds, and *Star Wars*' Expanded Universe (which is also the name of all the licensed fictional background used in spin-offs, merchandise, and other media – an indication if ever there was one of the conflation between centripetal and centrifugal dynamics in the dispersible text that is the *Star Wars* franchise).

Many critics of cult blockbusters use the formulaic application of the above-mentioned inspirations, and indeed the implications these have for representations of groups of people as an argument against their acceptance as "legitimate cults." It is worth bearing in mind that this formula is not so much the result of the exhaustion of inspiration. Rather, it is the effect of the overly systematic use of a small array of textbooks that condense the diversity of myths into *monomyths*. This term describes the process of reducing the common denominator of known myths to one single narrative, in particular that of the "hero's journey." Eileen Meehan and Deborah Tudor (2010) argue that post-1990s cult blockbusters' reliance on monomyths is indicative of, and runs parallel with, the political perspective of neo-liberalism, reflected in numerous references to class distinctions, for instance in *Titanic*, *Star Trek*, *Harry Potter*, and *The Lord of the Rings*.

As important as their story-worlds' cult potential is the "look" of cult blockbusters. Generally speaking, cult blockbusters provide spectacle – and indeed make a spectacle of themselves – through visual excess or cinematic trickery, dazzling the audience by showing vertiginous, breathtaking imagery through camera pyrotechnics and special effects. According to theories of film aesthetics, excess is an element of style that falls outside the regular framework because it does not occur in support of the story world or the plot (Thompson 1977). It works separately, often overshadowing other elements of a film. In the case of cult blockbusters, where regularities are already skewed because of factors such as size, the stylistic overkill produced by excess not only augments the story, it becomes its substitute, demanding a high degree of emotive involvement from the viewer. Reviewers often employ the metaphors of a rollercoaster or a car chase to refer to this mechanism. Aggregates of excess become spectacles. Just like the arenas of the theme park or the racing circuit within which the ride or chase happen, they connect to the wider affective range of experience and impression of excess, to its mode of reception. Cult blockbusters excel in spectacle. The canal chase in *Terminator II: Judgment Day*, and the flight from the Orcs in Moria and the Balrog on the Bridge of Khazad Dum in *The Lord of the Rings* are good examples. In each of these examples, movement, tricks, speed, and a quick succession of situations dictate a rhythm and pace that Murray Pomerance regards as all-engrossing. Here is how he describes its occurrence during a *Stars Wars* screening for a thousand-strong audience on Times Square:

> We are always sacrificing the progression of a story by succumbing to fascination. When the Millennium Falcon slips into hyperdrive, we choose to forget where we are, how we have come to be here, what has been happening, where we are going, all in the name of gaining the fullest possible consideration of the myriad stars stretching themselves swiftly into light beams against the black, black curtain of space ("WO!" screamed that audience, in unison) (Pomerance 2007: 22–23).

Such a description fits neatly that of the phenomenal experience we highlighted in Chapter 1. One or two such instances do not suffice to abandon attention for narrative progression for longer than a few moments, argues Pomerance. The "effects chain" of blockbusters, as he calls it, does not eliminate the story. With cultist viewers, however, who are already familiar with the story, who will take the spectacle not for what it stands for but as a goal in itself, and who might even have seen the film before, indulgence in vertiginous moments such as the one Pomerance describes *will* replace attention for the story as a focus of attention.

As can be deduced from Pomerance's example, the main tool here is the use of special effects, a core element of cult blockbusters ever since *Star Wars*. In Chapters 2, 18 and 19 we have devoted some special attention to the cult of special effects. Here, we will concentrate solely on the so-called "Big effects" that are so typical for cult blockbusters. Besides yet another reference to size, "big effects" are the kind that demand notice, not just for their quantitative presence, but for their dominance in the reception of the film they feature in. In their analysis of the unsuccessful blockbuster *Judge Dredd*, Barker and Brooks (1997: 283) observe how the young boy fans so dedicated to comic books and blockbusters appreciate just how much special effects are a "balancing act" that marries elements of the implied story-world with elements of the achievement: "[they] hover between being about the world their special effects imply ... and about special effects and the wizardry of the movies themselves." Further research on films such as *Titanic* and *Starship Troopers* suggests that the degree to which special effects dominate the reception of certain blockbusters is a key determinant in having them accepted as "big" – grand in size and certainly grand through their prevalence as a point of reference in the reception (Barker 2001). Overall, then, excessive demonstrativeness becomes a key attraction for cult blockbusters (Lichtenfeld 2007).

Turkey Plucking: The Critical Reception of Cult Blockbusters

At the Cannes festival of 1997, Bruce Willis caused uproar among the critical community by answering hostile comments on *The Fifth Element* with the suggestion that: "nobody up here pays attention to reviews ... most of the written word has gone the way of the dinosaur" (Boorman and Donahue 1998: 1). Besides yet another reference to size, Willis's reference to unfavorable criticism is a paramount element of cult blockbusters. With their supersized budgets and appeal, clichéd story-worlds, and overblown special effects cult blockbusters have been a particular target of reviewers, and, as such, their negative evaluations have aided their cult status. In fact, as "turkeys," they have come to occupy a critical category of their own. As Tom Shone writes: "In an age of marketing overload, the plucking, basting, and roasting of turkeys would become something of a cathartic public ritual, somewhere between an exorcism and a witch hunt, with the press in the role of witchmaster general" (Shone 2004: 211).

The main characteristics of the negative reviews of cult blockbusters are a frustration with waste, a refusal to acknowledge creative input (especially with regard to directors as *auteurs*), and a view on its audience as illiterate, indiscriminate, and shallow. The frustration with waste is – of course – connected to the supersize and excess of the films, and to the belief that anything so overly big, plump, glitzy, or extravagant could be "efficient," "good," or "proper cinema." The prime example here is *Titanic*, which was being prepared for what Shone has called "critical snobbery at its most knock-kneed" months before it was released (Shone 2004: 261). The industry press lambasted it for half a year before it was released, because it was so big – with cruel puns on the size and fate of the ship linked to that of the movie. Critics were mildly hostile towards the plumpness of the narrative (describing it as a "predictable" film with no "surprises"), or downright condescending towards its popularity with teenage girls' repeat viewing – another form of waste. Even when *Titanic* turned out to be a grand box office success, critics would reflect on what a shame such greed was for "real cinema." In the case of films such as *Heaven's Gate*, *Last Action Hero*, *Cutthroat Island*, *Waterworld*, or *Catwoman*, which were not only critical but also commercial failures, dismal critical ratings are often regarded (rightfully or wrongfully so) as the catalysis of the lack of popular appeal, reflecting the vox populi. In such cases, criticism takes on something of a performative element, decorating its frustration with the film with trivia, witty observations, descriptions of anachronisms, and even campy elements that all function to humiliate the film. Notably, female performers in cult blockbusters are given harsh criticism; infamous examples include Sharon Stone, Geena Davis, and Halle Berry (for her role in *Catwoman* which won her a Raspberry Award, see Chapter 3).

Creative labor in cult blockbusters in general is almost never accorded critical praise. This is perhaps most acutely visible through "adverse auteurism," or the snubbing of directors of cult blockbusters. This criticism is a logical consequence of the frustration with waste. Instead of auteurs cult blockbuster directors are called "dinosaurs" or "moguls" (yet more references to supersized-ness). High-profile directors such as Michael Cimino, John McTiernan, Renny Harlin, Kevin Reynolds, and Kevin Costner, have repeatedly been ridiculed for their box-office failures. Even perpetually successful directors and producers such as James Cameron, Michael Bay, and Luc Besson, who have made multiple blockbusters with cult followings, are permanently struggling to receive recognition for their work. Their mode of operation is often considered aggressive, bullish, and dictatorial, and their aesthetics are regarded as overly simplistic, even fascist. This vilification has given these directors and producers cultist reputations as the "men you'd love to hate," and it has given films such as *Rambo* (for which Cameron wrote the screenplay), *Terminator II: Judgment Day*, *The Fifth Element*, and the *Matrix* trilogy notoriously unhinged long-term receptions. The DVD receptions of these films, for instance the discussions surrounding the "place" of Michael Bay's films on the cinephile DVD label Criterion, or Cameron's entitlement to awards (especially with regard to *Avatar*), have a key place in these continuous contentions. Ironically, this criticism helps instigate a fractured trajectory that characterizes the reception of cult auteurs.

Added to disdain for their size and make up, glee about their potential failure, and misrecognition for their makers, critics view the spectators of cult blockbusters with contempt. This contempt is most often expressed in remarks about largesse, illiteracy, and shallowness. Critics assume readily that whoever displays a cultist fascination with blockbusters has not (yet) met the "proper films." Such remarks about cult blockbuster audiences are often peppered with observations about the average age of viewers (not yet considered to be mature enough), about their attention span (supposedly shorter than every other generation's), and about their addiction to fads and hypes. In often highly charged language, critics view audiences of blockbusters as susceptible to films presented as "hot" but without the faculties to turn them into something "cool."

The Audience Reception of Cult Blockbusters

If we look closely at those films most often called cult blockbusters it becomes clear that part of their audience make up – *within* the mass appeal as it were – exists of a core of devotees and followers whose actions are very cultist – if not in nature or intention then at least in their perception.

To begin with, there is a striking gender-uniformity in the cultist audience celebration of blockbusters. In our examples on special effects we have alluded to the appeal of these production values with young boys. Similarly, we have observed in Chapter 10 how the cult following of *Titanic* has a gender-specific element in that it was "not the huge number of fans that might make [it] cult but rather the way in which it was celebrated through all-girl repeat viewings" (Mathijs and Mendik 2008b: 5). Within the most devoted audience segments of *The Lord of the Rings*, too, gender-uniform constellations of "spiritual journey ladies" and "lonely epic males" stood out (Barker and Mathijs 2007). The research of Barker and Brooks on the reception of *Judge Dredd* has become paradigmatic, at least methodologically, for several other analyses of types of fandom that show cultist features, in which issues of gender and class are isolated. Research on mainly male fans of the *Resident Evil* franchise, fans of Sylvester Stallone, and female fans of Sharon Stone confirm such gender specificities (Lay 2007; Huffer 2007; Feasey 2003).

To an extent, these observations on cultism and blockbusters match sociological research on the tastes of lower-class audiences as "univorous." The opposite of "omnivorous taste," univorous taste is arranged around a narrow pattern of strong preferences for very few products, with the function of solidifying a group-identity (Peterson 1992; Bryson 1997).[3] Univorous taste confirms the position cult blockbusters hold as among the lowest possible in terms of cultural standing (even among cult films). It is a position they share with other types of cinema and media known for their solicitation of extreme emotion (soap, family life oriented reality TV, porn, extreme horror, hyperbolic melodrama). Among the most visible articulations of the cultist reception of blockbusters symptomatic for univorous taste are repeat group viewing, "swooning" (fanning adoration, often in the form of fake fainting) and "posturing" (prominent positioning of the body to indicate an ease with and control over the immediate social environment). All three are seen as group activities associated with unsophisticated puberty behavior. This negative connotation is a legacy from the use of the term to describe 1950s and 1960s youth culture, when it was used in connection to unruly and deviant gang, crowd or mass behavior (Cohen 1972). From that legacy also comes a connotation with gender-uniformity: repeat-viewing groups are usually made up of same-sex pals; swooning is for girls, and posturing for boys. When such terms and connotations are adopted in current debates about girl groups repeatedly watching *Titanic*, teenage girls voicing their adoration for *The Lord of the Rings*, or young boys expressing their fascination with *300* or *Robocop* through posturing, those forms of celebrations are portrayed as a sort of disruptive behavior typical of hardcore cults, a threat to "normal" society even.

Much of the cultism around blockbusters is more elusive than the category of "univorous taste" leads us to believe, and it is extremely hard to research. The release strategy of blanket market saturation makes it hard to discern cultist activities during the first months of release. Only in the longer term, when prolonged runs at theaters are accompanied by reports of demographic oddities in attendance does cultism become a term of reference. Even then it remains difficult to assess, and in most cases evidence remains either anecdotal or impossible to separate from the cultural mainstream – as we remarked in Chapter 1, it led reviewers of *The Lord of the Rings* to comment that the oft-used term "geekdom" does not fully capture what is no longer a subculture "but a formative force in the cultural imagination of our times" (Biltereyst, Mathijs, and Meers 2007: 46).

There are only two real moments that enable the measurement of cultist receptions of blockbuster, and both are open to manipulation. The first preempts the film's general release. As we have outlined above, blockbusters try to attract extra attention to their upcoming release through a range of prefigurative initiatives. One such initiative with high cultist potential is the premiere. Blockbusters aiming for a

Figure 20.1 Fans of *The Lord of the Rings* dressed up to attend the premiere of the Firefly fanseries at the Norwescon 33 convention in April 2010. Photo by Michael Hanscom of Norwescon (www.norwescon.org).

cult following often receive unusual slots at multiplex theaters. In keeping with the legacy of cult cinema traditions these are frequently midnight screenings, occasionally coupled to marathons sessions of previous installments in the franchise. In the case of cult blockbusters such premieres are known to attract dress-up attendance, as has been the case with *Star Wars*, *The Lord of the Rings*, or *Indiana Jones* premieres. The combination of the midnight hour and the dress-up occasion gives audiences an opportunity to publicly display their cultism. The second moment occurs years after the initial release, at specially staged activities such as conventions or fan gatherings. Here too, screenings of the film are organized at times and venues already indicative of devoted following. Often it has members-only or exclusive access. Both moments have two characteristics common for cultist gatherings: they pair a common cause with a high degree of "camaraderie." Indeed, research on the networks of repeat viewers of *The Lord of the Rings* stressed "friendship" as a prime marker for cultist blockbuster viewing (Biltereyst, Mathijs, and Meers 2007: 57) (Figure 20.1).

One final aspect of the audience reception of cult blockbusters that deserves attention is its celebration through performative actions, including tongue-in-cheek parodies of fandom. These performances build on the public's general knowledge of, and ambiguous feeling towards, blockbusters to create outrageous and hilarious interpretations and re-imaginations. In a sense, these performances use the imagery of excess

blockbusters are known for and give it a twist. As such, these performances of fandom build on the concepts of appropriation and bricolage singled out in Chapter 5. But, just like the blockbusters they use as their point of departure, they often go a few steps further in the hyperbole efforts – and their ridicule. The two most visible types of such outings are "queering" and "slash-fiction." We discussed queering in Chapter 10, as a cultist appropriation of meanings that enabled the performance of gendered receptions. Its main aim is to point to ambiguous portrayals of masculinity (and the ideologies these embed) in blockbuster cinema by using highly sophisticated strategies of interpretation on films that were purportedly single-minded, straightforward (with the pun on the word "straight" intended), and crude in their presentation of masculinity. As we have indicated in Chapter 5, slash fiction is, like fan fiction, the creation of fictional tales based on the characters, narratives and story-worlds of blockbusters. But it combines the reverent tone towards the original that is typical for much fan fiction with a mocking attitude and the rearrangement of meanings of the original through same-sex and pornographic innuendo. Since such alterations are often laid out in new products (online stories, prints, posters, re-edits of clips, etc., and even some newly shot work) there is a creative and productive aspect to slash fiction. Because slash fiction enhances visibility, adds to the liveliness of reception, and challenges taste norms and standards of industrial practice (including copyright) blockbusters that are frequently slashed are more likely to develop cult reputations – as if slash fiction uncovers their "dark side" and gives them a more rebellious attitude. Among the most consistently slashed are the *Harry Potter* franchise, *Star Trek*, *The Lord of the Rings*, and *Star Wars*. Each of these series has been criticized for its conservative politics, and in each case slash fiction has given it a somewhat more edgy and less conformist reputation.

Conclusion: Calculation and Spontaneity

The methods used by slash fiction and ironic performances are, of course open to endorsement or adoption by the industry. This is often part of an attempt to gain some form of control over those forms of celebration, and to invite audiences of new work to accept it as cultist – but "cultist" as labeled by the industry instead of by audiences. In a sense, then, self-ridiculing instances in films such as *Men in Black* (where Will Smith is appalled to find his "super weapon" is actually tiny), or in advertisements in which director Michael Bay demands everything to be "awesome" (while blowing up his pool and barbeque), signal a continuation of struggles between the industry and audiences over the legitimacy of terms such as cult and blockbuster, and their combinations. It is even addressed in erotic spoofs of blockbusters, such as *Lord of the G-Strings* (Hunter 2006; also see Chapter 10).

This overt danger of reappropriation explains perhaps why, even amid the acrimony towards the cult appeal of some blockbusters, only a few of them are easily accepted into the cult canon. *Waterworld*, *Showgirls*, or *Judge Dredd* are such commercial disasters, and *The Lord of the Rings* and *Star Wars* have such devoted followings, and all of these are bathed in such visual excess and mythical story-worlds, that their cultist receptions cannot be ignored. Curiously, however, when faced with such evident cultism, most critics and fans appear to want to save themselves from the potentially negative connotations of the term "blockbuster," so they drop the term altogether and *only* employ the label cult.

Notes

1. Many of the contributions to *Cineaste*'s 2008 symposium on cult cinema expressed this concern.
2. Martin Barker has called such dynamics "ancillary materials," and Ernest Mathijs refers to them as "ancillary discourses" (Barker 2004; Mathijs 2005b).
3. We should note that research that identifies univorous taste is frequently methodologically ill-equipped to detect complex patterns of interpretation among audiences because it cannot probe beyond audiences' utterances, which might not always be perfectly formulated. It is a problem similar to the anxiety of cult consumption we observed in Chapter 10.

21

Intertextuality and Irony

The last two chapters in this book discuss modes and themes that revolve around the self-consciousness of film cultism, as a knowing mode of engagement with both the film text and the audience that, frequently, leads to *performed* cultism. In this chapter we focus on intertextuality and irony. Both have appeared several times in the course of this book, most prominently as viewing positions or modes of reception that are significant elements in establishing cult status. We discussed ironic viewing positions particularly in Chapter 8, while intertextuality in classical Hollywood cults, in the cult of horror, and in meta-cultism is addressed in Chapters 17, 18, and 22. Throughout this chapter we will mainly focus on cult film texts (the films themselves), though we cannot totally extract textual workings from their contextual surroundings, so the role of the reader will still assume an important position.

Among the most prominent terms that play a role within cult cinema are parody, pastiche, irony, and related terms such as satire. These modes, to varying degrees, can be understood as forms of intertextuality: where one text refers to another text or, more frequently, to a number of other texts. For Umberto Eco, in a seminal essay on the cult film, this form of intertextual quotation was a crucial element of cult films: if a film is made up of a number of intertextual references it becomes a patchwork in which any part of that film can be dislocated from the whole. This process gives rise to the "glorious ricketiness" that Eco saw as a particularly important quality of the cult film (1984: 198–199). More recently, Matt Hills has argued that the self-conscious interrogation of

genre conventions is one particular "modality" recurrent across a number of cult film texts, particularly through a "display of intertextual subcultural capital" (2008a: 44).

Let us start by outlining some of the terms that we will be using in this chapter: many of them are related, but they also have been distinguished in particular ways. *Parody* is a process of reworking a text, or textual elements, in a manner that attempts to mock the reworked text(s). As Dan Harries has pointed out, parody depends on an oscillation between similarity and difference: there needs to be a recognizable congruence between the text referred to and the new text for parody to function, but a disparity between the texts must be apparent for the parodic effect to be successful (Harries 2000: 6; 25). *Satire*, by contrast, tends to refer not so much to the mocking of aesthetic forms recurrent across prior texts, but of social attitudes and/or behaviors (Dyer 2007: 41). The terms need not be mutually exclusive, as parodic discourse can also be satiric: for example, an artwork may parody and mock a former text (or set of texts) *and* also critique social attitudes related to such texts. Another concept related to parody is *pastiche*: like parody, pastiche depends upon imitation of other texts and relies upon the reader to "get it" in order to fully work, but unlike parody it does not mock or satirize; it is, as Frederic Jameson pointed out, "blank parody" (1983: 114). *Irony* refers to a mode of discourse in which an utterance is double-coded: a conventional sentence may be spoken which actually means something else, but only an initiated audience will understand this other meaning, while the uninitiated may only interpret the overt meaning.

Cult Cinema: An Introduction. Ernest Mathijs and Jamie Sexton.
© 2011 Ernest Mathijs and Jamie Sexton. Published 2011 by Blackwell Publishing Ltd.

Irony overlaps with parody, pastiche, and satire to the extent that all these processes involve transforming conventionalized codes into other codes, "an activity that results in the possible recognition of incongruity between the two codes" (Harries 2000: 30).

Cult Parody

It should be pointed out that the functions of parodic art can vary a great deal. Even though there has been a tendency for critics to focus on the subversive nature of parody it is, as Simon Dentith argues, "politically and socially multivalent" (2000: 28). Parody can be used for socially progressive or conservative purposes, or it may be wielded for primarily comic intent. Actually gauging the purpose of parodic content can itself be difficult, as such an assessment will need to be cognizant of the social context within which the work was produced and the intentions of the parodist(s). Furthermore, the purpose of the content may not always be successful due to the range of interpretive possibilities that any work can generate. Nevertheless, to parody another work, or other works, does often entail an evaluative stance towards the material being referred to, as it generally involves mockery. Within this mocking cultural mode there nevertheless exist degrees of criticism, from gentle mockery to acerbic ridicule. Such mockery can, however, exist alongside a more loving stance toward the object being mocked on occasions. An example of such loving mockery can be found in the cult film *This Is Spinal Tap*; while the film makes fun of some of the ridiculous aspects associated with heavy metal music, there is also an evident fondness for the culture and, in particular, for the characters. The film is, therefore, "mocking, yet reverent" (de Seife 2007: 9).

According to Harries, film parody creates an oscillation between similarity and difference through three central categories: *lexical*, *syntactic*, and *stylistic* (2000: 9).[1] The lexical refers to the iconographic elements of a film, such as setting, costumes, and characters; the syntactic refers to the plot and structure of the film; the stylistic refers to the expressive cinematic techniques used, such as camera movement, editing, sound. It is often the case in parody, Harries

argues, that at least one of these category levels needs to be retained (in order to produce a resemblance to the parodied text), while at least one other level is altered. Similarity and difference can also occur within the same category, so that a dominant referent can be evoked and then disrupted. Harries provides an example of this in *Blazing Saddles* where a pack of cowboys riding through open plains (evoking, through costume and landscape, the Western) eventually come across a toll booth, a lexical unit incongruous with the genre and which therefore is intended to produce a comic effect.

Much of Mel Brooks's oeuvre relies on spoof and parody, and his earlier films in particular have garnered a cult status. His directorial debut, *The Producers*, undertook a typical cult journey in becoming a cultural phenomenon after initial hostile reviews and a disappointing box-office performance. Although the film is, overall, more of a farce than a parody, it does contain parodic components. In particular, the Broadway musical featured within the film, *Springtime for Hitler*, relies on the incongruity of generic expectations to create its comedy. The encasing of serious content (the Nazi invasion of Europe) within the syntactic and stylistic confines of a musical was, at the time it was made, comic because the manner in which it combined these generic units was considered to be outrageously inappropriate. After this film Brooks moved much more into a spoof-parody mode, in particular creating comic material out of specific genres (horror with *Young Frankenstein*, the Western with *Blazing Saddles*, science-fiction with *Spaceballs*), a particular mode of cinema (silent filmmaking conventions in *Silent Movie*) and techniques primarily associated with a respected film director (Hitchcock in *High Anxiety*).

Another Jewish American comedian with cult appeal who – at least earlier in his career – utilized parody on numerous occasions is Woody Allen (in particular, he has a solid cult reputation in France, with many small Paris cinemas regularly screening films from his catalog). Allen often incorporated parodic sketches both within his films at certain moments, and sometimes across whole films. In the latter category we could include both *Sleeper*, which parodies science fiction filmmaking, and also the "mockumentary" *Zelig*. The latter film concerns a "human chameleon" and inserts Allen's eponymous character into actual documentary footage to provide a convincing illusion of his actual presence at historical events. The generic simulation is further enhanced by the inclusion of real public figures, such as Susan Sontag and Saul Bellow, providing commentary on the figure of Zelig. Allen had already used the technique of having a real, extratextual figure entering the narrative (and thus pulling the narrative out of its textuality as it were) in *Annie Hall*, a film Danny Peary (1989: 20) sees as Allen's most beloved cult picture. In a scene in which the philosophy of Marshall McLuhan is briefly discussed, an annoyed Allen stops the narrative, pulls McLuhan into the frame and asks him to give his view on the matter. Other Allen films are more diffuse parodies: *Love and Death*, for example, mainly targets Russian novelists such as Tolstoy and Dostoevsky, but also includes numerous references to other films, in particular the works of Ingmar Bergman; whereas the compendium film *Everything You Always Wanted to Know about Sex (But Were Afraid to Ask)* contains send-ups of a variety of different artists and forms, including Shakespeare, Antonioni and television game shows. *Stardust Memories*, which French and French (1999: 202) regard as the "key film in the cult of the Woodman" parodies the system of art house cinema, and puts the films of Federico Fellini, in particular his already self-reflexive *8½*, through the mangle.

Parody's importance as a cultic form of filmic expression is that it relies upon broader cultural knowledge to function effectively. In this sense, it can sometimes appeal to a prominent sector of cult cinephiles: viewers with an extensive knowledge about cinema as a whole, gained through heavy viewing and associated information seeking. Extensive use of parody will more likely be fully understood by such viewers, who will have an increased likelihood of spotting the allusions at work in a parodic text. This would indicate that there is an elitist dimension to parody and associated intertextual forms which rely upon knowledge of other texts in order to be fully understood. To some extent this may be the case, though it is a point which needs qualification. First, as Richard Dyer has argued in discussing pastiche (which we will come to later), this elitist dimension (which also applies to parody) does not overlap with elites as socially defined: pastiche (and parody) occurs as much in popular and mass culture as it does in middle and high-brow culture. It could be posited, then, that it is a kind of populist/popular elitism: this relates to a number of processes connected to cultism, particularly the ways in which cultism often revolves around substantial knowledge and understanding of a range of popular texts. Secondly, we also need to understand the ways in which an appeal to people who "get it" works by a matter of degrees. It is not often the case that one set of viewers "gets" a parody and another set doesn't. This is because there will often be a number of references to other works within a given parodic film, which means that the amount of references recognized may vary a great deal from viewer to viewer. It is often the case that many parodic films will tend to function in a manner that minimizes the exclusivity of their operations: this is achieved through scattering references so that a film does not necessarily depend on the recognition of one referent text, and also by creating scenes that can function effectively even if the parodic referent is not spotted. A typical instance of the latter case is to create a comic scene which parodies another film, but which also can be interpreted as comic by viewers who do not possess the knowledge of the parodied text. It may be the case that certain parodic functions may fail if a crucial referent is not identified: for example, would *Zelig* "work" without knowledge that it is parodying the documentary? Would *Blazing Saddles* "work" without any knowledge of the Western film? They would probably not, though we would not want to rule out the possibility that "naïve" appreciation of these films cannot occur. This process of "getting it" is, however, only an extension of the intertextual regime upon which everyday film viewing depends. If we do not possess broader generic knowledge then it may also be the case that we may not "get" "straight" genre movies, because genres depend on a set of conventions which "specify the ways in which the individual work is to be read and understood, forming the implicit context in which that work acquires significance and meaning" (Ryall 1997: 328). This itself is an extension of culture in general, because no text (whether it be a film, a piece of writing, even an everyday utterance) can be understood in isolation, but "always appears to us as emerging from some other text" (Iampolski 1998: 15).

Parody often draws attention to the generic codes that viewers often take for granted. Many parodic films are created when particular generic conventions have become routine to the point of cliché. If, at the broadest level, parody operates by spoofing the most clichéd examples of generic formulae, one could postulate that "cult" parodic films will tend to send up more specialist material, or at least material that itself has a particularly marked relation to cult cinema. This is certainly the case regarding one of the most well-known cult films, *The Rocky Horror Picture Show*, which contains a number of parodic references to cult films including *Frankenstein* and *King Kong*, as well as referencing a slew of cheap science-fiction pictures. It is also the case with *Play it Again, Sam*, which sends up the cult classic *Casablanca* and is all about the cultic fascination that the film, in particular Bogart's character, exerts on Allan Felix (Woody Allen). Inevitably, comic results are produced by the gap between what Allan is (a neurotic nerd) and what he aspires to be (tough and cool). John Carpenter's *Dark Star*, meanwhile, spoofs science-fiction cinema, including the portentous cult film *2001: A Space Odyssey*. Nevertheless, the often unpredictable quotient involved in cult cinema means that, while lampooning other cult and/or obscure material may be more likely to lead to cult status, this is not necessarily the case.

Often, it is hard to tell whether the high amount of tongue-in-cheek plagiarism of story-worlds, costumes or props, characters, and broad narrative lines is the result of comic genius, an attempt to tap into the eagerness of cultist audiences, a form of homage to the original, or just plain laziness. The cult status of the films of the British comedy team Monty Python, especially *Monty Python and the Holy Grail* (a spoof of the Arthur myth) and *Life of Brian* (a spoof of the life of Jesus Christ), has, over the years, been considered a mix of each of these components. For some, Monty Python is ridiculous, for others silly, for others yet it is ultra-clever, and for many it is all of that – cult because of how it unhinges notions of humor. Since the 1990s, films such as *Mars Attacks!*, *Men in Black*, and *Galaxy Quest* have proved that mainstream audiences can sustain and even celebrate mockery. Even the cheekiest spoofs, such as erotic spoofs of blockbusters, have adopted the parody mode. In fact, their existence, and the degree of fidelity, crassness, or lack of production-value can be regarded as an indication of the cult appeal of the blockbuster they are spoofing. Production

company Seduction Cinema, which labels itself as "cult" in its marketing, has made a name for itself as producer of erotic spoofs. Among the most visible have been *Lord of the G-Strings*, *Spiderbabe*, and *Batbabe: The Dark Nightie* (see Hunter 2006).

Cult Pastiche

Pastiche is closely related to parody: both modes draw attention to the conventions of generic discourse through a combination of imitation and discrepancy. Yet, while the two forms often overlap and are sometimes employed similarly, pastiche does not tend to contain the satirical, mocking nature of parody. Richard Dyer (2007: 47–48) has argued that three main factors need to be taken into account when distinguishing between pastiche and parody: *paratextual* factors, which relates to how a film is presented (for example, advertising and critical reaction may point out that a film is a pastiche); *contextual* factors, where we need to work out, for example, what decisions informed the work; and *textual* factors. Of course, there may be difficulties in arriving at any straightforward decision even when considering these elements because contradictory evidence may exist: a film may be advertised as a pastiche while more commonly identified as a parody by critics; different people who worked on the film may provide conflicting information about the reasons behind particular imitative strategies; while, as Dyer has pointed out, the textual distinctions between pastiche and parody are often not clearly marked but are a matter of degree. Ultimately, Dyer argues that whether we treat a text as pastiche or parody is a matter of how particular readers draw upon paratextual, contextual, and textual evidence to construct valid arguments which illuminate the texts concerned (2007: 48). We should point out here, though, that Dyer himself draws a distinction between *pasticcio* and *pastiche* (the latter word deriving from the former).

Pasticcio refers to a work that incorporates a number of references to, or quotations from, heterogeneous works, creating a multivocal play of competing textualities. An example of this would be the conscious placing of generic clues and cues in a film in order to provide a wink to the in-the-know audience. Two examples of this with great currency in cult cinema are rabbits and chainsaws. Over the years, the referencing of rabbits has become a key component of cult films, from *Harvey* over *Rabbit's Moon*, *Weekend*, *El Topo*, *Monty Python and the Holy Grail*, *Night of the Lepus*, *Nekromantik*, *Akira*, *Bill and Ted's Bogus Journey*, to *The Lord of the Rings*.[2] The genealogy of this reference can probably be traced, for instance, to Lewis Carroll's *Alice in Wonderland* (see Brooker 2004) or performance artist Joseph Beuys' use of rabbits as symbolic figures (and many folkloric uses of the animal well before that), but that genealogy matters less than the inter-relationships and associations these references generate. By the time *Donnie Darko*, *Gummo*, *House of a 1000 Corpses*, and *Inland Empire* referenced rabbits, the trope had become a key marker in cult cinema. With chainsaws, a genealogy runs from *The Texas Chainsaw Massacre*, over films such as *Motel Hell*, *Scarface*, *The Evil Dead*, *Bad Taste*, and *The Hollywood Chainsaw Hookers*, to *Pulp Fiction*, *American Psycho*, and *Chainsaw Sally*. In each of its appearances in these films – most of which are spoofs of some kind – the chainsaw signals a moment of pasticcio, of simultaneously acknowledging a solid place in a generic tradition started by *The Texas Chainsaw Massacre* (as is observed by Kermode 2001), yet also pulling it out of this narrow generification. In *Pulp Fiction*, the chainsaw is one of a series of weapons Butch (Bruce Willis) considers using to liberate someone from torture. In the end Butch settles for a samurai sword – a weapon with a similar function as pasticcio.

For the larger part of his study, Dyer focuses on a specific form of pastiche, where instead of specific tools or moments, the overall work itself is signaled as imitative of other work(s) in some way (2007: 9–48). One particular genre that Dyer characterizes as marked by pastiche, and which has also spawned a number of cult films, is the spaghetti western. He argues: "The very fact of a Western being made not in the American West or even North America, and at a time when Hollywood Western production was considerably diminished, may suggest that at the very least it is apt to be pastiche, to be not the real thing and evidently conscious of it" (Dyer 2007: 102). Many spaghetti westerns, he argues, produce displays of "generic form qua generic form" (2007: 102), char-

acteristically "take a standard formal procedure of the Western and then exaggerate and intensify it, to the point that it is carrying most of the force rather than the action it is disclosing" (2007: 105). We can relate such remarks to the frequency of stylistic excess within a number of cult films, because many such films intensify standard generic Western traits, heightening elements such as violence and formal expressiveness (for example, exaggerated close-ups, music that incorporates "extra-musical" sounds such as gunshots and cracking whips). It is perhaps this playful renegotiation of traditional Western traits which led to the critical dismissal of these films at the height of their production (in the 1960s), but also led to them building up a cult following. They were dismissed on the one hand, but perversely appreciated on the other, for being mere stylistic exercises that stripped the western of its moral dimensions to create cynical, nihilistic works.

The works of Leone are the best known spaghetti westerns, and it is his rather lavish *The Good, the Bad and the Ugly* and, even more so, *Once Upon a Time in the West* that have, in particular, come to earn critical respect over the years while also maintaining a cult status. *Once Upon a Time in the West*, in particular, is a film built from the history of the American Western, but which transforms previous motifs, themes and moments into something distinctive. According to Christopher Frayling, the film "is an anthology of great sequences from the Hollywood Western, lovingly re-created before being turned inside out" (2008: 55): the film includes a large number of citations from other westerns, including *High Noon*, *The Iron Horse*, *Johnny Guitar*, *Man of the West*, *The Man Who Shot Liberty Valance*, *The Searchers*, and *Shane* (2008: 59–63). This citational pastiche running through the film also informs Morricone's score, which quotes from Mozart's *Don Giovani* and Beethoven's *Seventh Symphony* (French and French 1999: 157). Spaghetti western producers themselves showed awareness of how their films were pastiches too. *Once Upon a Time in the West* and *My Name Is Nobody* used iconic actor Henry Fonda against type. In *Once Upon a Time in the West* Fonda's character is killed dramatically, in a duel, after it is revealed just how cruel he was. In *My Name Is Nobody* his demise is presented as much more matter-of-fact, a riddance without even the generic convention of a decent duel. Alex Cox (2010: 8) gives a good illustration of spaghetti westerns' pastiche awareness folding onto itself in his discussion of the cult reputation of *Rita of the West*, a spaghetti western that was intended to emulate *Django* – and which introduced Terrence Hill (who would go on to *My Name Is Nobody*) to the genre. In *Rita of the West*, Django reappears as a character, as does a character resembling Clint Eastwood from Leone's films, mixed into a structure that is as much a musical (with Italian pop star Rita Pavone) as it is a western.

Dyer, in analyzing relationships between pastiche, genre, and history, also analyzes the concept of *neo-noir*: films that consciously rework the visual style and/or mood of the film noir of the 1940s and 1950 and which emerged in the 1980s. It was the first cycle of neo-noir that Frederik Jameson focused on in his discussion of postmodern pastiche. Neo-noir has continued to be used up until the current date, and a number of such films have gained cult status, including *Lost Highway*, *Memento*, *Pulp Fiction*, and *The Usual Suspects*, as well as the noir-inflected science fiction film *Blade Runner*. As film noir is itself a controversial genre – in that it defines a body of films that were never identified as such at the time of their release – the increasing appeal of neo-noir not only functions in cultifying films that serve as crucial reference points, but actually plays a part in strengthening the existence of film noir as a generic category. As Dyer argues, "pastiche contributes not only to fixing the perception of the genre that it pastiches but to identifying its very existence. Moreover, in the case of neo-noir, it contributes to making the case for something whose existence is in fact problematic" (2007: 128–129).

The director and production team of Joel and Ethan Coen, who enjoy a cult reputation, have been most drawn to noir as an influence in their filmmaking. The Coens are often identified with genre pastiche (e.g. screwball comedy in *The Hudsucker Proxy*, the gangster film in *Miller's Crossing*) and have included a vast range of intertextual references within their films. The noir-inflected crime film has, however, been one of the most prominent generic features of their work and informs, in different ways, *The Big Lebowski*, *Blood Simple*, *Fargo*, and *The Man Who Wasn't There*. While their debut feature *Blood Simple*, which established their reputation, was a fairly "straight" take on hard-boiled crime, their biggest cult favorite *The Big Lebow-*

ski can be considered a noir in disguise (as a buddy comedy). *Lebowski* uses a noir-ish plot influenced by Raymond Chandler, and twists it into absurd, incongruous directions. As J.M. Tyree and Ben Walters (2007: 48) have pointed out, Robert Altman's *The Long Goodbye* had already updated Chandler by replacing the cool, cynical, witty detective typified by Bogart with the rambling, laidback, and rather dim Elliot Gould. Altman's film is among the Coen brothers' favorite and also informs their film, but *The Big Lebowski* takes the initial plot mechanics of Chandler further into uncharted, and comic, territory by placing the most incongruous and reluctant character at the heart of its story (the Dude, a dope-smoking slacker who likes to bowl). The film is very much informed by the twin processes of pastiche and incongruity. Situations, imagery, and characters that are often borrowed, share the same space without any apparent logic. For Tyree and Walters, though, the film is not merely an "empty" exercise in pastiche; rather, the film is actually about pastiche, for within the film many of the characters are not who they seem and "put on" an identity (2007: 38). In a similar way, *The Big Lebowski* is a film that "puts on" the surface accoutrements of a buddy comedy while structurally adhering to a noir-type thriller. Surface appearances throughout the film are deceptive, apart from the Dude and Walter, who end the film by going bowling, unchanged by their adventures in deceptive pastiche.

The Cult of Irony and "Smart" Film

One film director who has often used pastiche within his work is Todd Haynes, who established a reputation as a cult director with *Superstar: The Karen Carpenter Story*, a film that gained cult status after it was removed from public exhibition (due to infringing the copyright of the Carpenters' music) and went on to gain an enthusiastic following among those who exchanged bootleg copies of the film on VHS cassette (Davis 2008; Hilderbrand 2009). *Superstar* itself relied on intertextual irony through using a well-known children's toy product – the Barbie doll – to act out the life and times of Karen Carpenter (from mainstream 1970s chart-toppers The Carpenters). Haynes played upon the knowledge of Barbie's wholesome reputation by inserting such dolls within a story that focused on bulimia and anxiety, thus producing a satiric comment on fame and beauty within American society. This cultish reputation has tended to stay with Haynes, and he has gone on to create films which very much draw on a variety of intertextual devices. For example, his Sirk-inspired *Far from Heaven* told a 1950s story in a style influenced by a number of 1950s Hollywood melodramas, but with a few differences – such as its explicit tackling of homosexuality, its swifter editing pace, its musical score (Dyer 2007: 175). Haynes also makes use of pastiche in his film *Poison*, both in the segment "Hero" – which pastiches documentary reconstruction – and "Horror," which recreates the stylistic ambience of a 1950s low-budget, science fiction/horror film. His music-themed films *Velvet Goldmine* and *I'm Not There*, meanwhile, use a number of pastiche moments to evoke the times that they recreate, such as music videos, references to David Bowie and Marc Bolan, and *Citizen Kane* in the former, and the Dylan documentary *Don't Look Back* in the latter.

Haynes has been linked to a mode of filmmaking that Jeffrey Sconce (2002) has labeled "smart cinema." Sconce argued that a number of recent American films, existing on the fringes of the independent and the mainstream industry (and which some would perhaps term as belonging to the hybrid territory of "indiewood"), are marked by a sense of ironic distance, as well as by a "predilection for irony, black humour, fatalism, relativism and ... nihilism" (Sconce 2002: 350). The importance of this "smart" corpus of film-making to cult cinema is through its mode of address. Sconce argues:

> To speak in an ironic tone is instantly to bifurcate one's audience into those who "get it" and those who do not. The entire point of ironic address is to ally oneself with sympathetic peers and to distance oneself from the vast "other" audience, however defined, which is often the target of the speaker's or artist's derision. (2002: 352)

These films, then, tend to create an "us" and "them" mentality, which extends to the way they are marketed: to young, educated "bohemian" audiences and contrasted to mainstream Hollywood fare (positioned as smarter). This very much fits into a cult mentality: an "us versus them" mentality incorporated into the texts and aimed at niche audiences. Such audiences may very well enjoy the privileged position that they assume when watching such films; these films may, in their "smartness," assure viewers that they are superior to the average audience (often labeled as mainstream).

Pastiche and the ironic distance that marks smart films are connected to the extent that both speak in a language of quotation marks. Though they are often perceived as symptoms of postmodernity, they are expressive techniques that have rich histories, stretching back long before the mid twentieth century. It has been argued, nevertheless, that ironic discourse has increased in more recent times: Nicholas Rombes argues that it has grown in tandem with the rise of television (2005: 73), while Harries contends that since the 1970s we have been living in an "age of irony" (2000: 21). The particular form of ironic discourse evident in a number of American independent films from the 1990s onwards is often (though not always) a sarcastic and cynical form of irony. Sconce, in his analysis of smart cinema, claims that many critics have linked this cynical, disenchanted ironic mode to "Generation X." Generation X was a term lifted from the title of Douglas Coupland's eponymous 1991 novel and which referred, in the early 1990s, to smart, highly educated men and women who had missed out on the economic growth enjoyed by baby boomers and who were accused by the older generation of laziness, cynicism, sarcasm, and of being apolitical. Such laziness and cynicism, however, was often linked to the fact that this generation saw their elders as selling out to the forces they once claimed to fight (Sconce 2002: 355). Distrustful of consumer capitalism yet also resigned to it, this generation were seen to practice a form of "ironic cultural consumption," in which popular culture was discussed in quotation marks: it could be enjoyed yet one could also distance oneself from it at the same time (Sconce 2002: 356). Among the films that drew at least part of their cult status from this, are *Slacker* and the slightly more hyperbolic *Office Space* and *Idiocracy* (all hailing from Austin, Texas; see Macor 2010).

One movie that would seem to encapsulate "ironic cultural consumption" is *Ghost World*. Adapted from Daniel Clowes's graphic story, the film concerns two female school-leavers negotiating their identities, futures, and culture. Both Enid (Thora Birch) and Rebecca (Scarlett Johansen) approach almost everything ironically, through which they can express their disgust with contemporary culture, but also enjoy a modicum of sarcastic satisfaction. An example is their visit to a 1950s diner, an establishment that rather lamely attempts ersatz simulation and which ironically appeals to them through its "badness." However, when Enid and Rebecca have to get jobs they are placed much more within cultural milieus that they are used to mocking from a distance. This leads to a split between the characters: Rebecca starts to take her job more seriously in her attempts to save money to move out of her parents', and thus adopts a more mature, less ironic approach. Enid, though, continues to adopt her sarcastic mien, which leads to increasing alienation (she is sacked from a cinema she works at as such an attitude is not countenanced). Their friendship is further tested when Enid begins to hang around the elder Seymour, in whom she detects – with his love for old 78 rpm records and hatred of modern culture – an authenticity lacking in her current generation.

Ghost World concerns the difficulties that some people have relating to aspects of modern life, but also the difficulty in relating to aspects of it when surrounded by people who will knock you down for doing so. Ironic sarcasm can liberate people from such pitfalls, but it also offers its own problems, namely an inability to identify with anything and thus an increasing alienation from life. It is difficult to detect an ultimate standpoint of the film: while Enid's excessive irony is seen as problematic, it also offers its pleasures and the film would seem to side with her over Rebecca, whose increasing conventionality is presented as rather staid and unattractive. Seymour's retreat from modern life does not seem to offer an answer, either, as he ends the film by moving back with his mother. The film appears to adopt a somewhat distanced, even ironic, mode of narration itself, not identifying firmly with any figure, and perhaps hinting at the complexities of negotiating modern life.

The idea of "distanced" narration links with Sconce's assertion that many "smart films" employ a *blank style*: "an attempt to convey a film's story, no matter how sensationalistic, disturbing, or bizarre, with a sense of *dampened affect*" (2002: 359). Such a

technique is evident in the work of Todd Solondz, whose work is typified by an aggressively sarcastic distancing from characters. Solondz presents his material in a thoroughly mocking way, to the extent that many of his films are drenched in irony. In *Happiness*, for example, distance occurs both among characters and between characters and viewers: through sarcastic remarks, awkward silences, character placement within frames, and through the "ironic" use of music (such as light, breezy muzak accompanying scenes that are often anything but light and breezy in tone). The effect is to undercut the positive surface sheen of suburban America as empty, alienating, and demoralizing (hence the ironic title of the film itself). While satires of middle-class suburbia are nothing new, *Happiness* intensifies many themes to a generally uncomfortable degree through its cruel humor and bleak outlook. This has led some critics to bemoan Solondz as nihilistic and misanthropic. Even in more tender moments, where we are perhaps meant to sympathize with characters, the overall tone is often infused with ironic distance. For example, when Allen (Philip Seymour Hoffman) and Kristina (Camryn Manheim) form a bond and dance, the potential tenderness of the scene is undermined through Air Supply's "All Out of Love" playing over the speakers. It may be the case that Solondz was not deliberately using this song ironically, but as a rather over-sentimental, 1980s ballad the song would seem to represent the rather gauche, middle-class values that he is attacking.

Solondz was increasingly referred to as a cult director within film magazines and other critical writing after releasing *Happiness*, a film which pushed smart cinema into particularly uncomfortable, cringe-inducing places and therefore gained extra cult kudos for its ability to disgust some audiences. The film invited a large amount of controversy (another factor common among cult reputations) for its pedophilia theme and this limited its distribution (Sundance Film Festival even refused to accept the film due to its controversial themes). Solondz was promoted as a nerd who was nevertheless cool and savvy, a figure who fitted into the "geek chic" trends that emerged in the late 1990s. He continues to create rather hermetically sealed filmic worlds that tend to relate to other films he has made: thus, the character of Mark Weiner from *Welcome to the Dollhouse* reappears in *Palindromes*, while Solondz's *Life during Wartime* is a sequel to *Happiness* which uses different actors to play the same characters from that film.

Conclusion: Reflexivity and Anti-illusionism

During the 1970s and into the 1980s there emerged a kind of academic cult around reflexive films. One particular genre that made extensive use of the possibilities of reflexivity is the horror genre. Because of its peculiarities we have expanded on this particular application in Chapter 18. Reflexivity influenced cult cinema well beyond the horror genre, especially through the influence by the ideas of Brecht. Among sections of academic film studies there was an interest in left-wing politics and how film could be used in a "progressive" direction. Many academics considered a large percentage of commercial filmmaking ideological in the sense that it represented an illusory world that people were encouraged to become absorbed in for merely escapist purposes. It was against such illusory practices that reflexive strategies became of interest, as reflexivity was a process that drew attention to the film itself and therefore went against the general illusory processes at work in many narrative films. As Robert Stam has argued, "While illusionist art strives for an impression of spatio-temporal coherence, anti-illusionist art calls attention to the gaps and holes and seams in the narrative tissue. To the suave continuities of illusionism, it opposes the rude shocks of rupture and discontinuity" (1992: 7).

While theorists saw differences among particular reflexive strategies – between, for example, the stark "structural-materialist" films of Peter Gidal and the playful reflexivity of Chuck Jones's animated *Duck Amuck* – reflexive techniques nevertheless demanded attention because of their ability to disrupt the illusory flow of narrative fiction. As such, Hollywood films that were particularly reflexive accrued interest for the ways that they tapped into the concerns of the film studies agenda. One prominent mode – which would also have appealed to those studying film to the extent that it mirrored their own discipline – is films either about filmmaking or film spectatorship. *Sunset Boulevard*, *Singin' in the Rain*, *Rear Window*, and *Peeping Tom*,

for example, became important films in this respect, and could be classed as "academic cults" for the widespread analyses they inspired within university research and teaching. In *Rear Window*, Jeffries (James Stewart) is immobilized in a wheelchair and watches different people in the flats opposite. Jeffries is both a model of spectatorship because of his immobile gazing, but also a metaphor for the director in that he chooses different lenses to watch and chooses which scenes to focus on (Stam 1992: 46). *Peeping Tom* concerns the serial-killer cameraman Mark Lewis (Karlheinz Böhm) and probes into the sadistic, dark side of filmmaking. As a film that was critically mauled on its release and which later became acclaimed it also underwent a reception trajectory common to many cult films. Another cult film concerning filmmaking is Peter Bogdanovich's *Targets*. This Roger Corman production features Boris Karloff as an ageing actor (Byron Orlok – the surname recalling Graf Orlok, aka "Nosferatu") who feels that his films have become redundant in the modern, violent world. Intertwined with this plot is a story of a man who randomly kills people with his shotgun. At the end of the movie the two strands collide at a drive-in screening (of Karloff in *The Terror*), and the meeting of "old" and "new" horror come face to face, with Orlok eventually emerging triumphant.

While interest in reflexive techniques largely stemmed from a political interest in filmmaking, the 1980s saw a wider interest in reflexive techniques with the rise of postmodernism in the academy. As reflexive, intertextual, and ironic techniques proliferated, it became somewhat difficult to uphold a belief that such techniques were themselves necessarily radical or critical. David Foster Wallace bemoaned the increasing use of ironic techniques in relation to consumerist lifestyles within literature in 1993 as being empty rather than critical. Such techniques may have once proved critical devices that drew attention to the hollowness of consumer culture, but these devices had since been appropriated by that very culture: many advertisements, for example, employ a self-mocking irony (Wallace 1997: 52). Likewise, within cinema, the proliferation of parody and irony has led Harries to contend that we now live in a "culture steeped in irony; an era where postmodern activity has become more the norm than any sort of alternative practice," a process he terms "ironic supersaturation" (Harries 2000: 3). It is clear, then, that in an age when parody, irony, and associated modes have become so common, such techniques will vary in status and intention: they will not necessarily become cult films, but some of them will; they are not necessarily going to be critical of the status quo, though the adoption of irony does not render them incapable of criticism.

Notes

1. He is here drawing on the work of Rick Altman (1986 and 1999).
2. For a list of almost 100 cult movies with rabbits, see the thread "rabbits and cult cinema," at: http://cultmedias- tudies.ning.com/forum/topics/rabbits-and-cult-cinema? id=2098248%3ATopic%3A7829&page=1#comments.

22

Meta-cult

Our final chapter is an attempt to think about the ways in which "cult" has increasingly and consciously been used within various realms of culture – including reviewing, marketing, film production – so that cultural artifacts positioned as cult have become much more commonplace. In his book *Metaculture*, Greg Urban (2001: 3) writes that "metaculture is culture about culture," and argues that metaculture is important in aiding the circulation of cultural objects: it can, for example, draw attention to art works and help overcome the "forces of dissipation to which culture, moving through the world, is subject" (2003: 38). In a similar manner, we can think of the idea of "meta-cult" (used by Eco in his classic 1986 article, but here used in a slightly broader sense) as not only related to discourses which frame a particular work as cult, but also more generally to works which self-consciously draw on cult – *cult as performing cult* as it were. There has undoubtedly been an increase in such meta-cultural processes in recent times, and these can be grouped into three broad categories. First, the discursive uses of "cult" in relation to films by critics, academics, and other types of audiences; secondly, filmmakers who self-consciously draw on cult and who may also become important commentators on cult cinema; thirdly, industrial mechanisms which employ cult as a categorical and/or marketing tool. We will deal with these three issues in more detail before moving on to reflect upon some changes that have resulted in the emergence of these trends.

Cult Discourses

Historically, the term "cult" was employed sporadically in relation to movie-going as far back as the 1920s, usually to negatively describe particular audiences without relation to specific films. The actual term "cult film" (or "cult movie") began to be employed around the mid 1970s to describe films that were being watched repeatedly, usually at either college venues or at midnight screenings (present knowledge points towards this phrase being applied first within the United States, though more research arguably needs to be undertaken to investigate this issue).

This is also the time when the word "cult" itself became present in the marketing of films, as a tool to attract audiences and capture a place in the market (we addressed this partly in Chapter 2). *Harold and Maude*, for instance, had been dismissed by critics, but had managed to "hang on by word of mouth for two years in Detroit, and over three at the Westgate theatre in suburban Minneapolis, largely *because* the studio had invested little or no publicity in the film" writes Greg Taylor (1999: 119). He continues: "Encouraged, Paramount revived *Harold and Maude*, carefully marketing it as a cultist gem (starting with test-runs at New York's counterculture Thalia and Elgin)." That was 1974. Two years later, the poster for John Carpenter's *Assault on Precinct 13* (1976) announced it as the "cult film of the year".[1] *The Rocky Horror Picture Show* too, was

Cult Cinema: An Introduction. Ernest Mathijs and Jamie Sexton.
© 2011 Ernest Mathijs and Jamie Sexton. Published 2011 by Blackwell Publishing Ltd.

explicitly marketed as cult, as was the release of *Eraserhead*.

By and large, films that gained cult followings tended to be older films (which may or may not have been popular in their day) which had found a new audience, or newer films that had taken time to build up a small, devoted following. These processes reflect Telotte's distinction between the "classical cult film" and the "midnight movie" (1991a: 10–11), though this designation is slightly too neat, as Telotte focuses on once-mainstream Hollywood movies in the former category and low-budget, newer movies in the latter. This overlooks newer, larger budget films that gained cult followings (such as *2001: A Space Odyssey*) as well as more obscure, older films (such as *Detour*).

The 1980s were a period when the term was employed on a more regular, albeit gradual, basis. Alongside the increasing utilization of the phrase there was a gradual broadening of its application: this may have resulted partially from semantic circulation (i.e. the increasing spread of the term led to some using it in different ways than others, either through vagueness of explication and understanding, or through deliberately employing it in a novel manner), but we also need to be aware of the rise of home video during the 1980s, which offered a new platform by which films could gain cult reputations. Cult was now a process not merely limited to the public sphere of the cinema theater, but which had now spilled over into domestic space. This process further alerted some commentators to think about cult films in relation not just to video, but also to television. This was particularly so within the United States, where the variety of cable channels led to a number of specialized – or niche – channels. Thus, in 1984, *New York Times* critic Peter Kerr noted that the cable channel Bravo (formed in 1980) specialized in cult films (Kerr 1984: 28). Notably, he used cult to refer to "obscure" and "offbeat" fare, so that it signified a text's cultural status and broad textual qualities. This semantic expansion resulted from people observing how a number of films with cult reputations also shared certain qualities, thus leading to cult being employed in some contexts as a label describing a certain kind of film.

The 1980s was a period when a few academic studies of cult film emerged and this increased throughout the 1990s, alongside the continued pro-

liferation of the concept more generally. This was also a decade that saw the emergence of two particularly important technologies which would impact upon the phenomenon of the cult film: the internet and DVDs. While the internet had existed for some time, it was only in the early 1990s – with the emergence of the World Wide Web – that it became available to the general public, though it would take time to filter into many people's lives. DVDs entered the consumer marketplace in the late 1990s and outstripped home video in terms of rapid take-up. Both the internet and DVDs would increase in popularity in the 2000s, a decade which gave rise to further developments that impacted upon the phenomenon of cult cinema. These include: increasingly fast broadband connections, which further led to a growth in file sharing; blogging; social networking sites; and YouTube, to name only a few examples. Discursively, the web has been host to an even greater proliferation of writings on cult cinema (mentioned in Chapters 4 and 5) which enables people to encounter such talk on a more regular basis (particularly if they are, as researchers, looking for cult film discussions), and therefore creates a kind of loop: the more that people witness a particular term being employed, the more likely it is to seep into their vocabulary and potentially infuse their talk.

Self-conscious Cultism

We use the term "self-conscious cultism" to refer to the ways in which filmmakers themselves can actively draw upon cult film history to imbue their own films with cult value. Such maneuvers may not necessarily guarantee cult status as it is traditionally conceived, but the continual mutations of cult cinema as a discourse should alert us to the importance of such processes. In this sense, cult film could be viewed as having moved beyond its origins as referring to particular receptions of films, shooting off in a number of different directions. As Matt Hills has argued, accounts which construct cult as merely a matter of audience response "fail to consider the duality of cult: that is, 'cult' status can arise both through audiences' discourses and through production or textual strategies" (2008a: 448). He goes on to claim that cult's meanings have developed historically, and that we now need to consider its use as:

> a category and discourse by filmmakers and publicists, as well as its wider circulation as a discourse in scholarly and journalistic work. What "cult" demonstrates, rather well, is that a film category may emerge as an audience/critical discourse, but can then mutate into a form of generic contract, or a form of interpellative marketing, or a series of production/textual strategies. (2008a: 449)

In this sense, the self-conscious cultism of filmmakers should be considered an important part of the cult film phenomenon, marking a stage in cult cinema history whereby the term has infused film culture to a significant extent.

As briefly mentioned in Chapter 6, both Joe Dante and Tim Burton can be seen as notable examples of filmmakers who have self-consciously drawn upon cult cinema within their own work. They both, for example, employ references to a number of films that have themselves been considered as cult films. Dante himself has a background steeped in cult-related activities: he not only gained filmmaking experience working with cult auteur Roger Corman, he also wrote reviews for the *Castle of Frankenstein* – a journal devoted to horror film and related culture – in the early 1960s. His knowledge of a wide range of films, particularly more exploitation fare, has fed into his filmmaking practice. His first film was actually a compilation of clips assembled from films, commercials, and trailers, entitled *Movie Orgy*, and this compulsion to reference other filmmaking would feed into his later work. His first film for Corman's New World Pictures – *Hollywood Boulevard* (co-directed with Allan Arkush, 1976) – would continue this trend by pastiching low-budget pictures and incorporating stock footage from other films. Even when he made more commercial films for the studios, his parading of cult knowledge has continued: from *Innerspace*, a virtual remake of *Fantastic Voyage*, to the William Castle-inspired *Matinee*, and his regular employment of cult actors such as Dick Miller, Kevin McCarthy and Kenneth Tobey. As Martyn Bamber has written (2003): "Dante's love of movies – particularly B-movies – oozes off the screen and you get the sense that he wants to share that love with his audience as well."

This is also the case with Burton, another filmmaker who grew up loving exploitation films, many of which have since become associated with cult cinema. His short film *Vincent* was about his obsession with cult star Vincent Price, who would later appear in Burton's feature *Edward Scissorhands*, in what would turn out to be his last appearance. Christopher Lee is another cult actor who has appeared in Burton's movies, one of which – *Sleepy Hollow* – was a homage to the Gothic horror films produced by Hammer Studios. Burton would revisit his love for low-budget, disreputable sci-fi films in his *Mars Attacks!*, but it his more loving homage to cult director Ed Wood – *Ed Wood* – which perhaps stands as his ultimate meta-cult statement. Burton's films are not only infused with particular references to the cult films that he grew up with, they are also more generally permeated with "cultishness" on a textual level: his tendency to create strange, fantastical worlds (particularly notable at the level of design) and his thematic obsession with outsiderness, for example, are both features that have been considered important in many cult films.

A number of other directors can be seen as self-consciously cult in a similar manner. Quentin Tarantino, in particular, has drawn on his film-going experiences within his own work and peppered his films with a number of filmic references. In his more recent films, in particular, he has almost been engaged in a form of cult fan filmmaking on a large scale, from the martial arts-inspired *Kill Bill Vol. 1* and *Kill Bill Vol. 2*, his homage to grindhouse cinema *Death Proof* – occasionally presented as a double "grindhouse" package alongside Robert Rodriguez's *Planet Terror* – and his most recent *Inglourious Basterds*, a "revisioning" of Enzo Castellari's movie *Inglorious Bastards*. Tarantino also plays the part of the cultist more generally, in expressing his adoration for the phenomenal experience of watching cult movies:

> I always remember back in the days when I was a film-geek, hanging out with my friends, how we were always trying to see the sort of film that you couldn't see, like Jodorowsky's *El Topo*: it was completely out of circulation, there was no way you could see it ... One of us would get a copy, a horrible screwed up one – the more screwed up it was the cooler it was – we'd sit around and watch this bad copy, (oh man, so cool, get this ripped, crappy, old copy of *El Topo*, look at that, oh boy! You know!) (Tarantino 1995)

Tarantino also presents himself as a cultist by appearing in many documentaries on cult films and filmmakers: these include a documentary on Sam Fuller, *The Typewriter, the Rifle and the Movie Camera*, and a film about Australian exploitation cinema, *Not Quite Hollywood: The Wild, Untold Story of Ozploitation!*. He has also set up a short-lived company in 1995, Rolling Thunder Pictures, with Bob and Harvey Weinstein, to release older exploitation films and market them to new audiences. Though this was short-lived – releasing a few films such as *Switchblade Sisters*, *The Beyond*, and *Mighty Peking Man* – the films were subsequently released on DVD with Tarantino's name and face on the covers. All these activities show that Tarantino himself is a meta-cult director: not only does he enjoy his own cult following, but through his films and other activities he attempts to draw attention to the cult movies that he admires and thus broaden their viewership. While this does not always work out as intended (hence the short life of Rolling Thunder Pictures), Tarantino is nevertheless an important figure who has the potential to draw attention to more obscure cult movies. In short, he can use his (large) cult status to further create cult auras around other (smaller cult) films. He is among a number of filmmakers who also comment upon, and therefore contribute to, the values associated with particular cult films. Joe Dante is a similar figure in this regard, having contributed to DVD extras of cult films: for example, he discusses the cult status of *Spider Baby* on MPI's 2007 DVD (in a featurette titled "The Hatching of Spider Baby"). Dante has also drawn attention to a number of older films – some already established cult films, others perhaps potential cults – through his *Trailers from Hell* web site, in which himself and a number of other directors (such as Eli Roth, Larry Cohen, and Allison Anders) introduce and comment on film trailers and outline the personal significance of the film under discussion.

Less established directors can also draw upon, and contribute to the field of, cult cinema, in a bid to gain an audience within a competitive film market. This is not an entirely new phenomenon – Richard Elfman's *Forbidden Zone*, for example, drew upon a variety of disreputable genre traditions and mixed them together in a particularly self-conscious manner – but it does seem to be increasing in line with the growing awareness of cult cinema. While it is not possible to exhaustively outline films which self-consciously draw on cult film, we will devote brief attention to three more recent examples. First, Don Coscarelli's *Bubba Ho-tep*, a film based on a story by a cult writer (Joe R. Lansdale), featuring an actor with a dedicated cult following (Bruce Campbell), and based around a dead star (Elvis Presley) with a huge cult aura. It draws on the horror genre but mixes this with very quirky humor and a bizarre form of alternate history: Elvis is still alive and living in a retirement home (having swapped identities with an Elvis impersonator) and then becomes involved in a battle with an evil Egyptian entity. In its genre mixing and incorporation of different cult personalities, the film seems designed to be "cultish." Secondly, *Viva* is a film that consciously mimics elements of 1970s sexploitation films, incorporating colorfully gaudy decor and costumes, deliberately campy acting, and drawing upon the work of directors such as Russ Meyer and Radley Metzger. The result is a pastiche that acknowledges the cult reputation that many films from this subgenre of filmmaking have garnered. It can thus be considered a film which reflects upon the cult of a particular type of film from a particular era, but in doing so also positions itself as a potential cult itself. Such positioning was certainly aided by its UK DVD release, which was released on the Cine-Excess imprint of Nouveaux Pictures, a label aiming to release cult films aimed at both the general consumer and the educational sector. Thirdly, *In Bruges*, the feature debut of theater maker Martin McDonagh, is a homage to numerous cult elements, most notably cult cinema's obsession with grotesque and disabled bodies (see Chapter 9). Jordan Prentice plays the role of a foul-mouthed, womanizing, and arrogant dwarf-actor in a European horror movie filmed in Bruges (very much in the tradition of *Daughters of Darkness* it seems), the shooting of which is upset by a war between Irish gangsters. In general, dwarves in cult films merely figure as "being there," but in *In Bruges*, the emphasis is instead placed on how non-cute and ill-tempered Prentice's character is. This makes *In Bruges* both a pastiche and a critique. Soon after its release, *In Bruges* was being touted as a cult film on the website "The Cult," the official site of *Fight Club* writer Chuck Palahniuk.

Cult Positioning

The idea of positioning or framing films as cult is the final important consideration that we will discuss in this chapter, and it is a process that is occurring on a number of different levels. First, "cult" is now being used by the industry as a term by which to promote and/or to categorize films. This can occur within the marketing of films for theatrical screenings and DVD release, as well as by retail outfits. The aforementioned *Viva*, for example, not only parades its cult references within the film text but also through associated promotional discourse. Thus, press for the film claims that: "VIVA is a cult freak-out retro 1970's spectacle ... VIVA is a highly stylized film that draws on classic exploitation cinema for its look and characters" (www. lifeofastar.com/viva.html). And to use a non-exploitation example as well: upon the DVD release of Peter Watkins's *Punishment Park*, Chris Fujiwara in the Boston Phoenix referred to it as a "cult hit waiting to happen," a claim that was promptly put on the cover of subsequent editions of the DVD.

The use of the term "cult" within promotion is certainly growing, as is the use of the term within critical reviews. If cult is designated by reviewers then this can itself feed back into promotional discourse. An example of this can be detected in the DVD release of *Christmas on Mars*, a low-budget science fiction film featuring music act The Flaming Lips. A film that only had a limited theatrical release, it was nevertheless positioned as a cult movie by *New York Times* writer Andy Webster, who placed it in a lineage of music-related films such as *Head* and *Led Zeppelin: The Song Remains the Same*, and wrote that these "were endearingly ragged projects, destined for cult status" (2008: 10). Cult cinema was further evoked through referencing other cult films such as *2001: A Space Odyssey*, *Dark Star* and cult filmmaker David Lynch. The quote "destined for cult status" was then used on some of the posters that accompanied the DVD release of the film, while promotion for the DVD used the same quote as one of "3 reasons to buy this film."

It is not just films themselves that are subject to cult positioning: DVD companies, for example, are increasingly adopting cult as a category to use within their catalogs. Thus, one of the most prestigious DVD companies, Criterion – well known for its high-quality transfers and extra materials – includes a set of "themes" within its online catalog, one of which is "cult movies." The introduction to its range of cult movies claims that, with the wane of drive-ins and midnight movie screenings, the DVD has become a key means to access cult cinema, and continues to offer a short description: such films are considered to be "boundary-testing" and "delicately ride the line between pulp and art, always landing firmly in the latter camp." Criterion is a label that does not merely categorize films as cult, however: it is arguably a label that has itself become subject to a cult following. Many DVD collectors praise the label for the care that it puts into its releases and its reputation is reflected in the reliably high prices that it charges for its DVDs, a price that leaves those outside of the "Criterion cult" puzzled as to why anyone would pay so much. Thus, on an AV Forums discussion about rare DVDs, a poster comments:

> some peeps are just looney toons for the Crit label and will pay way above the odds for a version of a movie released by them just to add to their collection – doesn't matter if there's another version that's just as good/better available at a much lower price, it's the Criterion name that's all important! (Crazy Horse 2005)

It should come as no surprise that many of the DVDs cited as belonging to the rare – and therefore collectible and expensive – category are out-of-print Criterion releases. Further evidence of Criterion's cult status can be found in fan activities, which include a blog entitled "The Criterion Contraption," a series of writings based around the idea of watching every DVD in the Criterion collection, and an emerging trend to create imaginary Criterion DVD covers for films either not released in the series, or as alternate covers for those that have been released. Most of these can be found on Criterion's own forum, "The Auteurs," though they also appear on other forums and blogs, and have become a popular pastime among a certain section of cinema enthusiasts (Figure 22.1).

While other DVD companies may not enjoy the cult following enjoyed by Criterion, many do use cult, or cultish components, to either distinguish themselves and/or categorize products. This can take the simple

Figure 22.1 A piece of Criterion fan art: an imaginary cover for Russ Meyer's *Faster Pussycat! Kill! Kill!*

means of using "cult" as a generic category within their catalogs (this is used, for example, by Kino and Image Entertainment, both American companies), or it can take the form of companies that specialize in cult cinema, or have imprints that devote themselves to such fare. Companies such as Blue Underground (US), Mondo Macabro (US, with a UK arm), Synapse (US), Cult Epics (US), Fantoma (US) and Something Weird (US) can all be seen as specializing in cult cinema. Most of these companies specialize in lower-budget, exploitation films: Something Weird is dedicated to releasing obscure, unreleased titles from the 1930s–1970s; Blue Underground presents itself as continuing the tradition of grindhouse cinemas for a home movie age, though does not limit itself to a specific era of film production; Mondo Macabro focuses on global genre cinema, the majority of which is not well known by Western audiences. Not all films released by such companies are considered to be

exploitation films, however: Fantoma, for example, has released films by Kenneth Anger; Synapse has released Leni Riefenstahl's controversial propaganda film *Triumph of the Will*, and Cult Epics has released films by Fernando Arrabel and Jean Genet. While the word "cult" is not used by all of these companies, it often is: Blue Underground has a category entitled "Cult Classics"; Synapse has a range of films which it releases under the "Asian Cult Cinema Collection." Even when not explicitly used, it is hinted at in language that evokes cult.

There are also imprints of labels that attempt to position products as cult objects. These include, for example, Tartan's "Asia Extreme" imprint (UK, now defunct), and BFI's "Flipside" (UK). Tartan's "Asia Extreme" imprint grew out of its releases of *Ringu*, *Audition*, and *Battle Royale*, in 2001. After the films – in particular *Audition* – caused some controversial press responses, Tartan rebranded the films "Tartan Asia Extreme" in order to capitalize on such notoriety. This then led to a number of subsequent releases under the imprint, which by March 2005 constituted almost a third of Tartan's entire DVD output (Drew 2007: 53–54). Drew argues that Tartan targeted what it saw as an existing cult fan following for Asian genre films, but also marketed these films for "art-house" audiences (seen as favoring less obviously generic output and emphasizing stylistic appreciation, particularly through the lens of authorship). While these audience segments are not mutually exclusive, this twin demographic targeting could help maximize the films' appeal to specialized audiences within the UK. The BFI's "Flipside" label can also be seen as manifesting a growing awareness of the overlaps between cult/art-house audiences (Figure 22.2). The BFI has long been considered to be an institution that has nurtured the appreciation of film as art, but its recent DVD imprint focuses on obscure, and often eccentric, films from British cinema history. The press release for Flipside mentions "cult" twice and further illustrates how the BFI sees this series as broadening its audience by claiming that it "is likely to appeal to a diverse range of film fans, many of whom may be unfamiliar with the BFI's more traditional DVD and Blu-ray output."

While these smaller companies attempt to frame films as cult in order to appeal to a broader, albeit still "specialized" audience, major companies have also

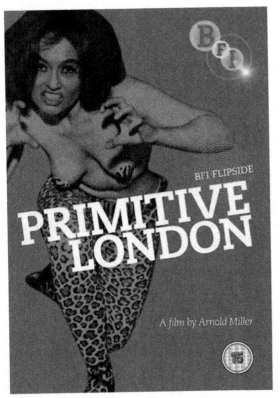

Figure 22.2   Cover of *Primitive London* DVD, part of the BFI Flipside DVD and Blu-ray collection. © 2009 BFI. Courtesy of the British Film Institute.

targeted films at cult film fans. These include: Universal's "Cult Cinema Collection," Warner's "Cult Camp Classics," and Twentieth Century Fox's/MGM's "Midnite Movies." The adoption of cult as a marketing strategy by major companies demonstrates a broader attempt to maximize audience appeal across their large range of titles. The majors will still pay most attention to marketing what they consider their "top" titles: contemporary, larger budgeted films, often featuring major stars. Nevertheless, it has been noted by many commentators that while such "hits" are still extremely important, there is now a growing market for "niche" cultural products, a phenomenon dubbed "The Long Tail" by Chris Anderson (2006). The growth of the internet has provided an ever-expanding network of online retail outlets which, because they do not need to store products in a single, physical retail outlet, can offer increasing amounts of goods (which

people around the globe can order if they have access to the net and a suitable account with which to make payment). In addition to the proliferation of cultural information, the ability to share knowledge, and the emergence of recommendation suggestions (based on personal searches and purchases, on what other consumers have purchased in conjunction with particular products, and through consumer lists, for example), the internet provides enhanced opportunities to stumble upon a range of cultural objects.

Usually niches are heterogeneous and small. Anderson argues that because audiences are aware that pretty much everything is available to them at any time the aggregate of small sales can make a difference. He writes: "the combined value of modest sellers and quirky titles equals the sales of top hits" (2006: 1). The issue, then, becomes a matter of accessing audiences as "partners" in helping the marketplace distinguish between "kinds" of things wanted – to let the audience assist in selecting the categories of the catalog, and to allow for products to have a "long tail" and let them be available for extended periods of time, in small amounts. This comes very close to the situation of cult cinema, where there is constant demand in a relatively small market, and where there is a high insistence on self-selection of categories (such as underground, indie, countercultural, gore, splatter, camp, sex, chic, cool, hot, mondo, nasty, "head," "mindfuck," "rubber reality," etc.). Most online retailers have started marketing their "special interest" products in exactly these ways. Anderson argues that the "crap" that accumulates in this approach is necessary to separate the good from the bad stuff (a selection each audience segment makes differently), and because it gives recognition – it is as little fun to flip through a selection of films of which no one is even remotely familiar as it is to see only well-known titles (Anderson 2006: 116). "Niche culture" thus becomes increasingly important on both a cultural and an economic level: Drew (2007: 55) cites a Film Council report which claims that DVD sales of non-mainstream titles within the UK grew from 10 to 30% in 2005, a trend that is likely to continue. In such a climate, cult cinema could be considered a particularly notable concept through which the importance of niche culture is made sense of by consumers and retailers.

The "Midnite Movies" range of titles – drawing on a founding cult cinema exhibition context and usually packaged as double bills – is another case of a DVD series gaining its own cult following. Not only has the series given rise to its own Yahoo discussion group – founded in 2004 and currently with over 700 members – but it has also led to a petition for reviving the series. In 2005, after a lengthy period in which nothing was released in the series, a petition was organized and advertised at the web site "DVD Drive-in." After almost 5000 online signatures were collected, Fox (who handle MGM's home video releases) decided to issue a new batch in the series in 2007 (making reference to the petition in a press release). No films in the series have been released since then, however, so the petition has been revived in order to request more releases (in the knowledge that a large number of titles owned by MGM have yet to see DVD releases). This process demonstrates the growth of what has been dubbed "consumer activism" (Jenkins 1992: 278), by which fans lobby media producers (or, in this case, distributors) to make changes in line with fans' wishes. Although such activities have long existed, the ability to connect with a large range of other fans over the internet has led to them becoming much more frequent. Companies may not always react to such activism in the ways that fans always wish, but there is an increased tendency to listen, and cater to, cult fans, particularly considering they are often heavy consumers of media consumables and early adopters of new technologies (Drew 2007: 61). Such awareness of the importance of the "cult consumer" is another reason as to why cult is increasingly incorporated into marketing strategies.

Alongside the growth of cultish DVD labels and series, cult is also utilized by some retail stores to categorize films, while many magazines and journals also position themselves as cult, or at least have cultish sections within their pages. While retail categorization is a relatively recent phenomenon, cult-inflected magazines and journals have existed for a long period. As mentioned in Chapters 4, 11 and 19, a number of fanzines were demonstrative of cult fandom, and such activities fed into a number of specialist prozines. Publications such as *Fangoria*, *Video Watchdog*, and *Asian Cult Cinema,* are just a small selection of specialist magazines which have catered to cult tastes for a number of years. In more recent times, a number of

cult-related web sites have also emerged to expand such coverage. These include DVD news and review sites such as *DVD Drive-In*, *Mondo Digital* and *Eccentric Cinema*; a number of cult cinema blogs (e.g. *Mondo Esoterica*, *Moon in the Gutter*), plus ezines and ejournals which include a substantial focus on cult movies (including *Bright Lights Film Journal* and *Wormwood*). There also exist forums, discussion groups, and podcasts devoted to aspects of cult cinema that can be accessed via the web.

Conclusion

The examples of self-conscious cultist filmmakers, the rise in cult being employed as a discursive category within criticism and other forms of film writing, and the use of cult as an industrial category to position cultural products within the marketplace, demonstrate that cult has started to infiltrate film culture on a number of levels. As it has done so, its actual meanings have also broadened: this is because different agents may utilize the concept for different purposes (e.g. companies using it to market products; critics employing it to place a film within a specific tradition), and also because some will conceive of its meanings differently from others (so, for example, while some may use the term in a strict manner in an attempt to refer to a specific process, others may adopt it in a vaguer, looser manner).

Some critics and academics have expressed skepticism about the continued usefulness of "cult" as a concept because of these developments. In a 2008 symposium on cult film in the journal *Cineaste*, Jonathan Rosenbaum, Jeffrey Sconce, and Peter Stanfield all doubted whether the concept actually meant anything anymore. Stanfield, for example, writes:

> I am struck by how redundant the term has become. What once defined a rarefied, albeit often perverse set of critical practices that lay far beyond the purview of any officially sanctioned notion of "good taste," cult, like the now innocuous concept of "alternative" when affixed to a life style or consumption choice, is simply a term for any product or activity that can be pitched by commercial agencies as existing outside the mainstream. (2008: 49)

Such a comment, however, assumes that cult was never a commercial concept and that it is now merely a commercial category. While the concept has become increasingly used by commercial bodies to sell products, we hope to have shown that it is not *merely* a commercial term. And, while the commercialization of the term has undoubtedly intensified, it is historically inaccurate to claim that the concept has never previously been tainted by commercial interests. Such a view, also detectable within Sconce's comments in the symposium, suggests a nostalgic longing for a more "authentic" period in which cult cinema was the preserve of an elite few, and/or a more "personal memory" period that reflects the link between audiences' "moments of access" of certain movies and their own personal narratives (a parallel between critics' example of when cult films were "more authentic" and their teenage or college years is easily drawn).

We started our book with a discussion of the midnight movie as a paradigmatic exemplar of cult cinema. By the end of our book the picture regarding the midnight movie has become a lot more complex. Before jumping to the conclusion that the "golden period" of midnight movie screenings was a manifestation of a pure "bottom-up" process, whereby audiences themselves made a film cult without commercial influences, we should consider at least the following two processes. First, *Eraserhead*, now considered a seminal midnight movie, originally found it difficult to find *any* audiences: it was only because Elgin Theatre owner Ben Barenholtz continued to show it, that it eventually found an audience and developed a cult following. Without Barenholtz's role here, the film may not have become a cult film in the way that it

did, thus alerting us to the importance not merely of audiences, but also of distributors, in the construction of a cult film. Barenholtz may have been an idiosyncratic, non-corporate business man, but he was a business man nonetheless. Secondly, *Pink Flamingos,* another seminal midnight movie, was marketed at midnight venues by its distributor New Line, and after it began to find an audience on this circuit New Line created a trailer for the film in which audiences were interviewed about their impressions of the film. A similar strategy underpinned New Line's re-release of *Night of the Living Dead*, a film it presented in its 1978 catalog as "that rare phenomenon, a film that found its audience entirely through word-of-mouth" (New Line Cinema 1978: 58).[2] Here, then, we can see that even by the late 1970s, films could be deliberately marketed at cult audiences and that such audiences could be "co-opted" for commercial purposes. The commercialization of cult may not have existed on the same scale as today, but then neither did the concept of cult circulate to the same extent as it does today. Its discursive proliferation and escalating commercialization have developed in tandem: we should not merely dismiss this and retreat into uncritical nostalgia, but instead seek to understand the increasing complexity of cult as a concept, the ways in which it is now used, in what contexts, and for what purposes.

We hope to have shown that cult is a term that now has more currency than ever, hence our assertion that we are now living in a "meta-cult" world, in which cult is used in increasingly self-conscious ways and in a number of different contexts. This is a process which does not extinguish its meanings but rather extends them and therefore requires of scholars further research into this important area of film culture.

Notes

1. With thanks to IQ Hunter for drawing our attention to this.
2. We would like to thank April Green and Dana Keller for their research into the New Line Cinema catalogs, and the University of Michigan's library for granting us access to that collection. This ongoing research project is supported by the University of British Columbia's Arts Undergraduate Research Grant RPB-12R46755.

Filmography

$8\frac{1}{2}$ (Fellini, Italy, 1963)
$9\frac{1}{2}$ Weeks (Lyne, USA, 1986)
24 Hour Party People (Winterbottom, UK, 2002)
The 36th Chamber of Shaolin (Liu, Hong Kong, 1978)
42nd Street (Bacon, USA, 1933)
200 Motels (Palmer/Zappa, USA, 1971)
300 (Snyder, USA, 2006)
2000 Maniacs (Lewis, USA, 1964)
2001: A Space Odyssey (Kubrick, UK/USA, 1968)
Aag/Flames (Varma, India, 2007)
The Abyss (Cameron, USA, 1989)
The Acid Eaters (Mabe, USA, 1968)
The Act of Seeing with One's Own Eyes (Brakhage, USA, 1971)
The Adventures of Baron Munchausen (Gilliam, UK/West Germany, 1988)
L'Âge d'or (Buñuel/Dali, France, 1930)
Aguirre, Wrath of God (Herzog, West Germany, 1972)
Akira (Ôtomo, Japan, 1988)
Alfred Packer: The Musical (aka Cannibal! The Musical) (Parker, USA, 1993)
Ali Baba and the Forty Thieves (Lubin, USA, 1944)
Alice in Acidland (Donne, USA, 1969)
Alice's Restaurant (Penn, USA, 1969)
Alien (Scott, USA/UK, 1979)
Aliens (Cameron, USA/UK, 1986)
All about Eve (Mankiewicz, USA, 1950)
All that Heaven Allows (Sirk, USA, 1955)
Allures (Belson, USA, 1961)
Alone. Life Wastes Andy Hardy (Arnold, Austria, 1998)
Alphaville (Godard, France/Italy, 1965)
The Amazing Transparent Man (Ulmer, USA, 1960)

American Psycho (Harron, USA, 2000)
Angel Heart (Parker, USA, 1987)
The Animatrix (Chung/Jones/Kawajiri/Koike/Maeda/Morimoto/Watanabe, USA, 2003)
Annie (Huston, USA, 1982)
Annie Hall (Allen, USA, 1977)
The Anniversary (Baker, UK, 1968)
Antonio das Mortes (Rocha, BRA, 1969)
Anthropophagus (D'Amato, Italy, 1980)
The Arena (Carver/D'Amato, USA, 1974)
Artificial Intelligence: AI (Spielberg, USA, 2001)
Ashes of Time (Kar Wai, Hong Kong, 1994)
Assault on Precinct 13 (Carpenter, USA, 1976)
Astro Boy (Tezuka, Japan, 1963)
Atamé (Almodovar, Spain, 1990)
Attack of the Crab Monsters (Corman, USA, 1957)
Audition (Miike, South Korea/Japan, 1999)
Avatar (Cameron, USA/UK, 2009)
Awakening of the Beast (Marins, Brazil, 1970)
Back to the Future (Zemeckis, USA, 1985)
Bad Taste (Jackson, New Zealand, 1987)
Baise-moi (Despentes/Coralie, France, 2000)
Barfly (Schroeder, USA, 1987)
Barbarella (Vadim, France/Italy, 1968)
Basic Instinct (Verhoeven, USA/France, 1992)
Batbabe: The Dark Nightie (Bacchus, USA, 2009)
Batman (Burton, 1989)
The Battle of Brazil (Matthews/Criterion, USA, 1996)
Battle Royale (Fukasaku, Japan, 2000)
Battlefield Earth (Christian, USA, 2000)
Battleship Potemkin (Eisenstein, Soviet Union, 1925)
Be Kind Rewind (Gondry, UK/USA, 2008)

Beat the Devil (Huston, USA, 1953)

The Beast from 20,000 Fathoms (Lourié, USA, 1953)

Begotten (Merhige, USA, 1990)

Behind the Green Door (Mitchell/Mitchell, USA, 1972)

The Believers (Schlesinger, USA, 1987)

Belle de jour (Buñuel, France, 1967)

The Beyond (Fulci, Italy, 1981)

Beyond the Time Barrier (Ulmer, USA, 1960)

Beyond the Valley of the Dolls (Meyer, USA, 1970)

The Big Heat (Lang, USA, 1953)

The Big Lebowski (Coen/Coen, USA/UK, 1998)

The Big Silence (Corbucci, Italy, France, 1968)

The Big Sleep (Hawks, USA, 1946)

The Bigamist (Lupino, USA, 1953)

Bill and Ted's Bogus Journey (Hewitt, USA, 2001)

The Bishop's Wife (Koster, USA, 1947)

Black Caesar (Cohen, USA, 1973)

The Black Cat (Ulmer, USA, 1934)

Black Emanuelle (Albertini, Italy, 1975)

Black Mama White Mama (Romero, USA, The Philippines, 1973)

Black Sunday (Bava, Italy, 1960)

Blackboard Jungle (Brooks, USA, 1955)

Blacula (Crain, USA, 1972)

Blade Runner (Scott, USA/Hong Kong, 1982)

The Blair Witch Project (Myrick/Sánchez. USA. 1999)

Blast! (Williams, USA, 1972)

The Blank Generation (Kral/Poe, USA, 1976)

Blazing Saddles (Brooks, USA, 1974)

The Blob (Yeaworth Jr/Doughten Jr, USA, 1958)

Blood Feast (Lewis, USA, 1963)

Blood from the Mummy's Tomb (Holt/Carreras, UK, 1971)

Blood on Satan's Claw (Haggard, UK, 1971)

Blood Simple (Coen/Coen, USA, 1984)

The Blood Splattered Bride (Aranda, Spain, 1972)

Blow Job (Warhol, US, 1963)

Blue Steel (Bigelow, 1990)

Blue Sunshine (Lieberman, USA, 1978)

Blue Velvet (Lynch, USA, 1986)

The Blues Brothers (Landis, USA, 1980)

Body Snatchers (Ferrara, USA, 1993)

Bolero (Derek, USA, 1984)

The Boogeyman (Lommel, USA, 1980)

Born in Flames (Borden, USA, 1983)

À bout de souffle (Godard, France, 1960)

Boyz N the Hood (Singleton, USA, 1991)

Braindead (Jackson, New Zealand, 1992)

Bram Stoker's Dracula (Coppola, USA, 1992)

Branded to Kill (Suzuki, Japan, 1967)

Brazil (Gilliam, UK, 1985)

The Bride of Frankenstein (Whale, USA, 1935)

Bring me the Head of Alfredo Garcia (Peckinpah, USA/ Mexico, 1974)

Bringing up Baby (Hawks, USA, 1938)

The Brood (Cronenberg, Canada, 1979)

The Brother from another Planet (Sayles, USA, 1984)

Bubba Ho-tep (Coscarelli, USA, 2002)

Bubblegum Crisis (Akiyama/Gôda/Hayashi/Obari/ Takayama, Japan, 1987)

A Bullet for the General (Damiani, Italy, 1966)

Burden of Dreams (Blank, USA, 1982)

The Cabinet of Dr. Caligari (Wiene, Germany, 1920)

Café Flesh (Sayadian, US, 1982)

La cage aux folles (Molinaro, France, 1978)

Caged Heat (Demme, USA, 1974)

Caligula (Brass/Guccione, Italy/USA, 1979)

Cannibal Ferox (Lenzi, Italy, 1981)

Cannibal Holocaust (Deodato, Italy, 1979)

Cannibal Girls (Reitman, Canada, 1973)

The Cannibal Man (de la Iglesia, Spain, 1972)

Captain Blood (Curtiz, USA, 1935)

Carnival of Souls (Harvey, USA, 1962)

Carrie (De Palma, USA, 1976)

Casablanca (Curtiz, USA, 1942)

Cat People (Tourneur, USA, 1942)

Catwoman (Pitof, USA, 2004)

Chafed Elbows (Downey Sr., US, 1966)

Chainsaw Sally (Burril, USA, 2004)

Un Chant d'Amour (Genet, France, 1950)

Chelsea Girls (Morrissey/Warhol, USA, 1966)

Un Chien Andalou (Buñuel/Dali, France, 1920)

Child's Play III (Bender, USA, 1991)

A Chinese Ghost Story (Ching, Hong Kong, 1987)

Chinese Opium Den (Edison, USA, 1894)

Christiane F (Edel, West Germany, 1981)

Christmas on Mars (Coyne/Beesley/Salisbury, USA, 2008)

Ciao! Manhattan (Palmer/Weisman, USA, 1972)

Citizen Kane (Welles, USA, 1941)

City of the Living Dead (Fulci, Italy, 1980)

City on Fire (Lam, Hong Kong, 1987)

Clockers (Lee, USA, 1995)

A Clockwork Orange (Kubrick, UK/US, 1971)

Close Encounters of the Third Kind (Spielberg, USA, 1977)

The Cobra Woman (Siodmak, USA, 1944)

Coffy (Hill, USA, 1973)

College (Keaton/Horne, USA, 1927)

Conan the Barbarian (Milius, US, 1982)

The Connection (Clarke, USA, 1963)

Control (Corbijn, UK/USA/Australia/Japan, 2007)

The Cook, the Thief, his Wife, and her Lover (Greenaway, UK/The Netherlands, 1989)

The Cool and the Crazy (Witney, USA, 1958)

Crash (Cronenberg, Canada/UK, 1996)

Cry-Baby (Waters, USA, 1990)

Cry of the Banshee (Hessler, UK, 1970)

Cube (Natali, Canada, 1997)

Cure (Kurosawa, Japan, 1997)

Cutthroat Island (Harlin, USA, 1995)

Dance, Girl, Dance (Arzner, USA, 1940)

Dark City (Proyas, Australia/USA, 1998)

The Dark Knight (Nolan, USA, 2008)

Dark Star (Carpenter, USA, 1974)

Dark Water (Nakata, Japan, 2002)

Daughters of Darkness (Kümel, Belgium/France/West Germany, 1971)

Dawn of the Dead (Romero, USA, 1978)

Day of the Dead (Romero, USA, 1985)

The Day the Earth Stood Still (Wise, USA, 1951)

Day the World Ended (Corman, USA, 1955)

Dazed and Confused (Linklater, USA, 1993)

Dead or Alive (Miike, Japan, 1999)

Deadly Weapons (Wishman, USA, 1972)

Death Proof (Tarantino, USA, 2007)

Death Race 2000 (Bartel, USA, 1975)

The Decline of Western Civilization (Spheeris, USA. 1981)

Debbie Does Dallas (Clark, USA, 1978)

Deep Throat (Damiano, USA, 1972)

Deliverance (Boorman, USA, 1972)

Demon Seed (Cammell, USA, 1977)

Desperate Living (Waters, USA, 1977)

Detour (Ulmer, USA, 1975)

The Devil in Miss Jones (Damiano, USA, 1973)

The Devils (Russell, UK, 1971)

Le Diable est parmi nous (Beaudin, Canada, 1972)

Die Hard (McTiernan, USA, 1988)

Dirty Dancing (Ardolino, USA, 1987)

Django (Corbucci, Italy/Spain, 1966)

La Dolce Vita (Fellini, Italy, 1960)

Don't Look Back (Pennebaker, USA, 1967)

Donnie Darko (Kelly, USA, 2001)

Dr Strangelove or: How I Stop Worrying and Learned to Love the Bomb (Kubrick, UK, 1964)

Dracula (Browning, USA, 1930)

Driller Killer (Ferrara, USA, 1979)

Drugstore Cowboy (Van Sant, USA, 1989)

Duck Amuck (Jones, USA, 1953)

Duck Soup (McCarey, USA, 1933)

Dune (Lynch, USA, 1984)

East of Borneo (Melford, USA, 1931)

Easy Rider (Hopper, USA, 1969)

Ecstasy (Machaty, Czech Republic, 1933)

Ed Wood (Burton, USA, 1994)

Edward Scissorhands (Burton, USA, 1990)

El Topo (Jodorowsky, Mexico, 1970)

The Elephant Man (Lynch, USA, 1980)

Emanuelle and the Last Cannibals (D'Amato, Italy, 1977)

Emmanuelle (Jaeckin, France, 1973)

Emperor Tomato Ketchup (Terayama, Japan, 1971)

Empire (Warhol, USA, 1964)

Enter the Dragon (Clouse, Hong Kong/USA, 1973)

Equinox (Woods/Muren/McGee, USA, 1970)

Eraserhead (Lynch, USA, 1976)

Even Dwarfs Started Small (Herzog, Germany, 1970)

Everything You Always Wanted to Know about Sex (But Were Afraid to Ask) (Allen, USA, 1972)

The Evil Dead (Raimi, USA, 1981)

Evil Dead II (Raimi, USA, 1987)

eXistenZ (Cronenberg, Canada/UK, 1999)

Eyes without a Face (Franju, France, 1958)

The Exorcist (Friedkin, USA, 1973)

Faces of Death (Le Cilaire, USA, 1979)

Fascination (Rollin, France, 1979)

Fame (Parker, US, 1980)

The Fan (Schmidt, Germany, 1982)

Fantastic Voyage (Fleischer, USA, 1966)

Fantômas (Feuillade, France, 1917-19)

Far from Heaven (Haynes, USA, 2002)

Fargo (Coen/Coen, USA, 1996)

Faster Pussycat! Kill! Kill! (Meyer, USA, 1965)

Female Trouble (Waters, USA, 1974)

Ferris Bueller's Day Off (Hughes, US, 1986)

Fight Club (Fincher, USA/Germany, 1999)

The Fifth Element, (Besson, France, 1997)

Final Fantasy (Sakaguchi, Japan, 2001)

The Final Comedown (Williams, USA, 1972)

Fist of Fury (Lo, Hong Kong 1972)

Fitzcarraldo (Herzog, Peru/West Germany, 1982)

Five Deadly Venoms (Cheh, Hong Kong, 1978)

Flaming Creatures (Smith, USA, 1963)

Flavia the Heretic (Mingozzi, Italy/France, 1974)

Flesh (Morrissey, USA, 1968)

The Flower Thief (Rice, USA, 1960)

Footlight Parade (Bacon, USA, 1933)

For Y'ur Height Only (Nicart, The Philippines, 1981)

Forbidden Planet (Wilcox, USA, 1956)

Forbidden Zone (Elfman, USA, 1982)

Foxy Brown (Hill, USA, 1974)

Frankenstein (Whale, USA, 1931)

Freaks (Browning, USA, 1932)

Freddy vs. Jason (Yu, USA, 2003)

Freeway Mad II: Confessions of a Trickbaby (Bright, USA, 1999)

Friday the 13th (Cunningham, USA, 1980)

From Dusk 'till Dawn (Rodriguez, US, 1995)

Fullmetal Alchemist (Mizushima, Japan, 2003-2004)

Full Metal Yakuza (Miike, Japan, 1997)

Galaxy Quest (Parisot, USA, 1997)

Game of Death (Clouse, Hong Kong/USA, 1978)

Gas! – Or – How it Became Necessary to Destroy the World in Order to Save it (Corman, USA, 1970)

George Lucas in Love (Nussbaum, USA, 1999)

Gestapo's Last Orgy (Canevari, Italy, 1977)

Ghost in the Shell (Oshii, Japan/USA, 1995)

Ghost in the Shell 2: Innocence (Oshii, Japan, 2004)

Ghost World (Zwigoff, USA, 2001)

Gimme Shelter (Maysles/Maysles, USA, 1970)

The Giant Claw (Sears, USA, 1957)

Ginger Snaps (Fawcett, Canada, 2000)

Ginger Snaps II: Unleashed (Sullivan, Canada, 2003)

Ginger Snaps III: Ginger Snaps Back (Harvey, Canada, 2004)

The Girl Can't Help it (Tashlin, USA, 1956)

Glen or Glenda (Wood Jr, USA, 1953)

Go Fish (Troche, USA, 1994)

The Godfather (Coppola, USA, 1972)

The Gods Must Be Crazy (Uys, Botswana/South Africa, 1980)

Godzilla (Honda, Japan, 1954)

Gold Diggers of 1933 (LeRoy, USA, 1933)

Gone with the Wind (Fleming, USA, 1939)

The Good, the Bad and the Ugly (Leone, Italy/Spain/West Germany, 1966)

Gordon's War (Davis, USA, 1973)

The Gospel According to St. Matthew (Pasolini, Italy, 1964)

La grande bouffe (Ferreri, France/Italy, 1973)

Grease (Kleiser, USA, 1978)

Grease 2 (Birch, USA, 1982)

The Great Rock 'n' Roll Swindle (Temple, UK, 1980)

Grindhouse (Rodriguez/Roth/Tarantino/Wright/Zombie, USA, 2007)

Groove (Harrison, USA, 2000)

Gummo (Korine, USA, 1997)

Gun Crazy (Lewis, USA, 1950)

Habit (Larry Fessenden, USA, 1997)

Hairspray (Waters, USA, 1988)

Halloween (Carpenter, USA, 1978)

Hallucination Generation (Mann, USA, 1966)

Hannibal (Scott, USA, 2001)

Happiness (Solondz, USA, 1998)

The Happiness of the Katakuris (Miike, Japan, 2001)

Happy Together (Kar Wai, Hong Kong, 1997)

Hard Boiled (Woo, Hong Kong, 1992)

A Hard Day's Night (Lester, UK, 1964)

The Harder They Come (Henzell, Jamaica, 1972)

Harlis (Van Ackeren, Germany, 1972)

Harold & Kumar Go to White Castle (Leiner, USA/Canada/Germany, 2004)

Harold & Kumar Escape from Guantanamo Bay (Hurwitz/Schlossberg, USA, 2008)

Harold and Maude (Ashby, USA, 1971)

Harry Potter and the Philosopher's Stone (Columbus, USA, 2001)

Harry Potter and the Chamber of Secrets (Columbus, USA, 2002)

Harry Potter and the Prisoner of Azkaban (Cuarón, USA, 2004)

Harvey (Koster, USA, 1950)

Häxan: Witchcraft through the Ages (Christensen, Denmark/Sweden, 1922)

Head (Refelson, USA, 1968)

Heart of Glass (Herzog, West Germany, 1976)

Heat (Morrissey, USA, 1972)

Heaven's Gate (Cimino, US, 1981)

Heavy Metal (Potterton, Canada, 1981)

Hedwig and the Angry Inch (Mitchell, USA, 2001)

Heimat (Reitz, Germany, 1984)

Help! (Lester, UK, 1965)

Hellraiser (Barker, UK, 1987)

Hellzapoppin' (Potter, USA, 1941)

Henri-Georges Clouzot's Inferno (Bromberg/Medrea, France, 2009)

Henry and June (Kaufman, USA, 1990)

Henry, Portrait of a Serial Killer (McNaughton, USA, 1990)

High Anxiety (Brooks, USA, 1977)

High Noon (Zinnemann, USA, 1952)

High School Confidential! (Arnold, USA, 1958)

The Hills Have Eyes (Craven, USA, 1977)

Hiroshima Mon Amour (Resnais, France, 1958)

Histoire d'O (Jaeckin, France, 1975)

The Hitcher (Harmon, USA, 1985)

The Hitch-Hiker (Ida Lupino, USA, 1953)

Holiday (Cukor, USA, 1938)

Hollywood Boulevard (Arkush/Dante, USA, 1976)

The Hollywood Chainsaw Hookers (Ray, USA, 1988)

The Holy Mountain (Jodorowsky, Mexico/USA, 1973)

House of a 1000 Corpses (Zombie, USA, 2003)

House on Haunted Hill (Castle, USA, 1959)

House on the Edge of the Park (Deodato, Italy, 1980)

The Hudsucker Proxy (Coen/Coen, UK/Germany/USA, 1994)

Human Traffic (Kerrigan, UK/Ireland, 1999)

I Drink your Blood (Durston, USA, 1970)

I Saw What You Did (Castle, USA, 1965)

I Spit on your Grave (Zarchi, USA, 1978)

I Walked with a Zombie (Tourneur, USA, 1943)

I Was a Teenage Werewolf (Fowler Jr., USA, 1957)

I Will Walk Like a Crazy Horse (Arrabal, France, 1973)

Ichi the Killer (Miike, Japan, 2001)

Idiocracy (Judge, USA, 2006)

If.... (Anderson, UK, 1968)

Ilsa, She Wolf of the SS (Edmonds, USA/West Germany, 1975)

I'm Not There (Haynes, USA/Germany, 2007)

Imitation of Life (Sirk, USA, 1959)

In a Lonely Place (Ray, USA, 1950)

In Bruges (McDonagh, UK/USA, 2008)

In the Realm of the Senses (Oshima, Japan, 1976)

Inauguration of the Pleasure Dome (Anger, USA, 1954)

Indiana Jones and the Temple of Doom (Spielberg, USA, 1984)

Indiana Jones and the Last Crusade (Spielberg, USA, 1989)

Inferno (Argento, Italy, 1980)

Inglorious Bastards (Castellari, Italy, 1978)

Inglourious Basterds (Tarantino, USA/Germany, 2009)

Inland Empire (Lynch, France/Poland/USA, 1996)

Innerspace (Dante, USA, 1987)

The Invasion (Hirschbiegel, USA/Australia, 2007)

Invasion of the Body Snatchers (Siegel, USA, 1956)

Invasion of the Body Snatchers (Kaufman, USA, 1976)

Invocation of my Demon Brother (Anger, USA, 1969)

The Iron Horse (Ford, USA, 1924)

Irréversible (Noé, France, 2002)

The Isle (Ki-Duk, Korea, 2000)

It's Alive (Cohen, USA, 1974)

It's a Wonderful Life (Capra, USA, 1946)

Jackie Brown (Tarantino, USA, 1997)

Jailhouse Rock (Thorpe, USA, 1957)

Jaws (Spielberg, USA, 1975)

Jeanne Dielman, 23 Quai du Commerce, 1080 Bruxelles (Akerman, Belgium, 1975)

La Jetée (Marker, France, 1962)

Joe's Apartment (Payson, USA, 1996)

Johnny Guitar (Ray, USA, 1954)

Jubilee (Jarman, UK, 1978)

Judge Dredd (Cannon, USA, 1995)

Ju-on: The Grudge (Shimizu, Japan, 2002)

Jurassic Park (Spielberg, USA, 1993)

Justine De Sade (Pierson, France, 1972)

Kill Bill Vol. 1 (Tarantino, USA, 2003)

Kill Bill Vol. 2 (Tarantino, USA, 2004)

The Killer (Woo, Hong Kong, 1989)

Killer Nun (Berruti, Italy, 1978)

The Killing (Kubrick, USA, 1956)

Kimba, the White Lion (Yamamoto/Tezuka, Japan, 1966/1994)

King Kong (Cooper/Schoedsack, USA, 1933)

King Lear (Godard, USA, 1987)

King of New York (Ferrara, USA, 1990)

King Solomon's Mines (Thompson, USA, 1985)

Kiss Me Deadly (Aldrich, USA, 1955)

Koyaanisqatsi (Reggio, USA, 1982)

Lady Terminator (Djalil, Indonesia, 1988)

Lapis (Whitney, USA, 1966)

Last Action Hero (John McTiernan, USA, 1993)

Last House on the Left (Craven, USA, 1972)

Last Tango in Paris (Bertolucci, Italy, 1972)

Led Zeppelin: The Song Remains the Same (Clifton/Massot, UK/USA, 1976)

Legend of the Overfiend (Takayama, Japan, 1987-1995)

The Legend of the Seven Golden Vampires (Baker, UK/
  Singapore, 1974)
Life during Wartime (Solondz, USA, 2009)
Life of Brian (Jones, UK, 1979)
Lightning over Water (aka *Nick's Movie*) (Ray, Sweden/
  West Germany, 1980)
Liquid Sky (Tsukerman, USA, 1982)
Lisa and the Devil (Bava/Leone, Italy/Germany/Spain,
  1974)
The Living End (Araki, USA, 1992)
Living in Bondage (Rapu, Nigeria, 1992)
London after Midnight (Browning, USA, 1927)
The Long Goodbye (Altman, USA, 1973)
The Lord of the Rings: The Fellowship of the Ring
  (Jackson, USA/New Zealand, 2001)
The Lord of the Rings: The Two Towers (Jackson, USA/
  New Zealand/Germany, 2002)
The Lord of the Rings: The Return of the King (Jackson,
  USA/New Zealand/Germany, 2003)
Lord of the G-Strings: Femaleship of the String (West,
  USA, 2003)
Lords of Dogtown (Hardwicke, USA, 2005)
Lost Highway (Lynch, France/USA, 1997)
Love and Death (Allen, France/USA, 1975)
Love Me Tender (Webb, USA, 1956)
Lucifer Rising (Anger, USA, 1980)
M (Lang, Germany, 1931)
À ma soeur (Breillat, France, 2003)
Macabre (Castle, USA, 1958)
Mad Max (Miller, Australia, 1979)
Mad Max 2: The Road Warrior (Miller, Australia, 1981)
Mädchen in Uniform (Sagan/Froehlich, Germany,
  1931)
Magic Boy (Daikuhara/Yabushita, Japan, 1959)
Magical Mystery Tour (Harrison/Knowles/Lennon/
  McCartney/Starr, UK, 1967)
The Maltese Falcon (Huston, USA, 1941)
Man Bites Dog (Belvaux/Bonzel/Poelvoorde,
  Belgium, 1992)
Man of the West (Mann, USA, 1958)
Man Facing Southeast (Subiela, Argentina, 1986)
The Man from Planet X (Ulmer, USA, 1951)
The Man Who Fell to Earth (Roeg, UK, 1976)
The Man Who Shot Liberty Valance (Ford, USA, 1962)
The Man Who Wasn't There (Coen/Coen, USA/UK,
  2001)

The Man with the Golden Arm (Preminger, USA, 1955)
Maniac (Esper, USA, 1934)
Manos, the Hands of Fate (Warren, USA, 1966)
Mariken van Nieumeghen (Stelling, The Netherlands,
  1974)
Mars Attacks! (Burton, USA, 1996)
Martin (Romero, USA, 1977)
Matinee (Dante, USA, 1993)
The Matrix (Wachowski/Wachowski, USA/Australia,
  1999)
Mean Streets (Scorsese, USA, 1973)
Medea (Pasolini, Italy, 1969)
Meet me in St. Louis (Minnelli, USA, 1944)
Memento (Nolan, USA, 2000)
Men in Black (Sonnenfeld, USA, 1997)
Metropolis (Lang, Germany, 1927)
Mighty Peking Man (Ho, Hong Kong, 1977)
Mildred Pierce (Curtiz, USA, 1945)
Miller's Crossing (Coen/Coen, USA, 1990)
Miracle on 34th Street (Seaton, USA, 1947)
The Misfits (Huston, USA, 1961)
Mommie Dearest (Perry, USA, 1991)
Mondo Cane (Cavara/Jacopetti/Prosperi, Italy, 1962)
Mondo Hollywood (Cohen, USA, 1967)
Monterey Pop (Pennebaker, USA, 1968)
Monty Python and the Holy Grail (Gilliam/Jones, UK,
  1975)
More (Schroeder, West Germany/France/
  Luxembourg, 1969)
Mortal Inheritance (Amenechi, Nigeria, 1996)
Motel Hell (Connor, USA, 1980)
Movie Orgy (Dante, USA, 1968)
Mr. Nice Guy (Kam-Bo, Hong Kong, 1997)
Ms. 45 (Ferrara, USA, 1981)
My Best Fiend (Herzog, UK/Germany/Finland/USA,
  1999)
My Bloody Valentine (Mihalka, Canada, 1981)
My Darling Clementine (Ford, USA, 1946)
My Name Is Bruce (Campbell, USA, 2007)
My Name Is Nobody (Valerii/Leone, Italy/France/
  West Germany, 1973)
My Neighbor Totoro (Miyazaki, Japan, 1988)
My Own Private Idaho (Van Sant, USA, 1992)
Myra Breckenridge (Sarne, USA, 1970)
Naked Killer (Yiu-Leung, Hong Kong, 1992)
The Nanny (Holt, UK, 1965)

Narcotic (Esper/Sodar't, USA, 1933)

Nausicaa of the Valley of the Wind (Miyazaki, Japan, 1984)

Near Dark (Bigelow, USA, 1987)

Nekromantik (Buttgereit, West Germany, 1987)

Nekromantik 2: Der Todesking (Buttgereit, Germany, 1991)

Neon Genesis Evangelion (Anno, Japan, 1995)

New Jack City (Van Peebles, USA, 1991)

New Wave Hookers (Dark, USA, 1985)

Night of the Hunter (Laughton, USA, 1955)

Night of the Lepus (Claxton, USA, 1972)

Night of the Living Dead (Romero, USA, 1968)

The Night Porter (Cavani, Italy, 1974)

Nightmare on Elm Street (Craven, USA, 1984)

Nightmare on Elm Street II: Freddy's Revenge (Sholder, USA, 1985)

Nosferatu: Symphonie des Grauens (Murnau, Germany, 1922)

Not Quite Hollywood: The Wild, Untold Story of Ozploitation! (Hartley, Australia/USA, 2008)

Nothing (Natali, Canada, 2003)

Les Nuits Fauves (Collard, France, 1991)

Oedipus Rex (Pasolini, Italy, 1967)

Of Freaks and Men (Balabanov, Russia, 1998)

Office Space (Judge, USA, 1999)

Oldboy (Park, Korea, 2003)

Once Upon a Time in the West (Leone, Italy/USA, 1968)

Ong-bak (Pinkaew, Thailand, 2003)

The Opening of Misty Beethoven (Metzger, USA, 1976)

Orphée (Cocteau, France, 1950)

Otaku No Video (Mori, Japan, 1991)

Out of the Past (Tourneur, USA, 1947)

Outrageous! (Benner, Canada, 1977)

Owo Blow: The Genesis (Ogidan, Nigeria, 2007)

Palindromes (Solondz, USA, 2004)

Pandora's Box (Pabst, Germany, 1927)

The Panic in Needle Park (Schatzberg, USA, 1971)

Paranormal Activity (Pelti, USA, 2007)

The Passion of Joan of Arc (Dreyer, France, 1928)

The Passion of the Christ (Gibson, USA, 2004)

Peeping Tom (Powell, UK, 1960)

Peggy Sue Got Married (Coppola, USA, 1986)

Performance (Cammell/Roeg, UK, 1970)

Personal Best (Towne, USA, 1982)

Le petit amour (Varda, France, 1988)

Phantom of the Opera (Julian, USA, 1924)

Pink Flamingos (Waters, USA, 1972)

Pink Floyd: The Wall (Parker, UK, 1982)

Piranha (Dante, USA, 1978)

The Pirate (Minnelli, USA, 1948)

Pirates of the Caribbean: The Curse of the Black Pearl (Verbinski, USA, 2003)

Pirates of the Caribbean: Dead Man's Chest (Verbinski, USA, 2006)

Pirates of the Caribbean: At World's End (Verbinski, USA, 2007)

Plan 9 from Outer Space (Wood Jr., USA, 1959)

Planet of the Apes (Schaffner, USA, 1968)

Planet Terror (Rodriguez, USA, 2007)

Play it Again, Sam (Ross, USA, 1972)

Point Break (Bigelow, USA, 1991)

Poison (Haynes, USA, 1991)

Porcile (Pasolini, Italy, 1969)

Predator (McTiernan, USA, 1987)

Primer (Carruth, USA, 2004)

Prince of Darkness (Carpenter, USA, 1987)

Primitive London (Miller, UK, 1965)

Princess Mononoke (Miyazaki, Japan, 1997)

Priscilla, Queen of the Desert (Elliott, Australia, 1994)

The Producers (Brooks, USA, 1968)

Prophecy (Frankenheimer, USA, 1979)

Psycho (Hitchcock, USA, 1960)

Psych-Out (Rush, USA, 1968)

Psychomania (Sharp, UK, 1973)

Pull My Daisy (Frank/Leslie, USA, 1959)

Pulp Fiction (Tarantino, USA, 1994)

Punishment Park (Watkins, USA, 1971)

Quadrophenia (Roddam, UK, 1979)

Quatermass and the Pit (Baker, UK, 1967)

Queen of Sheba Meets the Atom Man (Rice, US, 1963)

A Question of Silence (Gorris, The Netherlands, 1982)

Rabbit's Moon (Anger, USA, 1950)

Race with the Devil (Starrett, USA, 1975)

The Rainbow Thief (Jodorowsky, UK, 1990)

Raiders of the Lost Ark (Spielberg, USA, 1981)

Rambo: First Blood Part II (Cosmatos, USA, 1985)

Rape of the Vampire (Rollin, France, 1968)

Rear Window (Hitchcock, USA, 1954)

Rebel without a Cause (Ray, USA, 1955)

Reefer Madness (aka *Tell Your Children*) (Gasnier, USA, 1936)

Re-Animator (Gordon, USA, 1985)

Re-Entry (Belson, USA, 1964)

Repo Man (Cox, USA, 1984)

Reservoir Dogs (Tarantino, USA, 1992)

Resident Evil (Anderson, UK/France/Germany, 2002)

Return of the Living Dead (O'Bannon, USA, 1985)

Ride Lonesome (Boetticher, USA, 1959)

Ride the High Country (Peckinpah, USA, 1962)

Ringu (Nakata, Japan, 1998)

Rio Bravo (Hawks, USA, 1959)

Rita of the West (Baldi, Italy, 1967)

Robocop (Verhoeven, USA, 1987)

Robot Monster (Tucker, USA, 1953)

Rock 'n' Roll High School (Arkush, USA, 1979)

Rock around the Clock (Sears, USA, 1956)

Rock, Rock, Rock! (Price, USA, 1956)

The Rocky Horror Picture Show (Sharman, UK/USA, 1975)

Romance (Breillat, France, 1999)

The Room (Wiseau, USA, 2003)

Rose Hobart (Cornell, USA, 1936)

Rosemary's Baby (Polanski, USA, 1969)

Sailor Moon (Sato, Japan, 1992)

Salò, or the 120 Days of Sodom (Pasolini, Italy, 1975)

Salon Kitty (Brass, Italy, Germany, 1976)

Santa Fe Satan (McGoohan, UK/USA, 1974)

Santa Sangre (Jodorowsky, Mexico/Italy, 1989)

The Saragosa Manuscript (Has, Poland, 1965)

Scanners (Cronenberg, Canada, 1981)

Scarface (De Palma, USA, 1983)

Schoolgirl Report (Hofbauer, GER, 1971–1975)

Scorned (Stevens, USA, 1994)

Scorpio Rising (Anger, USA, 1964)

SCUM Manifesto (Seyrig/Roussopoulos, France, 1976)

The Searchers (Ford, USA, 1956)

The Serpent and the Rainbow (Craven, USA, 1987)

Se7en (Fincher, USA, 1995)

Seven Samurai (Kurosawa, Japan, 1954)

Sex and Zen (Mak, Hong Kong, 1991)

Sex and Zen III (Chang, Hong Kong, 1998)

Sex: The Annabel Chong Story (Lewis, USA, 1999)

Shaft (Parks, USA, 1971)

Shaft in Africa (Guillerman, USA, 1973)

Shake, Rattle and Rock! (Cahn, USA, 1956)

Shakespeare in Love (Madden, USA/UK, 1998)

Shane (Stevens, USA, 1953)

Shaun of the Dead (Wright, UK/France, 2004)

Shivers (Cronenberg, Canada, 1975)

Shogun Assassin (Houston, Japan/USA, 1980)

Sholay (Sippy, India, 1975)

The Shooting (Hellman, USA, 1967)

Showgirls (Verhoeven, France/USA, 1995)

Sick: The Life and Death of Bob Flanagan, Supermasochist (Dick, USA, 1997)

Silence of the Lambs (Demme, USA, 1991)

Silent Movie (Brooks, USA, 1976)

Singin' in the Rain (Donen/Kelly, USA, 1952)

Sins of the Fleshapoids (Kuchar, USA, 1965)

Sissi (Marischka, 1955)

Sissi, the Young Empress (Marischka, Austria, 1956)

Sissi, Fateful Years of an Empress (Marischka, Austria, 1957)

Skidoo (Preminger, USA, 1968)

Slacker (Linklater, USA, 1991)

Sleep (Warhol, USA, 1963)

Sleep with Me (Kelly, USA, 1994)

Sleeper (Allen, USA, 1973)

Sleepy Hollow (Burton, USA/Germany, 1999)

Smithereens (Seidelman, USA, 1982)

Snakes on a Plane (Ellis, USA, 2006)

Snuff (Findlay/Fredriksson/Nuchtern, US, 1976)

Some Like it Hot (Wilder, USA, 1963)

Suicide Club (Sono, Japan, 2002)

The Sound of Music (Wise, USA, 1965)

Space Is the Place (Coney, USA, 1974)

Spaceballs (Brooks, USA, 1987)

Spartacus (Kubrick, USA, 1960)

Speed (de Bont, USA, 1994)

Spider Baby (Hill, USA, 1968)

Spiderbabe (Crash, USA, 2003)

Spirits of the Dead (Vadim/Malle/Fellini, France/Italy, 1968)

Splice (Natali, Canada/France, 2010)

A Star Is Born (Cukor, USA, 1954)

Star Trek (Desilu Productions, Norway Productions, Paramount Television, USA, 1966–1969)

Star Wars (Episode I: The Phantom Menace) (Lucas, USA, 1999 US)

Star Wars (Episode II: Attack of the Clones (Lucas, USA, 2002)

Star Wars (Episode III: Revenge of the Sith) (Lucas, USA, 2005)

Star Wars (Episode IV: A New Hope) (Lucas, USA, 1977)

Star Wars (Episode V: The Empire Strikes Back) (Kershner, USA, 1980)

Star Wars (Episode VI: Return of the Jedi) (Marquand, USA, 1983)

Stardust Memories (Allen, USA, 1980)

Starship Troopers (Verhoeven, USA, 1997)

Starship Troopers 2: Hero of the Federation (Tippett, USA, 2004)

Stop Making Sense (Demme, USA, 1984)

Strange Days (Bigelow, USA, 1995)

Straw Dogs (Sam Peckinpah, USA, 1971)

Streets of Fire (Hill, USA, 1984)

Successive Slidings of Pleasure (Robbe-Grillet, France, 1974)

Suicide Club (Sono, JAP, 2001)

Sullivan's Travels (Sturges, USA, 1941)

Sunset Boulevard (Wilder, USA, 1950)

Super Fly (Parks Jr, USA, 1972)

Super Fly T.N.T. (O'Neal, USA, 1973)

Superstar: The Karen Carpenter Story (Haynes, USA, 1988)

Suspiria (Argento, Italy, 1977)

Sweet Sweetback's Baadasssss Song (Van Peebles, USA, 1971)

Switchblade Sisters (Hill, USA, 1975)

Sylvia Scarlett (Cukor, USA, 1935)

Sympathy for Mr. Vengeance (Park, Korea, 2002)

The Tall T (Boetticher, USA, 1957)

Tank Girl (Talalay, USA, 1995)

Targets (Bogdanovich, USA, 1968)

Tarzan the Ape Man (Van Dyke, USA, 1932)

Tarzan and his Mate (Gibbons, USA, 1934)

Taxi Driver (Scorsese, USA, 1976)

Teenage Zombies (Warren, USA, 1957)

The Tenderness of the Wolves (Lommel, Germany, 1973)

Tenebrae (Argento, Italy, 1982)

Terminal Island (Rothman, USA, 1973)

Terminator II: Judgment Day (Cameron, USA, 1991)

The Terror (Corman, USA, 1963)

Tesis (Amenabar, Spain, 1996)

Tetsuo, Man of Iron (Tsukamoto, Japan, 1989)

The Texas Chainsaw Massacre (Hooper, USA, 1974)

Them! (Douglas, USA, 1954)

They Live (Carpenter, USA, 1988)

The Thing (Carpenter, USA, 1982)

Thirteen (Hardwicke, USA, 2003)

This Filthy World (Garlin, USA, 2006)

This Is Spinal Tap (Reiner, USA, 1982)

Thriller – A Cruel Picture (Vibenius, Sweden, 1973)

Thundercrack! (McDowell, USA, 1975)

The Tingler (Castle, USA, 1959)

Titanic (Cameron, USA, 1997)

Tokyo Decadence (Murakami, Japan, 1992)

Tommy (Russell, UK, 1975)

Top Gun (Scott, USA, 1986)

Top Hat (Sandrich, USA, 1935)

Touch of Evil (Welles, USA, 1958)

A Touch of Zen (Hu, Hong Kong, 1969)

Towering Inferno (Guillermin/Allen, USA, 1974)

Trainspotting (Boyle, UK, 1996)

Trash (Morrissey, USA. 1970)

The Trip (Corman, USA, 1967)

Triumph of the Will (Riefenstahl, Germany, 1935)

Trog (Francis, UK, 1970)

Troll 2 (Fragasso, Italy, 1990)

Tron (Lisberger, USA/Taiwan, 1982)

Troops (Rubio, USA, 1998)

Trouble Every Day (Denis, France/Germany/Japan, 2001)

Trouble Man (Dixon, USA, 1972)

Turkish Delight (Verhoeven, The Netherlands, 1973)

Tusk (Jodorowsky, France, 1980)

Twelve Monkeys (Gilliam, USA, 1995)

Twilight (Hardwicke, USA, 2008)

The Typewriter, the Rifle and the Movie Camera (Simon, USA/UK, 1996)

Two Lane Blacktop (Hellman, USA, 1971)

Unico (Hirata/Tezuka, Japan, 1981)

The Unknown (Browning, USA, 1927)

Up in Smoke (Adler, USA, 1978)

The Usual Suspects (Singer, USA, 1995)

Vampire Princess Miyu (Hirano, Japan, 1988)

Vampyr (Dreyer, France/Germany, 1932)

Vampyros Lesbos (Franco, West Germany/Spain, 1971)

Velvet Goldmine (Haynes, UK/USA, 1998)

The Velvet Vampire (Rothman, USA, 1971)

Videodrome (Cronenberg, Canada, 1983)

Vincent (Burton, USA, 1982)

Vinyl (Warhol, USA, 1965)

Violent Cop (Kitano, Japan, 1989)

Visitor Q (Miike, Japan, 2001)
Viva (Biller, USA, 2007)
Viva la muerte (Arrabal, France/Tunisia, 1971)
Wanda, the Sadistic Hypnotist (Coraito, USA, 1969)
The War Game (Watkins, UK, 1965)
The War of the Worlds (Haskin, USA, 1956)
The Warriors (Hill, USA, 1979)
Waterworld (Reynolds, USA, 1995)
We Can't Go Home Again (Ray, USA, 1976)
Weekend (Godard, France/Italy, 1967)
Welcome Home Brother Charles (Fanaka, USA, 1975)
Welcome to the Dollhouse (Solondz, USA, 1995)
Wes Craven's New Nightmare (Craven, USA, 1994)
What Ever Happened to Baby Jane? (Aldrich, USA, 1962)
When Harry Met Sally (Reiner, USA, 1989)
When Night Is Falling (Rozema, Canada, 1994)
The Wicker Man (Hardy, UK, 1973)
The Wild Angels (Corman, USA, 1966)
The Wild Bunch (Peckinpah, USA, 1969)

Wild at Heart (Lynch, USA, 1990)
The Wild One (Benedek, USA, 1953)
Wild in the Streets (Shear, USA, 1968)
Wings of Desire (Wenders, Germany, 1987)
Witchfinder General (Reeves, UK, 1968)
The Wizard of Oz (Fleming, USA, 1939)
Woodstock (Wadleigh, USA, 1970)
The World's Biggest Gang Bang (Bone, USA, 1995)
WR: Mysteries of an Organism (Makaveyev, Yugoslavia, 1971)
X: The Man with the X-Ray Eyes (Corman, USA, 1963)
Yantra (Whitney, USA, 1957)
Yojimbo (Kurosawa, Japan, 1961)
Young Frankenstein (Brooks, USA, 1974)
Zelig (Allen, USA, 1983)
Zero de conduite (Vigo, France, 1933)
Ziegfried Follies (Ayers/Del Ruth/Lewis/Minnelli/Pye/Sidney/Walters, USA, 1945)
Zombie Flesh Eaters (Fulci, Italy, 1979)

References

Abercrombie, Nicholas, and Brian Longhurst (1998), *Audiences: A Sociological Theory of Performance and Imagination* (London: Sage).

Acland, Charles (2007), "Introduction," in C. Acland (ed.), *Residual Media* (Minneapolis: University of Minnesota Press), xiii–xxvii.

Adams, Michael (2010), *Showgirls, Teen Wolves and Astro Zombies: A Film Critic's Year-Long Quest to Find the Worst Movie Ever Made* (New York: It Books – Harper Collins).

Agterberg, Bas (2004), "Mariken Van Nieumeghen," in Ernest Mathijs (ed.), *The Cinema of the Low Countries* (London: Wallflower Press), 121–128.

Alliez Eric (1996), *Capital Times: Tales from the Conquest of Time* (Minneapolis: University of Minnesota Press).

Altman, Rick (1986), "A semantic/syntactic approach to film genre," in Barry KeithGrant (ed.), *Film Genre Reader* (Austin, TX: University of Texas Press), 26–39.

Altman, Rick (1999), *Film/Genre* (London: British Film Institute).

An, Jinsoo (2001). "*The Killer*: Cult film and transcultural (mis) reading," in Esther Yau (ed.), *At Full Speed; Hong Kong Cinema in a Borderless World* (Minneapolis: University of Minnesota Press), 95–113.

Anderson, Benedict (1983), *Imagined Communities: Reflections on the Origin and Spread of Nationalism* (London: Verso).

Anderson, Chris (2006), *The Long Tail* (London: Random House).

Andrew, Dudley (1985), "The neglected tradition of phenomenology in film theory," in: Bill Nichols (ed.), *Movies and Methods II* (Berkeley: University of California Press), 625–632.

Anger, Kenneth (1975), *Hollywood Babylon* (San Francisco: Straight Arrow Books).

Apers, Michel (2004), "De Monty: Laatste Cinema voor de Autostrade," in Willy Magiels and Robbe De Hert (eds), *Magie van de Cinema* (Antwerp: Facet), 143–147.

Arthur, Paul (2005), "Routines of emancipation: Jonas Mekas and alternative cinema in the ideology and politics of the sixties," in Paul Arthur, *A Line of Sight: American Avant-garde Films since 1965* (Minneapolis: University of Minnesota Press), 1–23.

Atkinson, Michael (2001), "Hobbit forming: Fan boys line up for 'ring'-side seats," *Village Voice* (June 5), online at: www.villagevoice.com/2001-06-05/news/hobbit-forming/ (accessed August 18, 2010).

Atkinson, Michael (2009), "The wild bunch: Seijun Suzuki," *Sight and Sound* 19(9), 34.

Aubry, Danielle and Gilles Visy (eds) (2009), *Les Œuvres Cultes: Entre la Transgression et la Transtextualité* (Paris: Editions Publibook Université).

Auslander, Philip (1997), *From Acting to Performance* (London: Routledge).

Austin, Bruce (1981a), "Portrait of a cult film audience: *The Rocky Horror Picture Show*," *Journal of Popular Communication*, 31 (Spring), 43–54.

Austin, Bruce (1981b), "Film attendance: Why college students chose to see their most recent film," *Journal of Popular Film and Television*, 9 (Spring), 43–49.

Austin, Bruce (1983), "Critics' and consumers' evaluations of motion pictures: A longitudinal test of the taste culture and elitist hypotheses," *Journal of Popular Film*, 10(4), 156–167.

Austin, Bruce (1984), "Portrait of an art film audience," *Journal of Communication*, 34 (Winter), 74–87.

Austin, Thomas (2002), *Hollywood, Hype, and Audiences: Selling and Watching Popular Film in the 1990s* (Manchester: Manchester University Press).

Bacon-Smith, Camille (1992), *Enterprising Women: Television Fandom and the Creation of Popular Myth* (Philadelphia: University of Pennsylvania Press).

Bacon-Smith, Camille (2000), *Science Fiction Culture* (Philadelphia: University of Pennsylvania Press).

Bainbridge, William Sims and Rodney Stark (2003), "Cult formation: Three compatible models," in Lorne Dawson, ed., *Cults and New Religious Movements: A Reader* (London: Blackwell Publishing), 59–70; originally published in 1979 in *Sociological Analysis*, 40, 283–295.

Bakhtin, Mikhail (1965, 1984), *Rabelais and his World* (trans. Héléne Iswolsky; Bloomington: Indiana University Press).

Balun, Chas (1992). *More Gore Score: Brave New Horrors* (Key West: Fantasma Books).

Bamber, Martyn (2003), "Joe Dante," *Senses of Cinema*, 26 (May–June), online at: http://archive.sensesofcinema. com/contents/directors/03/dante.html (accessed November 18, 2010).

Barbas, Samantha (2001), *Movie Crazy: Fans, Stars and the Cult of Celebrity* (New York: Palgrave).

Barcinski, André (2003), "Coffin Joe and José Mojica Marins: Strange men for strange times," in Steven Jay Schneider (ed.), *Fear without Frontiers: Horror Cinema across the Globe* (Godalming: FAB Press), 27–38.

Barker, Martin (1984), *The Video Nasties: Freedom and Censorship in the Media*, (London: Pluto Press).

Barker, Martin (2004), "News, reviews, clues, interviews and other ancillary materials – a critique and research proposal," in James Burton (ed.), *21st Century Film Studies: A Scope Reader*, online at: www.scope .nottingham.ac.uk/reader/index.php (accessed March 7, 2010).

Barker, Martin (2005), "Loving and hating *Straw Dogs*: The meanings of audience responses to a controversial film," *Participations* 2 (2), online at: www.participations.org/ (accessed August 18, 2010).

Barker, Martin (2006), "Loving and hating *Straw Dogs*: The meanings of audience responses to a controversial film, Part 2,"*Participations* 3 (1), online at: www.participations. org/ (accessed August 18, 2010).

Barker, Martin, Jane Arthurs and Ramaswami Harindranath (2001), *The Crash Controversy: Censorship Campaigns and Film Reception* (London: Wallflower Press).

Barker, Martin with Thomas Austin (2001), *From Antz to Titanic* (London: Pluto Press).

Barker, Martin and Kate Brooks (1997), *Knowing Audiences: Judge Dredd, Its Friends, Fans and Foes* (Luton: University of Luton Press).

Barker, Martin and Ernest Mathijs (eds) (2007), *Watching The Lord of the Rings: Tolkien's World Audiences* (New York: Peter Lang).

Barker, Martin, Ernest Mathijs and Xavier Mendik (2006), "Menstrual monsters: The reception of the Ginger Snaps cult horror franchise," *Film International*, 4(3), 68–77.

Barker, Martin, Ernest Mathijs, Jamie Sexton *et al.* (2008), Report to the British Board of Film Classification upon completion of the research project: "Audiences and Reception of Sexual Violence in Contemporary Cinema," Aberystwyth: University of Wales, Aberystwyth, March 2007, online at: www.bbfc.co. uk/downloads/index.php (accessed March 7, 2010).

Barral, Etienne (1999), *Otaku: Les enfants du virtuel* (Paris: Denoel).

Barratt, Jim (2008), *Bad Taste* (London: Wallflower Press).

Baudrillard, Jean (1981), *For a Critique of the Political Economy of the Sign* (St. Louis, MO: Telos Press).

Baudrillard, Jean (1990), *Fatal Strategies* (London: Pluto).

Bazin, André (2009) [1955], "The festival viewed as a religious order," in Richard Porton (ed.), *Dekalog 3: On Film Festivals* (London: Wallflower Press), 13–19.

Beauchamp, Cari and Henri Béhar (1992), *Hollywood on the Riviera: The Inside Story of the Cannes Film Festival* (New York: William Morrow and Co.).

Becker, Howard P. (1932), *Systematic Sociology on the Basis of the Beziehungslehre and Gebildelehre of Leopold Von Wiese* (New York: John Wiley & Sons, Ltd).

Becker, Howard S. (1963), *Outsiders: Studies in the Sociology of Deviance* (New York: The Free Press).

Beckford, James (2003), *Social Theory and Religion* (Cambridge: Cambridge University Press).

Bell, David (2006), *Cyberculture Theorists: Manuel Castells and Donna Haraway* (London: Routledge).

Benjamin, Walter (1936), "The work of art in the age of mechanical reproduction," in *Illuminations* (1969) (New York: Schocken Books).

Benshoff, Harry (1997) *Monsters in the Closet: Homosexuality in the Horror Film* (Manchester: Manchester University Press).

Benshoff, Harry M. (2001), "The short-lived life of the Hollywood LSD film," *Velvet Light Trap*, 47 (Spring), 29–44.

Benshoff, Harry M. (2007), "Camp," in Barry Keith Grant (ed.), *Schirmer Encyclopedia of Film* (Detroit: Schirmer), 201–205.

Bermel, Albert (1977), *Artaud's Theatre of Cruelty* (London: Methuen).

Berra, John (ed.) (2010), *Directory of World Cinema: Japan* (Bristol: Intellect).

Betz, Mark (2003) "Art, exploitation, underground," in Mark Jancovich *et al.* (eds), *Defining Cult Movies: The Cultural Politics of Oppositional Taste* (Manchester: Manchester University Press), 202–222.

Biltereyst, D. (2005), "Youth, moral panics and the end of cinema: On the reception of *Rebel without a Cause* in Europe," in J. David Slocum (ed.), *Rebel without a Cause:*

Approaches to a Maverick Masterwork (New York: SUNY Press), 171–189.

Biltereyst, Daniel, Ernest Mathijs and Philippe Meers (2007), "An avalanche of attention: The prefiguration and reception of *The Lord of the Rings*," in Martin Barker and Ernest Mathijs (eds), *Watching The Lord of the Rings: Tolkien's World Audiences* (New York: Peter Lang), 37–59.

Bissell, Tom (2010), "Cinema crudite: The mysterious appeal of the post-camp cult film," *Harper's Magazine*, 321(1923), 58–65.

Blake, Linnie (2004), "Jörg Buttgereit's Nekromantiks: Things to do in Germany with the dead," in Ernest Mathijs and Xavier Mendik (eds), *Alternative Europe: Eurotrash and Exploitation Cinema Since 1945* (London: Wallflower Press), 191–202.

Bloch, Ernst (1918, 2000), *The Spirit of Utopia* (Stanford, CA: Stanford University Press).

Bloch, Ernst (1949, 1986), *The Principle of Hope* (Boston, MA: MIT Press).

Bode, Lisa (2010), "Transitional tastes: Teen girls and genre in the critical reception of *Twilight*," *Continuum: Journal of Media and Cultural Studies*, 24(5), 707–720.

Bogdan, Robert (1988) *Freak Show: Presenting Human Oddities for Amusement and Profit* (Chicago: University of Chicago Press).

Bolton, Christopher (2005), "Anime Horror and its Audience: *3x3 Eyes* and *Vampire Princess Miyu*," in Jay McRoy (ed.), *Japanese Horror Cinema* (Edinburgh: University of Edinburgh Press), 66–76.

Boorman, John and Walter Donahue (eds) (1998), *Projections 8; Film-makers on Film-making* (London: Faber & Faber).

Bordwell, David, Janet Staiger and Kristin Thompson (1985), *The Classical Hollywood Cinema: Film Style and Mode of Production to 1960* (London: Routledge).

Bordwell, David (1989), *Making Meaning: Inference and Rhetoric in the Interpretation of Cinema* (Cambridge, MA: Harvard University Press).

Bordwell, David (2000), *Planet Hong Kong* (Cambridge, MA: Harvard University Press).

Borneman, Ernest (1977), "United States versus Hollywood: The case study of an antitrust suit," in Tino Balio (ed.), *The American Film Industry* (Madison, WI: University of Wisconsin Press), 332–345.

Botting, Fred and Scott Wilson (eds) (1997), *The Bataille Reader* (Oxford: Blackwell).

Bourdieu, Pierre (1984), *Distinction: A Social Critique of the Judgment of Taste* (New York: Routledge).

Bourdieu, Pierre (1986), "The forms of capital" (trans. Richard Nice), in J.G. Richardson (ed.), *Handbook for Theory and Research for the Sociology of Education* (Westport, CT: Greenwood Press), 241–258.

Bowman, Paul (2010), *Theorizing Bruce Lee: Film-Fighting-Fantasy-Philosophy* (New York/Amsterdam: Editions Rodopi).

Boym, Svetlana (2001), *The Future of Nostalgia* (New York: Basic Books).

Brake, Mike (1980), *The Sociology of Youth Culture and Youth Subcultures* (London: Routledge & Keegan Paul).

Britton, Piers D. (2009), "Design for screen SF," in Mark Bould, Andrew M. Butler, Adam Roberts and Sherryl Vint (eds), *The Routledge Companion to Science Fiction* (London: Routledge), 341–349.

Brook, K. (2006), "Puce modern moment: Camp, postmodernism and the films of Kenneth Anger," *Journal of Film and Video*, 58(4), 3–15.

Brooker, Will (2002), *Using the Force: Creativity, Community and "Star Wars" Fans* (New York: Continuum).

Brooker, Will (2004), *Alice's Adventures: Lewis Carroll in Popular Culture* (London: Continuum).

Brooks, Xan (2007), " 'I'm the last crazy artist'," *The Guardian*, Features Section (April 5), 28.

Brophy, Philip (1986), "Horrality: The textuality of contemporary horror films," *Screen*, 27(1), 2–13.

Brophy, Philip (2004), *100 Modern Soundtracks* (London: British Film Institute).

Brophy, Philip (2005), *100 Anime* (London: British Film Institute).

Brottman, Mikita (1997), *Offensive Films: Towards an Anthropology of Cinema Vomitif* (Westport, CT: Greenwood Press).

Brottman, Mikita (2000), "Star cults/cult stars: Cinema, psychosis, celebrity, death," in Xavier Mendik and Graeme Harper (eds), *Unruly Pleasures: The Cult Film and its Critics* (Guildford: FAB Press), 104–119.

Brottman, Mikita, Carel Rowe and Anna Powell (2001), *Moonchild: The Films of Kenneth Anger. Persistence of Vision Volume 1* (ed. Jack Hunter; London: Creation Books).

Broughton, James (1964). "Knokke-le-Zoute," *Film Quarterly* 17(3), 13–15.

Bryson, Bethany (1997), "What about the univores? Musical dislikes and group-based identity construction among Americans with low levels of education," *Poetics* 25, 141–156.

Budd, Mike (ed.) (1990), *The Cabinet of Dr. Caligari: Texts, Contexts, Histories* (Piscataway, NJ: Rutgers University Press).

Burkert, Walter (1987), *Ancient Mystery Cults* (Cambridge, MA: Harvard University Press).

Buruma, Ian (1995), "A case of overkill: Legend of the overfiend," *Index on Censorship*, 6: 46–47.

Butler, Judith (1990), *Gender Trouble: Feminism and the Subversion of Identity* (London: Routledge).

Caldwell, John Thornton (2008), *Production Culture: Industrial Reflexivity and Critical Practice in Film and Television* (Durham, NC: Duke University Press).

Cammaer, Gerda Johanna (2005), "EXPRMNTL 3/ Knokke-le-Zoute 1963: *Flaming Creatures*, raving features," *Synoptique* 8, online at: www.synoptique.ca/ (accessed March 14, 2010).

Campbell, Colin (1977), "Clarifying the cult', *British Journal of Sociology*, 28(3), 375–388.

Caine, Andrew (2001), "The A.I.P. beach movies – cult films depicting subcultural activities," *Scope* (December), online at: www.scope.nottingham.ac.uk/article.php?issue=dec2001&id=277&section=article (accessed November 18, 2010)

Cairns, Lucille (2006), *Sapphism on Screen: Lesbian Desire in French and Francophone Cinema* (Edinburgh: Edinburgh University Press).

Card, James (1991), "Confessions of a Casablanca cultist: An enthusiast meets the myth and its flaws," in J.P. Telotte (ed.), *The Cult Film Experience* (Austin, TX: University of Texas Press), 66–78.

Carroll, Noel (1990), *The Philosophy of Horror: Paradoxes of the Heart* (London: Routledge).

Carroll, Noel (1998), *Interpreting the Moving Image* (Cambridge: Cambridge University Press), 240–264.

Cary, Diana Serra (1979), *Hollywood's Children: An Inside Account of the Child Star Cult* (New York: Houghton Mifflin).

Castells, Manuel (1996), The Rise of the Network Society, *The Information Age: Economy, Society and Culture Vol. I* (Cambridge, MA: Blackwell).

Castells, Manuel (1997), *The Power of Identity, The Information Age: Economy, Society and Culture Vol. II* (Cambridge, MA: Blackwell).

Castells, Manuel (1998), *End of Millennium, The Information Age: Economy, Society and Culture Vol. III* (Cambridge, MA: Blackwell).

Castle, Robert (2004), "The interpretative odyssey of 2001," *Bright Lights Film Journal* (Issue 46), online at: www.brightlightsfilm.com/46/2001.htm (accessed November 18, 2010)

Catterall, Ali, and Simon Wells (2002), *Your Face Here: British Cult Movies since the Sixties* (London: Fourth Estate).

Chamberlin, Philip (1960), "Allies, not enemies: Commercial and nontheatrical experience on the West Coast," *Film Quarterly*, 14 (Winter), 36–39.

Châteauvert, Jean and Tamara Bates (2002), "Films et cultistes," in Philippe Le Guern (ed.), *Les cultes médiatiques: culture fan et oeuvres cultes* (Rennes: Presses Universitaires Rennes), 87–96.

Cherry, Brigid (1999), "Refusing to refuse to look: Female viewers of the horror film," in Richard Maltby and Melvyn Stokes (eds), *Identifying Hollywood Audiences* (London: British Film Institute), 187–203.

Cherry, Brigid (2010), *Horror* (London: Routledge).

Chibnall, Steve (1997), "Double exposures: Observations on *The Flesh and Blood Show*," in Deborah Cartmell, I.Q. Hunter, Heidi Kaye and Imelda Whelehan (eds), *Trash Aesthetics: Popular Culture and its Audience* (London: Pluto Press), 84–102.

Chibnall, Steve (1998), *Making Mischief: The Cult Films of Pete Walker* (Godalming: FAB Press).

Chibnall, Steve (2007), *Quota Quickies: The Birth of the British "B" Film* (London: British Film Institute).

Chriss, James J. (1993), "Durkheim's Cult of the Individual as Civil Religion: Its Appropriation by Erving Goffman," *Sociological Spectrum* 13(2), 251–275.

Church, David (2005), "Examining the role of disability in Herzog's *Even Dwarves Started Small*," *The Film Journal*, 13, online at: www.thefilmjournal.com/issue13/herzog.html (accessed August 18, 2010).

Church, David (2009), "Of manias, shit, and blood: The reception of *Salò* as a 'sick film'," *Participations* 6(2), online at: www.participations.org/ (accessed August 18, 2010).

Church, David (2011), "Freakery, cult films, and the problem of ambivalence," *Journal of Film and Video*, 63(1),3–17.

Cineaste (2009), "Editorial," *Cineaste* 35(1), 2.

Cleto, Fabio (1999), "Introduction: Queering the Camp,' in Fabio Cleto (ed.), *Camp: Queer Aesthetics and the Performing Subject: A Reader* (Edinburgh: Edinburgh University Press), 1–42.

Click, Melissa (2009), " 'Rabid', 'obsessed', and 'frenzied': Understanding *Twilight* fangirls and the gendered politics of fandom," *FlowTV* 12, online at: http://flowtv.org/2009/12/ (accessed August 5, 2010).

Cohen, Alain J.-J. (2003), "12 Monkeys, Vertigo and La Jetée: Postmodern mythologies and cult films," *New Review of Film and Television*, 1(1): 149–164.

Cohen, Stanley (1972), *Folk Devils and Moral Panics* (London: MacGibbon & Kee).

Conrich, Ian (1997), "Seducing the subject: Freddy Krueger, popular culture and the Nightmare on Elm Street Films," in Deborah Cartmell, I.Q. Hunter, Heidi Kaye and Imelda Whelehan (eds), *Thrash Aesthetics: Popular Culture and its Audience* (London: Pluto Press), 118–131.

Conrich, Ian (2000) "An aesthetic sense: Cronenberg and neo-horror film culture," in Michael Grant (ed.), *The Modern Fantastic: The Films of David Cronenberg* (Trowbridge: Flicks Books), 35–50.

Conrich, Ian (2005), "Metal-morphosis: Post-industrial crisis and the tormented body in the *Tetsuo* films," in Jay McRoy (ed.), *Japanese Horror Cinema* (Edinburgh: University of Edinburgh Press), 95–106.

Conrich, Ian (2006), "Musical performance and the cult film experience," in Ian Conrich and Estella Tincknell (eds), *Film's Musical Moments* (Edinburgh: Edinburgh University Press), 115–131.

Conrich, Ian, and Estella Tincknell (2006), "Introduction," in Ian Conrich and Estella Tincknell (eds), *Film's Musical Moments* (Edinburgh: Edinburgh University Press): 1–13.

Cook, David A. (2000), *Lost Illusions: American Cinema in the Shadow of Watergate and Vietnam, 1970–1979* (Berkeley, CA: University of California Press).

Cooper, Ian (2011), *Bring me the Head of Alfredo Garcia* (London: Wallflower Press).

Corman, Roger (1990), *How I Made a Hundred Movies in Hollywood and Never Lost a Dime* (London: Muller).

Cornea, Christine (2007), *Science Fiction Cinema: Between Fantasy and Reality* (Edinburgh: Edinburgh University Press).

Corrigan, Timothy (1991), "Film and the culture of cult," in J.P.Telotte (ed.), *The Cult Film Experience: Beyond all Reason* (Austin, TX: University of Texas Press), 26–37.

Corrigan, Timothy (2003), "The commerce of auteurism," in Virgina Wright Wexman (ed.), *Film and Authorship* (Piscataway, NJ: Rutgers University Press): 96–111.

Couldry, Nick (2003), *Media Rituals: A Critical Approach* (London: Routledge).

Cova, Bernard, Robert Kosinets and Avi Shankar (eds) (2007), *Consumer Tribes* (Amsterdam: Elsevier).

Cowan, Douglas E. (2003), *Bearing False Witness? An Introduction to the Christian Countercult* (Westport, CT: Praeger).

Cowan, Douglas and David Bromley (2008), *Cults and New Religions* (Oxford: Wiley-Blackwell).

Cox, Alex (2000), "My kind of woman," *The Guardian* (September 15), online at: www.guardian.co.uk/film/2000/dec/15/filmcensorship.culture (accessed August 18, 2010).

Cox, Alex (2006), "A study in sexual violence," *The Guardian*, Film and Music Section (July 14), 14.

Cox, Alex (2010), "Refrain on the range: *Rita of the West*," *Film Comment*, 46(2), 8.

Cox, Alex and Nick Jones (1990), *Moviedrome: The Guide* (London: BBC).

Cox, Alex and Nick Jones (1993), *Moviedrome 2: The Guide* (London: BBC).

Cox, Harvey (1969), *The Feast of Fools: A Theological Essay on Festivity and Fantasy* (Cambridge, MA: Harvard University Press).

Crawford, Christina (1978), *Mommie Dearest* (New York: William Morrow).

Crawford, Travis (2003), "The urban techno-alienation of Sion Sono's *Suicide Club*," in Steven Jay Schneider (ed.), *Fear without Frontiers: Horror Cinema across the Globe* (Godalming: FAB Press), 305–311.

Crazy Horse (2005), "Comment to: Top 10 rarest DVDs in the world," *AVForums* (February 20), online at: www.avforums.com/forums/movies-cinema/190033-top-10-rarest-dvds-world.html (accessed November 20, 2010).

Creed, Barbara (1987), "Horror and the monstrous-feminine: An imaginary abjection," *Screen*, 27(1), January–February.

Creed, Barbara (1993), *The Monstrous-Feminine: Film, Feminism, Psychoanalysis* (London: Routledge).

Cubitt, Sean (2005), *Ecomedia* (New York/Amsterdam: Editions Rodopi).

Curci, Loris (1996), *Shock Masters of the Cinema* (Key West: Fantasma Books).

Curtis, James (1998), *James Whale* (London: Faber & Faber).

d'Allondans, Thierry Goguel (2009), "Du côté de l'amour: Digressions sur Les Nuits Fauves de Cyril Collard,' in Jocelyn Lachance, Hugues Paris and Sébastien Dupont (eds), *Films Cultes et Culte du Film chez les Jeunes* (Québec: Presses de l'Université Laval), 77–84.

Danvers, Louis (1984), "La chair et le câble," *Visions*, 19, 12.

Daugherty, Rebecca (2002), "The spirit of '77: Punk and the girl revolution," *Women and Music*, 6: 27–32.

Davis, Darrell and Yeh Yueh-Yu (2001), "Warning! Category III: The other Hong Kong cinema," *Film Quarterly* 54(4): 12–26.

Davis, Glyn (2008), *Superstar: The Karen Carpenter Story* (London: Wallflower Press).

DeCordova, Richard (1991), "The emergence of the star system in America," in Christine Gledhill (ed.), *Stars: Industry of Desire* (London: Routledge), 17–29.

De Kock, Ivo (1983), "1st International Fantasy Film Festival," *Andere Sinema*, 51, 35–37.

Denison, Rayna (2006), "Global markets for Japanese film: Miyazaki Hayao's *Spirited Away*," in Alastair Phillips and Julian Stringer (eds), *Japanese Cinema: Texts and Contexts* (London: Routledge).

Denison, Rayna (2008), "The language of the blockbuster: Marketing, Princess Mononoke and the Daihitto in Japanese film culture," in Leon Hunt and Leung Wing-Fai (eds), *East Asian Cinemas: Transnational Connections on Film* (London: IB Tauris).

Dentith, Simon (2000), *Parody* (London: Routledge).

de Picciotto, Miriam Dagan (2003), "Oppositional spaces: Kenneth Anger and sixties counterculture," Master's dissertation, Humboldt University, Berlin.

Desai, Jigna and Rajinder Dudrah (2008), "The essential Bollywood," in Rajinder Dudrah and Jigna Desai (eds), *The Bollywood Reader* (Maidenhead: Open University Press), 1–20.

De Seife, Ethan (2007), *This Is Spinal Tap* (London: Wallflower Press).

Desser, David (2005), "Hong Kong film and the new cinephilia," in Meaghan Morris, Siu Leung Li and Stephen Chan Ching-kiu (eds), *Hong Kong Connections: Transnational Imagination in Action Cinema* (Durham: Duke University Press; Hong Kong: Hong Kong University Press), 205–222.

Dethier, Hubert (1994–2002), *De Beet Van de Adder* (4 volumes) (Brussels: VUB Press).

De Valck, Marijke (2005), "Drowning in popcorn at the International Film Festival Rotterdam ? The festival as multiplex of cinephilia," in Marijke de Valck and Malte Hagener (eds), *Cinephilia: Movies, Love, Memory* (Amsterdam: Amsterdam University Press): 97–109.

Dika, Vera (2003), *Recycled Culture in Contemporary Art and Film: The Uses of Nostalgia* (Cambridge: Cambridge University Press).

Diken, Bülent and Carsten Bagge Laustsen (2002), "Enjoy your fight: *Fight Club* as a symptom of the network society," *Cultural Values* 6(4), 349–367.

Dion, Elise (2009), "Vampyros Lesbos de Jess Franco: voyeurisme baroque," in Danielle Aubry and Gilles Visy (eds), *Les Œuvres Cultes: Entre la Transgression et la Transtextualité* (Paris: Editions Publibook Université), 161–74.

Dissanayake, Wimal and Malti Sahai (1992), *Sholay, a Cultural Reading* (New Delhi: Wiley Eastern Limited).

Dixon, Wheeler Winston (2006), "Movies and postwar recovery," in Wheeler Winston Dixon (ed.), *American Cinema of the 1940s* (Piscataway, NJ: Rutgers University Press), 162–182.

Doherty, Thomas (1999), *Pre-Code Hollywood: Sex, Immorality and Insurrection in American Cinema 1930–1934* (New York: Columbia University Press).

Doherty, Thomas (2002), *Teenagers and Teenpics: The Juvenilization of American Movies in the 1950s* (Revised and expanded edition; Philadelphia: Temple University Press).

Donnelly, K.J. (2005), *The Spectre of Sound: Music in Film and Television* (London: British Film Institute).

Doty, Alexander (2000), *Flaming Classics: Queering the Film Canon* (London: Routledge).

Douglas, Mary (1966), *Purity and Danger* (London: Routledge).

Drew, Oliver (2007), "'Asia Extreme': Japanese cinema and British hype," *New Cinemas: Journal of Contemporary Film*, 5(1), 53–73.

Dunn, Stephane (2008), *"Baad Bitches" and Sassy Supermamas: Black Power Action Films* (Chicago: University of Illinois Press).

Durkheim, Emile (1915/1995), *The Elementary Forms of the Religious Life* (London: Allen & Unwin).

Dwyer, Rachel (2005), *100 Bollywood Films* (London: British Film Institute).

Dyer, Richard (1979), *Stars* (London: British Film Institute).

Dyer, Richard (1986), *Heavenly Bodies: Film Stars and Society* (Basingstoke: Macmillan).

Dyer, Richard (2003), *Now You See It: Historical Studies on Lesbian and Gay Film* (London: Routledge).

Dyer, Richard (2007), *Pastiche* (Abingdon: Routledge).

Eagleton, Terry (1984), *The Function of Criticism* (London: Verso).

Earnest, Olen J. (1985), "*Star Wars*: A case study of motion picture marketing," *Current Research in Film*, 1, 1–18.

Eberwein, Robert (1998), "The erotic thriller," *Post Script* 17(3),25–33.

Eco, Umberto (1984) "The frames of comic 'freedom'" in Thomas A. Sebeok (ed.), *Carnivale! Approaches to Semiotics* (Berlin: Mouton).

Eco, Umberto (1986), "Cult movies and intertextual collage," in Eco, *Travels in Hyperreality* (London: Picador), 197–211.

Egan, Kate (2007), *Trash or Treasure? Censorship and the Changing Meanings of Video Nasties* (Manchester: Manchester University Press).

Eleftheriotis, Dimitris (2001), *Popular Cinemas of Europe: Studies of Texts, Contexts and Frameworks* (London: Continuum).

Eleftheriotis, Dimitris and Gary Needham (2006), "Bruce Lee: Stardom and Identity," in Dimitris Eleftheriotis and Gary Needham (eds), *Asian Cinemas: A Reader and Guide* (Honolulu: University of Hawaii Press), 406–409.

Eliade, Mircea (1961), *The Sacred and the Profane: The Nature of Religion* (New York, Harper Torchbooks).

Eliade, Mircea (1963), *Myth and Reality* (New York: Harper and Row).

English, James (2005), *The Economy of Prestige: Prizes, Awards, and the Circulation of Cultural Value* (Cambridge, MA: Harvard University Press).

Erb, Cynthia (1998), *Tracking King Kong: A Hollywood Icon in World Culture* (Detroit: Wayne State University Press).

Eshun, Kodwo (1995), "From blaxploitation to rapsploitation," in Jonathan Romney and Adrian Wootton (eds), *Celluloid Jukebox: Popular Music in the Movies since the 50s* (London: British Film Institute), 52–59.

Espinosa, Shirlita (2009), "Filipino pito-pito films and digital piracy: The beginning of an end," paper presented at the

B for Bad Cinema Conference (Monash University, Melbourne, April, 15–17).

Everman, Welch (1993), *Cult Horror Films* (New York: Citadel Press/Virgin Books).

Falicov, Tamara (2004), "U.S.-Argentine Co-productions 1982–1990: Roger Corman, Aries Productions, "Schlockbuster Movies," and the international market," *Film and History*, 34(1), 31–39.

Farber, Manny (1998), "Underground films," in *Negative Space: Manny Farber on the Movies* (New York: Da Capo), 12–24.

Fay, Jennifer (2004), "The Schoolgirl Reports and the guilty pleasure of history," in Ernest Mathijs and Xavier Mendik (eds), *Alternative Europe: Eurotrash and Exploitation Cinema since 1945* (London: Wallflower Press), 39–52.

Feasey, Rebecca (2003), "Sharon Stone: Screen diva: Stardom, femininity, and cult fandom," in Mark Jancovich et al. (eds), *Defining Cult Movies: The Cultural Politics of Oppositional Taste* (Manchester: Manchester University Press), 172–184.

Feigenbaum, Anna (2007), "Remapping the resonances of Riot Grrrl: Feminisms, postfeminisms, and 'processes' of punk," in Yvonne Tasker and Diane Negra (eds), *Interrogating Postfeminism: Gender and the Politics of Popular Culture.* (Durham, NC: Duke University Press), 132–152.

Fenner, David (2008), *Art in Context* (Athens, OH: Ohio University Press/Swallow Press).

Fiedler, Leslie (1978), *Freaks: Myths and Images of the Secret Self* (New York: Simon & Schuster).

Fiedler, Leslie (1996), "Foreword," in Rosemary Garland Thomson (ed.), *Freakery: Cutural Spectacles of the Extraordinary Body* (New York: New York University Press), xiii–xvii.

Fischer, Lucy (2001), "Ecstasy: Female sexual, social, and cinematic scandal," in Adrienne McLean and David Cook (eds), *Headline Hollywood: A Century of Film Scandal* (Piscataway, NJ: Rutgers University Press), 129–142.

Fischer, Lucy and Marcia Landy (2004), "General introduction: Back story," in Lucy Fischer and Marcia Landy (eds), *Stars: The Film Reader* (New York: Routledge), 1–9.

Fiske, John (1989), *Understanding Popular Culture* (London: Routledge).

Fiske, John (1992), "The Cultural Economy of Fandom," in Lisa A. Lewis (ed.), *Adoring Audiences: Fan Culture and Popular Media* (New York: Routledge), 30–49.

Flam, Leopold (1973), *Filosofie van de Eros* (Antwerp: Ontwikkeling).

Flynn, Charles, and Todd McCarthy (1975), "The economic imperative: Why was the B movie necessary?," in Todd McCarthy and Charles Flynn (eds), *Kings of the Bs: Working within the Hollywood System* (New York: E.P. Dutton & Co.), 13–43.

Franco, Judith (2003), "Gender, genre and female pleasure in the contemporary revenge narrative: *Baise-Moi* and *What it Feels Like for a Girl*," *Quarterly Review of Film and Video*, 21(3), 1–10.

Frank, Nino (1999), "A new kind of police drama: The criminal adventure," in Alain Silver and James Ursini (eds), *Film Noir Reader 2* (New York: Limelight Editions), 15–19.

Frank, Thomas (1997), *The Conquest of Cool: Business Culture, Counter Culture and the Rise of Hip Consumerism* (Chicago: University of Chicago Press).

Frayling, Christopher (2007), *Sergio Leone: Once Upon a Time in Italy* (London: Thames and Hudson).

French, Karl, and Philip French (1999), *Cult Movies* (London: Pavilion Books).

Friedrich, Otto (1986), *City of Nets* (London: Headline).

Gamson, Joshua (1996) "The organizational shaping of collective identity: The case of lesbian and gay film festivals in New York," *Sociological Forum*, 11: 231–262.

Garcia Bardon, Xavier (2002), "Exprmntl. Festival hors normes. Knokke 1963, 1967, 1974," *Revue Belge du Cinéma*, 43.

Garner, Ken (2001), " 'Would you like to hear some music?' Music in-and-out-of-control in the films of Quentin Tarantino," in K.J. Donnelly (ed.), *Film Music: Critical Approaches* (Edinburgh: Edinburgh University Press), 188–203.

George, Peter (1958), *Red Alert* (New York: Ace Books).

Gerow, Aaron (2009), "The homelessness of style and the problems of studying Miike Takashi," *Canadian Journal of Film Studies*, 18(1), 24–43.

Gerstner, David A. and Janet Staiger (eds) (2003), *Authorship and Film* (New York: Routledge).

Girard, Rene (1972), *La Violence et le Sacré* (Paris: Grasset).

Gladwin, Stephen (2003), "Witches, spells and politics: The horror films of Indonesia," in Steven Jay Schneider (ed.), *Fear without Frontiers: Horror Cinema across the Globe* (Godalming: FAB Press), 219–230.

Godin, Marc (1994), "David Cronenberg," in *Gore: autopsie d'un cinéma* (Paris: Editions du collectioneur), 110–113.

Goodall, Mark (2006), *Sweet and Savage: The World through the Shockumentary Film Lens* (Manchester: Headpress).

Gorfinkel, Elena (2000), "The body as apparatus: Chesty Morgan takes on the academy," in Xavier Mendik and Graeme Harper (eds), *Unruly Pleasures: The Cult Film and its Critics* (Godalming: FAB Press), 155–170.

Gorfinkel, Elena (2008), "Cult film: Or cinephilia by any other name," *Cineaste*, 34(1), 33–38.

Graham, Alison (1991), "Journey to the center of the fifties: The cult of banality," in J.P. Telotte (ed.), *The Cult Film Experience: Beyond all Reason* (Austin, TX: University of Texas Press), 107–121.

Grahame-Smith, Seth (2009), *Pride and Prejudice and Zombies* (Philadelphia: Quirk Books).

Grant, Barry Keith (ed.) (1984), *Planks of Reason: Essays on the Horror Film*, (Metuchen, NJ: Scarecrow Press).

Grant, Barry Keith (1991), "Science-fiction double feature: Ideology in the cult film," in J.P. Telotte (ed.), *The Cult Film Experience: Beyond all Reason* (Austin, TX: University of Texas Press), 122–137.

Grant, Barry Keith (1999), "'Sensuous elaboration': Reason and the visible in the science-fiction film," in Annette Kuhn (ed.), *Alien Zone II: The Spaces of Science Fiction Cinema* (London: Verso), 16–30.

Grant, Barry Keith (2000), "Second thoughts on double features: Revisiting the cult film," in Xavier Mendik and Graeme Harper (eds), *Unruly Pleasures: The Cult Film and its Critics* (Godalming: FAB Press), 13–27.

Grant, Catherine (2008), "Auteur machines? Auteurism and the DVD," in James Bennett and Tom Brown (eds), *Film and Television after DVD* (Abingdon: Routledge), 101–115.

Gray, Beverley (2004), *Roger Corman: Blood-Sucking Vampires, Flesh-Eating Cockroaches, and Driller Killers* (New York: Thunder's Mouth Press).

Gray, Stephen (2003), "Nigeria on-screen: 'Nollywood' films' popularity rising among emigres," *The Washington Post* (November 8), Financial Section, E01.

Green, Bill, Ben Peskoe, Will Russell and Scott Shuffitt (2007), *I'm a Lebowski You're a Lebowski* (New York: Bloomsbury).

Greenberg, Clement (1986), "Avant-garde and kitsch," in Clement Greenberg, *Collected Essays and Criticism, Volume 1: Perceptions and Judgments 1939–1944* (ed. John O'Brian; London and Chicago: University of Chicago Press), 5–22.

Grenier, Cynthia (1960), "Ill-starred thirteenth Festival of Cannes," *Film Quarterly*, 13(4), 15–19.

Gresset, Julie (2009), "Je pense donc je suis . . . une cyborg; Du mecha au cyberpunk dans Ghost in the Shell de Mamoru Oshii," in Danielle Aubry and Gilles Visy (eds), *Les Œuvres Cultes: Entre la Transgression et la Transtextualité* (Paris: Editions Publibook Université), 129–140.

Griffin, Sean (2009), *Hetero: Queering Representations of Straightness* (New York: SUNY Press).

Grossberg, Lawrence (2002), "Cinema, postmodernity and authenticity," in Kay Dickinson (ed.), *Movie Music: The Film Reader* (London: Routledge), 83–97. Originally published in Simon Frith et al. (eds), *Sound and Vision: The Music Video Reader* (London: Routledge, 1993).

Guare, John (1994), *Six Degrees of Separation* (New York: Vintage).

Guerrero, Edward (1990), "AIDS as monster in science fiction and horror films," *Journal of Popular Film and Television*, 18(3), 86–93.

Guins, Raiford (2005), "Blood and black gloves on shiny discs: New media, old tastes, and the remediation of Italian horror films in the United States," in Steven Jay Schneider and Tony Williams (eds), *Horror International* (Detroit: Wayne State University Press), 15–32.

Gwenllian Jones, Sara (2002), "Phantom Menace: Killer fans, consumer activism and digital filmmakers," in Xavier Mendik and Steven Jay Schneider (eds), *Underground USA: Filmmaking beyond the Hollywood Canon* (London: Wallflower Press), 169–179.

Haas, Charles (1983), "Headsploitation," *Film Comment*, 19(3),67–71.

Hagener, Malte (2007), *Moving Forward, Looking Back: The European Avant-garde and the Invention of Film Culture 1919–39* (Amsterdam: Amsterdam University Press).

Hagman, Hampus (2007), "'Every Cannes needs its scandal": Between art and exploitation in contemporary French films," *Film International*, 5(5), 32–41.

Halberstam, Judith (2003), "What's that smell: Queer temporalities and subcultural lives," *International Journal of Cultural Studies*, 6(3), 313–333.

Hall, Kenneth (2009), *The Killer* (Hong Kong: Hong Kong University Press).

Hall, Phil (2004), *The Encyclopaedia of Underground Movies: Films from the Fringes of Cinema* (Studio City: Michael Wiese Productions).

Hamilton, John (2005), *Beasts in the Cellar: The Exploitation Film Career of Tony Tenser* (Godalming: FAB Press).

Hammond, Paul (ed.) (2000), *The Shadow and its Shadow: Surrealist Writing on the Cinema* (San Francisco: City Lights Books).

Hansen, Rob (1994), *Then: Rob Hansen's History-in-Progress of British Science-Fiction Fandom*, online at: http://fanac.org/Fan_Histories/Then/ (accessed November 22, 2010)

Hantke, Steffen (2005), "The dialogue with American popular culture in two German films about the serial killer," in Steven Jay Schneider and Tony Williams (eds), *Horror International* (Detroit: Wayne State University Press), 56–80.

Harbord, Janet (2002), *Film Cultures* (London: Sage).

Harper, Sue and Vincent Porter (1996), "Moved to tears: Weeping in the cinema in post-war Britain," *Screen* 37(2), 152–173.

Harries, Dan (2000), *Film Parody* (London: British Film Institute).

Harries, Dan (2004), "Camping with Lady Divine: Star Persona and Parody," in Lucy Fischer and Marcia Landy (eds), *Stars: The Film Reader* (New York: Routledge), 151–161.

Harris, Marvin (1981), "Why the cults are coming," in *America Now* (New York: Simon and Schuster), 141–165.

Harris, Marvin (1987), *Cultural Anthropology* (2nd edn; New York: Harper and Row).

Havis, Allan (2008), *Cult Films: Taboo and Transgression* (New York: University Press of America).

Hawkins, Joan (1996), "One of us: Tod Browning's freaks," in Rosemarie Garland Thomson (ed.), *Freakery: Cultural Spectacles of the Extraordinary Body* (New York: New York University Press), 265–277.

Hawkins, Joan (2000), *Cutting Edge: Art Horror and the Horrific Avant-garde* (Minneapolis: University of Minnesota Press).

Hawkins, Joan (2003), "Midnight sex horror movies and the downtown avant-garde," in Mark Jancovich et al. (eds), *Defining Cult Movies: The Cultural Politics of Oppositional Taste* (Manchester: Manchester University Press), 223–234.

Hawkins, Joan (2010), "Culture wars: Some new trends in art horror," in Ian Conrich (ed.), *Horror Zone: The Cultural Experience of Contemporary Horror Cinema*, (London: IB Tauris), 125–138.

Heath, Joseph and Andrew Potter (2004), *The Rebell Sell: Why Culture Can't Be Jammed* (Chichester: Capstone Publishing, Wiley).

Hebdige, Dick (1979), *Subculture: The Meaning of Style* (London: Methuen).

Heffernan, Kevin (2004), *Ghouls, Gimmicks and Gold: Horror Films and the American Movie Business, 1953–1968* (Durham, NC: Duke University Press).

Heffernan, Kevin (2007), "Art house or house of exorcism? The changing distribution and reception contexts of Mario Bava's Lisa and the Devil," in Jeffrey Sconce (ed.), *Sleaze Artists: Cinema at the Margins of Taste, Style and Politics* (Durham, NC: Duke University Press), 144–164.

Hentzi, Gary (1993), "Little cinema of horrors," *Film Quarterly*, 46(3), 22–27.

Herzogenrath, Bernd (ed.) (2008), *The Cinema of Tod Browning: Essays of the Macabre and Grotesque* (Jefferson, NC: McFarland).

Herzogenrath, Bernd (ed.) (2009), *Edgar G. Ulmer: Essays on the King of the B's* (Jefferson, NC: McFarland).

Higashi, Sumiko (2005), "Movies and the paradox of female stardom," in Murray Pomerance (ed.) *American Cinema of the 1950s* (Piscataway, NJ: Rutgers University Press), 65–88.

Hilderbrand, Lucas (2009), *Inherent Vice: Bootleg Histories of Videotape and Copyright* (Durham, NC: Duke University Press).

Hill, Annette (1997), *Shocking Entertainment: Viewer Responses to Violent Movies* (Luton: University of Luton Press).

Hills, Matt (2002a) *Fan Cultures* (London: Routledge).

Hills, Matt (2002b) "Transcultural Otaku: Japanese representations of fandom and representations of Japan in anime/manga fan cultures," paper presented at Media in Transition 2: globalization and convergence (MIT, May).

Hills, Matt (2003), "*Star Wars* fandom, film theory and the museum: The cultural status of the cult blockbuster," in Julian Stringer (ed.), *Movie Blockbusters* (London: Routledge), 178–189.

Hills, Matt (2005), "Ringing the changes: Cult distinctions and cultural differences in US fans' readings of Japanese horror cinema," in Jay McRoy (ed.), *Japanese Horror Cinema* (Edinburgh: University of Edinburgh Press), 161–174.

Hills, Matt (2006a) "Fandom and fan studies," in Glen Creeber (ed.), *Tele-Visions: An Introduction to Studying Television* (London: British Film Institute) 100–106.

Hills, Matt (2006b) "Realising the cult blockbuster: Lord of the Rings fandom and residual/emergent cult status in 'the mainstream'" in Ernest Mathijs (ed.), *The Lord of the Rings: Popular Culture in Global Context* (London: Wallflower Press), 160–171.

Hills, Matt (2007), "Para-paracinema: The *Friday the 13th* film series as other to trash and legitimate film cultures," in Jeffrey Sconce (ed.), *Sleaze Artists: Cinema at the Margins of Taste, Style and Politics* (Durham, NC: Duke University Press), 219–239.

Hills, Matt (2008a) "The question of genre in cult film and fandom: Between contract and discourse," in James Donald and Michael Renov (eds), *The Sage Handbook of Film Studies* (London: Sage), 436–453.

Hills, Matt (2008b) "Cult film: A critical symposium," *Cineaste* 34(1), online at: www.cineaste.com/articles/cult-film-a-critical-symposium (accessed August 18, 2010).

Hills, Matt (2011) *Blade Runner* (London: Wallflower Press).

Hills, Matt (2010b) "Attending horror film festivals and conventions: Liveness, cultural capital and 'flesh and blood genre communities'" in Ian Conrich (ed.), *Horror Zone, the Cultural Experience of Contemporary Horror Cinema* (London: IB Tauris), 87–102.

Hoberman, J. (1980), "Bad cinema," *Film Comment* (July), reprinted in Philip Lopate (ed.), *American Movie Critics* (New York: The Library of America), 517–528.

Hoberman, J., and Jonathan Rosenbaum (1991) [1983] *Midnight Movies* (New York: Da Capo).

Holderness, Graham (2005), "Animated icons: Narrative and liturgy in *The Passion of the Christ,*" *Literature and Theology*, 19(4), 384–401.

Holthof, Marc (1980), "It's alive," *Andere Sinema*, 21: 14–17.

Hollows, Joanne (2003), "The masculinity of cult," in Mark Jancovich et al. (eds), *Defining Cult Movies: The Cultural Politics of Oppositional Taste* (Manchester: Manchester University Press), 35–53.

Horak, Jan-Christopher (1995), "The first American film avant-garde, 1919–1945" in Jan-Christopher Horak (ed.), *Lovers of Cinema: The First American Film Avant-garde 1919–1945* (Madison, WI: University of Wisconsin Press), 14–66.

Horton, Donald and Richard Wohl (1956), "Mass communication and para-social interaction," republished online in *Participations* 3 (1) (2006) www.participations.org/volume%203/issue%201/3_01_hortonwohl.htm (accessed August 18, 2010).

Hoxter, Julian (2000), "Taking possession: Cult learning in *The Exorcist,*" in Graeme Harper and Xavier Mendik (eds), *Unruly Pleasures: The Cult Film and its Critics* (Guildford: FAB Press), 171–186.

Huag, K. (1996) "An interview with Kenneth Anger," *Wide Angle*, 18(4), 74–92.

Huffer, Ian (2007), "I wanted to be Rocky, but I also wanted to be his wife!': Heterosexuality and the (re)construction of gender in female film audiences' consumption of Sylvester Stallone,"*Participations* 4 (2), online at: www.participations.org/ (accessed August 18, 2010)

Hulme, John, and Michael Wexler (1996), *Baked Potatoes: A Pot Smoker's Guide to Film and Video* (New York: Main Street).

Hunt, Leon (1998), *British Low Culture: From Safari Suits to Sexploitation* (London: Routledge).

Hunt, Leon (2000). "Han's Island revisited: *Enter the Dragon* as a transnational cult film," in Xavier Mendik and Graeme Harper (eds), *Unruly Pleasures: The Cult Film and its Critics* (Guildford: FAB Press), 75–85.

Hunt, Nathan (2003), "The importance of trivia: Ownership, exclusion and authority in science fiction fandom," in Mark Jancovich et al. (eds), *Defining Cult Movies: The Cultural Politics of Oppositional Taste* (Manchester: Manchester University Press), 185–201.

Hunter, I.Q. (2000), "Beaver Las Vegas: A fan boy's defence of showgirls," in Xavier Mendik and Graeme Harper (eds), *Unruly Pleasures: The Cult Film and its Critics* (Guildford: FAB Press), 189–201.

Hunter, I.Q. (2006), "Tolkien dirty," in Ernest Mathijs (ed.), *The Lord of the Rings: Popular Culture in Global Context* (London: Wallflower Press), 317–333.

Hunter, Russ (2009), *The Cross-Cultural Reception of Dario Argento* (PhD thesis, University of Wales, Aberystwyth).

Hunter, Russ (2010), "'Didn't you used to be Dario Argento?': The cult reception of Dario Argento," in William Hope (ed.), *Italian Film Directors in the New Millennium* (Cambridge: Cambridge Scholars Press), 63–74.

Hutchings, Peter (2003), "The Argento effect," in Mark Jancovich et al. (eds), *Defining Cult Movies: The Cultural Politics of Oppositional Taste* (Manchester: Manchester University Press), 127–141.

Iampolski, Mikhail (1998), *The Memory of Tiresias: Intertextuality and Film* (Berkeley, CA: University of California Press).

Imanjaya, Ekky (2009), "The other side of Indonesia: New Order's Indonesian exploitation cinema as cult films," paper presented at the B for Bad Cinema Conference (Monash University, Melbourne, April, 15–17).

Isenberg, Noah (2004), "Perennial detour: The cinema of Edgar G. Ulmer and the experience of exile," *Cinema Journal* 43(2), 3–25.

Jameson, Frederik (1983), "Postmodernism and consumer capitalism," in Hal Foster (ed.), *The Anti-Aesthetic: Essays on Postmodern Culture* (Port Townsend, WA: Bay Press).

Jäckel, Anne (2003), *European Film Industries* (London: British Film Institute).

Jancovich, Mark (1996), *Rational Fears: American Horror in the 1950s* (Manchester: Manchester University Press).

Jancovich, Mark (2002), "Cult fictions: Cult movies, subcultural capital and the production of cultural distinctions," *Cultural Studies*, 16(2), 306–322.

Jancovich, Mark (2009), "Shadows and bogeymen: Horror, stylization and the critical reception of Orson Welles during the 1940s," *Participations*, 6(1), online at: www.participations.org/Volume%206/Issue%201/jancovich.htm (accessed November 18, 2010).

Jancovich, Mark, Lucy Faire and Sarah Stubbings (2003), *The Place of the Audience: Cultural Geographies of Film Consumption* (London: British Film Institute).

Jancovich, Mark, Antonio Lázaro Reboll, Julian Stringer and Andrew Willis (2003a) "Introduction," in Mark Jancovich et al. (eds), *Defining Cult Movies: The Cultural Politics of Oppositional Taste* (Manchester: Manchester University Press), 1–13.

Jancovich, Mark, Antonio Lázaro Reboll, Julian Stringer, and Andy Willis (eds) (2003b) *Defining Cult Movies: The Cultural Politics of Oppositional Taste* (Manchester: Manchester University Press).

Jarvis, Brian (2007), "Monsters Inc.: Serial killers and consumer culture," *Crime, Media, Culture*, 3(3), 326–344.

Jenkins, Henry (1992), *Textual Poachers: Television Fans and Participatory Culture* (London: Routledge).

Jenkins, Henry (2002), "Interactive audiences? The collective intelligence of media fans," online at: http://web.mit.edu/cms/People/henry3/collective%20intelligence.html (accessed November 18, 2010)

Jenkins, Henry (2003), "Quentin Tarantino's Star Wars? Digital cinema, media convergence, and participatory culture," online at: http://web.mit.edu/cms/People/henry3/starwars.html (accessed November 18, 2010).

Jenkins, Henry (2006), *Convergence Culture: Where Old and New Media Collide* (New York: New York University Press).

Jennings, David (2007), *Net, Blogs and Rock 'n' Roll* (London: Nicholas Brealey).

Jennings, Wade (1991), "The Star as Cult Icon: Judy Garland," in J.P. Telotte (ed.), *The Cult Film Experience: Beyond all Reason* (Austin, TX: University of Texas Press), 90–101.

Jerslev, Anne (1992), "Semiotics by instinct: 'Cult film' as a signifying practice between film and audience," in Michael Skovmand and Kim Schroder (eds), *Media Cultures: Reappraising Transnational Media* (London: Routledge), 181–198.

Joly-Corcoran, Marc (2009), "*The Matrix*: Cult Fandom, Neo, et l'affect adolescent," in Jocelyn Lachance, Hugues Paris and Sébastien Dupont (eds), *Films Cultes et Culte du Film chez les Jeunes* (Québec: Presses de l'Université Laval), 123–130.

Kael, Pauline (1961), "Fantasies of the art-house audience," *Sight and Sound*, 31(1), 4–9; reprinted in *I Lost it at the Movies* (Boston: Little Brown, 1965), 31–44.

Kael, Pauline (1969), "Trash, art, and the movies," *Harper's Magazine*, February, 65–83.

Karpovich, Angelina (2007), *Hyperactive Audiences: Media Fandom Online* (PhD thesis, Aberystwyth University).

Kaufman, Gerald (1994), *Meet me in St. Louis* (London: British Film Institute).

Kawin, Bruce (1991), "After midnight," in J.P. Telotte (ed.), *The Cult Film Experience: Beyond all Reason* (Austin, TX: University of Texas Press), 18–25.

Kawin, Bruce (1992), *How Movies Work* (Berkeley, CA: University of California Press).

Keesey, Pam (2003), "Madmen, visionaries and freaks: The films of Alejandro Jodorowsky," in Steven Jay Schneider (ed.), *Fear without Frontiers: Horror Cinema across the Globe* (Godalming: FAB Press), 15–25.

Kelman, Ken (1970), "Smith myth," in P. Adams Sitney (ed.), *Film Culture Reader* (New York: Cooper Square Press), 280–284.

Kent, Stephen E. (2001), *From Slogans to Mantras: Social Protest and Religious Conversion in the Late Vietnam Era* (Syracuse, NY: Syracuse University Press).

Kerekes, David, and David Slater (2000), *See No Evil: Banned Films and Video Controversy* (Manchester: Critical Vision).

Kerényi, Karl (1976), *Dionysos: Archetypical Image of Indestructible Life* (Princeton, NJ: Princeton University Press).

Kermode, Mark (1995), "Out on the edge: Interview with John Waters," *Index on Censorship* 6 (June), 10–19.

Kermode, Mark (2001), "I was a teenage horror fan: or, how I learned to stop worrying and love Linda Blair," in Martin Barker and Julian Petley (eds), *Ill Effects: The Media/Violence Debate* (2nd edn; London: Routledge), 126–134.

Kern, Stephen (1983), *The Culture of Time and Space, 1880–1918* (Cambridge, MA: Harvard University Press).

Kerr, Peter (1984), "Cable TV notes: Mini-series and comedies kick off the new season," *New York Times* (Section 2), 28.

Kinder, Marsha (1977), "Reflections on 'Jeanne Dielman'," *Film Quarterly*, 30(4), 2–8.

King, Geoff (2007), *Donnie Darko* (London: Wallflower Press).

King, Stephen (1981), *Danse Macabre* (New York: Everest House).

Kinkade, Patrick T., and Michael A. Katovich (1992), "Toward a sociology of cult films: Reading *Rocky Horror*," *Sociological Quarterly*, 33(2), 191–209.

Kinski, Klaus (1989), *All I Need Is Love* (London: Random House).

Klinger, Barbara (1989), "Digressions at the cinema: Reception and mass culture," *Cinema Journal*, 28(4), 3–18.

Klinger, Barbara (1994), *Melodrama and Meaning: History, Culture and the Films of Douglas Sirk* (Bloomington, IN: Indiana University Press).

Klinger, Barbara (1997), "Film history: Terminable and interminable: Recovering the past in reception studies," *Screen* 38(2), 107–128.

Klinger, Barbara (2010a), "Contraband cinema: Piracy, *Titanic*, and Central Asia," *Cinema Journal* 49(2), 106–124.

Klinger, Barbara (2010b), "Becoming cult: *The Big Lebowski*, replay culture and male fans," *Screen* 51(1), 1–20.

Knee, Adam (2005), "Thailand haunted: The power of the past in the contemporary Thai horror film," in Steven Jay Schneider and Tony Williams (eds), *Horror International* (Detroit: Wayne State University Press), 141–161.

Koehler, Robert (2009), "Cinephilia and film festivals," in Richard Porton (ed.), *Dekalog 3: On Film Festivals* (London: Wallflower Press), 81–97.

Koller, Michael (2001), "Un Chien Andalou," *Senses of Cinema*, 12 (February–March), online at: http://archive.sensesofcinema.com/contents/cteq/01/12/chien.html (accessed November 18, 2010).

Koven, Mikel (2006), *La Dolce Morte: The Italian Giallo Film* (Metuchen: Scarecrow Press).

Kracauer, Siegfried (1926), "The cult of distraction," from *The Mass Ornament* (Cambridge, MA: Harvard University Press), 323–328.

Kracauer, Siegfried (1959), *From Caligari to Hitler* (Princeton, NJ: Princeton University Press).

Kreitman, Norman (2006), "The varieties of aesthetic disinterestedness," *Contemporary Aesthetics*, 4, online at: www.contempaesthetics.org/newvolume/pages/article.php?articleID=390 (accessed August 10, 2010).

Kristeva, Julia (1974), *La Révolution du Langage Poétique* (Paris: Éditions du Seuil).

Kristeva, Julia (1982), *The Powers of Horror: An Essay on Abjection* (New York: Columbia University Press).

Kultermann, Udo (1970), *Leben und Kunst: zur Funktion der Intermedia* (Tübingen: Ernst Wasmuth Verlag).

Kyrou, Ado (2000) [1963], "The marvelous is popular," in Paul Hammond (ed.), *The Shadow and its Shadow: Surrealist Writing on the Cinema* (San Francisco: City Lights Books), 68–71.

Lachman, Gary (2001). *Turn off your Mind: The Mystic Sixties and the Dark Side of the Age of Aquarius* (New York: Disinformation).

Lafond, Frank (2004), "Man Bites Dog," in Ernest Mathijs (ed.), *The Cinema of the Low Countries* (London: Wallflower Press), 215–222.

Lamarre, Thomas (2009), *Anime Machine: A Media Theory of Animation* (Minneapolis: University of Minnesota Press).

Lane, Christina (2000), *Feminist Hollywood: From Born in Flames to Point Break* (Detroit: Wayne State University Press).

Lapper, Craig (2005), "All fixed up: The story of 'trash' and the BBFC" (booklet accompanying DVD box set *Three Films Written and Directed by Paul Morrissey)* (London: Tartan).

Larsen, Robert and Beth A. Haller (2002). "Public reception of real disability: The case of freaks," *Journal of Popular Film and Television* 29(4), 164–172.

Lavery, David (1991), "Gnosticism and the cult film," in J.P. Telotte (ed.), *The Cult Film Experience* (Austin, TX: University of Texas Press), 187–199.

Lay, Samantha (2007), "Audiences across the divide: Game to film adaptation and the case of *Resident Evil*," *Participations* 4(2), online at: www.participations.org/ (accessed August 18, 2010).

Lebbing, Mike, and Bart Van Der Put (2000), "Italian drug cinema: A selective overview," in Jack Stevenson (ed.), *Addicted: The Myth and Menace of Drugs in Film* (New York: Creation Books), 151–165.

Le Breton, David (2009), "Sur Thirteen: Adolescence et Cinéma," in Jocelyn Lachance, Hugues Paris and Sébastien Dupont (eds), *Films Cultes et Culte du Film chez les Jeunes* (Québec: Presses de l'Université Laval), 137–146.

Le Cain, Maximilian (2002a) "Jean Vigo," *Senses of Cinema*, 21 (July–August), online at: http://archive.sensesofcinema.com/contents/directors/02/vigo.html (accessed November 18, 2010)

Le Cain, Maximilian (2002b) "Fresh blood: *Baise-moi*," *Senses of Cinema*, 22(2), online at: http://archive.sensesofcinema.com/contents/02/22/baise-moi_max.html (accessed August 18, 2010)

Lee, David (1992), *Competing Discourses: Perspective and Ideology in Language* (London: Longman).

Leeson, Peter (2009), *The Invisible Hook: The Hidden Economics of Pirates* (Princeton, NJ: Princeton University Press).

Le Guern, Philippe (2004) "Toward a constructivist approach to media cults," in Sara Gwenllian Jones and Roberta E. Pearson (eds), *Cult Television* (Minneapolis: University of Minnesota Press), 3–26.

Leiva, Antonio Dominguez (2008), "Sex Heil! Apogée et chute du sado-masochisme psychotronique," in D. Leiva and S. Hubier (eds), *Délicieux Supplices et cruauté en Occident* (Dijon: Editions du murmure).

Lichtenfeld, Eric (2007), *Action Speaks Louder: Violence, Spectacle and the American Action Movie* (Middletown, CT: Wesleyan University Press).

Lippit, Akira Mizuta, Noel Burch, Chon Noriega et al. (2003), "Round table: *Showgirls*," *Film Quarterly*, 56(3), 32–46.

LoBrutto, Vincent (1999), *Stanley Kubrick: A Biography* (Cambridge, MA: Da Capo).

Locks, Adam (2010), "Ripped mass monsters: Professional bodybuilding and the cult(ivation) of the freak," paper presented at Cine Excess IV, London, April 2010.

Loudermilk, A. (2003), "Eating 'dawn' in the dark: zombie desire and commodified identity in George Romer's *Dawn of the Dead*," *Journal of Consumer Culture*, 3, 83–108.

Lucas, Tim (2007), *Mario Bava: All the Colors of the Dark* (New York: Video Watchdog).

Lucas, Tim (2008), *Videodrome* (Centipede Press).

Lucas, Tim (2010), "Henri-Georges Clouzot's Inferno," *Video Watchdog* (No. 157, July/August), 70–73.

Luckett, Moya (2003), "Sexploitation as feminine territory: the Films of Doris Wishman," in Mark Jancovich et al. (eds), *Defining Cult Movies: The Cultural Politics of Oppositional Taste* (Manchester: Manchester University Press), 142–156.

MacCormack, Patricia (2004), "Masochistic cinesexuality: The many deaths of Giovanni Lombardo Radice," in

Ernest Mathijs and Xavier Mendik (eds), *Alternative Europe: Eurotrash and Exploitation Cinema since 1945* (London: Wallflower Press), 106–116.

Macdonald, Susan (1969), "Pasolini: Rebellion, art and a new society," *Screen* 10: 19–34.

Macias, Patrick (2001), *Tokyoscope: The Japanese Cult Film Companion* (Viz Media LCC).

MacKenzie, Scott (2002), "*Baise-moi*, feminist cinemas and the censorship controversy," *Screen* 43(3), 315–324.

MacKinnon, Kenneth (2005) "The mainstream AIDS movie prior to the 1990s," in Graeme Harper and Andrew Moor (eds), *Signs of Life: Medicine and Cinema* (London: Wallflower Press), 33–44.

Macor, Alison (2010), *Chainsaws, Slackers and Spy Kids* (Austin, TX: University of Texas Press).

Macpherson, Kenneth (1930), "As is," *Close Up*, 6(1), 2.

Maffesoli, Michel (1993a) [1985] *The Shadow of Dionysus: A Contribution to the Sociology of the Orgy* (New York: State University of New York Press).

Maffesoli, Michel (1993b) , "The social ambience," *Current Sociology*, 41(2), 7–15.

Maffesoli, Michel (1993c) , "The imaginary and the sacred in Durkheim's sociology," *Current Sociology*, 41(3),59–67.

Maffesoli, Michael (1996a) [1988] *The Time of the Tribes: The Decline of Individualism in Mass Society* (London: Sage Publications).

Maffesoli, Michel (1996b) *The Contemplation of the World: Figures of Community Style* (Minneapolis: University of Minnesota Press).

Maffesoli, Michel (2005), "Dionysus and the ideals of 1968," in Alan de Sica and Stephen Turner (eds), *The Disobedient Generation: Social Theorists in the Sixties* (Chicago: University of Chicago Press), 196–204.

Maffesoli, Michel (2007), "Tribal aesthetic," in Bernard Cova, Robert Kosinets and Avi Shankar (eds), *Consumer Tribes* (Amsterdam: Elsevier), 27–34.

Magiels, Willy (2004), "Festival fantastische film in Antwerpen," in Willy Magiels and Robbe De Hert (eds), *Magie van de Cinema* (Antwerp: Facet), 161–162.

Maland, Charles (2007), "Movies and American culture in the Annus Mirabilis," in Ina Rae Hark (ed.), *American Cinema in the 1930s* (Piscataway, NJ: Rutgers University Press), 227–252.

Maltby, Richard (1996), "A brief romantic interlude: Dick and Jane go to 3½ seconds of the classical Hollywood cinema," in David Bordwell and Noel Carroll (eds), *Post-Theory: Reconstructing Film Studies* (Madison, WI: University of Wisconsin Press), 434–459.

Mannheim, Karl (1936), *Ideology and Utopia* (London: Routledge).

Marchetti, Gina (1985), "Subcultural studies and the film audience: Rethinking the film viewing context," in Bruce Austin (ed.), *Current Research in Film, Volume 2* (Norwood, NJ: Ablex), 61–79.

Marcuse, Herbert (1964), *One-Dimensional Man* (Boston: Beacon Press).

Marcuse, Herbert (1966), *Eros and Civilization* (London: Routledge).

Marx, Karl (1976), "The fetishism of the commodity and its secret," in *Capital (Volume 1)* (London: Penguin), 163–177.

Martin, Adrian (2008), "What's cult got to do with it? In defense of cinephile elitism," *Cineaste*, 34(1), 39–42.

Mathijs, Ernest (2002), "The wonderfully scary monster and the international reception of horror: Ridley Scott's Hannibal," *Kinoeye* 2(19), online at: www.kinoeye.org/ (accessed August 10, 2010).

Mathijs, Ernest (2003a). "The making of a cult reputation: Topicality and controversy in the critical reception of Shivers," in Mark Jancovich et al. (eds), *Defining Cult Movies: The Cultural Politics of Oppositional Taste* (Manchester: Manchester University Press), 109–126.

Mathijs, Ernest (2003b) , "AIDS references in the critical reception of David Cronenberg: It may not be such a bad disease after all," *Cinema Journal*, 42(4), 29–45.

Mathijs, Ernest (2004), "Daughters of Darkness," in *The Cinema of the Low Countries* (London: Wallflower Press), 97–108.

Mathijs, Ernest (2005a) Man Bites Dog and the critical reception of Belgian horror (in) cinema," in Steven Jay Schneider and Tony Williams (eds), *Horror International* (Detroit: Wayne State University Presss), 315–335.

Mathijs, Ernest (2005b) , "Bad reputations: The reception of trash cinema," *Screen*, 46(4), 451–472.

Mathijs, Ernest (2006), "To die for: The fan and the reception of sexuality and horror in early 1980s German cinema," in Steffen Hantke (ed.), *Caligari's Heirs: The German Cinema of Fear after 1945* (Lanham, MD: Scarecrow Press), 129–144.

Mathijs, Ernest (2007), "Tijd, Cultcinema en de jaren Tachtig: *Back to the Future* en *Peggy Sue Got Married* via *Donnie Darko* en *It's a Wonderful Life*,' in Daniel Biltereyst and Christel Stalpaert (eds), *Filmsporen, Opstellen over film, Verleden en Geheugen* (Ghent: Academia Press), 180–198.

Mathijs, Ernest (2008), *The Cinema of David Cronenberg: From Baron of Blood to Cultural Hero* (London: Wallflower Press).

Mathijs, Ernest (2009), "Threat or treat: Film, television and the ritual of Halloween," *Flow TV* 11(1), online at: http://flowtv.org/?p=4486 (accessed August 18, 2010)

Mathijs, Ernest (2010a) "Television and the yuletide cult," *Flow TV* 11(5), online at: http://flowtv.org/?p=4683 (accessed August 18, 2010)

Mathijs, Ernest (2010b) , "Time wasted," *FlowTV*, 11(10) (March 29), online at: http://flowtv.org/2010/03/time-wasted-ernest-mathijs-the-university-of-british-columbia/ (accessed August 18, 2010)

Mathijs, Ernest (2010c) , "They're here! Special effects in horror cinema of the 1970s and 1980s," in Ian Conrich (ed.), *Horror Zone, the Cultural Experience of Contemporary Horror Cinema* (London: IB Tauris), 153–172.

Mathijs, Ernest (2011a) "Referential acting and the ensemble cast," *Screen* 52(1), forthcoming.

Mathijs, Ernest (2011b) "From being to acting: Performance in cult cinema," in Aaron Taylor (ed.), *Playing to the Critics: Film Acting and Theory* (Detroit: Wayne State University Press, forthcoming).

Mathijs, Ernest, and Xavier Mendik (eds) (2004), *Alternative Europe: Eurotrash and Exploitation Cinema since 1945* (London: Wallflower Press).

Mathijs, Ernest, and Xavier Mendik (eds) (2008a) *The Cult Film Reader* (New York: Open University Press).

Mathijs, Ernest, and Xavier Mendik (2008b) "What is cult film?," in Ernest Mathijs and Xavier Mendik (eds), *The Cult Film Reader* (New York: Open University Press), 1–11.

Mathijs, Ernest and Bert Mosselmans (2000), "Mimesis and the representation of reality: A historical world view," *Foundations of Science* 5(1), 61–102.

McCarty, John (ed.) (1995), *The Sleaze Merchants: Adventures in Exploitation Filmmaking* (New York: St. Martin's Press).

McCarthy, Soren (2003), *Cult Movies in Sixty Seconds* (London: Fusion Press).

McCarthy, Todd and Charles Flynn (1975), "Interview: Herschell Gordon Lewis," in Todd McCarthy and Charles Flynn (eds), *Kings of the Bs: Working within the Hollywood System* (New York: E.P. Dutton & Co.), 347–360.

McKelly, James (2005), "Youth cinema and the culture of rebellion: *Heathers* and the *Rebel* archetype," in J. David Slocum (ed.), *Rebel without a Cause: Approaches to a Maverick Masterwork* (New York: SUNY Press), 209–216.

McRobbie, Angela and Jenny Garber (1991), "Girls and subcultures," in Angela McRobbie (ed.), *Feminism and Youth Culture* (Basingstoke: Macmillan), 1–15.

McRoy, Jay (2010), "Parts is parts: Pornography, splatter films and the politics of corporeal disintegration," in Ian Conrich (ed.), *Horror Zone, the Cultural Experience of Contemporary Horror Cinema* (London: IB Tauris), 191–204.

Medved, Harry, and Michael Medved (1980), *The Golden Turkey Awards* (London: Harper Collins).

Medved, Michael, Harry Medved and Randy Dreyfuss (1978), *The Fifty Worst Movies of all Time* (New York: Putnam).

Meehan, Eileen R. (1991), " 'Holy commodity fetish, Batman!': The political economy of a commercial intertext," in Roberta E. Pearson and William Uricchio (eds), *The Many Lives of the Batman* (New York: Routledge), 47–65.

Meehan, Eileen and Deborah Tudor (2010), "Star Trek's prime directive: To exploit and protect," paper presented at the Annual Society for Cinema and Media Studies, Los Angeles, 20 March.

Mendik, Xavier (2000), *Tenebrae* (London: Flicks Books).

Mendik, Xavier, and Graeme Harper (eds) (2000a) *Unruly Pleasures: The Cult Film and its Critics* (Godalming: FAB Press).

Mendik, Xavier, and Harper, Graeme (2000b) "The chaotic text and the Sadean audience: Narrative transgressions of a contemporary cult film," in Xavier Mendik and Graeme Harper (eds), *Unruly Pleasures: The Cult Film and its Critics* (Guildford: FAB Press), 235–249.

Mendik, Xavier, and Steven Jay Schneider (2002), "A tasteless art: Waters, Kaufman and the pursuit of 'pure' gross-out," in Xavier Mendik and Steven Jay Schneider (eds), *Underground USA: Filmmaking beyond the Hollywood Canon* (London: Wallflower Press), 204–220.

Mendik, Xavier (2004), "Black sex, bad sex: Monstrous ethnicity in the Black Emanuelle films," in Ernest Mathijs and Xavier Mendik (eds), *Alternative Europe: Eurotrash and Exploitation Cinema since 1945* (London: Wallflower Press), 146–159.

Mes, Tom (2004), *Agitator: The Films of Takashi Miike* (Guildford: FAB Press).

Metz, Walter (2003), "John Waters goes to Hollywood: A poststructuralist authorship study," in David A. Gerstner and Janet Staiger (eds), *Authorship and Film* (New York: Routledge).

Meyrowitz, Joshua (2002), "The majority cult: Love and grief for media friends," in Philippe Le Guern (ed.), *Les cultes médiatiques: culture fan et oeuvres cultes* (Rennes: Presses Universitaires Rennes), 133–162.

Mikalson, John (2010), *Ancient Greek Religion* (2nd edn; Oxford: Wiley-Blackwell).

Miller, Daniel (2010), *Stuff* (Cambridge: Polity Press).

Modleski, Tania (2007), "Women's cinema as counter-phobic cinema: Doris Wishman as the last auteur," in Jeffrey Sconce (ed.), *Sleaze Artists: Cinema at the Margins of Taste, Style and Politics* (Durham: Duke University Press), 47–70.

Moine, Raphaelle (2008), *Cinema Genre* (Oxford: Wiley-Blackwell).

Morris, Meaghan, Siu Leung Li and Stephen Chan Ching-kiu (eds) (2005), *Hong Kong Connections: Transnational Imagination in Action Cinema* (Durham, NC: Duke University Press; Hong Kong: Hong Kong University Press).

Mulvey, Laura (1975), "Visual pleasure and narrative cinema," *Screen* 16(3), 6–18.

Mulvey, Laura (2006), *Death 24x a Second: Stillness and the Moving Image* (London: Reaktion).

Nakahara, Tamao (2004), "Barred nuns: Italian nunsploitation films," in Ernest Mathijs and Xavier Mendik (eds), *Alternative Europe: Eurotrash and Exploitation Cinema since 1945* (London: Wallflower Press), 124–133.

Nakahara, Tamao (2010), "Making up monsters: Set and costume design in horror films," in Ian Conrich (ed.), *Horror Zone, the Cultural Experience of Contemporary Horror Cinema* (London: IB Tauris), 139–152.

Napier, Susan (2006), "The world of anime fandom in America," in Frenchy Lunning (ed.), *Emerging Worlds of Anime and Manga (Mechademia 1)* (Minneapolis: University of Minnesota Press), 47–64.

Napier, Susan (2007), *From Impressionism to Anime: Japan as Fantasy and Fan Cult in the Mind of the West* (Basingstoke: Palgrave Macmillan).

Ndalianis, Angela (1994), "Muscles, hybrids and new bad futures," *World Art*, 1(1), 76–81.

Ndalianis, Angela (1995), "Muscle, excess and rupture: Female body building and gender construction," *Media Information Australia*, 75, February: 13–23.

Needham, Gary (2002) "Playing with genre: An introduction to the Italian Giallo," in *Kinoeye* 2(11), online at: www.kinoeye.org/ (accessed August 18, 2010).

Needham, Gary (2006), "Japanese cinema and orientalism," in Dimitris Eleftheriotis and Gary Needham (eds), *Asian Cinemas: A Reader and Guide* (Honolulu: University of Hawaii Press), 8–16.

Negra, Diane (1999), "Titanic, survivalism and the millennial myth," in Kevin Sandler and Gaylyn Studlar (eds), *Titanic: Anatomy of a Blockbuster* (Piscataway, NJ: Rutgers University Press), 220–238.

New American Cinema Group, The (2000), "First Statement of the New American Cinema Group," in P. Adams Sitney (ed.), *Film Culture Reader* (New York: Cooper Square Press 79–83. Originally published in *Film Culture*, 22–23, Summer 1961.

New Line Cinema (1978), *New Line Cinema 1978 Catalogue* (New York: New Line Cinema).

Newitz, Annalee, (1995), "Magical girls and atomic bomb sperm: Japanese animation in America," *Film Quarterly*, 49(1), 2–15.

Nietzsche, Friedrich, (1968), *Twilight of the Idols/The Anti-Christ* (trans. R.J. Hollingdale; Harmondsworth: Penguin).

Noriega, Chon, (1987), "Godzilla and the Japanese nightmare: When *Them* is U.S.," *Cinema Journal*, 27(1),63–77.

O'Pray, Michael, (2003), *Avant-garde Film: Forms, Themes and Passions* (London: Wallflower).

Orbaugh, Sharalyn, (2002), "Sex and the single cyborg: Japanese pop culture experiments in subjectivity," *Science Fiction Studies* 29(3), 436–452.

O'Toole, Lawrence, (1979), "The cult of horror," *Maclean's*, 16 July, 46–47, 49–50.

Otto, Walter, (1965), *Dionysus: Myth and Cult* (Bloomington, IN: Indiana University Press).

Paszylk, Bartlomiej, (2009), *The Pleasure and Pain of Cult Horror Films* (Jefferson: McFarland).

Pearson, Michelle, (2002), *Special Effects: Still in Search of Wonder* (New York: Columbia University Press).

Peary, Danny, (1981), *Cult Movies: The Classics, The Sleepers, The Weird and the Wonderful* (New York: Gramercy).

Peary, Danny, (1983), *Cult Movies II* (New York: Delta Books).

Peary, Danny, (1989) *Cult Movies III* (London: Sidgwick and Jackson).

Perlmutter, Dawn, (1999), "The sacrificial aesthetic: Blood rituals from art to murder," *Anthropoetics*, 5(2), online at: www.anthropoetics.ucla.edu/ap0502/blood.htm (accessed November 16, 2010).

Peterson, Richard, (1992), "Understanding audience segmentation: From elite and mass to omnivore and univore," *Poetics*, 21, 243–258.

Pitzl-Waters, Jason, (2007), "Musical influence of The Wicker Man soundtrack," *A Darker Shade of Pagan* (June 22), online at: www.adarkershadeofpagan.com/labels/The%20Wicker%20Man.html (accessed November 18, 2010).

Plunka, Gene, (2005), "John Guare and the popular culture hype of celebrity status," in David Krasner, (ed.), *A Companion to Twentieth Century American Drama* (Oxford: Blackwell), 352–369.

Polan, Dana, (1978), "A Brechtian cinema? Towards a politics of self-reflexive film," *Jump Cut* 17.

Pomerance, Murray, (2007), *The Horse Who Drank the Sky: Film Experience beyond Narrative and Theory* (Piscataway, NJ: Rutgers University Press).

Potamkin, Harry Allan, (2008), "Film cults," in Ernest Mathijs and Xavier Mendik (eds), *The Cult Film Reader*

(Maidenhead: Open University Press). Originally published in Modern Thinker and Author's Review, November 1933.

Powell, Anna, (1994), Blood on the borders – *Near Dark* and *Blue Steel*," *Screen* 35(2), 136–156.

Puchalski, Steven, (1996), *Slimetime: A Guide to Sleazy, Mindless Movies* (Manchester: Headpress).

Puchalski, Steven, (2002), *Slimetime: A Guide to Sleazy, Mindless Movies* (rev. and updated edn; Manchester: Headpress).

Ragas, Matthew, (2002), *The Power of Cult Branding* (New York: Random House).

Randall, Richard, (1976), "Censorship from The Miracle to Deep Throat," in Tino Balio (ed.), *The American Film Industry* (Madison, WI: University of Wisconsin Press), 432–457.

Rayns, Tony, (2009), "The Wild Bunch: Nobuo Nakagawa," *Sight and Sound* 19(9), 31–32.

Read, Jacinda, (2003), "The cult of masculinity: From fan-boys to academic bad boys," in Mark Jancovich et al. (eds), *Defining Cult Movies: The Cultural Politics of Oppositional Taste* (Manchester: Manchester University Press), 54–70.

Reboll, Antonio Lazaro (2009), " 'Perversa América Latina': The reception of Latin American exploitation cinemas in Spanish subcultures," in Victoria Ruétalo and Dolores Tierney (eds), *Latsploitation, Latin America, and Exploitation Cinema* (London: Routledge), 37–54.

Redmond, Sean and Deborah Jermyn (eds), (2003) *The Cinema of Kathryn Bigelow, Hollywood Transgressor* (London: Wallflower Press).

Reid, Craig (1994), "Fighting without fighting: Film action fight choreography," *Film Quarterly* 47(2), 30–35.

Reynaud, Bérénice (2002), "*Baise-moi* – A personal angry-yet-feminist reaction," *Senses of Cinema* 2(22), online at: http://archive.sensesofcinema.com/contents/02/22/baise–moi.html (accessed August 18, 2010)

Reynolds, Dawn (2007), "Disability and BDSM: Bob Flanagan and the case for sexual rights," *Sexuality Research and Social Policy*, 4(1), 40–52.

Rich, B. Ruby (1998), "Lady killers: A question of silence," in *Chick Flicks: Theories and Memories of the Feminist Film Movement* (Durham, NC: Duke University Press), 319–325.

Rich, B. Ruby (1999), "Lesbian and gay film festivals' *GLQ: A Journal of Lesbian and Gay Studies*, 5: 73–93.

Richardson, Niall (2009), *The Queer Cinema of Derek Jarman* (London: IB Tauris).

Robertson, William Preston (2006), "Hey, nice marmot," *The Guardian* Culture Section, online at: http://arts.guardian.co.uk/filmandmusic/story/0,1920449,00.html (accessed June 2008)

Rombes, Nicholas (2005), "The rebirth of the author," *Ctheory.net* (10 June), online at: www.ctheory.net/articles.aspx?id=480 (accessed November 18, 2010).

Romney, Jonathan (2007), "*La Jetée:* Unchained melody," *The Criterion Collection:* www.criterion.com/current/posts/485 (accessed November 18, 2010).

Rosenbaum, Jonathan (1980), "Le Rocky Horror Picture Show: Cult-film," *Cahiers du cinema*, 307: 33–38.

Ross, Andrew (1989), *No Respect: Intellectuals and Popular Culture* (New York: Routledge).

Ross, Andrew (2008), "Uses of camp," in Ernest Mathijs and Xavier Mendik (eds), *The Cult Film Reader* (New York: Open University Press), 53–66.

Ross, Jonathan (1993), *The Incredibly Strange Film Book* (London: Simon & Schuster).

Ross, Karen, and Virginia Nightingale (2003), *Media Audiences: New Perspectives* (Maidenhead: Open University Press).

Rowe, Carel (1974), "Illuminating Lucifer," *Film Quarterly*, 27(4), 24–33.

Ruh, Brian (2004). *Stray Dog of Anime: The Films of Mamoru Oshi* (Basingstoke: Palgrave Macmillan).

Ryall, Tom (1997), "Genre and Hollywood," in John Hill and Pamela Church Gibson (eds), *The Oxford Guide to Film Studies* (Oxford: Oxford University Press).

Said, Edward (1978), *Orientalism* (New York: Vintage Books).

Samuels, Stuart (1983), *Midnight Movies* (New York: Macmillan).

Sandahl, Carrie (2000), "Bob Flanagan: Taking it like a man," *Journal of Dramatic Theory and Criticism*, 15(1), 97–103.

Sandahl, Carrie and Philip Auslander (eds) (2005), *Bodies in Commotion: Disability and Performance* (Ann Arbor, MI: University of Michigan Press).

Sandell, Jillian (1996), "The spectacle of male intimacy in the films of John Woo," *Film Quarterly*, 49(4), 23–34.

Sandler, Kevin and Gaylyn Studlar (eds) (1999), *Titanic: Anatomy of a Blockbuster* (Piscataway, NJ: Rutgers University Press).

Sandler, Kevin (2001), "The naked truth: Showgirls and the fate of the X/NC-17 Rating," *Cinema Journal*, 40(3), 69–93.

Sandvoss, Cornel (2005), *Fans: The Mirror of Consumption* (Cambridge: Polity Press).

Sanjek, David (1990), "Fans' notes: The horror film fanzine," *Literature/Film Quarterly* 18(3), 150–160.

Sargeant, Jack (1999), *Deathtripping: The Cinema of Transgression* (London: Creation).

Sarris, Andrew (1962), "Notes on the auteur theory in 1962," Film Culture, 27. Reprinted in P. Adams

Sitney (ed.), *Film Culture Reader* (New York: Cooper Square Press, 2000), 121–135.

Sarris, Andrew (1970), *Confessions of a Cultist: On the Cinema 1955–1969* (New York: Simon & Schuster).

Schaefer, Eric (1999), *"Bold! Daring! Shocking! True!" A History of Exploitation Films, 1919–1959* (Durham, NC: Duke University Press).

Schaefer, Eric (2002), "Gauging a revolution: 16mm film and the rise of the pornographic feature," *Cinema Journal*, 41(3), 3–26.

Schneider, Steven Jay (ed.) (2003), *Fear without Frontiers: Horror Cinema across the Globe* (Godalming: FAB Press).

Schneider, Steven Jay (2006), "Movies and the march to war," in Wheeler Winston Dixon (ed.), *American Cinema of the 1940s* (Piscataway, NJ: Rutgers University Press), 74–93.

Schneider, Steven Jay and Tony Williams (eds) (2005), *Horror International* (Detroit: Wayne State University Press).

Schoell, William (1985), *Stay out of the Shower: 25 Years of Shocker Films* (New York: Dembner Books), 81–87.

Schreck, Nicolas (2002), "Atom age AntiChrist: Satanic cinema in the 1950s," in Jack Hunter (ed.), *The Bad Mirror: 19 Illustrated Features on Exploitation and Underground Cinema* (London: Creation Books), 249–260.

Sconce, Jeffrey (1995), "Trashing the academy: Taste, excess and an emerging politics of cinematic style," *Screen*, 36(4), 371–393.

Sconce, Jeffrey (2002), "Irony, nihilism and the new American 'smart' film," *Screen*, 43(4), 371–393.

Sconce, Jeffrey (ed.) (2007), *Sleaze Artists: Cinema at the Margins of Taste, Style and Politics* (Durham, NC: Duke University Press).

Selfe, Melanie (2008), "Inflected accounts and irreversible journeys," *Participations*, 5(1) Special Edition, online at: www.participations.org/ (accessed August 18, 2010).

Seltzer, Mark (1998), *Serial Killers: Death and Life in America's Wound Culture* (London: Routledge).

Sexton, Jamie (2006), "A cult film by proxy: Space Is the Place and the Sun Ra Mythos," *New Review of Film and Television Studies*, 4(3), 197–215.

Sexton, Jamie (2008a) *Alternative Film Culture in Inter-War Britain* (Exeter: Exeter University Press).

Sexton, Jamie (2008b), "Cult film: A critical symposium," *Cineaste* 34(1), online at: www.cineaste.com/articles/cult-film-a-critical-symposium (accessed August 18, 2010).

Sexton, Jamie (2011), "Cult cinema: From bad to good and back to 'bad' again," in Constantine Verevis, Claire Perkins and Alexia Kannas (eds), *B for Bad Cinema* (Detroit: Wayne State University Press).

Shary, Timothy (2005), "The Stark Screen Teen: Echoes of James Dean in Recent Young *Rebel* Roles,' in J. David Slocum (ed.) *Rebel without a Cause: Approaches to a Maverick Masterwork* (New York" SUNY Press).

Shaviro, Steven (2004), "The life, after death, of postmodern emotions," *Criticism*, 26(1), 125–141.

Shone, Tom (2004), *Blockbuster* (London: Simon & Schuster).

Siegel, Mark (1980), " 'The Rocky Horror Picture Show': More than a lip service," *Science Fiction Studies*, 7(3), 305–312.

Sims, Yvonne (2006), *Women of Blaxploitation* (Jefferson, NC: McFarland).

Skal, David (1993), *The Monster Show: A Cultural History of Horror* (Basingstoke: Macmillan).

Smith, Iain Robert (2010a) "You're really a miniature bond: Weng Weng and the transnational dimensions of cult fandom," paper presented at Cine Excess IV, London, April.

Smith, Iain Robert (2010b) "Spiderbabe," in Xavier Mendik (ed.), *Peepshows: Cult Film and the Cine-Erotic* (London Wallflower Press, forthcoming).

Smith, Jack (1962/3), "The perfect filmic appositeness of Maria Montez," *Film Culture*, 27 (Winter), 28–33.

Smith, Jacob (2007), "Sound and performance in Stephen Sayadian's Night Dreams and Café Flesh," *Velvet Light Trap*, 59, 15–29.

Smith, Jeff (1998), *The Sounds of Commerce: Marketing Popular Film Music* (New York: Columbia University Press).

Smith, Justin T. (2006), *Cult Films and Film Cults in British Cinema 1968–86* (PhD thesis, University of Portsmouth).

Smith, Justin (2010), *Withnail and Us: Cult Films and Film Cults in British Cinema* (London: IB Tauris).

Smith, Murray (2002), *Trainspotting* (London: British Film Institute).

Smoodin, Eric (2004), *Regarding Frank Capra: Audience, Celebrity, and American Film Studies, 1930–1960* (Durham, NC: Duke University Press).

Smythe, Dallas, Parker B. Lusk and Charles A. Lewis (1953), "Portrait of an art-theater audience," *The Quarterly of Film Radio and Television*, 8(1), 28–50.

Snelders, Stephen (2005), *The Devil's Anarchy* (New York: Autonomedia).

Sobchack, Vivian (1999), "Cities on the edge of time: The urban science-fiction film," in Annette Kuhn (ed.), *Alien Zone II: The Spaces of Science Fiction Cinema* (London: Verso), 123–143.

Sobchack, Vivian (2001), *Screening Space: The American Science Fiction Film* (Piscataway, NJ: Rutgers University Press).

Sobchack, Vivian (2004), *Carnal Thoughts: Embodiment and Moving Image Culture* (Berkeley, CA: University of California Press).

Sontag, Susan (2008), "Notes on camp," in Ernest Mathijs and Xavier Mendik (eds), *The Cult Film Reader* (New York: Open University Press), 41–52. Originally published in Susan Sontag, *Against Interpretation and Other Essays* (1964).

Sorfa, David (2000), "No spectators: Four films on ecstasy," in Jack Stevenson (ed.), *Addicted: The Myth and Menace of Drugs on Film* (New York: Creation Books), 258–262.

Springer, Claudia (2005), "In the shadow of *Rebel without a Cause*: The postcolonial rebel," in J. David Slocum (ed.), *Rebel without a Cause: Approaches to a Maverick Masterwork* (New York: SUNY Press).

Springer, Claudia (2007), *James Dean Transfigured: The Many Faces of Rebel Iconography* (Austin, TX: University of Texas Press).

Sragow, Michael (2008), "The invasion of the body snatchers," in David Sterritt and John Anderson (eds), *The B List* (Cambridge, MA: Da Capo Press), 77–78.

Staiger, Janet (1990), "Announcing wares, winning patrons, voicing ideals: Thinking about the history and theory of film advertising," *Cinema Journal*, 29(3), 3–31.

Staiger, Janet (1992), *Interpreting Films: Studies in the Historical Reception of American Cinema* (Princeton, NJ: Princeton University Press).

Staiger, Janet (1999), "Future noir: Contemporary representations of visionary cities," in Annette Kuhn (ed.), *Alien Zone II: The Spaces of Science Fiction Cinema* (London: Verso), 97–122.

Staiger, Janet (2000), *Perverse Spectators: The Practices of Film Reception* (New York: New York University Press).

Staiger, Janet (2005a) *Media Reception Studies* (New York: New York University Press).

Staiger, Janet (2005b) "Cabinets of transgression: Collecting and arranging Hollywood images," *Participations*, 1(3), online at: www.participations.org/volume%201/issue%203/1_03_staiger_article.htm#_ednref13 (accessed November 18, 2010).

Stam, Robert (1985), *Reflexivity in Film and Literature* (Ann Arbor, MI: UMI Research Press).

Stam, Robert (1992), *Reflexivity in Film and Literature* (repr. with new preface; New York: Columbia University Press).

Stam, Robert (1999), *Film Theory: An Introduction* (Oxford: Blackwell).

Stanfield, Peter (2008), "Cult film: A critical symposium," *Cineaste* 34(1), 49–50.

Stark, Rodney and William Sims Bainbridge (1985), *The Future of Religion: Secularization, Revival and Cult Formation* (Berkeley, CA: University of California Press).

Starks, Michael (1982), *Cocaine Fiends and Reefer Madness: An Illustrated History of Drugs in the Movies* (New York: Cornwall Books).

Stevenson, Jack (1996), *Desperate Visions: The Films of John Waters and the Kuchar Brothers* (London: Creation Books).

Stevenson, Jack (2000), "Highway to hell: The myth and menace of drugs in American cinema," in Jack Stevenson (ed.), *Addicted: The Myth and Menace of Drugs on Film* (New York: Creation Books), 11–62.

Stevenson, Jack (2003a) "A million frightened teenagers," in Stevenson, *Land of a Thousand Balconies: Discoveries and Confessions of a B-Movie Archaeologist* (Manchester: Headpress), 21–26.

Stevenson, Jack (2003b) "Trash ain't garbage: Identifying a new aesthetic in cinema," in Stevenson, *Land of a Thousand Balconies* (Manchester: Headpress), 125–130.

Stevenson, Jack (2003c) "The actor who wouldn't die: A tribute to ham," in Stevenson, *Land of a Thousand Balconies* (Manchester: Headpress), 69–71.

Stevenson, Jack (2003d) "The passionate plastic pleasure machine: Or, on camp film about to turn fat and forty," in Stevenson, *Land of a Thousand Balconies* (Manchester: Headpress), 113–124.

Stevenson, Jack (2003e) "A secret history of cult movies," in Stevenson, *Land of a Thousand Balconies* (Manchester: Headpress), 47–57.

Stevenson, Jack (2006), *Witchcraft through the Ages* (Guildford: FAB Press).

Stolnitz, Jerome (1960a) "On objective relativism in aesthetics," *Journal of Philosophy*, 57(8), 261–276.

Stolnitz, Jerome (1960b) *Aesthetics and the Philosophy of Art Criticism* (Boston: Riverside Press).

Straayer, Chris (1996), *Deviant Eyes, Deviant Bodies* (New York: Columbia University Press).

Strasberg, Lee (1987), *Lee Strasberg: A Dream of Passion* (New York: Plume Books).

Straw, Will (1997), "Sizing up record collections: Gender and connoisseurship in rock music culture," in Sheila Whiteley (ed.), *Sexing the Groove: Popular Music and Gender* (London: Routledge), 3–16.

Stringer, Julian (1999), "Category 3: Sex and violence in postmodern Hong Kong," in Christopher Sharrett (ed.), *Mythologies of Violence in Postmodern Media* (Detroit: Wayne State University Press), 361–379.

Studlar, Gaylyn (1991), "Midnight s/excess: Cult figurations of femininity and the perverse," *Journal of Popular Film and Television*, 17(1), 2–14.

Suarez, Juan A. (2002), "Pop, queer, or fascist? The ambiguity of mass culture in Kenneth Anger's *Scorpio Rising*," in Wheeler Winston Dixon and Gwendolyn Audrey Foster (eds), *Experimental Cinema: The Film Reader* (London: Routledge), 115–137.

Syder Andrew and Dolores Tierney (2005), "Importation/mexploitation, or, how a crime-fighting, vampire-slaying, Mexican wrestler almost found himself in an Italian sword-and-sandals epic," in Steven Jay Schneider and Tony Williams (eds), *Horror International* (Detroit: Wayne State University Press), 33–55.

Talalay, Rachel (2010), "Bigelow's best director award doesn't help women in film – it may hurt them, *Vancouver Sun* (April 17), online at: www.vancouversun.com/ (accessed August 18, 2010).

Tarantino, Quentin (1995), "It's cool to be banned," *Index on Censorship* 6 (June), 56–58.

Tateishi, Ramie (2003), "The Japanese horror film series: Ring and Eko Eko Azarak," in Steven Jay Schneider (ed.), *Fear without Frontiers: Horror Cinema across the Globe* (Godalming: FAB Press), 295–304.

Taubin, Amy (2008), "Primer," in David Sterritt and John Anderson (eds), *The B List* (Cambridge, MA: Da Capo Press), 79–82.

Taves, Brian (1995), "The B film: Hollywood's other half," in Tino Balio, *Grand Design: Hollywood as a Modern Business Enterprise, 1930–1939* (Berkeley, CA: University of California Press), 313–350.

Taylor, Frank J. (2002), "Big boom in outdoor movies," in Gregory A. Waller (ed.), *Moviegoing in America* (Oxford: Blackwell). Originally published in the *Saturday Evening Post* (September 15, 1956).

Taylor, Greg (1999), *Artists in the Audience: Cults, Camp and American Film Criticism* (Princeton, NJ: Princeton University Press).

Telotte, J.P. (1991a) "Beyond all reason: The nature of the cult," in J.P. Telotte (ed.), *The Cult Film Experience* (Austin, TX: University of Texas Press), 5–17.

Telotte, J.P. (1991b) "*Casablanca* and the larcenous cult film," in J.P. Telotte (ed.), *The Cult Film Experience* (Austin, TX: University of Texas Press), 43–54.

Telotte, J.P. (1995), *Replications: A Robotic History of Science Fiction Film* (Urbana: University of Illinois Press).

Telotte, J.P. (2001), "*The Blair Witch Project* project: Film and the internet," *Film Quarterly*, 54(3), 32–39.

Teo, Stephen (1997), *Hong Kong Cinema* (London: British Film Institute).

Teo, Stephen (2007), *A Touch of Zen* (Hong Kong: Hong Kong University Press).

Thomas, Sarah (2007), "Playing 'Peter Lorre': The self-reflexive performance strategies of a cult actor," paper presented at the *Cine-Excess Conference on International Cult Film* (London, May 3–5).

Thompson, Ben (1995), "Pop and film: The charisma crossover," in Jonathan Romney and Adrian Wootton (eds), *Celluloid Jukebox: Popular Music in the Movies Since the 50s* (London: British Film Institute), 32–41.

Thompson, Dave (1999), *Better to Burn out: The Cult of Death in Rock 'n' Roll* (New York: Thunder's Mouth Press).

Thompson, Kristin (1977), "The concept of cinematic excess," *Ciné-Tracts*, 2 (Summer), 54–63.

Thompson, Kristin (1990), "Dr. Caligari at the Folies-Bergère, or the success of an early avant-garde film," in Mike Budd (ed.), *The Cabinet of Dr. Caligari: Texts, Contexts, Histories* (Piscataway, NJ: Rutgers University Press), 121–169.

Thomson, Rosemary Garland (ed.) (1996), *Freakery: Cutural Spectacles of the Extraordinary Body* (New York: New York University Press).

Thornton, Sarah (1995), *Clubcultures: Music, Media and Subcultural Capital* (Cambridge: Polity Press).

Tombs, Pete (1997), *Mondo Macabro: Weird and Wonderful Cinema around the World* (London: Titan).

Tombs, Pete (2003), "Oddball kinkiness and intellectual conceits," in Harvey Fenton (ed.), *Flesh and Blood Compendium* (Godalming: FAB Press), 352–356.

Totaro, Donato (2001), "Time, Bergson, and the cinematographical mechanism," *Offscreen*, online at: www.horschamp.qc.ca/new_offscreen/Bergson_film.html (accessed August 18, 2010).

Troeltsch, Ernst (1931), *The Social Teaching of the Christian Churches* (London: MacMillan).

Tseëlon, Efrat (2001), "From fashion to masquerade: Towards an ungendered paradigm," in Joanne Entwistle and Elizabeth Wilson (eds), *Body Dressing* (London: Berg), 103–117.

Tudor, Andrew (1989), *Monsters and Mad Scientists: A Cultural History of the Horror Movie* (Oxford: Blackwell).

Tulloch, John, and Henry Jenkins (1995), *Science Fiction Audiences: Watching Doctor Who and Star Trek* (London: Routledge).

Tumbocon Mauro Feria , (2003), "In a climate of terror: The Fillipino monster movie," in Steven Jay Schneider (ed.), *Fear without Frontiers: Horror Cinema across the Globe* (Godalming: FAB Press), 255–264.

Turcan, Robert (1996), *The Cults of the Roman Empire* (Oxford: Blackwell).

Turnbull, Sue (2007), "Beyond words: The return of the king and the pleasures of the text," in Martin Barker and Ernest Mathijs (eds), *Watching Lord of the Rings: Tolkien's World Audiences* (New York: Peter Lang), 181–190.

Tyler, Parker (1963), "Orson Wells and the big experimental film cult," *Film Culture*, No. 29. Reprinted in P. Adams Sitney (ed.), *Film Culture Reader* (New York: Cooper Square Press, 2000), 376–386.

Tyler, Parker (1969), *Underground Film: A Critical History* (New York: Grove Press).

Tyree, J.M. and Ben Walters (2007), *The Big Lebowski* (London: British Film Institute).

Tzioumakis, Yannis (2006), *American Independent Cinema: An Introduction* (Edinburgh: Edinburgh University Press).

Udris, Jan (2004), "A question of silence," in Ernest Mathijs (ed.), *The Cinema of the Low Countries* (London: Wallflower Press), 157–166.

Ulman, Erik (2003), "Edgar G. Ulmer," *Senses of Cinema*, 24 (January–February), online at: http://archive. sensesofcinema.com/contents/directors/03/ulmer.html (accessed November 18, 2010).

Urban, Greg (2001), *Metaculture: How Culture Moves through the World* (Minneapolis: University of Minnesota Press).

Vale, V. and Andrea Juno (eds) (1986), *Incredibly Strange Films* (San Francisco: Re/Search Publications).

Van Extergem, Dirk (2004), "A Report on the Brussels International Festival of Fantastic Film," in Ernest Mathijs and Xavier Mendik (eds), *Alternative Europe; Eurotrash and Exploitation Cinema since 1945* (London: Wallflower Press), 216–227.

Van Laer, Patrick (2004), "Brussels Internationaal Festival van de Fantastische Film," in Willy Magiels and Robbe De Hert (eds), *Magie van de Cinema* (Antwerp: Facet), 163–165.

Vonalt, Larry (1991), "Looking both ways in *Casablanca*," in J. P. Telotte (ed.), *The Cult Film Experience* (Austin, TX: University of Texas Press), 55–65.

Wagstaff, Christopher (1992), "A forkful of westerns: Industry, audiences, and the Italian western," in Richard Dyer and Ginette Vincendeau (eds), *Popular European Cinema* (London: Routledge), 245–261.

Walker, David, Andrew Rausch and Chris Watson (2009), *Reflections on Blaxploitation: Actors and Directors Speak* (Lanham, MD: Scarecrow Press).

Wallace, David Foster (1997), "E Unibus Pluram: Television and U.S. fiction," in *A Supposedly Fun Thing I'll Never Do Again* (London: Abacus), 21–82.

Wallace, David Foster (2006) "Big red son," in *Consider the Lobster and Other Essays* (New York: Little Brown), 3–50.

Waller, Gregory A. (1991), "Midnight movies, 1980–1985: A market study," in J. P. Telotte (ed.), *The Cult Film Experience: Beyond all Reason* (Austin, TX: University of Texas Press), 167–186.

Waters, John (2003), "Whatever happened to showmanship?" in *Crackpot: The Obsessions of John Waters* (expanded edn; New York: Scribner), 13–23.

Waters, John (2005), *Shock Value: A Tasteful Book about Bad Taste* (New York: Thunder's Mouth Press).

Wathen, Mike (1994), "For adults only! Home grown British crud, 1954–1972" in Stefan Jaworzyn (ed.), *Shock Xpress 2* (London: Titan Books), 91–101.

Watson, Paul (1997), "There's no accounting for taste: Exploitation cinema and the limits of film theory," in Deborah Cartmell, I.Q. Hunter, Heidi Kay and Imelda Wheleyan (eds), *Trash Aesthetics: Popular Culture and its Audience* (London: Pluto Press).

Webster, Andy (2008), "Films in review," *New York Times* (September 12, Section E), 10.

Weinstock, Jeffrey (2007), *The Rocky Horror Picture Show* (London: Wallflower Press).

Weinstock, Jeffrey (ed.) (2008), *Reading Rocky Horror: The Rocky Horror Picture Show and Popular Culture* (Basingstoke: Palgrave MacMillan).

Weisser, Thomas (1997), *Asian Cult Cinema* (New York: Boulevard Books).

Weisser, Thomas and Yuko Mihara (1997), *Japanese Cinema Encyclopedia* (New York: Vital Books).

Weldon, Michael (1983), *The Psychotronic Encyclopedia of Film* (New York: Balanatine Books).

Wexman, Virginia (ed.) (2003), *Film and Authorship* (Piscataway, NJ: Rutgers University Press).

Whelehan, Imelda and Esther Sonnet (1997), "Regendered reading: Tank Girl and postmodern intertextuality," in Deborah Cartmell, I.Q. Hunter, Heidi Kaye and Imelda Whelehan (eds), *Trash Aesthetics* (London: Pluto Press), 31–47.

Wilinsky, Barbara (2001), *Sure Seaters: The Emergence of Art House Cinema* (Minneapolis: University of Minnesota Press).

Williams, Linda (1982), "Women in love: Personal best," *Jump Cut*, 27(1), 11–12.

Williams, Linda (1994), "Learning to Scream," *Sight and Sound*, 4(12), 14–17.

Williams, Linda (1999). *Hard Core: Power, Pleasure, and the Frenzy of the Visible* (Berkeley, CA: University of California Press).

Williams, Linda Ruth (2005), *The Erotic Thriller in Contemporary Cinema* (Bloomington: Indiana University Press).

Williams, Sophy (2000), "L'Âge d'or: faux-raccord (false match)," *Senses of Cinema*, 5 (April), online at: http://archive.sensesofcinema.com/contents/cteq/00/5/age.html (accessed (November 18, 2010)

Williams, Tony (2005), "Hong Kong social horror: Tragedy and farce in Category III," in Steven Jay Schneider and Tony Williams (eds), *Horror International* (Detroit: Wayne State University Press) 203–218.

Williamson, Milly (2005), *The Lure of the Vampire from Bram Stoker to Buffy* (London: Wallflower Press).

Willis, Paul E. (1976), "The cultural meaning of drug use," in Stuart Hall and Tony Jefferson (eds), *Resistance through Rituals: Youth Subcultures in Post-War Britain* (London: Hutchinson & Co.), 106–118.

Wilson, Angela (2008), "The galaxy is gay": Examining the networks of lesbian punk rock subculture," in Susan Driver (ed.), *Queer Youth Cultures* (New York: SUNY Press).

Wilson, Robert (2005), "Spectral critiques: Tracking "uncanny" filmic paths towards a bio-poetics of trans-pacific globalization," in Meaghan Morris, Siu Leung Li and Stephen Chan Ching-kiu (eds), *Hong Kong Connections: Transnational Imagination in Action Cinema* (Durham, NC: Duke University Press; Hong Kong: Hong Kong University Press), 249–268.

Winge, Theresa (2006), "Costuming the imagination: Origins of anime and cosplay," in Frenchy Lunning (ed.), *Emerging Worlds of Anime and Manga (Mechademia 1)*, (Minneapolis: University of Minnesota Press), 65–77.

Wood, Robert E. (1991), "Don't dream it: Performance and *The Rocky Horror Picture Show,*" in J.P. Telotte (ed.), *The Cult Film Experience* (Austin, TX: University of Texas Press), 156–166.

Wood, Robin (1979), "An introduction to the American horror film," in Andrew Britton, Robin Wood, Richard Lippe and Tony Williams (eds), *The American Nightmare* (Toronto: Festival of Festivals), 7–28.

Wong, Cindy Hing-Yuk (2007), "Film festivals and the global projection of Hong Kong cinema," in Gina Marchetti and Tan See Kam (eds), *Hong Kong Film, Hollywood and New Global Cinema* (London: Routledge), 177–192.

Wu, Harmony H. (2003), "Trading in horror, cult and matricide: Peter Jackson's phenomenal bad taste and New Zealand's fantasies of inter/national cinematic success," in Mark Jancovich et al. (eds), *Defining Cult Movies: The Cultural Politics of Oppositional Taste* (Manchester: Manchester University Press), 84–108.

Yoshimoto, Mitsuhiro (1993), "The difficulty of being radical: The discipline of film studies and the postcolonial world order," in Masao Miyoshi and H.D. Harootunian (eds), *Japan in the World* (Durham, NC: Duke University Press), 338–353.

Youngblood, Gene (1970), *Expanded Cinema* (New York: Dutton).

Zerzan, John (1994), "Time and its discontents," in *Running on Emptiness: The Pathology of Civilization* (Los Angeles: Feral House).

Zimmer, Jacques (2002), *Le Cinéma X* (Paris: La muscardine).

Credits and Sources

The authors and publisher gratefully acknowledge the permission granted to reproduce the copyright material in this book.

Figure 1.1 *Sources:* DVD frame grabs: *El Topo* (from ABKCO/Anchor Bay USA DVD, 2007) Year – 1970; Country – Mexico; Producers – Mick Gochanour, Robin Klein, Juan Lopez Moctezuma, Moshe Rosemberg, Robert Viskin; Director – Alejandro Jodorowsky. *The Rocky Horror Picture Show* (from 20th Century Fox USA DVD, 2000) Year – 1975; Country – United Kingdom, United States; Producers – Lou Adler, John Goldstone, Michael White; Director – Jim Sharman. *Donnie Darko* (from 20th Century Fox USA DVD, 2004) Year – 2001; Country – USA; Producers – Adam Fields, Nancy Juvonen, Sean McKittrick; Director – Richard Kelly.

Figure 1.2 *Sources:* DVD frame grabs: (from Oddbod Productions/City Heat Productions CANADA/USA DVD, 2003) Year – 2000; Country – Canada; Producers - Karen Lee Hall, Steven Hoban; Director – John Fawcett.

Figure 2.1 *Superstar: The Karen Carpenter Story*, 1987; Country – United States; Producers – Todd Haynes/Cynthia Schneider; Director – Todd Haynes.

Figure 3.1 UPI Photo/Barbara Wilson/Golden Raspberry Award Foundation. *Source:* United Press International.

Figure 3.2 *Sources:* © BIFFF/Buzzelli, courtesy of PeyMey Diffusion and the Brussels International Festival of Fantastic Film; © BIFFF/Mauricet, courtesy of PeyMey Diffusion and the Brussels International Festival of Fantastic Film; © BIFFF/Michetz, courtesy of PeyMey Diffusion and the Brussels International Festival of Fantastic Film; © BIFFF/Sokal, courtesy of PeyMey Diffusion and the Brussels International Festival of Fantastic Film.

Figure 4.1 *Sources:* DVD frame grabs: *Cannibal Holocaust* (from Grindhouse Releasing USA DVD, 2008) Year – 1979; Country – Italy; Producers – Franco Di Nunzio, Franco Palaggi; Director – Ruggero Deodato. *The Beyond* (from Anchor Bay USA DVD, 2000) Year – 1981; Country – Italy; Producers – Fabrizio De Angelis; Director – Lucio Fulci. *Evil Dead* (from Anchor Bay USA DVD, 2002) Year – 1981; Country – USA; Producers – Robert Tapert, Irvin Shapiro; Director – Sam Raimi.

Figure 5.1 Image used with permission of Lebowskifest.

Figure 7.1 Year – 1936; Country – USA; Produced and directed by Joseph Cornell.

Cult Cinema: An Introduction. Ernest Mathijs and Jamie Sexton.
© 2011 Ernest Mathijs and Jamie Sexton. Published 2011 by Blackwell Publishing Ltd.

Figure 7.2   Year – 1959; Country – USA; Produced and directed by William Castle.

Figure 8.1   Year – 1939; Country – USA; Producers – Mervyn LeRoy; Director – Victor Fleming.

Figure 9.1   *Sources: Emmanuelle* (from Lions Gate Entertainment USA DVD, 2007) Year – 1974; Country – France; Producer – Yves Rousset-Rouard; Director – Just Jaeckin; *The Brood* (from MGM Home Entertainment USA DVD 2003): Year – 1979; Country – Canada; Producers – Pierre David, Claude Héroux, Victor Solnicki; Director – David Cronenberg; *Showgirls* (from MGM Home Entertainment/Twentieth Century Fox Home Entertainment USA DVD 2007): Year – 1995; Country – United States.

Figure 9.2   DVD frame grab: (from New Line Home Entertainment USA DVD, 2004) *Pink Flamingos.* Year – 1972; Country – USA; Director and Producer – John Waters.

Figure 10.1   DVD frame grab: (from Warner Home Video USA DVD, 2009) *Fame.* Year – 1980; Country – USA; Producers – David De Silva, Alan Marshall; Director – Alan Parker.

Figure 11.1   Publicity still, courtesy Royal Film Archive of Belgium.

Figure 13.1   Courtesy Kathleen Dow, Robert Shaye Papers, Special Collections Library, University of Michigan.

Figure 13.2   Year – 1974; Country – USA; Producer: Buzz Feitshans; Director – Jack Hill.

Figure 14.1   Image courtesy of Royal Film Archive of Belgium. Year – 1920; Country – Germany; Producers – Rudolph Meinert, Erich Pommer; Director – Robert Wiene.

Figure 14.2   Year – 1970; Country – USA; Produced by Andy Warhol; Directed by Paul Morrissey.

Figure 15.1   Year – 1968; Country – UK/USA; Produced and directed by Stanley Kubrick.

Figure 16.1   *The Sound of Music* Year – 1965; Country – USA; Produced and Directed by Robert Wise. *The Happiness of the Katakuris* – courtesy of Palisades Tartan.

Figure 17.1   DVD frame grab: (from Paramount Home Entertainment CANADA DVD, 2007) Year – 1946; Country – USA; Producer and Director – Frank Capra.

Figure 19.1   DVD frame grab: (from Warner Bros. Entertainment UK DVD Release, 2007) Year – 1982; Country – USA/Hong Kong; Producers - Michael Deeley/Ridley Scott; Director – Ridley Scott.

Figure 20.1   Photo by Michael Hanscom of Norwescon (www.norwescon.org). *Source*: Michael Hanscom, used with permission.

Figure 22.2   © 2009 BFI. Courtesy of the British Film Institute.

Every effort has been made to trace copyright holders and to obtain their permission for the use of copyright material. The publisher apologizes for any errors or omissions in the above list and would be grateful if notified of any corrections that should be incorporated in future reprints or editions of this book.

Index

Page numbers in italics refer to illustrations.

Cult Cinema: An Introduction. Ernest Mathijs and Jamie Sexton.
© 2011 Ernest Mathijs and Jamie Sexton. Published 2011 by Blackwell Publishing Ltd.

Ulmer, Edgar G.: 146, 193n, 208
Umiliani, Piero: 179
Un Chant d'Amour: 160
Un Chien Andalou: 158
Underground film: 8, 13–14, 15, 27, 32, 52, 61, 63, 72, 81, 88, 92, 95, 96n, 106, 107, 112, 140, 151, 155, 158–63, 164, 167, 168, 169, 174, 175, 240
Ungawa: 90
Unico: 127
Universal Pictures: 203, 204, 210, 240
Unknown, The: 198
Up in Smoke: 169
Urban, Greg: 234
Utopian thought: 20, 24, 54, 131–41

Vadim, Roger: 168
Vale, V.: 67, 91
Valentino, Rudolph: 79, 137
Vampire film: 14, 74, 114, 126, 128, 197, 199, 200, 201, 203
Vampire Princess Miyu: 128
Vampyr: 92
Vampyros Lesbos: 114, 181
Van Der Put, Bart: 168
Van Extergem, Dirk: 43, 44, 45, 203
Van Laer, Patrick: 44
Van Peebles, Melvin: 151
Vangelis: 180
Varda, Agnes: 74
Vaughan, James: 169
V-cinema: 152
Velvet Goldmine: 230
Velvet Underground, The: 169
Velvet Vampire: 74, 109
Verhoeven, Paul: 28, 38, 49, 104
Vertov, Dziga: 157
Vidal, Gore: 89
Video/VHS/VCR/videocassette: 4, 6, 15, 17, 33–4, 46, 63, 65, 69, 72, 85, 107, 117, 118, 122, 123, 124, 126, 127, 128, 140, 152, 161, 168, 169, 177, 197, 199, 202, 203, 229, 235, 241
Video nasties: 4, 5, 19, 23, 47–8, *48*, 49, 63, 107, 118, 199, 202
Video Watchdog: 32, 63, 93, 241
Videodrome: 42, 54, 198, 202
Vieux Colombier cinema, Paris: 156
Vigo, Jean: 51, 71, 72
Village Voice (periodical): 158, 217
Vincent: 72, 236
Vinton, Bobby: 175
Vinyl: 161

Violence: 14, 40–1, 44–5, 46–9, 190–1, 79, 83, 109, 114, 116–17, 121, 122, 125, 126, 128–9, 134, 137, 138, 140, 141n, 150, 153, 163, 185, 190–1, 195, 196, 198–9, 201, 204, 211, 228, 232
Vipco: 197
Visitor Q: 152
Visy, Gilles: 23
Viva: 237, 238
Viva La Muerte: 14, 138
Vogel, Amos: 158, 159, 164
Vonalt, Larry: 187

Wagstaff, Christopher: 28
Walker, David: 105
Walker, Pete: 151
Wallace, David Foster: 37, 232
Waller, Gregory A.: 4, 7, 25n, 120, 172
Walsh, Raoul: 52
Walters, Ben: 229
Wanda, the Sadistic Hypnotist: 166
War Game, The: 91, 97
Warhol, Andy: 69, 79, 89, 160, 161, 169
Warner Bros: 153
Waste/wasteful: 18, 22, 27, 196, 220
Waters, John: 30, 55, 68–9, 73, 74, 75n, 81, 88, 89, 99, 101, 104, 106, *107*, 111, 177
Waterworld: 27, 215, 220, 223
Wathen, Mike: 151
Watkins, Peter: 91, 238
Watson, Chris: 105
Watson, Paul: 153
We Can't Go Home Again: 34, 75n
Weaver, Sigourney: 207
Webster, Andy: 238
Weekend: 228
Weiner, Norbert: 181
Weinstein, Harvey: 237
Weinstock, Jeffrey: 15, 31, 101, 111, 115, 176
Weisser, Tom: 123, 130
Welcome Home Brother Charles: 105
Welcome to the Dollhouse: 231
Weldon, Michael: 90
Welles, Orson: 28, 70
Wells, Simon: 173, 179
Welsh, Irvin: 170, 179
Wenders, Wim: 75n
Weng Weng: 104
Wes Craven's New Nightmare: 200
West, Mae: 80, 84, 87
Wexler, Michael: 168
Wexman, Virginia: 75

CPSIA information can be obtained at www.ICGtesting.com
Printed in the USA
BVOW09s1052190816

459246BV00008BA/3/P